Studien zum Bank-, Börsen- und Kapitalmarktrecht

Edited by
Prof. Dr. Dr. h.c. Ulrich Immenga
Prof. Dr. Lars Klöhn, LL.M. and
Prof. Dr. Daniel Zimmer

Volume 86

Matthias Hausdorf

Dark Liquidity

Conflicts between Transparency and Anonymity
in Financial Markets Law

Nomos

Onlineversion
Nomos eLibrary

The Deutsche Nationalbibliothek lists this publication in the Deutsche Nationalbibliografie; detailed bibliographic data are available on the Internet at http://dnb.d-nb.de

a.t.: Basel, Univ., Diss., 2023

ISBN 978-3-7560-2229-8 (Print)
978-3-7489-4881-0 (ePDF)

1st Edition 2025

To my parents, my wife, and my daughter.

Preface

This manuscript was accepted as a thesis for the degree of Doctor of Law by the Faculty of Law of the University of Basel in the winter term of 2023. The thesis strives to include the law and legal literature on the topic as of June 2023.

My deepest gratitude goes to my academic advisor – Professor Dr. iur. Ulrich G. Schroeter – who introduced me to academic research in law during our time at the University of Mannheim and kindly offered me the chance as a German scholar to work and teach in Switzerland. I consider my time in Switzerland as a privilege I would not have had without him. Professor Schroeter always encouraged me to find my field of interest and supported me in exploring it in-depth. I greatly enjoyed the discussions we had and the freedoms I was granted.

I am also deeply grateful for the support of my secondary academic advisor Professor Dr. iur. Peter Jung. He provided me with invaluable insights into Swiss financial markets law both in- and outside of the classroom, a source of knowledge I greatly appreciated.

As a doctoral examination committee in Basel would not be complete without an external expert in the field, I am especially thankful for Dr. iur. Philipp Henneberg, LL.B. who assumed the task of reading the over 500 pages of my manuscript and preparing for the oral disputation in Basel besides his professional obligations as an esteemed attorney-at-law in the field of capital markets law in Frankfurt am Main, Germany.

This book also rests on the support and resources provided by the renowned academic institutions and the brilliant minds of their faculty members: I am honored to have studied at the University of Mannheim, a university combining both excellence in law and the adjacent fields of business and economics. Furthermore, having conducted research at the oldest university in Switzerland fills me with pride. The welcoming but rigorous academic environment at the University of Basel allowed me to explore my academic interests on an unparalleled level. It was here, that I received ample support from many people, among them Professor Dr. iur. Sabine Gless who gave my dissertation many inspiring impulses and, together with Professor Schroeter, supported me in pursuing my Master of Laws at Georgetown University. During my time in Switzerland, I also benefitted from the Swiss National Bank's Study Center at Gerzensee where I attended a seminar on "Behavioral Law and Economics" by Professor Ryan Bubb (New York University) who sacrificed his spare time outside the seminar to discuss topics of my thesis.

I am also deeply honored by the wonderful time I had at Georgetown University Law Center which was generously supported by the Heinrich von Kronstein Foundation. In Washington, D.C., I met many distinguished scholars as well as practitioners in US securities regulations and financial markets law among them my distinguished law school Professors Chris Brummer, Donald Langevoort, Gregory A. Scopino, and Joshua C. Teitelbaum. It was also my pleasure to be a fellow at the Institute of International Economic Law at Georgetown University and participate in the many discussions on current legal and regulatory topics impacting the US and the world at large.

Even though much time has been allocated to my academic work, my life would not be complete without the people with whom I spend my spare time: I am very thankful for my closest friends, Marina Seizov and Oliver Friedrich, and their families. My deep gratitude also extends to my parents, Stefanie and Ulrich Nägele, who always supported me in pursuing my academic endeavors, provided me with great advice, and have been great role models in many ways.

The most important person deserving the highest praise is my dearest wife, Tamara Hausdorf, LL.M. (The George Washington University). She has been (and still is) my greatest supporter (and critic). She gave me the time I needed to write this book and lent me her brilliant mind for endless discussions of my thoughts in many places spanning from Freiburg to Washington, D.C. to Los Angeles. Without her support, this book would not have been possible. I am deeply honored and grateful to have you in my life.

To conclude, I want to thank the person who put this achievement into perspective: my daughter, Sophie Elisabeth Hausdorf. She was born before this manuscript was even printed showing me that much more complicated endeavors can be achieved in far less time. As I learned on the day my doctoral degree was conferred that my wife and I are soon to be parents, my daughter heralded a new chapter in our lives we are happy to begin.

This book is dedicated to my parents, my wife, and my daughter.

Frankfurt am Main, August 2024 Matthias Hausdorf

Table of Contents

Abbreviations

AG	Die Aktiengesellschaft – Zeitschrift für deutsches, europäisches und internationales Aktien-, Unternehmens- und Kapitalmarktrecht
AMAFI	L'Association française des marchés financiers (French Financial Markets Association)
AMEX	American Stock Exchange
AMF	Autorité des Marchés Financiers
APA	Approved Publication Arrangement
ATS	Alternative Trading System
AVT	Average Value of Transaction
BaFin	Bundesanstalt für Finanzdienstleistungsaufsicht (German Federal Financial Supervisory Authority)
BATS	Better Alternative Trading System
BB	Betriebs-Berater
BCN	Broker Crossing Network
BEHG	Bundesgesetz über die Börsen und den Effektenhandel (Swiss Stock Exchange Act)
BIS	Bank for International Settlement
BKR	Zeitschrift für Bank- und Kapitalmarktrecht
BörsG	Börsengesetz (German Stock Exchange Act)
CapLaw	Swiss Capital Markets Law
CAPM	Capital Asset Pricing Model
CB	Compliance-Berater
CCP	Central Counterparty
CCZ	Corporate Compliance Zeitschrift
CDR	Commission Delegated Regulation
CESR	Committee of European Securities Regulators
CFTC	Commodity Futures Trading Commission
CHF	Swiss Franc
CH-MTF	Swiss Multilateral Trading Systems
CH-OTF	Swiss Organized Trading Systems

COD	Commission: ordinary legislative procedure (*ordentliches Gesetzgebungsverfahren*)
COFIA	Classes of Financial Instruments Approach
COM	Commission Document
CQS	Consolidated Quotation System
CTA	Consolidated Tape Association
CTS	Consolidated Tape System
DLT	Distributed Ledger Technology
Draft-FinfraG	Vernehmlassung FinfraG (Draft version of FinfraG)
Draft-FinfraV	Vernehmlassung FinfraV (Draft version of FinfraV)
DVC	Double Volume Cap
DVCM	Double Volume Cap Mechanism
EBBO	European Best Bid and Offer
EC	European Community
ECB	European Central Bank
ECMH	Efficient Capital Market Hypothesis
ECN	Electronic Communication Network
EFD	Eidgenössisches Finanzdepartement (Swiss Department of Finance)
EFSF	European Financial Stability Facility
EMIR	European Market Infrastructure Regulation (Regulation (EU) No 648/2012 of the European Parliament and of the Council of 4 July 2012 on OTC derivatives, central counterparties and trade repositories)
ESM	European Stability Mechanism
ESMA	European Securities and Markets Authority
ESMA-Regulation	Regulation (EU) No 1095/2010 of the European Parliament and of the Council of 24 November 2010 establishing a European Supervisory Authority (European Securities and Markets Authority), amending Decision No 716/2009/EC and repealing Commission Decision 2009/77/EC
ETF	Exchange Traded Fund
EU	European Union
EUR	Euro
EuZ	Zeitschrift für Europarecht
FCA	Financial Conduct Authority (UK)
FIDLEG	Finanzdienstleistungsgesetz (Swiss Financial Services Act)

FinfraG	Finanzmarktinfrastrukturgesetz (Swiss Financial Market Infrastructure Act)
FinfraV	Finanzmarktinfrastrukturverordnung (Swiss Financial Market Infrastructure Ordinance)
FINIG	Finanzinstitutsgesetz (Swiss Financial Institutions Act)
FINMA	Eidgenössischen Finanzmarktaufsicht (Swiss Financial Market Supervisory Authority)
FINRA	Financial Industry Regulatory Authority
FOMC	Federal Open Market Committee of the Federal Reserve System
Form ATS-N	Form Alternative Trading System-New
FR	Federal Register (US National Archives)
FRBNY	Federal Reserve Bank of New York
FSB	Financial Stability Board
GesKR	Schweizerische Zeitschrift für Gesellschafts- und Kapitalmarktrecht
GG	Grundgesetz (German Constitution)
HFT	High Frequency Trader
Index CDS	Index Credit Default Swaps
IOI	Indications Of Interest
IOSCO	International Organization of Securities Commissions
ITS	Intermarket Trading System
KWG	Kreditwesengesetz (German Banking Act)
LIS	Large In Scale
LIS-Waiver	Large In Scale Waiver
LLC	Limited Liability Company
MAD	Market Abuse Directive
MAR	Market Abuse Regulation
MiFID I	Markets in Financial Instruments Directive I (Directive 2004/39/EC of the European Parliament and of the Council of 21 April 2004 on markets in financial instruments amending Council Directives 85/611/EEC and 93/6/EEC and Directive 2000/12/EC of the European Parliament and of the Council and repealing Council Directive 93/22/EEC)
MiFID II	Markets in Financial Instruments Directive II (Directive 2014/65/EU of the European Parliament and the of the Council of 15 May 2014 on markets in financial instru-

	ments and amending Directive 2002/92/EC and Directive 2011/61/EU)
MiFIR	Markets in Financial Instruments Regulation (Regulation (EU) No 600/2014 of the European Parliament and of the Council of 15 May 2014 on markets in financial instruments and amending Regulation (EU) No 648/2012)
MTF	Multilateral Trading Facility
NASD	National Association of Securities Dealers
NASDAQ	National Association of Securities Dealers Automated Quotations
NBBO	National Best Bid and Offer
NCA	National Competent Authority
NGT-Waiver	Negotiated Trade Waiver
NJW	Neue Juristische Wochenschrift
NMS	National Market System
NYSE	New York Stock Exchange
NZG	Neue Zeitschrift für Gesellschaftsrecht
OJ	Official Journal of the European Union
OMF-Waiver	Order Management Facility Waiver
OPRA	Options Price Reporting Authority
OTC	Over The Counter
OTF	Organized Trading Facility
PBBO	Primary Best Bid and Offer
Q&A	Questions and Answers
RdF	Recht der Finanzinstrumente
Regulation ATS	Regulation Alternative Trading System
Regulation NMS	Regulation National Market System
RIW	Recht der internationalen Wirtschaft
RM	Regulated Market
RP-Waiver	Reference Price Waiver
SEC	US Securities and Exchange Commission
SI	Systematic Internalizer
SIF	Staatssekretariat für Internationale Finanzfragen (Swiss State Secretariat for International Finance)
SIP	Securities Information Processor
SJZ	Schweizerische Juristen-Zeitung

SME	Small and Medium Enterprises
SNB	Swiss National Bank
SRO	Self-Regulatory Organizations
SSM	Single Supervisory Mechanism
SRIEL	Swiss Review of International and European Law
SSTI	Size Specific to the Financial Instrument
SSTI-Waiver	Size Specific to the Financial Instrument Waiver
SVC	Single Volume Cap
SZW	Schweizerische Zeitschrift für Wirtschafts- und Finanzmarktrecht
TFEU	Treaty on the Functioning of the European Union
TOTV	Traded on a Trading Venue
UBS	Union de Banques Suisses
UK	United Kingdom
US	United States
USA	United States of America
USD	United States Dollar
WL	WestLaw
WM	Zeitschrift für Wirtschafts- und Bankrecht: Wertpapier-Mitteilungen
WpHG	Wertpapierhandelsgesetz (German Securities Trading Act)
WpIG	Wertpapierinstitutsgesetz (German Securities Institutions Act)
ZBB	Zeitschrift für Bankrecht und Bankwirtschaft
ZGR	Zeitschrift für Unternehmens- und Gesellschaftsrecht
ZHR	Zeitschrift für das gesamte Handelsrecht und Wirtschaftsrecht

Part I: The Origins and Theory of Dark Liquidity

§ 1. Challenges of Dark Trading

A. Transparency and Dark Trading

Transparency of financial markets is regarded both as a *'hallmark'* of financial market regulation[1] and an internationally *'shared principle'* across multiple jurisdictions.[2] It aims to foster a level-playing-field among different market participants, ranging from individual retail investors to large institutional investors. Transparency calls market participants to order and provides for information that fuels the fundamental market functions, such as price formation.[3] While transparency is generally provided by subjecting market participants and market infrastructures to disclosure rules, the amount of transparency in a market is highly sensitive to shifts in market infrastructure.[4]

---

1 Chair Mary Jo White, 'SEC Enhancing Our Equity Market Structure' (5 June 2014). But see for Swiss law the mentioning of transparency as a regulatory objective under Article 1(2) FinfraG.

2 See Recital 1 MiFIR.

3 Cf. Louis D Brandeis, *Other People's Money and How the Bankers Use It* (Stokes 1914) 92: *'Publicity is justly commended as a remedy for social and industrial diseases. Sunlight is said to be the best disinfectants; electric light the most efficient policeman.'*; IOSCO, 'Objectives and Principles of Securities Regulation' (May 2017) 12, I. 35: *'Regulation should promote transparency of trading.'* See also: IOSCO, 'Transparency and Market Fragmentation: Report from the Technical Committee of the International Organization of Securities Commissions' (November 2001) 4; Niamh Moloney, 'EU Financial Governance and Transparency Regulation: A Test for the Effectiveness of Post-Crisis Administrative Governance' in Danny Busch and Guido Ferrarini (eds), *Regulation of the EU Financial Markets: MiFID II and MiFIR* (1st edn, Oxford University Press 2017) para 12.10ff; Ruben Lee, *Running the World's Markets: The Governance of Financial Infrastructure* (Princeton University Press 2011) 352–3; Rolf Sethe and others (eds), *Kommentar zum Finanzmarktinfrastrukturgesetz FinfraG* (SK FinfraG, 1st edn, Schulthess 2017) Art 1 para 28.

4 IOSCO, 'Transparency and Market Fragmentation' (n 3) 4, 12; CESR, 'CESR Technical Advice to the European Commission in the Context of the MiFID Review - Equity Markets: Consultation Paper' (CESR/10-394, April 2010) 27; Peter Gomber and Axel Pierron, 'MiFID: Spirit and Reality of a European Financial Markets Directive' (September 2010) 56; Christoph Kumpan and Finn Schmidt in Matthias Lehmann and Christoph Kumpan (eds), *European Financial Services Law: Article-by-Article Commentary* (1st edn, Nomos; CH Beck; Hart Publishing 2019) Foreword MiFIR paras

In the last decades, innovation in technology and regulation reshaped the landscape of financial markets.[5] First, markets transformed from the manual trading environment of exchanges populated by floor traders into highly automated computer-driven infrastructures dominated by algorithms enabling traders to trade at lightning speed or being replaced by artificial intelligence eventually.[6] Subsequently, market infrastructure heavily shifted when traditional exchanges lost their quasi-monopoly on securities trading to the evolving alternative trading systems (ATS).[7] ATS are computerized electronic communication networks able to bring together buyers and sellers in securities and thereby compete with traditional exchanges.[8] These

---

1–2; Niamh Moloney, *EU Securities and Financial Markets Regulation* (3rd edn, Oxford University Press 2016) 446.

5 Erik Banks, *Dark Pools: Off-Exchange Liquidity in an Era of High Frequency, Program, and Algorithmic Trading* (2nd edn, Palgrave Macmillan UK 2014) 7–8; Hans Degryse and others, 'Dark Trading' in H. K Baker and Halil Kiymaz (eds), *Market Microstructure in Emerging and Developed Markets: Price Discovery, Information Flows, and Transaction Costs* (John Wiley & Sons, Inc 2013) 213; David Easthope and Arin Ray, 'Dark Pools: In the Eye of the Storm' (April 2014) 5; Monica Petrescu and Michael Wedow, 'Dark Pools in European Equity Markets: Emergence, Competition and Implications' (Occasional Paper Series No. 193, European Central Bank, July 2017) 7.

6 SEC, 'Concept Release on Equity Market Structure' (17 CFR Part 242, Release No. 34-61358, File No. S7-02-10, 21 January 2010) 75 FR 3594; Committee on Capital Markets Regulation, 'The U.S. Equity Markets: A Plan for Regulatory Reform' (July 2016) 3–4; FCA, 'UK Equity Market Dark Pools: Role, Promotion and Oversight in Wholesale Markets' (Thematic Review TR 16/5, July 2016) 7; Foresight, 'The Future of Computer Trading in Financial Markets: An International Perspective' (Final Project Report, The Government Office for Science, London, 2012) 28ff. See also James Angel, Lawrence Harris and Chester S Spatt, 'Equity Trading in the 21st Century' (Marshall Research Paper Series, Working Paper FBE 09-10, 18 May 2010) 4; Christian Hoops, *Verborgene Liquidität im Marktordnungsrecht der MiFID* (Ph.D.-Thesis Johann Wolfgang Goethe-University Frankfurt 2018, Peter Lang 2018) 3. On the application of artificial intelligence in the trading process see: ESMA, 'ESMA TRV Risk Analysis: Artificial Intelligence in EU Securities Markets' (ESMA50-164-6247, 1 February 2023) 12ff.

7 SEC, 'Concept Release on Equity Market Structure' (n 6) 75 FR 3594ff. See also Angel, Harris and Spatt (n 6) 5; Carole Gresse, 'Market Fragmentation in Europe: Assessment and Prospects for Market Quality' (UK Government's Foresight Project, Government Office for Science, Driver Report DR 19, London, 30 March 2012) 4, 9; Simone F Fioravanti and Monica Gentile, 'The Impact of Market Fragmentation on European Stock Exchanges' (Working Paper No 69, Commissione Nazionale per le Società e la Borsa (CONSOB), Rome, July 2011) 5, 12.

8 SEC, 'Concept Release on Equity Market Structure' (n 6) 75 FR 3599; CESR, 'Proposed Standards for Alternative Trading Systems: Paper for final Consultation' (CESR/02-001, 14 January 2002) 4; Christoph Kumpan, *Die Regulierung außerbörslicher*

trading systems are often run by market intermediaries such as broker-dealers, who offer clients better execution prices than incumbent exchanges, but are also often less regulated than exchanges.[9] While ATS are able to provide transparency in a similar manner exchanges do, their appearance left a rift in the regulatory framework of many jurisdictions since not all ATS were subject to the same transparency rules applicable to exchanges, allowing some ATS to offer a certain form of trading - so-called dark trading - to grow rapidly in the respective markets.[10] Dark trading is securities trading in secondary markets that does not provide trade transparency to other market participants, and therefore remains hidden from the public.[11]

B. Historical Rise of Dark Trading

However, dark trading is not a new phenomenon: In the era of manual trading, an early form of dark trading was so-called *upstairs trading* in which brokers agreed upon transactions for large orders of securities in

Wertpapierhandelssysteme im deutschen, europäischen und US-amerikanischen Recht (Ph.D.-Thesis University of Hamburg 2005, De Gruyter 2006) 5; Daniela Cohn-Heeren, *Kapitalmarktrechtliche Regulierungskonzepte für Alternative Handelssysteme* (Ph.D.-Thesis University of Freiburg 2004, Duncker & Humblot 2006) 30ff; Cally Jordan, *International Capital Markets: Law and Institutions* (Jeffrey Golden ed, 1st edn, Oxford University Press 2014) 258.

9 SEC, 'Concept Release on Equity Market Structure' (n 6) 75 FR 3599ff; CESR, 'Proposed Standards for Alternative Trading Systems' (n 8) 4; Kumpan, *Die Regulierung außerbörslicher Wertpapierhandelssysteme im deutschen, europäischen und US-amerikanischen Recht* (n 8) 5; Cohn-Heeren (n 8) 30ff.

10 Cf. SEC, 'Concept Release on Equity Market Structure' (n 6) 75 FR 3599.

11 ibid 75 FR 3599; CESR, 'CESR Technical Advice to the European Commission in the Context of the MiFID Review - Equity Markets' (n 4) 27; IOSCO, 'Issues Raised by Dark Liquidity: Consultation Report' (CR05/10, October 2010) 4; see also Rainer Baisch, Simone Baumann and Rolf H Weber, '"Shades of grey" in Dark Pools' [2014] GesKR 183, 184; Banks (n 5) 3; Carole Comerton-Forde, 'Current Issues in Market Design' in H. K Baker and Halil Kiymaz (eds), *Market Microstructure in Emerging and Developed Markets: Price Discovery, Information Flows, and Transaction Costs* (John Wiley & Sons, Inc 2013) 191; Degryse and others (n 5) 213ff; Thomas Hochstrasser, 'Dark Pools im Spannungsfeld zwischen Transparenz und Anonymität' [2016] AJP 305, 307; Peter Kasiske, 'Compliance-Risiken beim Wertpapierhandel in Dark Pools' [2015] BKR 454.

private negotiations on the top floors of brokerage firms.[12] However, the rise of entire trading systems dedicated to dark trading, so-called *dark pools*, is a new form of dark trading. It expanded a marginal phenomenon into a rapidly growing dark market that is accessible not only to bespoke large orders but also to more standardized orders of smaller size.[13]

Since the late 1990s and early 2000s, dark trading has widely spread in financial markets and accounts for an estimated market share of 31 %[14] to 40 %[15] in the United States (US). After its early success in the US, dark trading soon became popular in Europe as well. While dark trading accounted for only 1 % in 2009, its market share grew rapidly and is currently estimated at around 8 % in the European Union (EU).[16] However, the Tabb Group found in its European Equities Liquidity Matrix Report for January 2020 that *'(...) Dark MTFs[17] executed €4.4bn per day in January, up from €3.6bn in December 2019. This represents 10.4 % of on-venue volume, a record market share of dark MTFs (...)'*.[18]

While the US and the EU shared similar experiences with dark trading, Switzerland went another way. Swiss dark trading is much more centralized and tied to the one major exchange operator, SIX Swiss Exchange. Currently, SIX runs its third generation of dark pool, *SwissatMid*, which is the largest dark pool in the country and commands a market share of 45 %, four times the volume of its closest competitor.[19]

---

12 IOSCO, 'Issues Raised by Dark Liquidity' (n 11) 4 fn 4; IOSCO, 'Principles for Dark Liquidity: Final Report' (FR06/11, May 2011) 11; Ryan J Davies and Erik R Sirri, 'The Economics and Regulation of Secondary Trading Markets' in Merritt B Fox and others (eds), *Securities Market Issues for the 21st Century* (Columbia University 2018) 166; Baisch, Baumann and Weber (n 11) 185; Hochstrasser (n 11) 307.

13 FCA, 'UK Equity Market Dark Pools' (n 6) 6; IOSCO, 'Principles for Dark Liquidity' (n 12) 11.

14 Rhodri Preece, 'Dark Pools, Internalization, and Equity Market Quality' (CFA Institute, October 2012) 1.

15 Valerie Bogard, 'TABB Equity Digest: Q2-2016, TABB Group' (8 December 2016).

16 Petrescu and Wedow (n 5) 22. See also Carole Comerton-Forde, 'Shedding Light on Dark Trading in Europe' (August 2017) 3.

17 'MTF' is short for 'multilateral trading facility' and denotes a regulatory category for alternative trading venues under EU law discussed below in Part II § 6.B.II.2.

18 Tim Cave, 'European Equities Liquidity Matrix January 2020'.

19 SIX Swiss Exchange, 'SwissAtMid: Ihre Liquiditätsquelle für Schweizer Aktien' (Factsheet, 2023). See also Hayley McDowell, 'The Only Game in Town' (The Trade News 6 January 2020).

C. Tightening of Regulatory Scrutiny over Dark Trading

The success of the new form of dark trading in dark pools drew regulatory scrutiny that culminated in regulatory action in the aftermath of the Global Financial Crisis of 2008-09.[20] First, the International Organization of Securities Commissions (IOSCO) examined the phenomenon and suggested five principles for the regulation of dark trading in 2011.[21] Then, the US, the EU, and Switzerland discussed and launched new regulatory frameworks to address an increasing dark market in their respective jurisdictions.[22] While legislators and regulators in those three jurisdictions were determined to formulate and enforce new rules on dark pools, it was, and still is, unclear – in both, regulatory practice and academia – what the proper regulation of dark trading should look like.[23]

D. Effects of Dark Trading

I. Individual Gains

The uncertainty over proper regulation of dark trading is rooted in the ambivalent effects that dark trading may have on traders and the financial market as a whole. By dispensing the need to display trade transparency, dark pools offer advantages for their users which traditional exchanges do not, such as price improvements, protection from information leakage, reduction of market impact costs as well as avoiding interaction with *'harmful traders'* like high frequency traders (HFTs) who use algorithms

---

20 Cf. Recital 1 MiFIR; Moloney, *EU Securities and Financial Markets Regulation* (n 4) 446.

21 IOSCO, 'Issues Raised by Dark Liquidity' (n 11) 4, 24ff; IOSCO, 'Principles for Dark Liquidity' (n 12) 25ff.

22 In the United States: SEC, 'Regulation of Non-Public Trading Interest: Proposed Rules and Amendments to Joint-industry Plans' (17 CFR Part 242, Release No. 34-60997, File No. S7-27-09, 23 November 2009) 74 FR 61208; SEC, 'Regulation of NMS Stock Alternative Trading Systems: Proposed Rule' (17 CFR Parts 240, 242, 249, Release No. 34-76474, File No. S7-23-15, 28 December 2015) 80 FR 80998, 81001ff. In the European Union, MiFID II/MiFIR was implemented, see Moloney, *EU Securities and Financial Markets Regulation* (n 4) 455ff. In Switzerland FinfraG was implemented, see Bundesrat, 'Botschaft zum Finanzmarktinfrastrukturgesetz (FinfraG)' (3 September 2014) BBl. 2014, 7483, 7485.

23 On the advantages and disadvantages of dark trading

to find and use any available price difference for opportunistic trading at the expense of others.[24]

II. Collective Costs

However, more and more trading systems in the market that command an ever-growing number of orders which do not display trade transparency may ultimately jeopardize the concept of transparency as a mainstay of financial market regulation. Erosion of transparency in secondary markets may have adverse effects on fundamental market functions such as price formation as well as fair access to information and to trading opportunities. An increase in the number of trading venues, especially dark pools, can further propel market fragmentation since competition among different trading systems is no longer counter-balanced by transparency which displays trading opportunities on all marketplaces and thereby consolidates a market fragmented among many venues together as one.[25]

Another issue is that providers of dark trading services do not always keep promises to their clients: especially in the US, this led to an array of enforcement measures by both the US Securities and Exchange Commission (SEC) and the Attorney General of New York.[26] In some cases, for ex-

24 IOSCO, 'Principles for Dark Liquidity' (n 12) 11–12. On the advantages of dark trading see also below Part I § 3.D.III.

25 IOSCO, 'Principles for Dark Liquidity' (n 12) 20ff. On the disadvantages of dark trading see below Part I § 3.D.IV.

26 *Pipeline Trading Systems LLC* (2011) Exchange Act Release No. 65609, 102 SEC Docket 1062, 2011 WL 5039038 (SEC); *EBX, LLC* (2012) Exchange Act Release No. 67969, 104 SEC Docket 2844, 2012 WL 4580151 (SEC); *Liquidnet, Inc.* (2014) Exchange Act Release No. 72339, 109 SEC Docket 10, 2014 WL 2547522 (SEC) paras 16–17, 41ff; SEC, *Press Release: SEC Charges New York-Based Dark Pool Operator With Failing to Safeguard Confidential Trading Information* (2014); *UBS Securities LLC* (2015) Exchange Act Release No. 74060, 110 SEC Docket 3471, 2015 WL 179551 (SEC); SEC, *Press Release: SEC Charges UBS Subsidiary With Disclosure Violations and Other Regulatory Failures in Operating Dark Pool* (2015); *ITG Inc.* (2015) Exchange Act Release No. 75672, 112 SEC Docket 887, 2015 WL 4748216 (SEC); SEC, *Press Release: SEC Charges ITG With Operating Secret Trading Desk and Misusing Dark Pool Subscriber Trading Information* (2015); *Barclays Capital Inc.* (2016) Exchange Act Release No. 77001, 113 SEC Docket 1548, 2016 WL 369813 (SEC); SEC, *Press Release: Barclays, Credit Suisse Charged With Dark Pool Violations: Firms Collectively Paying More Than $150 Million to Settle Cases* (2016); *Deutsche Bank Securities Inc.* (2016) Exchange Act Release No. 79576, 115 SEC Docket 4333, 2016 WL 7324405 (SEC); SEC, *Press Release: Deutsche Bank Settles Charges of Misleading Clients About*

ample, the dark pool operators deceived their clients so the clients thought they were protected from HFTs in a respective dark pool while there was plenty of HFT-interaction with their orders.[27] In another instance, dark pool operators exploited their superior knowledge to trade against their customers' orders harming the customers' execution quality.[28] An extensive discussion of such market manipulation and fraud matters, however, would exceed the scope of this study and will therefore only be discussed in aspects where it supports the institutional approach of this study to unveil the conflicts of interest that furthered the fraudulent behavior subject to such enforcement measures.

E. Methodology and Examined Jurisdictions

I. Statutory Interpretation as Means to Define the Scope of Regulation

This study examines the regulatory framework that shapes both transparent and non-transparent trading. Whether a regulatory framework demands transparency or leaves certain aspects of trading in the dark is essentially a matter of the scope of transparency requirements. This in turn is a legal question because, in this context, transparency is created by subjecting market participants to disclosure rules. To assess the scope of individual transparency rules and the scope of exemptions from trade transparency, one must interpret the laws and rules of the respective transparency regime.

Even though this study examines both common and civil law jurisdictions – namely the US, the EU, Germany, and Switzerland – the fundamental methodology for interpreting the law is similar. This is because the common law judges' interpretative powers are limited in a similar manner to civil law judges because the US securities regulation comprises of statuto-

---

Order Router (2016); *Citigroup Global Markets, Inc.* (2018) Exchange Act Release No. 84124, 2018 WL 4382852 (SEC); SEC, *Press Release: SEC Charges Citigroup for Dark Pool Misrepresentations* (2018).

27 SEC, *Press Release: Barclays, Credit Suisse Charged With Dark Pool Violations* (n 26); SEC, *Press Release: SEC Charges UBS Subsidiary With Disclosure Violations and Other Regulatory Failures in Operating Dark Pool* (n 26); see also Kasiske (n 11) 456–7.

28 *Pipeline Trading Systems LLC* (n 26); Sal Arnuk and Joseph Saluzzi, *Broken Markets: How High Frequency Trading and Predatory Practices on Wall Street Are Destroying Investor Confidence and Your Portfolio* (2nd edn, Addison Wesley 2014) 125ff; SEC, 'Shedding Light on Dark Pools: Statement by Commissioner Luis A. Aguilar' (18 November 2015); see also Kasiske (n 11) 456.

ry law complemented by administrative rules. The methodology used can be broken down into the following methods:

II. Statutory Interpretation in Common Law Jurisdictions

Since common law primarily rests on case law, statutory law is considered an exception and only exists where the legislature deemed it necessary to correct a social or economic mischief.[29] From this exceptional character stems the most striking difference to civil law jurisdictions which is the tendency of common law judges to apply a rather literal understanding of a statute's text in order to limit its scope of application.[30]

1. The Literal Rule

Statutory interpretation in common law jurisdictions begins with the 'literal rule' to which all other rules are subordinate. It is the judge's or legal scholar's task to distill the intent of the lawmaker from the written word by examining the language and the statute as a whole.[31]

2. The Golden Rule

While the legal scholar ought to adhere to the grammatical and ordinary sense of the word under the literal rule, the golden rule allows for a deviating interpretation if the literal interpretation would lead to some absurdity, repugnance, or inconsistency with the rest of the instrument. However, to respect the separation of powers between the lawmaker and the judicial branch, lawyers and judges ought not to go farther than to resolve the abovementioned issues.[32]

---

29 Mathias M Siems, *Comparative Law* (3rd edn, Cambridge University Press 2022) 53; Konrad Zweigert and Hein Kötz, *Introduction to Comparative Law* (Tony Weir tr, 3rd edn, Oxford University Press 1998) 265.

30 Siems (n 29) 54; Zweigert and Kötz (n 29) 266.

31 Gerard Carney, 'Comparative Approaches to Statutory Interpretation in Civil Law and Common Law Jurisdictions' (2015) 36(1) Statute Law Review 46, 55; Siems (n 29) 54.

32 Carney (n 31) 55; Siems (n 29) 54.

3. The Mischief Rule

Under the 'mischief rule', the judge will interpret the law with regard to the legal and factual situation that existed when the law was passed and the reason for its initial implementation or later amendment.[33]

While there may be slight differences between common law textualists and purposivists,[34] those three rules of statutory interpretation in common law have their civil law counterparts that operate in a similar manner. Even the strict literal interpretation has been softened for a more contextual and teleological method shifting the weight of the interpretation from a mere literal interpretation towards a more purposive approach asking for the goal of the law.[35]

III. Statutory Interpretation in Civil Law Jurisdictions

In civil law jurisdictions, four methods of statutory interpretation can be distinguished:

1. Language of the Statute

A civil law scholar will begin their interpretation of a statute like a common law colleague by examining the language of the statute. The literal meaning of a term used in a provision informs the legal scholar about the scope of the rule at hand and the possible meaning in and of itself.[36]

2. Genesis of the Statute

The interpretation however goes beyond merely distilling the literal meaning from a legal text and also looks at its genesis. An insightful interpretation of a statute also asks why the rule was adopted in the first place and

33 Carney (n 31) 55; Siems (n 29) 54.

34 See on the discussion: Valerie C Brannon, 'Statutory Interpretation: Theories, Tools, and Trends' (Congressional Research Service, 18 May 2022) 10ff with further references.

35 Siems (n 29) 54; Zweigert and Kötz (n 29) 266–7.

36 Siems (n 29) 53.

what is the legislative history of its adoption, comparable to common law jurisdictions.[37]

3. Context of the Statute

Furthermore, a word or phrase in a provision or even the provision itself does not stand in isolation, but rather must be interpreted in the context of the other rules surrounding it and the (statutory) body of law as a whole. This contextual interpretation also informs about the meaning of the law and allows for a uniform body of law without internal contradictions.[38] In common law jurisdictions, this is regarded as part of the literal rule.

4. Purpose and Extra-Legal Value of the Statute

The fourth rule of statutory interpretation in civil law is to interpret a provision in light of its purpose and extra-legal value. Laws are meant to solve social problems. If a particular interpretation of a word, a phrase, or provision manages to solve an issue, whereas another does not, it is fair to assume that the one solving the issue is the preferable one. This also holds true in less obvious cases in which one interpretation of a word leads to a more socially balanced solution or merely avoids significant harm that another interpretation might cause.[39] This step combines aspects the golden and the mischief rule.

In conclusion, despite the different monikers for their rules, the rules of statutory interpretations are very similar in both common and civil law.

IV. Additional Methods

Both common and civil law jurisdictions complement these classical methods with two additional methods: the economic analysis of law (economic analysis of the law approach) and the comparative analysis of law (comparative law approach).

---

37 ibid 53.
38 ibid 53.
39 ibid 53.

1. Economic Analysis of the Law

The economic analysis of law is a method that uses economic theories (e.g., price theory and game theory) and methods (e.g., statistics and econometrics) to analyze the effects of implicit prices laws attached to behavior.[40]

Adopting an economic perspective to analyze the issue of transparency and dark trading is insightful since economics aims to explain whether a behavior enhances the overall goal of efficiency.[41] Since this study analyzes the regulation of transparency and dark trading on financial markets and the effects of both ways of trading on market efficiency, the economic perspective appears compelling. Economics unveils the incentives which laws have on market participants' behavior by assigning implicit prices to the respective behavior and provides guidance to steer laws to the policy objective of efficiency.[42]

That said, it becomes apparent that the economic analysis of the law feeds the abovementioned methods of legal interpretation in multiple ways: in the context of financial markets regulation, economics plays an important role in interpreting the literal meaning of a term because the terms are generally such that economists use and attach with a certain meaning. Hence, economic studies on the topic of dark trading inform the understanding of the economic terms used in legal texts to regulate the issue (language of the statute).

Moreover, economic research is more extensive than legal research on this topic and often pre-dates the regulations to be examined.[43] Since the legislative and regulatory process has been informed by economic research, the economic terminology partly found access into the legal texts. Thus, an interpretation of the legal language should consider the economic research on this topic and the meaning attached to it in those studies (genesis).

While the economic research has no direct bearing on the contextual interpretation of the law, economic studies inform legal scholars about the policy goals of a certain provision; in this case, it is market efficiency as

---

40 Robert Cooter and Thomas S Ulen, *Law and Economics* (6th edn, Addison-Wesley 2012) 3.

41 ibid 7.

42 ibid 9.

43 For an overview of economic research on the topic, see Peter Gomber and Ilya Gvozdevskiy, 'Dark Trading under MiFID II' in Danny Busch and Guido Ferrarini (eds), *Regulation of the EU Financial Markets: MiFID II and MiFIR* (1st edn, Oxford University Press 2017) paras 14.24ff.

a fundamental goal of economics (purpose and extra-legal value of the statute).

A combination of legal and economic analysis of the issue of dark trading in financial markets is therefore favorable because law illustrates the institutional framework in which dark trading occurs and economics provides an understanding why certain behavior occurs and its consequences on the policy goal of efficiency.[44] The latter again informs legal scholars about the adjustments necessary in the legal texts to achieve a specific policy goal.[45]

2. Comparative Law

In addition to the economic analysis of the law, the comparative law approach is an important method to understand the issue of dark trading. This study will examine the federal securities laws of the United States as the dominant common law jurisdiction in financial markets law. US laws will be compared with the laws of the European Union and Germany, which will serve as a specimen of a member state to the EU as well as an example of a civil law jurisdiction. Furthermore, it represents the largest economy in the EU. Moreover, the laws of the United States and the European Union will be compared to the laws of Switzerland as another civil law jurisdiction that is not an EU-member state.

This choice of jurisdictions is compelling due to the historical appearance of both the phenomenon of dark trading and its subsequent regulation, which began in the United States, then occurred in the European Union and finally made its way to Switzerland. The regulation followed the same path, and each of the subsequent jurisdictions took the preceding jurisdiction's regulations as its blueprint but made significant adaptations. Thus, the comparison allows for an analysis of similarities and differences in the regulatory framework and the reasons for the variations.

44 For the relation between law and finance see Katharina Pistor, 'A Legal Theory of Finance' (Columbia Law School Public Law & Legal Theory Working Paper Group, 9 May 2013) 2–3.

45 Cooter and Ulen (n 40) 9. See also Maureen O'Hara, *Market Microstructure Theory* (Blackwell Publishing 1995) 9: *'(...) What determines the operation of the market is this not its location, but rather the rules by which trades occur. These rules, (...), dictate what can be traded, who can trade, when and how orders can be submitted, who may see or handle the orders, how orders are processed, and how the prices are set. (...) In any case, however, the rules determine how the mechanism works, and thus how the outcome of the trading game is decided.'*

The reason for selecting highly developed economies with thriving financial markets that have well-established market regulations facilitates rather than hinders the comparative research approach because dark trading is most prevalent in highly developed financial markets, whereas it is only a minor issue in less developed financial markets.[46] The level playing field between the economies allows for an undistorted comparison because it avoids comparing 'apples with oranges.'[47]

This is particularly true for the financial markets of the US and EU, which are comparable in size and in their attractiveness for domestic and international investors. The comparison between the regulatory approaches chosen by the US and the EU for regulating dark liquidity may also shed new light on the discussion of whether the EU focusses more on a public-interest regulation, like other civil law jurisdictions; while the US, as a common law jurisdiction, takes a regulatory approach that is rather issue-driven, aiming to protect individual rights and merely correct market-failures, eventually producing a less coherent regulatory framework than the ones observed in continental Europe.[48]

If the assumption made above is correct, we should find a rather extensive regulatory framework in the EU in the sense that it would aim for a rather broad regulatory perimeter to capture all relevant economic activity and would tie regulatory demands to dark trading depending on the risk it poses to the regulatory goals. By contrast, in the US one might expect a leaner regulatory framework that is more permissive unless there is an actual market failure that needs to be corrected.

In this comparison, Switzerland is an important jurisdiction because it is, on the one hand, a civil law country in continental Europe which, according to the hypothesis above, should gravitate towards a public-interest regulation with a rather detailed regulatory apparatus. On the other hand, Switzerland is not a member state to the EU and, thus, can choose to employ different regulatory techniques, for example, such that focus primarily on correcting market failures, like the US is often said to do.

---

46 IOSCO, 'Principles for Dark Liquidity' (n 12) 10–1.

47 Siems (n 29) 18.

48 ibid 53; Anthony I Ogus, 'Comparing Regulatory Systems: Institutions, Processes and Legal Forms in Industrialised Countries' in Paul Cook and others (eds), *Leading Issues in Competition, Regulation and Development* (Edward Elgar 2004) 149; Zweigert and Kötz (n 29) 260.

Comparing Switzerland with the US and the EU is also interesting because it shows whether there is a so-called *'Brussels effect'* on regulating dark trading, which describes a situation in which the EU unilaterally sets high standards adopted by third countries.[49] This may be the case if Switzerland also adopts strict regulations that resembling those found in the EU.

Furthermore, Swiss law has a sound regulatory framework that incorporates a historically developed tradition of self-regulation which rather resembles the regulatory approach by the US, also incorporating elements of self-regulation, whereas the EU rather frowns upon self-regulation.

Although there is a noticeable difference in market size between Switzerland, on the one hand, and the United States and the European Union, on the other hand, Switzerland fits into the comparison because its market is equally developed and well-regulated. While Switzerland is rather a niche market for financial services, its services are sought after by domestic and international investors similar to the large-scale markets in the US and EU. Moreover, Switzerland is particularly interesting because it is a highly centralized market, while the US and EU markets are rather decentralized.

Those structural differences may have a significant impact on the regulatory scrutiny necessary to grapple with the effects of dark trading. This mix of resemblances and difference warrants a thorough comparison.

F. Research Questions

With regard to the examined jurisdictions, the following research questions shall be answered:

The first question to be answered is how to define the concept of trade transparency and dark trading. Moreover, the purpose of trade transparency and dark trading in the context of financial markets must be identified before the backdrop of the regulatory goals of the three examined jurisdictions.

The second question to be answered is what issue can be identified with dark trading that call for regulatory attention.

In a third step, each jurisdiction will be examined for its trading infrastructure regime, the transparency regime, and the access regime. This

49 Anu Bradford, 'The Brussels Effect' (2012) 107(1) Northwestern University Law Review 1, 3ff; Anu Bradford, *The Brussels Effect: How the European Union rules the world* (Oxford University Press 2020) 1ff.

shows where transparent trading is required, and under which circumstances dark trading can occur in each jurisdiction. It will be examined whether allowing for dark trading in a particular instance serves a regulatory purpose or is rather an exploitation of a loophole or regulatory gaps by way of regulatory arbitrage.

In a fourth step, the regulatory regimes will be compared and contrasted to identify differences and similarities. In this comparison, the regulatory responses will be put in context with the respective jurisdiction's structural characteristics and regulatory goals. This way, it shall be identified whether the variations are caused by different problem sets that demanded for different regulatory responses among the jurisdictions or if the problem sets among the jurisdictions are similar and the variation is a sign of a superior regulatory response found by one jurisdiction.

In a final step, the comparison shall be used to identify whether one jurisdiction has found a regulatory regime, or aspects of it, that are superior to all others, in the sense of an *'ideal'* regulatory framework that should serve as a blueprint for others to properly regulate dark trading. If not, it shall be asked if there are common principles of regulation that may serve as a standard for proper regulation of dark trading in a more generalized manner.

§ 2. Trade Transparency, Dark Trading and the Role of Market Infrastructure

A. *Manifestations of Transparency: Transparency about Fundamental Information and Trade Transparency*

While the fundamental distinction between 'lit' and 'dark' trading is the presence or absence of transparency, the concept of transparency itself remains a matter of legal interpretation.[50] In general, transparency can be described as a status of a financial market in which information relevant for the investment decision is fully disclosed to the market and market participants.[51] However, the nature and extent of information shared can vary significantly and needs to be further defined.

---

50 Urs Kägi in Rolf Watter and Rashid Bahar (eds), *Basler Kommentar Finanzmarktaufsichtsgesetz, Finanzmarktinfrastrukturgesetz* (3rd edn, Helbing & Lichtenhahn Verlag 2019) FinfraG Art 28 para 39; Claude Humbel, *Die Regelung der Vor- und Nachhandelstransparenz in der Europäischen Union und der Schweiz* (Ph.D.-Thesis University of Zurich 2019, Schulthess 2019) 7.

51 IOSCO, 'Transparency and Market Fragmentation' (n 3) 3; Laura N Beny, 'U.S. Secondary Stock Markets: A Survey of Current Regulatory and Structural Issues and a Reform Proposal to Enhance Competition' (2002) 2002(2) Columbia Business Law Review 399, 435–4; Nis J Clausen and Karsten E Sørensen, 'Reforming the Regulation of Trading Venues in the EU under the Proposed MiFID II: Levelling the Playing Field and Overcoming Market Fragmentation?' (2012) 9(3) European Company and Financial Law Review 275, 293; Frank Fernholz, *Börse und ihre Alternativen: Eine Transaktionskostensicht* (Josef Eul Verlag 2005) 84; Humbel, *Die Regelung der Vor- und Nachhandelstransparenz in der Europäischen Union und der Schweiz* (n 50) 7; Markus Lenenbach, *Kapitalmarktrecht und kapitalmarktrelevantes Gesellschaftsrecht* (2nd edn, RWS-Verlag 2010) para 3.157; Ananth Madhavan, 'Market Microstructure: A Survey' (2000) 3 Journal of Financial Markets 205, 207; Christoph Kumpan, 'Transparenz als Mittel der Kapitalmarktregulierung: Die neuen Transparenzvorschriften der Richtlinie über Märkte für Finanzinstrumente' [2006] WM 797, 798; Bernd Rudolph and Heiner Röhrl, 'Grundfragen der Börsenorganisation aus ökonomischer Sicht' in K. Hopt, B. Rudolph and H. Baum (eds), *Börsenreform: Eine ökonomische, rechtsvergleichende und rechtspolitische Untersuchung* (Schäffer-Poeschel 1997) 183–4; Dieter Zobl and Stefan Kramer, *Schweizerisches Kapitalmarktrecht* (Schulthess 2004) para 61.

I. Fundamental Information about the Issuer

With respect to financial markets, transparency information can be distinguished according to the sources of the information. On the one hand, there is transparency about fundamental information, which is also called material or background information. It provides information about exogenous factors of market valuation.[52] Fundamental information is about the issuer of a financial instrument on topics that influence the expectation of its current and future cashflows which enter the computation of the net present value of the respective financial instrument.[53] Thus, fundamental information informs the market and the investing public about the characteristics and quality of both the issuer and its financial instrument.[54]

II. Technical Information about the Market

On the other hand, there is trade transparency, sometimes referred to as market transparency, which is created by disclosure of endogenous market information about the process of trading itself.[55] As *O'Hara* described it: *'Market transparency refers to the ability of market participants to observe the information in the trading process.'*[56] The information provided by trade transparency is crucial to determine the supply and demand and thus the

52 Kägi (n 50) BSK FinfraG Art 29 para 4; Fernholz (n 51) 84–5.; Humbel, *Die Regelung der Vor- und Nachhandelstransparenz in der Europäischen Union und der Schweiz* (n 50) 8.

53 Lars Klöhn in Heribert Hirte and Thomas M J Möllers (eds), *Kölner Kommentar zum WpHG* (2nd edn, Carl Heymanns Verlag 2014) WpHG § 13 paras 150ff; Lars Klöhn in Lars Klöhn (ed), *Marktmissbrauchsverordnung: Verordnung (EU) Nr. 596/2014 über Marktmissbrauch* (1st edn, CH Beck 2018) MAR Art 7 paras 160ff; Merritt B Fox, 'MiFID II and Equity Trading: A US View' in Danny Busch and Guido Ferrarini (eds), *Regulation of the EU Financial Markets: MiFID II and MiFIR* (1st edn, Oxford University Press 2017) para 18.12. See also Kägi (n 50) BSK FinfraG Art 29 paras 4, 7; Fernholz (n 51) 84–5; Humbel, *Die Regelung der Vor- und Nachhandelstransparenz in der Europäischen Union und der Schweiz* (n 50) 8.

54 Kägi (n 50) BSK FinfraG Art 29 para 7.

55 ibid BSK FinfraG Art 29 para 4; Fernholz (n 51) 84; Rudolph and Röhrl (n 51) 204.

56 O'Hara, *Market Microstructure Theory* (n 45) 252.

market price for a financial instrument.[57] It enables trading, and thus, the information provided is also called technical or functional information.[58]

B. Relevance of Market Information Compared to Fundamental Information

The following chapters will focus solely on technical market information disclosed via trade transparency, because it is the difference between lit trading, where trade transparency is present, and dark trading, where it is absent.

In legal scholarship, however, the focus rather rests on transparency rules concerned with fundamental information, for example, the issuer's obligation to disclose information in a prospectus when issuing financial instruments or the obligations to make periodic and ad hoc disclosures.[59]

This focus of legal scholarship on fundamental information[60] implicitly follows the assumption of neo-classical economics that draws from the *Efficient Capital Market Hypothesis (ECMH)* by *Eugene Fama.*[61] In very general terms, the ECMH states that having all fundamental information in the market is sufficient to reach a market price that is equal to the fair value of the traded instrument.[62]

---

57 Ansgar Schott and Peter Sester, 'Organisation und Betrieb einzelner Finanzmarktinfrastrukturen' in Peter Sester and others (eds), *St. Galler Handbuch zum Schweizer Finanzmarktrecht: Finanzmarktaufsicht und Finanzmarktinfrastrukturen* (1st edn, Dike 2017) § 22 paras 97–8; IOSCO, 'Principles for Dark Liquidity' (n 12) 20.

58 Kägi (n 50) BSK FinfraG Art 29 para 4; Fernholz (n 51) 84–5; Humbel, *Die Regelung der Vor- und Nachhandelstransparenz in der Europäischen Union und der Schweiz* (n 50) 8.

59 Cf. Heinz-Dieter Assmann and Petra Buck-Heeb, 'Kapitalanlagerecht im Regelungsgefüge des Kapitalmarkt- und Finanzmarktrechts' in Heinz-Dieter Assmann, Rolf A Schütze and Petra Buck-Heeb (eds), *Handbuch des Kapitalanlagerechts* (5th edn, CH Beck 2020) § 1 para 95; Kägi (n 50) BSK FinfraG Art 29 para 7.

60 Cf. Kägi (n 50) BSK FinfraG Art 29 para 7.

61 The *ECMH* is discussed in further detail below in Part I § 3.A.I.1.a).

62 Eugene F Fama, 'Efficient Capital Markets: A Review of Theory and Empirical Work' (1970) 25(2) The Journal of Finance 383ff; Eugene F Fama, 'The Behavior of Stock-Market Prices' (1965) 38(1) The Journal of Business 34ff; Eugene F Fama, 'Efficient Capital Markets: Reply' (1976) 31(1) The Journal of Finance 143ff; Eugene F Fama, 'Efficient Capital Markets: II' (1991) 46(5) The Journal of Finance 1575ff; Eugene F Fama and others, 'The Adjustment of Stock Prices to New Information' (1969) 10(1) International Economic Review 1ff; Eugene F Fama and Arthur B Laffer, 'Information and Capital Markets' (1971) 44(3) The Journal of Business 289ff. See also John Armour and others, *Principles of Financial Regulation* (1st edn, Oxford University

Despite the undisputed importance of fundamental information for price discovery, even the ECMH acknowledges the importance of trade transparency since having a displayed price that becomes the agreed upon price for every transaction in a marketplace protects those traders who are uninformed about the latest fundamental information from being taken advantage of by traders in possession of such information.[63] This builds on *Hayek's* insight that one important function of displayed market prices is to carry and communicate information.[64]

The importance of trade transparency, however, even goes beyond that understanding. Even if fundamental information was equally distributed among all market participants, it is very unlikely that individual market participants would understand and interpret it in the same manner. Transparency about fundamental information provides merely the raw data about the financial situation of an issuer. Fundamental information does not explicitly tell the recipients about the future cashflows or the net present value of the financial instrument, nor does it tell them whether to sell, buy, or hold.[65]

Instead, the exogenous information must be interpreted by the recipients. This interpretation involves knowledge, skill, and a certain amount of (educated) guesswork, because market participants not only factor objective facts in the processing of financial information, but also their subjective expectations about the future.[66] These expectations are always implicitly contained in their investment decisions revealed to others only by trade transparency displaying market information when they trade upon new

Press 2016) 104; Ronald J Gilson and Reinier H Kraakman, 'The Mechanisms of Market Efficiency' (1984) 70 Virginia Law Review 549, 555–6.

63 Jacek Bak and Jochen Bigus, 'Kapitalmarkteffizienz versus zwingender Anlegerschutz im Aktienrecht' (2006) 18(6) ZBB 430, 431.

64 Friedrich A Hayek, 'The Use of Knowledge in Society' (1945) 35 The American Economic Review 519; Esteban F Thomsen, *Prices and Knowledge: A Market-Process Perspective* (Routledge 1992) 16, 29ff. See also Milan Bayram, *Manipulative Handelspraktiken gem. Art. 12 MAR* (Ph.D.-Thesis University of Erlangen-Nuremberg 2019, Duncker & Humblot 2020) 17; Holger Fleischer, *Informationsasymmetrie im Vertragsrecht: Eine rechtsvergleichende und interdisziplinäre Abhandlung zu Reichweite und Grenzen vertragsschlussbezogener Aufklärungspflichten* (Habilitation-Thesis University of Cologne 1999, CH Beck 2001) 91ff.

65 Cf. Bak and Bigus (n 63) 431. See also Klaus J Hopt, *Der Kapitalanlegerschutz im Recht der Banken: Gesellschafts-, bank- und börsenrechtliche Anforderungen an das Beratungs- und Verwaltungsverhalten der Kreditinstitute* (Habilitation-Thesis University of Munich 1973, CH Beck 1975) 89.

66 Gilson and Kraakman (n 62) 561–2.

fundamental data. Furthermore, when market participants trade, they create another source of information, i.e., information about current demand in a financial instrument.

Therefore, focusing on trade transparency is crucial to understand how fundamental information is processed and understood in the market as well as how additional information is sampled into the cocktail of fundamental information moving the price away from or closer to its calculated net present value. Thus, while fundamental information is always fueling the transparency process, market information may enhance or alter the way it is perceived.

C. Classification of Trade Transparency

Knowing about the importance of trade transparency for the market as the distinguishing feature between lit and dark trading, several clarifications are necessary: what information can be observed through trade transparency, what purpose does such information serves, how detailed and recent should it be, and who may be able to observe the information.[67] To answer these questions it is necessary to divide trade transparency into such pieces of information provided before a transaction occurs, i.e., pre-trade transparency, and such pieces of information provided after a transaction has taken place, i.e., post-trade transparency.[68]

67 O'Hara, *Market Microstructure Theory* (n 45) 252.

68 Kägi (n 50) BSK FinfraG Art 29 para 5; Fernholz (n 51) 84ff; Thierry Foucault, Marco Pagano and Ailsa Röell, *Market Liquidity: Theory, Evidence, and Policy* (Oxford University Press 2013) 279; Lars Klöhn, '§ 6 Kapitalmarktrecht' in Katja Langenbucher (ed), *Europäisches Privat- und Wirtschaftsrecht* (5th edn, Nomos 2022) § 6 para 55; Rudolph and Röhrl (n 51) 193, 208ff; Christian Vollmuth and Julius Seifert, 'Handelstransparenz differenziert nach Marktform: geregelte Märkte, multilaterale Handelssysteme, systematische Internalisierer' in Peter Clouth and Volker Lang (eds), *MiFID Praktikerhandbuch: Neue Verhaltenspflichten für Banken und Sparkassen durch Gesetzgeber und Bankenaufsicht* (Bank-Verlag Medien 2007) 371 para 856; Julius Seiffert and Laura A Lembke, 'Handelstransparenz' in Jürgen Ellenberger and Peter Clouth (eds), *Praktikerhandbuch Wertpapier- und Derivategeschäft* (5th edn, Finanz Colloquium Heidelberg 2018) para 2368.

I. Pre-Trade Transparency

When a trader sends an order into a market place, pre-trade transparency informs others whether this order is a sell or a buy order and about the price and volume of the order.[69] It informs traders about trading opportunities available in a trading system by showing unfilled orders in a specific financial instrument, the order's price and volume.[70] On the other hand, sellers who submit orders to a trading system that shows pre-trade transparency can attract interested buyers or, in the case of a buy order, sellers can be attracted.[71] In addition, pre-trade transparency information tells traders whether there currently is an imbalance of supply and demand in the market, from which traders can infer whether there is new fundamental data that they are yet unaware of.[72]

Pre-trade and post-trade transparency are crucial for the functioning of a trading system as well as for modern financial markets comprising of multiple trading systems operating in juxtaposition.[73] Pre-trade transparency

69 Klöhn, '§ 6 Kapitalmarktrecht' (n 68) § 6 para 55; Moloney, 'EU Financial Governance and Transparency Regulation' (n 3) para 12.10.

70 Bundesrat, 'Botschaft zum Finanzmarktinfrastrukturgesetz (FinfraG)' (n 22) BBl. 2014, 7532; for the EU see: Recital 44 MiFID I; Recital 1 MiFIR; Tanja Bošković, Caroline Cerruti and Michel Noël, 'Comparing European and U.S. Securities Regulations: MiFID versus Corresponding U.S. Regulations' (World Bank Working Paper No. 184, The World Bank, Washington, D.C., 2009) 24; Moloney, 'EU Financial Governance and Transparency Regulation' (n 3) para 12.10; Klöhn, '§ 6 Kapitalmarktrecht' (n 68) § 6 para 54; Ansgar Schott and Markus Winkler in Rolf Sethe and others (eds), *Kommentar zum Finanzmarktinfrastrukturgesetz FinfraG* (SK FinfraG, 1st edn, Schulthess 2017) Art 29 paras 8, 14ff.

71 IOSCO, 'Transparency and Market Fragmentation' (n 3) 3; Foucault, Pagano and Röell (n 68) 280ff; Pierre Francotte, Diego Valiante and Karel Lannoo, *MiFID 2.0 - Casting New Light on Europe's Capital Markets: Report of the ECMI-CEPS Task Force on the MiFID Review* (Centre for European Policy Studies (CEPS) 2011) 44; Kumpan, 'Transparenz als Mittel der Kapitalmarktregulierung' (n 51) 798; Lenenbach (n 51) para 3.157; Rudolph and Röhrl (n 51) 204ff; Seiffert and Lembke (n 68) para 2369.

72 Kägi (n 50) BSK FinfraG Art 29 para 5; Clausen and Sørensen (n 51) 293; Foucault, Pagano and Röell (n 68) 280, 284ff; Humbel, *Die Regelung der Vor- und Nachhandelstransparenz in der Europäischen Union und der Schweiz* (n 50) 35; Kumpan, 'Transparenz als Mittel der Kapitalmarktregulierung' (n 51) 798; Polly Nyquist, 'Failure to Engage: The Regulation of Proprietary Trading Systems' (1995) 13 Yale Law & Policy Review 281, 285; Vollmuth and Seifert (n 68) paras 855–7.

73 IOSCO, 'Transparency and Market Fragmentation' (n 3) 2; Jan Liersch, 'Nachteile für den Finanzplatz durch außerbörslicher Wertpapiergeschäfte' [2003] WM 473, 475; Moloney, 'EU Financial Governance and Transparency Regulation' (n 3) para 12.10; Vollmuth and Seifert (n 68) para 855. See also SEC, 'Regulation NMS: Proposed rules

allows traders to compare prices and volumes, i.e., market depth, in different trading systems.[74] Thereby, traders can overcome market fragmentation that may arise when more than one trading system exists in a market.[75] In this regard, pre-trade transparency is crucial to reduce transaction costs for traders.[76]

However, the extent to which those purposes are achieved depends on the amount of detail and the recency of the information provided by pre-trade transparency. The degree of detail depends on two factors: First, on the kind of trading system a trader uses, and second, on the kind of order submitted.

1. Trading System: Order-Driven or Quote Driven Trading Systems

The price for a financial instrument can be derived in different ways: the simplest of them is a bilateral negotiation between a buyer and a seller. While this price might represent the fair value of the financial instrument, it is more likely that there may be other aspects that determined the transaction price.[77]

The transaction price is more informative with respect to the actual market price if there are several buyers and sellers pooled in one market competing for transaction.[78] Trading systems can choose whether they run

and amendments to joint industry plans' (17 CFR Parts 200, 230, 240, 242, and 249, Release No. 34-49325, File No. S7-10-04, 9 March 2004) 69 FR 11126; Section 11A(a)(1)(D) Exchange Act (15 U.S.C. 78k-1(a)(1)(D)).

74 Seiffert and Lembke (n 68) para 2369.

75 IOSCO, 'Transparency and Market Fragmentation' (n 3) 2; Moloney, 'EU Financial Governance and Transparency Regulation' (n 3) para 12.10; Vollmuth and Seifert (n 68) para 857.

76 IOSCO, 'Transparency and Market Fragmentation' (n 3) 3ff. See also Francotte, Valiante and Lannoo (n 71) 44; Humbel, *Die Regelung der Vor- und Nachhandelstransparenz in der Europäischen Union und der Schweiz* (n 50) 34–5; Kumpan, 'Transparenz als Mittel der Kapitalmarktregulierung' (n 51) 798; Klöhn, '§ 6 Kapitalmarktrecht' (n 68) § 6 para 54; Lenenbach (n 51) para 3.157; Rudolph and Röhrl (n 51) 204ff; Vollmuth and Seifert (n 68) para 855.

77 Arnold Picot, Christine Bortenlänger and Heiner Röhrl, *Börsen im Wandel: Der Einfluß von Informationstechnologie und Wettbewerb auf die Organisation von Wertpapiermärkten* (Knapp 1996) 55.

78 ibid 56.

an order-driven or a quote-driven market or a hybrid-system combining elements of both systems.[79]

a) Order-Driven Trading Systems

In an order-driven trading system, traders directly compete for transaction with each other.[80] They submit their orders to a central order book, which is a ledger containing all currently unfilled orders waiting for execution. The order matching can either occur by means of a periodic auction call or a continuous call.[81]

aa) Periodic Auction Call

In a periodic auction call, the trading venue collects several buy- and sell-orders for a certain period of time before it matches the order batch. For matching, the trading system selects a price at which most orders can be executed.[82] A periodic auction call system is often used in illiquid financial instruments to concentrate order flow over time and to allow for a price discovery closer to the fair value.[83] However, periodic auction call systems are also beneficial for financial instruments trading in a liquid but

---

79 Cf. Klöhn, '§ 6 Kapitalmarktrecht' (n 68) § 6 para 52 summarizing the regulatory options under EU law according to Art 2 (CDR) Commission Delegated Regulation (EU) 2017/566 of 18 May 2016: '*Trading venues shall calculate the ratio of unexecuted orders to transactions effectively entered into the system by each of their members and participants for every financial instrument traded under an electronic continuous auction order book or a quote-driven or a hybrid trading system.*'

80 Picot, Bortenlänger and Röhrl (n 77) 56; Rudolph and Röhrl (n 51) 208; Seiffert and Lembke (n 68) para 2369; Vollmuth and Seifert (n 68) para 857.

81 Picot, Bortenlänger and Röhrl (n 77) 56; Rudolph and Röhrl (n 51) 211; Moloney, *EU Securities and Financial Markets Regulation* (n 4) 427; Peter von Hall, 'Vorhandelstransparenzpflichten für Systematische Internalisierer' [2015] GesKR 497, 499. See also Larry Harris, *Trading and exchanges: Market microstructure for practitioners* (Oxford University Press 2003) 92.

82 FCA, 'Periodic Auctions: With MiFID II Altering the Landscape of Equity Markets, We Take a Look at this Emerging Trading Format – With the Help of Data' (25 June 2018); Hall (n 81) 499; Picot, Bortenlänger and Röhrl (n 77) 56; Rudolph and Röhrl (n 51) 211.

83 Picot, Bortenlänger and Röhrl (n 77) 57.

volatile market or where large order sizes are traded, since the aggregation of several orders avoids erratic price movements.[84]

bb) Continuous Call

Trading systems that use a continuous call mechanism match orders on a price-time-priority-basis: once there are two or more best-priced orders that correspond with each other, the trading system will match them immediately, regardless of a better priced order coming into the market momentarily after the first one.[85] This system is most commonly used for highly liquid markets since it allows for a high degree of immediacy, however, it also invites more volatility into the market.[86]

cc) Hybrid Systems

While periodic auction call mechanisms and continuous call mechanisms are archetypical, a combination of both systems is common. Often in predefined periods at the beginning, the middle and the end of the trading day as well as in times of low liquidity, auctions are held to aggregate liquidity, whereas, for the remainder of the trading day, continuous calls are used.[87]

dd) Order Type: Market or Limit Order

In all three forms of order-driven trading systems, traders must place their orders before the transaction price is determined. To allow traders to either influence their transaction price or their transaction probability, they can choose between two order types: market or limit orders.

A market order is an executable order that only shows which instrument shall be traded and at which volume. For the transaction price, the trader

84 ibid 57.

85 Hall (n 81) 499; Picot, Bortenlänger and Röhrl (n 77) 57; Rudolph and Röhrl (n 51) 211.

86 Picot, Bortenlänger and Röhrl (n 77) 57.

87 See for instance the trading periods on SIX Swiss Exchange: SIX Swiss Exchange, 'Directive 3: Trading' (10 March 2021) 5, 9ff.

is willing to accept whatever price results from the interplay of supply and demand in the order book.[88]

With limit orders, traders can determine the price at which they are willing to trade, however, at the expense that a transaction will not occur if the price is outside of their preferred price range.[89]

There are also hybrid forms and special order types that traders can submit. Nevertheless, the choice between market and limit orders illustrates the basic trade-off between execution certainty at the cost of price certainty and vice versa a trader faces when placing an order in an order-driven system.[90]

ee) Ambiguity of the Visibility of Depth of Order Book

When several orders on both the buy- and the sell-side enter the order book over the course of the trading day, the degree of pre-trade transparency also depends on the visibility of the depth of the order book. If the trading system only shows the best buy-order and the best sell-order, it shows minimal pre-trade transparency since those orders often have small volumes. Larger orders cannot be placed with certainty that there is sufficient liquidity in the market to achieve an attractive transaction price.[91] A trading venue offers maximum transparency if the entire order book is visible to traders, even the worst priced orders.[92] This, however, exposes worse priced orders, which are often larger-sized orders, to opportunistic behavior by other traders, and may therefore incentivize those block traders to withdraw their liquidity from the market altogether.[93] Thus, it is common to provide

---

88 Merritt B Fox, Lawrence R Glosten and Gabriel V Rauterberg, 'The New Stock Market: Sense and Nonsense' (2015) 65(2) Duke Law Journal 191, 208; Harris (n 81) 73; Petrescu and Wedow (n 5) 16.

89 Fox, Glosten and Rauterberg, 'The New Stock Market' (n 88) 208–9; Harris (n 81) 73; Petrescu and Wedow (n 5) 16.

90 See for further detail on special order types: Martin Monsch, *Hochfrequenzhandel: Eine rechtsökonomische Analyse des Phänomens sowie eine rechtsdogmatische Betrachtung des schweizerischen Aufsichtsrechts unter funktionaler Berücksichtigung des europäischen Rechts* (Ph.D.-Thesis University of Zurich 2018, Schulthess 2018) 38–9.

91 Rudolph and Röhrl (n 51) 208.

92 ibid 208.

93 ibid 208.

pre-trade transparency for some initial best-priced buy- and sell-orders in the order book, usually the top five buy- and sell-orders.[94]

ff) Impact of Order-Driven Systems on Pre-Trade Transparency

Thus, pre-trade transparency in an order-driven system depends on the type of trading system, visibility of the depth of the order book, and the order type. Often pre-trade transparency can only inform about the volume and the price preferences specified in limit orders, but not the ultimate transaction price, which is only available after the matching.[95] While this lack of certainty falls short of the goal of maximum pre-trade transparency, it benefits traders because their orders are less likely to be taken advantage of prior to matching. This problem is more prevalent with quote-driven systems.

b) Quote-Driven Trading Systems

In contrast to order-driven trading systems, quote-driven systems depend on market makers who are special market participants continuously offering quotes for buying and selling financial instruments.[96] Quote-driven markets therefore have no auction, but sellers and buyers can sell immediately to or buy from a market maker who is the counterparty to every transaction (for a specific instrument). Quote-driven systems are more common in markets with low levels of liquidity.[97]

As professional liquidity suppliers, market makers set the bid-price for buying an instrument below and ask-prices for selling an instrument above

94 See under EU law: Art 3(1) and Table 1 Annex I of Delegated Regulation 2017/587; Martin Gebauer in Heinz-Dieter Assmann, Uwe H Schneider and Peter O Mülbert (eds), *Wertpapierhandelsrecht: Kommentar* (7th edn, Otto Schmidt 2019) MiFIR Art 3 para 24; see under Swiss law: Art 27(2) FinfraV; Schott and Winkler (n 70) SK FinfraG Art 29 para 27.

95 Rudolph and Röhrl (n 51) 208.

96 Jens Ekkenga, '§ 7. Wertpapierhandel' in Carsten P Claussen and Roland Erne (eds), *Bank- und Kapitalmarktrecht* (6th edn, CH Beck 2023) § 7 para 140c. See also under German law Section 2(8) No. 2 lit a of the German Securities Trading Act (*Wertpapierhandelsgesetz*).

97 Moloney, *EU Securities and Financial Markets Regulation* (n 4) 427; Picot, Bortenlänger and Röhrl (n 77) 58–9; Rudolph and Röhrl (n 51) 208–9, 211. Cf. Seiffert and Lembke (n 68) para 2369; Vollmuth and Seifert (n 68) para 857.

the current market price in order to earn a profit.[98] When market makers anticipate that their estimate of the current market price is inaccurate, because a trader is constantly buying from them, even though the price is higher than the current market price, they widen their bid-ask-spread to insure themselves against adverse selection risk, i.e., the risk of being taken advantage of.[99]

c) Hybrid Trading Systems

There are also systems that use a combination of both order-driven and quote-driven systems where traders can interact with each other and, especially in periods with low liquidity levels, with a market maker.[100]

2. Time of Disclosure

The degree of pre-trade transparency also depends on the time of disclosure. A trading system can either immediately disclose the information about placed orders or delay that information for a certain period of time. The longer it takes until the information is disclosed to other potential traders, the less useful it becomes, because the price preference of the order may be stale or other traders may have chosen another trading venue instead.[101]

---

98 Fox, 'MiFID II and Equity Trading' (n 53) para 18.07; Merritt B Fox, Lawrence R Glosten and Gabriel V Rauterberg, *The New Stock Market: Law, Economics, and Policy* (Columbia University Press 2019) 64–5; Merritt B Fox, Lawrence R Glosten and Gabriel V Rauterberg, 'Stock Market Manipulation and Its Regulation' (2018) 35 Yale Journal on Regulation 67, 90; Harris (n 81) 158.

99 Fox, 'MiFID II and Equity Trading' (n 53) paras 18.13ff; Fox, Glosten and Rauterberg, 'Stock Market Manipulation and Its Regulation' (n 98) 91–2; Merritt B Fox, Lawrence R Glosten and Gabriel V Rauterberg, 'Informed Trading and Its Regulation' (2018) 43(4) The Journal of Corporation Law 817, 846. For further details on adverse selection see: George A Akerlof, 'The Market for "Lemons": Quality Uncertainty and the Market Mechanism' (1970) 84(3) The Quarterly Journal of Economics 488; Fox, Glosten and Rauterberg, *The New Stock Market* (n 98) 65–6.

100 Moloney, *EU Securities and Financial Markets Regulation* (n 4) 427; Picot, Bortenlänger and Röhrl (n 77) 59.

101 Cf. Recital 14 MiFIR.

3. Recipient of Disclosure

Additionally, the circle of eligible recipients determines the degree of pre-trade transparency in a trading system. The trading system can choose not to disclose this information at all, disclose it to only a few traders, or disclose it to the entire trading public (unless the applicable law requires otherwise). The legal requirements for determining the recipients of the disclosure are discussed in the subsequent chapters.[102]

II. Post-Trade Transparency

1. Disclosed Information and Purpose of Disclosure

'Post-trade transparency is the dissemination of the information about trades to the public after the trade has occurred.'[103] In general, under post-trade transparency the price and volume of the executed transactions are provided, and, depending on the legal requirements or self-regulatory rules, post-trade transparency information also encompasses the time of the transaction and the trading system.[104] It informs the parties of the transaction about the specifics of the concluded transaction and allows them to monitor the execution quality.[105] This is especially important for investors who depend on intermediaries for trading since it reduces the principle-agent-conflict inherent in such situations.[106]

Moreover, post-trade transparency serves an integral purpose in price discovery, price accuracy, and overall market efficiency.[107] By informing the market and the investing public about prices at which traders were

102 Cf. Art 1(1)(a) MiFIR. See Part II below.

103 IOSCO, 'Principles for Dark Liquidity' (n 12) 28; see also Bošković, Cerruti and Noël (n 70) 24; Humbel, *Die Regelung der Vor- und Nachhandelstransparenz in der Europäischen Union und der Schweiz* (n 50) 14; Klöhn, '§ 6 Kapitalmarktrecht' (n 68) § 6 para 55; Madhavan (n 51) 240; Seiffert and Lembke (n 68) para 2371.

104 Gebauer (n 94) MiFIR Art 6 para 1; Kägi (n 50) BSK FinfraG Art 29 para 36; Schott and Winkler (n 70) SK FinfraG Art 29 para 48; different under US law, where Rule 600(b)(14) Regulation NMS (17 CFR § 242.600(b)(14)) only requires to display price, volume and market identifier; cf. Humbel, *Die Regelung der Vor- und Nachhandelstransparenz in der Europäischen Union und der Schweiz* (n 50) 14, fn 37.

105 Schott and Winkler (n 70) SK FinfraG Art 29 para 8.

106 Kägi (n 50) BSK FinfraG Art 29 para 5; Fernholz (n 51) 86; Rudolph and Röhrl (n 51) 205.

107 IOSCO, 'Principles for Dark Liquidity' (n 12) 28.

able to match orders, post-trade transparency is a valuable and reliable source for the price discovery process and, thus, caters to the pre-trade transparency information of future orders and transactions of others.[108] It also reduces information asymmetry among traders and mitigates of the adverse effects of market fragmentation by revealing which market offers the best transaction prices and conditions.[109]

In fragmentated markets, post-trade transparency unveils execution prices on other trading systems which allows for a consolidation of price relevant information and a convergence of the market price across all venues.[110]

2. Time and Granularity of Disclosure

While the quality of pre-trade information is also important, trading systems often provide it in a sufficient manner since it is in their interest to attract traders paying fees for their service to their trading venue. Unfortunately, the interests of the market and the trading systems are not always aligned with regard to post-trade transparency as with pre-trade transparency.[111] While trading systems prefer to either keep their post-trade information undisclosed or reveal it at a later time, often as multiple transactions batched together in indiscernible packages,[112] market efficiency generally benefits from timely publication of data on a trade-by-trade basis.[113] The degree of post-trade transparency is certainly enhanced when post-trade information is provided as close to real-time as possible and on a trade-by-trade basis.[114]

3. Recipient of Disclosure

The circle of eligible recipients of post-trade transparency information also depends on the choice of the trading system within the boundaries set by

108 Kägi (n 50) BSK FinfraG Art 29 para 5; Fernholz (n 51) 86ff.
109 IOSCO, 'Principles for Dark Liquidity' (n 12) 28.
110 Klöhn, '§ 6 Kapitalmarktrecht' (n 68) § 6 para 54; Moloney, 'EU Financial Governance and Transparency Regulation' (n 3) para 12.10.
111 Madhavan (n 51) 240–1.
112 IOSCO, 'Principles for Dark Liquidity' (n 12) 21; Madhavan (n 51) 240–1.
113 IOSCO, 'Principles for Dark Liquidity' (n 12) 21.
114 Recitals 13, 14 MiFIR.

the applicable law that is examined in the subsequent chapters, as is the case with pre-trade transparency. In contrast to pre-trade transparency, the collection of post-trade transparency data in a central data service, also called a *consolidated tape*, is considered crucial by IOSCO to ensure wide dissemination of post-trade information.[115]

D. Addressees of Trade Transparency Requirements

I. Central Role of Trading Systems

Transparency is not a natural characteristic of financial markets. Instead, financial markets are by default dark, non-transparent markets. To create transparency about fundamental data, for instance, financial markets regulations require the issuer (as the originator) as well as the offerors of the financial instrument to publish information about the financial instrument in a prospectus.[116]

For trade transparency a parallel choice would be to require the trader to publish trade transparency information, but this would greatly burden financial market actors who are as heterogenous as retail investors and investment banks. To avoid this, regulators centralized the task and require the operator of the trading system to publish trade transparency information.[117]

Therefore, publication of trade transparency data is required from trading systems such as exchanges, alternative trading systems, as well as large market participants which trade so intensively that they create a market-like environment. Such intermediaries are, for example, investment banks

115 IOSCO, 'Principles for Dark Liquidity' (n 12) 28.

116 Cf. Armour and others (n 62) 163ff; James D Cox and others, *Securities Regulation: Cases and Materials* (8th edn, Wolters Kluwer 2017) 134ff; Anna Heidelbach in Eberhard Schwark and Daniel Zimmer (eds), *Kapitalmarktrechts-Kommentar: Börsengesetz mit Börsenzulassungsverordnung, Wertpapierprospektgesetz, Wertpapierhandelsgesetz, Wertpapiererwerbs- und Übernahmegesetz, Europäische Marktmissbrauchsverordnung* (5th edn, CH Beck 2020) WpPG § 8 paras 5ff; Alexander Vogel, Christoph Heiz and Reto Luthiger, *OFK FIDLEG/FINIG Kommentar: Bundesgesetz über die Finanzdienstleistungen und Bundesgesetz über die Finanzinstitute* (Orell Füssli Kommentar (OFK), 1st edn, Orell Füssli Verlag 2020) FIDLEG Art 35 para 8.

117 Cf. US law: Rules 602, 604 Regulation NMS (17 CFR §§ 242.602 and 242.604); EU law: Art 3ff MiFIR; Swiss law: Art 29 FinfraG.

that internalize large amounts of order flow against their own book by trading against their proprietary capital.[118] Apart from such internalizing investment banks, trading activity occurring outside trading systems, i.e., over-the-counter-trading (OTC-trading), therefore remains (unregulated) dark trading, because no pre-trade transparency is displayed.[119]

II. Categorization of Trading Systems

To capture trading systems as addressees of trade transparency rules, the law needs to find generalized categories to distinguish the pluralism of market providers. This is why the following examination of the three jurisdictions also focuses on the trading infrastructure. For categorization purposes, all three jurisdictions follow a categorization similar to the following:

1. Trading Systems and Information Systems

First, *'trading systems'* must be distinguished from mere *'information systems'*, often called *'bulletin boards'*.[120]

a) Information Systems

An information system or bulletin board is a set of rules that merely allows for the communication of buy and sell interests, whereas the contract formation appears outside of the rules provided by the operator of the system.[121] Thus, an information system can range from a passive system which only allows the posting of buy and sell interests, where interested parties can only inform themselves but have to find the trading partner on

118 Kumpan, *Die Regulierung außerbörslicher Wertpapierhandelssysteme im deutschen, europäischen und US-amerikanischen Recht* (n 8) 18–9; Paul Mahoney and Gabriel Rauterberg, 'The Regulation of Trading Markets' in Merritt B Fox and others (eds), *Securities Market Issues for the 21st Century* (Columbia University 2018) 228–9.

119 Cf. Recital 10 MiFIR; Moloney, *EU Securities and Financial Markets Regulation* (n 4) 461.

120 Recital 8(2) MiFIR; Kumpan, *Die Regulierung außerbörslicher Wertpapierhandelssysteme im deutschen, europäischen und US-amerikanischen Recht* (n 8) 19.

121 Recital 8(2) MiFIR; Kumpan, *Die Regulierung außerbörslicher Wertpapierhandelssysteme im deutschen, europäischen und US-amerikanischen Recht* (n 8) 19.

their own,[122] to partially active, in which the operator provides the contact data of the buyers and sellers,[123] to an active information system, in which the operator provides a (virtual) room in which a buyer can negotiate with a seller about a trade, but the operator neither provides rules for this negotiation nor does it provide any additional matching infrastructure.[124]

b) Trading Systems

A trading system is a set of rules that allows the interaction between buyer and seller of a financial instrument in a way that it can result in a sales contract of the financial instrument, i.e., a trade.[125] In contrast to an information system, trading systems provide the infrastructure for buyers and sellers to match their interests in buying and selling within its system. Trading systems therefore do not leave the question of when and how a trade may occur to the discretion of the traders but offer the matching mechanism to perform this function.[126]

2. Parameters to Categorize Trading Systems

Trading systems can be distinguished along two pairs of parameters: multilateral vs. bilateral and non-discretionary vs. discretionary trading systems.

---

122 Paul D Cohen, 'Securities Trading via the Internet' (1999) 4 Stanford Journal of Law, Business & Finance 1, 7–8; Kumpan, *Die Regulierung außerbörslicher Wertpapierhandelssysteme im deutschen, europäischen und US-amerikanischen Recht* (n 8) 20.

123 Cohen (n 122) 7–8; Kumpan, *Die Regulierung außerbörslicher Wertpapierhandelssysteme im deutschen, europäischen und US-amerikanischen Recht* (n 8) 20.

124 Kumpan, *Die Regulierung außerbörslicher Wertpapierhandelssysteme im deutschen, europäischen und US-amerikanischen Recht* (n 8) 20–1; Gerald Spindler, 'Elektronische Finanzmärkte und Internet-Börsen - Teil I: Grundlegende Risiken und Reform des nationalen Kapitalmarktrechts' [2002] WM 1325, 1326.

125 Christoph Kumpan in Eberhard Schwark and Daniel Zimmer (eds), *Kapitalmarktrechts-Kommentar: Börsengesetz mit Börsenzulassungsverordnung, Wertpapierprospektgesetz, Wertpapierhandelsgesetz, Wertpapiererwerbs- und Übernahmegesetz, Europäische Marktmissbrauchsverordnung* (5th edn, CH Beck 2020) WpHG § 2 para 138; Kumpan, *Die Regulierung außerbörslicher Wertpapierhandelssysteme im deutschen, europäischen und US-amerikanischen Recht* (n 8) 223ff, 270ff.

126 Kumpan (n 125) WpHG § 2 para 138.

a) Multilateral Trading Systems

A multilateral trading system is a system or facility in which multiple buying and selling interests in financial instruments are able to interact in a manner that a contract is formed under the rules of the system or facility.[127] Such systems include trading systems with the power to first admit financial instruments to trading (listing),[128] such as exchanges like *Frankfurter Wertpapier Boerse* (run by *Deutsche Boerse AG*) or *SIX Swiss Exchange*, and systems without listing power, like most alternative trading systems that allow their traders to interact with each other to make trades.[129]

b) Bilateral Trading Systems

A bilateral trading system is a system or facility which deals on its own account when executing client orders.[130] While a bilateral trading system may have multiple clients who are buying from and selling to it, the bilateral trading system always forms the counterparty to every seller and every buyer.[131] Unlike multilateral trading systems, bilateral trading systems cannot

127 Cf. Art 4(1)(19) MiFIR; Daniela Cohn, 'Alternative Handelssysteme: Ein Beitrag zur Neufassung der §§ 58 ff BörsG' [2002] ZBB 365, 367–8; Kumpan, *Die Regulierung außerbörslicher Wertpapierhandelssysteme im deutschen, europäischen und US-amerikanischen Recht* (n 8) 13.

128 See definitions under EU law under Article 4(1)(19), (21) MiFID II and under Swiss law under Article 26(a), (b) FinfraG. Moloney, *EU Securities and Financial Markets Regulation* (n 4) 463; Schott and Winkler (n 70) SK FinfraG Art 26 paras 23, 25.

129 See definitions under EU law under Article 4(1)(19), (22) MiFID II and under Swiss law under Article 26(a), (c) FinfraG. Moloney, *EU Securities and Financial Markets Regulation* (n 4) 464; Schott and Winkler (n 70) SK FinfraG Art 26 para 35.

130 Cf. Art 4(1)(20) MiFID II on systematic internalizers; see also Heinz-Dieter Assmann in Heinz-Dieter Assmann, Uwe H Schneider and Peter O Mülbert (eds), *Wertpapierhandelsrecht: Kommentar* (7th edn, Otto Schmidt 2019) WpHG § 2 para 113; BaFin, 'Hinweise zu den Tatbeständen des Eigenhandels und des Eigengeschäfts' (22 March 2011, changed on 15 May 2019) para 1. b) aa); Kumpan (n 125) WpHG § 2 para 103. See also Stephanie M Bialluch, 'Systematische Internalisierung de lege lata' [2015] WM 2030; Cohn (n 127) 368; Kumpan, *Die Regulierung außerbörslicher Wertpapierhandelssysteme im deutschen, europäischen und US-amerikanischen Recht* (n 8) 18; Siegfried Kümpel and Arne Wittig (eds), *Bank- und Kapitalmarktrecht* (4th edn, Otto Schmidt 2011) para 17.120.

131 Assmann (n 130) WpHG § 2 para 164; Kumpan (n 125) WpHG § 2 para 142; Mariam Güllner, 'MiFID II: Die neue Handelsplatzarchitektur in der EU' [2017] WM 938, 941; Christian Hoops, 'Bedeutung des organisierten Handelssystems in der gegenwärtigen Marktinfrastruktur' [2017] RdF 14, 16; Christoph Kumpan and Hendrik

directly match client orders, thus, bilateral trading systems assume proprietary market risk by actively trading with their clients as either seller or buyer.[132] Those bilateral trading systems include for example broker-dealers who act as OTC-market makers internalizing large amounts of customer order flow.[133]

c) Non-Discretionary and Discretionary Trading Systems

Both, multilateral and bilateral trading systems can either be non-discretionary or discretionary. Under non-discretionary rules, the trading system sets up pre-defined rules for order matching but when it comes to the matching decision for a specific transaction, neither the trading system operator nor the traders can alter whether, when or how a specific buying interest matches with a specific selling interest.[134]

However, a system operates under discretionary rules if the trading system operator or the traders have discretion over whether an order can be placed on a trading system, whether and when it matches with another

---

Müller-Lankow, 'Ein-Market-Maker-Systeme in der neuen Kapitalmarktregulierung - Abgrenzung zwischen multilateralen und bilateralen Systemen' [2017] WM 1777, 1783. See also Jochen Hoffmann, 'Elektronische Handelssysteme nach dem 4. Finanzmarktförderungsgesetz' [2003] WM 2025, 2028; Gerald Spindler, 'Elektronische Finanzmärkte und Internet-Börsen - Teil II: Regulierungsvorhaben auf der europäischen Ebene' [2002] WM 1365, 1369, 1372; Fabian Reuschle and Andreas M Fleckner, 'Börsenähnliche Einrichtungen - die privatrechtliche Organisation einer Börse im materiellen Sinne' [2002] BKR 617, 621; Peter O Mülbert, 'Empfiehlt es sich, im Interesse des Anlegerschutzes und zur Förderung des Finanzplatzes Deutschland das Kapitalmarkt- und Börsenrecht neu zu regeln?' [2002] JZ 826, 829.

132 Kumpan (n 125) WpHG § 2 para 103. Cf. Recital 6(2) MiFID I; Bialluch (n 130) 2030; Jochen Seitz, 'Die Regulierung von Wertpapierhandelssystemen in der EU' [2004] AG 497, 502.

133 Kumpan, *Die Regulierung außerbörslicher Wertpapierhandelssysteme im deutschen, europäischen und US-amerikanischen Recht* (n 8) 18–9; Mahoney and Rauterberg (n 118) 228–9.

134 Recital 7(2)(3) MiFIR and Recital 6(8) MiFID I; Kumpan (n 125) WpHG § 2 para 141. See also BaFin, 'Merkblatt: Tatbestand des Betriebs eines multilateralen Handelssystems gemäß § 1 Abs. 1a Satz 2 Nr. 1b KWG' (7 December 2009, changed on 27 April 2023) para 1. d); Gerald Spindler and Roman A Kasten, 'Der neue Rechtsrahmen für den Finanzdienstleistungssektor - die MiFID und ihre Umsetzung - Teil I -' [2006] WM 1749, 1754.

order, and whether it is fully or only partially executed against another order.[135]

d) Systems with a Price Formation Mechanism and Price Importing Systems

Although regulators do not use the characteristic of a trading system having a proprietary price formation mechanism as a distinctive feature *per se*, it plays a significant role when discussing dark trading, as will be shown in the subsequent chapters. A trading system can therefore run its own price formation mechanism in which it uses the information from its clients' orders to derive the current market price of a specific instrument from its supply and demand.[136] While this is a primary function of an exchange, alternative trading systems can also operate a proprietary price formation mechanism.[137] In its Order Handling Rule of 1997, the SEC named the alternative trading systems which offer a price formation mechanism 'electronic communication networks' (ECNs). This connotation has been adopted internationally and is still in use today when an off-exchange trading system is used that offers a price formation mechanism.[138]

The opposite of systems with price formation are price importing systems. These systems do not run a proprietary price formation mechanism but take, or import, the price(s) from one or more trading venue(s) that entertain such a mechanism.[139] Often, price importing systems use the

135 Kumpan (n 125) WpHG § 2 para 150; Moloney, *EU Securities and Financial Markets Regulation* (n 4) 462, 464–5.

136 Schott and Sester (n 57) § 22 para 97ff; Kumpan, *Die Regulierung außerbörslicher Wertpapierhandelssysteme im deutschen, europäischen und US-amerikanischen Recht* (n 8) 16.

137 Kumpan, *Die Regulierung außerbörslicher Wertpapierhandelssysteme im deutschen, europäischen und US-amerikanischen Recht* (n 8) 16; Mahoney and Rauterberg (n 118) 228.

138 SEC, 'Order Execution Obligations: Final Rules' (17 CFR Part 240, Release No. 34–37619A, File No. S7–30–95, 12 September 1996) 61 FR 48290; SEC, 'Regulation of Exchanges and Alternative Trading Systems: Final Rules' (17 CFR Parts 202, 240, 242 and 249, Release No. 34–40760, File No. S7–12–98, 22 December 1998) 63 FR 70844; Kumpan, *Die Regulierung außerbörslicher Wertpapierhandelssysteme im deutschen, europäischen und US-amerikanischen Recht* (n 8) 16; Mahoney and Rauterberg (n 118) 228.

139 Kumpan, *Die Regulierung außerbörslicher Wertpapierhandelssysteme im deutschen, europäischen und US-amerikanischen Recht* (n 8) 17; Jonathan R Macey and Maureen O'Hara, 'Regulating Exchanges and Alternative Trading Systems: A Law and

midpoint price between the best bid and best ask price on another trading system, i.e., the midpoint of the bid-ask-spread, or the closing price of another trading system.[140] These systems are generally called 'crossing-systems' or 'broker crossing networks' (BCNs) which allow traders to execute their orders at prices uninfluenced from the market impact of that order, which means that the order does not move the market price when it hits the order book. Furthermore, BCNs allow their traders to keep the volume of their order undisclosed to other traders in- and outside of the trading system preventing information leakage.[141]

III. Implications of Trading Infrastructure on Trade Transparency

The production and dissemination of trade transparency information is a complicated task for which the trading system operators as part of the market infrastructure are better suited than the individual traders. Given that trading systems are the producers of trade transparency information, it becomes evident that the law regulating the trading infrastructures influences the amount of trade transparency in a similar manner as the trade transparency rules themselves.

A first distinction the trading infrastructure regime draws is the one between on-venue trading and off-venue trading, also known as OTC-trading. Since all trade transparency rules need to address either a trading system operator (or internalizing investment firm), off-venue trading between traders is not subject to trade transparency rules and falls in the unregulated, dark OTC-space. Only on-venue trading organized by an operator can be subject to (broad) transparency rules. Thus, without a proper trading infrastructure regime, the best trade transparency regime is futile. To create the necessary pre-condition of a functioning trade transparency regime, legislators and regulators need to aim for a trading infrastructure regime

---

Economics Perspective' (1999) 28(1) The Journal of Legal Studies 17, 46 fn 62; Nyquist (n 72) 303; Kari Korhonen, 'Securities Market ATSs Concepts, Their Roles and Related Policy Issues' (Bank of Finland Discussion Papers 24/2001, Helsinki, 20 November 2001) 15.

140 Kumpan, *Die Regulierung außerbörslicher Wertpapierhandelssysteme im deutschen, europäischen und US-amerikanischen Recht* (n 8) 17; Gabriel Matus, 'The Regulation of Alternative Trading Systems: Market Fragmentation and the New Market Structure' (2000-2001) 44 New York Law School Law Review 583, 586.

141 Kumpan, *Die Regulierung außerbörslicher Wertpapierhandelssysteme im deutschen, europäischen und US-amerikanischen Recht* (n 8) 17.

that defines regulatory categories – i.e., define venue-categories – capable to catch all organized trading. If it fails that task, organized trading can slip into the dark off-venue OTC-space as well.

The second calibration of the trading infrastructure regime which influences the trade transparency regime is the one between non-discretionary, multilateral and discretionary, bilateral trading systems. Legislators and regulators should aim to calibrate the transparency regime for the different incentive structures on multilateral and bilateral trading systems. For example, multilateral and bilateral trading should be distinguished into separate trading systems to avoid conflicts of interest between the system operator and its clients which ensures a more informative price formation process on multilateral trading venues expressing only the equilibrium of third-party supply and demand.[142] If the trading infrastructure regime blends non-discretionary, multilateral and discretionary, bilateral trading in one trading system, the trade transparency regime will not be able to unravel multilateral and bilateral order flows later on. That way, the production of insightful information is much harder.[143]

On a multilateral trading system, trade transparency can reach further than on bilateral trading systems, because multilateral systems do not assume principal risk, whereas bilateral systems do. So, bilateral systems are vulnerable to strategic behavior when they take on large positions because operators of bilateral trading systems need to unwind these large positions into the market after a buy transaction to balance their book again.[144] A bilateral system therefore aims to avoid other traders who depress its transaction prices by trading against it.[145] This aversion to position risk may legitimize an exception from extensive trade transparency, especially

142 EG-Kommission, 'Vorschlag für neue Wertpapierdienstleistungsrichtlinie' [2002] ZBB 518, 550–1; Güllner (n 131) 941; Moloney, *EU Securities and Financial Markets Regulation* (n 4) 427–8; cf. Spindler, 'Elektronische Finanzmärkte und Internet-Börsen - Teil I: Grundlegende Risiken und Reform des nationalen Kapitalmarktrechts' (n 124) 1333.

143 Cf. Guido Ferrarini and Niamh Moloney, 'Reshaping Order Execution in the EU and the Role of Interest Groups: From MiFID I to MiFID II' (2012) 13(4) European Business Organization Law Review 557, 592–3; Güllner (n 131) 941; Spindler, 'Elektronische Finanzmärkte und Internet-Börsen - Teil I: Grundlegende Risiken und Reform des nationalen Kapitalmarktrechts' (n 124) 1333.

144 Moloney, *EU Securities and Financial Markets Regulation* (n 4) 431, 484–5; O'Hara, *Market Microstructure Theory* (n 45) 258.

145 Moloney, *EU Securities and Financial Markets Regulation* (n 4) 431; O'Hara, *Market Microstructure Theory* (n 45) 258.

given that bilateral systems are most common in markets with low levels of liquidity.[146]

Nevertheless, multilateral systems also need some calibration for their operation model: even though multilateral systems usually do not assume principal risk, they are dependent on traders providing sufficient liquidity to the trading system to allow for a certain network effect[147] so the trading system can earn its fees from a sufficiently large order flow. Traders who place large orders are providing a substantial source of liquidity but are also particularly vulnerable to trade transparency because of market impact costs.[148] To account for this issue, some exceptions from trade transparency are necessary for multilateral systems as well.

Consequently, trading infrastructure and trade transparency cannot be discussed in isolation from each other. If and how exceptions are reasonable and what exceptions the national regulations deem appropriate, will be discussed subsequently to the forms of dark trading as well as its advantages and disadvantages.

E. The Phenomenon of Dark Trading

I. Difference between 'Lit' and 'Dark' Trading, Pools, Orders, and Liquidity

1. 'Lit' and 'Dark' Trading

After having discussed the crucial aspects of trade transparency and trading infrastructure, it can be concluded that the difference between so-called 'lit' and 'dark' trading is the presence of trade transparency in lit trading, whereas dark trading is characterized by the absence of trade transparency.[149] More specifically, dark trading is trading in financial instruments

146 Moloney, *EU Securities and Financial Markets Regulation* (n 4) 431–2, 484–5.

147 Harris (n 81) 535–6; Hoops, *Verborgene Liquidität im Marktordnungsrecht der MiFID* (n 6) 109–10; Steven McNamara, 'The Stock Exchange as Multi-Sided Platform and the Future of the National Market System' (2019) 2018(5) Brigham Young University Law Review 969, 993ff; Rudolph and Röhrl (n 51) 180; Martin K Thelen, *Dark Pools: Schattenbörsen im Lichte US-amerikanischer, europäischer und deutscher Kapitalmarktregulierung* (Ph.D.-Thesis University of Bonn 2019, Duncker & Humblot 2019) 52.

148 IOSCO, 'Principles for Dark Liquidity' (n 12) 27.

149 SEC, 'Concept Release on Equity Market Structure' (n 6) 75 FR 3599; Easthope and Ray (n 5) 3; Christopher Mercurio, 'Dark Pool Regulation' (2013-2014) 33 Review

with no pre-trade transparency.[150] However, dark trading can also display reduced, incomplete, or deferred post-trade transparency.[151]

The emphasis on pre-trade transparency is unsurprising because, first and foremost, dark trading serves traders' need that use it: those traders wish to remain anonymous and keep their order confidential, so other traders are unable to alter the price of their orders in the respective financial instrument to the detriment of the dark trader.[152] In this regard, pre-trade transparency about unfilled orders is of paramount importance since only price alterations before a trade occurs have a direct effect on the trader's transaction price. In return, a trader using dark trading needs to accept that their order may need longer to execute since contra-side liquidity cannot find them as quickly as an order that raises market attention by showing pre-trade transparency, and often times trading rules favor lit over dark orders that entered the market at the same time.[153]

There are, however, instances where dark traders are also interested in keeping their anonymity and confidentiality after a trade has occurred. This is the case when, in an initial dark trade, a large order position is taken over by a buyer who needs to unwind their position into the market after the trade but wants to conceal their current position from the market. If a regulatory regime seeks to protect the buyer of the initial transaction, it often allows for extended dark trading by delaying post-trade transparency as well.[154] This is a common strategy to protect market makers in quote-driven markets.[155] Thus, while dark trading always lacks pre-trade transparency, it may also lack, limit or defer post-trade transparency.

---

of Banking & Financial Law 69; Gary Shorter and Rena S Miller, 'Dark Pools in Equity Trading: Policy Concerns and Recent Developments' (Congressional Research Service, 26 September 2014); Committee on Capital Markets Regulation, 'The U.S. Equity Markets' (n 6) 3.

150 FCA, 'UK Equity Market Dark Pools' (n 6) 14 para 2.8; IOSCO, 'Principles for Dark Liquidity' (n 12) 4; Banks (n 5) 3.

151 Baisch, Baumann and Weber (n 11) 184; Davies and Sirri (n 12) 167; Hochstrasser (n 11) 306.

152 IOSCO, 'Principles for Dark Liquidity' (n 12) 4; Petrescu and Wedow (n 5) 17; Shorter and Miller, 'Dark Pools in Equity Trading' (n 149) 2, 5.

153 Shorter and Miller, 'Dark Pools in Equity Trading' (n 149) 2.

154 O'Hara, *Market Microstructure Theory* (n 45) 258.

155 Moloney, *EU Securities and Financial Markets Regulation* (n 4) 431–2, 484–5, 487–8.

2. 'Lit' and 'Dark' Pools

While lit and dark trading describe the action of transparent and non-transparent trading, lit and dark pools connotate the institutions for such trading. A lit pool is a trading system for financial instruments which shows trade transparency.[156] The archetypical example of a lit pool is an exchange such as the New York Stock Exchange (NYSE), London Stock Exchange, Deutsche Boerse, and SIX Swiss Exchange.

A dark pool is a trading system for financial instruments that does not display pre-trade transparency, and in some instances, displays reduced, incomplete, or deferred post-trade transparency.[157]

3. 'Lit' and 'Dark' Orders

On the transactional level, we find the pair of term of lit and dark orders, where a lit order means an order that is showing trade transparency, whereas the term dark order describes an order displaying no pre-trade transparency.[158] As its counterparts before, a dark order may also display reduced, incomplete, or deferred post-trade transparency.[159]

While dark orders are the smallest unit of dark trading, they are not confined to only dark pools. Dark orders can also occur on otherwise pre-trade transparent trading systems, like exchanges or outside of a dark pool in the less regulated OTC-space.[160] On otherwise lit trading systems, dark orders offer certain traders, for example large block traders, the chance to use an exchange without the adverse market impact associated with trade transparency.[161] This way, not only does the trader placing a dark order benefit from the higher levels of liquidity, but the lit pool benefits by keep-

156 Petrescu and Wedow (n 5) 4; Mahendrarajah Nimalendran and Sugata Ray, 'Informational Linkages Between Dark and Lit trading Venues' (2014) 17 Journal of Financial Markets 230, 231.

157 IOSCO, 'Principles for Dark Liquidity' (n 12) 4; Banks (n 5) 3; Baisch, Baumann and Weber (n 11) 184; Bošković, Cerruti and Noël (n 70) 11; Easthope and Ray (n 5) 4; Hochstrasser (n 11) 306; Petrescu and Wedow (n 5) 4; Shorter and Miller, 'Dark Pools in Equity Trading' (n 149) 2.

158 IOSCO, 'Principles for Dark Liquidity' (n 12) 4–5; Hoops, *Verborgene Liquidität im Marktordnungsrecht der MiFID* (n 6) 92ff.

159 Baisch, Baumann and Weber (n 11) 184; Hochstrasser (n 11) 306.

160 IOSCO, 'Principles for Dark Liquidity' (n 12) 5.

161 Hans Degryse and others, 'Two Shades of Opacity: Hidden Orders and Dark Trading' (June 2021) 2ff.

ing the block trader from migrating to dark pools and thus retaining their additional liquidity supply. However, the remainder of unaware traders may consider dark orders disadvantageous if they happen to misjudge the supply and demand for an instrument due to large amounts of dark orders that would have shifted the price in their favor.[162] Resolving this conundrum is a question of the individual jurisdiction's regulation and will therefore be discussed in the subsequent chapters.

4. 'Lit' and 'Dark' Liquidity

The last piece of terminology is the difference between lit and dark liquidity. Lit liquidity is the sum of all lit orders, i.e., the orders showing trade transparency. Dark liquidity is the sum of all dark orders, i.e., the orders that display no pre-trade transparency but may also display reduced, incomplete, or deferred post-trade transparency.[163] Both terms are therefore umbrella terms to refer to the extent to which lit and dark trading can be found in the market.

II. Dark Trading and the Law

Dark trading and its related 'dark' phenomena are commonly used in academia, media, or regulatory discourse to describe the phenomenon of non-transparent trading. While regulators and legislators also use the term in their discussion papers, they refrain from using them when formulating the law. A reason for this is certainly that dark trading is a phenomenon where different legal regimes, first and foremost the trading infrastructure and transparency regime, interact and create spaces, sometimes even loopholes, in which dark trading can flourish. Therefore, the terms 'dark trading', 'dark pools' and 'dark orders' may be absent from legal texts, but nevertheless are certainly important terms for the following examination of the laws of the US, EU, Germany, and Switzerland, since they have been the target of regulatory action.

---

162 Cf. Stefan Frey and Patrik Sandås, 'The Impact of Iceberg Orders in Limit Order Books' (CFR-Working Paper No. 09-06, 17 May 2009) 24ff.

163 Cf. IOSCO, 'Principles for Dark Liquidity' (n 12) 4–5.

III. Classification of Dark Trading

Due to the wide proliferation of dark trading, it has become a heterogenous phenomenon in today's financial markets.[164] A categorization of dark trading services shall provide an overall structure of the realm of dark trading services before dealing with their regulation. For this purpose, the following two categorization approaches shall be used: first, the approach by *Gomber/Gvozdevskiy*, who use the operating entity as the structuring principle,[165] and second, the approach by *Thelen*, who uses a sort of 'family-resemblance' test to the archetype of an exchange to map the dark trading realm.[166]

According to *Gomber/Gvozdevskiy*, dark trading services can be divided into 'regulated' and 'unregulated' dark pools.[167] Regulated dark pools include trading services provided by regulated trading infrastructures, such as, exchanges and alternative trading systems, whereas the realm of unregulated dark pools means transactions conducted in the over-the-counter market.[168]

1. Regulated Dark Pools

Regulated dark pools or dark trading services on exchanges and alternative trading systems are considered 'regulated' since they fall into the regulatory perimeter of the trading infrastructure regime.[169] As mentioned above, this provides the legislator and regulator with an addressee to direct their transparency requirements.[170]

164 Baisch, Baumann and Weber (n 11) 188; Humbel, *Die Regelung der Vor- und Nachhandelstransparenz in der Europäischen Union und der Schweiz* (n 50) 16.

165 Gomber and Gvozdevskiy (n 43) paras 14.16ff.

166 Thelen (n 147) 59ff.

167 Gomber and Gvozdevskiy (n 43) paras 14.17ff.

168 ibid paras 14.17ff; NB: Although the terms *'exchange'*, *'alternative trading system'* and *'broker-dealer'* also have a regulatory meaning within US law as discussed later, in the categorization at hand, those terms shall merely describe the incumbent trading venues for financial instruments (*'exchanges'*), the new, electronic off-exchange trading systems (*'alternative trading systems'*) and the trading systems of a market intermediary, often an investment bank (*'broker-dealer'*).

169 ibid paras 14.17ff.

170 See above Part I § 2.D.

a) Partially Dark

Dark trading on regulated dark pools can appear either partially or completely dark.[171] An exchange or otherwise lit alternative trading system that allows for some dark orders falls into the category of only partially dark systems.[172] Those dark orders are usually available for specific order types, such as orders that are large in scale while the remainder of the (smaller) orders displays trade transparency.[173] Therefore, dark trading depends on specific exceptions from a generally applicable trade transparency rule. Dark trading is not a result of evading trade transparency altogether because the transparency rules would just not apply.[174]

Regulated dark pools that are only partially dark also have their own price discovery mechanism.[175] Since those trading systems also operate a multilateral market, proprietary trading against proprietary capital of the trading system operator does not occur.[176] The market operator can thus remain in a neutral position and avoid conflicts of interests.[177] This form of dark pool raises few regulatory concerns as long as the exceptions from trade transparency do not become overly broad.

b) Completely Dark

Regulated dark pools can also be completely dark if no order within their system displays pre-trade transparency.[178] These dark pools are often regulated as alternative trading systems and manage to evade trade transparency requirements either through specific exceptions, for example, for large orders or for reference pricing the publicly displayed exchange prices, or by

171 Thelen (n 147) 60ff.
172 ibid 60.
173 IOSCO, 'Principles for Dark Liquidity' (n 12) 5, 11; Hoops, *Verborgene Liquidität im Marktordnungsrecht der MiFID* (n 6) 92ff; Thelen (n 147) 60.
174 IOSCO, 'Principles for Dark Liquidity' (n 12) 11; Kumpan, 'Transparenz als Mittel der Kapitalmarktregulierung' (n 51) 798.
175 Thelen (n 147) 60.
176 Banks (n 5) 65ff; Thelen (n 147) 60.
177 Recital 7 MiFIR; Moloney, *EU Securities and Financial Markets Regulation* (n 4) 464–5.
178 Thelen (n 147) 61ff.

means of a minimal threshold for the application of the trade transparency regime.[179]

Specific exceptions are advantageous from a regulatory perspective, because the regulator can define specific cases in which it deems orders and transactions vulnerable to trade transparency. However, it must also ensure that the exceptions are not misused by arbitrageurs for an unintended purpose and that the exceptions are not overbroad or outdated.[180]

A regulatory approach where all trading in a financial instrument below a certain percentage of turnover in an instrument, for instance 5 %, compared to the aggregate market remains outside the scope[181] has the advantage of being less in need to be adapted to changes in trading as specific exceptions. However, it has the disadvantage of being less precise. Since a minimal threshold applies to all transactions below the threshold, the market may miss order information from orders it would not want to exempt in the first place. This way of creating darkness is also prone to arbitrageurs keeping the turnover just below the threshold.[182] However, such a measure is often an attempt by the regulator to lift the heavy burden of trade transparency from small trading systems and to grant them a competitive advantage over incumbent exchanges. The regulator also indicates that it does not consider turnover under a specific rate a valuable contribution to the price formation process.[183]

Dark pools that only offer trading in instruments that are not subjected by trade transparency rules use an even wider exception. This is often the case in jurisdictions in which trade transparency is only mandatory for shares or equity instruments but not for bonds and derivatives since their markets often suffer from low levels of liquidity. Regulators often fear that such markets would dry out if the bright light of transparency shone on

179 Bošković, Cerruti and Noël (n 70) 10; Chris Brummer, 'Disruptive Technology and Securities Regulation' (2015) 84 Fordham Law Review 977, 1010; IOSCO, 'Principles for Dark Liquidity' (n 12) 16; Thelen (n 147) 61.

180 Ferrarini and Moloney (n 143) 588ff; IOSCO, 'Principles for Dark Liquidity' (n 12) 21, 31–2.

181 See under US law: Rule 301(b)(3) Regulation ATS (17 CFR § 242.301(b)(3)); Bošković, Cerruti and Noël (n 70) 10.

182 Edwin Batista, 'A Shot in the Dark: An Analysis of the SEC's Response to the Rise of Dark Pools' (2014) 14 Journal of High Technology Law 83, 109.

183 SEC, 'Regulation of Exchanges and Alternative Trading Systems' (n 138) 63 FR 70844, 70867.

them.[184] Such exchanges and alternative trading systems only count among regulated dark pools because they are regulated with regard to their infrastructure which would allow the regulator to introduce trade transparency by simply extending the trade transparency regime to those instruments not yet within the regulatory perimeter.[185]

Dark pools that are completely dark can either have their own internal price formation process or operate as crossing networks that import prices from another lit trading system.[186]

More critical is the distinction between dark pools refraining from and those actively engaging in proprietary trading. Proprietary trading on a dark pool allows the system operator to provide liquidity in illiquid market circumstances by forming the opposite side of the trade with a client. However, in a dark pool, the system operator is the only one who can see all the order information, which invites conflicts of interest into the trading process. Even separated trading desks and Chinese Walls may not prevent information leakage from the system operator to its proprietary trading desk as the SEC enforcement measure against Pipeline LLC has shown.[187]

c) Examples

Examples of dark pools provided by exchanges include Smartpool of Euronext, SwissAtMid of SIX Swiss Exchange, and formerly Xetra Midpoint of Deutsche Börse. These exchanges entered the dark pool market after the success of dark pools run by alternative trading systems as a response to the resulting liquidity loss.[188]

Despite the attempt to win back order-flow, the number of dark pools operated by alternative trading systems is still significant. Examples of such dark pools are the services provided by Liquidnet, ITG POSIT, Turquoise, and Normura.[189]

---

184 See for Swiss law: Art 29 FinfraG. See also Schott and Winkler (n 70) SK FinfraG Art 29 para 39.

185 Cf. Schott and Winkler (n 70) SK FinfraG Art 29 para 39.

186 Thelen (n 147) 61ff.; Haoxiang Zhu, 'Do Dark Pools Harm Price Discovery?' (2014) 27(3) Review of Financial Studies 747, 753–4.

187 Amy Kwan, Ronald Masulis and Thomas H McInish, 'Trading Rules, Competition for Order Flow and Market Fragmentation' (2015) 115 Journal of Financial Economics 330, 333; *Pipeline Trading Systems LLC* (n 26) 1, 16.

188 Gomber and Gvozdevskiy (n 43) para 14.17.

189 ibid para 14.17, figure 14.5.

2. Unregulated Dark Pools

a) Completely Dark, Price Importing, with Proprietary Trading

Among the unregulated dark pools are those operated by entities, often broker-dealers, in the less regulated over-the-counter market. Although broker-dealers are also generally captured by the regulatory perimeter, their duties resemble those of an intermediary rather than of a marketplace, like those of exchanges and alternative trading systems. Since the role of market intermediaries is to be a market actor rather than a provider of the market infrastructure, broker-dealers are not subject to marketplace specific regulation. Especially with regard to trade transparency, broker-dealers are often subject to less restrictive regulations than exchanges and alternative trading systems. For this reason, broker-dealers fall in the category of 'unregulated dark pools' in this classification.[190]

Unregulated dark pools, so-called crossing networks, provide for completely anonymous dark trading because they are subject to no or more permissive pre-trade transparency requirements or operate under far-reaching exemptions from pre-trade transparency.[191] Those trading systems generally import prices from lit trading venues like an exchange.[192] Since broker-dealers provide bilateral trading, the dark trading service is a proprietary trading service in which each trader trades against the trading system operator who becomes an interested party in the transaction. This internalization of order flow is widely used in the OTC-space, where brokers route the order flow of their clients to specific broker-dealer internalizers for consideration in so-called 'payment for order-flow'-schemes.[193]

---

190 ibid paras 14.02, 14.19ff.

191 Hans Degryse, Mark von Achter and Gunther Wuyts, 'Shedding Light on Dark Liquidity Pools' [2008] TILEC Discussion Paper, 6; Gomber and Pierron (n 4) 49–50; Thelen (n 147) 61ff.

192 Degryse, Achter and Wuyts (n 191) 6; Thelen (n 147) 62.

193 SEC, 'Concept Release on Equity Market Structure' (n 6) 75 FR 3599f; Gomber and Pierron (n 4) 49–50; Mahoney and Rauterberg (n 118) 259–62; Thelen (n 147) 63–4. See also SEC, 'Memorandum to Equity Market Structure Advisory Committee: Certain Issues Affecting Customers in the Current Equity Market Structure' (Division of Trading and Markets, 26 January 2016) 6: '*(...) the concept of payment for order flow encompasses a wide variety of cash or in-kind compensation structures that a broker may receive for directing its customers' orders to a particular broker-dealer or trading venue.*' See also current research by BaFin that paints a more nuanced picture that payment for order flow may have positive effects for smaller orders but

b) Examples

Examples of broker-dealer run dark pools include multiple trading systems offered by investment banks, for instance, SigmaX by Goldman Sachs, Crossfinder by Credit Suisse, and SuperX by Deutsche Bank.[194]

3. Conclusion

In the course of this study, this differentiation will provide context to regulatory changes, especially in the European Union. After having discussed those recent reforms, it will become apparent that some formerly unregulated dark pools now fall within the category of regulated dark pools. Thus, among others, Goldman Sachs SigmaX, and Liquidnet MTF are currently regulated as multilateral trading facilities (MTFs), which is the regulatory category for off-exchange alternative trading systems in the European Union under the Markets in Financial Instruments Directive II and Markets in Financial Instruments Regulation (MiFID II/MiFIR), which will be discussed below.[195]

negative effects for large orders: BaFin, 'Studie zur Ausführung an ausgewählten deutschen Handelsplattformen: WA-Datenanalyseeinheit' (11 April 2022) 1, 7–9.

194 Gomber and Gvozdevskiy (n 43) para 14.19.

195 See below Part II § 6. See also Annabel Smith, 'Goldman Sachs to go live with SIGMA X Europe MTF on 21 December: The SIGMA X EU MTF will launch on 21 December in Paris at Goldman Sachs ahead of the end of the Brexit transition period on 31 December' (The Trade News 17 December 2020); Aziz Abdel-Qader, 'Dark Pool Operator Liquidnet Activates Dublin MTF Ahead of Brexit: Liquidnet began preparations to open an EEA-based presence as a post-Brexit base of operations in early 2017' (Finance Magnates 2 December 2020).

§ 3. Goals of Financial Regulation, Transparency as a Driver of Market Efficiency, and the Role of Dark Trading

This chapter will discuss the common goals of financial regulation in the United States, the European Union, Germany, and Switzerland. Embarking from the common goals, this chapter will explore how market efficiency is measured by economists and how trade transparency can enhance or potentially even harm market efficiency in certain instances. Those findings will be contrasted with the role dark trading plays in achieving market efficiency, evaluating both the advantages dark trading can offer to its users and to the market at large as well as the adverse effects it may entail.

A. Goals of Financial Regulation

Although the United States, the European Union, Germany, and Switzerland have their distinct approaches to financial markets regulation, the primary goals of their respective financial markets laws are very similar. These goals are, on the one hand, promoting and protecting the functioning of fair and orderly markets, and on the other hand, ensuring investor protection.[196] While there may be a varying emphasis on one goal or the other

196 For US law: Section 2 Exchange Act (15 USC § 78b); SEC, 'Order Execution Obligations' (n 138) 61 FR 48290, 48291; Bošković, Cerruti and Noël (n 70) 15; Cox and others (n 116) 12; Eric J Pan, 'Organizing Regional Systems: The US Example' in Niamh Moloney, Eilís Ferran and Jennifer Payne (eds), *The Oxford Handbook of Financial Regulation* (Oxford University Press 2015) 190ff; For EU law: Christian Bumke, 'Regulierung am Beispiel der Kapitalmärkte' in Klaus J Hopt, Rüdiger Veil and Jörn A Kämmerer (eds), *Kapitalmarktgesetzgebung im europäischen Binnenmarkt* (Mohr Siebeck 2008) 107, 118–9; Rüdiger Veil, '§ 2 Concept and Aims of Capital Markets Regulation' in Rüdiger Veil (ed), *European Capital Markets Law* (3rd edn, Hart Publishing 2022) § 2 paras 7–14; For German law: Petra Buck-Heeb, *Kapitalmarktrecht* (12th edn, C.F. Müller Verlag 2022) § 1 para 6; Matthias Lehmann, 'Internationales Finanzmarktrecht' in Jan von Hein (ed), *Münchener Kommentar zum Bürgerlichen Gesetzbuch: Internationales Privatrecht II, Internationales Wirtschaftsrecht, Einführungsgesetz zum Bürgerlichen Gesetzbuche (Art. 50-253)* (vol. 13, 8th edn, CH Beck 2021) paras 2–3; Lenenbach (n 51) para 1.48; Dörte Poelzig, *Kapitalmarktrecht* (2nd edn, CH Beck 2021) 11; For Swiss law: Christoph Winzeler in Rolf Watter and Rashid Bahar (eds), *Basler Kommentar*

and some specificities of each jurisdiction,[197] all examined jurisdictions aim to maintain fair and orderly markets for the investors' benefit.

Since the Global Financial Crisis of 2008-09, a third goal of financial markets law has gained importance, i.e., the goal of protecting financial stability.[198] While some consider it a goal in its own right,[199] it could also be considered as merely a subcategory of the goal to promote the functioning of fair and orderly markets.[200] In the discussion about dark trading, this question can remain unresolved because the matter of trade transparency is certainly crucial for the functioning of financial markets and investor protection but does not jeopardize customers' savings in the same manner as collapsing banks would, and is therefore less critical in this context.[201]

I. Functions of Prices on Capital Markets

In order to evaluate whether capital markets are operating as they are supposed to when determining prices, it is important to have a fundamental understanding of the purpose of market prices. According to economic theory, prices at capital markets shall achieve three main functions: an information function, a valuation function, and an allocation function.[202]

Finanzmarktaufsichtsgesetz, Finanzmarktinfrastrukturgesetz (3rd edn, Helbing & Lichtenhahn Verlag 2019) FINMAG Art 5 paras 11ff; Rolf Watter in Rolf Watter and Rashid Bahar (eds), *Basler Kommentar Finanzmarktaufsichtsgesetz, Finanzmarktinfrastrukturgesetz* (3rd edn, Helbing & Lichtenhahn Verlag 2019) FinfraG Art 1 para 11; Rolf Sethe in Rolf Sethe and others (eds), *Kommentar zum Finanzmarktinfrastrukturgesetz FinfraG* (SK FinfraG, 1st edn, Schulthess 2017) Art 1 para 3.

197 For example, under Swiss law, Art 4(2) FINMAG (formerly Art 5(2) FINMAG) also considers protecting the reputation, competitiveness and sustainability of Switzerland's financial market as a regulatory goal. As the commentators however correctly assess, it is rather an effect of proper functioning markets and investor protection than a goal in its own right, cf. Winzeler (n 196) BSK FINMAG Art 5 para 14.

198 Veil, '§ 2 Concept and Aims of Capital Markets Regulation' (n 196) § 2 para 15.

199 Lehmann, 'Internationales Finanzmarktrecht' (n 196) para 4.

200 Veil, '§ 2 Concept and Aims of Capital Markets Regulation' (n 196) § 2 para 16.

201 ibid § 2 paras 15–19.

202 Bayram (n 64) 17; Annemarie Sapusek, *Informationseffizienz auf Kapitalmärkten: Kozepte und empirische Ergebnisse* (Gabler Verlag 1998) 14–5.

1. Informational Function

a) Information Function according to the ECMH

The informational function of prices is most prominently described by the *Efficient Capital Market Hypothesis* by *Eugene Fama*, postulating that all information is reflected in the market price. This means that an individual trader, on the one hand, cannot gain a profit from a new piece of information, but also on the other hand, the trader does not have to be aware of the information to trade at an informed price.[203] However, the ECMH is rather a heuristic model than an absolute rule. Even *Fama* distinguishes between three forms of his hypothesis: the weak form, where merely all information about historic price movements is reflected in an instrument's current market price; the semi-strong form, where all past movements and all current publicly announced information is reflected; and the strong form, where also the information possessed only by insiders is reflected in the publicly displayed price.[204]

Empirical testing of the hypothesis, however, has often only proven the weak form of the ECMH in actual market settings, raising major criticism from other economists on its explanatory value.[205] In the well-developed US capital markets and to some degree in the German capital markets,

203 Fama, 'Efficient Capital Markets' (n 62) 383ff; Fama, 'The Behavior of Stock-Market Prices' (n 62) 34ff; Fama, 'Efficient Capital Markets' (n 62) 143ff; Fama, 'Efficient Capital Markets' (n 62) 1575ff; Fama and others (n 62) 1ff; Fama and Laffer (n 62) 289ff.

204 Fama, 'Efficient Capital Markets' (n 62) 363ff; Fama, 'The Behavior of Stock-Market Prices' (n 62) 34ff; Fama, 'Efficient Capital Markets' (n 62) 143ff; Fama, 'Efficient Capital Markets' (n 62) 1575ff; Fama and others (n 62) 1ff; Fama and Laffer (n 62) 289ff. See also Armour and others (n 62) 104; Gilson and Kraakman (n 62) 555–6.

205 Picot, Bortenlänger and Röhrl (n 77) 23; Thomas S Y Ho and Roni Michaely, 'Information Quality and Market Efficiency' (1988) 23(1) Journal of Financial and Quantitative Analysis 53-5; Humbel, *Die Regelung der Vor- und Nachhandelstransparenz in der Europäischen Union und der Schweiz* (n 50) 27. See further: J. B De Long and others, 'Noise Trader Risk in Financial Markets' (1990) 98 Journal of Political Economy 703ff; Donald C Langevoort, 'Theories, Assumptions, and Securities Regulation: Market Efficiency Revisited' (1992) 140 University of Pennsylvania Law Review 851, 866ff; Stephen F LeRoy, 'Efficient Capital Markets and Martingales' (1989) 27 Journal of Economic Literature 1583ff; Andrei Shleifer and Lawrence H Summers, 'The Noise Trader Approach to Finance' (1990) 4 The Journal of Economic Perspectives 19ff.

some studies show that a level of information efficiency is reached which fulfills the requirements of the semi-strong form of the ECMH.[206]

Moreover, the statements of the ECMH need to be understood with a long-term equilibrium in mind which allows for short-term deviations from the ideal: while an ideal market would instantly reflect all information in the displayed price, it is acknowledged that a new piece of information takes a certain amount of time to be imported by the price discovery process. The faster this process is, the higher the level of relative informational efficiency.[207]

b) Behavioral Finance on ECMH

As a recent strand of economic research, behavioral finance evolved as a response to neo-classical economics and its difficulties in describing market failures due to human characteristics.[208] According to behavioral finance, the ECMH's assumptions that all market participants are rational actors who are searching for pricing errors to gain a profit through informational arbitrage strategies is unrealistic.[209] While some market actors may well be rational actors, especially professional traders,[210] it is more likely that unsavvy retail investors have insufficient command over fundamental data analysis techniques to employ proper information arbitrage strategies. Those so-called *noise traders* or *myopic traders* are steered by hunches, emotions, and intuitions rather than fundamental information.[211] Noise

206 Bak and Bigus (n 63) 434.

207 Gilson and Kraakman (n 62) 560; Klöhn, '§ 6 Kapitalmarktrecht' (n 68) § 6 para 6.

208 See Nicholas Baberis and Richard H Thaler, 'A Survey of Behavioral Finance' in Richard H Thaler (ed), *Advances in Behavioral Finance* (Princeton University Press 2005) 1; Christine Jolls, Cass R Sunstein and Richard H Thaler, 'A Behavioral Approach to Law and Economics' in Cass R Sunstein (ed), *Behavioral Law and Economics* (Cambridge University Press 2000) 14ff; Andrei Shleifer, *Inefficient Markets: An Introduction to Behavioral Finance* (Oxford University Press 2000) 10ff, 175.

209 Bayram (n 64) 23; Lars Klöhn, 'Wertpapierhandelsrecht diesseits und jenseits des Informationsparadigmas' (2013) 177 ZHR 349, 359ff; Johannes Köndgen, 'Effizienzorientierung im Kapitalmarktrecht?' in Holger Fleischer and Daniel Zimmer (eds), *Effizienz als Regelungsziel im Handels- und Wirtschaftsrecht* (Verlag Recht und Wirtschaft 2008) 104–5; Shleifer (n 208) 10.

210 However, even institutional investors appear on the side of the rational investors as well as on the side of myopic investors or noise traders, see Langevoort (n 205) 868; cf. Robert J Shiller, *Market Volatility* (MIT Press 1989) 379ff, 399.

211 Langevoort (n 205) 868. See also Fischer Black, 'Noise' (1986) 41 The Journal of Finance 529-30; Albert S Kyle, 'Continiuous Auctions and Insider Trading' (1985)

traders can cause a deviation of the displayed market price from the fair value.[212] While informed traders can steer the market back to the fair value by arbitrage strategies, the informed traders may also decide to adapt to the market's overall direction when there is too much noise trading.[213]

In spite of the ongoing debate between neo-classicists and behavioralists, this study will take the insights of behavioral finance to refine the theories of neo-classical economics to explain the matter of dark trading but will not elaborate on the discussion about the two strands of economics.

2. Valuation Function

Prices on capital markets also serve a valuation function when the displayed market price is equal to the underlying fair value.[214] The fair value can only be determined if the fundamental information is conveyed into the market via disclosure about fundamental information and disclosure of informed traders using this information to trade on it, i.e., trade transparency. The quality of the valuation function is dependent on a high degree of information efficiency.[215] If either the source of fundamental information or the conveyer belt of trade transparency is missing or impaired, the process of importing new pieces of information is distorted. This bears the risk of a market price deviating from the fair value suggested by the fundamental data,[216] and might result in misguided investments and unnoticed risks for investors, which ultimately translates into transaction costs.[217]

---

53 Econometrica 1315ff; Jürgen Oechsler, 'Das Verbot der Marktmanipulation durch Aktienrückkauf im Licht der neueren Kritik an der klassischen Kapitalmarkttheorie' in Jens C Dammann, Wolfgang Grunsky and Thomas Pfeiffer (eds), *Gedächtnisschrift für Manfred Wolf* (CH Beck 2011) 291, 292ff; John L Teall, *Financial Trading and Investing* (2nd edn, Elsevier Academic Press 2018) 148.

212 Bak and Bigus (n 63) 435.

213 Bayram (n 64) 23; Langevoort (n 205) 870; Oechsler (n 211) 291, 295.

214 Bayram (n 64) 19; Heinz Bremer, *Grundzüge des deutschen und ausländischen Börsenrechts* (Enzyklopädie der Rechts- und Staatswissenschaft, Springer 1969) 85–6; Harris (n 81) 223.

215 Bayram (n 64) 19; Horst Bienert, *Der Marktprozeß an Aktienbörsen: Bewertungseffizienz und Umverteilung* (Gabler Verlag 1996) 19; James Tobin, 'On the Efficiency of the Financial System' [1984] Lloyds Bank Review 1, 2.

216 Bayram (n 64) 19.

217 Alexander Hellgardt, 'Europäisches Kapitalmarktrecht und Corporate Governance' in Harald Baum and others (eds), *Perspektiven des Wirtschaftsrechts: Deutsches, europäisches und internationales Handels-, Gesellschafts- und Kapitalmarktrecht.*

Since the fair value of a financial instrument is hard to determine, it is generally determined by the *Capital Asset Pricing Model* (CAPM)[218] which uses the sum of the net present value of the future dividends (or other payouts) and the sale proceeds of a given financial instrument.[219] However, the future development of the market and the wider economy is hard to foresee and cannot be known beforehand,[220] therefore, there is a certain amount of prediction and guesswork involved.[221] With far-reaching trade transparency, the findings and interpretations of information by the individual traders can be tested and inter-subjective consensus can be found through the trading mechanism.[222]

Whenever traders find evidence that the fair value is higher than the displayed price, they will buy the instrument, and sell it when their interpretation of the fundamental data suggests that it is the other way around.[223] Eventually, an equilibrium should be established with regard to a single piece of information.

For regulatory purposes, it is important to bear in mind, that the fair value is a non-observable, rather theoretical target that is very hard to aim for because no one knows what the future cashflows will be.[224] Trying to reach price accuracy at the cost of an attractive incentive structure for such traders who provide liquidity and/or information to the market may not be a preferable regulatory strategy.

Beiträge für Klaus J. Hopt aus Anlass seiner Emeritierung (De Gruyter 2008) 397, 405–6; Picot, Bortenlänger and Röhrl (n 77) 22.

218 Richard Brealey, Stewart Myers and Franklin Allen, *Principles of Corporate Finance* (12th edn, McGraw Hill Education 2016) 192ff; Raphael Stahl, *Capital Asset Pricing Model und Alternativkalküle: Analyse in der Unternehmensbewertung mit empirischem Bezug auf die DAX-Werte* (Springer Gabler 2016) 3ff.

219 Bayram (n 64) 19; Baruch Lev and Meiring de Villiers, 'Stock Price Crashes and 10b-5 Damages: A Legal, Economic, and Policy Analysis' (1994) 47(1) Stanford Law Review 7, 35; Martin Weber, 'Börsenkursbestimmung aus ökonomischer Perspektive' [2004] ZGR 280, 281.

220 Ekkenga (n 96) § 7 para 135.

221 Gilson and Kraakman (n 62) 561–2. See also Black (n 211) 533–4.

222 Harris (n 81) 222–3; Lars Klöhn, *Kapitalmarkt, Spekulation und Behavioral Finance: Eine interdisziplinäre und vergleichende Analyse zum Fluch und Segen der Spekulation und ihrer Regulierung durch Recht und Markt* (Ph.D.-Thesis University of Göttingen 2006, Duncker & Humblot 2006) 49; Klöhn, 'Wertpapierhandelsrecht diesseits und jenseits des Informationsparadigmas' (n 209) 353.

223 Bayram (n 64) 21; Klöhn, 'Wertpapierhandelsrecht diesseits und jenseits des Informationsparadigmas' (n 209) 354, 357–8.

224 Ekkenga (n 96) § 7 para 135.

3. Allocative Function

The allocative function builds upon the information and the valuation function.[225] The allocative function of financial markets describes how well a market can distribute capital to the capital demander who needs capital most urgently and distribute risk to the investor who can bear the risk most efficiently.[226] To make this choice among multiple market participants, trade transparency is also an essential component. Investors will only invest their money in the financial markets if they trust in the market's fairness, stability, and integrity.[227] Moreover, in the decentralized market setting, the allocation process of capital and risk is guided by price incentives. Without trade transparency the price formation process stalls and investors cannot observe the available investment opportunities.[228]

II. Promoting and Ensuring Investor Protection

The second goal of financial markets law is investor protection. Investor protection can be divided into protection of the entirety of investors, the investing public (collective investor protection), and the protection of the individual investor (individual investor protection).[229] Investor protection shall enable investors to make an informed investment decision aligned with their risk profile, for which the investor needs current, comprehensive,

225 Bayram (n 64) 22; Buck-Heeb (n 196) § 1 para 10.

226 Buck-Heeb (n 196) § 1 para 10.

227 Eberhard Schwark and Daniel Zimmer in Eberhard Schwark and Daniel Zimmer (eds), *Kapitalmarktrechts-Kommentar: Börsengesetz mit Börsenzulassungsverordnung, Wertpapierprospektgesetz, Wertpapierhandelsgesetz, Wertpapiererwerbs- und Übernahmegesetz, Europäische Marktmissbrauchsverordnung* (5th edn, CH Beck 2020) WpHG § 1 para 5; Sethe (n 196) SK FinfraG Art 1 para 23; Buck-Heeb (n 196) § 1 para 12; Merritt B Fox and Kevin S Haeberle, 'Evaluating Stock-Trading Practices and Their Regulation' (2017) 42 The Journal of Corporation Law 887, 904; Hellgardt (n 217) 397, 403–4; Poelzig, *Kapitalmarktrecht* (n 196) 12; Veil, '§ 2 Concept and Aims of Capital Markets Regulation' (n 196) § 2 paras 8ff.

228 Hans-Joachim Cremer, 'Regulierung und Freiheit' in Michael Fehling and Matthias Ruffert (eds), *Regulierungsrecht* (Mohr Siebeck 2010) § 5 para 14.

229 Sethe (n 196) SK FinfraG Art 1 paras 11ff; Buck-Heeb (n 196) § 1 paras 11ff; Cox and others (n 116) 12.

and correct information about the market situation through pre- and post-trade transparency.[230]

The rationale of investor protection, and particularly collective investor protection, is that financial markets will only function properly if the investing public trusts the integrity and stability of the market. Thus, collective investor protection is strongly intertwined with the goal of protecting the functioning of financial markets as a whole. This becomes apparent with respect to disclosure and transparency rules which serve both purposes.[231] Trade transparency is not only a core element of the markets intermediating function between supply- and demand-side, but also increases the investors' monitoring power of both their intermediaries and the marketplace enhancing actual and perceived fairness of financial markets.[232]

B. Role of Transaction Costs and the Economic Operationalization of Transaction Costs

I. Role of Transaction Costs

If financial markets were able to fulfil their information, valuation and allocation function, the goals of protecting the functioning of fair and orderly markets and the investors would be achieved and regulators would not have to intervene. Due to incomplete information, limited rationality, and opportunistic behavior of actors on financial markets, transactions fail

230 Sethe (n 196) SK FinfraG Art 1 para 11; Peter O Mülbert, 'Anlegerschutz und Finanzmarktregulierung: Grundlagen' (2013) 177 ZHR 160, 164–5; Thelen (n 147) 75.

231 Gebauer (n 94) MiFIR Art 3 para 7; Schwark and Zimmer (n 227) WpHG § 1 para 6; Buck-Heeb (n 196) § 1 para 12; Klaus J Hopt, 'Grundsatz- und Praxisprobleme nach dem Wertpapierhandelsgesetz – insbesondere Insidergeschäfte und Ad-hoc-Publizität' (1995) 159 ZHR 135, 159; Christian Hoops, 'Die Regulierung von Marktdaten nach der MiFID II' [2018] WM 205; Poelzig, *Kapitalmarktrecht* (n 196) 14. See also Recital 117 of MiFID II and Recitals 8, 18 MiFIR under EU law reflect that the primary purpose of trade transparency is to serve the functioning of the market and the trust of the collective of investors, but EU law refrains from interpreting trade transparency rule as rules that provide a subjective right for individual investors.

232 Schwark and Zimmer (n 227) WpHG § 1 para 4; Brandon Becker and others, 'Automated Securities Trading' (1992) 6(4) Journal of Financial Services Research 327, 331–2; Picot, Bortenlänger and Röhrl (n 77) 24.

to be as efficient as suggested by the ideal outlined above.[233] Some sources of such inefficiencies are pointed out by *Coase*:

> *'In order to carry out a market transaction it is necessary to discover who is that one wishes to deal with, to inform the people that one wishes to deal and on what terms, to conduct negotiations leading to a bargain, to draw up a contract, to undertake the inspection needed to make sure that the terms of the contract are being observed, and so on.'*[234]

A market solution to the issues *Coase* outlined is the implementation and use of a trading system, for instance an exchange, that handles those problems for the traders.[235] Trading systems and the market at large can still fail at fully achieving the three abovementioned functions of capital markets and investor protection at the same time. Whenever a market deviates from the optimum, friction comes into the trading process which is operationalized as transaction costs. The level of transaction costs expresses how well a market or trading system is achieving its intermediation task for their traders.[236] Thus, the central concept of efficiency with regard to financial markets is the one of transaction costs.[237] It is the goal of regulation to keep transaction costs at the lowest level possible.

Transaction costs in financial markets can be classified as explicit or implicit. Explicit transaction costs comprise of fees and other overtly charged costs for trading.[238] Implicit transaction costs are all indirect charges for trading that result in a difference between the fair value and the achieved transaction price.[239] Examples include the liquidity premium caused by

---

233 Humbel, *Die Regelung der Vor- und Nachhandelstransparenz in der Europäischen Union und der Schweiz* (n 50) 23; Picot, Bortenlänger and Röhrl (n 77) 18ff; Rudolph and Röhrl (n 51) 161–2.

234 Ronald H Coase, 'The Nature of the Firm: Origin' (1988) 4(1) Journal of Law, Economics, and Organization 3, 9.

235 Rudolph and Röhrl (n 51) 162–3.

236 Kägi (n 50) BSK FinfraG Art 28 para 32; Fernholz (n 51) 64ff; Picot, Bortenlänger and Röhrl (n 77) 18ff.

237 Kägi (n 50) BSK FinfraG Art 28 para 32; Fernholz (n 51) 64ff; Humbel, *Die Regelung der Vor- und Nachhandelstransparenz in der Europäischen Union und der Schweiz* (n 50) 24; Picot, Bortenlänger and Röhrl (n 77) 18ff. On the fundamental insights on transaction costs, see Ronald H Coase, 'The Nature of the Firm' (1937) 4(16) Economica 386ff; Ronald H Coase, 'The Problem of Social Cost' (1960) 3(1) The Journal of Law & Economics 1ff.

238 Picot, Bortenlänger and Röhrl (n 77) 20; Rudolph and Röhrl (n 51) 170.

239 Fernholz (n 51) 66ff; Gernot Hinterleitner and Philipp Hornung, *Marktqualität und Insiderhandel auf Kapitalmärkten: Eine experimentelle Untersuchung unter-*

bridging the bid-ask-spread for instantaneous liquidity as well as market impact costs (especially for larger orders).[240]

While the trading system operator or the intermediary, who charge explicit transaction costs, set their prices due to their operation costs, profit targets and, first and foremost, by restraints set by competitors,[241] implicit transaction costs cannot be directly observed and, thus, are difficult to measure. However, the underlying efficiency criteria described in the following help to identify where implicit transaction costs arise.[242]

II. Operationalization of Transaction Costs by Efficiency Criteria

Different forms of market organization influence the efficiency criteria, which in turn effect transaction costs.[243] When regulation aims to change market organization in order to reduce transaction costs for increased market efficiency, the success of the regulatory measure can be observed by the effect it has on the efficiency criteria.[244] While there are multiple efficiency criteria,[245] three of those efficiency criteria are of pivotal importance for transaction costs in financial markets and will therefore be discussed more

---

schiedlicher Handelsformen (Springer Gabler 2016) 28ff; Humbel, *Die Regelung der Vor- und Nachhandelstransparenz in der Europäischen Union und der Schweiz* (n 50) 24; Picot, Bortenlänger and Röhrl (n 77) 18ff; Rudolph and Röhrl (n 51) 170ff.

240 Picot, Bortenlänger and Röhrl (n 77) 20; Rudolph and Röhrl (n 51) 170.

241 Picot, Bortenlänger and Röhrl (n 77) 144ff; cf. also Guido Ferrarini, 'Exchange Governance and Regulation: An Overview' in Guido Ferrarini (ed), *European Securities Markets: The Investment Services Directive and Beyond* (Kluwer Law International 1998) 245, 247; Kumpan, *Die Regulierung außerbörslicher Wertpapierhandelssysteme im deutschen, europäischen und US-amerikanischen Recht* (n 8) 21–2; Moloney, *EU Securities and Financial Markets Regulation* (n 4) 437. See further Peter Gomber and others, 'Competition Between Equity Markets: A Review of the Consolidation Versus Fragmentation Debate' (2017) 31 Journal of Economic Surveys 792, 807–8; Peter Gomber and Benedikt Jäger, 'MiFID: Eine systematische Analyse der Zielerreichung' (2014) 26 ZBB 40, 46ff.

242 Humbel, *Die Regelung der Vor- und Nachhandelstransparenz in der Europäischen Union und der Schweiz* (n 50) 25; Picot, Bortenlänger and Röhrl (n 77) 18ff.

243 Picot, Bortenlänger and Röhrl (n 77) 21–2.

244 ibid 21–2.

245 See for a comprehensive overview: Picot, Bortenlänger and Röhrl (n 77) 21ff; Rudolph and Röhrl (n 51) 169ff.

closely. Those three efficiency criteria are informational efficiency, market transparency, and market liquidity.[246]

1. Informational Efficiency

Informational efficiency is closely related to the informational function of prices in capital markets discussed above.[247] Information efficiency is high when the assumptions by the ECMH are met. This means that the displayed market prices display all available information, so they are equal to the fair value. Moreover, the displayed market price shall reflect new pieces of information instantaneously.[248]

That those criteria are met to their full extent is illusory because information production is, in contrast to the assumption made by the ECMH, a costly endeavor. Someone must incur the expenses of finding new pieces of information, interpret them, and trade with them.

The *Information Paradox* described by *Grossman/Stiglitz* suggests that failing to achieve complete informational efficiency is not a flaw but (to some extent) essential for the market to function properly in the first place.[249] Unlike the ECMH, *Grossman/Stiglitz* operate with the assumption that information production and publication raises costs for market participants.[250]

If traders have to raise costs for research of still private information, these so-called *'informed traders'* will only do so if they can off-set their costs by trading against so-called *'uninformed traders'* for a profit (*information*

246 Humbel, *Die Regelung der Vor- und Nachhandelstransparenz in der Europäischen Union und der Schweiz* (n 50) 25ff; Picot, Bortenlänger and Röhrl (n 77) 22ff.

247 See above Part I § 3.A.I.1.

248 See above Part I § 3.A.I.1.

249 Sanford J Grossmann and Joseph E Stiglitz, 'Information and Competitive Price Systems' (1976) 66(2) The American Economic Review 246ff; Sanford J Grossmann and Joseph E Stiglitz, 'On the Impossibility of Informationally Efficient Markets' (1980) 70(3) The American Economic Review 393ff; Gilson and Kraakman (n 62) 577ff.

250 Grossmann and Stiglitz, 'Information and Competitive Price Systems' (n 249) 248; Grossmann and Stiglitz, 'On the Impossibility of Informationally Efficient Markets' (n 249) 393–4; Sanford J Grossmann, 'On the Efficiency of Competitive Stock Markets: Where Traders Have Diverse Information' (1976) 31(2) The Journal of Finance 573.

arbitrage).[251] In a market showing complete informational efficiency, in accordance with the strong form of the ECMH, the market price would already reflect all information and no market participant would invest in research for new information since they cannot offset their costs through information arbitrage.[252] Over time however all traders would become uninformed, while the likelihood would increase that new private information would become available which is not yet reflected in the market price. Thus, the state of all traders being uninformed is also not a competitive equilibrium, since some traders would start to search for information again until the profits approximate zero.[253]

Since under complete informational efficiency no stable equilibrium can be reached, *Grossman/Stiglitz* conclude that a certain amount of opacity in the market, a certain informational inefficiency, is necessary to keep the conveyer belt of information arbitrage moving to fuel the price formation process.[254]

An equilibrium can only be reached if the costs of finding information are equal to the marginal utility of the information itself.[255] The marginal utility depends on the turnover and the liquidity of the financial instrument, because the more financial instruments are traded, without moving the price, the higher the potential utility of intensive research activity is. Thus, an informed trader can place large orders gaining a large profit when

251 Grossmann and Stiglitz, 'On the Impossibility of Informationally Efficient Markets' (n 249) 394. See also Klöhn (n 53) WpHG Vor §§ 12–14 paras 84ff; Klöhn (n 53) MAR Vor Art 7 paras 84ff; Klöhn, 'Wertpapierhandelsrecht diesseits und jenseits des Informationsparadigmas' (n 209) 355ff; Klöhn, *Kapitalmarkt, Spekulation und Behavioral Finance* (n 222) 26ff; Lynn A Stout, 'Irrational Expectations' (1997) 3 Legal Theory 227; Lynn A Stout, 'Why the Law Hates Speculators: Regulation and Private Ordering in the Market for OTC Derivatives' (1999) 48 Duke Law Journal 701, 737.

252 Grossmann and Stiglitz, 'On the Impossibility of Informationally Efficient Markets' (n 249) 393, 401, 404; Grossmann and Stiglitz, 'Information and Competitive Price Systems' (n 249) 246, 247ff.

253 Grossmann and Stiglitz, 'On the Impossibility of Informationally Efficient Markets' (n 249) 393, 401, 404; Grossmann and Stiglitz, 'Information and Competitive Price Systems' (n 249) 246, 247ff.

254 Grossmann and Stiglitz, 'On the Impossibility of Informationally Efficient Markets' (n 249) 393, 401–2; Grossmann and Stiglitz, 'Information and Competitive Price Systems' (n 249) 246ff; Gilson and Kraakman (n 62) 577ff.

255 Cf. Grossmann and Stiglitz, 'Information and Competitive Price Systems' (n 249) 246ff; Grossmann and Stiglitz, 'On the Impossibility of Informationally Efficient Markets' (n 249) 393ff. See also Gilson and Kraakman (n 62) 578; Picot, Bortenlänger and Röhrl (n 77) 23 fn 78.

the price remains stable for the time the transaction needs to be completed. The degree of research and processing of information, and with it the degree of information efficiency, crucially depend on turnover and liquidity in a financial instrument.[256]

However, the degree of informational efficiency is problematic as a guiding principle for regulatory decision-making because it depends on the difference between the currently displayed price and the fair value of a financial instrument.[257] While the currently displayed price can be observed, the fair value cannot. A better suited indicator is the observable degree of market transparency and liquidity.[258]

2. Market Transparency

The degree of market transparency, or trade transparency, is determined by the kind and scope of information about trading that is made public as well as the time and the addressees of the publication.[259] Trade transparency is crucial for creating efficient financial markets.[260]

Trade transparency should not be confused with informational efficiency, but it is the necessary – although not the sufficient – condition for informational efficiency.[261] While trade transparency only requires that trade information is published to the investing public, informational efficiency also requires that the information is properly processed and properly reflected in the displayed market price.[262]

When it comes to the amount of trade transparency, one must consider the insights of the *Information Paradox* and allow for some degree of opacity and darkness because otherwise the market might become unsta-

256 Picot, Bortenlänger and Röhrl (n 77) 23 fn 78.
257 Kägi (n 50) BSK FinfraG Art 28 paras 33ff.
258 ibid BSK FinfraG Art 28 para 39.
259 Picot, Bortenlänger and Röhrl (n 77) 23.
260 Schott and Winkler (n 70) SK FinfraG Art 29 para 9; Humbel, *Die Regelung der Vor- und Nachhandelstransparenz in der Europäischen Union und der Schweiz* (n 50) 28.
261 Christine Bortenlänger, *Börsenautomatisierung: Effizienzpotentiale und Durchsetzbarkeit* (Gabler Verlag, Deutscher Universitätsverlag 1996) 46; Humbel, *Die Regelung der Vor- und Nachhandelstransparenz in der Europäischen Union und der Schweiz* (n 50) 28; Klöhn, *Kapitalmarkt, Spekulation und Behavioral Finance* (n 222) 155–6; Picot, Bortenlänger and Röhrl (n 77) 23–4; Thelen (n 147) 71.
262 Picot, Bortenlänger and Röhrl (n 77) 23–4.

ble.[263] Since information production and publication is costly and done by informed traders who want to offset their costs for this endeavor, full disclosure of all their trading activity would deprive them of this benefit since everybody could detect the information and use it for their own benefit while the market price adapts to the new equilibrium price. This would render the new piece of information worthless.[264]

Another adverse effect of an overabundance of trade transparency are so-called market impact costs. Market impact costs are the costs traders incur when they place a large order, i.e., a block order, into the order book of a trading system and receive a price inferior to the price displayed shortly before.[265] This effect is driven by three distinct phenomena: the liquidity premium, adverse price movement, and the information effect.

Firstly, a trader that places a market order while there is no contra-side market order has to execute against the best priced limit order on the other side of the midpoint of the bid-ask-spread. Overcoming this price difference for instant liquidity leads to a price worse than the displayed midpoint price (*liquidity premium*).[266]

Secondly, while all traders demanding instant execution have to pay the liquidity premium, even those trading in retail sizes, block traders are more vulnerable to suffer also from *adverse price movement* because the best-priced sell-order may not be of sufficient volume to fill a large buy-order. Block traders have to buy from multiple sell-orders with gradually rising prices, depressing their overall transaction price even further.[267]

Thirdly, the situation of block traders becomes even worse when the *information effect* sets in: when a block-sized buy-order hits the order book, sellers will immediately cancel their orders and set new orders with higher prices because they anticipate an imbalance in demand and expect it to be a sign of an informed trader trading upon a newly-acquired piece of

---

263 ibid 24–5; Bernd Rudolph, 'Computerbörse für den Finanzplatz Deutschland' [1994] Die Betriebswirtschaft 426, 427; Rudolph and Röhrl (n 51) 206ff.

264 Grossmann and Stiglitz, 'Information and Competitive Price Systems' (n 249) 246ff; Grossmann and Stiglitz, 'On the Impossibility of Informationally Efficient Markets' (n 249) 393ff; Picot, Bortenlänger and Röhrl (n 77) 24–5; Rudolph (n 263) 427; Rudolph and Röhrl (n 51) 206ff.

265 Rudolph and Röhrl (n 51) 172. See also Gomber and Gvozdevskiy (n 43) para 14.12; Peter Gomber and Uwe Schweickert, 'Der Market Impact: Liquiditätsmaß im elektronischen Wertpapierhandel' [2002] Die Bank 485, 486; Picot, Bortenlänger and Röhrl (n 77) 24.

266 Gomber and Gvozdevskiy (n 43) para 14.12; Gomber and Schweickert (n 265) 486.

267 Gomber and Gvozdevskiy (n 43) para 14.12; Gomber and Schweickert (n 265) 486.

private price information.[268] It becomes apparent that transaction costs can accrue easily to a point where they become prohibitive. For this reason, block traders favor less trade transparency. Under complete transparency, they would not provide their much-needed liquidity to the market.[269]

On the other hand, too little trade transparency raises transaction costs, as well. Market participants, especially retail investors with limited capabilities and resources, face high search and information costs and find it harder to assess their execution quality since they lack the information of other traders. Thus, '*(...) [t]ransparency, or the dissemination of both quotations and trading reports, enhances investor protection and increases the actual and perceived fairness of securities markets.*'[270]

Thus, minimizing transaction costs by manipulating the degree of trade transparency is not a maximization problem but an optimization problem.[271] The optimum of trade transparency lies where the cost of information research is equal to the marginal utility of the information itself.[272] Since this equation is dependent on many other variables that are constantly changing, it is difficult if not impossible to target the optimum by regulation, given that regulation is a pre-defined set of rules.[273] To find a proper level of trade transparency, at least close to the optimum, the degree of liquidity in the market may be taken as an indicator. Insofar, market transparency is an observable characteristic of financial markets since the scope of information made public can be monitored,[274] and the degree of liquidity provides an approximate indicator whether the level

---

268 Gomber and Gvozdevskiy (n 43) para 14.13; Gomber and Schweickert (n 265) 486; Jan Liersch, *Regulierung des Blockhandels an den organisierten Aktienmärkten der Vereinigten Staaten, Großbritanniens und Deutschlands* (Ph.D.-Thesis Johann Wolfgang Goethe-University Frankfurt 2001, Peter Lang 2002) 62ff.

269 Liersch, *Regulierung des Blockhandels an den organisierten Aktienmärkten der Vereinigten Staaten, Großbritanniens und Deutschlands* (n 268) 64.

270 Becker and others (n 232) 331.

271 Fernholz (n 51) 85; Humbel, *Die Regelung der Vor- und Nachhandelstransparenz in der Europäischen Union und der Schweiz* (n 50) 29; Picot, Bortenlänger and Röhrl (n 77) 25; Rudolph and Röhrl (n 51) 207–8.

272 Picot, Bortenlänger and Röhrl (n 77) 23 fn 78; cf. Grossmann and Stiglitz, 'Information and Competitive Price Systems' (n 249) 246ff; Grossmann and Stiglitz, 'On the Impossibility of Informationally Efficient Markets' (n 249) 393ff.

273 Kägi (n 50) BSK FinfraG Art 28 para 39; Picot, Bortenlänger and Röhrl (n 77) 25; Rudolph and Röhrl (n 51) 207–8.

274 Kägi (n 50) BSK FinfraG Art 28 para 39.

of transparency is approaching its optimal amount or may have already surpassed it.[275]

3. Liquidity

The third efficiency criterion is the level of liquidity in the market. A market is considered liquid if market participants can place buy- and sell-orders of all sizes, small and larger orders, and receive fast execution at a price close to its fair value.[276] A high level of liquidity is crucial for the well-functioning of the market, since especially institutional investors choose trading systems with regard to their level of liquidity. On a market with a low level of liquidity, transaction speeds are slower and even smaller orders are more susceptible to suffer market impact costs.[277]

Liquidity is a criterion that is determined by four, partially interdependent characteristics: first, market breadth, which means that there is a significant number of orders close to the midpoint price;[278] second, market depth, which requires that also large order sizes can be executed at prices at least close to the midpoint price;[279] third, a liquid market shows immediacy, which is the capacity of a market to execute even large orders in a timely

275 Cf. Matteo Aquilina and others, 'Aggregate Market Quality Implications of Dark Trading' (FCA Occasional Paper No. 29, FCA, August 2017) 8. See also Sabrina Buti, Barbara Rindi and Ingrid M Werner, 'Diving Into Dark Pools' (Fisher College of Business Working Paper Series, June 2010) 10; James Brugler, 'Into the Light: Dark Pool Trading and Intraday Market Quality on the Primary Exchange' (Staff Working Paper No. 545, Bank of England, September 2015) 2, 6, 26; Rhodri G Preece and Sviatoslav Rosov, 'Dark Trading and Equity Market Quality' (2014) 70(6) Financial Analysts Journal 33, 36.

276 Foucault, Pagano and Röell (n 68) 8; Picot, Bortenlänger and Röhrl (n 77) 26: 'close at its consensus value' means at low transaction costs.

277 Picot, Bortenlänger and Röhrl (n 77) 25.

278 Gomber and Schweickert (n 265) 485; Picot, Bortenlänger and Röhrl (n 77) 26; Rudolph and Röhrl (n 51) 177; Raymund Scheffrahn, *Gestaltung einer wettbewerbsfähigen Börse Schweiz* (Ph.D.-Thesis University of Zurich, P. Haupt 1992) 39.

279 Gomber and Schweickert (n 265) 485; Picot, Bortenlänger and Röhrl (n 77) 26; Rudolph and Röhrl (n 51) 178.

manner;[280] and fourth, liquid markets show resilience, which means that prices react elastically to short-term imbalances in the order book.[281]

The level of liquidity is influenced by several parameters, among them is trade transparency. For this reason, liquidity can guide the trading system operator and regulators in the question whether there is too little, optimal or already too much transparency in the marketplace.[282] However, setting an amount of trade transparency matching the optimum[283] in every instance may not be possible because this optimum is a moving target.[284]

III. Effect of Liquidity and Trade Transparency on Transaction Costs

The three aspects of transaction costs in financial markets – commissions and fees, bid-ask-spread, and market impact costs – can be reduced if the efficiency criteria are calibrated properly.

1. Reduction of Fees

The positive effect of competition on commissions and fees for a service such as offering a trading system are evident because of the economic studies on monopolies[285] and the historical example of (high) commissions and

280 Picot, Bortenlänger and Röhrl (n 77) 26; Rudolph and Röhrl (n 51) 178. See also Gomber and Schweickert (n 265) 485; Olaf Oesterhelweg and Dirk Schiereck, 'Meßkonzepte für die Liquidität von Finanzmärkten' [1993] Die Bank 390.

281 Gomber and Schweickert (n 265) 485; Picot, Bortenlänger and Röhrl (n 77) 26; Rudolph and Röhrl (n 51) 178; Robert A Schwartz, *Reshaping the Equity Markets: A Guide for the 1990s* (Harper Collins 1991) 127.

282 Humbel, *Die Regelung der Vor- und Nachhandelstransparenz in der Europäischen Union und der Schweiz* (n 50) 25.

283 Optimum as defined by *Grossman and Stiglitz* as a competitive equilibrium of information arbitrage in an informationally incomplete market where the costs of finding information are equal to the marginal utility of the information itself. Cf. Grossmann and Stiglitz, 'Information and Competitive Price Systems' (n 249) 246ff; Grossmann and Stiglitz, 'On the Impossibility of Informationally Efficient Markets' (n 249) 393ff; Picot, Bortenlänger and Röhrl (n 77) 23 fn 78.

284 Kägi (n 50) BSK FinfraG Art 28 para 39; Picot, Bortenlänger and Röhrl (n 77) 25; Rudolph and Röhrl (n 51) 207–8.

285 Alexander Morell, '§ 3 - Nachfrage, Angebot und Märkte' in Emanuel V Towfigh and Niels Petersen (eds), *Ökonomische Methoden im Recht: Eine Einführung für Juristen* (2nd edn, Mohr Siebeck 2017) 72, § 3 para 154.

fees at, for instance, the NYSE when it had a dominant market position.[286] If there is only one provider in the market for a good or a service, it will most likely charge fees above its production costs.[287] In an environment with viable competitors, excess fees of one supplier will lead to a migration of the demander to the others.[288] Thus, competition is a useful means to moderate commissions and fees of services like offering a trading system. However, since there are no attempts by regulators to move back to centralized markets, the issue of fee reduction is not the primary issue of this study and can be neglected in the following.

2. Reduction of the Bid-Ask-Spread

The transaction costs resulting from a wide bid-ask-spread can be reduced by increasing the level of liquidity. A wide bid-ask-spread means that the best-priced buy-orders and the best-priced sell-orders are far from each other in the order book, thus the liquidity premium for a trader who wants to trade instantly is high. A higher level of liquidity is characterized by market breadth, which means that there is a significant number of orders close to the midpoint price.[289] This means that the bid-ask-spread is narrow and therefore also the transaction costs associated with the liquidity premium are low.[290]

High levels of liquidity do not require a maximum but rather an optimal amount of trade transparency. Thus, reducing transaction costs associated with the bid-ask-spread requires an optimally calibrated trade transparency regime.

3. Reduction of Market Impact Costs

Transaction costs caused by market impact costs are also reduced by higher liquidity. A high level of liquidity also depends on market depth, immediacy, and resilience. If those factors are high, large block orders can be absorbed quickly while barely moving the market price at the trader's

286 Mahoney and Rauterberg (n 118) 232–3.
287 Morell (n 285) 72ff, § 3 paras 154ff.
288 ibid 72ff, § 3 paras 154ff.
289 Picot, Bortenlänger and Röhrl (n 77) 26; Rudolph and Röhrl (n 51) 177; Scheffrahn (n 278) 39.
290 Ekkenga (n 96) § 7 para 138a.

detriment. To induce liquidity and avoid the information effect with other traders in the market, trade transparency should neither be too high nor too low; it, again, needs to be calibrated optimally.

IV. Conclusions for Further Analysis

The functioning of financial markets and investor protection guide financial markets regulation but need further interpretation and specification to be applied in a specific context such as the regulation of lit and dark trading. Economics informs the legal discussion with efficiency criteria of informational efficiency, market transparency and liquidity as measuring sticks for proper regulation. The *Information Paradox* theorizes that the relationship of transparency and dark trading may not be maximization but an optimization problem. In this regard, trade transparency serves as an observable variable that is interrelated with liquidity in a manner that regulators can align their regulation to the amount of transparency that provides sufficiently high levels of liquidity.

C. Influence of Pre- and Post-Trade Transparency on Market Efficiency

I. Pre-Trade Transparency

1. Positive Effects of Pre-Trade Transparency on Market Efficiency

In general, trading systems that have a high level of pre-trade transparency also show higher levels of liquidity which reduces transaction costs for their traders and enhances market efficiency.[291] Pre-trade transparency reduces transaction costs in several ways. For traders searching for available liquidity, pre-trade transparency reduces search costs because they can see other limit orders sitting in the order book. Pre-trade transparency is also beneficial for traders whose orders are sitting in the order book waiting for contra-side liquidity because the market becomes aware of the available

291 Humbel, *Die Regelung der Vor- und Nachhandelstransparenz in der Europäischen Union und der Schweiz* (n 50) 34; Kumpan, 'Transparenz als Mittel der Kapitalmarktregulierung' (n 51) 798; cf. Akerlof (n 99) 488; Joseph E Stiglitz, 'Information and the Change in the Paradigm in Economics' (2002) 92(3) The American Economic Review 460, 468.

liquidity.[292] While this insight is obvious in financial markets with only one exchange, visibility of orders becomes an essential market driver in fragmented markets where liquidity is dispersed across an array of trading systems.[293]

The comparability between trading systems created by pre-trade transparency supports the 'law of one price' for one product as prices converge across different trading systems.[294] This convergence lowers negotiation costs for traders and reduces arbitrage risks across the market.[295]

Pre-trade transparency also fuels the price formation mechanism on trading venues. Having a centralized price lowers the bargaining costs between traders, which is especially beneficial for smaller traders who otherwise would not be able to trade at the same prices as larger traders with greater bargaining power.[296] Additionally, pre-trade transparency supports informational efficiency by reducing information asymmetries because it conveys information from informed traders to uninformed traders.[297]

---

292 Francotte, Valiante and Lannoo (n 71) 44; Humbel, *Die Regelung der Vor- und Nachhandelstransparenz in der Europäischen Union und der Schweiz* (n 50) 34–5; Kumpan, 'Transparenz als Mittel der Kapitalmarktregulierung' (n 51) 789; Lenenbach (n 51) para 3.157; Rudolph and Röhrl (n 51) 204ff.

293 Humbel, *Die Regelung der Vor- und Nachhandelstransparenz in der Europäischen Union und der Schweiz* (n 50) 35; Kumpan, 'Transparenz als Mittel der Kapitalmarktregulierung' (n 51) 798; Lenenbach (n 51) para 3.157; Rudolph and Röhrl (n 51) 204.

294 Stephen J Lubben, *Corporate Finance* (2nd edn, Wolters Kluwer Law & Business 2017) 75: '*(...) the law of one price–the idea that an asset should have but one price, no matter how many forms or locations it might be sold in (...)*'.

295 Clausen and Sørensen (n 51) 293; Humbel, *Die Regelung der Vor- und Nachhandelstransparenz in der Europäischen Union und der Schweiz* (n 50) 35; Kumpan, 'Transparenz als Mittel der Kapitalmarktregulierung' (n 51) 798; Lenenbach (n 51) para 3.157; Nyquist (n 72) 285–6; Seitz (n 132) 502.

296 Humbel, *Die Regelung der Vor- und Nachhandelstransparenz in der Europäischen Union und der Schweiz* (n 50) 35; Kumpan, 'Transparenz als Mittel der Kapitalmarktregulierung' (n 51) 798; Lenenbach (n 51) para 3.157; Rudolph and Röhrl (n 51) 204ff.

297 Foucault, Pagano and Röell (n 68) 295; Humbel, *Die Regelung der Vor- und Nachhandelstransparenz in der Europäischen Union und der Schweiz* (n 50) 36. See also: Karl-Burkhard Caspari, 'Anlegerschutz in Deutschland im Lichte der Brüsseler Richtlinie' [2005] NZG 98, 99; Kumpan, 'Transparenz als Mittel der Kapitalmarktregulierung' (n 51) 798; Lenenbach (n 51) para 3.157; Marco Pagano and Ailsa Röell, 'Transparency and Liquidity: A Comparison of Auction and Dealer Markets with Informed Trading' (1996) 51(2) Journal of Finance 579ff; Rudolph and Röhrl (n 51) 205; Seitz (n 132) 502.

Thus, pre-trade transparency is an essential pre-requisite for the functioning of financial markets, and it increases investor trust in the market. This incentivizes investors to invest their excess funds into the financial market which enhances market liquidity and, ultimately, market efficiency.[298]

2. Economic Studies

Economists reached varying results in their analysis of pre-trade transparency's influence on market efficiency.

Flood et al. (1999)[299] and *Henderschott/Jones (2005)*[300] found positive effects of pre-trade transparency on the market. *Flood et al. (1999)* observed that '*(...) pre-trade transparency significantly reduces search costs, thus alleviating some uncertainty and facilitating trade. As a result, market liquidity, measured by spreads and volume, is greater in transparent markets.*'[301] In their study of dealer markets, *Flood et al (1999)* also revealed that rationally speculating dealers use less aggressive price adjustments in transparent markets in comparison to dealers in non-transparent markets.[302] This means price discovery in transparent markets was slower than in non-transparent markets, which renders transparent markets less informationally efficient than dark markets.[303] This observation is, however, unsurprising given that dealers could observe their competitors' prices which lead to locked-in prices similar to prices at gas stations on the opposite side of the

298 Francotte, Valiante and Lannoo (n 71) 46–7; Humbel, *Die Regelung der Vor- und Nachhandelstransparenz in der Europäischen Union und der Schweiz* (n 50) 35–6; IOSCO, 'Transparency and Market Fragmentation' (n 3) 3–4; Kumpan, 'Transparenz als Mittel der Kapitalmarktregulierung' (n 51) 798; Lenenbach (n 51) para 3.157; Nyquist (n 72) 285; Robert A Schwartz and Reto Francioni, *Equity Markets in Action: The Fundamentals of Liquidity, Market Structure & Trading* (John Wiley & Sons 2004) 195; Seitz (n 132) 502.

299 Mark D Flood and others, 'Quote Disclosure and Price Discovery in Multiple-Dealer Financial Markets' (1999) 12(1) Review of Financial Studies 37, 57.

300 Terrence Hendershott and Charles M Jones, 'Island Goes Dark: Transparency, Fragmentation, and Regulation' (2005) 18(3) The Review of Financial Studies 743, 787.

301 Flood and others (n 299) 57.

302 ibid 57.

303 ibid 57.

road.[304] This shows the *Information Paradox* when information travels too easily.

Henderschott/Jones (2005) examined the effects of a formerly lit market becoming a dark pool for certain Exchange Traded Funds (ETFs): they found that the trading system became less efficient as it began to operate as a dark pool because spreads widened and price discovery slowed down.[305]

The studies by *Baruch (2005)* and *Boehmer/Saar/Yu (2005)* underline the findings of *Flood et al. (1999)* and *Henderschott/Jones (2005)* that the NYSE's step to provide an open order book showed the positive effect that enhanced pre-trade transparency has on price-discovery.[306] Both studies also found that the liquidity seekers benefitted from increased transparency, whereas liquidity providers suffered and rather preferred closed order books.[307]

Negative effects of pre-trade transparency were found by *Madhavan/Porter/Weaver (2008)*,[308] *Bortoli et al. (2006)*,[309] *Kovaleva/Iori (2015)*[310] and *Bloomfield/O'Hara/Saar (2015)*.[311] While *Madhavan/Porter/Weaver (2008)* and *Bortoli et al. (2006)* found adverse effects of full order book transparency, i.e., the order book shows not only the best-priced buy- and sell-orders but also the inferiorly priced orders in the order book. Market quality suffered because the inferiorly priced orders in part cancelled their orders and posted new orders at even worse prices, broadening the bid-ask-spread and in part because those traders left the lit market for dark pools. Those liquidity suppliers fear adverse effects if informed traders trade

---

304 ibid 57.

305 Hendershott and Jones (n 300) 787.

306 Shmuel Baruch, 'Who Benefits from an Open Limit-Order Book?' (2005) 78(4) The Journal of Business 1267ff; 1295; Ekkehart Boehmer, Gideon Saar and Lei Yu, 'Lifting the Veil: An Analysis of Pre-trade Transparency at the NYSE' (2005) 60(2) The Journal of Finance 783ff, 812.

307 Baruch (n 306) 1267ff, 1295; Boehmer, Saar and Yu (n 306) 783ff, 812.

308 Ananth Madhavan, David Porter and Daniel Weaver, 'Should Securities Markets Be Transparent?' (2005) 8(3) Journal of Financial Markets 265, 269ff, 286–7.

309 Luke Bortoli and others, 'Limit Order Book Transparency, Execution Risk, and Market Liquidity: Evidence from the Sydney Futures Exchange' (2006) 26(12) Journal of Future Markets 1147ff, 1157ff, 1165–6.

310 Polina Kovaleva and Giulia Iori, 'The Impact of Reduced Pre-Trade Transparency Regimes on Market Quality' (2015) 57 Journal of Economic Dynamics and Control 145, 157.

311 Robert Bloomfield, Maureen O'Hara and Gideon Saar, 'Hidden Liquidity: Some New Light on Dark Trading' (2015) 70(5) The Journal of Finance 2227ff, 2254ff.

against their limit orders.[312] *Kovaleva/Iori (2015)* support these finding by stating that full quote transparency leads to higher transaction costs and less efficient markets.[313]

On the contrary, *Bloomfield/O'Hara/Saar (2015)* found robust liquidity levels on non-transparent markets, and call into doubt the role of pre-trade transparency for increased levels of liquidity and reduced transaction costs.[314]

Eom/Ok/Park (2007) found an ambivalent effect of pre-trade transparency. First, market efficiency increases with increases of pre-trade transparency, but the increases in efficiency have a decreasing growth rate, i.e., the function of growth in market efficiency is concave.[315] Above a certain threshold, further increases in pre-trade transparency see declines in market efficiency.[316]

These diverse findings may, in part, result from the different data sets used in those studies but can also be seen as evidence of the *Information Paradox* by *Grossman/Stiglitz.*

II. Post-Trade Transparency

1. Positive Effects of Post-Trade Transparency on Market Efficiency

Post-trade transparency allows investors of recently executed transactions to monitor their intermediaries and the trading systems regarding the execution quality they received compared to their peers who traded at a similar time. This reduces the principal-agent-conflict between investors and market intermediaries while building investor trust.[317]

---

312 Madhavan, Porter and Weaver (n 308) 269ff, 286–7; Bortoli and others (n 309) 1147ff, 1157ff, 1165–6.

313 Kovaleva and Iori (n 310) 157.

314 Bloomfield, O'Hara and Saar (n 311) 2227ff, 2254ff.

315 Kyong S Eom, Jinho Ok and Jong-Ho Park, 'Pre-Trade Transparency and Market Quality' (2007) 10(4) Journal of Financial Markets 319ff, 340.

316 ibid 319ff, 333ff.

317 Kägi (n 50) BSK FinfraG Art 29 para 5; Schott and Winkler (n 70) SK FinfraG Art 29 para 50; Kumpan and Schmidt (n 4) MiFIR Art 6 para 1; Timo Holzborn and Alexander Israel, 'Die Neustrukturierung des Finanzmarktrechts durch das Finanzmarktrichtlinienumsetzungsgesetz (FRUG)' [2008] NJW 791, 796; Humbel, *Die Regelung der Vor- und Nachhandelstransparenz in der Europäischen Union und der*

Moreover, post-trade transparency fuels the price formation process because it informs the market at which prices traders were willing to trade in the market.[318] Insofar, post-trade transparency serves similar purposes to pre-trade transparency when traders use the information of currently executed transactions as a benchmark for their upcoming transactions.[319]

2. Issues with Post-Trade Transparency

In quote-driven markets, market makers buy and sell the same financial instruments into the market and seek to have as little inventory risk as possible.[320] When market makers buy large orders, they need to dispose of them into the market and aim to do so with as little market impact as possible.[321] Under far-reaching post-trade transparency, traders will anticipate the subsequent transactions of the market makers and will only buy from them at an increased price.[322] This may exhaust the bid-ask-spread of the market makers, eliminating their profit from the initial block transaction. In anticipation of this, market makers will not buy the block order in the first place and thereby reduce liquidity in the market rendering it less efficient.[323]

Schweiz (n 50) 47; Kumpan, 'Transparenz als Mittel der Kapitalmarktregulierung' (n 51) 798, 801; Lenenbach (n 51) para 3.157; Seitz (n 132) 503.

318 Gebauer (n 94) MiFIR Art 6 para 2; Kägi (n 50) BSK FinfraG Art 29 para 5; Humbel, *Die Regelung der Vor- und Nachhandelstransparenz in der Europäischen Union und der Schweiz* (n 50) 47.

319 Kägi (n 50) BSK FinfraG Art 29 para 5; Fernholz (n 51) 86–7; Humbel, *Die Regelung der Vor- und Nachhandelstransparenz in der Europäischen Union und der Schweiz* (n 50) 47.

320 Kumpan and Schmidt (n 4) MiFIR Art 7 para 1; Moloney, *EU Securities and Financial Markets Regulation* (n 4) 484–5, 487; O'Hara, *Market Microstructure Theory* (n 45) 258.

321 Humbel, *Die Regelung der Vor- und Nachhandelstransparenz in der Europäischen Union und der Schweiz* (n 50) 48; Kumpan, 'Transparenz als Mittel der Kapitalmarktregulierung' (n 51) 799; Lenenbach (n 51) para 3.158; Rudolph and Röhrl (n 51) 209; Schwartz and Francioni (n 298) 193ff.

322 Humbel, *Die Regelung der Vor- und Nachhandelstransparenz in der Europäischen Union und der Schweiz* (n 50) 48; Kumpan, 'Transparenz als Mittel der Kapitalmarktregulierung' (n 51) 799; Lenenbach (n 51) para 3.158; Rudolph and Röhrl (n 51) 209.

323 Humbel, *Die Regelung der Vor- und Nachhandelstransparenz in der Europäischen Union und der Schweiz* (n 50) 48; Kumpan, 'Transparenz als Mittel der Kapitalmarktregulierung' (n 51) 799; Lenenbach (n 51) para 3.158; Rudolph and Röhrl (n 51) 209. See also on the vulnerability of market makers in highly transparent

3. Economic Studies

While pre-trade transparency received wide attention by economic scholars, post-trade transparency has less so. *Bloomfield/O'Hara (1999)*, however, found that a post-trade transparent market indeed shows wider bid-ask-spreads in an initial period, but, in a second period, those spreads narrow again. Thus, there are no clear empirical results on post-trade transparency.[324]

In the special instance of a market maker taking on a large position, post-trade transparency functions as pre-trade transparency for the subsequent disposal, therefore, the insights of the studies examining pre-trade transparency can be harnessed. These studies agree that large block orders should be exempt from pre-trade transparency to avoid market impact costs and incentivize block traders to provide valuable liquidity to the market.[325]

D. The Role of Dark Trading for Market Efficiency

Dark trading can alleviate the high transaction costs traders and trading systems face under broad trade transparency requirements. By sparing those traders and trading systems from the bright glare of extensive trade transparency regimes in modern markets, dark trading allows for additional liquidity to arise that would otherwise have withdrawn from the market and thereby enhances overall market efficiency.

---

markets: IOSCO, *Transparency on Secondary Markets: A Synthesis of the IOSCO Debate* (Il Sole 24 Ore Libri 1993) 14.

324 Robert Bloomfield and Maureen O'Hara, 'Market Transparency: Who Wins and Who Loses?' (1999) 12(1) Review of Financial Studies 5ff; Robert Bloomfield and Maureen O'Hara, 'Can Transparent Markets Survive?' (2000) 55(3) Journal of Financial Economics 425ff, 428ff; cf. O'Hara, *Market Microstructure Theory* (n 45) 258; Humbel, *Die Regelung der Vor- und Nachhandelstransparenz in der Europäischen Union und der Schweiz* (n 50) 48–9.

325 See below Part II § 5 E.II, § 6 C.V., § 7 C.II.5.

I. Lit Market's Attempts to Cure Adverse Effects of Trade Transparency

1. Veiling the Identity of Traders

Far-reaching transparency has been especially problematic for informed traders, since their informational advantage could easily be 'picked-off' by others who did not invest in information research when the informed traders' orders hit the order book showing pre-trade transparency.[326]

Although no trader in the market is an informed or an uninformed trader in every instance but finds himself for one order in the one group and for the next in the other, other market participants expect professional traders to be informed traders because they conduct extensive information research, and thus have a better understanding of market functions.[327] When other market participants, for instance, notice the broker identifier and realize that an incoming order is one by a professional trader, they picked off the (perceived) informational advantage of that order by bandwagoning the professional trader's order. Such market reactions can lower the incentive of professional traders to conduct market research for new information.[328]

326 Carole Comerton-Forde, Alex Frino and Vito Mollica, 'The Impact of Limit Order Anonymity on Liquidity: Evidence from Paris, Tokyo and Korea' (2005) 57(6) Journal of Economics and Business 528ff, 532ff; Carole Comerton-Forde and Kar M Tang, 'Anonymity, Liquidity and Fragmentation' (2009) 12(3) Journal of Financial Markets 337, 339ff, 365; Thierry Foucault, Sophie Moinas and Erik Theissen, 'Does Anonymity Matter in Electronic Limit Order Markets?' (2007) 20(5) The Review of Financial Studies 1707, 1708ff, 1739–40; Yusif Simaan, Daniel G Weaver and David K Whitcomb, 'Market Maker Quotation Behavior and Pretrade Transparency' (2003) 58 The Journal of Finance 1247ff; M. Á de Frutos and Carolina Manzano, 'Market transparency, market quality, and sunshine trading' (2014) 17 Journal of Financial Markets 174, 175, 180ff, 191; Humbel, *Die Regelung der Vor- und Nachhandelstransparenz in der Europäischen Union und der Schweiz* (n 50) 40–1.

327 Comerton-Forde and Tang (n 326) 338ff, 364–5; Foucault, Moinas and Theissen (n 326) 1708ff; 1739–40; Humbel, *Die Regelung der Vor- und Nachhandelstransparenz in der Europäischen Union und der Schweiz* (n 50) 40–1.

328 Juhani T Linnainmaa and Gideon Saar, 'Lack of Anonymity and the Inference from Order Flow' (2012) 25(5) The Review of Financial Studies 1414ff; Humbel, *Die Regelung der Vor- und Nachhandelstransparenz in der Europäischen Union und der Schweiz* (n 50) 40.

To protect the identity of professional traders as well as the conveyer belt of information production into the price formation process, most trading systems no longer display the identity of traders.[329]

2. No Full Order Book Transparency

As discussed before, a fully transparent order book would show not only the best-priced buy and sell orders but also all inferiorly priced orders.[330] Since inferiorly priced orders are more vulnerable to information traders, those orders would be withdrawn and routed to dark pools, which would mean less liquidity and higher transaction costs for the lit market.[331]

To avoid this, economists argue that only the best-priced orders need to be published because they have the most significant impact on price discovery whereas inferior orders have very little influence. Studies have shown that broadening the order book transparency to five orders on each side would (only) increase the price accuracy by 22 %.[332] While this shows that the best-priced orders certainly have the most significant impact, it remains a matter of regulatory decision-making if additional 22 % of accuracy are worth the risk.[333]

329 Comerton-Forde, Frino and Mollica (n 326) 528ff, 532ff, 538; Comerton-Forde and Tang (n 326) 364–5; Foucault, Moinas and Theissen (n 326) 1708ff, 1739–40; Frutos and Manzano (n 326) 180ff, 191; Humbel, *Die Regelung der Vor- und Nachhandelstransparenz in der Europäischen Union und der Schweiz* (n 50) 40–1.

330 See above Part I § 2.C.I.a).ee).

331 Kovaleva and Iori (n 310) 157.

332 Charles Cao, Oliver Hansch and Xiaoxin Wang, 'The Information Content of an Open Limit-Order Book' (2009) 29(1) Journal of Futures Markets 16, 23ff, 27ff, 39–40; cf. Kovaleva and Iori (n 310) 145ff; Yaling Lin, Tai Ma and Hsiu-Kuei Chen, 'Does Information Content Necessarily Increase with Greater Pre-Trade Transparency?' (2008) 11(4) Review of Pacific Basin Financial Markets and Policies 531ff, 535, 552.

333 See Ryuichi Yamamoto, 'Order Aggressiveness, Pre-Trade Transparency, and Long Memory in an Order-Driven Market' (2011) 35(11) Journal of Economic Dynamics and Control 1938, 1940ff finding no influence of the depth of order book transparency on volume, volatility and other signals. cf. Humbel, *Die Regelung der Vor- und Nachhandelstransparenz in der Europäischen Union und der Schweiz* (n 50) 41–2.

3. Introduction of Special-Order Types

Economists, regulators, and trading systems agree that large orders are susceptible to significant market impact costs in a transparent trading environment but are also vital liquidity providers for both lit and dark markets.[334] Consequently, large orders shall have access to some sort of dark trading, not only on dedicated dark pools, but also on otherwise lit venues to boost liquidity levels.[335]

To reduce transaction costs for large orders, transparent markets use special order types, such as *'hidden orders'* and *'iceberg orders'*.[336] Hidden order is simply another name for a dark order, i.e., an order with no pre-trade transparency. Iceberg orders are more sophisticated since they take a large order, slice it into multiple child orders and send one child order into the market showing pre-trade transparency. This child order can execute without the high market impact costs of a large order, and then the next child order follows into the market until the entire order has been executed over a prolonged period.[337]

While those measures are forms of dark trading that are still in use today, modern dark trading would not have risen to its current extent had the market not shifted. Those shifts in the market environment will be discussed next.

II. A New Market Environment

Even though the rise of dark trading was due to an interaction of a complex set of factors, for the purpose of this study two main developments shall be discussed that drove the rise of dark trading. Those two main drivers were more liberal regulation which caused market fragmentation and technological developments that gave rise to algorithmic trading and high frequency trading.[338]

---

334 Cf. IOSCO, 'Principles for Dark Liquidity' (n 12) 11–2.

335 Kovaleva and Iori (n 310) 151ff; Humbel, *Die Regelung der Vor- und Nachhandelstransparenz in der Europäischen Union und der Schweiz* (n 50) 42.

336 Kovaleva and Iori (n 310) 157.

337 Banks (n 5) 17.

338 Baisch, Baumann and Weber (n 11) 184; Banks (n 5) 8; Easthope and Ray (n 5) 5; Hochstrasser (n 11) 307; Humbel, *Die Regelung der Vor- und Nachhandelstransparenz in der Europäischen Union und der Schweiz* (n 50) 52; Monsch (n 90) 25–6.

1. Fragmentation of the Trading Landscape

In the late 1990s and early 2000s, the financial markets in the United States and Europe were dominated by exchanges that had a dominant market position over the institutionalized trading in the instruments listed with them.[339] Although concentration of liquidity in one trading system supported market efficiency, the lack of competitive pressure induced incumbent exchanges to postpone investment into modern trading infrastructures and enabled them to charge higher fees.[340]

In the United States, competition was introduced with the implementation of Regulation Alternative Trading System (Regulation ATS) in 1998 and Regulation National Market System (Regulation NMS) in 2005 which allowed broker-dealers to operate a trading venue as either an ECN, providing for trade transparency, or as an ATS, operating a dark pool.[341]

The European Union followed this policy of market liberalization with the introduction of the Markets in Financial Instruments Directive I (MiFID I) in 2007 which abolished the concentration rules in many Member States that protected the quasi-monopolies of national exchanges.[342] MiFID I introduced a three-pronged trading landscape consisting of regulated markets (RMs), MTFs, and systematic internalizers (SIs) to ensure competition and to lower transaction costs.[343]

---

339 Banks (n 5) 28; Gresse (n 7) 4, 19; Moloney, *EU Securities and Financial Markets Regulation* (n 4) 435–6.

340 Gresse (n 7) 3; See, for instance, fixed commission fees at NYSE under former Rule 390: Mahoney and Rauterberg (n 118) 237–8. For the EU, see also: Commission of the European Communities, 'Proposal for a Directive of the European Parliament and of the Council on Investment Services and Regulated Markets, and amending Council Directives 85/611/EEC, Council Directives 93/6/EEC and European Parliament and Council Directive 2000/12/EC' (COM(2002) 625 final, 2002/0269 (COD), Brussels, 19 November 2002) 9–10; for the US, see: SEC, 'Regulation NMS: Final Rules' (17 CFR Parts 200, 201, 230, 240, 242, 249, and 270, Release No. 34–51808, File No. S7–10–04, 29 June 2005) 70 FR 37496, 37498ff; cf. Humbel, *Die Regelung der Vor- und Nachhandelstransparenz in der Europäischen Union und der Schweiz* (n 50) 52.

341 Rules 300ff Regulation ATS (17 CFR § 242.300ff); Rules 600ff Regulation NMS (17 CFR § 242.600ff); Banks (n 5) 9–10; Humbel, *Die Regelung der Vor- und Nachhandelstransparenz in der Europäischen Union und der Schweiz* (n 50) 53; Mahoney and Rauterberg (n 118) 240ff, 254–5.

342 Gresse (n 7) 4; Moloney, *EU Securities and Financial Markets Regulation* (n 4) 435–6.

343 Gresse (n 7) 4ff; Humbel, *Die Regelung der Vor- und Nachhandelstransparenz in der Europäischen Union und der Schweiz* (n 50) 53.

The result of this 'market for markets' approach[344] was, however, the fragmentation of the once concentrated body of liquidity across an ever-growing number of trading systems with each trading system having a lower market share while, however, the level of liquidity, measured by the bid-ask-spread, did not necessarily suffer.[345] Those effects were most visible with incumbent exchanges which lost their monopoly and, with it, large amounts of liquidity: for instance, *Angel/Harris/Spatt (2010)* found that NYSE's market share dropped from 80 % in 2003 to 25 % in 2009.[346] *Gress (2012)* found a similar decline in market share for Euronext and Deutsche Börse, with both losing approximately 22 % of market share in their flagship-index stocks, and LSE's market share in FTSE 100 securities fell by almost 28 %, while the new market entrants Chi-X, Turnquoise, and Better Alternative Trading System (BATS) ramped up their business in Europe.[347]

It is commonly held that the resulting market fragmentation could best be cured by introducing broad trade transparency to consolidate the market on an informational level.[348] Traders should be able to see which market offers the best prices and tap into its liquidity.[349] In practice, traders split their orders and entered multiple markets at once to skim the best-priced orders on top of the order book. This left inferiorly priced orders even more vulnerable to market impact costs because liquidity thinned and execution

344 See Gresse (n 7) 5.

345 Kern Alexander, 'Market Structures, Technologie and European Regulation' in Brigitte Strebel-Aerni (ed), *Finanzmärkte im Banne von Big Data: Einfluss der modernen Informations- und Kommunikationstechnologie auf die Geschäftsmodelle der Finanzdienstleister und auf die Finanzmärkte, die Politik, Regulierungsbehörden und die Souveränität der Schweiz* (Schulthess 2012) 33, 36; Hans Degryse, Frank de Jong and Vincent van Kervel, 'The Impact of Dark Trading and Visible Fragmentation on Market Quality' (2015) 19(4) Review of Finance 1587, 1589, 1602; Gomber and Pierron (n 4) 29ff; Gresse (n 7) 4ff, 19ff; Güllner (n 131) 939; Humbel, *Die Regelung der Vor- und Nachhandelstransparenz in der Europäischen Union und der Schweiz* (n 50) 53–4; Foresight (n 6) 118.

346 Angel, Harris and Spatt (n 6) 24.

347 Gresse (n 7) 9.

348 Cf. Kumpan, 'Transparenz als Mittel der Kapitalmarktregulierung' (n 51) 798; Lenenbach (n 51) para 3.157; Rudolph and Röhrl (n 51) 204.

349 Humbel, *Die Regelung der Vor- und Nachhandelstransparenz in der Europäischen Union und der Schweiz* (n 50) 54.

quality further off the mid-point price plummeted.[350] While fragmentation paired with higher trade transparency already imposed challenging market conditions on traders, the rise of a new breed of market participants exacerbated the situation further.

2. Rise of High Frequency Traders

In recent years, not only changes in the market infrastructure drove the growth of dark trading, but also technological changes, especially the rise of high frequency traders.[351] HFT is a complex term and a certain overlap to familiar terms, such as, electronic trading,[352] algorithmic trading,[353] or low latency trading.[354] For the purpose of this study, algorithmic trading shall

---

350 Degryse, Jong and van Kervel (n 345) 1587ff; Gresse (n 7) 19ff; Humbel, *Die Regelung der Vor- und Nachhandelstransparenz in der Europäischen Union und der Schweiz* (n 50) 54.

351 Easthope and Ray (n 5) 5.

352 The first electronic trading systems were Instinet (1969) and NASDAQ (1971), see Franca Contratto, 'Hochfrequenzhandel und systemische Risiken: Risikovorsorge im Finanzmarktrecht gestützt auf das Vorsorgeprinzip' [2014] GesKR 143, 145; Humbel, *Die Regelung der Vor- und Nachhandelstransparenz in der Europäischen Union und der Schweiz* (n 50) 55 fn 231. Cf. Alexander, 'Market Structures, Technologie and European Regulation' (n 345) 34; Peter Gomber and others, 'High-Frequency Trading' (April 2011) Policy Platform White Paper, 8; Claude Humbel, 'Beyond human response time - Prävention und Freiheitlichkeit im Hochfrequenzhandel' in Anna Coninx, Ege Gian and Julian Mausbach (eds), *Prävention und freiheitliche Rechtsordnung* (Dike 2017) 349, 352.

353 Algorithmic trading allows trading systems to handle large volumes of order flow, see Dave Cliff, Dan Brown and Philip Treleaven, 'Technology Trends in the Financial Markets: A 2020 Vision' (The Future of Computer Trading in Financial Markets Driver Review – DR 3, London, 2010) 7; Humbel, *Die Regelung der Vor- und Nachhandelstransparenz in der Europäischen Union und der Schweiz* (n 50) 55 fn 232. Cf. Irene Aldridge, *High-frequency trading: A practical guide to algorithmic strategies and trading systems* (2nd edn, Wiley 2013) 13ff; Alain P Chaboud and others, 'Rise of the Machines: Algorithmic Trading in the Foreign Exchange Market' (2014) 69(5) The Journal of Finance 2045f; Gomber and others (n 352) 13–4; Joel Hasbrouck and Gideon Saar, 'Low-Latency Trading' (2013) 16(4) Journal of Financial Markets 646, 652; Terrence Hendershott, Charles M Jones and Albert J Menkveld, 'Does Algorithmic Trading Improve Liquidity?' (2011) 66(1) The Journal of Finance 1ff; Humbel, 'Beyond human response time - Prävention und Freiheitlichkeit im Hochfrequenzhandel' (n 352) 353.

354 Gomber and others (n 352) 29–30; Humbel, *Die Regelung der Vor- und Nachhandelstransparenz in der Europäischen Union und der Schweiz* (n 50) 55; Monsch (n 90) 74.

denote trading in financial instruments in which a computer algorithm automatically determines the parameters of the order, for instance, where the order is routed as well as timing, price or volume of the order and how the order shall be handled when it reaches the trading system.[355]

High-frequency trading is a subcategory of algorithmic trading[356] characterized by

> *'(a) infrastructure intended to minimise network and other types of latencies, including at least one of the following facilities for algorithmic order entry: co-location, proximity hosting or high-speed direct electronic access;*
> *(b) system-determination of order initiation, generation, routing or execution without human intervention for individual trades or orders; and*
> *(c) high message intraday rates which constitute orders, quotes or cancellations.'*[357]

High frequency trading is thus characterized and often criticized for its short term trading strategies and low profit margins that often only create a sizable return due to economies of scale.[358] While high-frequency traders

---

355 Benedikt Coridaß and Dominik Dreyer, 'Hochfrequenzhandel - was ist noch erlaubt?: Anforderungen und Gefahren des Hochfrequenzhandels' in Ralf Temporale (ed), *Europäische Finanzmarktregulierung: Handbuch zu EMIR, MiFID II/ MiFIR, PRIIPs, MAD/MAR, OTC-Derivaten und Hochfrequenzhandel* (1st edn, Schäffer-Poeschel 2015) 55, 59ff; Monsch (n 90) 11; Violeta Sliskovic, 'MiFID II-Anforderungen an den algorithmischen Handel aus der Perspektive eines Energiehandelsunternehmens' [2020] CB 145, 146. See also Article 4(1)(39) MiFID II and the transposition into German law in Section 80(2)(1) WpHG.

356 IOSCO, 'Regulatory Issues Raised by the Impact of Technological Changes on Market Integrity and Efficiency: Final Report' (FR09/11, October 2011) 22; Contratto, 'Hochfrequenzhandel und systemische Risiken' (n 352) 146; Hendershott, Jones and Menkveld (n 353) 1 fn 1; Humbel, *Die Regelung der Vor- und Nachhandelstransparenz in der Europäischen Union und der Schweiz* (n 50) 55 fn 232; Tilman Schultheiß, 'Die Neuerungen im Hochfrequenzhandel' [2013] WM 596.

357 Article 4(1)(40) MiFID II. See also the transposition into German law in Section 80(2)(2) WpHG. See also Milan Bayram and Dominik Meier, 'Pinging, Front Running und Quote Matching - Verbotene Handelspraktiken nach der Marktmissbrauchsverordnung?' [2018] WM 1295; Contratto, 'Hochfrequenzhandel und systemische Risiken' (n 352) 145–6; Coridaß and Dreyer (n 355) 59ff; Daniel Mattig, 'Kurze Leitungswege für den Handel in Milli- und Mikrosekunden - Zu den latenzminimierenden Infrastrukturen an Börsen und multilateralen Handelssystemen' [2014] WM 1940; Maureen O'Hara, 'High Frequency Market Microstructure' (2015) 116(2) Journal of Financial Economics 257; Sliskovic (n 355) 146; Monsch (n 90) 10–1.

358 Contratto, 'Hochfrequenzhandel und systemische Risiken' (n 352) 145–6.

can use an array of trading strategies,[359] such as market making, statistical arbitrage, and directional trading,[360] their adverse effects on a lit trading system shall be outlined by the two strategies which have contributed most significantly to the rise of dark trading in recent years: '*electronic front running*' and '*slow-market arbitrage*'.[361]

a) Electronic Front Running

When high-frequency traders use electronic front running strategies, they exploit a host of technological advantages to outrun other market participants.[362] If, for instance, an institutional trader wishes to make a block trade on lit markets, they will usually split up the block order into multiple smaller child orders and send them to multiple trading systems to execute against the best priced orders in each of the order books. High-frequency traders can detect the first child order hitting the order book of the first trading venue in milli- or even microseconds due to co-location agreements with the trading system (e.g., an exchange) allowing them to set up the HFT's trading computer in the same data center right next to the computer operating the trading system's matching engine.[363]

The HFT infers from the incoming order that there is a chance that other child orders are under way to other trading systems.[364] To take advantage of this knowledge, the HFT's trading computer in the data center of the

359 Charles R Korsmo, 'High-Frequency Trading: A Regulatory Strategy' (2014) 48 University of Richmond Law Review 523.

360 Humbel, *Die Regelung der Vor- und Nachhandelstransparenz in der Europäischen Union und der Schweiz* (n 50) 57.

361 Fox, Glosten and Rauterberg, 'The New Stock Market' (n 88) 202; Thelen (n 147) 46.

362 Merritt B Fox, Lawrence R Glosten and Gabriel V Rauterberg, 'High-Frequency Trading and the New Stock Market: Sense And Nonsense' (2017) 29(4) Journal of Applied Corporate Finance 30, 35; Gary Shorter and Rena S Miller, 'High-Frequency Trading: Background, Concerns, and Regulatory Developments' (Congressional Research Service, 19 June 2014) 3.

363 Bayram and Meier (n 357) 1296; Fox, Glosten and Rauterberg, 'The New Stock Market' (n 88) 202, 233; Fox, Glosten and Rauterberg, 'High-Frequency Trading and the New Stock Market' (n 362) 35, 37; Kasiske (n 11) 455–6; Mattig (n 357) 1940; Shorter and Miller, 'High-Frequency Trading' (n 362) 3; Thelen (n 147) 46.

364 Bayram and Meier (n 357) 1296; Fox, Glosten and Rauterberg, 'The New Stock Market' (n 88) 202; Fox, Glosten and Rauterberg, 'High-Frequency Trading and the New Stock Market' (n 362) 35; Kasiske (n 11) 455–6; Mattig (n 357) 1940; Thelen (n 147) 46.

first trading system sends a signal through ultra-fast fiber optic cables to its second computer in the co-location of the second trading system's data center. Upon receipt of the signal, the second trading computer will cancel the limit orders at the former prices and either set new limit orders at a higher price for the incoming order to transact with or follow the incoming order's direction of trading, i.e., switch from sell to buy when then incoming order is a buy order.[365]

This way the HFT can ensure it does not sell at a price attractive for the block trader, but rather takes advantage of selling at a higher price than the incoming order. Electronic front running strategies are often criticized for the fact that institutional investors need to pay more for their transaction while HFTs can generate a risk-free profit.[366] Former New York Attorney General Eric Schneiderman even stated:

> *'[W]hen blinding speed is coupled with early access to data, it gives small groups of traders the power to manipulate market movements in their own favor before anyone else knows what's happening.'*[367]

b) Slow-Market Arbitrage

Another issue of high-frequency trading is slow-market arbitrage.[368] Suppose an HFT holds the best sell-order for 10,000 shares at a price of USD 10.15 in the market on trading system A which is publicly displayed on a common reporting tape where information of all of the trading systems in one financial market is consolidated. All incoming buy-orders should transact with the HFT's best offer at the quoted price.[369]

---

365 Fox, Glosten and Rauterberg, 'The New Stock Market' (n 88) 202, 206. Cf. Jacob Adrian, 'Informational Inequality: How High Frequency Traders Use Premier Access to Information to Prey on Institutional Investors' (2016) 14 Duke Law & Technology Review 256, 262; Hoops, *Verborgene Liquidität im Marktordnungsrecht der MiFID* (n 6) 60–1; Kasiske (n 11) 455–6; Shorter and Miller, 'High-Frequency Trading' (n 362) 3; Thelen (n 147) 47.

366 Bayram and Meier (n 357) 1298; Fox, Glosten and Rauterberg, 'The New Stock Market' (n 88) 202, 226; Shorter and Miller, 'High-Frequency Trading' (n 362) 3; Thelen (n 147) 46.

367 Linette Lopez, 'New York's Attorney General Has Declared War on Cheating High-Frequency Traders' *Business Insider* (24 September 2013).

368 Fox, Glosten and Rauterberg, 'The New Stock Market' (n 88) 202, 238.

369 ibid 238; Fox, Glosten and Rauterberg, 'High-Frequency Trading and the New Stock Market' (n 362) 38; Thelen (n 147) 48.

If, on trading system B, a retail investor posts a sell-order for USD 10.13, this offer is now the best sell-order and all incoming buy-orders should transact with this second order. However, because the consolidation of trade transparency information of several trading systems requires time and HFTs may learn about the new competing order early due to their co-location, the HFT's stale price of USD 10.15 will remain the best priced order displayed on the public tape for some milliseconds, and incoming buy orders will be routed to this order.[370] The HFT can meanwhile use their superior transaction speed to buy from the new competing sell order at its lower price of USD 10.13 on trading system B while selling at the higher price of USD 10.15 on trading system A. Provided that both orders are for 10,000 shares, the HFT makes a 'risk-free' profit of USD 200 (USD 0.02 for 10.000 shares). This strategy is, however, only 'risk-free' with regard to the superior information the single HFT possesses, while the risk of other HFTs engaging in similar arbitrage strategies snatching the profitable order at USD 10.13 prevails.[371]

In spite of the reputation of arbitrage strategies to increase market efficiency, slow-market arbitrage is a costly endeavor detrimental to uninformed and informed non-high-frequency traders alike.[372] In other forms of arbitrage, such as information arbitrage, one trader exploits their dominant position against another trader for their own personal benefit but also improves market quality at large, such as price accuracy in the case of information arbitrage.[373] In the case of slow-market arbitrage, the HFT absorbs the entire profits of USD 200 in the market, i.e., USD 0.02 for 10.000 shares, costing both the buyer and the seller the chance to receive a superior transaction. This strategy is insignificant to the market itself, since the price is not getting more accurate because the former best sell price of the HFT of USD 10.15 prevails. If anything, the market price

370 Fox, Glosten and Rauterberg, 'The New Stock Market' (n 88) 202; Fox, Glosten and Rauterberg, 'High-Frequency Trading and the New Stock Market' (n 362) 38; O'Hara, 'High Frequency Market Microstructure' (n 357) 258; Thelen (n 147) 48.

371 Fox, Glosten and Rauterberg, 'The New Stock Market' (n 88) 239; Fox, Glosten and Rauterberg, 'High-Frequency Trading and the New Stock Market' (n 362) 38. Cf. Aldridge (n 353) 35; Bayram and Meier (n 357) 1296; Gomber and others (n 352) 29–30; Kasiske (n 11) 456; Jeffrey G MacIntosh, 'Revisioning Revisionism: A Glance at HFT's Critics' in Greg N Gregoriou (ed), *Handbook of High Frequency Trading* (Academic Press/Elsevier 2015) 123, 138–39; Monsch (n 90) 74; Thelen (n 147) 48–9.

372 Fox, Glosten and Rauterberg, 'The New Stock Market' (n 88) 241–2; Fox, Glosten and Rauterberg, 'High-Frequency Trading and the New Stock Market' (n 362) 38.

373 Fox, Glosten and Rauterberg, 'The New Stock Market' (n 88) 241.

becomes less accurate because the HFT prevents the market price from adjusting to the new best-offer price of USD 10.13.[374] Those costs come at the benefit of insignificantly faster transaction times since the HFT acts as an inter-trading system market maker providing worse prices for increased immediacy.[375]

If traders prefer superior transaction prices for the cost of less immediacy, dark trading is a better choice than trading under pre-trade transparency. This is particularly interesting for block traders as well as non-HFT uninformed investors, like retail investors, and non-HFT informed investors seeking to protect their private information. Insofar, an abundance of trade transparency may increase transaction costs for traders.[376]

Investor trust is a cornerstone of financial market regulation and necessary pre-requisite for its proper functioning.[377] Electronic front running strategies and slow-market arbitrage by HFTs are only the most obvious examples that illustrate the need of other traders for more anonymity and safety. Other trading practices, such as, *quote sniffing, momentum ignition, spoofing, smoking,* or *order layering*[378] undermine the willingness of other market participants to participate in lit trading or any kind of trading in which HFTs participate.[379] While those other trading practices are not discussed in this study, but rather fall under the scope of research dedicated to market abuse, it still unveils a new force driving market participants into dark pools.[380]

374 Fox, Glosten and Rauterberg, 'High-Frequency Trading and the New Stock Market' (n 362) 38.

375 Fox, Glosten and Rauterberg, 'The New Stock Market' (n 88) 240ff.

376 ibid 240ff.

377 Humbel, *Die Regelung der Vor- und Nachhandelstransparenz in der Europäischen Union und der Schweiz* (n 50) 60; Thomas Werlen, *Konzeptionelle Grundlagen des schweizerischen Kapitalmarktrechts* (Ph.D.-Thesis University of Zurich 1994, Schulthess 1994) 22; Zobl and Kramer (n 51) para 18.

378 FINMA, 'Rundschreiben 2013/8 Marktverhaltensregeln: Aufsichtsregeln zum Marktverhalten im Effektenhandel' (Bern, 1 October 2013) paras 19ff; Kasiske (n 11) 455ff; Monsch (n 90) 88ff; Humbel, *Die Regelung der Vor- und Nachhandelstransparenz in der Europäischen Union und der Schweiz* (n 50) 60.

379 Humbel, *Die Regelung der Vor- und Nachhandelstransparenz in der Europäischen Union und der Schweiz* (n 50) 60.

380 ibid 60; O'Hara, 'High Frequency Market Microstructure' (n 357) 260.

III. Need for New Forms of Dark Trading

In a market environment with traders facing a greater risk of falling prey to HFT strategies due to lower levels of liquidity (influenced by increased fragmentation and transparency), dark trading offers advantages for block traders as well as traders of small- and medium-sized orders.[381]

1. Avoiding Information Leakage

Traders choose dark trading over lit trading to avoid information leakage about their orders.[382] Without pre-trade transparency, traders can protect their orders from the information effect.[383] When other market participants remain naïve about incoming orders, especially incoming block orders, they cannot react to them by cancelling opposite limit orders, posting new ones at an inferior price, or even follow the incoming order by trading in the same direction.[384] This protects dark traders from dwindling liquidity on the other side of the order book as well as adverse price selection in the

381 IOSCO, 'Principles for Dark Liquidity' (n 12) 4; Easthope and Ray (n 5) 6, 10; Gomber and Pierron (n 4) 28.

382 ASIC, 'Dark Liquidity and High-Frequency Trading' (Report 331, March 2013) 25 para 82, table 3; European Commission, 'Commission Staff Working Paper Impact Assessment EU Commission, Impact Assessment: Accompanying the document Proposal for a Directive of the European Parliament and of the Council on Markets in financial instruments [Recast] and the Proposal for a Regulation of the European Parliament and of the Council on Markets in financial instruments' (SEC(2011) 1226 final, Brussels, 20 October 2011) 130–1; IOSCO, 'Principles for Dark Liquidity' (n 12) 11; SEC, 'Regulation of Non-Public Trading Interest' (n 22) 74 FR 61220. See also Banks (n 5) 36–7; Batista (n 182) 110; Carole Comerton-Forde and Tālis J Putniņš, 'Dark Trading and Price Discovery' (2015) 118(1) Journal of Financial Economics 70, 78; Easthope and Ray (n 5) 3, 5; Gomber and Gvozdevskiy (n 43) para 14.13; Gomber and Pierron (n 4) 35–6; Allison Hintz, 'Lost in the Dark: An Analysis of the SEC's Regulatory Response to Dark Pools' (2015) 13(2) DePaul Business & Commercial Law Journal 329; Humbel, *Die Regelung der Vor- und Nachhandelstransparenz in der Europäischen Union und der Schweiz* (n 50) 51.

383 Ekkenga (n 96) § 7 para 142a; Liersch, *Regulierung des Blockhandels an den organisierten Aktienmärkten der Vereinigten Staaten, Großbritanniens und Deutschlands* (n 268) 62ff.

384 Liersch, *Regulierung des Blockhandels an den organisierten Aktienmärkten der Vereinigten Staaten, Großbritanniens und Deutschlands* (n 268) 62ff; cf. Shorter and Miller, 'Dark Pools in Equity Trading' (n 149) 5.

execution process, although they might still need to transact with several contra-side orders until their block order is entirely filled.[385]

Avoiding information leakage also enables dark traders to evade 'predatory' trading strategies of HFTs.[386] Electronic front running and slow-market arbitrage strategies build on the ability of HFTs to be the first to notice when an order is entering one specific marketplace and react on another.[387] Without pre-trade transparency, such orders would be undetectable, even for HFTs. Unfortunately for dark traders, HFTs would not be genuine arbitrageurs, had they not found a way to pierce the *'veil of ignorance'* to lure information out of dark pools as well. The strategy of *'pinging'* is discussed in the subsequent section on disadvantages of dark trading.[388] Nevertheless, for many traders dark trading is a means to avoid 'predatory' HFT trading strategies that would adversely affect their individual transaction costs.[389]

Insofar, dark trading can reduce the transaction costs associated with information leakage and enhance market efficiency as well as investor protection of those traders that would have otherwise fallen 'prey' to 'predatory' HTF strategies.

2. Allowing for Price Improvement

Another reason why the level of dark trading has increased significantly in the last years is that dark trading offers price improvements over lit trading. While dark trading in the form of 'upstairs trading' only offered price improvements for large orders and at the cost of immediacy, today's dark

---

385 European Commission, 'Commission Staff Working Paper Impact Assessment EU Commission, Impact Assessment' (n 382) 130–1; SEC, 'Regulation of Non-Public Trading Interest' (n 22) 74 FR 61219f; Ekkenga (n 96) § 7 para 142a; Shorter and Miller, 'Dark Pools in Equity Trading' (n 149) 5.

386 IOSCO, 'Principles for Dark Liquidity' (n 12) 12; Hintz (n 382) 329.

387 On 'electronic front running' and 'slow-market arbitrage' see above Part I § 3.D.II.2. Liersch, *Regulierung des Blockhandels an den organisierten Aktienmärkten der Vereinigten Staaten, Großbritanniens und Deutschlands* (n 268) 72.

388 See below Part I § 3.D.IV.2.b). Cf. ASIC, 'Dark Liquidity and High-Frequency Trading' (n 382) 29 para 88; *Pipeline Trading Systems LLC* (n 26) 2 no. 3–5; Hintz (n 382) 329–30.

389 Cf. Sean Foley and Tālis J Putniņš, 'Should We Be Afraid of the Dark?: Dark Trading and Market Quality' (2016) 122(3) Journal of Financial Economics 456, 459; Gomber and Pierron (n 4) 37.

pools offer price improvement for all order sizes, including small- and mid-sized orders, at a relatively high speed.[390]

a) Reasons for Price Improvement

aa) Mid-Point Pricing

The first reason for price improvement on dark pools is the manner in which they determine execution prices. Most dark pools do not maintain a price formation mechanism on their trading system, but rather import prices established on lit trading systems (so-called reference pricing).[391] However, dark pools which use reference pricing do not use the multiple price points of several buy and sell orders but only import the midpoint price of the lit trading system to match all their buy- and sell-orders.[392] This midpoint pricing saves traders half of the bid-ask-spread from the midpoint to the best sell price, in case of a buy-order, or to the best buy price, in case of a sell-order.[393] For example, provided a share on any given exchange has a bid price of USD 10.10 and an ask price of USD 10.20, then the midpoint price would be at USD 10.15. In a market not using the midpoint price, like a lit exchange, each party must pay the entire spread of USD 0.10 between the best bid and ask price if it wishes to trade immediately. In a dark pool with midpoint pricing, both traders only need to pay the difference between their price, either bid or ask, and the midpoint price, resulting in immediate trading costs of only USD 0.05. Although this price improvement may sometimes be a penny or even only a fraction of a penny, it can be enough to incentivize traders of small-, mid-

390 ASIC, 'Dark Liquidity and High-Frequency Trading' (n 382) 25, 27 paras 82 table 3, paras 85ff; IOSCO, 'Principles for Dark Liquidity' (n 12) 12; Easthope and Ray (n 5) 5–6; Gomber and Gvozdevskiy (n 43) para 14.12; Gomber and Pierron (n 4) 28, 36; Shorter and Miller, 'Dark Pools in Equity Trading' (n 149) 5.

391 IOSCO, 'Issues Raised by Dark Liquidity' (n 11) 12; IOSCO, 'Principles for Dark Liquidity' (n 12) 13; Sabrina Buti, Barbara Rindi and Ingrid M Werner, 'Dark Pool Trading Strategies, Market Quality and Welfare' (2017) 124(2) Journal of Financial Economics 244; Foley and Putniņš (n 389) 457, 459; Monsch (n 90) 18; Shorter and Miller, 'Dark Pools in Equity Trading' (n 149) 9; Zhu (n 186) 753.

392 IOSCO, 'Issues Raised by Dark Liquidity' (n 11) 12; IOSCO, 'Principles for Dark Liquidity' (n 12) 13; Buti, Rindi and Werner, 'Dark Pool Trading Strategies, Market Quality and Welfare' (n 391) 244; Preece (n 14) 12–3.

393 Easthope and Ray (n 5) 5; Gomber and Gvozdevskiy (n 43) para 14.12; Gomber and Pierron (n 4) 36.

and large-size orders to send their order to a dark pool instead of lit trading system because even miniscule savings add up to substantial amounts when hundreds or thousands of shares are traded.[394] From a market efficiency perspective, one can argue that a narrower bid-ask-spread compared to the lit market increases a measure of liquidity. Thus, dark pools can be considered efficiency enhancing.[395]

bb) Cost Savings

The absence of a price formation process in most dark pools also saves the dark pool operator the expenses of running a proprietary price formation mechanism. Considering the amount of order flow and price information pouring into a dark pool's systems coupled with resilience requirements for volatile market situations, running a price formation mechanism is an expensive endeavor. Even though dark pools often need to purchase private data feeds from lit trading systems that produce prices, they still save a significant amount of expenses that they can share with their users to offer even more attractive trading services.[396] Additionally, dark pools often charge lower per-share fees than exchanges making splitting up large orders into smaller ones more attractive for traders.[397]

Given the two sources for price improvements, dark pools are often able to lower transaction costs for their clients in this regard as well. This ultimately benefits market efficiency.

b) Pecking Order of Investors

Even though dark pools often offer price improvements, they generally have the disadvantage that they do not attract the same kind of traders as lit exchanges. For instance, dark pools generally do not have traditional market makers which leads to lower levels of liquidity on dark pools compared to exchanges. Nevertheless, traders choose to trade in a dark pool because the

394 ASIC, 'Dark Liquidity and High-Frequency Trading' (n 382) 23 para 77; IOSCO, 'Principles for Dark Liquidity' (n 12) 7, 20; Foley and Putniņš (n 389) 457ff.

395 Cf. Rudolph and Röhrl (n 51) 174ff.

396 Monsch (n 90) 331.

397 ASIC, 'Dark Liquidity and High-Frequency Trading' (n 382) 25 para 82, table 3; Shorter and Miller, 'Dark Pools in Equity Trading' (n 149) 5; Dave Michaels, 'Trading Rebates Skew Markets, NYSE and Allies Tell SEC' (Bloomberg 21 February 2014).

trade-off between less immediacy and price improvements renders those venues more beneficial for them.

In their study, *Mekveld/Yueshen/Zhu (2017)* have shown that there is a 'pecking order' of traders with three categories: the first category of traders prefer lowest cost and lowest immediacy trading venues, thus, they prefer dark pools which price at the midpoint; the second category of traders prefer medium cost and medium immediacy, thus, like to trade on dark pools which price off-side the midpoint; the third category of traders prefer high costs and high immediacy, thus, those traders prefer to trade on lit exchanges and other highly liquid lit venues.[398] Generally, uninformed traders find themselves more attracted to either of the two sorts of dark pools depending on their preference towards immediacy, whereas informed traders need to use their private information as quickly as possible to set off their search costs before someone else trades upon it. Thus, informed traders gravitate toward lit exchanges.[399]

Insofar, dark trading provides an addition to the overall trading landscape that can specifically cater to those (uninformed) traders who are willing to wait for better execution prices at the cost of immediacy.

3. Avoiding Adverse Price Selection due to Market Impact Costs

Furthermore, dark trading can reduce transaction costs by avoiding market impact costs.[400] In dark pools, block orders do not suffer adverse price selection by sweeping down the order book for two reasons.

The first reason is that traders need not fear the information effect when posting a large order at a competitive price because there is no pre-trade transparency.[401] This is particularly the case with dark pools that do not

398 Albert J Menkveld, Bart Z Yueshen and Haoxiang Zhu, 'Shades of Darkness: A Pecking Order of Trading Venues' (2017) 124(3) Journal of Financial Economics 503, 505.

399 Aquilina and others (n 275) 27; Menkveld, Yueshen and Zhu (n 398) 522.

400 ASIC, 'Dark Liquidity and High-Frequency Trading' (n 382) 25 para 82, table 3; Easthope and Ray (n 5) 5–6; Fox, 'MiFID II and Equity Trading' (n 53) para 18.97; Gomber and Gvozdevskiy (n 43) para 14.12; Gomber and Pierron (n 4) 35; Humbel, *Die Regelung der Vor- und Nachhandelstransparenz in der Europäischen Union und der Schweiz* (n 50) 51; Preece (n 14) 12–3; Shorter and Miller, 'Dark Pools in Equity Trading' (n 149) 5.

401 Liersch, *Regulierung des Blockhandels an den organisierten Aktienmärkten der Vereinigten Staaten, Großbritanniens und Deutschlands* (n 268) 72. See also Fox, 'MiFID II and Equity Trading' (n 53) para 18.97.

match orders at the midpoint, but rather allow traders to post their orders at their preferred limit price. In theory, orders should be much larger in dark pools than in lit markets. Statistics, however, show that the average order size has declined in recent years.[402] Only dedicated block crossing networks, which are trading platforms that only allow their traders to post large orders, can reliably offer the advantage of lower market impact costs due to larger order sizes.[403]

The second reason for the ability of dark pools to avoid market impact costs is that all orders – large and small – are executed regardless of their size: especially dark pools that match orders at the midpoint price provide large orders with price improvements since large orders are executed together with smaller orders at the midpoint. In lit markets, only small orders would execute close to the midpoint, whereas larger orders could only execute at more inferior prices. Sweeping down the order book is thus no longer an issue.[404]

By avoiding market impact costs, dark trading avoids the most significant burden for block traders and provides them with an efficient way to add their liquidity to the market. This is certainly one of the most important aspects in which dark trading enhances market efficiency and investor protection.

4. Protecting Market Makers

Dark trading not only protects the initial block trader, but also their trading partners who generally are market makers.[405] Market makers are in the business of supplying liquidity; thus, they have no interest in having large holdings of any financial instrument over a longer period of time.[406] Trading with a block trader would mean taking over such a large position, long or short, which must be disposed into the market in a timely manner. In this case post-trade transparency about the first transaction forms pre-trade

402 ASIC, 'Dark Liquidity and High-Frequency Trading' (n 382) 27 paras 85ff; Gomber and Pierron (n 4) 37.

403 Gomber and Pierron (n 4) 37 refer to Liquidnet, BlockCross and to a lesser extend ITG POSIT as dark pools dedicated to block trading.

404 Gomber and Gvozdevskiy (n 43) para 14.12; Preece (n 14) 12–3.

405 Thelen (n 147) 89.

406 Liersch, *Regulierung des Blockhandels an den organisierten Aktienmärkten der Vereinigten Staaten, Großbritanniens und Deutschlands* (n 268) 70, 118ff.

information for the subsequent disposal by the market maker which they want to avoid. Deferred post-trade transparency allows the market maker to both supply liquidity to block traders and be protected from adverse selection in subsequent transactions.[407]

IV. Concerns about Adverse Effects of Dark Trading

Besides the positive effects, dark trading is a departure from the principle of transparency that is considered fundamental for the functioning of financial markets and investor protection alike.[408] Intuitively, regulators as well as scholars were suspicious about the adverse effects of dark trading.

1. Price Accuracy and Liquidity

The complexity of the effects of dark trading is most pronounced with the issues of price accuracy and liquidity. Economic theory postulates that prices are determined by the equilibrium of aggregate supply and demand illustrated by two intersecting curves.[409] It is intuitively plausible that this mechanism will be disturbed if an increasing number of traders from either curve leave the lit market for dark trading.[410]

Dark trading can leave the market ignorant of the actual trading volumes and price preferences for a given instrument.[411] Even informed traders may have difficulties with retrieving information from dark pools and integrating it into the price formation process. Whether, however, this veiled information improves or harms market quality is debated among economists.[412]

---

407 ibid 70, 118ff; O'Hara, *Market Microstructure Theory* (n 45) 259; Thelen (n 147) 89.

408 Cf. Sethe (n 196) SK FinfraG Art 1 para 28.

409 Schott and Sester (n 57) § 22 para 97; Morell (n 285) 69 para 149.

410 Terrence Hendershott and Haim Mendelson, 'Crossing Networks and Dealer Markets: Competition and Performance' (2000) 55(5) The Journal of Finance 2071, 2104; Mao Ye, 'A Glimpse into the Dark: Price Formation, Transaction Cost and Market Share of the Crossing Network' (9 June 2011) 39.

411 Comerton-Forde and Putniņš (n 382) 72.

412 ibid 72; Hoops, *Verborgene Liquidität im Marktordnungsrecht der MiFID* (n 6) 71ff; Thelen (n 147) 93–4.

a) Theoretical Papers

The studies by *Hendershott/Mendelson (2000)* and *Ye (2011)* find a negative influence of dark trading on price accuracy. Both theoretical studies find that a migration of informed traders from lit markets to dark markets will deprive the price formation process of important pieces of information rendering the resulting prices less accurate.[413] *Hendershott/Mendelson (2000)* also find that spreads on lit dealer markets will widen since informed traders use the lit markets as a 'market of last resort' when they are unable to find liquidity in dark pools. Dealers on lit venues thus face an increased probability of adverse selection because they are more likely to interact with an informed trader than with uninformed traders who rather choose dark pools than lit pools for the dark pools' lower execution prices.[414] To insure themselves against the heightened adverse selection risk, dealers on lit markets widen their spreads, signaling less liquidity and less accurate prices.[415]

While *Ye (2011)* generally agrees with the findings of *Hendershott/Mendelson (2000)*, the study identifies the lower execution probability in dark pools compared to lit markets as a significant drawback for informed traders using dark pools.[416]

The theoretical work by *Zhu (2014)* picked up on the idea of informed traders remaining on lit exchanges due to the increased execution probability, while pre-dominantly uninformed traders are lured into dark pools because of their attractive costs structure and price improvements.[417] *Zhu (2014)* concluded that dark pools absorb uninformed '*noise trading*' which leads to a concentration of informed trading on lit exchanges eventually improving price discovery instead of harming it.[418] *Boulatov/George (2013)* also attested that dark trading had a positive effect on price accuracy since their model found that the presence of dark trading intensifies the compe-

413 Hendershott and Mendelson (n 410) 2104; Ye (n 410) 39.
414 Hendershott and Mendelson (n 410) 2102ff.
415 ibid 2104.
416 Ye (n 410) 39.
417 Zhu (n 186) 779.
418 ibid 779.

tition among liquidity providers forcing them to quote more aggressively which eventually leads to lower trading costs and more efficient prices.[419]

Degryse/de Jong/van Kervel (2015) found the same pattern as *Zhu (2014)* in their theoretical paper of informed traders clustering on lit markets while uninformed traders migrate to dark pools. In contrast to *Zhu (2014)*, *Degryse/de Jong/van Kervel (2015)* conclude that liquidity and price accuracy will be impaired due to increased adverse selection risk on lit markets.[420]

b) Empirical Papers

The different findings of theoretical papers called for empirical testing. While *Jiang/McInish/Upson (2012)*, *Comerton-Forde/Putniņš (2015)*, and *Aquilina et al. (2017)* confirm the findings of *Zhu (2014)* and *Degryse/de Jong/van Kervel (2015)* that dark orders often come from uninformed traders whereas informed traders rather populate the lit venues, the studies are divided with regard to the effects of dark trading on price accuracy.[421] *Jiang/McInish/Upson (2012)* conclude that a concentration of informed traders on lit venues increases price accuracy,[422] whereas *Comerton-Forde/Putniņš (2015)* stress that broad trade transparency diminishes the incentives for informed traders to search for new fundamental information.[423] *Comerton-Forde/Putniņš (2015)* also address the issue that dealers may widen their spreads due to an elevated probability of adverse selection when interacting with informed traders on lit markets.[424] Insofar, empirical studies appear to merely mirror the findings of the theoretical papers.

c) Empirical Findings on an Optimum of Dark Trading

The new insight first mentioned in *Comerton-Forde/Putniņš (2015)* and further developed in *Foley/Putniņš (2016)* and *Aquilina et al. (2017)* is that

419 Alex Boulatov and Thomas J George, 'Hidden and Displayed Liquidity in Securities Markets with Informed Liquidity Providers' (2013) 26(8) Review of Financial Studies 2095, 2098, 2120–1.

420 Degryse, Jong and van Kervel (n 345) 1587, 1592, 1619–20.

421 Aquilina and others (n 275) 27; Comerton-Forde and Putniņš (n 382) 70–1, 90; Christine X Jiang, Thomas H McInish and James Upson, 'Market Fragmentation and Information Quality: The Role of TRF Trades' (March 2012) 24.

422 Jiang, McInish and Upson (n 421) 3, 5, 24.

423 Comerton-Forde and Putniņš (n 382) 70–1, 90.

424 ibid 70–1, 90.

the effects of dark trading on price accuracy and liquidity are non-linear but quadratic: i.e., at first, moderate levels of dark trading have a positive effect on price accuracy as well as liquidity until an optimum is reached, however, any additional unit of dark trading past that optimum has adverse effects.[425]

Comerton-Forde/Putniņš (2015) found that dark orders and block orders had different optima in the Australian market. While a small number of dark orders had no adverse or even a slightly positive effect on information efficiency, price accuracy started to decline as the volume of dark trading surpassed 10 percent of the Dollar volume.[426] Dark trading in large block orders, on the other hand, had positive effects on information efficiency up to 40 percent of the trading volume.[427]

Even though *Foley/Putniņš (2016)* primarily examined the impact of the 'trade-at' rules in Canada and Australia, they found that one-sided dark pools, i.e., dark pools that price at the midpoint, have adverse effects on price accuracy and liquidity, whereas, two-sided dark pools, pricing at various price points besides the midpoint, generally have a positive effect on price accuracy and liquidity.[428] However, *Foley/Putniņš (2016)* indicated that this positive effect of two-sided dark pools may reverse into adverse effects when a certain threshold is surpassed.[429]

As the first comprehensive study on the effects of dark trading in the United Kingdom (UK) market, *Aquilina et al. (2017)* found that dark trading under MiFID I also had a positive effect on price accuracy and liquidity when levels of dark trading were moderate, but when an optimum was surpassed, additional dark trading began to impair both price accuracy and liquidity.[430] Unlike *Foley/Putniņš (2016)* but similar to *Comerton-Forde/Putniņš (2015), Aquilina et al. (2017)* identified different optima for different variables tested ranging from 11 to 17 percent, and overall market quality appeared to improve up to a level of dark trading of 15 percent across the examined instruments.[431]

425 Aquilina and others (n 275) 27; Comerton-Forde and Putniņš (n 382) 70, 88; Foley and Putniņš (n 389) 479.
426 Comerton-Forde and Putniņš (n 382) 70, 88.
427 ibid 70, 72, 88.
428 Foley and Putniņš (n 389) 456–7; 478–9.
429 ibid 479.
430 Aquilina and others (n 275) 27.
431 ibid 27.

d) Regulatory Conclusions

Even though, economic theories do not determine an exact amount at which dark trading becomes detrimental, the current economic research is still the best description of the functioning and the effects of dark markets that legislators and regulators can turn to as a reference point for action. In spite of the different findings and remaining uncertainties, the latest economic research appears to have found a reasonable explanation for the varying outcomes of early studies and points to a plausible interpretation of the effects of dark trading: Moderate levels of dark trading help to clear up the lit market because uninformed 'noise traders' migrate to dark pools where they no longer interfere with price discovery. This enables more accurate prices on the lit markets which not only reduce transaction costs for lit traders but through reference pricing also reduce transaction costs on dark markets.

Those findings raise two further issues: Firstly, it is uncertain where exactly the optimum for each instrument and each market lies. Determining such a threshold *a priori* from a regulatory perspective appears to be a huge burden if not an impossible task.[432]

The second issue is whether the regulator needs to intervene at all or whether the market participants can reach the optimum on their own. A study by *Daniëls/Dönges/Heinemann (2013)* suggests that dark trading will not entirely replace lit trading and an equilibrium between both will be established, but the study also finds that the market share of dark crossing systems is likely to rise if liquidity in the instrument rises.[433] The latter is consistent with the rise in dark trading witnessed in recent years which did not abruptly end even when it reached very high levels.[434]

This can be explained by the externalities that dark trading has on the market participants. While dark trades can internalize the entire cost

---

432 Rudolph and Röhrl (n 51) 207–8.

433 Tijmen R Daniëls, Jutta Dönges and Frank Heinemann, 'Crossing Network versus Dealer Market: Unique Equilibrium in the Allocation of Order Flow' (2013) 62 European Economic Review 41, 53.

434 Comerton-Forde and Putniņš (n 382) 72, 88; Gomber and Pierron (n 4) 3; Hoops, 'Bedeutung des organisierten Handelssystems in der gegenwärtigen Marktinfrastruktur' (n 131) 14; European Parliament, 'Report on Regulation of Trading in Financial Instruments – 'Dark Pools' etc. (2010/2075(INI))' (A7-0326/2010, Committee on Economic and Monetary Affairs, Rapporteur: Kay Swinburne, 16 November 2010) 4–5.

advantages and price improvements that dark pools have to offer, they do not have to fully bear the efficiency losses they cause by not providing pre-trade and post-trade transparency to the market and not supporting price discovery. Those costs are shared with traders on lit venues who support the price discovery process by showing transparency but do not receive any compensation from dark traders who use their efforts by referencing the market price.[435]

Consequently, from an economic perspective, dark trading should not be banned entirely because it can enhance market efficiency by providing price accuracy and liquidity. However, when dark trading rises beyond a certain volume, market failure may arise, and regulation may become necessary.

According to *Aquilina et al (2017)*, the efficiency gains from dark trading in retail-sized orders are exhausted by its detrimental effects when the level of dark trading ranges above 15 percent of the trading volume. After that, adverse selection risks on lit markets rise significantly leaving dealers no choice but to widen their spreads which can impair not only lit but also dark trading prices.[436]

For block orders, *Comerton-Forde/Putniņš (2015)* and *Aquilina et al (2017)* found that the quadratic interrelation between the amount of dark trading and market quality found for retail-sized orders is principally also valid. In contrast to retail-sized orders, however, the amount of dark trading can be relatively high, up to 40 % of the trading volume, until market quality begins to deteriorate.[437]

From a regulatory perspective, those findings call at least for regulatory attention, if not regulatory action, given that dark trading in small- and medium-sized orders is close to or even exceeds the optima. For block orders, however, the current amount of dark trading in each of the examined jurisdictions does not exceed the very high optimum, and thus less regulatory attention is warranted at the moment.[438]

435 ASIC, 'Dark Liquidity and High-Frequency Trading' (n 382) 26 para 83.
436 Aquilina and others (n 275) 27.
437 ibid 27; Comerton-Forde and Putniņš (n 382) 72, 88.
438 Comerton-Forde and Putniņš (n 382) 72, 88.

2. HFT Strategies in Dark Pools

As previously mentioned, the rise of high-frequency traders increased transaction costs for both informed traders and uninformed traders on lit markets.[439] That those traders prefer to use dark pools instead is therefore a reasonable response to this threat. However, HFTs are capable of piercing dark trading's *'veil of ignorance'* due to their superior trading strategies. They sometimes peak into the dark pools' order books even with the help of the dark pool operators.[440] This is a disadvantage for dark traders unaware of interacting with HFTs who make substantial gains when trading on dark pools.[441]

a) Exploitation of Midpoint Orders

In dark pools, HFTs engage in a strategy similar to *'slow-market arbitrage'*[442] called *'exploitation of midpoint orders'*.[443] When exploiting a midpoint order, an HFT uses the short time needed for the information about a price change to travel from the exchange to the dark pool using the midpoint price as the reference price to match the orders of its dark traders.[444] If, for example, the exchange shows USD 10.11 as the best buy-order and USD 10.15 as the best sell-order, the midpoint lies at USD 10.13 on the exchange and, by way of reference pricing, also on the dark pool. When a new best-sell order at USD 10.12 enters the exchange's order book, the midpoint price changes to USD 10.115 on the exchange. Since this information needs a certain amount of time to travel to the dark pool, the HFT, informed by its co-location service, can send an immediate-or-cancel sell-order at the stale midpoint price at USD 10.13 to the dark pool in hope of finding a sell-order there. When the order executes on the dark pool, the HFT can turn around and repurchase the security on the lit market for USD 10.12 making a small

439 See above Part I § 3.D.II.2.

440 ASIC, 'Review of High-Frequency Trading and Dark Liquidity' (Report 452, October 2015) 54–55 paras 234–5.

441 ibid 54 para 234: in 85 % HFT trades are on the winning side according to research presented by ASIC.

442 See above Part I § 3.D.II.2.b).

443 Fox, Glosten and Rauterberg, 'The New Stock Market' (n 88) 242ff; Fox, Glosten and Rauterberg, 'High-Frequency Trading and the New Stock Market' (n 362) 33.

444 Fox, Glosten and Rauterberg, 'The New Stock Market' (n 88) 242ff; Fox, Glosten and Rauterberg, 'High-Frequency Trading and the New Stock Market' (n 362) 33.

profit of USD 0.01 without any risk.[445] If there is no sell-order, the immediate-or-cancel order is cancelled and the HFT incurs no loss. The buyer on the dark pool, however, overpaid and can only sell at an inferior midpoint price of USD 10.115 when the changed midpoint price reaches the dark pool. Given the similarity to 'slow-market arbitrage' discussed above, dark traders often do not receive the protection from HFTs they are looking for when trading in dark pools to avoid 'slow-market arbitrage' on lit pools.[446]

b) Pinging and Electronic Front Running

Block traders use dark pools for their block orders to avoid HFTs engaging in electronic front running strategies on lit markets. HFTs, however, anticipate the likelihood of dark pools holding block orders. To retrieve or 'sniff' this information out of the dark pools, HFTs use 'pinging' strategies in which they send a small immediate-or-cancel sell-order, usually no larger than 100 shares, to test the waters.[447] If the order executes, the HFT sends a slightly larger immediate-or-cancel order to ensure a block buy order has been discovered. After having retrieved this information, the HFT buys large amounts of the security on the lit market driving up the price and subsequently sells it to the block trader at a now increased midpoint price. This strategy provides HFTs with an informational advantage they can turn into a profit. Additionally, pinging and electronic front running betrays the trust investors put into dark trading and increases transaction costs for block traders in dark pools.[448]

Thus, the degree to which dark pools can deliver on the promise to protect traders depends on two factors: On the one hand, the degree to which the trading system running the dark pool can exercise discretion over the access decision so they can exclude HFTs. On the other hand, dark pools will only efficiently exclude HFTs when their dependence on HFT

---

445 Fox, Glosten and Rauterberg, 'The New Stock Market' (n 88) 243–4; Fox, Glosten and Rauterberg, 'High-Frequency Trading and the New Stock Market' (n 362) 33.

446 Fox, Glosten and Rauterberg, 'The New Stock Market' (n 88) 244; Fox, Glosten and Rauterberg, 'High-Frequency Trading and the New Stock Market' (n 362) 33.

447 Adrian (n 365) 263; Banks (n 5) 150–1; Bayram and Meier (n 357) 1295–6; Hoops, *Verborgene Liquidität im Marktordnungsrecht der MiFID* (n 6) 133–4; Kasiske (n 11) 456; Klaus U Schmolke in Lars Klöhn (ed), *Marktmissbrauchsverordnung: Verordnung (EU) Nr. 596/2014 über Marktmissbrauch* (1st edn, CH Beck 2018) MAR Art 12 para 93; Thelen (n 147) 97.

448 Adrian (n 365) 264–5; Kasiske (n 11) 456; Thelen (n 147) 97–8.

liquidity is small. The fact that the latter is also a major cause of detrimental effects of dark trading is discussed in the following section.

c) Preferred Information Access via Dark Pool Operators

HFTs sometimes even receive information from dark pool operators because dark pool operators are in a conflict of interest that often plays out in favor of the HFTs. This was the case in the SEC enforcement measures against the dark pool operator Posit ITG.[449] Dark pools often have no dedicated market makers such as exchanges, thus, HFT presence generates a bulk of order flow which substitutes market makers and increases liquidity levels in dark pools. In this respect, HFT presence even benefits the other traders on dark pools because the increased liquidity cuts latency times significantly, allowing for faster order execution.[450]

However, a bulk of orders also generates plenty of fees for the dark pool operator who generally is a for-profit exchange or investment bank.[451] Thus, when the HFT demands privileged information to perform its quasi-market making service for the dark pool, and may even pay for the information, dark pool operators generally grant this information about their order flow.[452] Often, dark pools provide HFTs with *'indications of interest'* that reveal important data about orders waiting for execution in the dark pool and can be used to the other traders' disadvantage, as the case of Posit ITG showed.[453]

In the case of the US-domiciled dark pool Posit ITG, several HFTs received information about order flow in the dark pool by its operator. The HFTs used this information to buy up securities on the lit markets driving up the price. Then they turned to the dark pool where they knew that the routing mechanism would lead their sell-orders at the inflated midpoint price to the residing orders to which they sold their newly acquired securities for a profit.[454] Such a collusion between operators and HFTs not only creates an unlevel playing field between HFTs and non-HFT investors and

449 *ITG Inc.* (n 26) 9 paras 44–5; *ITG Inc.* (2018) Exchange Act Release No. 84548, 2018 WL 5818281 (SEC) 6ff paras 24ff.
450 Kasiske (n 11) 457.
451 ibid 457.
452 ibid 457.
453 *ITG Inc.* (n 26) 9 paras 44–5; *ITG Inc.* (n 449) 6ff paras 24ff.
454 *ITG Inc.* (n 26) 9 paras 44–5; *ITG Inc.* (n 449) 6ff paras 24ff.

raises questions under criminal law, but also raises the transaction costs for traders that chose to wait for better priced contra-side orders in dark pools instead of suffering market impact on lit markets.[455]

d) Evaluation of High-Frequency Trading in Dark Pools

The HFT strategies have shown that despite an increase of liquidity and consequently execution probability and speed for traders, the presence of HTFs in dark pools diminishes many advantages of dark trading. Especially uninformed traders face increased transaction costs due to HFT presence because HFTs take away profitable trading opportunities and may cause adverse price movements for uninformed traders by adversely affecting the midpoint price in the dark pool.[456]

For informed traders the effects of HFT presence in dark pools is ambivalent. HFT strategies can be harmful with regard to informed traders who use dark pools to protect their private information while exploiting it for their profit. With pinging and front running, HFTs identify private pieces of information and impound it into the price formation process depriving the informed traders of their profits to offset their information research costs. This slows down the process of information research especially for pieces of information that informed traders may consider too transient or vague for lit trading but still worthwhile for dark trading.[457] Such an information search is rendered unprofitable and will no longer occur under HFT presence.

Informed traders trading on lit markets, however, will indirectly benefit from HFT presence in dark pools provided that uninformed traders realize that they 'fell prey' to HFT strategies. Then, uninformed traders may abandon dark trading and return to lit markets where they then 'fall prey' to information arbitrage of informed traders supporting the price formation process.[458] Whether uninformed traders are able to realize that they have been taken advantage of remains doubtful. Thus, the discussed

455 Cf. Kasiske (n 11) 457.
456 Fox, Glosten and Rauterberg, 'The New Stock Market' (n 88) 244; Thelen (n 147) 102.
457 Linlin Ye, 'Understanding the Impacts of Dark Pools on Price Discovery' (October 2016) 44.
458 Fox, Glosten and Rauterberg, 'The New Stock Market' (n 88) 244; Thelen (n 147) 103.

HFT strategies have adverse effects on the functioning of the market since they increase transaction costs and betray investor trust.

3. Limited Access to Dark Liquidity

Since the trading strategies pursued by high-frequency traders and informed traders have adverse effects on block traders, it is unsurprising that dark pools wish to exclude HFTs by denying them access.[459] This raises the topic of the access regime for trading systems in the examined jurisdictions. While exchanges provide membership on a non-discriminatory basis as long as certain professionality requirements are met and grant universal access through brokerage services, dark pools operating off-exchange may be able to exercise discretion with regard to access rights.[460] Some dark pools actually take pride in excluding or limiting exposure to HFTs to minimize transaction costs for block traders.[461]

The issue with regard to access rights is that dark pools as off-exchange markets already create further fragmentation which is only integrated in the overall market system when post-trade transparency is provided.[462] If access is contingent on the operator's discretion, the market is not only fragmented, but in fact two-tiered, providing only a select group of traders with superior trading chances.[463] Such non-penetrable barriers among traders have not only adverse impacts on investor fairness but also on price accuracy.[464]

---

459 Leslie A Boni, David C Brown and J. C Leach, 'Dark Pool Exclusivity Matters' (19 December 2013) 7–8; Fox, Glosten and Rauterberg, 'The New Stock Market' (n 88) 251–2; Kevin S Haeberle, 'Discrimination Platforms' (2017) 42(4) The Journal of Corporation Law 809, 811.

460 Haeberle (n 459) 823. For access to exchanges, see: Section 6(b) Exchange Act (15 U.S.C. § 78f(b)(2)(1934)), Rule 610(a) Regulation NMS (17 CFR § 242.610(a)(2005)) under US law, Article 53(1) MiFID II under EU law; Sec. 30 BörsG under German law and Sec. 18(1), 34(1) FinfraG under Swiss law.

461 Boni, Brown and Leach (n 459) 7–10, 22; Jack Gannon, 'Developments in Banking and Financial Law 2009-2010: The Shadow Financial System' (2009) 29 Review of Banking & Financial Law 1, 90–1; Stanislav Dolgopolov, 'Securities Fraud Embedded in the Market Structure Crisis: High-Frequency Traders as Primary Violators' (2018) 9(3) William & Mary Business Law Review 551, 586ff.

462 IOSCO, 'Principles for Dark Liquidity' (n 12) 27–8.

463 ibid 23.

464 Haeberle (n 459) 825ff.

As mentioned above, the price formation process depends on informed traders trading against uninformed traders. In a two-tiered market, the uninformed traders are more likely to gravitate to dark pools than the informed.[465] This leaves an overabundance of informed traders on lit markets who only have the market makers left as their trading partners for information arbitrage. Those market makers are generally uninformed traders who do not possess the new piece of information which informed traders possess, but market makers are sophisticated enough to at least anticipate that they are more likely to trade against informed traders when other uninformed traders gravitate to dark pools. In anticipation of the increasing adverse selection risk, market makers will therefore widen their spreads which decreases overall market efficiency not only for lit traders but also for dark traders.[466]

Thus, if dark pools can choose an access regime, they will be overly selective which creates transaction costs that need to be borne by informed traders and HFTs. Eventually, informed traders may no longer be able to offset their search costs when trading against the market makers and cease their information search as well as their support of the price formation process. Information arbitrage by informed traders can also occur in the form of intermarket arbitrage. This means that informed traders can use their superior information and trade against uninformed traders on dark pools which reduces the adverse selection risk of market makers. Thus, market makers will not widen their spread as much even though uninformed traders gravitate to dark pools, rendering the market more liquid, and allowing informed traders to offset their search costs more profitably in both lit markets and dark pools.[467]

Regulation must therefore aim for a broad access regime to allow for information arbitrage by informed traders.[468] The specifics of the access regime of each jurisdiction will be discussed in the course of this study within each jurisdiction.

465 Aquilina and others (n 275) 27; Boni, Brown and Leach (n 459) 7–10, 22.

466 Haeberle (n 459) 826; Kevin Haeberle, 'Stock Market Law and the Accuracy of Public Companies' Stock Prices' (2015) 2015(1) Columbia Business Law Review 121, 154–5; Fox, Glosten and Rauterberg, 'Informed Trading and Its Regulation' (n 99) 846.

467 Haeberle (n 459) 829ff.

468 ibid 829ff; Haeberle (n 466) 158ff; Kumpan, *Die Regulierung außerbörslicher Wertpapierhandelssysteme im deutschen, europäischen und US-amerikanischen Recht* (n 8) 94–5, 98; Thelen (n 147) 93.

4. Fragmentation by Dark Trading Increases Transaction Costs

Another driver of transaction costs in modern financial markets is market fragmentation. Market fragmentation is an inevitable effect of market liberalization in which the dominant position of exchanges – often operating as (de facto) monopolies – was dissolved. Market liberalization was implemented to avoid market failure due to excessive market power of a single exchange. The benefits of dispersing liquidity to introduce competition in a 'market-for-markets' thus comes at the (transaction) cost of having to search for a proper marketplace for a specific execution.[469] Increases in transaction costs due to fragmentation occur among various lit marketplaces as well as lit and dark pools.[470]

Dark trading, however, exacerbates the issue of fragmentation because the rationale of trade transparency is to inform traders about current trading opportunities, help brokers to meet best execution requirements, and support the price formation process among an array of venues.[471] In dark markets, those goals are more difficult to achieve, especially when the dark market itself is fragmented among multiple trading venues, like in the United States with more than 30 dark pools and 200 broker dealers.[472]

5. Free-Riding of Information Production

Dark pools are also accused of free riding the price formation process of exchanges and other lit trading systems.[473] While this allegation cannot be raised against dark pools with endogenous price formation, the vast majority of dark pools is in fact price-importing.[474] From an economic point of view, the issue with price-importing dark pools is that they use exchange prices which share many properties of a public good. When dark pools

469 SEC, 'Concept Release on Equity Market Structure' (n 6) 75 FR 3597.

470 IOSCO, 'Principles for Dark Liquidity' (n 12) 21.

471 European Commission, 'Commission Staff Working Paper Impact Assessment EU Commission, Impact Assessment' (n 382) 12; IOSCO, 'Principles for Dark Liquidity' (n 12) 21.

472 IOSCO, 'Principles for Dark Liquidity' (n 12) 21; Menkveld, Yueshen and Zhu (n 398) 503.

473 IOSCO, 'Principles for Dark Liquidity' (n 12) 20. On free-riding, see: Michael Fritsch, *Marktversagen und Wirtschaftspolitik: Mikroökonomische Grundlagen staatlichen Handelns* (10th edn, Vahlen 2018) 94–6.

474 Monsch (n 90) 18.

use those exchange prices for their economic activity, they do so without contributing to it because their orders do not fuel the price formation process.[475]

Public goods are characterized by 'non-exclusivity' and 'non-rivalrous' as two independent factors that can be present in varying degrees.[476] Price information of any lit venue is characterized by non-rivalrous since one trader's consumption of the price information for their transaction does not diminish the consumption opportunities of others.[477] Literally thousands of traders match their orders at the same price if enough liquidity is present without 'exhausting' the price information.

With regard to the non-exclusivity of prices made by exchanges and other lit trading systems, some fear that the trading venue regime and the transparency regime are overbroad by requiring exchanges to broadly disseminate their prices.[478] Dark pools and their users could anticipate those prices for their trading without paying for the provided benefit (i.e., positive externality). This form of free riding of transparent markets may eventually draw even more traders to dark pools because they do not wish to bear the costs of providing trade transparency if they can have the benefits of a less costly transaction in dark pools.[479] Eventually, the free riding of the positive externality of the price formation process of exchanges creates a negative externality because the missing order information of the orders migrating to dark pools may render the price formation process less accurate, and may ultimately render the business of price formation unprofitable. This is a situation that resembles the economic textbook example of the *tragedy of the commons*.[480]

A cure for such public goods problems is to assign specific property rights, i.e., implement a mechanism that allows for a certain extent of exclusivity to charge a price for the positive externality created by the producers of the public good. In securities trading, either the trading venue regime and/or the transparency regime can contain provisions that allow for such 'property rights.' For instance, lit alternative trading systems may

---

475 IOSCO, 'Principles for Dark Liquidity' (n 12) 20.

476 Fritsch (n 473) 94, 96; Thomas A Lambert, *How to Regulate: A Guide for Policymakers* (Cambridge University Press 2017) 61ff.

477 Cf. Lambert (n 476) 61.

478 Fox, 'MiFID II and Equity Trading' (n 53) para 18.107.

479 IOSCO, 'Principles for Dark Liquidity' (n 12) 20.

480 On the tragedy of the commons see: Cooter and Ulen (n 40) 140; Fritsch (n 473) 96–8.

not be subject to the same strict rules requiring them to broadly disseminate their price information as exchanges usually are. Even exchanges – as the primary 'producer' of price information – may have the privilege to provide their data for compensation only or provide the price information for compensation when it is still recent and valuable (*'hot off the press'*).

To examine potential market failure caused by free riding of a public good, the following legal analysis of the individual jurisdictions must closely examine the trading venue regimes and the transparency regimes to assess each of the regulatory responses to this issue.

6. Free-Riding of Regulation and Moral Hazard

Dark pools also create a free-rider problem as well as a moral hazard problem[481] regarding market regulation.[482] Within the market oversight regime of some jurisdictions, exchanges assume a pivotal role in setting standards for behavior as self-regulatory bodies and assist the regulatory agencies in the enforcement of securities laws.[483] This role is particularly pronounced in jurisdictions that rely on self-regulation of securities trading instead of governmental oversight, such as the United States and Switzerland.

In contrast to exchanges, dark pools are often more lightly regulated and do not have to assume the same regulatory responsibilities, while they often cater to the same traders as exchanges where they are under supervision.[484] Especially in markets like the United States and Switzerland, dark pools free-ride the positive externality of the public good of market oversight and

481 IOSCO, 'Principles for Dark Liquidity' (n 12) 20.

482 Kumpan, *Die Regulierung außerbörslicher Wertpapierhandelssysteme im deutschen, europäischen und US-amerikanischen Recht* (n 8) 114–5; Yesha Yadav, 'Oversight Failure in Securities Markets' (2019) 104 Cornell Law Review 1799, 1845.

483 Yesha Yadav, 'The Failure of Liability in Modern Markets' (2016) 102 Virginia Law Review 1031, 1090–1; Yadav, 'Oversight Failure in Securities Markets' (n 482) 1819; Thelen (n 147) 115. Cf. SEC, 'Regulation Systems Compliance and Integrity' (17 CFR Parts 240, 242, and 249, Release No. 34-73639, File No. S7-01-13, 5 December 2014) 79 FR 72252.

484 Yadav, 'Oversight Failure in Securities Markets' (n 482) 1806–7. See on the unlevel playing field among regulated markets and MTFs under MiFID I and MAD: Kern Alexander, 'Market Structures and Market Abuse' in Gerard Caprio (ed), *Handbook of safeguarding global financial stability: Political, social, cultural, and economic theories and models* (1st edn, Elsevier 2013) 383: *'(...) unlike regulated markets, MTFs are not required under EU law to maintain market abuse surveillance systems and to have comprehensive suspicious transaction reporting systems.'*

its resulting market stability produced by exchanges due to their special role.[485]

In a competitive market environment in which liquidity is fragmented among multiple trading venues, the unlevel playing field among exchanges and dark pools incentivizes exchanges to exercise their monitoring role less zealously.[486] Despite their regulatory role, exchanges are for-profit enterprises competing for order flow from traders with their less regulated dark pool competitors. Monitoring traders is costly, especially in fragmented markets, where exchanges need to surveil traders' behavior across multiple venues.[487] While having to bear the expenses of monitoring by itself, the exchange does not exclusively enjoy the benefits of its monitoring, nor is the exchange insulated from lax monitoring by other trading venues because traders can freely travel from one venue to another.[488] It is likely that traders bring risky business with them or that traders even shop for the venues which provide favorable conditions to mask their fraudulent behavior.[489]

From an exchange's perspective this market mechanisms create a situation for moral hazard. If the exchange operator is not insulated from the effects of poor monitoring of others, others are not insulated from its poor monitoring either. To save costs and to exercise a *'light regulatory touch'* on important traders that provide liquidity and generate fees, such as HFTs, the exchange will exercise its regulatory role more generously which invites risks into the system for all market participants.[490]

This potential for market failure needs to be corrected by regulatory intervention. There are three possible ways to rectify the issue: First, fragmentation could be reduced or even eliminated by reducing the number of admissible trading venues, as has been the case under national concentration rules in many jurisdictions in the European Union, such as Germany

485 Yadav, 'Oversight Failure in Securities Markets' (n 482) 1809–10; Thelen (n 147) 115.

486 Yadav, 'Oversight Failure in Securities Markets' (n 482) 1806; Thelen (n 147) 115. See on the historical development of the competition between exchanges and dark pools: Andreas M Fleckner and Klaus J Hopt, 'Stock Exchange Law: Concept, History, Challenges' (2013) 7(3) Virginia Law & Business Review 513, 523ff.

487 Yadav, 'Oversight Failure in Securities Markets' (n 482) 1842–3; Thelen (n 147) 115.

488 Yadav, 'Oversight Failure in Securities Markets' (n 482) 1842; Thelen (n 147) 115.

489 Yadav, 'Oversight Failure in Securities Markets' (n 482) 1848ff; Thelen (n 147) 115.

490 Yadav, 'Oversight Failure in Securities Markets' (n 482) 1848ff; Yadav, 'The Failure of Liability in Modern Markets' (n 483) 1091–2; Thelen (n 147) 115.

prior to MiFID I.[491] This approach, however, eliminates investor benefits such as cost benefits and broader investor choice with a wider variety of suitable trading services in a competitive *'market for markets'*-system.[492]

Second, especially in jurisdictions with high levels of self-regulation, like the United States, exchanges enjoy immunity from investors' lawsuits, insulating exchanges from a significant amount of costs caused by poor monitoring. If this immunity was lifted, exchanges would internalize those costs and exercise increased monitoring efforts rendering the markets more stable again.[493]

However, the second approach would still not eliminate the free rider problem of dark pools and the cost pressure of exchanges which need to make monitoring expenses while competing with dark pools for order flow. Thus, thirdly, a sensible approach – also to complement the second approach – is to level the playing field by either demanding the same market monitoring efforts from all trading systems, regardless of whether they are exchanges or dark pools, or centralizing the task of market monitoring in the hands of government agencies.[494]

To assess whether the free-rider and moral hazard problems may occur and whether those situations need correction in the examined jurisdiction, the trading venue regime and the regulatory architecture need to be considered.

7. Information Asymmetries and Principal-Agent-Conflicts to Harm Investors

In an ideal dark pool that is equally opaque for all its users, at least one actor needs to oversee the order book: the dark pool operator. The concentration of information in the operator's hands entails a tremendous information asymmetry in comparison to its users that is prone to principal-agent-conflicts and moral hazard.[495] The conflict of interests for the

491 Yadav, 'Oversight Failure in Securities Markets' (n 482) 1858ff; Thelen (n 147) 115.
492 Yadav, 'Oversight Failure in Securities Markets' (n 482) 1858ff; Thelen (n 147) 115.
493 Yadav, 'The Failure of Liability in Modern Markets' (n 483) 1091–2; Yadav, 'Oversight Failure in Securities Markets' (n 482) 1861 ff; Thelen (n 147) 115.
494 European Commission, 'Commission Staff Working Paper Impact Assessment EU Commission, Impact Assessment' (n 382) 10–1, 33ff; CESR, 'CESR Technical Advice to the European Commission in the Context of the MiFID Review - Equity Markets' (CESR/10-802, 29 July 2010) 4, 16.
495 Kasiske (n 11) 456–7. On 'moral hazard' see Lambert (n 476) 190–1.

dark pool operator arises from its dual role as a 'neutral' infrastructure provider for traders while being a for-profit, private operation that is regularly owned by a large investment bank.[496] It is therefore unsurprising that there are a number of cases in which dark pools deviate from the 'ideal' of an equally opaque dark pool, providing deeper insights for some clients while leaving others ignorant.[497]

a) Principal-Agent-Conflict in Order Routing

One possible principal-agent-conflict that may harm investors can arise in the order routing process. When an investor turns to their investment bank for brokerage services, the investment bank might send the client order to its own dark pool first to save on exchange and handling fees and to increase liquidity on its own dark pool.[498] This can often be achieved via terms and conditions in the brokerage agreement to which the client pays little attention or fails to realize the impact of this broad leeway. Only if the order remains unfilled on the proprietary dark pool, will the broker send the order to an exchange or to another alternative trading system.[499] The information asymmetry between broker and customer regularly directs the order flow to dark pools, unless customers expressly instruct the broker to route the order to another venue, e.g., to an exchange for faster execution.[500]

While beneficial to the dark pool operating investment bank, this principal-agent-conflict may result in higher transaction costs and worse trading results for the investor if the investor forgoes a superior trading opportunity on another marketplace.[501] Even if the dark pool offers equally good or

---

496 FCA, 'UK Equity Market Dark Pools' (n 6) 26ff.

497 Kasiske (n 11) 456–7; Cf. CESR, 'CESR Technical Advice to the European Commission in the Context of the MiFID Review - Equity Markets' (n 494) 41.

498 FCA, 'UK Equity Market Dark Pools' (n 6) 26; Köndgen (n 209) 134ff; Cohn-Heeren (n 8) 209; Steffen Seibert, *Dark Pools - schwarze Goldgrube der Betreiber?: Eine Untersuchung verdeckter Liquiditätsplattformen im deutschen Aktienhandel* (GRIN Verlag 2010) 66.

499 FCA, 'UK Equity Market Dark Pools' (n 6) 26.

500 Menkveld, Yueshen and Zhu (n 398) 507; Thelen (n 147) 117; see also FCA, 'UK Equity Market Dark Pools' (n 6) 26ff.

501 Fox, Glosten and Rauterberg, 'The New Stock Market' (n 88) 252, 254; Kumpan, *Die Regulierung außerbörslicher Wertpapierhandelssysteme im deutschen, europäischen und US-amerikanischen Recht* (n 8) 95–6; Thelen (n 147) 116.

superior trading outcomes, such behavior can harm investor confidence in the brokerage service and result in funds being withdrawn from financial markets.[502]

The conflict of interests becomes even more pronounced when a broker not only routes an order to a dark pool to match it with another client's order but when it engages in (bilateral) proprietary trading where the dark pool operator forms the other side of the transaction. The dark pool leaves its neutral position as mere provider of a trading infrastructure and takes on a proprietary financial interest in the outcome of the transaction.[503] The opacity of the processes on a dark pool decreases the probability that the client or the regulator will discover the opportunistic conduct of the dark pool operator. Coupled with the financial interest of the dark pool operator, this situation is prone to misconduct at the detriment of the client.[504] To avoid this effect regulatory intervention is necessary.

b) Front Running

Front running strategies are another way in which investors may be harmed by information asymmetries. For instance, when the dark pool operator receives a block order to buy a certain stock from a user, the dark pool operator learns about the order imbalance and may infer that the block order is motivated by underlying private information. Before the dark pool matches the block order, the operator has a large incentive to buy stock in other venues at a lower price, turn around and sell it at the meanwhile increased price to the user waiting in the dark pool with their buy block order.[505] However, it is not necessary for the dark pool operator to act on this action himself to create the harm. The dark pool operator could also provide affiliated traders or valuable clients with this information hoping

502 Cf. Kumpan, *Die Regulierung außerbörslicher Wertpapierhandelssysteme im deutschen, europäischen und US-amerikanischen Recht* (n 8) 95–6.

503 Cohn-Heeren (n 8) 209; Gomber and Pierron (n 4) 56; Harris (n 81) 521; Seibert (n 498) 66; Thelen (n 147) 116–7.

504 FCA, 'UK Equity Market Dark Pools' (n 6) 9, 33; Thelen (n 147) 117.

505 Thelen (n 147) 117; cf. Banks (n 5) 201; George O'Malley, 'Diving into Dark Pools: An Analysis of Hidden Liquidity with Regard to the Proposed Markets in Financial Instruments Directive' (2014) 17 Trinity College Law Review 94, 107; Nicholas Crudele, 'Dark Pool Regulation: Fostering Innovation and Competition while Protecting Investors' (2015) 9 Brooklyn Journal of Corporate, Financial & Commercial Law 569, 586.

that they will generate revenue when selling the stock on his dark pool.[506] Due to the price increases in case of a buy block order and the price decreases in case of a sell block order, the initial block trader forgoes the superior execution prices in the dark pool by saving on market impact costs.[507] The block trader's loss is the dark pool's and/or the affiliated trader's gain. Those gains are generated at low risk because the block trader is unlikely to detect this form of misconduct.[508]

This form of *'front running'* is distinct from[509] the abovementioned *'electronic front running'*.[510] In this form of front running, the trader who exploits the informational advantage, i.e., the dark pool operator or one of its affiliates, did not gain the information by means of trading in the market, but rather obtained it from a fiduciary relationship. The dark pool operator breaches its fiduciary duty when trading upon this information or when tipping another trader. While this is considered illegal behavior in all three jurisdictions examined, further discussion here would exceed the scope of this study.[511]

Rather in a grey area is the question of *'indications of interest'*, or IOIs, which are messages sent by the dark pool operator on behalf of, for example, a block trader searching for liquidity to 'test the waters.' The block trader may give its authorization explicitly or implicitly by terms and conditions to the dark pool to inform appropriate counterparties.[512] Dark pool operators often provide this information to valuable clients, such as HFTs who can react on this information and depress the price for the block trader.[513] Given that block traders often choose dark pools because they

506 Kasiske (n 11) 456–7.
507 Crudele (n 493) 586; O'Malley (n 505) 107; Thelen (n 147) 117.
508 FCA, 'UK Equity Market Dark Pools' (n 6) 9, 33; Thelen (n 147) 117.
509 Fox, Glosten and Rauterberg, 'The New Stock Market' (n 88) 227.
510 See above Part I § 3.D.IV.2.b).
511 Fox, Glosten and Rauterberg, 'The New Stock Market' (n 88) 227. See for traditional front running under US law: *Opper v. Hancock Securities Corporation* (1966) 250 F. Supp. 668 (S.D.N.Y. 1966) (US District Court for the Southern District of New York) (holding front running to be illegal under principles of agency and federal law). SEC prosecutes front running as a violation of Section 10(b) Exchange Act and Rule 10(b)-5: *Securities and Exchange Commission v. Daniel Bergin* (2013) 2013 WL 2400793 (N.D.Tex.) (Trial Pleading) (US District Court for the Northern District of Texas Dallas Division) (charging trader for front running clients under Section 10(b)); SEC, 'Concept Release on Equity Market Structure' (n 6) 75 FR 3609.
512 Cf. Crudele (n 505) 586; O'Malley (n 505) 107; Thelen (n 147) 117.
513 Crudele (n 505) 586; O'Malley (n 505) 107; Thelen (n 147) 117.

wish to avoid HFTs, this conduct is contradictory to their aspirations. It amounts to highly problematic and even fraudulent behavior if dark pool operators promise that clients can protect themselves from HFT strategies or at least minimize exposure, when, in fact, HFTs count among the most active traders in dark pools and exposure-management tools are altered at the dark pool's discretion. This has been the subject of multiple enforcement measures in the United States.[514] The other jurisdictions not having such enforcement measures may in part be explained by the fact that many market participants are unaware of the actual operations in dark pool.[515]

The regulatory response to those issues should be to deem such fraudulent behavior illegal, which already is the case in the examined jurisdictions, and to counter the principal-agent-conflicts with proper conduct rules for dark pool operators. This depends on the trading venue regime. Moreover, market participants and regulators need to be able to identify breaches of fiduciary duties and other misconduct arising from principal-agent-conflicts. This requires disclosure by dark pools about their internal operations and their affiliation with other market actors, such as HFTs.[516]

V. Conclusion

In spite of the disreputable name, dark trading and dark pools have numerous positive effects on market efficiency. Dark pools allow vulnerable traders, such as block traders, to avoid information leakage and to minimize market impact costs. Traders can also realize price improvements due to midpoint pricing and cost saving on dark trading services. Dark trading protects market maker transactions and thereby increases market liquidity which ultimately reduces transaction costs. Those improvements of market efficiency are especially important in modern markets which

514 See *Barclays Capital Inc.* (n 26) paras 24ff; *Barclays Liquidity Cross and High Frequency Trading Litigation* (2015) 126 F. Supp. 3d 342 (S.D.N.Y. 2015) (US District Court for the Southern District of New York); *Pipeline Trading Systems LLC* (n 26) paras 26ff; *ITG Inc.* (2015) Exchange Act Release No. 75672, 112 SEC Docket 887, 2015 WL 4748216 (SEC) 6 paras 26ff.

515 See FCA, 'UK Equity Market Dark Pools' (n 6) 16 paras 2.19–20.

516 IOSCO, 'Principles for Dark Liquidity' (n 12) 30; Banks (n 5) 201; Fox, Glosten and Rauterberg, 'The New Stock Market' (n 88) 254, 274–5; Kumpan, *Die Regulierung außerbörslicher Wertpapierhandelssysteme im deutschen, europäischen und US-amerikanischen Recht* (n 8) 98; Thelen (n 147) 118–9.

are characterized by high HFT activity that puts investor trust at risk. An outright ban of dark trading may therefore not be prudent.

However, dark trading also bears many disadvantages that should not be underestimated. While some economists disagree as to whether dark trading has positive or negative effects on price accuracy, a third group of more recent studies finds an ambivalent result that is in accordance with both *Grossman/Stiglitz's* theory of the *Information Paradox* and the economic findings on the effects of trade transparency as the mirror image of dark trading: when dark trading is a small phenomenon, every increase in dark trading is beneficial for price accuracy. However, when an optimal amount is surpassed, each additional unit of dark trading is of decreasing utility for the market leading to a concave utility function. Unfortunately, an optimal amount of dark trading depends on multiple factors, for instance order size, and cannot be reliably determined a priori.

Furthermore, HFT activity in dark pools is often detrimental for other traders. HFTs, as liquidity providers, are often granted special rights that lead to an information advantage over other traders jeopardizing investor trust. Equally troubling are issues of limited market access to dark pools, market fragmentation as well as issues of free-riding, and informational asymmetry.

To conclude, dark trading is a phenomenon that is needed by many traders in vastly transparent and highly automated modern financial markets dominated by HFT strategies. Nevertheless, dark trading poses many risks that call for regulatory attention.

§ 4. Need for Regulation of Dark Trading

A. Pre-Requisites of Regulation and Market Failure

Dark trading has been subjected to different forms of regulation in the United States, the European Union, Germany, and Switzerland. Before turning to the question of *how* the jurisdictions regulate dark trading, the initial question of *whether to regulate* needs to be considered.

This question boils down to the conventional wisdom *'if it's not broken, don't fix it'*.[517] The important question that follows, however, is more difficult to answer: when is 'it' broken?

The *'it'* that needs to be fixed, if broken, is the financial markets. Market regulation is always a difficult endeavor, especially in liberal jurisdictions that respect the rule of law, individual freedoms, and the principle of proportionality as the examined jurisdictions do. Those factors are important for liberal market economies to thrive. Their governments ought to respect the coordinative functions of markets, while the markets themselves are not beyond the reach of regulatory authority.[518] Governments in liberal jurisdictions can and are expected to promote the market functioning by regulatory measures to limit unwanted and unintended market outcomes.[519]

The unwanted and unintended market outcomes describe the situation of a *'broken market'* in need of fixing. What qualifies as an unwanted or unintended outcome however is a normative question that is answered by the goals of financial markets regulations which are the protection and

---

517 Armour and others (n 62) 51.

518 Martin Eifert, 'Regulierungsstrategien' in Andreas Voßkuhle, Martin Eifert and Christoph Möllers (eds), *Grundlagen des Verwaltungsrechts Gesamtwerk: In 2 Bänden* (3rd edn, CH Beck 2022) § 19 para 16; Oliver Lepsius, 'Verfassungsrechtlicher Rahmen der Regulierung' in Michael Fehling and Matthias Ruffert (eds), *Regulierungsrecht* (Mohr Siebeck 2010) § 4 paras 10, 45ff; Kumpan, *Die Regulierung außerbörslicher Wertpapierhandelssysteme im deutschen, europäischen und US-amerikanischen Recht* (n 8) 46; Thelen (n 147) 67; Thomas Züll, *Regulierung im politischen Gemeinwesen: Zur demokratischen Legitimation von Wirtschaftsregulierung nach dem Grundgesetz und dem Europäischen Primärrecht* (Mohr Siebeck 2014) 41ff; cf. Bernd Grzeszick in Günter Dürig, Roman Herzog and Rupert Scholz (eds), *Grundgesetz: Kommentar* (99th edn, CH Beck 2022) GG Art 20 paras 107, 113.

519 Cremer (n 228) § 5 para 8.

promotion of the function of financial markets and investor protection.[520] Phrased differently, a new piece of financial markets regulations is warranted if there is market failure or other adverse effects on the investors.

Market failure describes a situation in which a market deviates from the economic model of perfect competition.[521] When regulating the availability and dissemination of market information, however, the model of perfect competition needs to be approached cautiously. Under the *Information Paradox*,[522] markets under perfect informational competition are markets that grant no profits to individual investors for possessing private information because all information is always reflected in the market price. Informationally complete markets, however, are unsustainable because the price formation process fundamentally relies on individual traders who can exploit private information and thereby import it into the public price formation process.

Thus, a government that achieves the goal of perfect market competition deprives the future traders of their profits to exploit their informational advantages which leads to no informational input, so the price is becoming stale in the long run. Hence, a certain degree of market opacity is inevitable if the regulator wants to achieve a stable informational equilibrium or, in other words, a stable influx of price information into the price formation process.

B. Dark Trading in Need of Regulation

Even though the need to intervene into the market with regulatory measures remains a matter of the individual jurisdiction, the preceding discussion of the disadvantages[523] made clear that dark trading can show several manifestations of market failure that call for correction. However, whether to regulate or to accept the inefficiency depends on a cost-benefit-analysis conducted for each regulatory measure. A regulatory measure shall only be implemented when its costs are outweighed by its benefits (*'If it's not broken, don't fix it.'*).

520 Sethe (n 196) SK FinfraG § 1 para 3; Buck-Heeb (n 196) § 1 para 6; Veil, '§ 2 Concept and Aims of Capital Markets Regulation' (n 196) § 1 paras 7ff.

521 Morell (n 285) § 3 para 153.

522 See above Part I § 3.B.II.1.

523 See above Part I § 3 D.IV.

A cost-benefit-analysis certainly weighs in favor of implementing a sound trading infrastructure and a trade transparency regime which provide a level-playing-field for all trading systems and grants specific exemptions for dark trading to prevent for unregulated dark trading.

Less clear, however, is the question of regulating the amount of dark trading, because experts disagree on the effects of dark trading on market quality.[524] Additionally, even those experts who agree on a concave utility curve with an optimal amount of dark trading at some point, cannot agree on where this optimum lies.[525] In this case, the legislator faces uncertainty in two ways: it is unclear whether dark trading is harmful at all and, if so, what amount is harmful to a degree that it legitimizes regulatory intervention with regard to a cost-benefit-analysis.[526]

In such situations of uncertainty, regulatory restraint may be a viable choice, wherein the regulator would only determine the pre-requisites of dark trading but refrain from steering the ultimate amount of permissible dark trading in the market.[527] Nevertheless, legislators may consider it necessary to go further and also regulate the permissible amount of dark trading. To do this properly, they must adhere to the principles of precautious regulation.[528]

---

524 See above Part I § 3 D.IV.2.

525 See above Part I § 3 D.IV.1.c).; cf. Rudolph and Röhrl (n 51) 207–8.

526 See above Part I § 3 D.IV.1.c)-d).; cf. Humbel, *Die Regelung der Vor- und Nachhandelstransparenz in der Europäischen Union und der Schweiz* (n 50) 63; Thelen (n 147) 121.

527 Commission of the European Communities, 'Communication from the Commission on the precautionary principle' (COM(2000) 1 final, Brussels, 2 February 2000) 15 para 5.2.1.: *'The decision to do nothing may be a response in its own right.'* Cf. Nina Reiser, *Durchsetzung heterogener börsengesellschaftsrechtlicher Normen* (Dike 2017) paras 91–2; Nina Reiser, 'Anlegerschutz durch Trennung?: Segregierung von Eigen- und Kundenbeständen bei der Drittverwahrung von Bucheffekten' [2017] SZW 452, 463; Hans C von der Crone, Matthias Maurer and Jan H Hoffmann, 'Revision Börsendelikte und Marktmissbrauch: Der Entwurf zur Änderung des Börsengesetzes' [2011] SZW 533, 534.

528 Cf. Christian Calliess, 'Finanzkrisen als Herausforderung der internationalen, europäischen und nationalen Rechtssetzung' in Christian Calliess, Georg Lienbacher and Bernd Grzeszick (eds), *Grundsatzfragen der Rechtsetzung und Rechtsfindung: Referate und Diskussionen auf der Tagung der Vereinigung der Deutschen Staatsrechtslehrer in Münster vom 5. bis 8. Oktober 2011* (Veröffentlichungen der Vereinigung der Deutschen Staatsrechtslehrer Band 71, De Gruyter 2012) 139–41; Udo Di Fabio, 'Gefahr, Vorsorge, Risiko: Die Gefahrenabwehr unter dem Einfluß des Vorsorgeprinzips' [1996] Jura 566, 572ff; Markus Thiel, *Die Entgrenzung der Gefahren-*

C. Principles of Precautious Regulation

The regulation of financial markets is generally law of risk prevention (‘*Gefahrenabwehrrecht*’). This requires the materialization of a specific risk before the government can intervene.[529] The principle of precautious regulation applies in cases in which a specific risk has not yet materialized, however, there is merely a (more distant) chance of a risk, but holding back would bear the risk of rendering the intervention futile when the risk ultimately materializes.[530] While the distinction between both ways of regulation may sometimes be blurred, precautious regulation is characterized by a lower threshold for intervention and thus considered more intrusive. This can only be justified under the principle of proportionality if the end of the intrusive measure is to protect a good of high significance and value, such as financial stability.[531]

This style of regulation is most common in environmental regulation where the regulatory objective – preservation of nature – is complex and causal links between human action and resulting damage are not straightforward.[532] Financial markets law has often shown similar complexity and unclear causal links between actions and resulting damage which legitimizes the use of precautious regulation in this field of law as well.[533] In both cases, when damage is done to the environment or to the financial markets to a larger extent, the damage is difficult to repair after the fact.

Under the principle of precaution, regulatory intervention is warranted when the cause for precautious regulation is clearly and narrowly defined,[534] when there is incomplete knowledge about the phenomenon that shall be regulated and when there is the chance of future harm created by this phenomenon.[535] In such a case, the factual uncertainty about the

---

abwehr: Grundfragen von Freiheit und Sicherheit im Zeitalter der Globalisierung (Mohr Siebeck 2011) 90–1.

529 Calliess (n 528) 139–41; Thiel (n 528) 94–5.

530 Calliess (n 528) 139–40; Thiel (n 528) 94–5.

531 Calliess (n 528) 140–1, 146; Contratto, ‘Hochfrequenzhandel und systemische Risiken’ (n 352) 154–5.

532 Calliess (n 528) 136–7.

533 ibid 137–9.

534 Humbel, *Die Regelung der Vor- und Nachhandelstransparenz in der Europäischen Union und der Schweiz* (n 50) 65–6. Cf. Calliess (n 528) 140–1; Di Fabio (n 528) 572ff; Thiel (n 528) 90–1.

535 Humbel, *Die Regelung der Vor- und Nachhandelstransparenz in der Europäischen Union und der Schweiz* (n 50) 66. Cf. Contratto, ‘Hochfrequenzhandel und sys-

risk propensity of economic activity transforms into a legislative mandate in which the legislator can decide whether a risk shall be accepted or be subjected to regulation.[536]

As has been shown by the current discussion in economics about the influence of dark trading on price accuracy, the issue of how much dark trading shall be allowed is a matter which can only be addressed by precautious regulation because there is no acute risk of market break-down due to dark trading (as an identifiable event that can be corrected for after the fact).[537] Thus, dark trading in its current form and size does not have the same bearing on systematic stability of the financial markets as, for instance, bank failures have.[538] However, once investors lose their trust in the price formation process, this damage is hard to repair. Whether the regulatory measures should be used to regulate the amount of dark trading – especially the volume cap mechanism under EU law – shall be discussed in the analysis of the respective jurisdiction.[539]

D. Government Regulation and Self-Regulation

After having established when to regulate, the question arises *who* should be the one responsible to regulate dark trading. Regulation is the implementation, monitoring, and enforcement of rules, which appears to be a principal function of the government.[540] Yet, in financial markets and other areas of business law, self-regulation is common. Self-regulation is

temische Risiken' (n 352) 154–5; Ernst Kutscheid, 'Immissionsschutzrechtliche Vorsorge und Drittschutz' in Bernd Bender and others (eds), *Rechtsstaat zwischen Sozialgestaltung und Rechtsschutz: Festschrift für Konrad Redeker zum 70. Geburtstag* (CH Beck 1993) 448.

536 Humbel, *Die Regelung der Vor- und Nachhandelstransparenz in der Europäischen Union und der Schweiz* (n 50) 66. See also Calliess (n 528) 140–1; Commission of the European Communities, 'Communication from the Commission on the precautionary principle' (n 527) 15 para 5.2.1: '*The appropriate response in a given situation is thus the result of an eminently political decision, a function of the risk level that is "acceptable" to the society on which the risk is imposed.*'

537 See above Part I § 3 A. and D.IV.

538 See above Part I § 3 A. and D.IV.

539 See below Part II § 6.C.III.1.c).

540 Christoph Winzeler, 'Selbstregulierung: Grenzen und Möglichkeiten' in Peter Sester and others (eds), *St. Galler Handbuch zum Schweizer Finanzmarktrecht: Finanzmarktaufsicht und Finanzmarktinfrastrukturen* (1st edn, Dike 2017) § 7 para 1.

the creation and monitoring of rules by a limited number of individuals or companies to exert control over their own members and their behavior.[541]

The advantages and disadvantages of government regulation and self-regulation have been studied broadly and are not discussed in full length in this study.[542] However, the differences between both types of regulation are important with regard to dark trading because the trading venue regime and the transparency regime were originally domains of self-regulation by exchanges and other self-regulatory bodies.[543] Over time, both regimes have come more and more under governmental supervision, however, to a varying degree in the United States, the European Union, Germany, and Switzerland. Especially in the United States and in Switzerland, self-regulation is still a central element of financial market regulation. For this reason, the primary advantages and drawbacks of self-regulation shall be outlined briefly.

I. Advantages of Self-Regulation

In financial markets, regulation often requires expertise in the subject matter which governmental agencies may lack. The individuals and companies operating in the area subjected to regulation have first-hand experience and can bring insight-knowledge to the regulatory process.[544] Moreover,

541 Robert Baldwin, Martin Cave and Martin Lodge, *Understanding Regulation: Theory, Strategy, and Practice* (2nd edn, Oxford University Press 2012) 137; Winzeler, 'Selbstregulierung' (n 540) § 7 para 2.

542 See for further detail: Gregor Bachmann, *Private Ordnung: Grundlagen ziviler Regelsetzung* (Mohr Siebeck 2006) passim; Petra Buck-Heeb and Andreas Dieckmann, *Selbstregulierung im Privatrecht* (Mohr Siebeck 2010) 217ff; Jan Damrau, *Selbstregulierung im Kapitalmarktrecht: Eine rechtsökonomische Analyse der Normsetzung der deutschen Börsen und ihrer Träger* (Ph.D.-Thesis University of Göttingen 2003, TENEA-Verlag 2003) 76; Martin Schmidhuber, *Verhaltenskodizes im nationalen und grenzüberschreitenden elektronischen Geschäftsverkehr: Zur Frage der Integration der Selbstregulierung durch Private in die staatliche Rechtsordnung* (Ph.D.-Thesis University of Heidelberg 2004, Peter Lang 2004) 134.

543 Barr, Jackson and Tahyar (n 516) 444ff.

544 Baldwin, Cave and Lodge (n 541) 139; Buck-Heeb and Dieckmann (n 542) 222–3; Damrau (n 542) 77; Eilís Ferran, 'Institutional Design: The Choices for National Systems' in Niamh Moloney, Eilís Ferran and Jennifer Payne (eds), *The Oxford Handbook of Financial Regulation* (Oxford University Press 2015) 110; Hopt, *Der Kapitalanlegerschutz im Recht der Banken* (n 65) 429; Sabine Kress, *Effizienzorientierte Kapitalmarktregulierung: Eine Analyse Aus Institutionenökonomischer Per-*

self-regulation is a leaner process which can react more quickly to innovation and market adaptation than governmental regulation.[545] Since self-regulation is not imposed by the government and more independent from current policy matters,[546] it also enjoys a high degree of acceptance by the regulated entities.[547] Finally, by outsourcing the regulatory task to the private sector, the government can save costs.[548]

II. Disadvantages of Self-Regulation

The disadvantages of self-regulation are the inherent conflicts of interest. Members of the same industry have a large incentive to exert a 'light touch'[549] regulation on each other to promote one's own and the industries' interests but may neglect the interest of the general public.[550] Self-regulatory standards usually do not have the authority of government-made law and therefore may have an enforcement deficit.[551] Additionally, self-regulation can also be overly restrictive to set up barriers for new market entrants.[552]

---

spektive (Ph.D.-Thesis Johann Wolfgang Goethe-University Frankfurt 1995, Gabler 1996) 100; Schmidhuber (n 542) 134; Winzeler, 'Selbstregulierung' (n 540) § 7 para 5.

545 Baldwin, Cave and Lodge (n 541) 140–1; Buck-Heeb and Dieckmann (n 542) 220–1; Damrau (n 542) 76; Ferran (n 544) 110; Schmidhuber (n 542) 134; Winzeler, 'Selbstregulierung' (n 540) § 7 para 5.

546 Ferran (n 544) 110.

547 Baldwin, Cave and Lodge (n 541) 140; Buck-Heeb and Dieckmann (n 542) 223–4; Damrau (n 542) 78; Winzeler, 'Selbstregulierung' (n 540) § 7 para 4.

548 Baldwin, Cave and Lodge (n 541) 140; Buck-Heeb and Dieckmann (n 542) 224–5; Damrau (n 542) 79; Ferran (n 544) 111; Schmidhuber (n 542) 134; Winzeler, 'Selbstregulierung' (n 540) § 7 para 5.

549 Ferran (n 544) 110.

550 Baldwin, Cave and Lodge (n 541) 145–6; Buck-Heeb and Dieckmann (n 542) 231ff; Damrau (n 542) 80–1; Ferran (n 544) 111; Kress (n 544) 98–9; Winzeler, 'Selbstregulierung' (n 540) § 7 para 5.

551 Buck-Heeb and Dieckmann (n 542) 229ff; Damrau (n 542) 81–2.

552 Ferran (n 544) 111. See also Boston Consulting Group, 'Securities and Exchange Commission: Organizational Study and Reform' (10 March 2011) 25.

III. Role of Self-Regulation in the Examined Jurisdictions

Among the examined regulatory regimes of this study, the United States and Switzerland rely on a self-regulatory regime that is a 'middle path' between pure governmental regulation and pure self-regulation. In this 'managed self-regulation'[553] (*'gesteuerte Selbstregulierung'*)[554], the self-regulator is 'enrolled' in the public oversight system by formal assignment or delegation of certain responsibilities and overseen by a government agency.[555]

With MiFID II/MiFIR, the European Union delegates more power to the European Securities and Markets Authority (ESMA), however, the oversight in the Member States is carried out by the national competent authority. According to Article 67(2) MiFID II, the national competent authority shall be a public authority. Consequently, German financial regulation is characterized by governmental regulation, not self-regulation.[556] The influence of governmental and self-regulation on the regulation of dark trading will be examined in the subsequent chapters.

E. Potential Market Failures of Dark Trading

After having described the pre-requisites of regulation and the forms of regulation, the last section before turning to the regulatory measures of the jurisdictions will focus on the potential market failures of dark trading that may need fixing. Here the goal of perfect competition plays an important

553 There is no common nomenclature for this form of self-regulation, see Ian Ayres and John Braithwaite, *Responsive Regulation: Transcending the Deregulation Debate* (Oxford University Press 1992) 103 who distinguish between '*co-regulation*' and '*enforced self-regulation*'.

554 Winzeler, 'Selbstregulierung' (n 540) § 7 paras 8, 12; Urs Zulauf, 'Koregulierung statt Selbstregulierung: Erfahrungen mit der Selbstregulierung im Schweizer Finanzmarktrecht seit der Finanzkrise von 2007' (Jusletter 4 November 2013) paras 22–3.

555 Ferran (n 544) 111; Julia Black, 'Enrolling actors in regulatory systems: Examples from UK financial services regulation' [2003] Public Law 63ff; Winzeler, 'Selbstregulierung' (n 540) § 7 paras 8, 12; Zulauf (n 554) paras 22–3.

556 Doris Döhmel in Heinz-Dieter Assmann, Uwe H Schneider and Peter O Mülbert (eds), *Wertpapierhandelsrecht: Kommentar* (7th edn, Otto Schmidt 2019) WpHG Einl. §§ 6–11 para 1; see also Section 1 FinDaG and Section 3 BörsG under German law.

role but needs to be taken with a grain of salt due to the *Information Paradox*.[557]

I. Market Power and Ruinous Competition

In perfect competition, no market participant has the power to set prices; prices result from the undisturbed interaction of supply and demand.[558] In the era before market liberalization in the late 20th century, incumbent exchanges occupied a quasi-monopoly position over organized order flow and charged excess fees for their services.[559] This position of market power was supposed to be remedied by the introduction of competition among new and old market places which led *inter alia* to the rise of dark pools.[560] In present markets, however, there is so much competition among trading venues that some observers even fear it may lead to ruinous competition.[561] If dark pools have an unfair price advantage because they can free-ride the information production of exchanges and operate under more permissive regulations, they may have lower operating costs compared to exchanges and other lit venues which would cause an unlevel playing field among competitors for the same order flow.[562]

II. Rationalization and Coordination

Every market transaction entails transaction costs.[563] Sometimes transaction costs may reach prohibitive levels so that market participants are unable to agree via privately negotiated contracts how to organize their

557 See above Part I § 4 A.
558 Cooter and Ulen (n 40) 28–9; Fritsch (n 473) 26, 163; Morell (n 285) 154–5; Thelen (n 147) 77.
559 Gresse (n 7) 4; Moloney, *EU Securities and Financial Markets Regulation* (n 4) 435–6.
560 Banks (n 5) 7ff; Petrescu and Wedow (n 5) 9.
561 Baldwin, Cave and Lodge (n 541) 19; Fritsch (n 471) 190; Thelen (n 147) 78.
562 Baldwin, Cave and Lodge (n 541) 19–20; Fritsch (n 473) 190; Arnd A Schulte, *Die Regulierung der deutschen Effektenbörsen: Eine Analyse staatlicher Maßnahmen im deutschen Börsenwesen seit der Währungsreform* (Ph.D.-Thesis University of Münster 1994, Peter Lang 1995) 26–7; Thelen (n 147) 78.
563 Cf. Coase, 'The Problem of Social Cost' (n 237) 15; Coase, 'The Nature of the Firm' (n 237) 391; Fritsch (n 473) 10–1; Thelen (n 147) 78.

behavior in an efficient manner.[564] In such instances, regulation can rationalize the 'production' or operation process.[565] A common means is standardization, for example standardization of financial instruments to allow comparison among different issuers.[566]

In an environment in which many marketplaces compete among each other for order flow, the service of providing a marketplace itself becomes the marketable good; a *'market for markets'* is created. In such a *'market for markets'* the rationale of standardization can aid consumers of the good 'market' – here the traders – to lower their search costs for the market that suits their needs. Therefore, marketplaces that serve a similar function or purpose should operate under a standardized set of rules.[567]

In the context of dark trading, this would require a cohesive regulation of the rules for trading infrastructures and trade transparency in order to create a level-playing-field among lit and dark venues that perform a comparable function for traders.[568] In this regard, unregulated dark pools operating outside the regulatory perimeter raise transaction costs, because they are not only hard for regulators to monitor but also hard for investors to compare and therefore should be avoided.[569] A similar problem is created when loopholes in the transparency regime lead to dark trading[570] or when

564 Coase, 'The Problem of Social Cost' (n 237) 2ff; Thelen (n 147) 78–9.

565 Baldwin, Cave and Lodge (n 541) 21.

566 Armour and others (n 62) 245–6. Cf. BaFin, 'Hinweise zu Finanzinstrumenten nach § 1 Abs. 11 Sätze 1 bis 5 KWG (Aktien, Vermögensanlagen, Schuldtitel, sonstige Rechte, Anteile an Investmentvermögen, Geldmarktinstrumente, Devisen, Rechnungseinheiten, Emissionszertifikate, Kryptowerte und Schwarmfinanzierungsinstrumente)' (20 December 2011, changed on 1 December 2022) 2. a) bb); Matthias Lehmann, *Finanzinstrumente* (Mohr Siebeck 2009) 315ff; Kumpan (n 125) WpHG § 2 para 7; Olivier Favre and Stefan Kramer in Rolf Sethe and others (eds), *Kommentar zum Finanzmarktinfrastrukturgesetz FinfraG* (SK FinfraG, 1st edn, Schulthess 2017) Art 2 lit b para 1.

567 IOSCO, 'Principles for Dark Liquidity' (n 12) 21; IOSCO, 'Transparency and Market Fragmentation' (n 3) 11.

568 CESR, 'CESR Technical Advice to the European Commission in the Context of the MiFID Review - Equity Markets' (n 4) 27; Moloney, *EU Securities and Financial Markets Regulation* (n 4) 446–7.

569 Recital 6 MiFIR; CESR, 'CESR Technical Advice to the European Commission in the Context of the MiFID Review - Equity Markets' (n 4) 28–9.

570 CESR, 'CESR Technical Advice to the European Commission in the Context of the MiFID Review - Equity Markets' (n 4) 27ff; Gomber and Pierron (n 4) 53–4; Mahoney and Rauterberg (n 118) 244; SEC, 'Regulation of Non-Public Trading Interest' (n 22) 74 FR 61214: *'Few if any dark pool ATSs exceed the 5 % threshold for any NMS stocks (…)'*.

there is incompatible post-trade information from exchanges and dark pools.[571] Standardized transparency requirements are important to create transparency on lit markets and to require dark pools to use the exemptions from pre-trade transparency the regulatory regime holds ready for this task.[572] Without standardization, transaction costs may rise to a prohibitive level for private transactions which is one form of market failure that has to be avoided.[573]

III. Externalities and Public Goods

1. Externalities

In perfect competition, each market actor pays for all costs caused by their economic activity and is compensated for the benefits they produce for others.[574] In reality, the effects of economic activity rarely remain between the parties of a transaction and often have effects on third parties.[575] Those external effects of economic activity can either be negative or positive externalities.[576] Negative externalities pass on costs to society as a whole, leading to lowered transaction prices between buyer and seller which induces production levels of the good to rise above the socially desirable quantity.[577] Positive externalities, on the other hand, pass on benefits of economic transactions to society, which means that the buyer will not enjoy all benefits of the transaction and will only be willing to pay a lower price which ultimately leads to production levels falling below the socially desirable level.[578]

571 SEC, 'Regulation of Non-Public Trading Interest' (n 22) 74 FR 61219.

572 CESR, 'CESR Technical Advice to the European Commission in the Context of the MiFID Review - Equity Markets' (n 4) 27ff; Gomber and Pierron (n 4) 53–4.

573 Cf. Fritsch (n 473) 10; Lawrence J White, 'International Regulation of Securities Markets: Competition or Harmonization?' in Andrew W Lo (ed), *The Industrial Organization and Regulation of the Securities Industry* (The University of Chicago Press 1996) 210.

574 Fritsch (n 473) 84.

575 Cremer (n 228) 251; Fritsch (n 473) 84.

576 White (n 573) 211.

577 Baldwin, Cave and Lodge (n 541) 18; Stephen G Breyer, *Regulation and Its Reform* (Harvard University Press 1982) 23ff; Cremer (n 228) 251–2; Fritsch (n 473) 84ff; Anthony I Ogus, *Regulation: Legal Form and Economic Theory* (Hart Publishing 2004) 35ff; White (n 573) 211–2.

578 Baldwin, Cave and Lodge (n 541) 20; Fritsch (n 473) 89–90; White (n 573) 212.

2. Public Goods

a) Public Goods and the Price Formation Process

The issue of positive externalities is most pronounced with public goods. Public goods are characterized by the non-exclusivity and non-rivalrous of their consumption.[579] Since consumers can enjoy the benefits of the public good without paying for it, they will free-ride the utility of the good without compensating the producer. The producer will therefore be unable to set-off its costs for producing the public good, which will lead to under-production.[580] An example of a public good is a lighthouse that provides the socially desirable service of keeping ships from sinking at night. No ship near the lighthouse can be excluded from seeing the light signal (non-exclusivity) and its utility is not diminished when one ship saw the light (non-rivalrous).[581]

Similar to the signal of a lighthouse, some also consider the price formation process on financial markets an example of a (quasi-)public good because the displayed price is a signal that can be observed by all market participants (non-exclusivity) and with its utility not being diminished when one trader observed it because other may still see and use it (non-rivalrous).[582] In this case, dark trading can be considered an overuse of the price formation process where the user of the dark pool is not contributing the information about one's own transaction made in the dark pool to the price formation process.

b) Distinction between Different Aspects of the Price Formation Process

This rationale, however, only describes one aspect of dark trading but falls short of an important distinction. On the issue of non-exclusivity, it is certainly a fact observed by many observers of the US, EU, and Swiss markets that prices are broadly available to both the traders and the public. However, it should not be forgotten that this is a circumstance in markets which already have far-reaching transparency rules and that would most

579 Baldwin, Cave and Lodge (n 541) 20; Cremer (n 228) 261; Fritsch (n 473) 81, 96; White (n 573) 212.

580 Cremer (n 228) 261. See also Baldwin, Cave and Lodge (n 541) 20; White (n 573) 212.

581 Cremer (n 228) 261.

582 White (n 573) 212.

likely not be the case without such rules. If traders and venue operators were free to choose their preferred level of transparency, markets would neither be fully opaque nor fully transparent. A likely outcome would be that traders and venue operators chose a level of transparency which would optimally support their trading needs (i.e., lower transaction costs to an optimal level), while leaving market outsiders with as little information as possible since they are not compensated for the dissemination of this information. That said, it is the very topic of this study to examine how far-reaching the transparency regimes of the jurisdictions in fact are and if the notion of broad availability of trade transparency information is actually founded in the law. Insofar, there may be good reason to consider the price information under the trade transparency regimes a non-exclusive good due to regulation.

aa) Post-Trade Information is Non-Rivalrous

More nuanced are the findings on the second prong – non-rivalrous – because there is a functional difference between different types of information. If a trader, as the consumer of price information, uses a displayed price merely to inform himself about current market prices, this is a non-rivalrous usage because any other market participant can still do the same without diminishing the utility of the piece of information. The same is true for a trader that uses said information to convince their counterparty that the price found on the market is a fair one for their transaction. This situation is most common with post-trade transparency information because the trading opportunity presented by two parties who recently made the trade has passed – they have just traded – there can no longer be rivalrous. Moreover, the information is more informative for other traders than pre-trade transparency information because it is not a merely reservation price of one trader but a price another trader was willing to agree upon. Thus, post-trade transparency information shares the features of a public good showing non-exclusivity and non-rivalrous to some extent.

bb) Pre-Trade Information is Rivalrous

For pre-trade transparency information, the situation is different. The issue of non-exclusivity is again a matter of the specific regulation in the particular jurisdiction. Here, the incentive to keep the information for oneself may be even higher because there is the issue of front running and information leakage leading to market impact costs. With regard to the non-rivalrous of pre-trade information the situation is different from post-trade information: if one trader reacts on the offer of another trader at a certain price, the offer's lot and price point cannot be used by a third trader to the extent the transaction is exhaustive. Even if the trader decides not to trade with the announcing trader, but rather to use the information of their competitive offer to buy up or sell off stock at another venue still displaying a stale price, the informational advantage will still be consumed. A third trader cannot gain an informational advantage on the same piece of price information again. Pre-trade transparency information appears to be rivalrous and, thus, unlike a public good. An uncompensated overuse may not be expected.

c) Only Post-Trade Information is a Public Good

As a result, it appears viable to expect different forms of regulation for pre-trade and post-trade transparency because the information they produce possesses different economic features: one is a (quasi-)public good whereas the other is not. The information about pre-trade transparency can therefore be limited with less concerns about market failure due to exploitation of a public good, while the limitation of post-trade transparency may result in issues related to public goods and should therefore be made more cautiously. This hypothesis remains to be examined in the actual regulatory environments of the jurisdictions.

IV. Information Asymmetry, Principal-Agent-Problems and Moral Hazard

1. Information Asymmetry

A major reason for markets to operate sub-optimally are information asymmetries among market actors.[583] *'Problems of 'asymmetric information' arise when a party on one side of a transaction has relevant information that the*

583 Cremer (n 228) 258; Martin Leschke, 'Regulierungstheorie aus ökonomischer Sicht' in Michael Fehling and Matthias Ruffert (eds), *Regulierungsrecht* (Mohr Siebeck 2010) 303ff.

other side does not have.'[584] If a market participant lacks relevant information for as investment decision, they may fall victim to a market participant who possesses an informational advantage. If the disadvantaged market participant is aware of his lack of information, the fear of another party exploiting its advantage can lead to a situation described by *George Akerlof's 'Market of Lemons*'[585] which depicts the issue of *adverse selection*:[586] The chance of engaging in a disadvantageous transaction incentivizes the trader who lacks information to lower his reservation price below the reservation price of the 'good-quality' market participants but above the reservation price of the 'poor-quality' market participants. Eventually, information asymmetry incentivizes the 'good-quality' market participants to leave the market while those offering 'poor-quality' remain.[587] The expectation of having only the chance to interact with 'poor-quality' market participants will incentivize uninformed traders, who cannot distinguish between good- and poor-quality offers, to withdraw from the market eventually.[588]

That said, some degree of information asymmetry is necessary to fuel the price formation process through of information arbitrage (*Information Paradox*).[589] However, in financial markets that have dark trading, traders are also aware of the fact that they have incomplete information about the aggregate order flow in the market which raises the issue of adverse selection. From a regulatory perspective, financial markets need to ensure that there is some opacity in the market to enable information traders to set-off their costs of information research, but enough transparency to induce sufficient investor trust to avoid adverse selection. Thus, in short,

584 White (n 573) 213.

585 Akerlof (n 99) 488ff.

586 See Lambert (n 476) 187 for a definition of 'adverse selection': *'Adverse selection occurs when something causes 'bad' market participants – those offering below-average value to their trading partners – to be overrepresented on a pool of buyers or sellers; that pool has been 'selected adversely'.'*
See also Fritsch (n 473) 253; Klaus U Schmolke, '§ 5 - Vertragstheorie und ökonomische Analyse des Vertragsrechts' in Emanuel V Towfigh and Niels Petersen (eds), *Ökonomische Methoden im Recht: Eine Einführung für Juristen* (2nd edn, Mohr Siebeck 2017) 138ff, § 5 paras 273ff.

587 Fritsch (n 473) 249–253; Morell (n 285) 75–6, § 3 para 160; Schmolke, '§ 5 - Vertragstheorie und ökonomische Analyse des Vertragsrechts' (n 586) 138ff, § 5 paras 273ff.

588 Fritsch (n 473) 252–3; Schmolke, '§ 5 - Vertragstheorie und ökonomische Analyse des Vertragsrechts' (n 586) 139–40, § 5 para 275.

589 See above Part I § 3.B.II.1. Cf. also Klöhn, 'Wertpapierhandelsrecht diesseits und jenseits des Informationsparadigmas' (n 209) 375–6.

financial markets need to accept short-term information asymmetry to allow for long-term information efficiency.[590]

2. Principal-Agent-Issues and Moral Hazard

Furthermore, dark trading raises principal-agent-issues and moral hazard problems when HFTs operate within dark pools.[591] For dark pool operators HFTs are a valuable source of order flow which increases the chances for other traders to find liquidity at any given time in the dark pool. This welcome effect of HFT presence may create an incentive to invite HFTs into dark pools or even grant them more insights into the order book as any other trader would have.[592] Given that the other traders trust in the equal application of the rule of not displaying their order information by the dark pool operator, there is a principal-agent-issue and a moral hazard problem, because most non-HFT-traders are unable to monitor whether the operator abides by the agreed upon rules.

After having shed light on the character and interrelation of lit and dark trading as well as their need for regulation, the next step is to analyze the approaches of regulating dark trading taken by the United States of America, the European Union, Germany, and Switzerland.

590 Thelen (n 147) 412. Cf. Klöhn, 'Wertpapierhandelsrecht diesseits und jenseits des Informationsparadigmas' (n 209) 375–6; Klöhn (n 53) MAR Vor Art 17 paras 35ff.
591 See above Part I § 3 D.IV.
592 Kasiske (n 11) 457.

Part II: Analysis of the Regulation of Dark Liquidity in the United States of America, the European Union, Germany, and Switzerland

§ 5. Regulation of Dark Trading under the Federal Securities Law of the United States of America

A. Introduction

The first regulatory regime to be examined is the federal securities law of the United States of America. Because the United States encountered the phenomenon of modern dark trading first through the emergence of new alternative trading systems as early as 1969 with Instinet,[593] the US regulators were also the first to regulate dark trading.[594] US regulation of dark trading has been highly influential on other jurisdictions, such as the European Union, Germany, and Switzerland, when they promulgated their regulatory regimes for dark trading.[595]

B. The Structure of US Securities Law and its Regulatory Bodies

I. The Structure of US Securities Law

The federal securities law in the United States rests on the Securities Act of 1933 and the Securities Exchange Act of 1934 (Exchange Act), which were both enacted in response to the Great Depression.[596] When examining dark trading and US trading infrastructure, regard is only given to the secondary

593 Peter Gomber, *Elektronische Handelssysteme: Innovative Konzepte und Technologien im Wertpapierhandel* (Ph.D.-Thesis Justus-Liebig-University Gießen 2000, Physica-Verlag 2000) 70–1; Kumpan, *Die Regulierung außerbörslicher Wertpapierhandelssysteme im deutschen, europäischen und US-amerikanischen Recht* (n 8) 121.

594 Banks (n 5) 19; Gerald Spindler and Mario Hüther, 'Börse ohne Parkett - oder: Alternative Trading Systems: Elektronische Handelssysteme in den USA' [2002] RIW 649 fn 6.

595 Cf. Bundesrat, 'Botschaft zum Finanzmarktinfrastrukturgesetz (FinfraG)' (n 22) BBl. 2014, 7483, 7493; Recital 1 MiFIR; Kumpan, *Die Regulierung außerbörslicher Wertpapierhandelssysteme im deutschen, europäischen und US-amerikanischen Recht* (n 8) 121.

596 Michael S Barr, Howell E Jackson and Margaret E Tahyar, *Financial Regulation: Law and Policy* (University Casebook Series, Foundation Press 2018) 444–5; Cox and others (n 116) 5ff; Nyquist (n 72) 290ff.

equity market, which is regulated under the Exchange Act.[597] The Exchange Act's approach to the regulation of trading systems is an institutional approach, in which certain types of market institutions are defined and the requirements for market participants to qualify as such institutions are outlined. The rationale behind defining such market institutions is to tie certain rights and duties to those institutions and to allow the regulator to address the market institutions with regulatory measures.[598]

In its institutional approach, the Exchange Act mirrors the market environment of the 1930s: While there was a certain amount of over-the-counter-trading, the Exchange Act's purpose was to regulate exchange trading.[599] For this purpose, it created two regulatory institutions or 'buckets', the *'national securities exchange'* as the marketplace (Section 3(a)(1)[600] and Section 6 Exchange Act)[601] and the *'broker-dealers'* as the actors on the marketplace (Section 3(a)(4),[602] (5)[603] and Section 15 Exchange Act).[604] With the emergence of new trading systems, this narrow regulatory approach left a regulatory gap that was soon populated by trading systems combining aspects of market actors and marketplaces in the same entity.[605]

597 Mahoney and Rauterberg (n 118) 230–1.

598 Ian Domowitz and Ruben Lee, 'On the Road to Reg ATS: A Critical History of the Regulation of Automated Trading Systems' (2001) 4(2) International Finance 279, 282; Kumpan, *Die Regulierung außerbörslicher Wertpapierhandelssysteme im deutschen, europäischen und US-amerikanischen Recht* (n 8) 122; Mahoney and Rauterberg (n 118) 230–1, 254–5.

599 Barr, Jackson and Tahyar (n 596) 445; Fox, Glosten and Rauterberg, *The New Stock Market* (n 98) 29; Macey and O'Hara, 'Regulating Exchanges and Alternative Trading Systems' (n 139) 40; George J Benston, 'Required Disclosure and the Stock Market: An Evaluation of the Securities Exchange Act of 1934' (1973) 63(1) The American Economic Review 132-3.

600 Section 3(a)(1) Exchange Act (15 U.S.C. § 78c(1)) defining the national securities exchange.

601 Section 6 Exchange Act (15 U.S.C. § 78f) regulating the national securities exchange.

602 Section 3(a)(4) Exchange Act (15 U.S.C. § 78c(4)) defining broker.

603 Section 3(a)(5) Exchange Act (15 U.S.C. § 78c(5)) defining dealer.

604 Section 15 Exchange Act (15 U.S.C. § 78o) registration and regulating broker and dealer.

605 *Board of Trade of the City of Chicago v. Securities and Exchange Commission* (1991) 923 F.2d 1270 (7th Cir. 1991) (US Court of Appeals for the 7th Circuit); Barr, Jackson and Tahyar (n 4) 543; Brian P Baxter, 'The Securities Black Market: Dark Pool Trading and the Need for a More Expansive Regulation ATS-N' (2017) 70 Vanderbilt Law Review 311, 315–6; Robert L Colby and Erik R Sirri, 'Consolidation and Competition in the US Equity Markets' (2010) 5 Capital Markets Law Journal 169, 183–4; Maria Zyskind, 'Fighting for Market Share: How a Trade-at Rule Can Improve Market Efficiency' (2016) 91(1) Chicago-Kent Law Review 411, 414.

II. Regulatory Bodies

1. Securities and Exchange Commission

Besides regulating secondary market trading, the Exchange Act also created the Securities and Exchange Commission as the federal supervisory agency for securities regulation.[606] While Congress only intervenes to set the regulatory course in more fundamental issues, especially in times of crisis, the SEC is entrusted to monitor the markets, enforce the federal securities laws, and promulgate new regulations defining the provisions of the Securities Act and Exchange Act.[607] When the SEC engages in rulemaking, it influences the course of securities trading significantly and, within the SEC, it is the Commissioners who have the ultimate power to approve a new regulation after the appropriate notice and comment period for public review.[608] On the working level of the SEC, it is the Division of Trading and Markets that '*(...) deals primarily with the regulation of the securities professionals associated with the public capital markets. As a part of its function, Trading and Markets regulates, among others, broker-dealers and the self-regulatory organizations.*'[609]

2. Self-Regulatory Organizations

US securities law also accepts and encourages self-regulation by market participants.[610] To provide an institutional framework for self-regulation, the Exchange Act allows for self-regulatory organizations to form and register with the SEC.[611] Self-regulatory organizations (SROs) are quasi-private regulatory bodies that provide an additional layer of investor protection.[612]

606 Stephen J Choi and Adam C Pritchard, *Securities Regulation* (5th edn, Foundation Press 2019) 43–4; Cox and others (n 116) 9.

607 Choi and Pritchard (n 606) 43–4; Cox and others (n 116) 9.

608 Choi and Pritchard (n 606) 45–6; Fox, Glosten and Rauterberg, *The New Stock Market* (n 98) 29.

609 Choi and Pritchard (n 606) 45.

610 Barr, Jackson and Tahyar (n 596) 449; Cox and others (n 116) 20–1; Joel Seligman, 'Cautious Evolution or Perennial Irresolution: Stock Market Self-Regulation During the First 70 Years of the Securities and Exchange Commission' (2004) 59(4) The Business Lawyer 1347.

611 See Section 6 and Section 15A Exchange Act (15 U.S.C. § 78f and § 78o-3); Cox and others (n 116) 20ff.

612 Choi and Pritchard (n 606) 46.

However, the reason for their absence in the 1933 Securities Act and their sudden appearance in the Exchange Act was that the political winds had changed in the meantime. Since the stringent regulatory system introduced by the 1933 Securities Act did not prevent the crisis from worsening, the exchanges argued vigorously when being subjected to SEC supervision that they should at least maintain some self-regulatory powers.[613] It is therefore not surprising that national exchanges count among the SROs.

However, according to Section 3(a)(26)[614] Exchange Act, registered securities associations also have the status of SROs and are entrusted with regulating broker-dealers. Initially lobbied for by the exchanges to extend the self-regulatory duties also to the formerly lightly regulated broker-dealer industry to level the playing field,[615] the National Association of Securities Dealers (NASD) was established in 1939 and is known today as the Financial Industry Regulatory Authority (FINRA).[616] FINRA operates as a private, non-profit, membership-based organization for the regulation of broker-dealers.[617] In this capacity, FINRA adopts rules designed to

> '(...) *prevent fraudulent and manipulative acts and practices, to promote just and equitable principles of trade, to foster cooperation and coordination with persons engaged in (...) processing information with respect to, and facilitating transactions in securities, to remove impediments to and perfect the mechanism of a free and open market and a national market system, and, in general, to protect investors and the public interest (...).*'[618]

FINRA also enforces its rules and the securities laws against its member broker-dealers and provides for dispute settlement by arbitration for customers, brokers, and brokerage firms.[619]

---

613 Barr, Jackson and Tahyar (n 596) 445.

614 Section 3(a)(26) Exchange Act (15 U.S.C. § 78c(26)).

615 Barr, Jackson and Tahyar (n 596) 446ff.

616 Choi and Pritchard (n 606) 46; John C Coffee, Hillary A Sale and M T Henderson, *Securities Regulation: Cases and Materials* (13th edn, Foundation Press 2015) 57, 72–7.

617 Choi and Pritchard (n 606) 46.

618 Section 15A(b)(6) Exchange Act (15 U.S.C. § 78o-3(b)(6)). Cf. Choi and Pritchard (n 606) 46–7.

619 ibid 47.

C. The Securities Acts Amendments of 1975 and The National Market System

I. Policy Considerations

In the years following the Exchange Act of 1934, national securities exchanges, especially the New York Stock Exchange, rose to power and dominated the market.[620] Congress, however, was troubled that several large trading systems in juxtaposition would allow those trading centers to gain market power and extract surplus rents from traders and investors.[621] Although the SEC managed to intervene in some important areas as, for example, when implementing Rule 19b-3 which banned the fixed commission system NYSE used to charge their traders high fees,[622] the SEC reached the boundaries of its rule making power and Congress had to step in. To modernize the regulatory environment and counter such a concentration of market power, Congress thus envisioned an integrated '*national market system*' (NMS) '*(...) with fair competition among brokers, dealers and markets, the availability to all of information on transaction prices and dealer quotes, the linking of markets and the ability to execute orders in the best market.*'[623]

With the national market system, Congress aimed to reduce barriers between trading systems set up by the incumbent exchanges by means of

620 Crudele (n 505) 572; Eric Czervionke, 'Making Markets Work: The Critical Role of Market Infrastructure' in Gary Strumeyer and Sarah Swammy (eds), *The Capital Markets: Evolution of the Financial Ecosystem* (John Wiley & Sons 2017) 128.

621 Roger D Blanc, 'Intermarket Competition and Monopoly Power in the U.S. Stock Markets' (2007) 1(2) Brooklyn Journal of Corporate, Financial & Commercial Law 273, 297–8; Crudele (n 29) 573.

622 Mark Borrelli, 'Market Making in the Electronic Age' (2001) 32(4) Loyola University Chicago Law Journal 815, 832ff; Gregg A Jarrell, 'Change at the Exchange: The Causes and Effects of Deregulation' (1984) 27 The Journal of Law & Economics 273, 276, 280; Mahoney and Rauterberg (n 118) 233. See for further detail: Barr, Jackson and Tahyar (n 596) 535ff.

623 Hans R Stoll, 'Electronic Trading in Stock Markets' (2006) 20(1) The Journal of Economic Perspectives 153, 169. See also Beny (n 51) 411ff, 450ff; Borrelli (n 622) 832ff; Crudele (n 505) 572ff; Macey and O'Hara, 'Regulating Exchanges and Alternative Trading Systems' (n 139) 28; Jonathan R Macey and David D Haddock, 'Shirking at the SEC: The Failure of the National Market System' (1985) 1985(2) University of Illinois Law Review 315, 321ff; Therese H Maynard, 'What is an "Exchange?" - Proprietary Electronic Securities Trading Systems and the Statutory Definition of an Exchange' (1992) 49(3) Washington and Lee Law Review 833, 857ff; John G Moon, 'Dangerous Territoriality of American Securities Law: A Proposal for an Integrated Global Securities Market' (2000) 21(1) Northwestern Journal of International Law & Business 131ff.

interlinking trading systems, to allow for fair access to their orders, and to increase inter-market competition.[624] To achieve this, Section 11A was introduced into the Exchange Act in 1975, in which Congress entrusted the SEC *'(...) to facilitate, but not design, the development of a National Market System.'*[625] In Section 11A(a)(1)(C) Exchange Act,[626] Congress provided the SEC with a broad mandate to pursue achieving five properties when regulating: *'(...) (1) economically efficient execution of securities transactions, (2) fair competition, (3) transparency, (4) investor access to the best markets, and (5) the opportunity for investors' orders to be executed without the participation of a dealer.'*[627] While these properties may be viewed as credentials of a securities market that is able to serve diverse needs of participants in an optimal way, they are not by themselves the end goal of regulation, which is investor protection and ensuring the proper functioning of the securities market.[628] The five properties may even conflict with each other at times and cannot be attained simultaneously in every instance. It is thus mandatory that the SEC interprets its mandate with discretion and implements regulation that is capable of approaching ever closer to an ideal securities market.[629]

As the following examination of the Commission's regulatory practice will show, finding a path towards a National Market System requires calibrating securities regulation with regard to multiple goals at any given time. However, the panacea of the 1960s and 1970s – competition among multiple trading facilities – turned out to create unwanted adverse effects when modern technology significantly reduced both the complexity and costs for setting up a new trading venue. Alternative trading systems drove a wedge in the two-tiered regulatory regime of exchanges and broker-dealers. Although Congress never changed the system fundamentally on the level of

624 Blanc (n 621) 297–8; Crudele (n 505) 573.

625 Macey and O'Hara, 'Regulating Exchanges and Alternative Trading Systems' (n 139) 28. Cf SEC, 'Market 2000 Report: An Examination of Current Equity Market Developments' (Washington, D.C., January 1994) 4; Section 11A(a)(2) Exchange Act (15 U.S.C. § 78k-1(a)(2)).

626 Section 11A(a)(1)(C) Exchange Act (15 U.S.C. § 78k-1(a)(1)(C)).

627 Macey and O'Hara, 'Regulating Exchanges and Alternative Trading Systems' (n 139) 28. Cf Anna-Carina Salger, *Dark Trading: Shedding Light on US and EU Regulation of the Securities Markets' Dark Sector* (Ph.D.-Thesis University of Freiburg 2018/19, De Gruyter 2020) 129; Crudele (n 505) 574.

628 See above Part I § 3 A.II. Bošković, Cerruti and Noël (n 70) 15.

629 Macey and O'Hara, 'Regulating Exchanges and Alternative Trading Systems' (n 139) 28.

the Exchange Act, the SEC has used its rulemaking power to keep a balance between competition and a regulatory level-playing field among trading facilities.[630]

II. Implemented Measures by the SEC: A Consolidated Tape

With regard to the 'plumbing of the market', the different marketplaces became interconnected through the electronic communication systems: the Consolidated Quotation System (CQS), the Intermarket Trading System (ITS), and the Consolidated Tape System (CTS).[631] The CQS serves pre-trade transparency by disseminating the quotation prices of traders among the trading systems.[632] It also informs the traders about the National Best Bid and Offer prices (NBBO) in NMS-stock.[633] The ITS allows for the

630 Mahoney and Rauterberg (n 118) 240–3; Salger (n 627) 129.

631 Kumpan, *Die Regulierung außerbörslicher Wertpapierhandelssysteme im deutschen, europäischen und US-amerikanischen Recht* (n 8) 125; Louis Loss, Joel Seligman and Troy Paredes, *Fundamentals of Securities Regulation* (7th edn, Wolters Kluwer Law & Business 2018) 691ff. See also Beny (n 51) 415ff; Borrelli (n 622) 835ff; Norman S Poser, 'Restructuring the Stock Markets: A Critical Look at the SEC's National Market System' (1981) 56 New York University Law Review 883, 915ff; Moon (n 623) 139–40; Morris Mendelson and Junius W Peake, 'Whose Market Is It Anyway? Intermediaries' or Investors'' (1994) 19 Journal of Corporate Law 443, 463–4.

632 17 CFR § 240.11Ac1–1(b)(1)(i) (for exchanges) and 17 CFR § 240.11Ac1–1(b)(1)(ii) (for trader associations); Kumpan, *Die Regulierung außerbörslicher Wertpapierhandelssysteme im deutschen, europäischen und US-amerikanischen Recht* (n 8) 126.

633 For the definition of NMS-stock see Rule 600 (57) Regulation NMS (17 CFR § 242.600 (57)): '*NMS stock means any NMS security other than an option.*'; Rule 600 (47) Regulation NMS (17 CFR § 242.600 (47)): '*NMS security means any security or class of securities for which transaction reports are collected, processed, and made available pursuant to an effective transaction reporting plan, or an effective national market system plan for reporting transactions in listed options.*'; for the definition of NBBO see Rule 607 (50) Regulation NMS (17 CFR § 242.600 (50)): '*National best bid and national best offer means, with respect to quotations for an NMS stock, the best bid and best offer for such stock that are calculated and disseminated on a current and continuing basis by a competing consolidator or calculated by a self-aggregator and, for NMS securities other than NMS stocks, the best bid and best offer for such security that are calculated and disseminated on a current and continuing basis by a plan processor pursuant to an effective national market system plan; provided, that in the event two or more market centers transmit to the plan processor, a competing consolidator or a self-aggregator identical bids or offers for an NMS security, the best bid or best offer (as the case may be) shall be determined by ranking all such identical bids or offers (as the case may be) first by size (giving the*

routing of orders between trading systems.[634] The CTS, on the other hand, serves post-trade transparency by disseminating the information of recently concluded transactions from several trading systems to one consolidated tape.[635]

The SEC approved three transaction reporting plans for the consolidated tape: (1) the Consolidated Tape Association (CTA) Plan which disseminated the data of the New York Stock Exchange in Network A; NYSE Arca, NYSE Amex, and other regional exchanges in Network B for listed common stock, long-term warrants, preferred stock, and American Depository Receipts; (2) the Over the Counter/Unlisted Trading Privileges (OTC/UTP) Plan for consolidated reporting of transactions for issues listed on the NASDAQ Stock Exchange; and (3) the Options Price Reporting Authority (OPRA) Plan for consolidated reporting of transactions in eligible options contracts listed and traded on national securities exchanges.[636] In accordance with those plans, the exchanges and FINRA show the price and volume of the recently closed transaction as well as the time of the transaction.

D. The Trading Infrastructure Regime under US Law

The trading infrastructure regime under US law comprises of three categories regulated as either broker-dealer, national securities exchange, or alternative trading system.

I. Broker-Dealers

1. Definition

Brokers, dealers, and the combined broker-dealers are the market actors defined under the Exchange Act. Section 3(a)(4) Exchange Act defines a

---

highest ranking to the bid or offer associated with the largest size), and then by time (giving the highest ranking to the bid or offer received first in time).'
Cf. also Banks (n 5) 10; Mahoney and Rauterberg (n 118) 236.

634 Beny (n 51) 416.

635 ibid 415.

636 See SEC, 'Responses to Frequently Asked Questions Concerning Large Trader Reporting' (2016) Section 1; Beny (n 51) 415–7.

broker as *'(...) any person engaged in the business of effecting transactions in securities for the account of others (...)'*,[637] whereas Section 3(a)(5) defines a dealer as *'(...) any person engaged in the business of buying and selling securities (...) for such person's own account through a broker or otherwise.'*[638]

According to those definitions, a broker is in the business of routing client orders to another market or a third person but will not act as either buyer or seller for their own client, and therefore is not *per se* interested in the outcome of the transaction.[639] A dealer, on the other hand, buys and sells securities on their own account to their clients and assumes an interest in the outcome of the transaction.[640] Despite the different roles performed by brokers and dealers, it is not only possible for one market actor to perform the broker- and the dealer-function simultaneously (if registered accordingly), but in fact it is so common that the market and the subsequent discussion refers to broker-dealers as a joint category.[641] Since brokers, dealers, and broker-dealers are subject to the same regulatory requirements under Section 15 Exchange Act,[642] the SEC acknowledged the blurred boundaries of the two regulatory categories of brokers and dealers by providing a joint form for registration. 'Form BD' is for any person registering either as broker, dealer, or broker-dealer.[643]

The scope of both the broker and the dealer definition – while very broad – excludes all investors who actively trade in securities but who are not *'in the business'* of intermediating in securities trading either as principal or agent.[644] Only those who engage in effecting transactions in securities on a regular basis rather than on an isolated basis and typically

---

637 Section 3(a)(4) Exchange Act (15 U.S.C. § 78c (a)(4)); Loss, Seligman and Paredes (n 631) 755ff.

638 Section 3(a)(5) Exchange Act (15 U.S.C. § 78c (a)(5)); Loss, Seligman and Paredes (n 631) 755ff.

639 Kumpan, *Die Regulierung außerbörslicher Wertpapierhandelssysteme im deutschen, europäischen und US-amerikanischen Recht* (n 8) 123. NB: certain compensation schemes can make the broker an interested party in the transaction but rather with regard to its fees, instead of the transaction price or quality.

640 ibid 123.

641 Cox and others (n 116) 1022; Kumpan, *Die Regulierung außerbörslicher Wertpapierhandelssysteme im deutschen, europäischen und US-amerikanischen Recht* (n 8) 122–3.

642 Section 15 Exchange Act (15 U.S.C. § 78o).

643 Bošković, Cerruti and Noël (n 70) 17; Mahoney and Rauterberg (n 118) 257; Section 15(b) Exchange Act (15 U.S.C. § 78o(b)); SEC, 'Form BD: Uniform Application for Broker-Dealer Registration'.

644 Cox and others (n 116) 1022; Mahoney and Rauterberg (n 118) 257.

make their services public fall within the definition of either broker or dealer.[645]

2. Functions of Broker-Dealers

In general, the function of broker-dealers can be described as controlling the institutionalized professional trading on secondary securities markets in the United States. Insofar, broker-dealers perform a gatekeeping function.[646] However, within this function they either act as a trader or as a marketplace themselves.

a) Trader-Function of Broker-Dealers

Broker-dealers play a large role as intermediaries between customers and trading facilities. As members or users of trading facilities, broker-dealers execute orders on exchanges and other trading facilities in return for a commission.[647] Some broker-dealers are, in fact, highly active participants of a trading facility; they even count among the market makers for such facility. A market maker is a person who continuously offers to buy and sell a specific security at a specific price (Section 3(a)(38) Exchange Act).[648] The business model of a market maker is to earn a profit from the spread between the bid and the ask price.[649]

---

645 Cox and others (n 116) 1022; see *Securities and Exchange Commission v. Robert L. Ridenour* (1990) 913 F.2d 515 (8th Cir. 1990) (US Court of Appeals for the 8th Circuit).

646 Cox and others (n 116) 1022.

647 SEC, 'Concept Release on Equity Market Structure' (n 6) 75 FR 3599; Cox and others (n 116) 1022.

648 Section 3(a)(38) Exchange Act (15 U.S.C. § 78c (a)(38)): *'The term 'market maker' means any specialist permitted to act as a dealer, any dealer acting in the capacity of block positioner, and any dealer who, with respect to a security, holds himself out (by entering quotations in an inter-dealer communications system or otherwise) as being willing to buy and sell such security for his own account on a regular or continuous basis.'*

649 Fox, 'MiFID II and Equity Trading' (n 53) paras 18.06ff.

b) Internalizer-Function of Broker-Dealers

Internalization is the other function of broker-dealers. Broker-dealers only route a minority of customer orders to external trading facilities like exchanges; while, the bulk of customers' orders are executed internally.[650] When a broker-dealer internalizes order flow, it either crosses a customer's order with a matching order of another customer or the broker-dealer steps in as principal and executes the trade against its proprietary capital, forming the counter-party to the trade, which qualifies as bilateral trading.[651]

Internalization resembles market making on trading venues, but instead of buying and selling securities on someone else's marketplace paying for access and quoting prices publicly, internalization happens within the broker-dealer's own systems.[652] Hence, under Rule 600(b)(52) Regulation NMS *'(...) any dealer that holds itself out as being willing to buy and sell to its customers, or others, in the United States, an NMS stock for its own account on a regular or continuous basis otherwise than on a national securities exchange in amounts of less than block size'* qualifies as an *'OTC market maker'*. According to Rule 600(b)(9) Regulation NMS, an order is of *'block size'* if it is either an order of at least 10,000 shares or an order of at least USD 200,000.[653] Broker-dealers who internalize block orders are called *'block positioners'* who – either as principal or agent – help their clients to execute such large order volumes.[654]

Internalization allows broker-dealers to save on fees as well as to keep the quotes private (i.e., not providing trade transparency) and also enables such broker-dealers to earn a profit from the bid-ask-spread with minimal

650 Committee on Capital Markets Regulation, 'Enhancing U.S. Equity Market Structure for Retail Investors' (September 2021) 2; Mahoney and Rauterberg (n 118) 228–9.

651 SEC, 'Concept Release on Equity Market Structure' (n 6) 75 FR 3599f; Mahoney and Rauterberg (n 118) 228.

652 Committee on Capital Markets Regulation, 'Enhancing U.S. Equity Market Structure for Retail Investors' (n 650) 2–5: It is also common practice for retail broker-dealers to pass on their clients' orders to wholesale broker-dealers in a payment for order flow-scheme where the majority of those orders are executed within the system of the wholesale broker-dealer. See also Mahoney and Rauterberg (n 118) 228–9.

653 SEC, 'Concept Release on Equity Market Structure' (n 6) 75 FR 3599f.

654 ibid 75 FR 3599f.

adverse selection risk.[655] Furthermore, the broker-dealers can gain information from the incoming order flow, can aggregate liquidity to offer better execution to their clients, and can even earn additional commissions when selling the internal order flow to dealers who offer *'payment for order flow'*-schemes instead of routing the orders to other facilities.[656] Payment for order flow-schemes have proven a strong incentive for routing decisions by broker-dealers and therefore raise concerns with regard to conflicts of interest and the duty of best execution.[657] Since this internalized trading volume is (currently) not quoted publicly, broker-dealer internalization qualifies as a form of dark trading.[658]

3. Regulatory Requirements

Brokers, dealers, and broker-dealers have to register with the SEC according to Section 15[659] Exchange Act.[660] Unless registered by filing Form BD with the SEC, broker-dealers cannot lawfully effectuate transactions in securities.[661]

4. Self-Regulatory Organization

Merely registering with the SEC, however, is not sufficient for broker-dealers to start with their trading business. Unlike exchanges, broker-dealers do not perform any market surveillance function. Therefore, brokers, dealers and broker-dealers have to become a member of an SRO before they can

655 Committee on Capital Markets Regulation, 'Enhancing U.S. Equity Market Structure for Retail Investors' (n 650) 4; Mahoney and Rauterberg (n 118) 228–9.

656 Mahoney and Rauterberg (n 118) 228–9, 260. See also SEC, 'Concept Release on Equity Market Structure' (n 6) 75 FR 3600; SEC, 'Memorandum to Equity Market Structure Advisory Committee' (n 193) 5ff.

657 SEC, 'Concept Release on Equity Market Structure' (n 6) 75 FR 3600.

658 Mahoney and Rauterberg (n 118) 229, 261; See also SEC, 'Concept Release on Equity Market Structure' (n 6) 75 FR 3599–3600.

659 Section 15 Exchange Act (15 U.S.C. § 78o).

660 Choi and Pritchard (n 606) 37; Cox and others (n 116) 1023.

661 Cox and others (n 116) 1024.

commence trading in securities pursuant to Section 15(b)(8) Exchange Act.[662] The only SRO for surveillance of broker-dealers is the FINRA.[663]

FINRA's responsibilities include the regulatory oversight of all broker-dealers, the training, testing and licensing of registered persons, arbitration and mediation of disputes, the market regulation for certain exchanges taken over by contract, and providing trade reporting and other utilities.[664] Insofar, FINRA functions as 'the first line of defense' in the conduct regulation of broker-dealers, whereas the SEC can step in if it deems it necessary to remedy a violation of the federal securities laws.[665] Moreover, *'[t]he SEC has the power to approve, disapprove or modify SRO rules as it 'deems necessary or appropriate to insure the fair administration of the self-regulatory organization' under § 19 of the Exchange Act.'*[666]

II. National Securities Exchanges

1. Definition

The second market infrastructure defined in the Exchange Act is the national securities exchange. According to Section 3(a)(1)

> *'[t]he term 'exchange' means any organization, association, or group of persons whether incorporated or unincorporated, which constitute, maintain, or provide a market place or facilities for bringing together purchasers and sellers of securities or for otherwise performing with respect to securities the functions commonly performed by a stock exchange as that term is generally understood, and includes the market place and the market facilities maintained by such exchange.'*[667]

---

662 Cf. Bošković, Cerruti and Noël (n 70) 17; Cox and others (n 116) 1022; Andrew F Tuch, 'Self-Regulation of Investment Bankers' (2014) 83 The George Washington Law Review 101, 104.

663 Barr, Jackson and Tahyar (n 596) 449–50; Choi and Pritchard (n 606) 46.

664 Barr, Jackson and Tahyar (n 596) 450.

665 Cox and others (n 116) 1024–6. See also the quote from Joel Seligman, *The Transformation of Wall Street: A History of the Securities and Exchange Commission and Modern Corporate Finance* (3rd edn, Aspen Publishing 2003) 185 citing Douglas in Dec 1937 on the SEC's role in the self-regulatory process: *'(...) Government would keep the shotgun, so to speak, behind the door, loaded, well oiled, cleaned, ready for use but with the hope it would never have to be used.'*

666 Choi and Pritchard (n 606) 46.

667 Section 3(a)(1) Exchange Act (15 U.S.C. § 78c(a)(1)).

In spite of this convoluted definition, Congress established national securities exchanges as a regulatory category capturing marketplaces for secondary securities trading characterized by the *'(...) bringing together of purchasers and sellers of securities (...)'* which circumscribes a trading venue allowing for multilateral, non-discretionary trading of third-parties on its system.[668] Registered national securities exchanges include institutions such as the New York Stock Exchange (NYSE), the trading system of National Association of Securities Dealers Automated Quotations (NASDAQ), American Stock Exchange (AMEX), as well as relatively recent competitors such as the trading system of Better Alternative Trading System (BATS).[669]

While in 1934, Congress was primarily concerned with bringing securities trading to secondary markets under federal law, it conceived securities trading as a dualism between institutionalized exchange trading and rather ad hoc over-the-counter-trading. The prong of the definition deeming all *'(...) functions commonly performed by a stock exchange as that term is generally understood (...)'*[670] to fall within the exchange definition subject to the regulation it entails was quite clearly understood at the time the definition was written and meant all trading systems similar to the NYSE which was the archetype of all exchanges.[671] In combination with the Securities Acts Amendments of 1975 and almost sixty years of regulatory and technological developments later, this 'generally understood'-test proved problematic in the emergence of alternative trading systems, allowed for a regulatory loophole and introduced a large number of unregulated dark trading systems into the US securities market. This issue of the exchange definition will be discussed in the subsequent section on the definition of alternative trading systems.[672]

668 Cf. Section 3(a)(1) Exchange Act (15 U.S.C. § 78c(a)(1)).

669 SEC, 'Concept Release on Equity Market Structure' (n 6) 75 FR 3598. BATS started its trading business as a US ECN in 2006 but registered as a national securities exchange in 2008 which makes it one of the more recent additions to the exchange landscape, see Banks (n 5) 87.

670 Section 3(a)(1) Exchange Act (15 U.S.C. § 78c(a)(1)).

671 Domowitz and Lee (n 598) 283.

672 See below Part II § 5.E.I.1.

2. Regulatory Requirements

When a trading facility falls within the scope of the exchange definition, it triggers the registration requirement of Section 5 Exchange Act. Under Section 5 Exchange Act, it is unlawful to use any facility of the exchange for securities trading unless (1) the exchange is registered as a national securities exchange under Section 6 Exchange Act (preemptive prohibition subject to authorization) or (2) the exchange is exempted from the registration requirement upon the exchange's application to the SEC. The SEC can only grant an exemption if the Commission is of the opinion that, due to the limited volume of transactions effected on such exchange, requiring registration is not practical and not necessary or appropriate in the public interest or for the protection of the investors (de minimis-exemption).[673] These statutory requirements are reflected in the SEC's rule-making power and the exception the SEC adopted for alternative trading systems the SEC made in Regulation ATS.[674]

By registering, the SEC can exercise its surveillance power and monitor the facility's fitness for the business of running an exchange by reviewing the documents filed along with Form 1.[675] This filing usually contains the rules of the exchange and other information and documents as the SEC sees necessary and appropriate for the public interest or for the protection of the investors (Section 6(a) Exchange Act). In contrast to exchanges in the EU, the SEC also assesses the exchanges' ability to discipline their members when their non-compliant with federal law or SRO rules which underlines the self-regulatory mandate of exchanges in the US.[676]

This rule/exception-pattern reveals the conflict US law is trying to resolve. The goal is to counteract the risk-prone operation of trading platforms for securities trading with a registration requirement and thus to ensure the maintenance of fair and orderly market operations and investor protection. On the other hand, in line with the idea of the national market system, the door to the market should be opened to small competitors by relieving them of the registration burden in order to make the market

673 Section 5 Exchange Act (15 U.S.C. § 78e).

674 See below Part II § 5.E.I.3.

675 Bošković, Cerruti and Noël (n 70) 18. See also SEC, 'Form 1: Application for, and Amendments to Application for, Registration as a National Securities Exchange or Exemption from Registration Pursuant to Section 5 of the Exchange Act'.

676 Bošković, Cerruti and Noël (n 70) 18, 20.

more economically efficient through competitive forces.[677] These efficiency gains are intended to serve as a meta-goal which in turn supports the superordinate goals of the functioning of financial markets and investor protection allowing investors to make their investment decisions unfettered by the market power and excess returns of incumbent exchanges.[678] This balancing act was initially accomplished by the introduction of the ATS, which will be discussed below, but at the same time it opened up the window of opportunity to exploit the regulatory regime for the widespread dissemination of dark pools.[679]

3. Self-Regulatory Organization

Even though the registration requirement established federal oversight of exchanges by the SEC, the United States introduced a large amount of self-regulation into its securities markets' regulation by deeming national securities exchanges, registered securities associations, and registered clearing agencies as self-regulatory organizations (Section 3(a)(26) Exchange Act[680]).[681] Historically, granting exchanges like the NYSE the status of self-regulatory organization was an acknowledgement of their ability to regulate trading and their members in an effective manner, giving exchanges a quasi-public status by fulfilling regulatory functions delegated by the SEC.[682]

The self-regulatory power requires exchanges to engage in market surveillance and regulation of their members to prevent fraudulent and manipulative acts and practices on their infrastructures (Section 6(b)(5) Exchange Act[683]). To effectuate this regulatory power, exchanges are given

677 Cf. SEC, 'Regulation of Exchanges and Alternative Trading Systems' (n 138) 63 FR 70844, 70856; Colby and Sirri (n 605) 183; Macey and O'Hara, 'Regulating Exchanges and Alternative Trading Systems' (n 139) 31.

678 See generally on the competition as a goal of the NMS: SEC, 'Market 2000 Report' (n 625) 13ff; Macey and O'Hara, 'Regulating Exchanges and Alternative Trading Systems' (n 139) 30–1.

679 Cf. Colby and Sirri (n 605) 183–4; Mahoney and Rauterberg (n 118) 243–4, 262–4.

680 Section 3(a)(26) Exchange Act (15 U.S.C. § 78c (a)(26)).

681 Barr, Jackson and Tahyar (n 596) 445; Cox and others (n 116) 21.

682 Barr, Jackson and Tahyar (n 596) 445; William Birdthistle and M T Henderson, 'Becoming a Fifth Branch' (2013) 99 Cornell Law Review 1, 5ff; Fox, Glosten and Rauterberg, *The New Stock Market* (n 98) 15.

683 Section 6(b)(5) Exchange Act (15 U.S.C. § 78f (b)(5)).

the power to sanction violations under Section 6(b)(6)[684] Exchange Act.[685] To tie this self-regulatory power back to the goals of federal securities regulation, the rules of the exchange on which it exercises its regulatory power over its members must meet the public interest standard and changes to the rules which require SEC approval to become effective.[686] The limitation of self-regulatory power by acts of consent on the part of the state supervisory authority is a typical containment mechanism in systems with strong self-regulatory tendencies, as is also shown by the example of Switzerland, where, pursuant to Article 27(4) FinfraG, the amendment of the trading regulations is also subject to the consent of FINMA as the state supervisory authority.[687]

III. Alternative Trading Systems

1. Definition: A Hybrid

The alternative trading system is the third trading infrastructure under US securities law. In the regulatory discussion, the market infrastructure of ATS is often used synonymous with the phenomenon of dark pools. While it is true that most dark pools are operated as ATS, not all ATS are dark pools. ATS can also be operated as lit pools and must therefore be considered separately from the phenomenon of dark pools.[688] However, the regulatory category of ATS was implemented to bring new electronic trading systems within the perimeter of US securities laws and to level the playing field for exchanges that experienced competitive pressure from the new market entrants also providing a marketplace for securities.[689]

---

684 Section 6(b)(6) Exchange Act (15 U.S.C. § 78f (b)(6)).

685 Mahoney and Rauterberg (n 118) 255.

686 ibid 255. For a more critical view, see: Birdthistle and Henderson (n 682) 59ff; Jonathan R Macey and Maureen O'Hara, 'From Markets to Venues: Securities Regulation in an Evolving World' (2005) 58 Stanford Law Review 563ff; Yadav, 'Oversight Failure in Securities Markets' (n 482) 1861ff.

687 See below Part II § 7 B.V.

688 Baxter (n 605) 314; Mahoney and Rauterberg (n 118) 228; Kirsten Zaza, 'A Fiduciary Standard as a Tool for Dark Pool Subscribers' (2013) 18 Stanford Journal of Law, Business & Finance 319, 324.

689 Brummer (n 179) 1006; Crudele (n 505) 571ff; Colby and Sirri (n 605) 183ff; Zaza (n 688) 325; Zyskind (n 605) 414–5.

a) Merging Markets and Market Participants

Beginning in 1969, when Instinet launched its first electronic trading system able to match incoming orders,[690] the two-tiered regulatory system of the Exchange Act – differentiating between marketplaces and market participants – came under pressure.[691] What was a small phenomenon in the early 1970s, experienced its first heydays in the 1980s when electronic order matching systems mushroomed in US securities markets.[692]

From a regulatory perspective, the rising number of electronic trading systems was on one hand, a success of the policy goals set out by Congress in the Securities Amendment Act of 1975, especially with regard to harnessing innovation and boosting competition; but, on the other hand, a challenge to the regulatory framework inherited from the 1930s in the Exchange Act.[693] The SEC intended to maintain the benefits of competition while preserving investor protection and a reliable price formation mechanism.[694]

Since ATS were at first primarily operated by investment banks and other entities who were registered as broker-dealers themselves, it almost came naturally that the SEC considered such ancillary services to fall within the broker-dealer regulation as well.[695] This regulatory framework, however, did not account for the fact that such electronic trading systems rather provided for a marketplace instead of broker-dealer services. Such electronic trading systems enabled users to trade multilaterally, a service that should fall within the exchange definition of Section 3(a)(1) Exchange Act rather than the broker-dealer definition of a market intermediary.[696] This tilted the playing field between exchanges, who had to provide for

690 Banks (n 5) 19.

691 Cf. SEC, 'Regulation of Exchanges and Alternative Trading Systems' (n 138) 63 FR 70844, 70845–6; Kumpan, *Die Regulierung außerbörslicher Wertpapierhandelssysteme im deutschen, europäischen und US-amerikanischen Recht* (n 8) 127; Nyquist (n 72) 309ff; Maynard (n 623) 835–6.

692 Cf. Mahoney and Rauterberg (n 118) 240ff. See also SEC, 'Market 2000 Report' (n 625) 10, 13 and Appendix IV (Description of Proprietary Trading Systems) 1–2.

693 SEC, 'Market 2000 Report' (n 625) 2, 5, 13; SEC, 'Regulation of Exchanges and Alternative Trading Systems' (n 138) 63 FR 70844, 70845–6; Crudele (n 505) 574ff.

694 SEC, 'Market 2000 Report' (n 625) 13; Crudele (n 505) 576.

695 SEC, 'Market 2000 Report' (n 625) 10; Kumpan, *Die Regulierung außerbörslicher Wertpapierhandelssysteme im deutschen, europäischen und US-amerikanischen Recht* (n 8) 127.

696 SEC, 'Regulation of Exchanges and Alternative Trading Systems' (n 138) 63 FR 70844, 70845; Borrelli (n 622) 851; Cohen (n 122) 24.

trade transparency, oversight as a self-regulatory organization, and, before the 2000s, for a membership-based corporate structure.[697]

b) The SEC's No-Action-Letters and the Delta Government Options Corp.-Case (*Board of Trade v. SEC*, 1991)

aa) No-Action-Letters

In the 1980s, the SEC began issuing no-action-letters to the new market entrants offering trading systems in the guise of the broker-dealer regime. In this procedure, the operators described in writing the nature and manner of operation of the proposed trading system to the SEC and delivered reasons why this trading system did not fall within the exchange definition.[698] The SEC staff – not the Commission itself – then merely conveyed an enforcement position, i.e., *'(...) whether the staff would recommend enforcement action to the full Commission if the transaction were undertaken in the manner described in the incoming letter. (...)'.*[699] The content of the issued no-action-letter, however, did not represent the Commissions' opinion nor was it legally binding.[700] By using the no-action-letter procedure, the SEC was able to decide on a case-by-case basis whether an electronic trading system fell within the exchange definition or could operate as a more permissively regulated broker-dealer instead.[701] Almost all trading systems that used this no-action-letter procedure were considered eligible to register

697 SEC, 'Market 2000 Report' (n 625) 2; Borrelli (n 622) 852.

698 Domowitz and Lee (n 598) 286.

699 Donna M Nagy, 'Judicial Reliance on Regulatory Interpretations in SEC No-Action Letters: Corrent Problems and a Proposed Framework' (1998) 83 Cornell Law Review 921, 923. See also Thomas P Lemke, 'The SEC No-Action Letter Process' (1987) 42 The Business Lawyer 1019ff; Kumpan, *Die Regulierung außerbörslicher Wertpapierhandelssysteme im deutschen, europäischen und US-amerikanischen Recht* (n 8) 128.

700 Nagy (n 699) 923–4. See also Lemke (n 699) 1019ff; Kumpan, *Die Regulierung außerbörslicher Wertpapierhandelssysteme im deutschen, europäischen und US-amerikanischen Recht* (n 8) 128.

701 Kumpan, *Die Regulierung außerbörslicher Wertpapierhandelssysteme im deutschen, europäischen und US-amerikanischen Recht* (n 8) 128; Spindler and Hüther (n 594) 650; Andrew R Thompson, 'Taming the Frontier?: An Evaluation of the SEC's Regulation of Internet Securities Trading Systems' (1999) 1999 Columbia Business Law Review 165, 172.

as broker-dealers,[702] which at least indicated that the SEC considered that the heavy burdens of self-regulation and transparency under the exchange regulation would stifle the rising competition by ATS.[703]

The SEC's discretionary evaluation of alternative trading systems was challenged in July 1988 when Delta Government Options Corp. applied for registration as a clearing agency under Section 17A Exchange Act.[704] Delta intended to issue options that could be traded on its fully electronic trading system and would subsequently be settled by its clearing agency.[705] For the first time, the SEC had to evaluate whether a fully automated trading system qualifies as an exchange, which ended in the landmark decision *Board of Trade v. SEC* in 1991.[706]

bb) *Board of Trade v. SEC* (1991)

(i) The Issue in *Board of Trade v. SEC* (1991)

In *Board of Trade v. SEC* (1991), the United States Court of Appeals for the Seventh Circuit had to decide whether the SEC's no-action-letter[707] to the operator of the Delta trading system stating that the trading system does not fall within the exchange definition under Section 3(a)(1) Exchange Act was in violation of the Exchange Act.[708] Delta's system was an electronic

702 SEC, 'Market 2000 Report' (n 625) 10; Kumpan, *Die Regulierung außerbörslicher Wertpapierhandelssysteme im deutschen, europäischen und US-amerikanischen Recht* (n 8) 128–9; Mahoney and Rauterberg (n 118) 241; F. C Vaupel, 'Die aufsichtsrechtliche Behandlung automatisierter Handelssysteme in den USA' [1995] RIW 568, 573.

703 Colby and Sirri (n 605) 183.

704 Kumpan, *Die Regulierung außerbörslicher Wertpapierhandelssysteme im deutschen, europäischen und US-amerikanischen Recht* (n 8) 129; Maynard (n 623) 896ff; Vaupel (n 702) 571ff.

705 Kumpan, *Die Regulierung außerbörslicher Wertpapierhandelssysteme im deutschen, europäischen und US-amerikanischen Recht* (n 8) 129. See also Ruben Lee, *What is an Exchange?: The Automation, Management, and Regulation of Financial Markets* (Oxford Universty Press 2000) 319–20; Vaupel (n 702) 571.

706 Kumpan, *Die Regulierung außerbörslicher Wertpapierhandelssysteme im deutschen, europäischen und US-amerikanischen Recht* (n 8) 129. See also Lee, *What is an Exchange?* (n 705) 319–20; Vaupel (n 114) 571.

707 Kumpan, *Die Regulierung außerbörslicher Wertpapierhandelssysteme im deutschen, europäischen und US-amerikanischen Recht* (n 8) 129.

708 *Board of Trade of the City of Chicago v. Securities and Exchange Commission* (n 605): the issue was '*(…) whether a system for trading options on federal government*

communication network that allowed buyers and sellers of securities to communicate their buy and sell offers within certain standardization parameters set by the trading system, and when offers matched, the computer system executed them. The buyers and sellers included securities dealers, banks, pension funds, and other institutional investors.[709]

For the SEC, qualifying Delta as an exchange would contradict the goals of supporting competition and enhancing the national market system as set out in Section 11A Exchange Act.[710] However, the Board of Trade and the Chicago Mercantile Exchange sued because they found that Delta offered a marketplace that competed with the Chicago Mercantile Exchange and should thus be subject to the same regulatory regime, i.e., the exchange regime.[711]

(ii) Majority Opinion Delivered by Judge Posner

In the majority opinion, Judge *Posner* held that the SEC's no-action-letter was lawful thus allowing the Delta system to operate outside the exchange regime of the Exchange Act.[712] Judge *Posner* summarized that *'(...) [t]here is no doubt that the Delta system creates an electronic marketplace for securities traders, and the petitioners say that no more is required to establish that the system must register as an exchange.'*[713] Nevertheless, the majority of the court dismissed this view for two reasons: First, the Exchange Act vested the SEC with wide discretion to interpret ambiguous definitions within the Exchange Act which includes the exchange definition. For this task, the SEC has the highest expertise and shall not be second-guessed by judges.[714] Second, within this discretion, the SEC as well as the court put

---

securities that has been put together by RMJ, a broker; Delta, a clearing agency; and SPNTCO, a bank (...) is an 'exchange' within the meaning of section 3(a)(1) of the [Exchange Act] (...)'.

709 ibid. NB: the users were strikingly similar to the ones of dark pools today.

710 ibid; Maynard (n 623) 898–9; Nyquist (n 72) 319ff; Vaupel (n 702) 572–3.

711 *Board of Trade of the City of Chicago v. Securities and Exchange Commission* (n 605); Colby and Sirri (n 605) 183–4; Maynard (n 623) 899ff.

712 *Board of Trade of the City of Chicago v. Securities and Exchange Commission* (n 605).

713 ibid.

714 ibid. Cf. Kumpan, *Die Regulierung außerbörslicher Wertpapierhandelssysteme im deutschen, europäischen und US-amerikanischen Recht* (n 8) 132; Maynard (n 623) 898ff; Vaupel (n 702) 572–3.

their emphasis on the 'general understood'-prong in the exchange definition under Section 3(a)(1) Exchange Act and employed a narrower exchange definition. An exchange can only be a trading system that resembles the traditional exchanges with regard to a trading floor, liquidity provision, standardization, access and transparency.[715] The wider definition of an exchange, supported by the plaintiffs, which only emphasizes the market-place-element in Section 3(a)(1) Exchange Act, was, in the eyes of the court, not superior to the narrower definition and stood in conflict with other definitions of the Exchange Act.[716]

(iii) Dissenting Opinion Delivered by Judge Flaum

Judge *Flaum* delivered the dissenting opinion arguing that the exchange definition under Section 3(a)(1) Exchange Act is unambiguous in leaving the SEC with no discretion.[717] While the prong *'as that term is generally understood'* may be open for interpretation, Judge *Flaum* concluded that the emphasis of the definition is on the first prong, i.e. the question whether *'(...) [a]n organization that 'constitutes, maintains, or provides a market place or facilitates for bringing together purchasers and sellers of securities' is an exchange.'*[718] *Flaum* held that this prong is crystal clear and when it is fulfilled, and it does not depend on whether bringing together both parties to a trade is *'generally understood'* to be a function of an exchange.[719] *Flaum* sees this feature as *'(...) a determinative characteristic, sufficient unto itself to confer exchange status.'*[720]

The dissent's preference for a broader exchange definition serves the purpose to close loopholes in the securities regulation framework between the broker-dealer and exchange regime. *Flaum* compares this issue with the exemption of the futures exchanges from securities regulation which

715 *Board of Trade of the City of Chicago v. Securities and Exchange Commission* (n 605).
716 ibid. Cf. Kumpan, *Die Regulierung außerbörslicher Wertpapierhandelssysteme im deutschen, europäischen und US-amerikanischen Recht* (n 8) 132; Maynard (n 623) 898ff; Vaupel (n 702) 572–3.
717 *Board of Trade of the City of Chicago v. Securities and Exchange Commission* (n 605).
718 ibid.
719 ibid.
720 ibid.

led to '*bucket shops*'[721] and massive fraud in derivatives until eventually a new regulatory regime was created by the enactment and amendments of the Commodity Exchange Act and the creation of the Commodity Futures Trading Commission (CFTC).[722]

c) Regulation ATS of 1998: Defining Exchange and ATS

In the years following *Board of Trade v. SEC* (1991), many more ATS entered the market and the SEC's no-action-letter approach became increasingly ill-suited for the market's needs.[723] While the no-action-letter approach allowed for high levels of flexibility, it proved to provide little orientation for an ever-growing market of ATS. And even the smallest of changes in an already reviewed trading system operating under a no-action-letter by the SEC staff required the issuance of a new one.[724] For this reason, the SEC eventually used its rule-making power and promulgated Regulation ATS in 1998.

aa) A Revised Exchange Definition under Rule 3b-16

In conjunction with Regulation ATS, the SEC also clarified the exchange definition of Section 3(a)(1) Exchange Act more closely in Rule 3b-16.[725] In this new rule, the SEC shifted from the broad exchange definition which emphasized the 'commonly understood'-prong to the narrow definition delivered in Judge *Flaum's* dissent in *Board of Trade v. SEC* (1991). Under Rule 3b-16, an exchange was characterized by only two aspects, i.e. (1)

721 Gregory Scopino, *Algo Bots and the Law* (Cambridge University Press 2020) 97–8; Jerry W Markham, '"Confederate Bonds," "General Custer," and the Regulation of Derivative Financial Instruments' (1994) 25 Seton Hall Law Review 1, 11; Brendan Sapien, 'Financial Weapons of Mass Destruction: From Bucket Shops to Credit Default Swaps' (2010) 19 Southern California Interdisciplinary Law Journal 411.

722 *Board of Trade of the City of Chicago v. Securities and Exchange Commission* (n 605).

723 SEC, 'Concept Release' (17 CFR Part 240, Release No. 34–38672, File No. S7–16–97, 4 June 1997) 62 FR 30485, 30486; Crudele (n 505) 576; Kumpan, *Die Regulierung außerbörslicher Wertpapierhandelssysteme im deutschen, europäischen und US-amerikanischen Recht* (n 8) 135.

724 Thompson (n 701) 172–3; David M Schizer, 'Benign Restraint: The SEC's Regulation of Execution Systems' (1992) 101(7) Yale Law Journal 1551, 1553–4.

725 17 CFR § 240.3b-16. SEC, 'Regulation of Exchanges and Alternative Trading Systems' (n 138) 63 FR 70844, 70847; Colby and Sirri (n 605) 182.

the bringing together of orders for securities of multiple buyers and sellers (multilateral trading), and (2) the use of non-discretionary methods, whether by providing a trading facility or by setting rules, under which such orders interact with each other (non-discretionary trading).[726]

In contrast to the wide exchange definition supported by the SEC in the Delta-Release and accepted by Judge *Posner*, the new definition under Rule 3b-16 no longer required liquidity provision, human intermediation on a floor, and, most importantly for dark trading, it did not require a price discovery mechanism in a trading system for it to be classified as an exchange.[727] This new exchange definition captured all multilateral, non-discretionary trading, i.e., all trading on a system with marketplace function, dispensing of any resemblance to incumbent exchanges. This broader definition also captured alternative trading systems, acknowledging their similarity to exchanges.[728] By promulgating this new definition, the SEC aimed to integrate ATS in the national market system to promote market fairness, efficiency, and transparency.[729] Nevertheless, the former exchange definition led to a sharp rise of ATS regulated as broker-dealers with only little to no trade transparency (i.e., dark pools) which turned out to be a fact which is hard to alter later on.

bb) Definition of ATS: Hybrid Systems Embedded in the Exchange Act's Framework

In 1998, Regulation ATS replaced the no-action-letter approach and the case-by-case definition with a clear-cut exchange definition in Rule 3b-16 and a blanket exemption for ATS under Rule 301 Regulation ATS guiding operators planning on setting up an ATS.[730] According to Rule 300(a) of Regulation ATS, an alternative trading system means any organization, association, person, group of persons, or system (1) that fulfills the exchange definition under Rule 3b-16, and (2) that does not (i) set rules governing

726 See definition under 17 CFR § 240.3b-16(a)(1), (2); cf. SEC, 'Regulation of Exchanges and Alternative Trading Systems' (n 138) 63 FR 70844, 70848, 70859.

727 Domowitz and Lee (n 598) 294.

728 SEC, 'Regulation of Exchanges and Alternative Trading Systems' (n 138) 63 FR 70844, 70848; Domowitz and Lee (n 598) 293.

729 SEC, 'Regulation of Exchanges and Alternative Trading Systems' (n 138) 63 FR 70900.

730 Domowitz and Lee (n 598) 294.

the conduct of subscribers other than the conduct of such subscribers' trading on such system, or (ii) discipline subscribers other than by exclusion from trading.[731] Thus, according to the definition under Rule 300 of Regulation ATS, an ATS performs the trading functions of an exchange and always fulfills the exchange definition but shall not act as a self-regulatory organization for its users.[732]

2. Registration: Still a Broker-Dealer

a) Registration Requirement under Rule 301 Regulation ATS

While the definition under Rule 300 Regulation ATS puts ATS in the realm of exchanges, Rule 301 Regulation ATS adheres to the practice of having ATS register as broker-dealers.[733] As before, a trading system can either, according to Section 5 Exchange Act, register as a fully-fledged national securities exchange under Section 6 Exchange Act which must assume its self-regulatory and transparency responsibilities;[734] or a trading system may be exempted from the requirement to register as an exchange under a de minimis-exemption if the trading system only handles limited transaction volumes. Granting this exemption is, however, at the discretion of the SEC.[735] The trading system can also refrain from its self-regulatory responsibilities and register as a broker-dealer under Section 15 Exchange Act as Rule 301(b) Regulation ATS requires.[736] This also entails the obligation to

731 See definition of ATS under 17 CFR § 242.300(a).

732 SEC, 'Regulation of Exchanges and Alternative Trading Systems' (n 138) 63 FR 70859; Committee on Capital Markets Regulation, 'The U.S. Equity Markets' (n 6) viii. Cf. Alexis L Collins, 'Regulation of Alternative Trading Systems: Evolving Regulatory Models and Prospects for Increased Regulatory Coordination and Convergence' (2002) 33 Law and Policy in International Business 481, 486, 488ff; Mark Klock, 'The SEC's New Regulation ATS: Placing the Myth of Market Fragmentation Ahead of Economic Theory and Evidence' (1999) 51 Florida Law Review 753, 765, 768; Spindler and Hüther (n 594) 652.

733 17 CFR § 242.301(b); Colby and Sirri (n 605) 183–4; Domowitz and Lee (n 598) 294.

734 17 CFR § 242.301(a). See Crudele (n 505) 577; Haeberle (n 459) 814.

735 Section 15(b)(8) Exchange Act (15 U.S.C. § 78o(b)(8)). Jordan M Marciello, 'Are You Afraid of the Dark: How the New York Attorney General is Shedding Light on Dark Pools and High Frequency Trading' (2016) 49 Suffolk University Law Review 163, 172; Salger (n 627) 132.

736 17 CFR § 242.301(b); Crudele (n 505) 577.

become a member of another self-regulatory organization, i.e., a registered national securities exchange or FINRA.[737]

With this approach, the SEC tried to continue its regulatory policy to enable competition to create a national market system for the benefit of investor, while providing a better framework for ATS.[738] It was the SEC's intention to allow new ATS to grow without the stifling burdens of regulatory and transparency requirements under the exchange regulation, but once they have grown to a substantial size, to adapt them to regulation under the exchange regime so they serve the national market system by providing regulatory security and information for a transparent market.[739]

To provide ATS with a facilitative environment, the SEC required trading systems with less than five percent of the trading volume in securities traded on the ATS compared to the entire market to do three things: (1) file a notice of operation and quarterly reports with the SEC, (2) maintain records, including an audit trail of transactions, and (3) refrain from using the words 'exchange', 'stock market', or similar terms in its name.[740]

When an ATS grows and surpasses the five percent threshold in overall trading volume, it can still register as a broker-dealer instead of an exchange, but the SEC will require it to integrate its trading activities into the national market system.[741] This is primarily done by the transparency obligation and rights of equal access to the system, which will be discussed below.[742]

The SEC adopted a catch-all provision (SEC under the Exchange Act) to avoid regulatory arbitrage by either ATS maintaining the status of a broker-dealer, although an exemption from self-regulatory responsibilities is no longer adequate due to its size and liquidity, or by exchanges opting to register as a broker-dealer to disentangle with expensive self-regulation.[743] The provision allows the SEC to require trading systems to fall within the scope of the ATS definition to register as an exchange if the public inter-

737 Marciello (n 735) 172; Salger (n 627) 133.

738 Colby and Sirri (n 605) 183–4.

739 ibid 183–4. See also Brummer (n 179) 1007; Committee on Capital Markets Regulation, 'The U.S. Equity Markets' (n 6) x; Crudele (n 505) 576.

740 17 CFR § 242.301(b); SEC, 'Regulation of Exchanges and Alternative Trading Systems' (n 138) 63 FR 70847; Crudele (n 505) 577.

741 SEC, 'Regulation of Exchanges and Alternative Trading Systems' (n 138) 63 FR 70847.

742 See below Part II § 5 F.

743 17 CFR § 240.3a1–1(b)(2).

est or investor protection renders it necessary and appropriate.[744] While this catch-all provision can also be used to subject large ATS to exchange regulation, the SEC rather wants to use it when ATS registered as broker-dealers engage in self-regulatory activities, regulating their members' and subscribers' behavior outside the ATS. To ensure that all self-regulatory organizations are registered as such with the SEC, pursuant to Section 19 Exchange Act, the SEC will not tolerate broker-dealers not registered accordingly to perform SRO powers.[745]

With regard to the growth of dark trading, Regulation ATS served as a catalyst rather than a hinderance for dark pools in the US. It manifested the practice of electronic trading systems operating under the lighter broker dealer regime compared to stricter regime incumbent exchanges had to comply with.[746] Coupled with the acceleration of automated trading, exchanges were no longer the sole source of immediate liquidity, and thus, the most attractive execution venue.[747] ATS could offer a comparable service, often at a lower price,[748] and since most ATS kept their volume below 5 % turnover compared to the entire market, the new competitors could also offer the anonymity of a dark pool.[749]

b) Form ATS-N as a Response to Market Conduct

aa) New Form ATS-N

In response to the fact that ATS are generally operated as dark pools and to address issues with market conduct in such ATS-dark pools, the SEC amended Regulation ATS on 18 July 2018.[750] At the center of this amend-

744 Salger (n 627) 132–3. Cf. SEC, 'Regulation of Exchanges and Alternative Trading Systems' (n 138) 63 FR 70844–70951, 70847; Klock (n 732) 765–6.

745 SEC, 'Regulation of Exchanges and Alternative Trading Systems' (n 138) 63 FR 70847.

746 Jennifer V C Dean, 'Paradigm Shifts & Unintended Consequences: The Death of the Specialist, the Rise of High Frequency Trading & the Problem of Duty-Free Liquidity in Equity Markets' (2012) 8 Florida International University Law Review 217, 233–4; Zyskind (n 605) 415.

747 Batista (n 182) 89; Zyskind (n 605) 415.

748 IOSCO, 'Principles for Dark Liquidity' (n 12) 12.

749 Baxter (n 605) 316; Mahoney and Rauterberg (n 118) 228.

750 SEC, 'Regulation of NMS Stock Alternative Trading Systems: Final Rule' (17 CFR Parts 232, 240, 242, and 249, Release No. 34-83663, File No. S7-23-15, 7 August 2018) 83 FR 38768.

ment was the registration and reporting of ATS.[751] The SEC replaced Form ATS with the extended Form ATS-N for most ATS to enhance disclosure on their internal operational matters that had been opaque to investors under the prior filings.[752] This heightened reporting standards, however, only applied to ATS that offer trading services in NMS stock, which is defined as all exchange traded securities other than debt and convertible debt securities, while an ATS solely offering trading services in non-NMS stocks can still use Form ATS.[753] An NMS Stock is a stock (other than an option) listed on a registered exchange.[754]

The disclosure under Form ATS meant a far-reaching privilege for ATS trading NMS stock compared to the filing requirements for national registered exchanges. Unlike exchanges, ATS did not have to file proposed rule changes with the SEC or publicly disclose the trading services or fee structure they offered.[755]

Because the SEC disapproved the discrepancy between exchanges and alternative trading venues since both were trading NMS stock, the Commission aimed to align both regimes by introducing Form ATS-N.[756] The Commission also saw investor choice jeopardized by the opacity of some ATS that did not inform investors about the kind of investors also present in the trading system, for instance high frequency traders.[757] Also, the SEC was

> *'(…) concerned that the lack of available information about the ATS-related activities of the broker-dealer operator and its affiliates may hinder the*

751 Baxter (n 605) 334–5.

752 SEC, 'Regulation of NMS Stock Alternative Trading Systems' (n 750) 83 FR 38768; Baxter (n 605) 334–5; Andre Owens and others, 'SEC Adopts Significant Changes to Regulation ATS' (Securities Alert, 11 September 2018) 1.

753 However, ATS trading in both NMS stock and non-NMS stock must use Form ATS-N since also filing Form ATS would be burdensome. See SEC, 'Regulation of NMS Stock Alternative Trading Systems' (n 750) 83 FR 38787 fn 256; Owens and others (n 752) 11 and n 80.

754 Rule 300(g) of Regulation ATS. See SEC, 'Memorandum to SEC Market Structure Advisory Committee: Rule 611 of Regulation NMS' (SEC Division of Trading and Markets, 30 April 2015) 3: *'An NMS stock generally means any exchange-listed security (other than listed options) for which consolidated market data is disseminated'.*

755 SEC, 'Concept Release on Equity Market Structure' (n 6) 75 FR 3599. This is, of course, still the case for ATS trading solely non-NMS stock.

756 SEC, 'Regulation of NMS Stock Alternative Trading Systems' (n 750) 83 FR 38768, 38776.

757 ibid 83 FR 38768, 38775. See also Chair Mary Jo White (n 1); Baxter (n 605) 334–5.

ability of market participants to evaluate potential conflicts of interest, and thus limit their ability to protect their interests (...).[758]

bb) Response to Market Conduct

These amendments are a response to the weaknesses in the regulatory system that have been revealed in the enforcement measures against some dark ATS.[759] The enforcement measures against the dark pools of Pipeline Trading Systems LLC and UBS Securities LLC will be examined as examples of such enforcement measures that revealed shortcomings in the regulatory regime:

(i) *Pipeline Trading Systems LLC*

In re Pipeline Trading Systems LLC, the SEC brought enforcement measures against Pipeline Trading Systems LLC operating a dark ATS and against its CEO and its chairman because Pipeline willfully violated Section 17(a)(2) Securities Act 1933, Rule 301(b)(2) Regulation ATS and Rule 301(b)(10) Regulation ATS, Sections 15(b)(6) and 21B(a)(3) Exchange Act.[760] Pipeline communicated to its customers and the public that it offered 'natural' liquidity in its ATS and that it would not entertain a proprietary trading desk to execute against customer orders. Moreover, Pipeline said it would deny access to arbitrageurs and high frequency traders. This should protect customers from being front-run.[761]

In fact, the overwhelming majority of customer orders were executed against orders by a wholly owned subsidiary of Pipeline, i.e., a proprietary trading desk. Although Pipeline disclosed to most of its customers that there was a possibility to interact with a Pipeline affiliate when trading on the ATS, it assured the customers that the affiliate would not receive preferential treatment or informational advantages. In fact, however, Pipeline shared information with the affiliate so the affiliate could predict customer

758 SEC, 'Regulation of NMS Stock Alternative Trading Systems' (n 750) 83 FR 38768, 38775. Chair Mary Jo White (n 1).

759 SEC, *Press Release: SEC Proposes Rules to Enhance Transparency and Oversight of Alternative Trading Systems* (2015); Baxter (n 605) 334–5.

760 *Pipeline Trading Systems LLC* (n 26) 2, 16–7.

761 ibid 2.

orders on the ATS and use this information to trade on the same market side on another marketplace before turning around to fill the customer's order and the affiliate made a profit. This was unforeseeable even for those customers who were informed about proprietary trading, and even less foreseeable for those left in the dark. In both instances, the customers' trust in the ATS-operator was harmed.[762]

(ii) *UBS Securities LLC*

In re UBS Securities LLC, the SEC brought enforcement for multiple violations of the federal securities laws. Among the allegations was the issue of UBS not giving notice to all subscribers of its dark pool UBS ATS that protection from algorithmic and high frequency trading can only be obtained by selecting a feature called 'natural-only crossing restriction'. By not selecting this feature, many of UBS's subscribers interacted with HFT firms giving away important order information they thought to be secure in UBS ATS.[763]

(iii) Remedying the former Shortfalls

Although both matters were settled with the SEC by imposing remedial sanctions and cease-and-desist orders upon Pipeline and UBS, these cases show that the reporting regime under Form ATS left both customers and the SEC in the dark about the internal functioning of dark pools operated in the form of an ATS. While the SEC was content with implementing disclosure requirements instead of choosing more intrusive measures, such as bans on proprietary trading on ATS, it should not be underestimated that reporting to the SEC or violations thereof are often used to bring enforcement measures. Nevertheless, more intrusive measures that regulate the conduct of ATS may also have been in order.

With regard to the latest amendments, Form ATS-N is the central instrument to inform subscribers and the SEC about potential conflicts of interest between the operator of the ATS and its customers as well as potential

762 ibid 2–3.
763 *UBS Securities LLC* (n 26) 3.

leakages of customers' trading information.[764] The operator must also outline in detail how orders may interact on their trading venue and how the operator can interact with client orders, for instance by proprietary trading. Furthermore, the ATS-operator must disclose potential arrangements that it has with unaffiliated trading centers, disclose the array of products and services the operator offers to its customers, and disclose the activities of service providers for the ATS.[765]

In the new Form ATS-N the operator must also disclose sensitive information about the

> *'(…) type of subscribers, eligibility for and exclusion from the ATS services, means of order entry, connectivity and co-location, order types and sizes, conditional orders and indications of interest, liquidity providers, order segmentation, counterparty restriction, fair access, and market data.'*[766]

Such information shall inform the investor and allow them to make an informed decision on whether to use this trading center or to route its order to a trading center more suitable for its individual trading needs.

To allow insights into Form ATS-N, the SEC posts them on its website EDGAR where they are publicly available free of charge.[767] To enhance the trust in such filings, the SEC has set out under Rule 304(b)(1) Regulation ATS that the new Form ATS-N constitutes a *'report'* pursuant to Sections 11A, 17(a), 18(a) and 32(a) Exchange Act.[768] Accordingly, *'(…) it would be unlawful for any person to willfully or knowingly make, or cause to be made, a false or misleading statement with respect to any material fact in Form ATS-N.'*[769] This serves as an incentive to ATS-operators to make truthful disclosures, induce trust by investors to base their order routing decision on this information and allow the SEC to bring enforcement measures against operators of ATS that violate disclosure rules to gain unfair information advantages.[770]

---

764 Owens and others (n 752) 2.
765 ibid 2.
766 ibid 2.
767 Baxter (n 605) 335.
768 Owens and others (n 752) 10–1.
769 SEC, 'Regulation of NMS Stock Alternative Trading Systems' (n 750) 83 FR 38810; see also Owens and others (n 752) 10–1.
770 SEC, 'Regulation of NMS Stock Alternative Trading Systems' (n 750) 83 FR 38810–1; see also Owens and others (n 752) 11.

With the latest amendments to Regulation ATS, the SEC has certainly strengthened regulatory scrutiny over ATS and aligned the reporting requirements of ATS trading NMS stock with national registered exchanges. Albeit through incremental steps, the SEC is determined to adapt the two-tiered system of exchanges and other market infrastructures under the Exchange Act to the new market environment with many trading centers fulfilling similar functions.[771]

3. Self-Regulatory Organization

The decision to register as an exchange or a broker-dealer is deeply intertwined with the issue of self-regulation.[772] If an ATS decides to register as an exchange, it qualifies as a self-organization and must surveil the conduct of its members not only within but also outside of the trading system. If an ATS, instead, registers as a broker-dealer, it is subject to the obligation to become a member of a self-regulatory organization, i.e., a registered exchange or FINRA, before it can start effecting transactions in securities (Section 15(b)(8) Exchange Act). In the latter case, the registered exchange or FINRA fulfill the self-regulatory duties so the broker-dealer may focus on its trading business, but at the cost of being supervised by an entity run either by competing peers, in case of FINRA, or a competing registered exchange, which may result in a conflict of interest between the supervisor and the supervised.[773]

E. The Transparency Regime under US Law

Transparency is a hallmark of US securities laws.[774] In order to advance trade transparency, the SEC promulgated Regulation NMS in 2005 which comprised in part of the re-organized Market Data Rules and Plan as well as new rules to moderate the effects of dark trading in the US securities markets.[775] When Congress tasked the SEC with implementing rules for a

771 Chair Mary Jo White (n 1).
772 Klock (n 732) 771.
773 Collins (n 732) 489; Czervionke (n 620) 130; Klock (n 732) 771.
774 Chair Mary Jo White (n 1).
775 SEC, 'Regulation NMS' (n 340) 70 FR 37496, 37503.

national market system, it required both competition and transparency.[776] While dark trading has spurred competition in a market comprising of multiple new ATS hungry for order flow, the SEC concluded that trade transparency had to be promoted since Congress considered it to be at the '*heart of the national market system*'.[777] The Commission intended to use increased trade transparency as a means to consolidate a market fragmented by competition among many market centers.[778]

The current US transparency regime is a combination of minimum standards for trade transparency and market practice exceeding these legal requirements for those willing to pay.[779] Regulation NMS distinguished between pre-trade transparency, referred to as 'quote' transparency that informs about the prices that traders are willing to transact at, and post-trade transparency, referred to as 'transaction' information that informs about the trades that were executed.[780]

The trade transparency regime ties its rules to the trading infrastructure and sets up different transparency requirements for national securities exchanges, broker-dealers, and alternative trading systems. Although the public considers exchanges to be widely transparent and ATS to be dark pools with no trade transparency at all,[781] the following section will show that all trading infrastructures can either operate under trade transparency or host considerable amounts dark trading.[782]

776 Section 11A Exchange Act (15 U.S.C. § 78k-1).
777 SEC, 'Regulation NMS' (n 340) 70 FR 37503; Baxter (n 605) 315.
778 Colby and Sirri (n 605) 185; Crudele (n 505) 577.
779 Haeberle (n 459) 819.
780 Fox, Glosten and Rauterberg, *The New Stock Market* (n 98) 29; Haeberle (n 459) 818.
781 Baxter (n 605) 315.
782 Haeberle (n 459) 818.

I. Pre-Trade Transparency

1. Exchanges

a) Rule

aa) Legal Requirements

(i) Rule 602 Regulation NMS

Pursuant to the public quoting requirement under Rule 602(a)(1)(i) of Regulation NMS, at all times during its trading hours, each national securities exchange must collect, process and make available to vendors the best bid, the best offer, and the aggregate quotation size for each security that is communicated through the system of the exchange.[783] This means that a national securities exchange must collect and publish the prices at which its traders are willing to transact and the corresponding volumes, but only with respect to the top of the order book, i.e., the number of shares posted at its highest displayed bid quote and the lowest displayed ask quote.[784] However, the law does not require publication of the price and volume of the inferiorly priced bids and offers in the order book.[785] Furthermore, Rule 602(a)(1)(i) Regulation NMS only requires the publication of displayed orders, i.e., orders which the traders sent to the open limit order book of the exchange for display to the other traders on the exchange.[786]

The exchange must provide such information to vendors. According to Rule 600(87) Regulation NMS, vendors are securities information processors (SIPs) engaged in the business of disseminating transaction reports, last sale data, or quotations with respect to NMS securities to brokers,

---

783 17 CFR § 242.602(a)(1)(i); SEC, 'Regulation of Non-Public Trading Interest' (n 22) 74 FR 61211f; Haeberle (n 459) 819; Robert Hatch, 'Reforming the Murky Depths of Wall Street: Putting the Spotlight on the Securities and Exchange Commission's Regulatory Proposal Concerning Dark Pools of Liquidity' (2010) 78 The George Washington Law Review 1032, 1035.

784 Barr, Jackson and Tahyar (n 596) 549–50; Bošković, Cerruti and Noël (n 70) 25; Fox, Glosten and Rauterberg, *The New Stock Market* (n 98) 30; Haeberle (n 459) 819.

785 Fox, Glosten and Rauterberg, *The New Stock Market* (n 98) 30; Haeberle (n 459) 819.

786 Haeberle (n 459) 819.

dealers, or investors on a real-time or other current and continuing basis, through the consolidated quotation system.[787] This way, pre-trade information becomes public.

(ii) Rule 604 Regulation NMS

Pursuant to Rule 604(a)(1) Regulation NMS, the exchange must display the pre-trade transparency information of customer limit orders it receives from its specialists[788] and broker-dealers admitted to the exchange (i.e., the 'Display Rule').[789] These specialists must immediately publish a bid or an offer that reflects the price and the full size of each customer limit order held by the specialist that is at a price that would improve or be equal to the bid or offer of such specialist in such security.[790] The information on price and volume of the customer limit order is subsequently processed and disseminated by the exchange to the vendors, who in turn disseminate the data to the public. Despite customer limit orders, quotes by market makers on an exchange are also displayed by the exchange if the quote represents the best bid or best offer on the exchange.[791] Through this process, pre-trade transparency is created for traders on the exchange and the public outside the exchange observing market movements.[792]

The intended effect of market consolidation by trade transparency despite market fragmentation is even further propelled by the duty for exchanges and national securities associations (i.e., FINRA) to disseminate their trade transparency information in consolidated form through the three tapes mentioned above.[793] Through those consolidated tapes, also post-trade transparency is disseminated.[794]

---

787 17 CFR § 242.600(87), § 242.605, § 242.610; Batista (n 182) 91; Fox, Glosten and Rauterberg, *The New Stock Market* (n 98) 30.

788 Those traders perform market making function, i.e., they quote on both sides of the market, buy- and sell-side, on a regular basis; cf. Section 3(38) Exchange Act (15 U.S.C. § 78c(38)).

789 SEC, 'Order Execution Obligations' (n 138) 61 FR 48290; Barr, Jackson and Tahyar (n 596) 549; Fox, Glosten and Rauterberg, *The New Stock Market* (n 98) 30.

790 Rule 604(a)(1)(i), (ii) of Regulation NMS (17 CFR § 242.604(a)(1)(i), (ii)).

791 SEC, 'Order Execution Obligations' (n 138) 61 FR 48295.

792 Colby and Sirri (n 605) 181.

793 See above Part II § 5.C.II.

794 Rule 603(b) of Regulation NMS (17 CFR § 242.603(b)).

bb) Private Data Feeds

(i) Nature of Private Data Feeds

Besides the public feeds, exchanges also disseminate private feeds with information on their proprietary trading data to clients willing to pay for an additional, timelier source of information.[795] The fact that such data is not available to everyone at the same time and is not published free of charge at a later point in time, does not trouble the SEC. The Commission rather considers private data feeds as a mere addition to the public data feeds which can only improve the availability of market information and sees no tilting effect of the level-paying field in those private data feeds.[796] Following the SEC's rationale, all trading centers provide additional information exceeding the legal requirements about prices and volumes of lower ranked orders in the order book, i.e., the depth of the order book, for those who are willing to pay for additional information.[797] The dissemination in a private feed – comprising of both the legally mandatory and additional information – is used by the purchasers of this service to construct the content of the publicly available data before it is published and enrich public data with additional private information to gain an informational advantage over the competitors.[798]

(ii) Issues with Private Data Feeds

It is common practice among institutional investors, especially high frequency traders, to use the combination of public and private data feeds to front-run the market. Under Rule 603(a) of Regulation NMS, exchanges and FINRA need to distribute trading data on terms that are 'fair and reasonable' and 'not unreasonably discriminatory'. The exchanges and FINRA comply with this rule by sending their data to the SIP for consolidation and dissemination to the public.[799] The SIP, however, is relatively slow so that some investment firms, such as high-frequency traders, rather buy the

795 Haeberle (n 459) 819.
796 SEC, 'Regulation NMS' (n 340) 70 FR 37503.
797 ibid 70 FR 37567.
798 Haeberle (n 459) 819.
799 Mahoney and Rauterberg (n 118) 235–6; Walter Mattli, *Darkness by Design: The Hidden Power in Global Capital Markets* (Princeton University Press 2019) 115.

private trading data from the venues with additional depth of the order book information to construct their own private version of the SIP.[800]

Although Rule 611 Regulation NMS prohibits trading centers from submitting trading data to clients of private data feeds before they submit the same information to the SIP for the public data feed, the provision does not specify how long the submission of the data of private data feeds may take, nor does it state that clients of private data feed services may not receive private trading data before the public data reaches the SIP for dissemination.[801]

In part, private clients are able to receive the data feed before the SIP due to lagging technology on the side of the SIP. However, the speed advantage of clients of private data feeds is also due to co-location arrangements that such clients have with the trading center operators. In such co-location agreements, clients of private feeds rent server space in the same server center where the main server of the trading center is located to shave off valuable milliseconds of transmission time.[802] By combining faster technology with physical proximity, private clients receive the data before the rest of the market can see it on the tape provided by SIPs. This leads to an uneven playing field and an unfair advantage among traders. Traders – especially HFTs – with access to private data feeds use their informational advantage to front-run other investors making the profitable trades before the rest of the market even knows about the trading opportunity (latency arbitrage).[803] For this reason, the SEC should consider amending Rule 611 Regulation NMS to require that the trading centers ensure that clients of private data feeds do not receive their data before the SIPs the data meant for public dissemination. This would, however, take away a lucrative business from trading centers.[804]

---

800 Michael Lewis, *Flash Boys* (Allen Lane 2014) 97–8; Mahoney and Rauterberg (n 118) 267–70; Haeberle (n 459) 819.

801 SEC, 'Memorandum to SEC Market Structure Advisory Committee' (n 754) 8, 20; Lewis (n 800) 97–8; Mahoney and Rauterberg (n 118) 267–70; Marciello (n 735) 174; Mattli (n 799) 114ff; Scott Patterson, *Dark pools: The Rise of the Machine Traders and the Rigging of the U.S. Stock Market* (1st edn, Crown Business 2013) 49ff; Salger (n 627) 142–3.

802 SEC, 'Memorandum to SEC Market Structure Advisory Committee' (n 754) 8, 20; Lewis (n 800) 97–8; Mahoney and Rauterberg (n 118) 267–70; Mattli (n 799) 115–6.

803 Lewis (n 800) 97–8; Mahoney and Rauterberg (n 118) 269–70; Mattli (n 799) 115ff.

804 Cf. SEC, 'Memorandum to SEC Market Structure Advisory Committee' (n 754) 8, 20; Lewis (n 800) 97–8; Mahoney and Rauterberg (n 118) 268; Marciello (n 735) 174; Mattli (n 799) 115ff; Patterson (n 801) 49ff; Salger (n 627) 142–3.

cc) Default Rule: Trade Transparency at the Top of the Order Book with Additional Information for Purchase

This examination of the pre-trade transparency requirement for exchanges has shown that the default rule for exchanges is to show pre-trade transparency. They are, indeed, lit markets but only with respect to the top of the order book and only with regard to orders that the respective trader dubs as 'displayed order'. As will be shown in the next section, exchanges can host a considerable amount of 'hidden orders' that fall outside the scope of the pre-trade transparency regime.

Moreover, the private data feeds bring additional light into the market with regard to the inferiorly priced orders but not to everyone. Only those willing and able to pay for the additional information will receive it. Even more troubling is the matter of front running due to longer latency times in the public tape compared to the private ones, which propels a sort of temporary dark trading in which the purchasers of the private data feed operate unnoticed by the rest of the market.

b) Exceptions

Dark trading on exchanges is important for vulnerable traders, such as block traders, who may suffer prohibitive transaction costs when subjected to pre-trade transparency.[805] Facing the competition of ATS-dark pools, it is only natural for exchanges to have their own exemptions from trade transparency to provide dark trading services. Today, the number of transactions in which dark orders are involved on exchanges accounts for 11 % to 14 % of the entire transaction volume.[806] Such dark orders are often priced at the midpoint of the exchanges' bid-ask-spread for a security. This midpoint price can be determined during most times of the trading day because there are orders available both on the bid and the ask side of the market.[807] During this time, the dark orders executed at the midpoint

805 See above Part I § 3 B.

806 Haeberle (n 459) 820; See Hidden Volume Ratios, SEC, 'Hidden Volume Ratios: Market Structure Data Highlight' (9 October 2013).

807 Haeberle (n 459) 820. See, e.g., NASDAQ, 'Midpoint Liquidity' (2018) 1 (advertising that '*Nasdaq has [hidden]midpoint liquidity for a large portion of the day in high volume securities*' and listing a number of securities for which hidden quotes at the midpoint of the bid-ask spread are posted for well over half of the trading day).

improve both the best buy and best sell offer significantly by half of the bid-ask-spread. This gives the dark order a price that a limit order in the lit order book could never obtain, because execution at the (arithmetical) midpoint between the best bid and the best ask order cannot be achieved in the transparent market due to the lack of a limit order placed at this (hypothetical) price.[808] At least the liquidity premium between the best bid and the best ask price must always be overcome if a trader wants to trade immediately.[809]

Such dark orders are also protected from being disseminated to the traders who are paying for additional information about the depth of the order book via private data feeds.[810] Pursuant to Rule 604(b) Regulation NMS, specialists and other broker-dealers do not have to publish order information of their own and customer limit orders in seven specified cases.[811]

Those seven cases can be grouped into either 'exceptions for bespoke order types' or 'exceptions for technical reasons':

aa) Exceptions for Bespoke Order Types

Rule 604(b)(2) Regulation NMS provides four exceptions from pre-trade transparency for bespoke order types:

(i) Customer Requests Broker-Dealer not to Display the Order

According to Rule 604(b)(2) Regulation NMS, the first of these exemptions applies to a customer limit order that is placed by a customer with the express request to the broker-dealer that their order shall not be displayed on the exchange.[812] Even though the SEC expected that most customers would like their limit orders to be displayed to attract contra-side liquidity and expedite the transaction, it figured that there may also be instances in which the customer would prefer anonymity.[813] Especially customers with

808 Haeberle (n 459) 820.
809 Gomber and Gvozdevskiy (n 43) para 14.12.
810 Haeberle (n 459) 820.
811 SEC, 'Order Execution Obligations' (n 138) 61 FR 48290, 48304.
812 17 CFR § 242.604(b)(2); SEC, 'Order Execution Obligations' (n 138) 61 FR 48304.
813 SEC, 'Order Execution Obligations' (n 138) 61 FR 48304.

large limit orders may want their broker-dealer to keep the order private to work it through the market bit by bit instead of displaying the order and suffering market impact costs.[814]

In spite of the SEC's reasonable motivation, the scope of the exception appears overly broad. The exception does not consider the public interest that limit orders should in principle be pre-trade transparent to maintain a functioning price formation. This is accomplished, for example, by limiting the applicability of the exception to very specific cases, for example large orders only. Since there is no restrictive element in the current exception, the broker-dealer faces a conflict at the cost of market quality between ensuring market quality on the one hand, e.g., by protecting price accuracy when using the exception rarely, and the interest of their customer on the other hand, to whom the broker-dealer owes best execution and who generally wants to receive the best price possible. The broker-dealer will always resolve this conflict in favor of the customer, which seems problematic in terms of maintaining market quality if the exception is used extensively. Moreover, given that there is also an exception for block orders, which are prone to suffer market impact costs, the purpose of this exception appears doubtful. This exception is a broad gateway for dark trading on exchanges.

(ii) Odd-lot Orders

Pursuant to Rule 604(b)(3) Regulation NMS, customer limit orders do not have to show pre-trade transparency information when they are an odd-lot order. Odd-lot orders are orders for purchase or sale of NMS stock in an amount less than a round lot.[815] The amount of a round lot order is defined by the trading system's regulations and is usually 100 instruments of a certain class. Odd-lot orders sometimes occur due to demand for a specific amount or because a round-lot order has only been partially executed; the remainder of such order often is an odd-lot. Contra-side liquidity for such orders is hard to find and pre-trade transparency may make finding it even more difficult, since the market will ask for a surplus to provide such specific order size forcing such orders off the venue.[816]

---

814 ibid 61 FR 48304.

815 Cf. Rule 600(51) of Regulation NMS (17 CFR § 242.600(51)).

816 SEC, 'Order Execution Obligations' (n 138) 61 FR 48304–5.

(iii) Block Orders

On the other end of the spectrum of those orders under 100 instruments are the customer limit are of block size, hence very large orders. Such block orders qualify for the exception under Rule 604(b)(4) Regulation NMS, unless a customer who is placing such an order specifically requests that the order shall be displayed.[817] In this regard, the block order exception reverses the default rule of pre-trade transparency to the default of no pre-trade transparency unless requested by the trader. Orders are of block size when the order comprises of at least 10,000 shares or is for a quantity of stock having a market value of at least USD 200,000.[818] Such large orders compared to the typical order size may suffer market impact costs either by sweeping down the order book in search of liquidity executing with orders of ever inferior prices or they may suffer market impact costs because traders change their prices or trade against the order in anticipation of the block order arriving on the market.[819] However, block orders inject large amounts of liquidity into the market and are often used by institutional investors like pension funds or other funds to adapt their portfolio to the current market situation.[820] Since these services are welcome in the securities markets and there is no specific interest in having large orders displayed, granting them an exemption for dark trading is reasonable.[821] Moreover, the SEC introduced the Display Rule to improve order handling and execution opportunities for investors who lack the power to negotiate better terms. However, according to the SEC's rationale, most investors who handle block orders have the power to negotiate better terms, therefore, they do not need the protection of pre-trade transparency.[822] Since block orders primarily originate from institutional investors, the SEC's rationale

817 Cf. Rule 604(b)(4) of Regulation NMS (17 CFR § 242.604(b)(4)); Thelen (n 147) 191.

818 Cf. Rule 600(10) of Regulation NMS (17 CFR § 242.600(10)).

819 SEC, 'Order Execution Obligations' (n 138) 61 FR 48305; Gomber and Schweickert (n 265) 486–7.

820 SEC, 'Concept Release on Equity Market Structure' (n 6) 75 FR 3599; SEC, 'Regulation of Non-Public Trading Interest' (n 22) 74 FR 61208–61209.

821 SEC, 'Order Execution Obligations' (n 138) 61 FR 48305; SEC, 'Concept Release on Equity Market Structure' (n 6) 65 FR 3599; Committee on Capital Markets Regulation, 'The U.S. Equity Markets' (n 6) 3–4; cf. IOSCO, 'Principles for Dark Liquidity' (n 12) 12.

822 SEC, 'Order Execution Obligations' (n 138) 61 FR 48305.

is certainly adequate for most of the block orders. In any other case, the client can insist on displaying the order.

(iv) 'All or None'-Orders ('Fill or Kill')

The fourth exception under Rule 604(b)(7) Regulation NMS exempts so-called 'all or none' orders from pre-trade transparency requirements on an exchange.[823] Also known as 'fill or kill' orders, such orders shall either be executed for their entire volume when they hit the order book (i.e., fill) or be cancelled immediately when the liquidity at the specific price point is insufficient (i.e., kill).[824] Fill or kill-orders can serve two purposes for traders: first, a trader may wish to trade a bespoke order volume that may suffer market impact costs if not executed at once, for instance, for an order size that is large but not block size or an informed order that will otherwise be front-run by HFTs when noticed after partial execution. The second purpose can be for arbitrage strategies employed by HFTs to unveil, for example, iceberg-orders residing in the exchange's order book.[825]

However, exempting 'all or none' orders from pre-trade transparency is also driven by a technical rationale. Such orders are not available for contra-side liquidity, thus, communicating such orders to other market participants serves no informational purpose. Providing pre-trade transparency about 'all or none' orders would rather mislead the market into believing there was more liquidity than there actually is.[826]

bb) Exceptions for Technical Reasons

The remaining exceptions from pre-trade transparency requirements under Rule 604(b) Regulation NMS serve a technical purpose rather than aiming to protect a trader vulnerable to costs associated with providing trade transparency.

823 17 CFR § 242.604(b)(7).
824 Monsch (n 90) 39.
825 ibid 39.
826 SEC, 'Order Execution Obligations' (n 138) 61 FR 48306.

(i) Already Filled Orders

Pursuant to Rule 604(b)(1) Regulation NMS, a customer limit order does not have to be published when it is executed upon receipt at the exchange. Displaying pre-trade transparency of already filled orders is futile because contra-side liquidity no longer needs to be attracted.[827]

(ii) Order already Sent On

Similarly, Rule 604(b)(5) and (6) Regulation NMS exempt orders that are sent on to another trading venue or broker-dealer immediately upon receipt. These orders never become available to the market at this trading system, thus, displaying them would create a kind of ghost liquidity since the order will re-appear in another marketplace where it will be displayed and available for trading.[828]

cc) Application of the Exceptions

The exceptions under Rule 604(b) Regulation NMS are not granted upon request by the SEC or the SROs – i.e., the exchange or FINRA – but rather are applied by the broker-dealers when handling customer limit orders. For some of the exceptions some sort of instruction by the customer is necessary, for example, the 'all or none' order; while other exceptions can be applied without customer involvement, for example, orders which are sent off to other market participants. While this allows for little regulatory involvement in the process, it also forfeits all regulatory control over the amount of dark trading that may occur and how the exceptions are eventually applied in practice. Such unregulated use of dark trading may cause problems with fairness and market quality, especially with the price formation process.

c) Dark Trading on Exchanges

This examination of the pre-trade transparency regime for exchanges has shown that exchanges are primarily transparent lit pools with only minimal

827 ibid 61 FR 48304.
828 ibid 61 FR 48305–6.

transparency standards for showing the top of the order book required by law. Additional and more timely information can only be purchased via private data feeds, thus tilting the level-playing field among traders.

However, exchanges can also host a considerable amount of dark trading in the form of hidden orders. The exceptions for odd-lot orders, block orders, and 'all or none'-orders serve a specific purpose which is also reflected in the legal requirements set out under Rule 604(b) Regulation NMS. While the exception from pre-trade transparency upon customer's request may have reasonable fields of application, it does not set out any limiting factors that would bind the use of the exception to any public interest in having the order dispense from supporting the price formation process. The practical use of this exception should be examined. It might be necessary to add restrictive features to this exception's definition. The technical exceptions, however, are reasonable to avoid market distortions.

2. Broker-Dealers

a) Rule

aa) Broker-Dealers as Market Actors and as Internalization Markets

Broker-dealers occupy the role of market actors, not marketplaces, according to the institutional design of the Exchange Act. For this reason, broker-dealers are not generally obliged to publish their quote information (i.e., pre-trade transparency).[829] Even when broker-dealers act as marketplaces from an investor's point of view by offering internalization services, the broker-dealer does not have to publish the price and volume at which they bought securities from one client, nor do they have to tell the market at which price they turned around and sold those securities to another client.[830] This is the case because, when internalizing order flow, broker-dealers may generally transact with client orders but if the order is unprofitable for them, they will refrain, thus, they do not offer market making services.[831] The pre-trade transparency default rule is therefore non-transparency or, in other words, dark trading.

829 Haeberle (n 459) 822; Mahoney and Rauterberg (n 118) 229.
830 Haeberle (n 459) 817–8, 822.
831 ibid 817–8, 822.

However, broker-dealers cannot transact at any price they want, the Order Protection Rule, Rule 611 of Regulation NMS requires them to transact at a price at least incrementally better than the best bid or the best-ask-price depending on whether they are selling or buying from clients. Some therefore argue that information about prices offered by broker-dealers can be inferred from the publicly displayed exchange prices, the NBBO, adding a minuscule price improvement of a tenth or a hundredth of a penny.[832] While this may be a practical way to reduce opacity, it is nevertheless important to know the exact price improvement offered to utilize this information in the price discovery process. This is even more vital given that this liquidity is often uninformed and is missing on exchanges, forcing market makers to widen their spread.[833]

bb) Broker-Dealers Acting as OTC-Market Maker

(i) Rule 602 Regulation NMS

Under Rule 602(a)(ii) Regulation NMS, FINRA, as the national securities association for broker-dealers, must collect, process, and make available to vendors the best bid, best offer, and quotation sizes communicated otherwise than on an exchange by each member of FINRA acting in the capacity of an OTC market maker, as well as the identity of the member, for each subject security. Only when the bid or offer is immediately executed after communication or during any suspension of over-the-counter trading activity by the broker-dealers, shall FINRA not publish pre-trade transparency information.[834] Furthermore, FINRA cannot publish pre-trade transparency information about bids and offers of OTC market makers who are members of an exchange.[835]

Pursuant to Rule 600(56) Regulation NMS, an OTC market maker is any dealer which holds itself out to be willing to buy from and sell to its customers, or others, an NMS stock for its own account on a regular or continuous basis, other than on a national securities exchange in amounts of less than block size. In other words, OTC market makers are bilaterally trading

832 ibid 822–3.
833 ibid 829–30. Fox and Haeberle (n 227) 911–2.
834 Rule 602(a)(1)(ii) of Regulation NMS (17 CFR § 242.602(a)(1)(ii)); Haeberle (n 459) 822–3.
835 Rule 602(a)(1)(ii) of Regulation NMS (17 CFR § 242.602(a)(1)(ii)).

providers trading against their proprietary capital with client orders. They only differ from the internalization services mentioned above because OTC market makers offer quotes regularly or continuously, whereas internalizers often reserve discretion on whether or not to transact with a client order.[836]

Since those services are functionally similar to a marketplace from an investor's point of view, it is reasonable to subject these platforms to some sort of pre-trade transparency.[837] However, OTC market makers are only required to publish pre-trade transparency data when their trading volume exceeds 1 % of the average daily trading volume in the entire market (so-called 'Mandatory Quote Rule').[838] Only a certain amount of internalization can be considered similar to the service of trading venues. Thus, in the OTC market maker context, this limitation is reasonable, otherwise, pre-trade transparency would also apply to sporadic trading.

(ii) Rule 604 Regulation NMS

Similar to the pre-trade transparency regime for exchanges, Rule 604(a)(2) Regulation NMS sets out that each registered broker or dealer that acts as an OTC market maker shall immediately publish a bid or offer that reflects the price and the full size of each customer limit order held by the OTC market maker that is at a price that would improve or is equal to the bid or offer of such OTC market maker in such security. This is a parallel provision to the transparency regime for exchanges and is unsurprising given that FINRA was designed as an SRO similar to an exchange for all broker-dealers operating in the OTC-space to create a playing field that is level with those broker-dealers registered with and supervised by an exchange as their SRO.[839]

---

836 Haeberle (n 459) 822–3.

837 SEC, 'Regulation NMS' (n 340) 70 FR 37496, 37538; SEC, 'Regulation of Non-Public Trading Interest' (n 22) 74 FR 61210.

838 SEC, 'Order Execution Obligations' (n 138) 61 FR 48290; Batista (n 182) 108–9; Barr, Jackson and Tahyar (n 596) 550.

839 Barr, Jackson and Tahyar (n 596) 446–7.

b) Exceptions

The exceptions from the requirement of displaying quotations of customer limit orders for broker-dealers qualifying as OTC market makers are the same as for broker-dealers on an exchange pursuant to Rule 604(b) Regulation NMS. For this reason, the outlines made above apply accordingly.[840]

However, it is worth mentioning that the definition of an OTC market maker only applies to orders that are less than block size, and therefore the entailing pre-trade transparency rule does not apply to block orders.[841] This limitation is very important for bilaterally trading broker-dealers since pre-trade transparency for the block order may impair their chances of unwinding the position taken over with a customer willing to sell a block order.[842]

c) Summary of Dark Trading with Broker-Dealers

Broker-dealers do not face the same strict pre-trade transparency rules as exchanges. They can use dark trading and offer such services to their customers either as market actors or as quasi-marketplaces when operating as an internalization platform. This form of dark trading is rather unregulated dark trading since it occurs outside of the scope of the transparency regime and therefore bears the risk of growing erratically.

Only when a broker-dealer falls within the definition of an OTC market maker does the transparency regime include their quote information in the price formation process. The exceptions granted by Rule 604(b) Regulation NMS as well as the exemption of block orders from the OTC market maker definition are deliberate regulatory choices bound to public policy reasons (i.e., avoiding market impact costs), and therefore can be considered regulated dark trading. Nevertheless, US law again only chooses to set out the basic principles for pre-trade transparency but does not make any regulatory decision about how much dark trading it is willing to accept, for example, through the means of a limiting device like a maximum quota of admissible dark trading. This question is left to be answered by the market.

---

840 See above Part II § 5 E.I.1.B).

841 See definition of OTC market maker Rule 600(56) of Regulation NMS (17 CFR § 242.600(56)).

842 Cf. SEC, 'Order Execution Obligations' (n 138) 61 FR 48305, referring to market impact more generally.

3. Alternative Trading Systems

a) Rule

Although the investing public considers ATS synonymous with dark pools, the regulatory framework draws a more nuanced picture.

aa) Rule 301 Regulation ATS and Rule 602 Regulation NMS

As already established, ATS are registered as broker-dealers and as such they are a member of either an exchange or FINRA as currently the only national securities association.[843] According to Rule 301(b)(3)(ii) Regulation ATS,

> '(…) *[an] alternative trading system shall provide to a national securities exchange or national securities association the prices and sizes of the orders at the highest buy price and the lowest sell price for (…) NMS stock, (…), for inclusion in the quotation data made available by the national securities exchange or national securities association to vendors pursuant to § 242.602.*'[844]

According to Rule 602(a) Regulation NMS, exchanges and FINRA are obliged to collect the quote data of its members through their respective quote-collection mechanisms and disseminate the pre-trade transparency data to the consolidated tapes.[845]

bb) Lit-ATS: Electronic Communication Networks (ECNs)

Such alternative trading systems that show the pre-trade transparency information qualify as lit pools and are referred to as ECN.[846] So far, the default rule for ATS appears to be that they need to provide pre-trade transparency. Unfortunately, the SEC found only few ATS operating as lit ECNs while most ATS operate as dark pools not surpassing the 5 %-threshold.[847]

843 Section 15(b)(1)(B) Exchange Act (15 U.S.C. § 78o(b)(1)(B)).
844 17 CFR § 242.301(b)(3)(ii).
845 Fox, Glosten and Rauterberg, *The New Stock Market* (n 98) 30; Haeberle (n 459) 821.
846 Mahoney and Rauterberg (n 118) 228.
847 SEC, 'Regulation of Non-Public Trading Interest' (n 22) 74 FR 61214.

Accord to the SEC, these dark-ATS represented about 7.9 % of the overall US market in 2010.[848]

b) Dark-ATS under Rule 301(b)(3)(i) Regulation ATS: Reversing the Default Rule to Dark Trading

The fact that US law set a minimal threshold for triggering the pre-trade transparency obligation has led to a wide proliferation of dark-ATS. Pursuant to Rule 301(b)(3)(i) Regulation ATS, ATS are only obliged to show pre-trade transparency of their system's quotes for NMS stock[849] and if

> '*(...) (A) the system displays the subscribers orders to any person (other than alternative trading system employees); and (B) During at least 4 of the preceding 6 calendar months, had an average daily trading volume of 5 percent or more of the aggregate average daily share volume for such NMS stock as reported by an effective transaction reporting plan.*'[850]

This means that an ATS can operate as a dark pool for as long as it does not exceed the 5 %-threshold of the entire market turnover in a specific stock for 4 of the past 6 months. Or, in case of exceeding this threshold, the ATS can still remain a dark pool if it does not show pre-trade transparency to anyone, not even their subscribers.[851] It should be noted that the 5 %-threshold is an instrument-specific threshold, meaning that an ATS can be a lit pool for one instrument if the turnover exceeds the 5 %-threshold while simultaneously remaining a dark pool for another instrument for which it does not exceed the 5 %-threshold of market turnover.[852] In practice, almost all ATS either remain under the 5 %-threshold or do not show quotes to any subscriber to benefit from this broad exemption from pre-trade transparency. In fact, most ATS remain just below the 5 %-threshold, which is striking since it is possible for one investment firm to operate several

848 SEC, 'Concept Release on Equity Market Structure' (n 6) 75 FR 3599.

849 Definition of NMS stock according to 17 CFR § 242.300(g): '*NMS stock shall have the meaning provided in § 242.600; provided, however, that a debt or convertible debt security shall not be deemed an NMS stock for purposes of this Regulation ATS.*' Definition of NMS stock according to § 242.600(54): '*NMS stock means any NMS security other than an option.*'

850 17 CFR § 242.301(b)(3)(i)(A), (B).

851 SEC, 'Concept Release on Equity Market Structure' (n 6) 75 FR 3602; Hatch (n 783) 1036; Mahoney and Rauterberg (n 118) 243.

852 Mahoney and Rauterberg (n 118) 243.

dark-ATS commanding slightly below 5 % of market turnover on each of the individual ATS, but exceeding the 5 %-threshold if the trading volume of all operated ATS would be consolidated.[853] However, the SEC does not evaluate such investment firms running several dark-ATS with regard to their consolidated turnover on the level of the master-operator but rather on an ATS-specific level, so that dark trading can grow without any limitation under US law.[854] This means that the actual default rule of pre-trade transparency for ATS is in fact dark trading.

It is therefore unsurprising that the public considers ATS and dark pools synonymous. Although some claim that the order protection rule, which requires quotes to be equal or slightly superior to the displayed NBBO, provides some information about prices in a dark pool.[855] Despite this notion of the prices on a dark pool, dark trading on ATS still keeps informed orders on dark pools outside of the price formation mechanism with respect to pre-trade transparency. Moreover, the practice to ping dark pools with 'fill or kill'-orders in order to retrieve information about the dark order flow and their prices is equally troubling, especially given that this technique is often used by HFTs.[856] The fact that HFTs can retrieve information from dark pools by pinging them with smaller orders that 'probe' the opaque order books casts doubt on the dark pools' ability to protect traders, especially block traders, who use dark pools to shield themselves from market impact costs often associated with HFT interaction.[857] It appears doubtful that US dark pools can actually deliver on the promises made to valuable liquidity providers that are vulnerable to pre-trade transparency.[858]

c) Unregulated and Unlimited Dark Trading in ATS

In spite of a pre-trade transparency rule generally applicable to ATS under Rule 301(b)(3)(ii) Regulation ATS, the broad exemption for ATS gathering less than 5 % of turnover and for ATS that do not display any quote infor-

853 SEC, 'Regulation of Non-Public Trading Interest' (n 22) 74 FR 61214; Mahoney and Rauterberg (n 118) 244.

854 Hatch (n 783) 1045–6; Thelen (n 147) 192.

855 Haeberle (n 459) 821.

856 ibid 821.

857 Batista (n 182) 111; Baxter (n 605) 323; Easthope and Ray (n 5) 6; Shorter and Miller, 'Dark Pools in Equity Trading' (n 149) 3, 5.

858 See the enforcement measures by the SEC due to misrepresentation with regard to HFT-presence in the pool above Part II § 5 D.III.2.

mation to anyone, dark trading is the default rule for ATS under US law.[859] While having a regulatory entity for dark trading is not troubling per se, the fact that the reason for dark trading is not tied to a public policy reason, such as, protecting block traders vulnerable to market impact costs, is a matter for concern: Regulation ATS considers incorporating quote information into the price discovery process less important than enhancing competition among trading systems for any dark-ATS that commands less than 5 % of turnover in a given instrument.[860] While this may have been a fair perspective when Regulation ATS was first promulgated, it is no longer necessary to provide ATS with such a competitive advantage over exchanges.[861] The fact that an investment firm can operate several dark-ATS just below the 5 %-threshold shows the arbitrariness of this rule and qualifies this form of dark trading as unregulated dark trading, since there is no actual public policy rationale justifying dark trading for those trading systems and the orders they host. With regard to ATS, US securities law again only lays out the fundamental principles for the scope of transparency as well as non-transparency but does not formulate any effective limits for dark trading under the ATS-regime.

II. Post-Trade Transparency

US securities law also requires post-trade transparency information to be published by the trading systems.

1. Exchanges

Under Rule 601 Regulation NMS, exchanges are required to collect information about post-trade information for the transactions they facilitate.[862] They collect the information about the volume and price of the transaction

859 SEC, 'Regulation of NMS Stock Alternative Trading Systems' (n 22) 80 FR 81057; Haeberle (n 459) 824.

860 SEC, 'Regulation of Exchanges and Alternative Trading Systems' (n 138) 63 FR 70844, 70856ff, 70865; Colby and Sirri (n 605) 183–4.

861 As can be seen by the SEC proposing to lower the 5 %- to a 0.25 %-threshold, since competition between ATS and exchanges appears to be healthy, see: SEC, 'Regulation of Non-Public Trading Interest' (n 22) 74 FR 61214f. Cf. Hatch (n 783) 1044ff.

862 17 CFR § 242.601. Haeberle (n 459) 819.

that occurred on their system and send the information in real time to SIPs. The SIPs publish the information on their tapes according to Rule 603 Regulation NMS.[863]

Parallel to pre-trade transparency, exchanges offer faster access to post-trade information through private data feeds for those market participants willing to pay for the timelier access.[864] This preferred access for some also tilts the playing field in favor of the purchasers of the post-trade information private data feeds to the disadvantage of to the pre-trade information private data feeds.[865]

With regard to post-trade transparency, US securities law is exceptionally strict. Unlike the European Union and Switzerland, which allow for a deferred publication of post-trade information under certain circumstances,[866] US law neither allows for an exception nor for a deferral from the default rule of publication of post-trade transparency data as close to real time as possible.[867] This strict approach results in a high degree of post-trade transparency which supports the price formation mechanism. Since the parties to a transaction have already filled their orders and no longer face adverse price movement, they generally do not bother sharing the transaction information with the market. However, for some transactions such a high degree of post-trade transparency with no deferrals may be disadvantageous: particularly, block traders in illiquid markets often need to turn to market makers and other institutional liquidity providers to receive order execution. If post-trade transparency is high and immediate, the liquidity provider might be reluctant to take on a block position that they will need to subsequently dispose in the market. Here, US law can only offer slicing the order or using ATS, as we will see below.

2. Broker-Dealers

The post-trade transparency requirement pursuant to Rules 601, 603 Regulation NMS apply to exchanges and FINRA.[868] Whether or not a broker-dealer is member to an exchange or FINRA will determine if either the

863 17 CFR § 242.603. Haeberle (n 459) 819.
864 ibid 819.
865 See above Part II § 5 E.I.1.A).bb).
866 See below on the EU Part II § 6 C.V., VI. and on Switzerland Part II § 7 C.II.5.
867 Haeberle (n 459) 819.
868 17 CFR § 242.601 and § 242.603. Haeberle (n 459) 822.

exchange or FINRA collects the post-trade information about size and price of the concluded transaction and sends it on to the SIP for publication on the respective tape.[869] This is the case when the broker-dealer internalizes the order flow.[870]

FINRA, on the other hand, ensures that it receives information from its member broker-dealers through FINRA Rules 6622,[871] 6380B,[872] and 6730;[873] this includes transactions of broker-dealers trading OTC.[874] Parallel to post-trade transparency rules for exchanges, there are no deferrals available for broker-dealers under US securities law.

869 Haeberle (n 459) 822.

870 ibid 822.

871 FINRA Rule 6622 for OTC Reporting Facility:
'(a) When and How Transactions are Reported
(1) OTC Reporting Facility Participants shall, as soon as practicable but no later than 10 seconds after execution, transmit to the OTC Reporting Facility, or if the OTC Reporting Facility is unavailable due to system or transmission failure, by telephone to the Operations Department, last sale reports of transactions in OTC Equity Securities executed during normal market hours. Transactions not reported within 10 seconds after execution shall be designated as late. (...)'

872 FINRA Rule 6380B for FINRA/NYSE Trade Reporting Facility:
'(a) When and How Transactions are Reported
(1) Trade Reporting Facility Participants shall, as soon as practicable but no later than 10 seconds after execution, transmit to the FINRA/NYSE Trade Reporting Facility or, if the FINRA/NYSE Trade Reporting Facility is unavailable due to system or transmission failure, by telephone to the FINRA/NYSE TRF Operations Department, last sale reports of transactions in designated securities executed during normal market hours. Transactions not reported within 10 seconds after execution shall be designated as late. (...)'

873 FINRA Rule 6730 for Trade Reporting and Compliance Engine (TRACE):
'(a) When and How Transactions are Reported
Each member that is a Party to a Transaction in a TRACE-Eligible Security must report the transaction. A member must report a transaction in a TRACE-Eligible Security as soon as practicable, but no later than within 15 minutes of the Time of Execution, except as otherwise specifically provided below. Transactions not reported within the specified timeframe will be designated as "late." A member must transmit the report to TRACE during TRACE System Hours. (...)'

874 Haeberle (n 459) 822; Thelen (n 147) 190.

3. Alternative Trading Systems

Since ATS are registered as broker-dealers, their post-trade transparency data is also collected by either the exchange they are member to or by FINRA.[875]

However, ATS benefitted from the reporting standards adopted by the Consolidated Tape Association which operates the Consolidated Tape. Its standards allowed for deferred post-trade transparency insofar as the reporting by ATS often appeared only at the end of the day, days or even weeks later.[876] While this does not support a timely utilization of the information on the price discovery process, it is beneficial for such liquidity providers facilitating block transactions for clients in illiquid markets. This way the market remains uninformed about the large order changing hands which allows the liquidity provider to dispose of their holdings without adverse price movements. This form of dark trading allows the liquidity provider to offer their much-needed service. Although clearer rules as to how long a liquidity provider can defer publication of post-trade transparency information may be preferable, a certain degree of dark trading with regard to post-trade data may be a vital part of a functioning market and explains the attraction of market participants towards dark-ATS.

III. Lit and Dark Trading under US law

The examination of the trade transparency regime under US securities law has shown that exchanges display pre-trade transparency information. Dark trading is only permissible if the transaction or order is in some way bespoke, for instance a block order or a negotiated transaction, that can be better served if there is no pre-trade transparency. These orders benefit from pre-defined exceptions under Regulation NMS.

Despite a general pre-trade transparency rule, ATS operate under a transparency regime that has a broad exemption which ultimately reverses the default rule of pre-trade transparency from lit to dark trading. For pre-trade transparency requirements to apply, the quotes on the ATS must be communicated to more than one person and the trading volume in the security must be at or above the 5 %-threshold. With such broad exemptions, ATS

875 Haeberle (n 459) 820.

876 SEC, 'Regulation of Non-Public Trading Interest' (n 22) 74 FR 61208, 61218; Hatch (n 783) 1036–7.

render non-pre-trade transparent trading their norm and are therefore a perfect vehicle for dark trading.

With regard to post-trade transparency, US securities law in combination with self-regulatory standards by exchanges and FINRA apply a strict and relatively homogenous standard across all trading infrastructures. Deferrals from immediate post-trade transparency for bespoke transactions – particularly such that are of block size – are not available under US securities law, despite their general acceptance in other jurisdictions such as the European Union and Switzerland.

The US transparency regime for trading systems aims to support trade transparency and provides exceptions for bespoke orders or, in the case of ATS, for 'small-sized' trading systems to facilitate their market access. However, the regulatory approach does not exceed a principle-based approach which sets out the minimum requirements for transparent trading as well as the broadly described cases when dark trading shall be permissible. There is however no mechanism to limit the amount of dark trading. This matter is rather left for the market to determine. This also means that there is no regulation that is based on the principle of precaution.[877] US securities law is rather satisfied with defining the basic rules of the market.

IV. Exceptions for Governmental Agencies

1. Scope

A general exemption from the provisions of the Exchange Act and its transparency regime is made by Section 3(c) Exchange Act. This section sets out that no provision of this title shall apply to any executive department or independent establishment of the United States acting in the course of its official duty, unless such provision makes specific reference to such department, establishment, or agency.[878]

877 See above Part I § 4 C.

878 Full text of Section 3(c) Exchange Act:
'No provision of this title shall apply to, or be deemed to include, any executive department or independent establishment of the United States, or any lending agency which is wholly owned, directly or indirectly, by the United States, or any office, agent, or employee of any such department, establishment, or agency, acting in the course of his official duty as such, unless such provision makes specific reference to such department, establishment, or agency.'

Under this provision, governmental departments and agencies can carry out their official duty without being bound to the requirements of the Exchange Act and the SEC Rules which further define the meaning and regulatory content of the Exchange Act. Hence, this also means that they are not bound by transparency requirements pursuant to Rule 301 Regulation ATS and Rules 601ff Regulation NMS. Due to such a broad exemption, neither pre-trade nor post-trade transparency must be provided when a governmental department or agency acts on the securities market making extensive use dark trading.

2. Eligible Entities

This exemption can be used by any executive department or independent establishment of the United States.[879] This very broad definition not only applies to government departments and agencies, such as the Treasury Department, but also to independent government agencies, such as the Federal Reserve. This means that the Board of Governors and the Federal Open Market Committee of the Federal Reserve System (FOMC) decide upon monetary policy measures which are eventually carried out by the Federal Reserve Bank of New York (FRBNY) through buying and selling securities without being subject to trade transparency requirements as authorized by the FOMC.[880] This is an important exemption to allow for transactions, such as open market transactions[881] as well as foreign exchange transactions,[882] which shall support a safer, more flexible, and more stable monetary and financial system in the United States.[883]

879 Cf. Section 3(c) Exchange Act 1934.

880 On the process of open market transactions see: The Federal Reserve System, 'Purposes & Functions' (10th edn, Federal Reserve System Publication, Washington, D.C., 2016) 32; On the Federal Reserve System, see also: Deutscher Bundestag - Wissenschaftliche Dienste, 'Das Federal Reserve System: Entstehungsgeschichte, Grundlagen, Aufbau' (2008) 4–5.

881 When the Federal Reserve carries out open market transactions it conducts purchases or sales of US government or agency securities in the open market, see: The Federal Reserve System (n 880) 41 fig. 3.4.

882 When the Federal Reserve carries out foreign exchange transactions it buys US dollar and sell foreign currency when it aims to support the value of the US dollar. It does the opposite transaction when it wants to decrease the value of US dollar to foreign currency. See description by Federal Reserve Bank of New York, 'Foreign Exchange Operations'.

883 The Federal Reserve System (n 880) 23.

3. Eligible Transactions

It is not further defined to what extent governmental departments and agencies can use the exemption under Section 3(c) Exchange Act and its entailing SEC Rules. With regard to the broad scope, the question arises whether the scope of this exemption is bound to the public purpose mission of the government body or whether mere fiscal transactions are also covered: In particular, whether the twelve Federal Reserve Banks can use Section 3(c) Exchange Act to fund themselves and programs like their employees' pension plans or are they bound to their public purpose when using dark trading.

Since US law does not provide an answer to this issue, a comparative approach may be insightful. EU law has a similar exception to Section 3(c) Exchange Act[884] but narrower in scope since only central banks in the European System of Central Banks can use it for carrying out monetary policy purposes. Due to Article 1(6) MiFIR providing similarly far-reaching exemptions, this provision also has a clause that restricts overuse. The rationale of this exemption is that trade transparency shall not interfere with the effectiveness of monetary policy measures by the central banks, for instance by suffering market impact if investors trade against the central bank or front-run it. Besides, the exception also prevents open market or foreign exchange transactions from sending misleading signals into the market and creating turmoil.[885] Therefore, only transactions that serve the public purpose of creating a stable and sound market, i.e., transactions made as measures of monetary policy, foreign exchange policy and financial stability policy fall within the exception under EU law. In contrast, transactions that serve a financing purpose, i.e., financing the government, the central bank, or their employees' pension plans, are not considered to serve the public purpose but rather a mere investment purpose. When pursuing investment purposes, central banks act in a functionally equivalent manner to any other investor, therefore, an exception from trade transparency is no longer justified.[886]

This differentiation between privileged dark trading for pursuing public purposes and non-privileged transparent trading when pursuing investment purposes is transferable from EU law to US law, so that govern-

884 Article 1(6) MiFIR but only applying to transparency matters of non-equity instruments under MiFIR.

885 Cf. Recitals 22, 23 of CDR (EU) 2017/583 (RTS 2).

886 For further detail see below on EU law Part II § 6 B.I.1.a).

ment departments and agencies are not exempt for all transactions they carry out. For instance, when the Federal Reserve carries out open market and foreign exchange transactions for monetary policy purposes, privileged dark trading should be possible to allow for the maximum effect of such measures, while avoiding turmoil on the markets. Insofar, government agencies may use Section 3(c) Exchange Act as an additional source of dark trading beyond the exceptions within the securities laws and regulations available to all investors. However, when conducting transactions for investment purposes, the government departments and agencies need to show trade transparency.

4. Open Market Transactions by FRBNY

In practice, the FRBNY conducts open market transactions with only with so-called primary dealers, i.e., dealers that are eligible to transact in treasury purchase operations directly with the Federal Reserve. Those dealers can submit offers for themselves and their customers.[887] The purchase of treasury securities is made through the FRBNY's proprietary trading system called FedTrade. This system uses a multiple-price, competitive auction system.[888]

The transactions on FedTrade are closed at prices close to the prevailing market prices at the close of the auction. There is thus no pre-trade transparency for the primary dealers in the FRBNY's proprietary trading system, which qualifies it as a dark pool. However, FedTrade offers post-trade transparency to a certain degree. It publishes operation results on the website of the FRBNY which includes data in the total amount of propositions received, the total amount of propositions accepted, and the amount purchased per issue. The primary dealers will receive the operation results together with their accepted propositions immediately after the auction through the FedTrade system. Public information about the prices, however, is released by the FRBNY no sooner than mid-month for the prior

887 Federal Reserve Bank of New York, 'FAQs Treasury Purchases' (11 February 2022).

888 See ibid: '*(…) A "multiple-price" auction is an auction in which securities are awarded at the price corresponding to the participant's offer in the operation, resulting in the security being awarded at multiple prices. The minimum auction amount, offer size, and offer increment are each $1 million. Participants can submit up to nine offers per security, with each offer reflecting both a price and par amount.*'

month.[889] Consequently, the monetary policy transactions by the FRBNY are carried out on a dark pool that shows no pre-trade transparency, but decent post-trade transparency for traders, whereas it shows heavily delayed post-trade transparency to the public.

F. Access Regime

While transparency is an important pre-requisite for finding the best bid or offer in the market, access to this liquidity is also vital to form efficient transactions.[890] However, with regard to access to their facilities, exchanges and off-exchange trading systems differ significantly from each other.[891] Regarding fair access, US securities law distinguishes between 'membership access', on the one hand, and 'order access' or 'quotation access', on the other hand.[892] The rules on membership access set out who can become a member of a trading system which effectively limits a trading system operator's discretion over who is admitted to the system. Order access, on the other hand, refers merely to the question of whether a trader can access a trading opportunity on a particular trading system through a member offering brokerage services if the trader is not a member themselves.[893]

I. Exchanges

Exchanges are the most open trading systems granting wide access to their system and their orders.[894]

1. Membership Access

With regard to membership access, exchanges have to grant fair access to all SEC-registered brokers and dealers according to Section 6(b) Exchange

889 Federal Reserve Bank of New York (n 887).
890 SEC, 'Regulation NMS' (n 340) 70 FR 37502; IOSCO, 'Principles for Dark Liquidity' (n 12) 22; IOSCO, 'Transparency and Market Fragmentation' (n 3) 16.
891 Haeberle (n 459) 823.
892 SEC, 'Regulation NMS' (n 340) 70 FR 37539.
893 Section 6(b) Exchange Act (15 U.S.C. § 78f(b)) and 17 CFR § 242.610(a). Haeberle (n 459) 823.
894 Haeberle (n 459) 823.

Act.[895] As long as this requirement is met, an exchange operator cannot exclude anyone at their discretion. This means an exchange cannot exclude HFTs to protect certain vulnerable traders, like block traders, who fear that HFTs would unveil their hidden orders to trade against them.[896]

2. Order Access

Order Access, however, is even broader since 2005 when Rule 610 Regulation NMS liberalized the former system to propel the goal of a truly integrated national market system.[897] Prior to 2005, exchanges only granted access to quotes to their members and their customers.[898] They, thus, could bar access to members of other trading systems when those traders wanted to transact through a brokerage service of one of their own members. In practice, this was often done by requiring one's own members to refrain from offering such services under the exchange regulations.[899]

The Access Rule set out in Rule 610 Regulation NMS liberalized the market and abolished such bans on brokerage services for other non-member broker-dealers. Under Rule 610(a) Regulation NMS, a national securities exchange (as well as the national securities associations FINRA) cannot impose unfairly discriminatory terms that prevent or inhibit any person from obtaining efficient access through a member of the national securities exchange or national securities association to the quotations in an NMS stock displayed through its SRO trading facility.[900] As a consequence, exchanges must grant access to its quotes through its members to any person regardless of whether or not the person is a member.

895 Section 6(b)(2) Exchange Act (15 U.S.C. § 78f(b)(2)); cf. Haeberle (n 459) 823.
896 Cf. Easthope and Ray (n 5) 6; Shorter and Miller, 'Dark Pools in Equity Trading' (n 149) 3, 5.
897 Mahoney and Rauterberg (n 118) 246–7.
898 SEC, 'Regulation NMS' (n 340) 70 FR 37539.
899 ibid 70 FR 37539.
900 17 CFR § 242.610.

II. Broker-Dealers

1. Membership Access

Fair membership access is required by Section 6(b) Exchange Act for national securities exchanges and by Rule 301(b)(5)(ii) Regulation ATS for ATS with a trading volume exceeding 5 % of the total trading volume in a security. Broker-dealers who offer internalization services, however, do not fall within the exchange or the ATS definition.[901] Since there is no specific rule for fair membership access for broker-dealer internalization systems, it is a matter of negotiation and discretion by the broker-dealer whether it grants a trader access to the liquidity hosted on the internalization system.[902]

2. Order Access

Broker-dealers are not required to offer fair order access under Rule 610 Regulation NMS, since they do not display quotes in the sense of firm offers.[903] When broker-dealers internalize order flow, they merely often – but not always – trade at a certain price. They retain a certain amount of discretion over whether or not they enter a customer order that comes their way.[904]

Broker-dealers use the discretion regarding member and order access extensively. Evidence supports that it is common practice that broker-dealers preferably choose retail orders for execution or that retail-brokers route retail-customers' orders in *'payment for order flow'*-schemes to large dealers which internalize the order flow. This strategy is considered very lucrative and is done to exclude institutional investors' orders as far as possible. The rationale is that institutional investors' orders are much more likely to be informed, meaning that informed traders possess information that indicates that the transaction at the said price with the broker-dealer is beneficial for informed traders but not for the internalizing broker-dealer who would transact at another price had it known the information. Generally, retail traders are uninformed traders who pose an insignificant adverse

901 See above Part II § 5 D.II.1 and III.1.
902 Haeberle (n 459) 825.
903 ibid 824.
904 ibid 822.

selection risk to broker-dealers, and therefore are welcome customers to earn a profit from the bid-ask spread and the fees charged.[905]

This exercise of freedom of contract does not sit comfortably when considering that broker-dealers are internalizing almost all retail order-flow, which is a tremendous market,[906] completely exempt from fair access rules; whereas exchanges must abide by fair access rules and are left with potentially informed institutional investors increasing the adverse selection risk for other traders on exchanges. It is therefore no surprise that exchanges want to compete with internalizing platforms in this market and file for permission to operate platforms that admits only retail investors.[907]

III. Alternative Trading Systems

1. Membership Access

ATS fall within the exchange definition but usually choose to register as broker-dealers instead, as a result the requirement to grant fair access to venue membership in Section 6(b) Exchange Act does not apply to ATS.[908] However, ATS have a special rule for fair membership access in Regulation ATS, acknowledging their middle ground position between an exchange and a broker-dealer. According to Rule 301(b)(5)(ii)(A) and (B) Regulation ATS, an ATS must establish written standards for granting access trading on its system and shall not unreasonably prohibit or limit any person's

905 SEC, 'Payment for Order Flow' (17 CFR Part 240, Release No. 34-33026, File No. S7-29-93, 13 October 1993) 58 FR 52934, 52936; Mahoney and Rauterberg (n 118) 259ff. Cf. Allen Ferrell, 'A Proposal for Solving the "Payment for Order Flow" Problem' (2001) 74 Southern California Law Review 1027.

906 SEC, 'Memorandum' (n 66) 2 fn 2 ('Internalization is believed to account for almost 100 % of all retail marketable order flow.'); Mahoney and Rauterberg (n 118) 259ff.

907 Haeberle (n 459) 825; e.g. SEC, 'Order Granting Approval to Proposed Rule Changes, as Modified by Amendments Nos. 1 and 2, Adopting NYSE Rule 107C to Establish a Retail Liquidity Program for NYSE-Listed Securities on a Pilot Basis until 12 Months From Implementation Date, and Adopting NYSE Amex Rule 107C to Establish a Retail Liquidity Program for NYSE Amex Equities Traded Securities on a Pilot Basis Until 12 Months From Implementation Date, and Granting Exemptions Pursuant to Rule 612(c) of Regulation NMS' (Release No. 34–67347, File Nos. SR–NYSE–2011–55, SR–NYSEAmex–2011–84, 3 July 2012, 10 July 2012) 77 FR 40673ff.

908 Haeberle (n 459) 823.

access by applying the established standards in an unfair or discriminatory manner.[909]

However, the significance of the fair access to membership is small in practice due to a minimum volume threshold for the requirement to apply. As with the pre-trade transparency requirements, the fair access requirement is not triggered for ATS that combine less than 5 % of the average daily turnover of a specific security or show no prices to their clients (Rule 301(b)(5)(i) Regulation ATS).[910]

Even broader is the exemption from the fair membership access in Rule 301(b)(5)(iii) Regulation ATS. According to this rule, an ATS is further exempted from the fair access requirement when it (A) matches two customers' orders, (B) does not display the customers' orders to any other person except for ATS employees, and (C) executes such orders at a price for such security disseminated by an effective transaction reporting plan or derived from such prices.[911] The rationale behind such exceptions can only be that the orders are not actionable because they are already matched with another customer and are executed at a price that does not improve the currently displayed price at the lit markets. Insofar, the access regime runs in tandem with the transparency regime. Unfortunately, for the transparency regime and for the fair access regime, the exception swallows the general rule making no pre-trade transparency as well as the lack of fair access to membership the default rule, since almost all ATS (99 %) use the exemptions and operate below the 5 %-threshold.[912]

2. Order Access

A similar situation can be observed with the requirement of fair order access. Rule 610(a) Regulation NMS covers ATS that are members of FINRA as the national securities association for broker-dealers. Alternative trading venues running an electronic communication network which provides for trade transparency cannot inhibit fair access of any person to their orders through their members. However, almost all ATS use the exemptions from pre-trade transparency, either by not exceeding the 5 %-threshold or by not

909 ibid 824; Mahoney and Rauterberg (n 118) 243.

910 Haeberle (n 459) 824; Mahoney and Rauterberg (n 118) 244.

911 Rule 301(b)(5)(ii) Regulation ATS (17 CFR § 242.301(b)(5)(iii)).

912 SEC, 'Regulation of NMS Stock Alternative Trading Systems' (n 22) 80 FR 80998, 81057; Haeberle (n 459) 824.

displaying any quotes to members, which allows them to circumvent the criterion of *'displayed'* quotation under Rule 610(a) of Regulation NMS. Falling outside the scope of this rule, the access to the orders hosted in those ATS is a matter of negotiation and unrestricted discretion on the side of the ATS.[913]

In practice, ATS running a dark pool even take pride in their discretion of both access to membership and orders. Most often they promise their customers that they keep HFTs away from the trading venue and only allow large scale orders into the facility. This advertises the venue's safeguards for customers against predatory trading practices by HFTs and shows their efforts to ensure market depth and liquidity in the pool.[914]

IV. Effects of Discriminatory Access in ATS

As the trade transparency regime influences price accuracy, so does the access regime.[915] From an individual perspective, it is reasonable for traders to seek dark trading if they are vulnerable to trade transparency either because they are handling block orders prone to market impact costs or because they are informed traders and want to exploit the private information for as long as possible. Since the rise of high frequency trading strategies, dispensing of trade transparency alone may no longer be sufficient. HFTs can use the predatory strategies discussed above,[916] such as pinging or electronic front running to unveil the order information in dark pools and earn a profit by trading faster than the remainder of the market.[917]

Under those circumstances, it is reasonable that traders prefer dark pools which are not only opaque but also selective with their access rules.[918] If HFTs do not have access to the trading system in the first place, they cannot retrieve the information. Within the US regulatory framework this is the case for ATS operating below the 5 %-threshold. Those dark pools can also select who can trade on their platform, and thereby offer not only protection from market impact for block traders but also offer a service

913 SEC, 'Concept Release on Equity Market Structure' (n 6) 75 FR 3614; Haeberle (n 459) 824.
914 Shorter and Miller, 'Dark Pools in Equity Trading' (n 149) 3, 5.
915 Haeberle (n 466) 150; Haeberle (n 459) 829ff.
916 See above Part II § 5 F.III.
917 Fox, Glosten and Rauterberg, 'The New Stock Market' (n 88) 230ff, 250–1.
918 ibid 250–1.

similar to an '*exclusive right of usage*' for private information in possession of informed traders on dark pools.

While this '*exclusive right of usage*' for price relevant information provides informed traders better chances to offset their costs of information production, denying HFTs access to trading systems inhibits intermarket arbitrage.[919] When HFTs and other traders engage in intermarket arbitrage by retrieving information through ping orders in a dark pool, they use this information generally on a lit pool for trading, and impound this information into the price formation process. Intermarket arbitrage thus enhances price accuracy in shorter periods of time and thereby decreases the transaction costs stemming from inaccurate prices for all traders.[920]

Although enabling informed traders to better offset their search costs for price relevant information by providing informed traders with exclusivity in the exploitation process is a purpose as viable as facilitating intermarket arbitrage to utilize information sooner to increase price accuracy, special attention must be given to this issue in the US market setting. Since almost all ATS choose to operate as dark pools below the 5 %-threshold,[921] a vast majority of dark pools can also have discriminatory access rights. Provided that a growing market share of trading service providers comprises of dark pools regulated as ATS, this means a major shift towards protection of informed traders who could also trade in the lit market supporting the price formation process leaving intermarket arbitrage a much smaller scope of application, which may adversely affect price accuracy and ultimately raise transaction costs rendering the market less efficient.[922]

G. Order Handling Rules under Regulation NMS

Adopted by the SEC in 2005, Regulation NMS has already been discussed with regard to its transparency regime and its access regime.[923] However, Regulation NMS also contains order handling rules that shape the market and introduce incentives for using lit and dark markets. Subsequently, three additional rules under Regulation NMS will be discussed: first, Rule 606

919 ibid 230ff, 250–1.

920 ibid 230ff, 250–1.

921 SEC, 'Regulation of NMS Stock Alternative Trading Systems' (n 22) 80 FR 81057; Haeberle (n 459) 824.

922 Haeberle (n 459) 830–1.

923 See above Part II § 5 E.I. and F.I.

on the disclosure of order handling, second, Rule 611 called the 'Order Protection Rule', and finally, Rule 612 dubbed the 'Sub-Penny Rule.'

I. Rule 606 Regulation NMS: Disclosure of Order Handling Information

1. Purpose and Functioning of Rule 606 Regulation NMS

Rule 606 Regulation NMS has a certain nexus to post-trade transparency since it requires disclosure of order handling information from broker-dealers.[924] Rule 606 Regulation NMS requires broker-dealers handling orders from their customers to inform them upon request about the routing of their orders.[925] Although this obligation already arises for broker-dealers due to their fiduciary duties as their customers' agents, the information requirement can be fulfilled in various different ways.[926] Rule 606 Regulation NMS requires standardized reports from broker-dealers about certain parameters of their order routing to their customers so they can inform themselves and compare different broker-dealers' services, ultimately sparking competition in the broker-dealer market for an efficient national market system.[927]

Order routing is a crucial factor for the agency relationship between customer and broker-dealer because information is leaked every time the order is routed to another trading system and broker-dealers may pursue their individual interests in the order routing process giving rise to principal-agent-problems.[928]

The principal-agent-problem becomes apparent in the order routing decisions by broker-dealers in which they maximize their own profits, instead of considering their customers' best interest. An example for this is the routing decision for marketable customers' limit orders versus non-marketable customers' limit orders: Broker-dealers usually route marketable retail or-

924 SEC, *Press Release: SEC Adopts Rules That Increase Information Brokers Must Provide to Investors on Order Handling* (2018);

925 SEC, 'Disclosure of Order Handling Information: Final Rules' (17 CFR Parts 240 and 242, Release No. 34-84528, File No. S7-14-16, 19 November 2018) 83 FR 58338, 58364; Fox, Glosten and Rauterberg, *The New Stock Market* (n 98) 30.

926 SEC, 'Disclosure of Order Handling Information' (n 925) 83 FR 58338, 58345.

927 ibid 83 FR 58338, 58339; SEC, 'Concept Release on Equity Market Structure' (n 6) 75 FR 3602.

928 SEC, 'Disclosure of Order Handling Information' (n 925) 83 FR 58338, 58344.

ders to other dealers who offer an internalization service for (uninformed) retail customers' orders under a payment-for-order-flow-scheme, whereas, non-marketable retail limit orders are often routed to exchanges that offer a maker-taker fee schedule.[929] While the first routing option often feeds the dark trading market due to the transparency regime for broker-dealers which does not require pre-trade transparency, the latter option feeds the lit market on exchanges.[930] Interestingly, the order decision is not based on the vulnerability of the order to pre-trade transparency, but merely on the profit-maximization of the broker-dealer which sends each order type to a venue that offers an additional incentive.[931] This, however, is not necessarily the customer's preference which means a principal-agent-conflict is inherent to this situation.[932] Thus, Rule 606 Regulation NMS aims to provide additional information about such underlying conflicts of interest to unveil hidden actions by the broker-dealer.[933]

To minimize the principal-agent-problem arising in such situations, Rule 606(a) Regulation NMS requires the broker-dealer to make publicly available quarterly reports about its routing practices to inform both customers and the public. Rule 606(b)(3) Regulation NMS provides deeper insights for customers on the order handling of their specific orders: upon request of the customer, a broker-dealer has to provide a report within seven business days disclosing the order handling of that customer's orders in NMS stock for the period of the prior six calendar months.[934] The report must include the total number of shares the customer sent to the broker-dealer during the period, the total number of shares executed on the broker-dealer's own account, and the total number of orders that the broker-dealer has exposed through sending actionable indications of interest including the venues and other customers to which such IOIs were sent.[935] However, the broker-dealer may not need to disclose the identity of such customers. With regard to the venues to which the broker-dealer sent customer orders, the broker-dealer must publish an array of information,

929 Beny (n 51) 432–3; Mahoney and Rauterberg (n 118) 261–2; Salger (n 627) 152.

930 SEC, 'Disclosure of Order Handling Information' (n 925) 83 FR58338, 58344.

931 Mahoney and Rauterberg (n 118) 261ff.

932 Lambert (n 476) 95ff; Schmolke, '§ 5 - Vertragstheorie und ökonomische Analyse des Vertragsrechts' (n 586) 151ff paras 304ff.

933 SEC, 'Disclosure of Order Handling Information' (n 925) 83 FR 58338, 58364.

934 Rule 606(b)(3) of Regulation NMS (17 CFR § 242.606(b)(3)); ibid 83 FR 58338, 58358–9.

935 ibid 83 FR 58338, 58364, 58366.

among which count the fill rate, the execution fee or rebate, the number of shares executed at the midpoint. Those details allow customers to assess their order handling quality and whether or not their order was sent to a dark pool, whether they interacted with high-frequency traders, and the incentives driving the broker-dealers routing decision.[936]

2. Two De Minimis Exceptions

In addition to the exemption for block orders, there are also two de minimis exemptions from the reporting rule. The first exemption focuses on the broker-dealer, relieving them from providing a customer-specific report if broker-dealer's order flow in NMS stock is less than 5 % of the total shares of NMS stock orders that the respective broker-dealer received from their customers in the last six months.[937] The second exemption focuses on the individual customer, by also not requiring a customer-specific report if the customer traded less than USD 1,000,000 of notional value of NMS stock through the broker-dealer in average each month for the prior six months.[938]

3. Criticism

With those exceptions, the reporting requirement may be less of a burden for the broker-dealer, but it is also basically ineffective for smaller-scale investors. However, the 5 %-threshold is a regulatory technique used by the SEC to delineate when an ATS needs to offer transparency and fair access. The 5 %-threshold serves the purpose of protecting small-scale broker-dealers that the SEC considers less significant.[939] Similar to the 5 %-threshold for ATS, this rule may incentivize broker-dealers who wish to avoid this reporting requirement to disperse their order-flow among many sub-systems to avoid the regulation completely. Despite its experience with ATS, the SEC has decided to operate with this technique once more.

In general, given that order routing by broker-dealers carries significant risks for conflicts of interest, the SEC chose a less intrusive path by impos-

936 ibid 83 FR 58338, 58366, 58421.

937 Rule 606(b)(4) of Regulation NMS (17 CFR § 242.606(b)(4)); ibid 83 FR 58338, 58346.

938 Rule 606(b)(5) of Regulation NMS (17 CFR § 242.606(b)(5)); ibid 83 FR 58338, 58346–7.

939 ibid 83 FR 58338, 58347

ing only disclosure requirements and not conduct regulation. Considering the de minimis exemptions and their potential for regulatory arbitrage, such less intrusive measures may not achieve the goal of a more transparent and more competitive market among broker-dealers.

II. Rule 611 Regulation NMS: Order Protection Rule

1. Purpose and Functioning of Rule 611 Regulation NMS

The Order Protection Rule under Rule 611 Regulation NMS shall provide intermarket price protection by charging trading centers to prevent trade-throughs of protected quotations within their trading systems.[940] A trade-through is the purchase or sale of securities at a price that is lower than a protected bid or higher than a protected offer, which usually is a limit order by an investor, on another trading center (Rule 600(81) Regulation NMS).[941] Protected bid or offer means a quotation in an NMS stock that (i) is displayed by an automated trading center, (ii) is disseminated in the consolidated market data feeds, and (iii) is the best bid (i.e., highest bid) or best offer (i.e., lowest offer) published by a national securities exchange or FINRA (Rule 600(61) Regulation NMS).[942] This means that Rule 611 Regulation NMS provides intermarket price protection only during the operating hours of the consolidated market feeds and only for the top of the order book quotations. There is no depth-of-book protection outside the best prices.[943]

Furthermore, a protected quotation has to be automatically accessible for immediate execution in another trading venue. This includes all quotations in electronic order books but excludes bids and offers on trading floors that need to be executed manually.[944]

The order protection rule protects the best-priced displayed orders in the market residing on one trading system from being side-stepped by infe-

940 SEC, 'Memorandum to SEC Market Structure Advisory Committee' (n 754) 2.

941 SEC, 'Regulation NMS' (n 340) 70 FR 37501; Mark Jickling, 'The Trade-Through Rule' (Congressional Research Service, 6 June 2005) 1; Preece (n 14) 26.

942 SEC, 'Memorandum to SEC Market Structure Advisory Committee' (n 754) 3; Salger (n 627) 137. Cf. Mahoney and Rauterberg (n 118) 245.

943 SEC, 'Memorandum to SEC Market Structure Advisory Committee' (n 754) 3–4.

944 SEC, 'Regulation NMS' (n 340) 70 FR 37504; Mahoney and Rauterberg (n 118) 244–5.

riorly priced orders on another trading system. This incentivizes traders to post best-priced orders since they know they will receive execution before anyone else, so long as no one posts a superiorly priced order.[945] Insofar, the rule supports the price discovery mechanism because it minimizes the position risk of best-priced orders. The order protection rule also protects orders entering the market because it ensures that those orders receive the best price in the market, even if it may reside in another trading system.[946]

In spite of the controversies raised by the Order Protection Rule among the market participants during the consultation for Regulation NMS, the SEC considered this rule an essential instrument to reach the goal of implementing the national market system.[947] The market research conducted before Regulation NMS showed that trade-throughs happened several times each trading day. This meant that in every other transaction a trader fell short of the price that was posted on the tape as the NBBO.[948] Besides the mere frequency of trade-throughs, the fact that traders received inferior prices may adversely affect investor confidence. Moreover, when the best market prices cannot be achieved, liquidity levels will suffer and transaction costs may rise thus rendering the market less efficient.[949] However, the rule does not require one marketplace to route the order to another for execution. It can comply with Rule 611 Regulation NMS by simply refraining from executing the residing order.[950] In many cases, the liquidity of investors using a broker as an agent will get routed to the trading venue with the best price displayed because the duty of best execution binds the broker to do so, unless the investor instructs the broker otherwise.[951] Only dealers acting as principles have to find the trading venue with the best prices on their own. As institutional investors, however, they are considered capable of fending for themselves.

This operating principle reveals that ensuring investors receive the best price available may be a welcome effect, but not the primary objective of the Order Protection Rule.[952] Regulation NMS implemented the Order Pro-

945 Mahoney and Rauterberg (n 118) 244–5.
946 ibid 244–5.
947 SEC, 'Regulation NMS' (n 340) 70 FR 37498.
948 ibid 70 FR 37498.
949 ibid 70 FR 37498.
950 SEC, 'Memorandum to SEC Market Structure Advisory Committee' (n 754) 4; Salger (n 627) 138.
951 Mahoney and Rauterberg (n 118) 244–5.
952 ibid 244–5.

tection Rule to incentivize investors to provide liquidity at the best price. The SEC's logic was that if investors can trust that their best priced limit order cannot be traded-through but received timely execution and thus they shall be more likely to post competitively priced limit orders which narrows the bid-ask-spread and elevates liquidity levels.[953] The primary goal was to improve market depth, liquidity and price discovery,[954] recognizing '*(...) that limit orders are the building blocks of public price discovery and efficient markets.*'[955] The order protection rule can therefore be considered one tool to minimize dark trading by raising the confidence that no adverse effects will be suffered when displaying limit orders in the open order book.[956]

2. Criticism on the Order Protection Rule

In practice, however, the adoption of the order protection rule coincides with a massive increase in dark trading.[957] Some see a causal link because the order protection rule requires also institutional investors trading in large orders to display their order or at least transact with the displayed best-priced order first.[958] Before Rule 611 Regulation NMS went into force, a trade-through protection was only in place for exchanges; and trade-throughs were not strictly forbidden, but rather to be avoided whenever possible.[959] Coupled with a duty of best execution that could be interpreted more broadly by taking also order size and immediacy into account, broker-dealers could execute a large order with a less competitively priced

953 SEC, 'Regulation NMS' (n 340) 70 FR 37505; Mahoney and Rauterberg (n 118) 244–5.

954 SEC, 'Regulation NMS' (n 340) 70 FR 37505.

955 ibid 70 FR 37501.

956 ibid 70 FR 37501: '*(...) The Commission agrees that strengthened protection of displayed limit orders would help reward market participants for displaying their trading interest and thereby promote fairer and more vigorous competition among orders seeking to supply liquidity (...)*'.

957 SEC, 'Memorandum to SEC Market Structure Advisory Committee' (n 754) 17ff; Crudele (n 505) 579; Mercurio (n 149) 71; Salger (n 627) 141.
SEC, 'Memorandum to SEC Market Structure Advisory Committee' (n 754) 7; cf. Crudele (n 505) 578.

958 SEC, 'Memorandum to SEC Market Structure Advisory Committee' (n 754) 17ff; Crudele (n 505) 578–9; Mercurio (n 149) 71; Salger (n 627) 141.

959 SEC, 'Memorandum to SEC Market Structure Advisory Committee' (n 754) 7; cf. Crudele (n 505) 578.

order but larger in size. Under the Order Protection Rule, this practice was severely curtailed.[960]

Rule 611 Regulation NMS puts more emphasis on factors such as speed, fees, and bespoke order types in the competition among lit venues; whereas factors more important to investors, such as liquidity and stability, could only be focused on if the quotes were not displayed. Thus, dark pools, especially ATS operating without trade transparency, catered to such investor needs, luring them away from traditional exchanges.[961] Moreover, with the new Order Protection Rule applying to automatically executable orders, the SEC did not see a direct causal link between the Order Protection Rule and the rise in dark trading. The Commission nevertheless acknowledged that the introduction of Rule 611 Regulation NMS and the increase in dark trading coincided, which *'(...) suggest that there might be some form of indirect causal connection between dark fragmentation and Rule 611 (...)'*.[962] It is therefore likely that ATS could exploit their speed advantage which caused a shift of order flow from exchanges to ATS.[963]

Although the SEC provided some exceptions, like the intermarket sweep orders, aimed at satisfying the needs of large orders, institutional investors feared being front-run by HFTs when pieces of their large order hit one marketplace and revealed that other fragments of this order will soon reach other marketplaces, thus giving HFTs time to move the market against them.[964]

Even though Rule 611 Regulation NMS may not be the sole reason for an increase in dark trading, empirical data by the SEC suggests that the Order Protection Rule had at least some influence on this development.[965] Thus, the Order Protection Rule may have failed its purpose to increase transparency, liquidity and the likelihood of displayed limit orders to execute against the full array of trading interest present in the market.[966]

960 Crudele (n 505) 578; cf. Jickling (n 941) 4–5.
961 SEC, 'Memorandum to SEC Market Structure Advisory Committee' (n 754) 17.
962 ibid 17.
963 Banks (n 5) 8, 11.
964 SEC, 'Memorandum to SEC Market Structure Advisory Committee' (n 754) 19–20; Marciello (n 735) 173–174; Salger (n 627) 142; Zaza (n 688) 326.
965 SEC, 'Memorandum to SEC Market Structure Advisory Committee' (n 754) 19–20.
966 ibid 17ff; Salger (n 627) 142.

III. Rule 612 Regulation NMS: Sub-Penny Rule

Rule 612 sets out the Sub-Penny Rule to protect liquidity, increase price transparency, and foster consistency. Under this rule, market participants are prohibited from displaying, ranking, or accepting quotations that are priced in increments of less than USD 0.01 if the price of the stock is currently USD 1.00 or above.[967] If, however, the price of the stock is currently below USD 1.00, the minimal increment for pricing an order cannot be less than USD 0.0001.[968]

The Sub-Penny Rule is the SEC's direct response to trading practices that became common after the decimalization of trading prices.[969] These practices included some traders sending orders into the open order book at economically insignificant improvements over the current best bid or offer price while ensuring their immediate execution (e.g., to step ahead of a USD 20.00 quotation, quote at USD 20.0000001 would have been sufficient).[970] This practice was particularly common among broker-dealer internalization services that wanted to attract retail investor orders of other brokerage firms under the duty of best execution.[971] This practice was problematic because broker-dealers do not have to show pre-trade transparency.[972] Also crossing networks, such as dark ATS, that matched incoming orders at the midpoint of the price displayed on lit markets surpassed the displayed price by only half of the bid-ask-spread, i.e. the midpoint, which was often merely half a penny.[973] Displayed limit orders, however, that provided their price information for the price discovery process did not get executed. To ensure execution for those who display limit orders to the market, the SEC implemented the Sub-Penny Rule. This Rule limited trading strategies in which traders front-run others by insignificant price improvements.[974]

967 SEC, 'Regulation NMS' (n 340) 70 FR 37503.
968 ibid 70 FR 37503; Mahoney and Rauterberg (n 118) 246–7.
969 Before decimalization of prices the NYSE, for example, priced in fractions, such as, 1/8 or 1/16 of a Dollar, see Banks (n 5) 15; Shorter and Miller, 'High-Frequency Trading' (n 362) 15.
970 SEC, 'Regulation NMS' (n 340) 70 FR 37551; Mahoney and Rauterberg (n 118) 246–7; Preece (n 14) 26.
971 Preece (n 14) 17.
972 See above Part II § 5 E.I.2.
973 Mahoney and Rauterberg (n 118) 246–7.
974 SEC, 'Regulation NMS' (n 340) 70 FR 37503.

H. Regulatory Incentives for Increased Use of Dark Trading

With a combination of push and pull factors, US securities law created incentives for traders to migrate from lit exchange trading to dark off-exchange trading since the adoption of Regulation ATS and Regulation NMS. While the burdensome regulation of exchanges made their services less attractive for many traders, the more lenient regulation of ATS and broker-dealer internalizers allowed their operators to position themselves as viable alternatives for multilateral exchange trading in an increasingly automated market environment.[975]

Under the Exchange Act, national securities exchanges are charged with self-regulatory and market surveillance tasks which add additional costs for operating a multilateral trading venue that are passed on to the traders.[976] Furthermore, performing the function of an SRO while operating a trading venue as a for profit business puts exchanges in a conflict of interest which hinders them from attracting clients as freely as they otherwise could.[977]

The regulatory decision to put ATS under the broker-dealer regime and require self-regulatory and market surveillance engagements only if an ATS exceeds the 5 %-threshold provided ATS operators with the opportunity to offer multilateral trading service – formerly monopolized by exchanges – without incurring the expenses from self-regulation and market surveillance.[978] The same is true for broker-dealer internalizers. Both ATS and broker-dealer internalizers outsource their self-regulatory and market surveillance tasks to FINRA as their SRO.[979]

In a similar vein, exchanges need to meet a public interest standard when setting up their rules. Any change to the rules of the trading system is subject to SEC approval. This is not the case for ATS operating below the 5 %-threshold or for broker-dealer internalizers.[980] Thus, ATS and bro-

975 Zyskind (n 605) 415. Cf. Zaza (n 688) 325ff.

976 Mahoney and Rauterberg (n 118) 255. See also Committee on Capital Markets Regulation, 'The U.S. Equity Markets' (n 6) 48ff.

977 Mahoney and Rauterberg (n 118) 255. See also Domowitz and Lee (n 598) 296–7.

978 Mahoney and Rauterberg (n 118) 255; Zyskind (n 605) 415.

979 See above Part II § 5 D.I4. and III.3.

980 See Sections 6(a), 3(a)(26) Exchange Act (15 U.S.C. §§ 78f(a), 78c(a)(26)); *Lanier v. BATS Exchange, Inc.* (2016) 838 F.3d 139 (2d Cir. 2016) (US Court of Appeals for the 2nd Circuit); Mahoney and Rauterberg (n 5) 255.

ker-dealer internalizers are less costly and less in conflict with their clients' interests as exchanges, which is more attractive for traders.[981]

Another crucial difference is the requirement to display pre-trade transparency. While exchanges are generally required to submit their quotes to the consolidated quotation system for display to the investing public, ATS only must disseminate their quotes if they display them to their users and, even if they do, only if the ATS exceeds the 5 %-threshold in turnover.[982] Since broker-dealer internalizers only have prices at which they often, but not always, prefer to transact with client orders, they do not quote prices, and, thus fall outside of the regulatory perimeter of the pre-trade transparency requirement.[983]

Although dark trading had already been attractive for traders before Regulation ATS and Regulation NMS was promulgated, the Order Protection Rule under Regulation NMS acted as an additional push-factor towards dark trading. The Order Protection Rule was intended to reward those traders who offered the best priced sell or buy orders in the market by protecting them from being skipped by a trade through.[984] However, the rule did not take into account that block traders in particular do not wish to trade with the best-priced orders in the market since best-priced orders are often rather small and would be insufficient to fill the large order entirely. The resulting transparency of the transaction and the order stub would be more costly than transacting with an inferiorly priced but larger order in the order book (market impact costs).[985] Thus, block traders often migrated to dark ATS and broker-dealer internalizers. Since liquidity attracts more liquidity, this was a self-reenforcing effect.[986]

The attractiveness of dark off-exchange trading was further increase by the differences in the access regime. Exchanges also have to grant fair access to every (qualified) person, whereas, ATS operating below the 5 %-threshold and broker-dealer internalizers can offer discriminatory access and choose their user base.[987] This power to guard access to their trading sys-

981 Cf. Domowitz and Lee (n 598) 297.

982 Mahoney and Rauterberg (n 118) 255; Zyskind (n 605) 417.

983 Haeberle (n 459) 822.

984 SEC, 'Regulation NMS' (n 340) 70 FR 37496, 37505.

985 SEC, 'Memorandum to SEC Market Structure Advisory Committee' (n 754) 19–20; Marciello (n 735) 173–174; Salger (n 627) 142; Zaza (n 688) 326.

986 SEC, 'Memorandum to SEC Market Structure Advisory Committee' (n 754) 17ff; Salger (n 627) 142.

987 Haeberle (n 459) 823ff; Mahoney and Rauterberg (n 118) 255.

tems proves a valuable selling point for ATS and broker-dealer internalizers in a market with rising HFT activity outpacing every other trader, because their trading venue is not only dark but also sealed off from predatory trading.[988]

This attraction to dark trading is further propelled by the fact that HFTs and institutional traders (often informed traders) ensure an informational advantage through private data feeds. Uninformed traders who do not purchase the costly private data feeds for faster and more detailed information anticipate this structural disadvantage and may see no reason to remain in the lit markets. Especially given that modern technology allowed ATS and broker-dealer internalizers to fill orders as quickly as exchanges, the former disadvantage of dark upstairs trading to be slower than exchange trading is no longer relevant. Dark pools run by ATS and broker-dealer internalizers often appear more attractive than lit trading which caused a massive increase in dark liquidity in the US securities market over the last decades.[989]

However, the fragmentation of liquidity led to a two-tiered market environment with informed traders predominantly gathering on lit exchanges and uninformed traders migrating to dark pools.[990] Some fear that this fragmentation can lead to a widening of the bid-ask-spread on exchanges since market makers need to insure themselves against the elevated adverse selection risk which renders the market less efficient.[991] Whether market quality is deteriorating with increased levels of dark trading is for the economists to evaluate, but appears to depend on the amount of dark trading in a specific market as the research previously discussed indicates.[992]

However, the practice of intermarket arbitrage, where informed traders tap uninformed traders' liquidity on dark pools to off-set their information-research costs by trading at the (uninformed) price,[993] casts doubt over the power of dark pools to protect their uninformed clients and may jeopardize investor trust. Thus, dark pools grew significantly in the US securities

988 Batista (n 182) 111; Baxter (n 605) 323.

989 See for instance SEC, 'Memorandum to SEC Market Structure Advisory Committee' (n 754) 17: '*(...) from February 2005 to February 2014, the collective share of dark venue trading in NYSE stocks increased from 13 % to 35 %, and the collective share of dark venue trading in NASDAQ stocks increased from 29 % to 39 % (...)*'.

990 Haeberle (n 459) 829ff; Mahoney and Rauterberg (n 118) 261.

991 Haeberle (n 459) 829.

992 See above Part I § 3.D.IV.

993 Haeberle (n 459) 829.

market due to regulatory incentives, but it remains unclear whether dark pools deliver on their promise or harm overall market quality and investor trust.

I. SEC Proposal for New Regulation in 2009

As early as 2009, the SEC proposed several measures to react to some of the most urgent issues raised by the increase of dark trading in US securities market, which shall be outlined in the following.[994]

I. Lowering the 5 %-Threshold for Alternative Trading Systems

Most of the dark trading in the United States occurs on alternative trading systems because they skillfully use the 5 %-threshold. As long as the average daily turnover remains below the 5 %-threshold, the ATS does not have to offer pre-trade transparency, nor does it have to grant fair access to all qualified traders.[995] The SEC identified this issue as contradicting with the goals of the national market system.[996] However, the SEC does not suggest entirely discarding the concept of a threshold that favors upcoming market entrants because the goals of the national market system also include fostering competition among trading venues.[997] Hence, small trading venues shall not be burdened with the full weight of regulation.

In an effort to find a decisive measure against the flourishing dark trading on ATS while maintaining low barriers for market entry, the SEC suggests lowering the 5 %-threshold to a 0.25 %-threshold.[998] This would mean that whenever an ATS meets or surpasses 0.25 % of average daily trading volume in four of the past six months it would not only have to display pre-trade transparency but also grant fair access to its systems.[999]

Even though it should be welcomed that the SEC is making a statement against this use of the 5 %-threshold, it is only half-hearted. At first glance, a reduction to 0.25 % appears vast and limiting the issue to a minimum.

994 SEC, 'Regulation of Non-Public Trading Interest' (n 22) 74 FR 61208ff.
995 Rule 301(b)(3)(i) of Regulation ATS (17 CFR § 242.301(b)(3)(i)).
996 SEC, 'Regulation of Non-Public Trading Interest' (n 22) 74 FR 61208, 61213ff.
997 Colby and Sirri (n 605) 189–90; Mahoney and Rauterberg (n 118) 244.
998 SEC, 'Regulation of Non-Public Trading Interest' (n 22) 74 FR 61208, 61213ff.
999 ibid 74 FR 61208, 61213; Hintz (n 382) 349–50.

However, the market has shown that as long as there is no absolute maximum amount of dark trading in the market or at least per entity holding the ATS, there will be arbitrage in the sense that multiple small ATS operating just below the 0.25 %-threshold will occur, most likely also in the hands of the same entity. This is particularly true given that setting up and running a new electronic marketplace has become increasingly inexpensive in recent years.[1000]

Lowering the 5 %-threshold to 0.25 % may even bias the competition between ATS and broker-dealers that qualify as OTC market makers.[1001] OTC market makers only have to display their quotes if their trading accounts for 1 % or more of the average daily turnover in the market.[1002] Those broker-dealers that operate a multilateral ATS today may operate a bilateral OTC market maker tomorrow if the thresholds are not aligned.[1003] Since bilateral trading means trading against the proprietary capital of the operator who accumulates risk in this process, the concentration of this risk in OTC market makers appears to be imprudent compared with dispersing it among many traders in multilateral trading only for the sake of achieving dark trading.

Given that ATS benefit from the same (broad) exemptions from the display rule pursuant to Rule 604(b) Regulation NMS, the 5 %-threshold exemption from displaying quotes should be discarded entirely.[1004] Making transparency the rule from which exceptions can be made in certain instances supports both transparency and competition as goals of the national market systems while allowing for (just) enough dark trading for the market to operate smoothly. With regard to the access rule, there may be a need for early ATS to distinguish between traders, and at the same time investors may also be interested in excluding for example HFTs. This should, however, be achieved by setting out clear regulations for access which should be reviewed and approved by the SEC to fulfill such specific, justified purposes and be administered by the ATS accordingly to protect traders from certain forms of trading if they so wish. A threshold only

1000 Hatch (n 783) 1045–6.
1001 Batista (n 182) 108–9.
1002 SEC, 'Regulation of Non-Public Trading Interest' (n 22) 74 FR 61208, 61227 fn 154; Batista (n 182) 108–9.
1003 Batista (n 182) 108–9.
1004 ibid 108–9.

causes regulatory arbitrage in which the motif and purpose of remaining below the threshold cannot be reviewed.[1005]

Consequently, the SEC should abolish the threshold altogether and subject ATS generally to the display rule and the access rule but provide for justified exceptions where necessary. Unfortunately, the SEC has neither lowered nor abolished the 5 %-threshold under Regulation ATS.[1006] The two-tiered market it produces continues to divide the US trading landscape today.

II. ATS should Identify Transactions on Tape

ATS are not only opaque due to their lack of pre-trade transparency, they also show less post-trade transparency than exchanges.[1007] This is primarily because ATS are not required to publish post-trade as detailed and granular information as exchanges.[1008]

Since ATS are regulated as broker-dealers, they have to become members of FINRA. As members, ATS have to report their post-trade information of executed transactions to FINRA. This information is eventually disseminated to the public.[1009] However, FINRA does not differentiate between transactions that occur on an ATS and those with a broker-dealer in the OTC-realm. Both trades will be reported as OTC trades.[1010] Such trades can be aggregated with other OTC-transactions and published as batches so that the information is less granular and less informative. Furthermore, OTC trade information can also occur with a significant delay often no sooner than at the end of the day.[1011]

This is problematic since ATS offer multilateral trading services comparable to exchanges and thus ATS garner a significant amount of market liquidity in their systems. When traders should be able to find this liquidity by looking at post-trade transparency data telling them which trading venue hosts enough liquidity, FINRA's data displaying ATS transactions as OTC transactions will not reveal this to the investing public. Thus, only investors

1005 ibid 109 in favor of a gradually decline of the threshold.
1006 Salger (n 627) 154.
1007 SEC, 'Regulation of Non-Public Trading Interest' (n 22) 74 FR 61208, 61219.
1008 Batista (n 182) 110.
1009 SEC, 'Regulation of Non-Public Trading Interest' (n 22) 74 FR 61208, 61219.
1010 ibid 74 FR 61208, 61219.
1011 Batista (n 182) 110; Baxter (n 605) 332–3.

who already know which one is the best ATS can tap its liquidity. The function of post-trade transparency to close the information gap between traders is not adequately fulfilled.[1012]

For this reason, the SEC proposed that ATS transactions should be identified in FINRA's data stream as such.[1013] The post-trade data should also be available in a timelier manner to the investing public.[1014] Again, to account for the threat of market impact, large block orders are exempted in the proposal.[1015]

Unfortunately, this proposal has also not been adopted, even though it would render post-trade information more informative and would aid with the distribution of knowledge about trading venues that offer attractive execution among traders. However, this rule would only make a significant difference if fair access rights would also be granted to investors that have been denied access so far.

III. Including Actionable Indications of Interest into the Definition of 'Best Bid and Offer'

The SEC further proposed broadening the definition of 'best bid and offer' under Regulation NMS to also include actionable IOIs.[1016] Actionable IOIs are often used in dark pools to attract attention in an order position residing in the dark pool. An actionable IOI informs about the volume and the direction (sell or buy) of the order in a specific security. Since pre-trade transparency is not available in dark pools to attract attention by other traders to fill a specific order, actionable IOIs are functionally similar to pre-trade transparency. However, unlike pre-trade transparency, an actionable IOI in a dark pool is not shown to all traders but only selected, particularly active traders that are likely to fill the order. However, those traders more often than not include traders against which most dark pool users want to shield their orders: being HFTs.[1017]

1012 SEC, 'Regulation of Non-Public Trading Interest' (n 22) 74 FR 61208, 61219–20.
1013 ibid 74 FR 61208, 61219–20; Hatch (n 783) 1044.
1014 SEC, 'Regulation of Non-Public Trading Interest' (n 22) 74 FR 61208, 61219–20.
1015 ibid 74 FR 61208, 61220.
1016 ibid 74 FR 61208, 61210.
1017 Baxter (n 605) 331–2; Hatch (n 783) 1047–8.

To avoid a two-tiered (dark) market with naïve traders and advantaged traders who receive IOIs, the SEC proposed including all actionable IOIs into the quoting requirement, i.e., into the pre-trade transparency regime under Regulation NMS.[1018] This was primarily motivated by the functional similarity of actionable IOIs and pre-trade transparent orders and the uneven playing-field that IOIs create among market participants.[1019] However, despite the general suspicion against actionable IOIs, the SEC considered them meritorious for block orders because orders with a volume of at least USD 200,000 or at least 10,000 shares may benefit from direct negotiation with a liquidity provider and may otherwise face difficulties in finding contra-side liquidity without moving the market to their detriment.[1020]

This amendment to Regulation NMS appears appropriate for the abovementioned reasons and long overdue given the international development. In 2011, IOSCO advised that actionable IOIs should be included in the bid and offer definition to subject them to pre-trade transparency to limit dark trading and avoid two-tiered markets.[1021] Both the European Union under MiFID II/MiFIR and Switzerland under FinfraG/FinfraV followed that advice.[1022] Yet, Regulation NMS still shows no amended definition including actionable IOIs into the bid and offer definition despite the SEC's proposal in 2009.

J. SEC Proposal of a Trade-At Rule in 2016

I. First Limiting Device under US Law

In 2016, the SEC addressed dark trading, among other issues, in its Tick Size Plan.[1023] In this plan, the SEC proposed a trade-at rule that aimed at limiting the amount of dark trading in the US securities markets.[1024] With regard to dark trading, the proposal of a limiting device such as the trade-

1018 SEC, 'Regulation of Non-Public Trading Interest' (n 22) 74 FR 61208, 61211.
1019 Baxter (n 605) 331–2.
1020 SEC, 'Regulation of Non-Public Trading Interest' (n 22) 74 FR 61208, 61212–3.
1021 IOSCO, 'Principles for Dark Liquidity' (n 12) 27.
1022 On EU law see Part II § 6.C.II.1.d).cc) and on Swiss law see Part II § 7.C.II.2.b).
1023 SEC, 'Order Directing the Exchanges and the Financial Industry Regulatory Authority to Submit a Tick Size Pilot Plan' (Release No. 34-72460, 30 June 2014)79 FR 36840, 36841, 36843-4.
1024 ibid 23–4.

at rule was the first measure where the SEC went beyond its regulatory approach of setting merely minimal standards and introduced a measure associated with precautious regulation of a market-shaping character.[1025]

II. Functioning of the Trade-At Rule

The trade-at rule is a tightened version of the Order Protection Rule, dubbed 'trade-through rule' by market jargon, pursuant to Rule 611 Regulation NMS.[1026] While the trade-through rule prohibited trading systems to match orders at a price inferior to the currently displayed NBBO, i.e., 'trading through' a best-priced order, it allowed a trading system to leave the best priced displayed order unfilled or to side-step this rule by using dark orders that do not have to be published as the new, protected NBBO since they do not qualify as 'displayed' orders.[1027]

The trade-at rule, on the other hand, requires trading systems displaying only quotes at prices inferior to the NBBO to either route an incoming order to the trading venue that displays orders at the NBBO or to offer a new, significantly improved NBBO on their trading system. Merely refraining from trading is no longer an option to avoid trading at the NBBO.[1028] An order can only be executed on a trading system if that trading system had been displaying the NBBO before the order arrived. Moreover, the SEC allows for exceptions for specific orders, such as block orders, to mitigate adverse effects caused by market impact costs.[1029]

1025 See above Part I § 4.C.
1026 See above Part II § 5.G.II.
1027 See above Part II § 5.G.II.
1028 SEC, 'Concept Release on Equity Market Structure' (n 6) 75 FR 3613; SEC, 'National Securities Exchanges and FINRA: Assessment of the Plan to Implement a Tick Size Pilot Program' (3 July 2018, revised 2 August 2018) 6–7.
1029 SEC, 'Order Directing the Exchanges and the Financial Industry Regulatory Authority to Submit a Tick Size Pilot Plan' (n 1023) 79 FR 36845-6; Mahoney and Rauterberg (n 118) 261–2; Salger (n 627) 149–50; Shorter and Miller, 'Dark Pools in Equity Trading' (n 149) 10; Daniel G Weaver, 'The Trade-At Rule, Internalization, and Market Quality' (17 April 2014) 28;

III. Trade-At Rule in Canada and Australia

The SEC's proposal of a trade-at rule as a device to limit dark trading in securities markets was inspired by regulatory measures in Canada and Australia, where similar versions of a trade-at rule were implemented in 2012 and 2013 respectively.[1030] In Canada, the trade-at rule reduced dark trading from 8.5 % to 5.3 %, while Australia saw a decline in dark trading from 15.2 % to 9.2 %.[1031] In both Canada and Australia, the amount of dark trading in the respective securities market had been relatively moderate before the trade-at rule was implemented compared to the United States, and was lowered even further after the introduction of the trade-at rule.[1032]

Although the trade-at rule achieved the sought-after reduction of dark trading, a study by *Foley/Putniņš (2016)* suggests that the trade-at rules in Canada and Australia did not improve but rather deteriorated market quality.[1033] The study suggests that this deterioration is caused by a shift away from beneficial two-sided dark trading towards more detrimental one-sided dark trading. While one-sided dark trading occurs at a uniform price point, i.e., the midpoint of the bid-ask-spread, two-sided dark trading allows for dark orders to reside at any price point that the trader launching the order prefers best. Thus, two-sided dark trading can offer liquidity off-side the midpoint of the bid-ask-spread. Two-sided dark trading is hence beneficial to market quality measures by supporting market liquidity, market depth, and market breadth; whereas the effects of one-sided dark trading tend to be detrimental.[1034] The *Foley/Putniņš (2016)* study considers one-sided dark trading matched at the midpoint price more detrimental, among other reasons, because it matches the liquidity of sellers and buyers almost instantaneously leaving only the overlapping buy- or sell-side liquidity in the dark pool.[1035] While most of the so-called 'balanced order flow' is likely to be uninformed, the overlap can either be a temporary overlap of uninformed liquidity or an overlap motivated by private information.[1036] For an overlap

1030 CFA Institute, 'Trade-At Rules in Australia and Canada: A Mixed Bag for Investors' (November 2014) 2.

1031 Foley and Putniņš (n 389) 462, 476; Shorter and Miller, 'Dark Pools in Equity Trading' (n 149) 11.

1032 Foley and Putniņš (n 389) 456.

1033 ibid 479.

1034 ibid 459–60.

1035 ibid 478–9.

1036 ibid 479.

motivated by private information, the one-sided dark pool is the inferior choice compared to an exchange because it often needs to wait for new uninformed liquidity to enter the dark pool. In the meantime, this overlap of an informed trader in a dark pool would easily be detected since the midpoint price is generally known by the market as the reference price of the exchange. If another trader were to probe the one-sided dark pool with a sell and a buy order at the midpoint price, they could infer the direction of the overlap by seeing which of the two orders receive execution.[1037]

Since one-sided dark pools are beneficial for uninformed traders because they allow fast execution at a superior price compared to a transaction with a market maker on an exchange by saving half the bid-ask-spread, uninformed traders prefer one-sided dark trading.[1038] Due to the position risk that informed traders face on one-sided dark pools, informed traders are more likely to route their orders to exchanges. In consequence, this segregation of order flow may force market makers on exchanges to widen their bid-ask-spread which renders the entire market less efficient.[1039]

IV. The Findings of Foley/Putniņš (2016)

Foley/Putniņš (2016) tested the impact of the trade-at rule in Canada and Australia under this theoretical framework: Before the trade-at rule was implemented in Canada and Australia, both one-sided and two-sided dark trading occurred in almost the same volume in both markets.[1040] The introduction of the trade-at rule tipped the scale in favor of one-sided dark trading rising from roughly 40 % to 99.8 % of all dark trading, whereas two-sided dark trading has effectively disappeared in the Canadian market.[1041]

By requiring a minimum price improvement over the NBBO, dark trading was possible at the midpoint of the NBBO almost exclusively as one-sided dark trading.[1042] As a consequence of the changed composition of dark trading, market quality suffered leading to the odd result that limiting dark trading by the trade-at rule has rendered both the Canadian and

1037 ibid 459–60.
1038 ibid 459–60.
1039 ibid 459–60.
1040 ibid 457–6.
1041 ibid 462–3. Foley and Putniņš found similar effects for the trade-at rule in Australia, see Foley and Putniņš (n 389) 477.
1042 CFA Institute (n 1030) 3–4; Foley and Putniņš (n 389) 471, 478.

Australian securities markets less liquid and less informationally efficient than before.[1043] The introduction of the trade-at rules had another adverse effect on a market quality metric: After the introduction of the trade-at rules, the quoted and effective[1044] spreads became wider in comparison to the spreads without the trade-at rule rendering the market less efficient and raising the trading costs for investors.[1045]

Furthermore, the trade-at rule did not lead to an increase of average order size on dark pools, which one might expect when the conditions for execution worsened for smaller orders. The trade-at rule did not have the effect that smaller dark orders were routed to exchanges for execution while dark block orders remained in the dark pools. In general, the trade-at rule merely showed a decrease in dark liquidity but no increase in lit liquidity.[1046] This should be a warning sign for the US market when adopting the trade-at rule.[1047]

V. Trade-At Rule in the United States

1. Tick Size Pilot Program

To find a response to a growing dark pool market, the SEC tested the trade-at rule in the Tick Size Pilot Program of October 2016 with regard to a limited number of securities.[1048] The Tick Size Pilot Program was conducted for two years, until October 2018, to assess the impact of wider minimum quoting and trading increments as well as the trade-at rule on common stock of small-capitalization companies. The pilot program comprised of three test groups and one control group of securities all having a market capitalization of USD 3 billion or less and a closing price of at

1043 Foley and Putniņš (n 389) 471, 478.
1044 CFA Institute (n 1030) 3 defines effective spreads as *'(...) as twice the difference between the actual execution price and the market quote at the time of order entry. The realized spread is based on twice the difference between the execution price and quote mid-point five minutes after the execution of the order.'*
1045 ibid 3–5; Foley and Putniņš (n 389) 465.
1046 CFA Institute (n 1030) 3, 5.
1047 Zyskind (n 605) 434–5.
1048 SEC, 'National Securities Exchanges and FINRA' (n 1028) 2; Mahoney and Rauterberg (n 118) 276; Zyskind (n 605) 423.

least USD 2.00.[1049] While Test Groups 1 and 2 were subjected to minimum quoting increments of different kinds, only Test Group 3 was subjected to both a minimum quoting increment of USD 0.05 and the trade-at rule requiring trading systems to either route an order to the trading system showing the NBBO or to provide for a price improvement to the NBBO for internal execution. The control group was subjected to no changes.[1050]

2. Assessment of the Tick Size Pilot Program

On 3 June 2018, the national securities exchanges and FINRA, in their capacity as SROs, submitted the joint 'Assessment of the Plan to Implement a Tick Size Pilot Program'-report summarizing the findings of this pilot program. With regard to the relevant Test Group 3 subject to the trade-at rule, the pilot showed that displayed liquidity at the NBBO rose significantly during the pilot's test period. In fact, the increase of displayed liquidity at the NBBO was most pronounced in Test Group 3 compared with Test Groups 1 and 2 as well as to the control group which was traced back to the trade-at rule.[1051]

On the other hand, the pilot also showed rather worrying results in Group 3 where the bid ask-spread of the quotes widened, and the displayed liquidity clustered at fewer price points. This was accompanied by a substantial decline in the use of dark liquidity in Group 3.[1052] The trade-at rule imposed substantial restrictions on liquidity providers to execute transactions in the non-displayed off-exchange realm away from the NBBO; Test Group 3 even experienced a decline in market makers per security during the pilot.[1053] While on its face this fulfills the purpose of limiting dark trading and supporting the displayed NBBO, the report's assessment echoes the findings of *Foley/Putniņš (2016)* in their assessment of the Canadian and Australian securities markets. Even though the report did not differentiate between one-sided and two-sided dark trading as *Foley/Putniņš (2016)*, it noted that midpoint dark trading increased, whereas, dark trading on

1049 SEC, 'National Securities Exchanges and FINRA' (n 1028) 6–7; Mahoney and Rauterberg (n 118) 277.

1050 SEC, 'National Securities Exchanges and FINRA' (n 1028) 6–7.

1051 ibid 6–7.

1052 ibid 10ff, 38, 41–2; Committee on Capital Markets Regulation, 'Enhancing U.S. Equity Market Structure for Retail Investors' (n 650) 7.

1053 SEC, 'National Securities Exchanges and FINRA' (n 1028) 38f, 42.

prices off-side the midpoint was made significantly more difficult by the trade-at rule.[1054] Thus, it is likely that the US version of the trade-at rule had similar effects to the Canadian and Australian trade-at rule, i.e., restricting beneficial two-sided dark trading severely while having only mild effects on harmful one-sided dark trading, which in total shows an overall limitation of dark trading coupled with the odd effect of deteriorating market quality when spreads are widening. Given that the trade-at rule had this effect, it would contradict the goal of the National Market System *'to assure economically efficient execution of securities transactions.'*[1055] Nevertheless, this *prima facie* analogy calls for empirical analysis by economists using the theoretical framework of *Foley/Putniņš (2016)*.

3. The Trade-At Rule in the NMS

Besides the considerations of market quality, the trade-at rule and its effects also contradict Section 11A Exchange Act's other goal of creating a National Market System. Even though the goals are enumerated in juxtaposition, the National Market System aims for competition among marketplaces which is undermined if a rule, like the trade-at rule, directs order flow to displayed exchanges and draws order flow away from ATS and broker-dealer internalization systems.[1056] Although the goal of transparency is strengthened, transparency, can only mitigate the effects of the resulting market fragmentation by consolidation of information from multiple marketplaces. Sacrificing competition, especially competition by ATS and broker-dealers with incumbent exchanges, for increased transparency levels contradicts this concept.[1057]

The trade-at rule in this regard bears some resemblance to the concentration rules fortifying the de facto monopolies of national exchanges in Europe preceding MiFID I.[1058] Such a rule would be in stark contrast to

---

1054 ibid 42.

1055 Section 11A(C)(i) Exchange Act of 1934.

1056 Zyskind (n 605) 413. See also Dave Michaels, 'U.S. Exchanges Get Test to Curb Dark Trading in SEC Program' (Bloomberg 25 June 2014); Bradley Hope, 'NYSE, Nasdaq Join to Push for Trading Rule' *The Wall Street Journal* (10 March 2014).

1057 Barr, Jackson and Tahyar (n 596) 539; Macey and O'Hara, 'Regulating Exchanges and Alternative Trading Systems' (n 139) 28, 30ff.

1058 Moloney, *EU Securities and Financial Markets Regulation* (n 4) 425–6; under German law see former version of Section 22 German Exchange Act (BörsenG) in the version before 1 November 2007.

the market design of US securities markets, which builds on cost-reducing forces of competition among trading venues.[1059] However, redirecting order flow away from dark pools and broker-dealer internalizers to incumbent exchanges would in theory consolidate order flow on one or only few trading venues. Having order flow concentrated would theoretically facilitate the price formation process since fragmentation is less of an obstacle. Consequently, this would render the market more efficient[1060] but the efficiency gains by concentrated order flow may be countered by losses of wider spreads and rising transaction costs due to less competitive pressure.[1061]

As appealing as this theoretical thought may be, the findings of *Foley/Putniņš (2016)* and of the exchanges and FINRA assessing the US Tick Size Pilot Program have shown that decreasing amounts of dark trading do not necessarily have to translate into corresponding increases in lit trading; even where lit trading increases, the increased costs caused by less two-sided dark trading can absorb all gains of increased lit trading.[1062] Despite its initial appeal, the SEC has not adopted the trade-at rule subsequent to the pilot program, and it is well advised to refrain from doing so in the future.[1063]

K. SEC Proposals in 2022

In December 2022, the SEC made four proposals that would significantly impact the US market structure if they came into law.[1064] All four amendments would have the potential to limit dark trading in a welcome manner.

1059 Sections 11A, 17A Exchange Act (15 U.S.C. §§ 78k-1, 78q-1); SEC, 'Memorandum to SEC Market Structure Advisory Committee' (n 754) 5–6; SEC, 'Regulation NMS' (n 340) 70 FR 37496, 37498–9: '*(…) Vigorous competition among markets promotes more efficient and innovative trading services, while integrated competition among orders promotes more efficient pricing of individual stocks for all types of orders, large and small. Together, they produce markets that offer the greatest benefits for investors and listed companies. (…)*'.

1060 Zyskind (n 605) 426ff, 435ff.

1061 Committee on Capital Markets Regulation, 'Enhancing U.S. Equity Market Structure for Retail Investors' (n 650) 7.

1062 Foley and Putniņš (n 389) 470–1.

1063 In favor of a trade-at rule: Zyskind (n 605) 435ff.

1064 SEC, 'SEC Proposals: Market Structure' (14 December 2022).

I. SEC Regulation Best Execution

The first proposal is to implement a best execution rule anchored in federal law in the proposed Regulation Best Execution.[1065] While broker-dealers are already bound by best execution requirements, those requirements are founded in self-regulatory rules such as the FINRA rules.[1066] Now, the SEC considers it necessary to promulgate a federal rule under proposed Regulation Best Execution to ensure better outcomes for customers by requiring more robust policies and procedures from broker-dealers to avoid conflicts of interest playing out for the detriment of the customer.[1067] The new rule would require broker-dealers who handle customer orders to review the execution quality at least quarterly as well as implement and maintain a review process of their best execution policies and procedures at least once a year which needs to be presented in a report.[1068] This new rule would be a fundamental shift further away from self-regulation towards more governmental regulation as the new SEC rule requires broker-dealers to make sure that customers receive the most favorable price under the given the market conditions.[1069] Thereby, the SEC leans more towards investor protection rather than merely ensuring the functioning of the market.

II. SEC Rule to Enhance Competition for Order Execution

The second proposal aims at regulating broker-dealers that internalize large amounts of retail order flow, so-called 'wholesalers.'[1070] Those wholesales are captured by the new regulatory category of 'restricted competition trading centers'. Such restricted competition trading centers are trading centers that do not meet the proposed requirements for transparency, access, and volume of their counterpart, the 'open competition trading centers', i.e., lit markets. The restricted competition trading centers are prohibited from

1065 SEC, 'Fact Sheet Regulation Best Execution' (Washington, D.C., 14 December 2022) 1.
1066 ibid 1.
1067 ibid 1.
1068 ibid 1–2.
1069 ibid 2.
1070 SEC, 'Fact Sheet Proposed Rule to Enhance Order Competition' (Washington, D.C., 14 December 2022) 1.

internally executing an order for an NMS stock right away.[1071] Such restricted competition trading centers first need to expose the order to competition in a qualified auction operated by an open trading center.[1072] This means that internalization of large amounts of order flow can no longer happen without sending it to an auction of a lit exchange or comparable trading system. Thus, directing most smaller retail client orders away from lit markets and thereby elevating the relative risk of adverse selection on lit markets through wholesalers, becomes much harder under the proposed rule. The reason for the SEC stepping in is that they found a 'competitive shortfall' in which the internalizers save on fees and adverse selection risk when internalizing customer order flow but only share a small amount of the profits with such customers.[1073]

III. SEC Proposed Tick Size Rule

The third proposal is a proposed amendment to Regulation NMS. Here, the SEC realized that the current minimum price increment of USD 0.01 for the bid-ask-spread for orders in NMS stock priced at or greater than USD 1 under Rule 612 Regulation NMS no longer reflects modern market forces.[1074] Many NMS stocks are constraint by this minimum quoting size which makes dark pools using a reference price that can also offer fractions of USD 0.01 as the current bid-ask-spread very attractive for traders in search of the best transaction price.[1075] Thus, to make lit markets more attractive, the SEC proposed a new tick size rule that has a tiered minimum price increment system reaching from USD 0.01 for stocks with a bid-ask-spread greater than USD 0.04 down to USD 0.001 for stocks with a bid-ask-spread at or below USD 0.008.[1076] This proposed rule change could make lit markets much more attractive as they have been in recent years compared to their dark pool competition.

1071 ibid 2.
1072 ibid 2.
1073 ibid 1.
1074 SEC, 'Fact Sheet Tick Size, Access Fees, and Transparency of Better Priced Orders' (Washington, D.C., 14 December 2022) 1.
1075 ibid 1.
1076 ibid 2.

IV. SEC Proposal on Disclosure of Order Execution Information

The fourth proposed rule concerns Rule 605 Regulation NMS. Comparable to the tick size rule, the SEC realized that the rule is no longer fit for the modern market environment.[1077] A particularly important change with regard to dark trading is the broadening of the scope of the post-trade transparency rule so it would also capture broker-dealers that carry 100,000 or more customer accounts, single dealer platforms, and entities that would operate proposed qualified auctions.[1078] Those entities, too, would be then required to publish standardized monthly quality reports.[1079] Furthermore, the scope with regard to the orders would be broadened because the new definition of 'covered orders' would also capture such orders submitted outside of regular trading hours and more bespoke order types like certain types of stop price-orders.[1080] This proposed rule would level the playing field between such trading systems currently operating under Rule 605 Regulation NMS, i.e., lit exchanges and lit ATS, and certain large broker-dealers, who currently offer some form of unregulated dark trading. Furthermore, it would prevent regulatory arbitrage to circumvent post-trade transparency by using order types currently not covered by Rule 605 Regulation NMS but equally interesting for the investing public to know about.[1081]

L. Conclusion and Criticism

The regulation of dark trading under US law rests on regulation of the trading systems, trade transparency, and access rights to trading systems. Since US securities law on secondary markets trading has long traditions dating back to the Exchange Act, it is unsurprising that the regulatory framework is, at times, rather patchwork instead of one coherent scheme. Nevertheless, the SEC, in its rule-making capacity, addressed the issues of dark trading and the rise of dark pools with two Regulations: Regulation ATS and Regulation NMS.

1077 SEC, 'Fact Sheet Disclosure of Order Execution Information' (Washington, D.C., 14 December 2022) 1.

1078 ibid 2.

1079 ibid 1–2.

1080 ibid 2.

1081 ibid 1.

Since the SEC, however, can only promulgate rules within the framework of the Exchange Act, it was and still is limited by the dualism of trading systems comprising of exchanges and broker-dealers. US securities law will therefore continue to have difficulties in covering all kinds of trading systems accurately until Congress decides to overhaul the Exchange Act. Accordingly, the introduction of the ATS-category was merely a balancing act between putting emerging trading systems in either the 'exchange-bucket' or leave them in the less regulated 'broker-dealer-bucket'.

While Regulation ATS complemented the new regulatory category with specific regulations to integrate ATS into the National Market System, the core of Regulation ATS is the 5 %-threshold which determines both the applicable regulatory regime – either the exchange or the broker-dealer regime – and the entailing trade transparency and access requirements. Guided and, at times, limited by the principles of a National Market System under Section 11A Exchange Act, the SEC had to opt for facilitative, competition-enhancing rules rather than more prescriptive, market-shaping rules when regulating the new ATS. Against this backdrop, a 5 %-threshold appears reasonable to protect new competition in a market dominated by quasi-monopolistic exchanges, like the NYSE in the 1990s.

However, since the 1990s, the NYSE has lost much of its market share and dominance to other exchanges as well as ATS. Leveling the playing field between exchanges and ATS would therefore be a welcome policy and has been proposed by the SEC which planned to reduce the 5 %-threshold to a 0.25 %-threshold. Even though this proposal did not make it into law, it would have been preferable to abandon a threshold-exemption all together.

Any threshold-exemption, be it 5 % or 0.25 %, opens a loophole for rather unregulated dark trading because it incentivizes trading venue operators to remain slightly below the threshold. This renders the reasonable above-the-threshold regulatory regime inapplicable for most ATS. For ATS below the threshold, no regulator or other institution can oversee whether orders in those dark pools actually need exemptions from pre-trade transparency, for instance because they qualify as a block order. Such loopholes allow for vast amounts of liquidity to bypass pre-trade transparency rendering the price formation process less informed. This is especially problematic when also post-trade transparency of ATS is less granular due to data aggregation in the reporting process compared to the post-trade information of exchanges. Aggregated information allows disguising price-relevant information which leaves price formation even less informed.

While it is already problematic to allow for one ATS to accrue slightly below 5 % turnover without providing pre-trade transparency, the fact that one operator can operate multiple ATS slightly below 5 % defeats any limiting purpose of this rule, practically allowing for unlimited dark trading and circumvention of all rules applicable for ATS above 5 %. Abandoning the threshold system would, very likely, not cause a steep increase in market impact costs due to an overabundance of pre-trade transparency since Rules 602 and 604 Regulation NMS allow for exemptions from pre-trade transparency in specific cases, among which is the very important exemption for block orders. Under these exemptions, the cases in which dark trading would be allowed can be regulated more precisely than under a broad 5 %-threshold.

Furthermore, regulating the operation of an ATS within the broker-dealer-regime introduces conflict of interest issues into the marketplace. When operating an ATS, broker-dealers generally execute matching client orders among each other, like exchanges, but also execute client orders against their proprietary capital which makes them an interested party in the transaction forfeiting their neutrality.

Additionally, the lack of neutrality with ATS is problematic with the provision of private data feeds which allow HFTs to exploit information leakages and engage in electronic front running strategies. The fact that the public SIPs operate at slow speed and that Regulation NMS only requires the simultaneous transmission but not simultaneous reception of the raw data of trading venues has enabled HFTs and other traders to produce their own price information system by purchasing private data feeds from trading venues. The faster transmission time of private data feeds has allowed HFTs to receive the information that was sent away by trading venues simultaneously, and shortly before the SIPs received and displayed it to the public. This provided HFTs with an information advantage worth paying considerable sums for, which, eventually, had a major impact on the interests of trading venues who discovered a lucrative source of income in selling trading information of their clients.

A similar problem occurs when HFTs function as liquidity providers for dark trading venues. In this constellation, dark pools often feed HFTs with information about order flow in the dark pool by means of indications of interest. This leads to an uneven playing field because HFTs have superior information about the liquidity in dark pools and put the trading venue operator in a conflict of interests because it earns fees when HFTs trade in the venue, but it should also preserve the interests of its other clients unaware of the IOI. It was therefore a reasonable proposal by the SEC to include IOIs into the trade transparency regime. However, this proposal did not make it into law either.

Consequently, US securities laws allow for dark trading in a wide variety of situations and shows only limited regulatory instruments that actually regulate dark trading. While the proposals by the SEC are generally positive, currently many of them have still not made it into law. However, the most recent proposals by the SEC in December 2022 may swing the pendulum back in favor of lit markets again since the new proposals would make lit markets much more attractive compared to dark pools as they currently are.

§ 6. Regulation of Dark Trading under European and German Law

A. The Rise of Dark Trading and Regulatory Efforts

I. The Rise of Dark Trading

In the European Union, dark trading began its rise soon after the first alternative trading systems appeared in the United States.[1082] Fully implemented in 2007, the paradigm-shifting Markets in Financial Instruments Directive of 2004 (MiFID I)[1083] played an important role in the rise of dark trading in Europe. MiFID I was an important step towards a pan-European trading market in financial instruments outlining a comprehensive regime for trading systems and trade transparency on which the current regulatory framework of MiFID II[1084]/MiFIR[1085] builds.[1086]

1082 European Commission, 'Commission Staff Working Paper Impact Assessment EU Commission, Impact Assessment' (n 382) 5 describing dark trading as *'(...) institutional investors increasingly seek to escape pre-trade transparency and hide their trading intentions from the public. (...)'*. See also CESR, 'CESR Technical Advice to the European Commission in the Context of the MiFID Review - Equity Markets' (n 4) 6–7; IOSCO, 'Principles for Dark Liquidity' (n 12) 4, 10; Gomber and Pierron (n 4) 29; Kumpan and Schmidt (n 4) Foreword MiFIR para 5; Moloney, *EU Securities and Financial Markets Regulation* (n 4) 441, 481, Petrescu and Wedow (n 5) 5, 26.

1083 MiFID I: Directive 2004/39/EC of the European Parliament and of the Council of 21 April 2004 on markets in financial instruments amending Council Directives 85/611/EEC and 93/6/EEC and Directive 2000/12/EC of the European Parliament and of the Council and repealing Council Directive 93/22/EEC.

1084 MiFID II: Directive 2014/65/EU of the European Parliament and the of the Council of 15 May 2014 on markets in financial instruments and amending Directive 2002/92/EC and Directive 2011/61/EU.

1085 MiFIR: Regulation (EU) No 600/2014 of the European Parliament and of the Council of 15 May 2014 on markets in financial instruments and amending Regulation (EU) No 648/2012.

1086 Banks (n 5) 12; Danny Busch, 'MiFID II and MiFIR: Stricter Rules for the EU Financial Markets' (2017) 11 Law and Financial Markets Review 126ff; Peter Gomber and Frank Nassauer, 'Neuordnung der Finanzmärkte in Europa durch MiFID II/MiFIR' (2014) 26 ZBB 250ff; Hoops, 'Bedeutung des organisierten Handelssystems in der gegenwärtigen Marktinfrastruktur' (n 131) 14; Moloney, *EU Securities and Financial Markets Regulation* (n 4) 435ff.

For instance, the categorization of trading systems into regulated markets referring to exchanges, multilateral trading facilities referring to alternative off-exchange trading systems, and systematic internalizers referring to broker-dealer internalization systems was introduced under MiFID I and is still used under MiFID II notwithstanding certain amendments analyzed below. Furthermore, the fundamental principles of today's trade transparency regime under MiFIR are rooted in the transparency regime introduced under MiFID I, even though it has been significantly expanded.[1087]

As a Member State of the European Union, EU law is also the law of the land in Germany. For regulations, such as MiFIR, it is directly applicable law without any implementation act by parliament (Article 288(2) Treaty on the Functioning of the European Union (TFEU)).[1088] With regard to directives, such as MiFID I and II, an act of the German parliament is necessary to transpose EU law into German law (Article 288(3) TFEU).[1089] For this reason, when EU regulations are discussed, this simultaneously is the law of the land in Germany and requires no additional discussion of German law. Insofar, as EU directives are discussed, the transposition in German law will be discussed, on the one hand, as an analysis of the German law and, on the other hand, as a specimen for a regulatory framework in an EU Member State.

1087 Busch (n 1086) 126ff; Gomber and Nassauer (n 1086) 251; Moloney, *EU Securities and Financial Markets Regulation* (n 4) 461, 480.

1088 Matthias Ruffert in Christian Calliess and Matthias Ruffert (eds), *EUV/AEUV-Kommentar: Das Verfassungsrecht der Europäischen Union mit Europäischer Grundrechtecharta* (6th edn, CH Beck 2022) AEUV Art 288 para 17; Markus Kotzur in Rudolf Geiger, Daniel-Erasmus Khan and Markus Kotzur (eds), *EUV - AEUV Kommentar: Vertrag über die Europäische Union - Vertrag über die Arbeitsweise der Europäischen Union* (6th edn, CH Beck 2017) AEUV Art 288 para 6; Gomber and Nassauer (n 1086) 252; Matthias Lehmann in Matthias Lehmann and Christoph Kumpan (eds), *European Financial Services Law: Article-by-Article Commentary* (1st edn, Nomos; CH Beck; Hart Publishing 2019) Introduction to MiFID II and MiFIR para 2; Rüdiger Veil, '§ 3 Legislative Power for Regulating and Harmonising Capital Markets in Europe' in Rüdiger Veil (ed), *European Capital Markets Law* (3rd edn, Hart Publishing 2022) 47, § 3 para 15.

1089 Ruffert (n 1088) AEUV Art 288 para 24; Kotzur (n 1088) AEUV Art 288 para 10; Gomber and Nassauer (n 1086) 253; Veil, '§ 3 Legislative Power for Regulating and Harmonising Capital Markets in Europe' (n 1088) 48, § 3 para 19.

II. The Role of MiFID I

1. A Pan-European Market

MiFID I was characterized by its facilitative elements that aimed to reduce transaction costs through competition.[1090] By abolishing the 'concentration rules' that protected the (quasi) monopolies of national exchanges in many Member States, the regulatory agenda aimed for a 'market for markets' approach in which trading systems compete for order flow comparable to the situation under the National Market System pursuant to Section 11 Exchange Act under US law.[1091]

According to the MiFID I review report, MiFID I was very successful in fostering competition because multiple new trading systems entered the market since 2007.[1092] However, similar to the situation in the United States, competition between multiple trading systems in the European Union came at the expense of market fragmentation. Thus, traders in European markets faced comparable issues with regard to finding information on available liquidity as well as the need to access multiple trading systems to gather relevant information.[1093] Like US law, EU law tried to consolidate fragmented markets by providing a pan-European regime of extensive trade transparency for shares.[1094] The instruments of pre- and post-trade transparency were

1090 Lehmann (n 1088) Introduction to MiFID II and MiFIR para 7; Gomber and Jäger (n 241) 6; Moloney, *EU Securities and Financial Markets Regulation* (n 4) 461; Marcus Lutter, Walter Bayer and Jessica Schmidt, *Europäisches Unternehmens- und Kapitalmarktrecht: Grundlagen, Stand und Entwicklung; nebst Texten und Materialien* (6th edn, De Gruyter 2018) § 32 para 32.34.

1091 EG-Kommission (n 142) 548–9; Bošković, Cerruti and Noël (n 70) 14; Gomber and Pierron (n 4) 7, 9; Gomber and Nassauer (n 1086) 251–2; Hoops, 'Bedeutung des organisierten Handelssystems in der gegenwärtigen Marktinfrastruktur' (n 131) 14; Peter Jung and Elias Bischof, *Europäisches Finanzmarktrecht: Die Regulierung von Märkten, Unternehmen und Dienstleistungen durch die Europäische Union* (Nomos 2015) para 70; Moloney, *EU Securities and Financial Markets Regulation* (n 4) 435–6; Martin Weber, 'Die Entwicklung des Kapitalmarktrechts im Jahre 2007' [2007] NJW 3688, 3689–90.

1092 European Commission, 'Proposal for a Directive of the European Parliament and of the Council Parliament and of the Council on markets in financial instruments repealing Directive 2004/39/EC of the European Parliament and of the Council (Recast)' (COM(2011) 656 final, 2011/0298 (COD), Brussels, 20 October 2011) 1; Gomber and Nassauer (n 1086) 252.

1093 IOSCO, 'Principles for Dark Liquidity' (n 12) 20–1; Banks (n 5) 12ff; Colby and Sirri (n 605) 173, 186ff; Gomber and Pierron (n 4) 29, 43.

1094 Colby and Sirri (n 605) 176; Gomber and Nassauer (n 1086) 251.

complemented by the duty of best execution to route an order to the best counter-order.[1095]

2. The Need for a New Market Regulation: Dark Trading under MiFID I

While MiFID I was a significant step forward, both its trading system regime as well as its transparency regime were prone to regulatory arbitrage, not only inviting new lit trading venues into the 'market for markets' but also propelling the growth of dark trading services.[1096]

a) Uneven playing field among RMs and MTFs

Like Regulation ATS under US law, MiFID I recognized the rise of alternative trading systems that operated similarly to incumbent exchanges.[1097] For these alternative trading systems, MiFID I introduced the category of an MTF for trading systems hosting multilateral trading, i.e., trading with multiple sellers and buyers other than the system operator, comparable to US-ATSs, and the category of SI for trading systems offering bilateral trading, i.e., trading with the trading system operator for both selling and buying, comparable to US-broker-dealers.[1098]

Since MTFs directly competed with incumbent exchanges regulated as RMs, RMs expressed their concerns that MiFID I imposed less stringent regulations on MTFs than on RMs.[1099] RMs claimed that such differences

1095 Hoops, 'Bedeutung des organisierten Handelssystems in der gegenwärtigen Marktinfrastruktur' (n 131) 14. On the current best execution requirement see Article 27(1)(1)(1) MiFID II: Lutter, Bayer and Schmidt (n 1090) § 32 para 32.29.

1096 CESR, 'CESR Technical Advice to the European Commission in the Context of the MiFID Review - Equity Markets' (n 4) 6–7; IOSCO, 'Principles for Dark Liquidity' (n 12) 4, 10; Kumpan and Schmidt (n 4) Foreword MiFIR para 5; Gomber and Pierron (n 4) 29; Petrescu and Wedow (n 5) 5, 26; Seitz (n 132) 498; Vollmuth and Seifert (n 68) 372–3 para 859.

1097 Bošković, Cerruti and Noël (n 70) 8; Seitz (n 132) 498; Vollmuth and Seifert (n 68) 372–3 para 859.

1098 Seitz (n 132) 498; Vollmuth and Seifert (n 68) 372–3 para 859. See Bošković, Cerruti and Noël (n 70) 7ff who see EU-RMs and US-Exchanges as equivalent but not EU-SI and US-Broker-Dealer. They consider US-Broker-Dealer as a broader category, which is not disputed in this study, but, nevertheless, SI and Broker-Dealer are functionally comparable regulatory concepts for bilateral trading.

1099 CESR, 'CESR Technical Advice to the European Commission in the Context of the MiFID Review - Equity Markets' (n 4) 25.

provided MTFs with more regulatory leeway and cost advantages over their competitors which resulted in an uneven playing field.[1100] Whether there were advantages for MTFs biasing competition with RMs under MiFID I and whether MiFID II/MiFIR corrected those issues will be discussed below in conjunction with the regulation of RMs and MTFs under MiFID II.[1101]

Nevertheless, the new MTFs lured liquidity away from RMs and introduced competition into the financial market that was formerly characterized by (quasi-)monopolies for national exchanges in many Member States.[1102] Some of those new MTFs operated as dark pools.[1103]

b) Regulatory Gaps between the MTF and SI regime into OTC-Space

Unlike US law, MiFID I did not allow for trading systems that combined multilateral and bilateral trading practices in a single trading system, but rather aimed to separate multilateral from bilateral trading by requiring each to use different trading systems, i.e., separate market institutions.[1104] To achieve this, MiFID I provided the RM- and MTF-category for multilateral systems and the SI-category for regular bilateral trading; whereas irregular bilateral trading as well as bilateral trading above standard market size remained for the less regulated OTC-space.[1105]

This segregation was to ensure that the operators of multilateral trading systems did not trade against proprietary capital because they should balance supply and demand of traders on their platform without any bias in order to support price formation undistorted by trading system operator's proprietary trading interest. When trading bilaterally against their proprietary capital, an operator's neutrality would be compromised by become a

---

1100 ibid 25. Cf. Alexander, 'Market Structures and Market Abuse' (n 484) 388.

1101 See below Part II § 6.B.II.3.

1102 Gomber and Nassauer (n 1086) 252.

1103 Gomber and Pierron (n 4) 29, 34.

1104 ibid 33, 48; Moloney, *EU Securities and Financial Markets Regulation* (n 4) 447.

1105 Recital 6 MiFID I. See Definitions of RM under Article 4(1)(14) MiFID I, MTF under Article 4(1)(15) MiFID I and SI under Article 4(1)(7) MiFID I. For details on trading system regime under MiFID I, see: Hoops, *Verborgene Liquidität im Marktordnungsrecht der MiFID* (n 6) 25ff. For unregulated dark trading in the OTC-space under MiFID I, see: CESR, 'CESR Technical Advice to the European Commission in the Context of the MiFID Review - Equity Markets' (n 494) 34–7; Hoops, *Verborgene Liquidität im Marktordnungsrecht der MiFID* (n 6) 37–8.

party who is interested in the outcome of the trade. This would introduce the risk of moral hazard into multilateral markets and ultimately elevate the traders' risk of suffering adverse selection when trading on a venue with an operator interested in the outcome of the transactions.[1106] While bilateral SI-trading was considered meritorious for rather illiquid markets where the fact of having an interested operator weighed less significantly than having no price formation in the first place, in liquid markets, on the other hand, the price formation should not be compromised by interested operators.[1107]

However, the scopes of the definitions of MTF and SI were not crafted well enough to prevent operators from eluding the regulatory perimeter and setting up shop in the unregulated OTC-space combining multilateral and bilateral trading in a single trading system.[1108] The most prominent example that kindled much of the MiFID II/MiFIR reform with respect to trading infrastructure and transparency were BCNs which were trading systems that did combine multilateral and bilateral trading to avoid the MTF-regulation and gamed the SI-definition in a manner that it qualified as unregulated OTC-trading. This way, BCNs which were primarily run by investment banks, similar to US-ATSs, could operate without providing any pre-trade and post-trade transparency while commanding a significant amount of market share of approximately 40 % of the trading volume under MiFID I.[1109] This drainage of liquidity in the OTC-space was one of the reasons why the European Union tightened the regulatory regime in the MiFID revision process.[1110] It shall be examined whether the new trading infrastructure regulation under MiFID II/MiFIR provides countermeasures

1106 Cf. Moloney, *EU Securities and Financial Markets Regulation* (n 4) 427.

1107 Cf. ibid 427–8.

1108 CESR, 'CESR Technical Advice to the European Commission in the Context of the MiFID Review - Equity Markets' (n 494) 34ff; Hoops, *Verborgene Liquidität im Marktordnungsrecht der MiFID* (n 6) 37–8.

1109 CESR, 'CESR Technical Advice to the European Commission in the Context of the MiFID Review - Equity Markets' (n 494) 34ff; Gomber and Nassauer (n 1086) 252; Gomber and Pierron (n 4) 33, 48; Hoops, *Verborgene Liquidität im Marktordnungsrecht der MiFID* (n 6) 37–8; Moloney, *EU Securities and Financial Markets Regulation* (n 4) 447–8.

1110 Hoops, 'Bedeutung des organisierten Handelssystems in der gegenwärtigen Marktinfrastruktur' (n 131) 14; Salger (n 627) 186; Christopher Bernard, 'MiFID II: The new market structure paradigm' (February 2014) 2. Cf. European Commission, 'Commission Staff Working Paper Impact Assessment EU Commission, Impact Assessment' (n 382) 4–5; Comerton-Forde (n 16) 2–3; Gomber and Gvozdevskiy (n 43) paras 14.02, 14.19, 14.36.

to avoid this drainage of liquidity into unregulated dark pools in the OTC-space.[1111]

The regulatory arbitrage strategy of BCNs is comparable to the one used by market actors (dark ATS) in the United States. While under US law, trading system operators needed to stay below a certain threshold to be exempt from transparency requirements, in the European Union, market actors needed to exceed a certain threshold to qualify for a transaction 'above standard market size' to be exempted from trade transparency.[1112]

c) Loophole in the Transparency Regime

Although the transparency regime introduced under MiFID I enhanced pre- and post-trade transparency for orders and transactions in shares on RMs, MTFs and SIs, significant amounts of dark trading could still occur under this regime as well. One reason for this was that orders in shares could be directed with relative ease to the OTC-space where pre-trade transparency rules did not apply.[1113] But even for trading within RMs, MTFs and SIs, the transparency regime was blind to orders and transactions in financial instruments other than shares and, under German law, also depositary receipts,[1114] leaving debt instruments, such as bonds and derivatives, within the realm of dark liquidity. This could also be used to game the transparency regime for shares as well. Where there was an instrument other than a share that could mimic the trading in shares, it could be used to achieve the same economic purpose without showing pre- and post-trade transparency.[1115]

Furthermore, the waiver regime from trade transparency under MiFID I – while institutionalizing dark trading and making it contingent on prior

---

1111 See below Part II § 6.B.III.1.a.iii.

1112 Bošković, Cerruti and Noël (n 70) 8–9.

1113 Gomber and Nassauer (n 1086) 252; Gomber and Pierron (n 4) 33, 48.

1114 While Articles 29(1) and 44(1) MiFID I were limited to shares only, the former Section 30 German Exchange Act (BörsG) and former Section 31g the German Securities Trading Act (WpHG) broadened the scope of pre-trade transparency to encompass both shares and depositary receipts. See Busch (n 1086) 130; Christian Duve and Moritz Keller, 'MiFID: Die neue Welt des Wertpapiergeschäfts' [2006] BB 2537, 2538–9; Holzborn and Israel (n 317) 795–6; Hoops, *Verborgene Liquidität im Marktordnungsrecht der MiFID* (n 6) 114–5; Kumpan, 'Transparenz als Mittel der Kapitalmarktregulierung' (n 51) 798; Lenenbach (n 51) para 3.156.

1115 See Recital 12 MiFIR.

regulatory approval – did not limit dark trading. Especially under waivers with a broad scope of application – such as the reference price waiver (RP-waiver) and negotiated trade waiver (NGT-waiver) – also orders of retail size could be traded showing no trade transparency.[1116] The reference price and negotiated trade waivers were particularly controversial because they exempted not only particularly large orders, like the order management facility or large in scale waiver (LIS-waiver), but also entire trading systems. This created parallel dark markets operating independently from lit markets draining liquidity from them.[1117]

d) Discretion in the Application of MiFID I Rules by the Member States' NCAs

Regulatory arbitrage also occurred because of not fully aligned regulatory practice by the National Competent Authorities (NCA) in the Member States. For the application of the transparency regime, the European Union had to rely on the NCAs that interpreted the qualitatively defined waivers with their broad scopes as they saw appropriate given the facilitative rationale of MiFID I to foster competition. Since each NCA is most familiar with the needs and usages of its financial market, different interpretations of the waiver rules have emerged.[1118] Most pronounced was the conflict between the United Kingdom, which was more permissive in granting particularly the reference price waiver than, and France, which followed a more restrictive agenda to boost market transparency.[1119] This deviation in the application of the waivers resulted in the acceptance of various reference prices like the volume-weighted average as a reference price or the so-called European Best Bid and Offer (EBBO), which was derived from multiple exchange prices.[1120] In the MiFID review process, the different opinions led to major discussions about maintaining or abolishing the ref-

1116 CESR, 'CESR Technical Advice to the European Commission in the Context of the MiFID Review - Equity Markets' (n 4) 10–11.
1117 Moloney, *EU Securities and Financial Markets Regulation* (n 4) 481.
1118 Cf. ESMA, 'Waivers from Pre-trade Transparency: CESR Positions and ESMA Opinions' (ESMA/2011/241h, 20 June 2016) 6ff.
1119 Moloney, *EU Securities and Financial Markets Regulation* (n 4) 456, 481.
1120 Cf. ESMA, 'Waivers from Pre-trade Transparency' (n 1118) 6ff.

erence price waiver altogether; a problem primarily caused by non-aligned, decentralized decision-making of national regulatory authorities.[1121]

3. Comparison to US law

Under both US law and MiFID I, dark trading was partly a phenomenon of unintended loopholes and regulatory gaps: While in the EU, the combination of MTF- and SI-elements allowed a bulk of trading systems to fall in neither category and operate in the OTC-space, US law created loopholes for orders on ATSs that are either below the 5%-threshold or that are not communicated internally. These exceptions were used much more vigorously as intended.[1122]

US law and EU law under MiFID I saw large amounts of dark trading for similar reasons, but such surge of dark trading was due to different weak spots in the respective systems. The US system can capture organized trading better within its trading system regime but has very broad exemptions with regard to pre-trade transparency remedied by a strong post-trade transparency obligation. MiFID I failed to capture all organized trading but managed to tie a solid transparency regime to the organized trading it was able to gather within the regulatory perimeter. The transparency regime also proved more flexible due to waivers and deferrals from pre- and post-trade transparency for clearly defined cases.

III. The Role of MiFID II/MiFIR

In the MiFID review process, the European Commission was generally content with the effects that MiFID I had on increased competition and reductions in transaction costs.[1123] The Commission attested that MiFID I was generally successful in creating *'(...) more competition, wider investor choice, a decrease on transaction costs, and deeper integration.'*[1124] Neverthe-

1121 Moloney, *EU Securities and Financial Markets Regulation* (n 4) 456, 481.

1122 See chapter on US law above, Part II § 5.E.I.3.b).

1123 European Commission, 'Proposal for a Directive of the European Parliament and of the Council Parliament and of the Council on markets in financial instruments repealing Directive 2004/39/EC of the European Parliament and of the Council (Recast)' (n 1092) 1; Gomber and Nassauer (n 1086) 252.

1124 Moloney, *EU Securities and Financial Markets Regulation* (n 4) 445; cf. European Commission, 'Commission Staff Working Paper Impact Assessment EU Commisless, in 2014, the Commission launched a successor Markets in Financial Instruments Directive II (MiFID II), this time accompanied by a Markets in Financial Instruments Regulation (MiFIR) which jointly replaced MiFID I on 3 January 2018 when MiFID II/MiFIR went into force.[1125]

The new tandem MiFID II/MiFIR was not only a reaction to the shortcomings of its predecessor, especially the rise of dark trading in the form of BCNs,[1126] but its consultations by the EU Commission also fell in the aftermath of the Global Financial Crisis of 2008-09. In response to the shifted views towards past regulatory approaches, the European Commission turned its back on the facilitative character of MiFID I, and rather looked for a more prescriptive regulatory framework to regulate European secondary markets.[1127] While it did not want to return to centralized markets under 'concentration rules' as in the pre-MiFID era, the Commission was looking to shape the market in a certain direction rather than granting considerable leeway for competition.[1128] The result is a vast regulatory apparatus split between, in large part, a fully harmonizing directive and a directly applicable regulation leaving little to no room for gold-plating by the Member States, but rather supporting the new policy of a 'single rulebook'.[1129]

With MiFID II/MiFIR, the European Union narrowed the discretion of the NCAs by switching from a regulatory approach that merely lays out the principles (principle-based regulation) to a regulation relying on a detailed

---

sion, Impact Assessment' (n 382) 5; European Commission, 'Proposal for a Regulation of the European Parliament and of the Council on markets in financial instruments and amending Regulation [EMIR] on OTC derivates, central counterparties and trade repositories' (COM(2011) 652 final, 2011/0296 (COD), Brussels, 20 October 2011) 3.

1125 Busch (n 1086) 126; Gomber and Nassauer (n 1086) 250–1; Lehmann (n 1088) Introduction to MiFID II and MiFIR para 2.

1126 Recital 6 MiFIR.

1127 Recitals 1 and 10 MiFIR; European Commission, 'Proposal for a Regulation of the European Parliament and of the Council on markets in financial instruments and amending Regulation [EMIR] on OTC derivates, central counterparties and trade repositories' (n 1124) 3; Lutter, Bayer and Schmidt (n 1090) § 32 para 32.24; Moloney, *EU Securities and Financial Markets Regulation* (n 4) 460f.

1128 Moloney, *EU Securities and Financial Markets Regulation* (n 4) 434, 461ff; Moloney, 'EU Financial Governance and Transparency Regulation' (n 3) paras 12.06, 12.16.

1129 Lehmann (n 1088) Introduction to MiFID II and MiFIR para 2.

set of rules (rule-based regulation).[1130] To influence the interpretation of MiFID II/MiFIR, ESMA assumed a new coordinating role, especially with regard to questions of trade transparency and dark trading.[1131]

Moreover, under MiFID II/MiFIR, no instrument can be unregulated including non-equity instruments. Hence, the regulatory perimeter was widened to also capture non-equity instruments after the G20 decided to bring organized derivatives trading from the OTC-space to trading venues to enhance transparency.[1132] With the introduction of the new category of a trading venue, the organized trading facility (OTF), and clearer delineation between MTF, SI and the OTC-space, MiFID II/MiFIR aims to limit dark trading and provide formerly unregulated dark BCNs with the choice of registering either as an MTF, OTF, or SI.[1133]

Although MiFID II/MiFIR has had some time to prove itself in practice, it nevertheless is a new generation of law for regulating secondary markets. Where appropriate in the analysis below, MiFID II/MiFIR provisions will be contrasted with MiFID I and the US regulations that rather represent a more facilitative regulatory paradigm.

On 8 October 2020, the European Parliament started the review process of MiFID II/MiFIR[1134] and on 25 November 2021, the EU Commission

---

1130 CESR, 'CESR Technical Advice to the European Commission in the Context of the MiFID Review - Equity Markets' (n 494) 9; Moloney, *EU Securities and Financial Markets Regulation* (n 4) 459–60.

1131 Moloney, *EU Securities and Financial Markets Regulation* (n 4) 483–4.

1132 Recitals 1, 12, 14 MiFIR; see also European Commission, 'Commission Staff Working Paper Impact Assessment EU Commission, Impact Assessment' (n 382) 12–3; European Commission, 'Proposal for a Regulation of the European Parliament and of the Council on markets in financial instruments and amending Regulation [EMIR] on OTC derivates, central counterparties and trade repositories' (n 1124) 11; CESR, 'CESR Response to Questions 1-14 and 19 of the European Commission Request for Additional Information in Relation to the Review of MiFID' (CESR/10-1254, October 2010) 9, 28ff; CESR, 'CESR Technical Advice to the European Commission in the Context of the MiFID Review: Non-Equity Markets Transparency' (CESR/10-799, 29 July 2010) 3ff; Rüdiger Veil and Marcus Lerch, 'Auf dem Weg zu einem Europäischen Finanzmarktrecht: die Vorschläge der Kommission zur Neuregelung der Märkte für Finanzinstrumente - Teil I -' [2012] WM 1557f, 1565.

1133 Recital 6 MiFIR; European Commission, 'Commission Staff Working Paper Impact Assessment EU Commission, Impact Assessment' (n 382) 122; Gomber and Nassauer (n 1086) 258.

1134 Issam Hallak, 'Amendments to MiFID II and MiFIR: The EU's Markets in Financial Instruments' (Briefing - EU Legislation in Progress, European Parliamentary Research Service, April 2023) 3.

announced a legislative proposal to 'ensure better data access and revamped investment rules.'[1135] This review process led to the proposal of a refit of MiFID II/MiFIR amending the 2014 MiFID II/MiFIR rather than promulgation a new, fully-overhauled version in a sense of a MiFID III/MiFIR II.[1136] The MiFID II/MiFIR refit instead aims to rectify some issues that surfaced under the 2014-MiFID II/MiFIR. While some parts of the MiFID II/MiFIR refit have already come into law, others are still in the making. Since the refit has not yet been fully implemented, the following analysis will take the 2014-MiFID II/MiFIR as the basis for its discussion but show the proposed or even agreed upon (and implemented) changes that already did or are most likely to come about under the MiFID II/MiFIR refit. In early March 2023, the trialogue between the European Parliament, the Commission and the Council began and, shortly after, the Committee on Economic and Monetary Affairs (ECON) adopted its report on the proposed refit of MiFIR for the first plenary reading.[1137]

B. Trading System Regime under MiFID II/MiFIR

The trading system regime under MiFID II/MiFIR can be found in the directive MiFID II outlining the trading landscape of the European financial markets. The directive needs to be transposed into national law (Article 288(3) TFEU) which can be found in the German Stock Exchange

1135 European Commission, *Press Release: Capital Markets Union: Commission proposes new measures to boost Europe's capital markets* (2021) para 4; Hallak (n 1134) 2.

1136 Hallak (n 1134) 2.

1137 ibid 1f, 9; Committee on Economic and Monetary Affairs, 'Report: on the proposal for a regulation of the European Parliament and of the Council amending Regulation (EU) No 600/2014 as regards enhancing market data transparency, removing obstacles to the emergence of a consolidated tape, optimising the trading obligations and prohibiting receiving payments for forwarding client orders (COM(2021)0727 - C9-0440/2021 - 2021/0385(COD))' (A9-0040/2023, European Parliament, Rapporteur: Danuta Maria Hübner, 2 March 2023) 5ff. See on the Trialogue in general: Doris König and Thomas Kleinlein, '§ 2 Gesetzgebung' in Reiner Schulze, André Janssen and Stefan Kadelbach (eds), *Europarecht: Handbuch für die deutsche Rechtspraxis* (4th edn, Nomos 2020) § 2 para 93; Fabian Walla, '§ 4 Rule-Making Process' in Rüdiger Veil (ed), *European Capital Markets Law* (3rd edn, Hart Publishing 2022) § 4 paras 9–13.

Act (‘*Börsengesetz*’ – BörsG) and in the German Securities Trading Act (‘*Wertpapierhandelsgesetz*’ – WpHG) under German law.[1138]

I. Ordering Principles for Categorizing Trading Systems

To categorize the realm of trading systems under EU financial markets law, MiFID II maintains the ordering principles first introduced under MiFID I spanning a continuum between multilateral and bilateral trading systems, on the one hand, and between non-discretionary and discretionary trading systems, on the other hand.[1139] However, MiFID II underlines and strengthens this distinction to avoid regulatory arbitrage, particularly in the form of BCNs.

1. Multilateral v. Bilateral Trading Systems

a) Multilateral Systems

MiFID II/MiFIR defines the ‘multilateral system’ as the anchor of its regulatory scheme. A multilateral system means any system or facility in which multiple third-party buying and selling trading interests in financial instruments are able to interact in the system.[1140] All multilateral systems can

1138 See Rüdiger Veil, ‘§ 5 Sources of Law and Principles of Interpretation’ in Rüdiger Veil (ed), *European Capital Markets Law* (3rd edn, Hart Publishing 2022) § 5 para 53.

1139 Cf. Guido Ferrarini and Paolo Saguato, ‘Regulating Financial Market Infrastructures’ in Niamh Moloney, Eilís Ferran and Jennifer Payne (eds), *The Oxford Handbook of Financial Regulation* (Oxford University Press 2015) 572; Guido Ferrarini and Paolo Saguato, ‘Reforming Securities and Derivatives Trading in the EU: from EMIR to MiFIR’ (2013) 13(2) Journal of Corporate Law Studies 319, 322–3; Ferrarini and Moloney (n 143) 565–6; Gomber and Nassauer (n 1086) 251; Moloney, *EU Securities and Financial Markets Regulation* (n 4) 427–8; Diego Valiante, ‘Setting an Institutional and Regulatory Framework for Trading Platforms: Is There a Case for a New Trading Venue Under MiFID?’ (2013) 21(1) Journal of Financial Regulation and Compliance 69, 71.

1140 Article 4(1)(19) MiFID II. See Section 2(21) WpHG for transposition into German law. Assmann (n 130) WpHG § 2 para 258; Kumpan (n 125) WpHG § 2 paras 138, 142.

only be operated in the form of a RM,[1141] MTF[1142] or the newly introduced OTF[1143].[1144]

Since the definition of multilateral trading marks the line between strictly regulated trading venues and more permissively regulated (bilateral) trading systems, the EU legislator saw the need to propose in 2021 to have the definition moved from Article 4(1)(19) MiFID II where it was initially placed under the MiFID II iteration of 2014 to Art 2(1)(11) MiFIR under the MiFID II/MiFIR refit proposal which has not yet come into law.[1145] The migration from the directive to the regulation aims to prevent Member States to apply different definitions due to deviating acts of transposition which would no longer be needed because the regulation is directly applicable in each Member State (Article 288(2) TFEU).[1146]

The common feature of such trading systems is that they are systems with a 'marketplace function' in which traders can interact and trade with each other.[1147] The marketplace function of multilateral systems also shows that the market operator does not interact with third party-trading interests on its system, but merely performs a neutral role as 'coordinator' of the order flow.[1148] To avoid conflicts of interest, investment firms and market op-

1141 Article 4(1)(21) MiFID II. See for exchange (*'Börse'*) Section 2(1) BörsG and for organized market (*'organisierter Markt'*) Section 2(11) WpHG for transposition into German law.

1142 Article 4(1)(22) MiFID II. See Section 2(8)(8) WpHG for transposition into German law.

1143 Article 4(1)(23) MiFID II. See Section 2(8)(9) WpHG for transposition into German law.

1144 Güllner (n 131) 941. Formerly, pursuant to Article 1(7)(1) MiFID II and Section 2(22) WpHG as its transposition under German law. Under the MiFID II/MiFIR refit the provision is moved to Article 1(7a) MiFIR which applies directly in the Member States with no transposition needed.

1145 Committee on Economic and Monetary Affairs, 'Report' (n 1137) 17.

1146 European Commission, 'Proposal for a Regulation of the European Parliament and of the Council amending Regulation (EU) No 600/2014 as regards enhancing market data transparency, removing obstacles to the emergence of a consolidated tape, optimising the trading obligations and prohibiting receiving payments for forwarding client orders' (COM(2021) 727 final, 2021/0385 (COD), Brussels, 25 November 2021) 14, 26.

1147 Cohn-Heeren (n 8) 28; Kumpan, *Die Regulierung außerbörslicher Wertpapierhandelssysteme im deutschen, europäischen und US-amerikanischen Recht* (n 8) 230ff, 270; Kumpan (n 125) WpHG § 2 para 142.

1148 Kumpan (n 125) WpHG § 2 para 138; Bialluch (n 130); Kumpan, *Die Regulierung außerbörslicher Wertpapierhandelssysteme im deutschen, europäischen und US-amerikanischen Recht* (n 8) 223ff, 270ff; Kumpan and Müller-Lankow (n 131) 1779;

erators operating a multilateral system cannot execute client orders against their proprietary capital.[1149] A limited exception applies for the OTF which may engage in matched principal trading.[1150]

By anchoring the regulatory system in this definition, MiFID II expresses its intention to subject all organized trading in financial instruments to regulation. Whenever a trading system brings together multiple trading interests in buying and selling of financial instruments, it can no longer operate in the OTC-space as a BCN or any other form of unregulated dark pool, but rather has to be regulated as an RM, MTF, or OTF instead.[1151]

b) Bilateral Systems

In contrast to multilateral systems are bilateral systems, which have not been expressly defined under MiFID II/MiFIR. Instead, bilateral systems are mentioned in Recital 7 MiFIR and are described as systems where an investment firm enters into every trade on own account, even as a riskless counterparty interposed between the buyer and seller.[1152] The only bilateral trading system defined in the provisions of MiFID II/MiFIR is the systematic internalizer according to Articles 1(7)(2), 4(1)(20) MiFID II.[1153] In bilateral trading, the trading system operator, i.e., the investment firm, becomes the counterparty to every seller and buyer on its system.[1154] Thus, the difference between multilateral and bilateral trading systems is deter-

Andreas Stefanski, *Eigenhandel für andere: Market-Making und Internalisierung im deutschen, europäischen und US-amerikanischen Recht* (Nomos 2009) 10.

1149 Cf. Articles 19(5), 47(2) MiFID II. Gomber and Nassauer (n 1086) 253; Kumpan and Müller-Lankow (n 131) 1784.

1150 Cf. Article 20(2) MiFID II. Matched principal trading allows for simultaneous matching of seller and buyer orders against the proprietary capital of the OTF operator. For further detail see below Part II § 6.B.II.4. Gomber and Nassauer (n 1086) 253.

1151 Recitals 6, 8 MiFIR; Güllner (n 131) 941.

1152 Assmann (n 130) WpHG § 2 para 112. Bialluch (n 130) 2030; Güllner (n 131) 942; Kumpan and Müller-Lankow (n 131) 1780; Holger Schelling, 'Die systematische Internalisierung in Nichteigenkapitalinstrumenten nach MiFID II und MiFIR' [2015] BKR 221, 222; Kümpel and Wittig (eds) (n 130) para 17.216.

1153 Güllner (n 131) 942.

1154 Kumpan (n 125) WpHG § 2 para 103; Bialluch (n 130) 2030; Kumpan and Müller-Lankow (n 131) 1780.

mined by the market operator's role in the system since it is assuming risk.[1155]

Bilateral trading systems have therefore no 'marketplace function' and cannot claim neutrality in coordinating the order flow of their clients. Since those systems trade against their proprietary capital, they are interested in the outcome of the transaction which may conflict with their clients' interest when trading with them.[1156] To distinguish the 'neutral' multilateral systems from the 'potentially conflicted' bilateral systems, MiFID II prohibits both characteristics from mingling in one system. Therefore, multilateral systems do not allow for proprietary trading, whereas bilateral systems do not allow for the matching of client orders with each other.[1157] However, there are two narrow exceptions to this rule: as mentioned above, the new category of OTF can perform matched principal trading. In this form of trading the operator steps between the buyer and the seller of a financial instrument if they wish to transact simultaneously. The OTF operator legally takes over the position as the contractual party for its traders but does not assume principal risk. An OTF-operator can only perform matched principal trading if the customer agreed to it.[1158] The second exception is that bilateral trading, for example with a systematic internalizer, does not qualify as multilateral trading merely because the SI-operator occasionally matches two client orders.[1159]

c) Characteristics of a Trading System

aa) Nothing but a 'Set of Rules'

So far, the focus was on the difference between multilateral and bilateral systems, however, MiFID II also assigns a certain meaning to the word 'system' itself. According to Recital 7(4) MiFIR, *'(...) [t]he term 'system'*

1155 Assmann (n 130) WpHG § 2 para 113; Kumpan (n 125) WpHG § 2 para 103; Güllner (n 131) 942; Seitz (n 132) 502.

1156 Güllner (n 131) 942; Kumpan and Müller-Lankow (n 131) 1784.

1157 Kumpan (n 125) WpHG § 2 paras 142ff; Güllner (n 131) 941; Kumpan and Müller-Lankow (n 131) 1779.

1158 Güllner (n 131) 944; Moloney, *EU Securities and Financial Markets Regulation* (n 4) 466–7.

1159 Recital 7(1) MiFIR; Kumpan, *Die Regulierung außerbörslicher Wertpapierhandelssysteme im deutschen, europäischen und US-amerikanischen Recht* (n 8) 286; Kumpan (n 56) WpHG § 2 para 103.

encompasses all those markets that are composed of a set of rules and a trading platform as well as those that only function on the basis of a set of rules.' It is therefore not necessary to operate a trading platform in order to qualify as a system. The required 'set of rules' need to govern aspects related to membership, admission of instruments to trading, trading between members, reporting and transparency obligations.[1160]

With the notion of a 'system', European law uses a technology neutral definition of a market which does not even rely on a physical presence as is common with electronic markets today. This neutrality also allows for the regulatory framework to be adaptable to new (technological) developments and avoids regulatory arbitrage as has been the issue with the exchange definition under US law in the *Delta* case.[1161]

bb) Trading Systems and Information Systems

While being adaptable to new forms of trading systems, the notion of a 'system' excludes mere information systems, also called 'bulletin boards' from the regulatory scope. Bulletin boards are information systems that display interests of traders in selling and buying a financial instrument but, in contrast to trading venues, traders cannot conclude their contracts through the bulletin board's infrastructure or under the bulletin board's rules.[1162]

Since mere information systems only help to initiate a transaction concluded outside of the rule of the system operator, those systems are a less significant risk to the functioning of financial markets and investor protection. The European legislator thus decided to exclude those information

1160 Recital 7 MiFIR; Kumpan (n 125) WpHG § 2 para 137. See also under the former MiFID I: Recital 6 MiFID I; Entwurf eines Gesetzes zur Umsetzung der Richtlinie über Märkte für Finanzinstrumente und der Durchführungsrichtlinie der Kommission (Finanzmarkt-Richtlinie-Umsetzungsgesetz) 12 January 2007, BT-Drucks. 16/4028 (Deutscher Bundestag) 56; BaFin, 'Merkblatt: Tatbestand des Betriebs eines multilateralen Handelssystems gemäß § 1 Abs. 1a Satz 2 Nr. 1b KWG' (n 134) para 1. a).

1161 See for the Delta-case above Part II § 5 D.III.1.b).bb).(i).

1162 Recital 7 MiFIR; Kumpan (n 125) WpHG § 2 para 103; Cohn-Heeren (n 8) 30; Güllner (n 131) 942; Kumpan, *Die Regulierung außerbörslicher Wertpapierhandelssysteme im deutschen, europäischen und US-amerikanischen Recht* (n 8) 19ff, 286.

systems from the notion of a '(trading) system' keeping them outside of the regulatory perimeter of MiFID II/MiFIR.[1163]

2. Non-Discretionary v. Discretionary Rules

The second organizing principle for trading systems is the dichotomy between non-discretionary and discretionary rules. Similar to the above-mentioned pair of opposites, MiFID II/MiFIR provides only guidance on 'non-discretionary' systems, so that 'discretionary' systems are negatively defined as any system not qualifying as 'non-discriminatory'.[1164]

As Recital 7(2) MiFIR points out,

> *'(...) [t]he term 'non-discretionary rules' means rules that leave the regulated market or the market operator or investment firm operating an MTF with no discretion as to how interests may interact. The definitions require that interests be brought together in such a way as to result in a contract which occurs where execution takes place under the system's rules or by means of the system's protocols or internal operating procedures.'*[1165]

This is reflected in the definitions of the regulated market and multilateral trading system according to Article 4(1)(21), (22) MiFID II. Consequently, the market operator or investment firm running a non-discretionary system has a certain discretion when promulgating its rules.[1166] However, in the ongoing trading process, the system operator enjoys no discretion on whether and how to match incoming orders. The system operator needs to obey its

1163 Recital 8(2) MiFIR; Kumpan (n 125) WpHG § 2 para 140; Güllner (n 131) 941–2; see also Kumpan, *Die Regulierung außerbörslicher Wertpapierhandelssysteme im deutschen, europäischen und US-amerikanischen Recht* (n 8) 19–20; Spindler, 'Elektronische Finanzmärkte und Internet-Börsen - Teil I: Grundlegende Risiken und Reform des nationalen Kapitalmarktrechts' (n 124) 1336; in result also: Spindler, 'Elektronische Finanzmärkte und Internet-Börsen - Teil II: Regulierungsvorhaben auf der europäischen Ebene' (n 131) 1369f.

1164 Humbel, *Die Regelung der Vor- und Nachhandelstransparenz in der Europäischen Union und der Schweiz* (n 50) 116.

1165 Recital 7(2) MiFIR. Cf. BaFin, 'Merkblatt: Tatbestand des Betriebs eines multilateralen Handelssystems gemäß § 1 Abs. 1a Satz 2 Nr. 1b KWG' (n 134) para 1. d); Kumpan (n 125) WpHG § 2 para 141.

1166 Humbel, *Die Regelung der Vor- und Nachhandelstransparenz in der Europäischen Union und der Schweiz* (n 50) 118; Valiante (n 1139) 71.

own rulebook.[1167] This restraint relieves the system operator from conflicts of interests when matching orders and ensure its neutrality.[1168]

The opposite of non-discretionary trading is discretionary trading in which the system operator can exercise discretion on whether and how an individual order is matched with another on a case-by-case basis.[1169]

It is therefore unsurprising that non-discretionary trading coincides with multilateral trading on RMs and MTFs. However, OTFs, while also generally falling in the category of multilateral trading, operate on the basis of discretionary rules. The discretionary character of OTFs is an important characteristic which differentiates this regulatory category from its peers, RMs and MTFs.[1170] With the exception of the OTF, discretionary trading is usually a hallmark of bilateral trading systems, such as systematic internalizers. In bilateral trading, the system operator trades against proprietary capital taking on principal risk, so it is unsurprising that the operator seeks to exercise discretion over whether and when to transact with a potential customer.[1171]

3. Ordering Principles in the further Discussion

The two dichotomies between multilateral versus bilateral trading and non-discretionary versus discretionary rules for trading are the underlying ordering principles of MiFID II/MiFIR. Those principles determine in which regulatory 'bucket' a trading system may fall and, thereby, with which rules the trading system must comply. Although the regulatory categories have to comply with a detailed catalogue of rules, the following section will briefly outline the trading systems with their key features under MiFID II/MiFIR. Thereafter, the trade transparency regime and access regime tied to each class of trading system will be discussed. This will illustrate the conditions

1167 Humbel, *Die Regelung der Vor- und Nachhandelstransparenz in der Europäischen Union und der Schweiz* (n 50) 118; Valiante (n 1139) 71.

1168 Recital 7(2) MiFIR; Humbel, *Die Regelung der Vor- und Nachhandelstransparenz in der Europäischen Union und der Schweiz* (n 50) 118; Valiante (n 1139) 71. On non-discretionary rules under MiFID I, see: Lenenbach (n 51) para 3.16–7, 3.19; Spindler and Kasten (n 134) 1754; Seiffert and Lembke (n 68) paras 2370, 2377.

1169 Recital 9(1) MiFIR; ESMA, 'Questions and Answers: On MiFID II and MiFIR Market Structures Topics' (ESMA70-872942901-38, 6 April 2021) 54, 5.2 Answer 20; Kumpan (n 125) WpHG § 2 para 150; Güllner (n 131) 943.

1170 Assmann (n 130) WpHG § 2 para 166; Kumpan (n 125) WpHG § 2 paras 141, 150; Güllner (n 131) 943.

1171 Cf. Kumpan (n 125) WpHG § 2 para 103; Güllner (n 131) 945.

under which dark trading may arise in the regulatory framework under European and German law. The assessment of whether dark trading is regulated well enough to avoid adverse effects while harnessing its advantages will focus on those key variables.

II. The Trading Venues under MiFID II

Following the structure of MiFID II/MiFIR, the analysis of the trading systems regime begins with multilateral systems. Under MiFID II, RMs, MTFs and OTFs qualify as 'multilateral systems.'[1172] According to Article 4(1)(24) MiFID II, the same three types of systems are summarized in the category of 'trading venues'[1173] which underlines their marketplace function once again. Moreover, the regulatory category of a 'trading venue' is used by the transparency regime under MiFIR to tie trade transparency obligations to trading venue operators.[1174]

From a regulator's perspective, the regulator needs someone to subject to trade transparency obligations. This person or institution is generally the trading system operator. Since the operator aggregates the order flow on its platform and is easier to monitor, this is the more efficient choice than demanding transparency from each individual trader. However, the experience with BCNs slipping through the regulatory cracks under MiFID I shows that it is important to provide a tailored trading system regime for the transparency regime to be effective.[1175] A regulatory scheme aiming for high levels of transparency requires a trading system regime that gathers all organized trading on platforms, in the first place, before the transparency regime can calibrate the light settings to a level comfortable for traders and the public alike. Before turning to the light settings, the different platforms and how they are furnished will be examined next.

1172 Lutter, Bayer and Schmidt (n 1090) § 32 para 32.35. Formerly pursuant to Article 4(1)(19) MiFID II and after the MiFID II/MiFIR refit pursuant to Article 2(1)(11) MiFIR.

1173 Jung and Bischof (n 1091) para 70.

1174 Cf. Articles 3ff MiFIR.

1175 Recitals 6, 11, 12, 14, MiFIR; Gomber and Nassauer (n 1086) 252; Gomber and Pierron (n 4) 33, 48.

1. Regulated Markets

a) EU Law

The first multilateral system is the regulated market. According to Article 4(1)(21) MiFID II,

> *'(...) 'regulated market' means a multilateral system operated and/or managed by a market operator, which brings together or facilitates the bringing together of multiple third-party buying and selling interests in financial instruments – in the system and in accordance with its non-discretionary rules – in a way that results in a contract, in respect of the financial instruments admitted to trading under its rules and/or systems, and which is authorised and functions regularly and in accordance with Title III of [Articles 44 ff MiFID II].'*[1176]

According to this definition, a regulated market is a non-discretionary, multilateral trading system operated and/or managed by a market operator.[1177] The aspect of 'multilateral trading' describes the market function of regulated markets bringing together the buying and selling interests of multiple third parties.[1178] To meet this requirement, the regulated market must have at least three active trading participants, otherwise the prong 'multiple' traders is not met.[1179] This also means that RMs are trading systems banned from bilateral trading against their proprietary capital and from matched principal trading.[1180] Being constituted as an uninterested party shall allow RMs to aggregate and consolidate the supply and demand in their market.[1181]

1176 Article 4(1)(21) MiFID II. See also Jung and Bischof (n 1091) para 70; Klöhn, '§ 6 Kapitalmarktrecht' (n 68) § 6 para 41; Lutter, Bayer and Schmidt (n 1090) § 32 para 32.36.

1177 Busch (n 1086) 127; Moloney, *EU Securities and Financial Markets Regulation* (n 4) 463. According to Article 4(1)(18) MiFID II *'(...) 'market operator' means a person or persons who manages and/or operates the business of a regulated market and may be the regulated market itself (...)'.*

1178 Kumpan (n 125) BörsG § 2 para 5; Kumpan, *Die Regulierung außerbörslicher Wertpapierhandelssysteme im deutschen, europäischen und US-amerikanischen Recht* (n 8) 272.

1179 Kumpan (n 125) BörsG § 2 para 9.

1180 Busch (n 1086) 127; Kumpan (n 125) BörsG § 2 para 5.

1181 Moloney, *EU Securities and Financial Markets Regulation* (n 4) 471.

However, being a strictly multilateral trading system also means that RMs cannot operate hybrid systems combining multilateral and bilateral aspects, like certain BCNs did. Nevertheless, RMs are not required to operate their own price formation process. Thus, as far as the transparency regime allows, RMs can host (regulated) dark liquidity.[1182]

RMs can either bring together multiple third-party interests in selling and buying of financial instruments or merely facilitate their bringing together. Due to this broad definition, the RM-regime not only catches systems that actively match buy and sell orders, but also those systems that merely display trading interests of their users leaving the initiation of the matching to the users, for example, via clicking on a counter-order in a display interface.[1183] This matching, either controlled by the market operator or the users themselves, must result in a contract.

For RMs, authorization with their national competent authority is a constitutive matter (Articles 4(1)(21), 44(1) MiFID II). In the matter *Nilaş*, the European Court of Justice decided that even an operating entity that merged with another operator already registered as regulated market must register for RM-status, because otherwise the strict authorization requirements could be circumvented.[1184] The authorization requirement, however, highlights the primary market function RMs play in the capital-raising process and the admission to trading of new financial instruments. Some issuers prefer to issue their financial instruments through the means of an RM to signal to investors that they passed the rigorous standards and, thus, benefit from lower transaction costs.[1185]

1182 Kumpan (n 125) BörsG § 2 para 4.

1183 ibid BörsG § 2 para 19; Markus Pfüller in Thomas Hoeren, Ulrich Sieber and Bernd Holznagel (eds), *Handbuch Multimedia-Recht: Rechtsfragen des elektronischen Geschäftsverkehrs* (date of issue: January 2018, CH Beck 2014) Chapter 13.7 para 152; Spindler, 'Elektronische Finanzmärkte und Internet-Börsen - Teil I: Grundlegende Risiken und Reform des nationalen Kapitalmarktrechts' (n 124) 1333f.

1184 *Nilaş and Others, ECLI:EU:C:2012:166* (2012) C-248/11 (CJEU) paras 48–9; Andreas von Bonin and Alexander Glos, 'Die neuere Rechtsprechung der europäischen Gerichte im Bereich des Bank- und Kapitalmarktrechts' [2013] WM 1201; Lutter, Bayer and Schmidt (n 1090) § 32 para 32.42.

1185 Moloney, *EU Securities and Financial Markets Regulation* (n 4) 169ff, 463.

b) Transposition into German Law

The German legislator transposed[1186] this definition of Article 4(1)(21) MiFID II into the definition of an *'exchange'* (*'Börse'*) under Section 2(1) BörsG and the definition of an 'organized market' (*'organisierter Markt'*) under Section 2(11) WpHG.[1187]

According to Section 4(1) BörsG, exchanges must register with the exchange supervisory agency (*'Börsenaufsichtbehörde'*), which is not a matter of federal but rather state administration (Articles 30, 83 of the German Constitution (*'Grundgesetz'* – GG)).[1188] For the largest securities exchange in Germany – the Frankfurt Stock Exchange – the exchange supervisory agency is the Ministry of Economy of Hesse.[1189]

2. Multilateral Trading Facilities

a) EU Law

The second category of trading venues under EU law is the multilateral trading facility which had already been adopted under MiFID I.[1190] The definition under Article 4(1)(22) MiFID II mirrors the definition under MiFID I setting out that

> *'(...) 'multilateral trading facility' or 'MTF' means a multilateral system, operated by an investment firm or a market operator, which brings together multiple third-party buying and selling interests in financial instruments*

1186 Klöhn (n 95) § 6 para 50.

1187 Klöhn, '§ 6 Kapitalmarktrecht' (n 68) § 6 paras 48f; Kumpan (n 125) BörsG § 2 para 1; Lenenbach (n 51) para 3.15ff.

1188 Wolfgang Groß, *Kapitalmarktrecht: Kommentar zum Börsengesetz, zur Börsenzulassungs-Verordnung, zum Wertpapierprospektgesetz und zur Prospektverordnung* (8th edn, CH Beck 2022) BörsG § 3 paras 3–7; Hoops, *Verborgene Liquidität im Marktordnungsrecht der MiFID* (n 6) 27; Klöhn, '§ 6 Kapitalmarktrecht' (n 68) § 6 para 48.

1189 Section 3(1) BörsG in conjunction with No. (*Ziffern*) 711, 733 of the resolution of the Hessian state government on the responsibilities of individual ministers pursuant to Art 104(2) of the Constitution of the State of Hesse dated 28 March 2014 (*des Beschlusses der hessischen Landesregierung über die Zuständigkeit der einzelnen Ministerinnen und Minister nach Art 104(2) der Verfassung des Landes Hessen vom 28. März 2014*); Hoops, *Verborgene Liquidität im Marktordnungsrecht der MiFID* (n 6) 27.

1190 Busch (n 1086) 126.

– in the system and in accordance with non-discretionary rules – in a way that results in a contract in accordance with Title II of (...) [MiFID II] (...).'[1191]

The definition of MTF resembles the definition of RMs discussed above and reflects the regulatory level playing field among functionally equivalent 'exchange platforms' and 'off-exchange platforms' competing with each other for which MiFID II was aiming.[1192]

As regulated markets, MTFs are non-discretionary, multilateral trading systems which are prohibited from conducting any discretionary bilateral trading within their system, either against their proprietary capital or matched principal trading.[1193] Like regulated markets, MTFs must have at least three active traders to ensure sufficient liquidity.[1194]

Despite the general familiarity, the definition of the MTF also differs from the definition of RMs to some extent. While it is sufficient for RMs to facilitate the bringing together of multiple third party buying and selling interests, the coordination function of MTFs needs to result in a contract in accordance with Title II of MiFID II.[1195] Although this represents a somewhat stricter threshold in theory, this requirement is generally met by trading systems since they offer execution within their system.

More significant is the difference between RMs and MTFs with regard to eligible system operators. The operation of an MTF qualifies as an investment service under Article 48(1)(2) and Section C(8) of Annex I MiFID II. When investment services are performed as regular occupation or business, as is the case with running an MTF, the operator qualifies as an investment firm. Investment firms must seek authorization from the national competent authority according to Article 5 MiFID II. Under Ger-

1191 Article 4(1)(22) MiFID II. See also Jung and Bischof (n 1091) para 70; Klöhn, '§ 6 Kapitalmarktrecht' (n 68) § 6 para 41.

1192 Assmann (n 130) WpHG § 2 paras 160ff; Kumpan (n 125) WpHG § 2 paras 136ff; Busch (n 1086) 126–7; Güllner (n 131) 938; Klöhn, '§ 6 Kapitalmarktrecht' (n 68) § 6 para 53; Kumpan, *Die Regulierung außerbörslicher Wertpapierhandelssysteme im deutschen, europäischen und US-amerikanischen Recht* (n 8) 190; Lenenbach (n 51) para 3.238.

1193 Article 19(5) MiFID II. See under German law: Section 74(5) WpHG; Kumpan (n 56) WpHG § 2 para 144.

1194 Article 18(7) MiFID II; Kumpan (n 125) WpHG § 2 para 145; Lutter, Bayer and Schmidt (n 1090) § 32 para 32.47.

1195 Humbel, *Die Regelung der Vor- und Nachhandelstransparenz in der Europäischen Union und der Schweiz* (n 50) 129; Lenenbach (n 51) para 3.238.

man law, the authorization requirement for investment firms operating an MTF can be found in Sections 32(1), 1(1a)(b) German Banking Act (*'Kreditwesengesetz'* – KWG) and in Sections 15(1), 2(2) no. 6 German Securities Institutions Act (*'Wertpapierinstitutsgesetz'* – WpIG) depending on the classification of the investment firm.[1196] The national competent authority for MTFs offering their trading services in Germany is the Federal Financial Supervisory Authority (*'Bundesanstalt für Finanzdienstleistungsaufsicht'* – BaFin).[1197]

The fact that investment firms can operate MTFs shows their origin as marketplaces run by market intermediaries such as investment banks.[1198] This is similar to the origin of ATS under US law.[1199] This difference demonstrates that an operating entity that complies with the requirements under Title II of MiFID II, i.e., Articles 5ff MiFIR, will receive authorization as an investment firm and can operate as many MTFs under this authorization as it sees fit.[1200] Market operators operating a RM, on the other hand, need to seek specific authorization for each RM they intend to operate. In contrast, investment firms and market operators that have obtained authorization in accordance with Article 5 MiFID II may operate several MTFs without the need for individual authorizations. Insofar, the supervision exercised through authorization for investment firms running multiple MTFs is a more general one, and therefore less granular than the supervision over market operators running a RM.[1201]

1196 For further detail see: Peggy Steffen in Urs B Lendermann, Heinrich Nemeczek and Ulrich G Schroeter (eds), *Wertpapierinstitutsgesetz: WpIG-Kommentar* (1st edn, CH Beck 2024) § 15 paras 29ff, 39ff.

1197 BaFin, 'Merkblatt: Tatbestand des Betriebs eines multilateralen Handelssystems gemäß § 1 Abs. 1a Satz 2 Nr. 1b KWG' (n 134) para 3; Lutter, Bayer and Schmidt (n 1090) § 32 para 32.10.

1198 Bošković, Cerruti and Noël (n 70) 8.

1199 See above Part II § 5.D.III.

1200 Humbel, *Die Regelung der Vor- und Nachhandelstransparenz in der Europäischen Union und der Schweiz* (n 50) 129. On the parallel situation under MiFID I: Kumpan, *Die Regulierung außerbörslicher Wertpapierhandelssysteme im deutschen, europäischen und US-amerikanischen Recht* (n 8) 191; Lenenbach (n 51) para 3.18.

1201 Humbel, *Die Regelung der Vor- und Nachhandelstransparenz in der Europäischen Union und der Schweiz* (n 50) 129; Kumpan, *Die Regulierung außerbörslicher Wertpapierhandelssysteme im deutschen, europäischen und US-amerikanischen Recht* (n 8) 191; Lenenbach (n 51) para 3.18; Moloney, *EU Securities and Financial Markets Regulation* (n 4) 469, 475.

This is often justified by the special listing power of RMs warranting more stringent oversight by the national competent authority.[1202] However, MTFs can also offer primary market trading but their service, while it may have standards similar to an (initial) public offering on an RM, does not possess a signaling power comparable to that of an RM.[1203] Since MTFs increasingly offer primary market services for small and medium enterprises (SME), Article 33 MiFID II introduces the subcategory of SME-growth market which is open to be used by MTF operators but is not obligatory.[1204]

b) Transposition into German Law

The German legislator transposed the requirements for MTFs under MiFID II into national under Sections 2(8) No. 8, 72 and 74 WpHG. Since there has been no deviation from EU law, no further discussion is required.[1205]

3. Differences between RMs and MTFs: An Uneven Playing Field?

In the MiFID I-review process, RMs reported to the Committee of European Securities Regulators (CESR) – the predecessor of ESMA – that they see an uneven playing field between RMs and MTFs.[1206] Due to lighter regulations, MTFs would gain a (cost) advantage and could therefore operate more competitively than RMs.[1207]

Under MiFID II/MiFIR, the regulation of RMs and MTFs may differ in some regards but, all in all, the regulatory regimes are closely aligned. While RMs can only be run by market operators, MTFs can be run by either an investment firm or a market operator.[1208] The conduct regime for market operators under Title III of MiFID II and for investment firms running an MTF under Title II is largely aligned with regards to secondary

1202 Moloney, *EU Securities and Financial Markets Regulation* (n 4) 463.
1203 ibid 463.
1204 Jung and Bischof (n 1091) para 70; Lutter, Bayer and Schmidt (n 1090) § 32 para 32.40; Moloney, *EU Securities and Financial Markets Regulation* (n 4) 463.
1205 Klöhn, '§ 6 Kapitalmarktrecht' (n 68) § 6 para 48.
1206 CESR, 'CESR Technical Advice to the European Commission in the Context of the MiFID Review - Equity Markets' (n 4) 25–6.
1207 ibid 25–6.
1208 Jung and Bischof (n 1091) para 70.

trading.[1209] The difference lies in the registration of RMs and MTFs. A market operator has to seek authorization for each RM on a case-by-case basis, whereas an investment firm can register once with the national competent authority and operate multiple MTFs.[1210]

This perceived disadvantage of market operators compared to investment firms is less severe for two reasons: First, RMs are much rarer than MTFs, and therefore the case-by-case authorization requirement is less of a burden to a market operator than it initially appears. It rather is justified by the central role RMs play in financial markets, both in the primary market listing financial instruments, and in the secondary market with regard to price formation.[1211] Second, market operators are only more strictly regulated with regard to RMs but, once authorized for operating an RM, they can also run MTFs without additionally registering as an investment firm. Just like investment firms, market operators can operate several MTFs under their authorization.[1212] Thus, there is a level playing field regarding the operation of MTFs between market operators and investment firms. Moreover, only market operators are eligible to operate an RM. Thus, market operators are not at a disadvantage, and the more stringent regulation of RMs accounts for their important primary market function. Both RMs and MTFs can admit securities to trading, but the listing function of RMs still signals that the issuer passed a more rigorous test than a (mere) admission to trading on an MTF. While some may regret the mingling of primary and secondary market functions, it still serves an important purpose for the public and warrants higher standards of transparency about fundamental data provided by the issuer to its investors. This important conveying mechanism fuels the market with information and is therefore a valid reason for higher standards since competition not only means competition for the lower price but also for better quality.

The only actual disadvantage between RMs and MTFs was that the former Market Abuse Directive (MAD), as a directive promulgated before MiFID I was passed, applied only to shares admitted to trading on RMs.

1209 Moloney, *EU Securities and Financial Markets Regulation* (n 4) 463.

1210 Humbel, *Die Regelung der Vor- und Nachhandelstransparenz in der Europäischen Union und der Schweiz* (n 50) 129; Kumpan, *Die Regulierung außerbörslicher Wertpapierhandelssysteme im deutschen, europäischen und US-amerikanischen Recht* (n 8) 191; Lenenbach (n 51) para 3.18; Moloney, *EU Securities and Financial Markets Regulation* (n 4) 469, 475.

1211 Cf. Moloney, *EU Securities and Financial Markets Regulation* (n 4) 463.

1212 ibid 475.

Consequently, MTFs that offered trading in non-listed shares did not have to fulfill anti-market abuse requirements under MAD. This was, however, changed with the introduction of MAD's successor.[1213] Thus, the perception of RMs of market regulation being an uneven playing field is incorrect. If there is a liquidity drainage to MTFs, either lit or dark, it is because specific MTF operators manage to offer more promising trading services to investors than their competitors.

4. Organized Trading Facilities

a) EU Law

aa) A New Trading System to Close the Regulatory Gaps

As the third multilateral trading venue under MiFID II, the OTF is an addition to the array of trading systems and did not already exist under MiFID I. The OTF is designed to ensure that all forms of organized trading in non-equities, especially of former OTC-dark pools, are captured on trading systems under MiFID II/MiFIR and that no liquidity slips through the gaps of the regulatory regime into the OTC-space.[1214] Furthermore, the introduction of the OTF aimed at bringing trading in non-equity instruments onto trading systems to shine on them the light of trade transparency and subject them to clearing obligations, especially derivatives which proved problematic in the Global Financial Crisis of 2008-09, and thus, became a focus of the G20.[1215]

1213 Alexander, 'Market Structures and Market Abuse' (n 484) 383, 388-9; Klöhn, '§ 6 Kapitalmarktrecht' (n 68) § 6 para 47; Dörte Poelzig, 'Insider- und Marktmanipulationsverbot im neuen Marktmissbrauchsrecht' [2016] NZG 528, 530.

1214 Recital 6 MiFIR; 'Opinion of the European Economic and Social Committee on the 'Proposal for a Regulation of the European Parliament and of the Council on markets in financial instruments and amending Regulation (EMIR) on OTC derivatives, central counterparties and trade repositories': COM(2011) 652 final — 2011/0296 (COD), (2012/C 143/14)' [2012] OJ C143/74, C143/75; Kumpan (n 125) WpHG § 2 para 147; Moloney, *EU Securities and Financial Markets Regulation* (n 4) 464; Gomber and Nassauer (n 1086) 253.

1215 Kumpan (n 125) WpHG § 2 para 147; Busch (n 1086) 127; Güllner (n 131) 940–1; Jung and Bischof (n 1091) para 70.

According to Article 4(1)(23) MiFID II

> *'(...) 'organised trading facility' or 'OTF' means a multilateral system which is not a regulated market or an MTF and in which multiple third-party buying and selling interests in bonds, structured finance products, emission allowances or derivatives are able to interact in the system in a way that results in a contract in accordance with Title II of (...) [MiFID II] (...).'*[1216]

As the definition shows, the OTF is meant as a broad trading system category that should catch all trading that would slip through the cracks of the RM-, MTF- and SI-regimes. Insofar, the introduction of the OTF addresses the issue of unregulated dark BCNs in the OTC-space at least to some extent.[1217]

bb) Criticism on the New OTF-Category

From the outset, however, the introduction of the OTF received criticism. Some scholars did not see any merit in a trading system that is very similar to the MTF, and viewed the new system as hindered by being subordinate to RMs and MTFs.[1218] Much of the criticism, however, originated from the initial proposal of the OTF which was designed to accommodate trading in equity and non-equity instruments alike.[1219] Bringing trading in shares and other equity instruments[1220] onto the OTF was rightfully criticized, since trading in those instruments is generally liquid and can sustain the strictly non-discretionary, multilateral trading environment of RMs and MTFs.[1221]

1216 Article 4(1)(23) MiFID II. See also Busch (n 1086) 127; Jung and Bischof (n 1091) para 70; Klöhn, '§ 6 Kapitalmarktrecht' (n 68) § 6 para 41.

1217 Kumpan (n 56) WpHG § 2 para 147; Güllner (n 131) 940–1; Hoops, 'Bedeutung des organisierten Handelssystems in der gegenwärtigen Marktinfrastruktur' (n 131) 15.

1218 Susann Funke, 'Reaktion auf die Finanzmarktkrise: Teil 2: MiFID und MiFIR machen das Frühwarnsystem perfekt!' [2012] CCZ 54, 55; Gomber and Nassauer (n 1086) 253; Hoops, 'Bedeutung des organisierten Handelssystems in der gegenwärtigen Marktinfrastruktur' (n 131) 20; Moloney, *EU Securities and Financial Markets Regulation* (n 4) 466.

1219 Ferrarini and Moloney (n 143) 591ff; Moloney, *EU Securities and Financial Markets Regulation* (n 4) 466.

1220 Other equity-like instruments are for instance depositary receipts, exchange traded funds, and certificates.

1221 Moloney, *EU Securities and Financial Markets Regulation* (n 4) 428, 431; Moloney, 'EU Financial Governance and Transparency Regulation' (n 3) para 12.15. See

The OTF with its softer requirements to multilateral trading and accommodation of discretionary elements could lure away the liquidity in equity instruments and undermine the price formation process on unbiased RMs and MTFs which contradicts the purpose and spirit of MiFID II/MiFIR.[1222]

With the limitation to non-equity instruments, such as bonds, structured finance products, emission allowances or derivatives, the OTF fulfills the requirements of the G20 and offers a tailored trading system for non-equity instruments that often trade in less liquid markets.[1223] For such purposes, the OTF regime allows for a softened understanding of multilateral trading and allows for discretion.[1224]

cc) A New Type of Multilateral Trading

Although Article 20(1) MiFID II forbids OTF operators – as with any multilateral trading system – from executing client orders against their proprietary capital of the operator or any other entity that is part of the same group or legal person, OTFs can deviate from the ideal of multilateral trading and perform matched principal trading (Article 20(2) MiFID II).[1225] A transaction qualifies as matched principal trading if the OTF operator facilitates the transaction between buyer and seller by interposing itself between both parties in a way that the operator is never exposed to any market risk throughout the execution of the transaction with both sides executed simultaneously.[1226] Since forming the buyer for the seller and vice versa, the trading pattern of an OTF indulging in in matched principal trading rather resembles those of systematic internalizers which are designed as the

also CESR, 'CESR's Response to the Commission on Non-Equities Transparency' (CESR/07-284b, July 2007) 4–5; London Economics, 'Quantification of the Macro-Economic Impact of Integration of EU Financial Markets: Final Report to The European Commission Directorate General for the Internal Market' (November 2002) 54–6.

1222 Ferrarini and Moloney (n 143) 591ff; Moloney, *EU Securities and Financial Markets Regulation* (n 4) 466; Moloney, 'EU Financial Governance and Transparency Regulation' (n 3) para 12.15.

1223 Moloney, *EU Securities and Financial Markets Regulation* (n 4) 466.

1224 Recital 9 MiFIR; Kumpan (n 125) WpHG § 2 para 150; Busch (n 1086) 127–8; Güllner (n 131) 943; Jung and Bischof (n 1091) para 70: Moloney, *EU Securities and Financial Markets Regulation* (n 4) 466.

1225 Lutter, Bayer and Schmidt (n 1090) § 32 para 32.50.

1226 Cf. Gomber and Nassauer (n 1086) 253; Lutter, Bayer and Schmidt (n 1090) § 32 para 32.50.

original trading system for bilateral trading under MiFID II.[1227] To avoid blurring the line between the OTF and SI regime, MiFID II also requires matched principal trading to occur at a price where the OTF operator makes no profit or loss, other than a previously disclosed commission, fee, or charge for the transaction (Article 4(1)(38) MiFID II). This reduces the chances of the OTF operator becoming an interested party in the outcome of the transaction and moderates potential conflicts of interest, so the OTF is similarly neutral to the other trading venues.[1228]

Matched principal trading allows a matching process comparable to the one employed by dark BCNs without generally allowing for a mingling of multilateral and bilateral elements compromising the regulatory framework which is designed along the differentiation of multilateral versus bilateral trading systems. For this reason, an OTF and an SI cannot be operated within the same legal entity. Neither can OTFs and SIs be connected with another OTF in a manner that may circumvent the limits of matched principal trading (Article 20(4) MiFID II).[1229] By implementing this limitation, EU law allows the OTF to be close but not quite like a BCN and thereby refrains from codifying the formerly existing BCNs as they operated under MiFID I, which would be close to the combination of multiple OTFs or an OTF combined with an SI. They also do not allow for a mingling of multilateral and bilateral trading such as the US-ATS permits, and therefore manage to avoid its inherent conflicts of interest.[1230] An OTF operator, however, should not engage in matched principal trading to execute client orders in derivatives eligible for clearing under Article 5 European Market Infrastructure Regulation (EMIR).[1231]

dd) Sovereign Debt Instruments

In contrast to the careful separation between multilateral matched principal trading and proprietary bilateral trading reserved for systematic in-

1227 Busch (n 1086) 128.

1228 Hoops, 'Bedeutung des organisierten Handelssystems in der gegenwärtigen Marktinfrastruktur' (n 131) 17.

1229 Busch (n 1086) 128.

1230 Cf. Kumpan (n 125) WpHG § 2 para 151; Güllner (n 131) 941, 944–5; Hoops, 'Bedeutung des organisierten Handelssystems in der gegenwärtigen Marktinfrastruktur' (n 131) 17.

1231 Article 20(2) subpara 2 MiFID II; Busch (n 1086) 128; Güllner (n 131) 944.

ternalizers, the EU dissolved its clear-cut framework for a rather crude privilege handed to sovereign issuers. According to Article 20(3) MiFID II, an OTF operator can engage in proprietary trading and deal on its own account assuming position risk and jeopardizing its neutrality with regard to sovereign debt instruments for which there is not a liquid market.[1232] This supports the illiquid sovereign bond markets allowing governments to broaden their fiscal capabilities. Given that this rule was promulgated at the height of the Euro Debt Crisis in which many countries' sovereign debt markets dried up, this provision must be considered as a concession to governments.[1233]

ee) A Discretionary Trading System

While OTFs are another multilateral trading system akin to RMs and MTFs with the exception of matched principal trading, OTFs are the only discretionary multilateral system.[1234] Since discretionary trading is generally reserved for bilateral trading systems, the exercise of discretion by the OTF operator is limited to two different aspects under Article 20(6)(a), (b) MiFID II:

> *'(…) (a) when deciding to place or retract an order on the OTF they operate;*
> *(b) when deciding not to match a specific client order with other orders available in the systems at a given time, provided it is in compliance with specific instructions received from a client and with its obligations in accordance with Article 27.'*[1235]

1232 Lutter, Bayer and Schmidt (n 1090) § 32 para 32.50; Lars Röh in Eberhard Schwark and Daniel Zimmer (eds), *Kapitalmarktrechts-Kommentar: Börsengesetz mit Börsenzulassungsverordnung, Wertpapierprospektgesetz, Wertpapierhandelsgesetz, Wertpapiererwerbs- und Übernahmegesetz, Europäische Marktmissbrauchsverordnung* (5th edn, CH Beck 2020) WpHG § 75 para 19.

1233 Moloney, *EU Securities and Financial Markets Regulation* (n 4) 465; Lutter, Bayer and Schmidt (n 1090) § 32 para 32.50.

1234 Recital 9(1) MiFIR; ESMA, 'Questions and Answers: On MiFID II and MiFIR Market Structures Topics' (n 1169) 48, 5.2 Answer 12 and 52, 5.2 Answer 19; Kumpan (n 125) WpHG § 2 para 150; Güllner (n 131) 943; Jung and Bischof (n 1091) para 70.

1235 Article 20(6)(a),(b) MiFID II; cf. Recital 9(1) MiFIR; Kumpan (n 125) WpHG § 2 para 150; Busch (n 1086) 127–8; Lutter, Bayer and Schmidt (n 1090) § 32 para 32.50.

According to Article 20(6) subpara. 2 MiFID II, it is in the operator's discretion – subject to client instructions – to decide whether an order shall be fully or only partially executed.[1236] ESMA therefore distinguishes between 'discretion at the order level' and 'discretion at the execution level.'[1237] The rationale of exercising discretion is to facilitate the negotiation between the clients of the OTF ultimately allowing for an increased number of trading interests matched in one transaction.[1238]

The limited scope of discretion – order-level and execution-level – is further limited by three principles, i.e., best execution (Article 20(6) MiFID II), non-discriminatory access (Article 18(3) MiFID II), and the duty to avoid conflicts of interest (Article 18(4) MiFID II).[1239] Additionally, the OTF's duty of accountability to its clients further curtails its discretion.[1240]

Moreover, the regulators may request either in the authorization process or on ad-hoc basis a detailed explanation why the system does not correspond to and cannot be operated as a regulated market, MTF or systematic internalizer, and may also request a detailed description as to how discretion will be exercised.[1241] This right of information is exercised by BaFin pursuant to Section 75(7) WpHG under German law and aims to prevent regulatory arbitrage by system operators. They cannot operate under the lighter regulatory framework of an OTF instead of an RM or MTF. However, the duty to explain why an operator chose to be regulated as an OTF instead of an SI is probably a new weakness in the regulatory framework since SI-regulation is lighter than OTF-regulation given that the SIs' transparency requirements for trading non-equity instruments are much more limited under Article 18 MiFIR compared to Articles 8, 9 MiFIR.[1242] This can only be explained by assuming the legislator prefers SIs over OTFs

---

1236 Kumpan (n 125) WpHG § 2 para 150; Lutter, Bayer and Schmidt (n 1090) § 32 para 32.50.

1237 ESMA, 'Questions and Answers: On MiFID II and MiFIR Market Structures Topics' (n 1169) 52–3, 5.2 Answer 19; Kumpan (n 125) WpHG § 2 para 150.

1238 Recital 9(2) MiFIR; Humbel, *Die Regelung der Vor- und Nachhandelstransparenz in der Europäischen Union und der Schweiz* (n 50) 132.

1239 Kumpan (n 125) WpHG § 2 para 150.

1240 Recital 9(2) MiFIR; Humbel, *Die Regelung der Vor- und Nachhandelstransparenz in der Europäischen Union und der Schweiz* (n 50) 132.

1241 Article 20(7) MiFID II; Röh (n 1232) WpHG § 75 para 28; Humbel, *Die Regelung der Vor- und Nachhandelstransparenz in der Europäischen Union und der Schweiz* (n 50) 132–3.

1242 Röh (n 1232) WpHG § 75 para 28. On the transparency regime see below Part II § 6.C.2.b. and Part II § 6.C.6.b.

because SI-operators need to take on market risk and thus (should) align their behavior accordingly.[1243] Nevertheless, this is an incoherence, given that the trading system regime generally prefers trading venues, i.e., RMs, MTFs and OTFs, over SIs and less regulated OTC-trading.

ff) Eligible Operating Entities

Unlike MTFs, the OTF definition does not mention the eligible operating entities. However, Article 20(1) MiFID II clarifies that both market operators and investment firms are eligible to operate an OTF. With respect to authorization, thus, the same applies as for MTFs discussed above since operating an OTF also qualifies as an investment service according to Article 4(1)(2) and Section C(9) of Annex I MiFID II.

b) Transposition into German law

The German legislator transposed the requirements for OTFs under MiFID II into national law under Sections 2(8) No. 9, 72 and 75 WpHG. Since there has been no deviation from EU law, no further discussion is required.

III. Investment Firms operating as Systematic Internalizers or OTC

Beyond the realm of multilateral trading venues lies the over-the-counter-space (OTC-space) in which investment firms trade bilaterally. It is, however, not hard to imagine that some investment firms trade more rigorously in a specific financial instrument than others. When investment firms trade so intensively in an instrument that they are functionally similar to a marketplace from a trader's perspective, the EU regulator considers it warranted to subject such investment firms to regulation.[1244]

1243 Röh (n 1232) WpHG § 75 para 28. Differently Gebauer (n 94) WpHG § 75 para 28.
1244 Assmann (n 130) WpHG § 2 para 112; Kumpan (n 125) WpHG § 2 para 102ff.

1. EU Law

a) Definition

The MiFID II/MiFIR framework accounts for those investment firms that internalize large amounts of order flow with the regulatory category of the systematic internalizer. According to Article 4(1)(20) MiFID II the term

> *'(...) 'systematic internaliser' means an investment firm which, on an organised, frequent systematic and substantial basis, deals on own account when executing client orders outside a regulated market, an MTF or an OTF without operating a multilateral system; (...).'*[1245]

b) Bilateral Trading

It is characteristic for systematic internalizers to trade bilaterally on their own account against client orders. This means that they are always the counterparty to a client's transaction and required to trade against their proprietary capital by which systematic internalizers assume position risk.[1246]

c) The Flaws under MiFID I and MiFID II/MiFIR's Response: Qualitative vs. Quantitative Approach

Besides the bilateral character of trading, which delineates systematic internalizers from multilateral trading venues, the SI-definition contains other criteria to distinguish SIs from mere OTC-trading.[1247] Even though MiFID II refrains from defining OTC-trading, the definition used in Recital 53 of MiFID I, which characterizes OTC transactions as being *'(...) ad-hoc and irregular (...)'*,[1248] can be used as guidance under MiFID II as well.

1245 Article 4(1)(20) MiFID II; Busch (n 1086) 129; Jung and Bischof (n 1091) para 69.

1246 ESMA, 'MiFID II Review Report: MiFID II Review Report on the Functioning of Organised Trading Facilities (OTF)' (ESMA70-156-4225, 23 March 2021) 19; Assmann (n 130) WpHG § 2 paras 112–3; Kumpan (n 125) WpHG § 2 para 103; Busch (n 1086) 129.

1247 Busch (n 1086) 129.

1248 Recital 53 MiFID I: *'It is not the intention of this Directive to require the application of pre-trade transparency rules to transactions carried out on an OTC basis, the characteristics of which include that they are ad-hoc and irregular and are carried out with wholesale counterparties and are part of a business relationship which is*

Thus, an investment firm is a systematic internalizer for an instrument if the firm's trading in this instrument is 'frequent systematic' and occurs on a 'substantial basis.'[1249] However, the broad categories of 'frequent systematic' trading on a 'substantial basis' need further specification to allow for a clear delineation of the systematic internalizer regime's scope and the OTC-space.

(i) Failure of the SI regime under MiFID I

In *Kay Swinburn's* report on the performance of MiFID I, she said that *'(...) it is hard to assess the SI regime for equities as anything other than a failure. Clearly the regime is not optimal for trading.'*[1250] This shows the difficulties that arose with the SI-definition under MiFID I.[1251] The major pitfall was that both prongs of the definition were further specified by qualitative criteria in Article 21 of the Commission Regulation (EC) 1287/2006, instead of quantitative ones. On the one hand, Article 21 sets out criteria defining which activities qualify as 'frequent and systematic' using qualitative criteria, such as that trading has to have a 'material commercial role for the firm', is carried out by dedicated 'personnel, or by means of an automated technical system' and is 'available to clients on a regular or continuous basis.'[1252] On the other hand, Article 21 defines the activities that do not qualify for the SI-definition, such as, that *'(...) the activity is performed on an ad hoc and irregular bilateral basis with wholesale counterparties as part of business relationships which are themselves characterised by dealings (...)'*[1253] and that *'(...) the transactions are carried out outside the systems habitually used by the firm concerned for any business that it carries out in the capacity of a systematic internaliser above standard market size (...)'.*[1254] When considering both qualitative criteria, it becomes apparent that trading systems could claim that they fell outside of the SI-regime and

---

itself characterised by dealings above standard market size, and where the deals are carried out outside the systems usually used by the firm concerned for its business as a systematic internaliser.'

1249 Article 4(1)(20) MiFID II. Busch (n 1086) 129.

1250 European Union Committee, *MiFID II: Getting it Right for the City and EU Financial Services Industry* (HL 2012-13, HL Paper 28) 22 para 40.

1251 See also Moloney, *EU Securities and Financial Markets Regulation* (n 4) 462–3.

1252 Article 21(1)(a)-(c) CR (EC) 1287/2006.

1253 Article 21(3)(a) CR (EC) 1287/2006.

1254 Article 21(3)(b) CR (EC) 1287/2006.

rather into the unregulated OTC-space if, for instance, they only operated with orders above standard market size for wholesale counter-parties.[1255]

This allowed dark pools, such as BCNs, to escape the regulatory perimeter under MiFID I entirely: First, the blending of multilateral and bilateral elements in the BCN disqualified the trading system from the exclusively multilateral MTF-regime. Second, dark broker dealer networks gamed the qualitative requirements of the SI-definition (especially the vague definition of trading orders 'above standard market size') to also fall outside this regulatory regime and operate unregulated in the OTC-space.[1256]

This form of dark trading qualifies as unregulated dark trading that is not exempted from trade transparency due to a waiver or other form of planned exemption, but rather simply falls outside the regulatory perimeter.[1257] However, since it combines several aspects of regulated behavior, it is reasonable to assume that there is even more cause for such trading to be regulated.[1258] Until the MiFID I revision process, the amount of OTC-trading grew significantly, up to 40 % of all trading in shares and depositary receipts with a large amount of this OTC-trading comprising of orders that were of standard market size. This drainage of liquidity from the OTC-space was one of the reasons why the EU tightened the regulatory regime in the MiFID revision process.[1259] The failure of the SI-regime to shrink the OTC-space can be seen in the fact that only 11 SIs initially registered under MiFID I.[1260]

This regulatory arbitrage strategy is comparable to the one used by market actors in the United States. While US trading system operators needed to stay below a certain threshold to be exempt from transparency requirements, EU market actors needed to exceed a certain threshold to

1255 Gomber and Pierron (n 4) 48–9; Moloney, *EU Securities and Financial Markets Regulation* (n 4) 467.

1256 Gomber and Pierron (n 4) 48–9, 56; Moloney, *EU Securities and Financial Markets Regulation* (n 4) 467; Spindler and Kasten (n 134) 1756.

1257 Gomber and Gvozdevskiy (n 43) para 14.19.

1258 Thelen (n 147) 130.

1259 European Parliament (n 434) 4; Hoops, 'Bedeutung des organisierten Handelssystems in der gegenwärtigen Marktinfrastruktur' (n 131) 14. See also: European Commission, 'Commission Staff Working Paper Impact Assessment EU Commission, Impact Assessment' (n 382) 4–5; Bernard (n 1110) 2; Comerton-Forde (n 16) 2–3; Salger (n 627) 186.

1260 CESR, 'Report: Impact of MiFID on equity secondary markets functioning' (CESR/09-355, 10 June 2009) 15–6; Moloney, *EU Securities and Financial Markets Regulation* (n 4) 443.

qualify for a transaction 'above standard market size' to be exempted from trade transparency.

(ii) MiFID II/MiFIR's Response

To remedy this issue, the SI-definition under MiFID II and its delegated regulation are no longer determined by qualitative but rather quantitative thresholds.[1261] This approach is not new, since the draft version of the MiFID I already relied on some quantitative criteria before they were given up for a purely qualitative approach.[1262] However, in the MiFID review process, CESR identified the blurry definition and called for an improved SI-definition to avoid regulatory arbitrage.[1263] If the low numbers of registered SIs under MiFID I tell a story of failure, the numbers under MiFID II, with currently 188 (as of July 2023) registered SIs compared to 11 initially registered when MiFID I commenced, might indicate that the SI-regime has been significantly improved.[1264]

d) Quantitative Definition of 'Frequent Systematic'

Under MiFID II, whether an investment firm is trading on a frequent and systematic basis is measured by the number of OTC trades in the financial instrument carried out by the investment firm on its own account when executing client orders.[1265] The specifics are set out in the Commission Delegated Regulation 2017/565 of 25 April 2016. In its calibration of the threshold for 'frequent systematic' trading, the level 2 measure accounts for the broadened scope of MiFID II/MiFIR and defines different thresholds for equity and non-equity instruments due to their varying trading patterns.[1266] Within those categories, the calibration also takes into account

1261 Kumpan (n 125) WpHG § 2 para 104; Gomber and Nassauer (n 1086) 253–4.

1262 Seitz (n 132) 501.

1263 CESR, 'Report' (n 1260) 15–6; CESR, 'CESR Technical Advice to the European Commission in the Context of the MiFID Review - Equity Markets' (n 494) 18ff; cf. Moloney, *EU Securities and Financial Markets Regulation* (n 4) 467; Humbel, *Die Regelung der Vor- und Nachhandelstransparenz in der Europäischen Union und der Schweiz* (n 50) 139.

1264 See ESMA Database on MiFID Infrastructures.

1265 Article 4(1)(20) subpara 2 MiFID II.

1266 Kumpan (n 125) WpHG § 2 para 105.

the trade-off between transparency and liquidity following ESMA's Classes of Financial Instruments Approach[1267] (COFIA) approach.[1268]

By way of example, Article 12(1)(a) CDR (EU) 2017/565 determines the threshold for frequent and systematic trading in equity instruments[1269] for which there is a liquid market where two requirements were met during the past 6 month: first, the number of OTC transactions carried out by the investment firm on its own account when executing client orders is equal to or larger than 0.4 % of the total number of transactions in the relevant financial instrument executed in the EU on any trading venue or OTC during the same period. Furthermore, the OTC transactions carried out by the investment firm on its own account when executing client orders in the relevant financial instrument take place on average on a daily basis.[1270]

Second, for financial instruments trading in illiquid markets, the requirement of 'frequent and systematic trading' is fulfilled if merely during the past 6 months the OTC transactions carried out by the investment firm on its own account when executing client orders takes place on average on a daily basis.[1271]

e) Role of Liquidity

The concept of liquidity and its interrelation with trade transparency has already been discussed above. As already noted, less liquid markets may suffer from an abundance of transparency while additional transparency may contribute little to market quality in illiquid markets.[1272]

For this reason, the subsequently discussed transparency regime under MiFIR is calibrated for liquidity levels in the market. Within the systematic internalizer regime, liquidity already becomes an issue on the trading system level although Article 4(1)(20) MiFID II does not tie the SI-definition

1267 For an in-depth description of COFIA see ESMA, 'Discussion Paper: MiFID II/ MiFIR' (ESMA/2014/548, 22 May 2014) 123ff.

1268 ESMA, 'Final Report: ESMA's Technical Advice to the Commission on MiFID II and MiFIR' (ESMA/2014/1569, 19 December 2014) 226.

1269 i.e., shares, depositary receipts, ETFs, certificates and other similar financial instruments.

1270 Article 12(a)(i), (ii) Commission Delegated Regulation (EU) 2017/565 of 25 April 2016; Kumpan (n 125) WpHG § 2 para 106.

1271 Article 12(b) Commission Delegated Regulation (EU) 2017/565 of 25 April 2016; Kumpan (n 125) WpHG § 2 para 106.

1272 See above Part I § 3 D.

to liquidity levels. In the level 2 process, however, ESMA considered it necessary to tie the very scope of the SI-regime to liquidity levels because the SI-definition primarily serves the purpose of obliging investments firms with significant turnovers to make firm quotes, i.e., to provide trade transparency, instead of operating as a dark pool.[1273]

To avoid adverse effects on bilateral liquidity provision by investment firms, ESMA suggested that the Commission use the same definition under Article 2(17)(a), (b) MiFIR to calibrate the scope of the SI-definition in its delegated commission regulation. The Commission followed this advice. For equity instruments, a liquid market is determined with regard to the free float, the average daily number of transactions, and the average daily turnover for the respective financial instrument (Article 2(1)(17)(b) MiFIR). In contrast, a liquid market for non-equity instruments is determined with regard to the average frequency and size of the transaction over a range of market conditions, having regard to the nature and life cycle of products within the class of financial instruments, the number and type of market participants, including the ratio of market participants to traded financial instruments in a particular product, and the average size of spreads, where available (Article 2(1)(17)(a) MiFIR). Both the transparency regime under MiFIR and the SI-definition in the level 2 measure can account for the differences in trading between equity and non-equity instruments by using this array of criteria to define a liquid market. Equity markets are often liquid and have a high rate of daily turnover, whereas certain non-equity classes, especially bonds, are traded very actively when issued and shortly before maturity but show only thin levels of liquidity in the meantime.[1274]

It is therefore sensible to adjust not only the trade transparency regime for liquidity but also the SI-definition because it primarily serves the purpose of demanding firm quotes from investment firms outside multilateral trading venues.

1273 Kumpan (n 125) WpHG § 2 para 106; Moloney, *EU Securities and Financial Markets Regulation* (n 4) 488–9.

1274 Moloney, *EU Securities and Financial Markets Regulation* (n 4) 431–2.

f) Quantitative Definition of 'Substantial Basis'

The second criterion that distinguishes systematic internalization from mere OTC-transactions is that its trading in a financial instrument occurs on a 'substantial basis.' According to Article 4(1)(20) subpara. 2 MiFID II,

> *'(...) [t]he substantial basis shall be measured either by the size of the OTC trading carried out by the investment firm in relation to the total trading of the investment firm in a specific financial instrument or by the size of the OTC trading carried out by the investment firm in relation to the total trading in the Union in a specific financial instrument.'*[1275]

To further exemplify the detailed level 2 calibration with the provision for equity instruments, Article 12(c) CDR (EU) 2017/565 defines trading on substantial basis as any trading

> *'(...) where the size of OTC trading carried out by [the investment firm] on own account when executing client orders is, during the past 6 months, equal to or larger than either:*
> *(i) 15 % of the total turnover in that financial instrument executed by the investment firm on own account or on behalf of clients and executed on a trading venue or OTC;*
> *(ii) 0,4 % of the total turnover in that financial instrument executed in the Union on a trading venue or OTC.'*[1276]

The thresholds are chosen in this manner to capture trading activity under the definition of systematic internalizer that has a material effect on price formation.[1277] This is crucial since systematic internalizers are OTC-investment firms which are subject to trade transparency requirements.[1278] The threshold, however, excludes those investment firms for which the systematic internalizer regime would impose disproportionate burdens.[1279]

1275 Article 4(1)(20) subpara 2 MiFID II. Cf. Ekkenga (n 96) § 7 para 144; Kumpan (n 125) WpHG § 2 para 106.

1276 Article 12(c) Commission Delegated Regulation (EU) 2017/565 of 25 April 2016; Kumpan (n 125) WpHG § 2 para 107.

1277 Recital 18 CDR (EU) 2017/565; Gebauer (n 94) MiFIR Art 14 para 14.

1278 On the trade transparency requirements see below Part II § 6 C.

1279 Recital 18 CDR (EU) 2017/565.

g) Cumulative Requirement and 'Opt-in'

To qualify as a systematic internalizer, the investment firm has to meet both the threshold for 'frequent systematic' trading and the threshold for trading on a 'substantial basis' for the respective instrument class.[1280] The calculation of both thresholds is a burdensome task for SI because it requires extensive information about market data that may not be easily accessible due to the (current) lack of consolidated post-trade transparency data and must be reassessed over the course of time when a consolidated tape may be implemented under the MiFID II/MiFIR refit.[1281] For this reason, MiFID II allows for a 'voluntary' opt-in by investment firms that do not (yet) meet the requirements of an SI but wish to comply with its regulations and register with the national competent authority as a systematic internalizer.[1282] ESMA explains the high levels of voluntary opt-ins as a result of clients' preference to delegate the reporting requirement of post-trade transparency onto the SI entirely, thus clients only want to transact with SIs rather than mere OTC-investment firms.[1283] However, it cannot be overlooked that the effort to monitor the regulatory thresholds may be too burdensome compared to opt-in the SI regime right away.

h) New Loopholes under MiFID II/MiFIR

The new fortification of the SI-regime with its shift from qualitative to quantitative requirements has pulled liquidity from OTC-BCNs into the

1280 Article 4(1)(20) subpara 2 MiFID II.

1281 Cf. Kumpan (n 125) WpHG § 2 para 104. A consolidated tape shall be implemented under the MiFID II/MiFIR refit, see European Commission, 'Proposal for a Regulation of the European Parliament and of the Council amending Regulation (EU) No 600/2014 as regards enhancing market data transparency, removing obstacles to the emergence of a consolidated tape, optimising the trading obligations and prohibiting receiving payments for forwarding client orders' (n 1146) 4.

1282 Cf. ESMA, 'Consultation Paper: MiFIR Report on Systematic Internalisers in Non-Equity Instruments' (ESMA70-156-1757, 3 February 2020) 12; ESMA, 'MiFIR report on Systematic Internalisers in Non-Equity Instruments' (ESMA70-156-2756, 16 July 2020) 11; Kumpan (n 125) WpHG § 2 para 104.

1283 Cf. ESMA, 'Consultation Paper: MiFIR Report on Systematic Internalisers in Non-Equity Instruments' (n 1282) 12; ESMA, 'MiFIR report on Systematic Internalisers in Non-Equity Instruments' (n 1282) 11; Kumpan (n 125) WpHG § 2 para 104.

regulatory perimeter.[1284] For equity instruments, this means less dark trading and more transparent liquidity because the trade transparency regime for equity trading on multilateral trading venues and systematic internalizers is rather strict, as will be discussed in the next section.[1285]

For trading in non-equity instruments, however, results may vary because the transparency regime is not equally aligned among multilateral trading venues and bilateral SIs and, even more important, the OTF-regime offers a structural loophole.

Per definition, systematic internalizers shall only buy and sell financial instruments to their clients. Therefore, the systematic internalizers may merely unwind their holdings or stock up their short positions over time, but they cannot match clients' selling and buying interests back-to-back in an organized manner. The latter would qualify for multilateral trading because the SI would no longer assume position risk, but rather would provide a marketplace for its clients to trade with each other using the systematic internalizer as a mere intermediary. Multilateral trading is however more strictly regulated because the operator's neutrality must be maintained for an unbiased balancing of supply and demand of third-party traders to achieve an informative price formation.[1286] Although ESMA acknowledges that according to Recital 17 of MiFID II, SIs only have to avoid bringing together third-party trading interest *'(...) in the same way as a trading venue (...)'*,[1287] a rule which may allow for an occasional matching of client orders,[1288] ESMA vigilantly observes recent market developments of so-called SI-networks.[1289]

In SI-networks, several SIs enter an arrangement that facilitates the execution of transactions between multiple buyers and sellers – blurring the

1284 Cf. AMAFI, 'Impact of the MiFIR Volume Cap Mechanism on the Microstructure of European Equity Markets' (Paris, 28 October 2019) AMAFI/19-103, 1, 12.

1285 See below Part II § 6.C. Cf. ibid 12.

1286 Moloney, 'EU Financial Governance and Transparency Regulation' (n 3) para 12.15.

1287 Recital 17 MiFID II.

1288 ESMA, 'MiFID II Review Report: MiFID II Review Report on the Functioning of Organised Trading Facilities (OTF)' (n 1246) 19. See also Recital (19) of the Commission Delegated Regulation (EU) 2017/565; Kumpan, *Die Regulierung außerbörslicher Wertpapierhandelssysteme im deutschen, europäischen und US-amerikanischen Recht* (n 8) 286; Kumpan (n 125) WpHG § 2 para 103.

1289 ESMA, 'MiFID II Review Report: MiFID II Review Report on the Functioning of Organised Trading Facilities (OTF)' (n 1246) 18–9; ESMA, 'MiFIR report on Systematic Internalisers in Non-Equity Instruments' (n 1282) 26–7.

line between bilateral and multilateral trading – without being authorized as a regulated market, an MTF, or OTF.[1290] Such de facto multilateral systems allow each SI participating in the network to carry out riskless back-to-back trading through arrangements with third-party liquidity providers while technically dealing on one's own account.[1291] This way, the SI-network can operate like a multilateral trading venue but under less restrictive transparency requirements, especially with regard to the rather light pre-trade transparency requirements for non-equity instruments under Article 18 MiFIR.[1292] Some market participants even suspect that those SI-networks are the new home of the liquidity pulled from the former BCNs in the OTC-space into the regulatory perimeter under MiFID II/MiFIR.[1293] While there is yet no conclusive evidence,[1294] this theory has merit insofar that one study by *Gomber et al.* predicted this outcome in its models before MiFID II/MiFIR was implemented.[1295]

Another study conducted by the association française des marchés financiers (French Financial Markets Association) (AMAFI) found data supporting the theory that the suspension of waivers does not have a measurable negative market impact at all.[1296] AMAFI theorizes that this lack of an effect may result from an increase in overall liquidity in lit markets during a halt in dark trading under the volume cap mechanism which provides a 'liquidity cushion' that softens market impact for larger orders that can no longer use dark trading.[1297]

Even though ESMA perceives that there is no room for regulatory arbitrage, or, at least, believes that it has already been fixed by introducing

---

1290 ESMA, 'MiFID II Review Report: MiFID II Review Report on the Functioning of Organised Trading Facilities (OTF)' (n 1246) 18–9. See also Steven Maijoor, 'Letter of Steven Maijoor to Olivier Guernsent - Ref: MiFID II - SIs Operating Broker Crossing Networks' (ESMA70-872942901-19, 1 February 2017) 1–2; Humbel, *Die Regelung der Vor- und Nachhandelstransparenz in der Europäischen Union und der Schweiz* (n 50) 138.

1291 ESMA, 'MiFID II Review Report: MiFID II Review Report on the Functioning of Organised Trading Facilities (OTF)' (n 1246) 19.

1292 Röh (n 1232) WpHG § 75 para 28. On the transparency regime see below Part II § 6.C.2.b. and Part II § 6.C.6.b.

1293 ESMA, 'MiFID II Review Report: MiFID II Review Report on the Functioning of Organised Trading Facilities (OTF)' (n 1246) 19–20.

1294 ibid 19–20.

1295 Peter Gomber and others, 'The MiFIR Trading Obligation: Impact on Trading Volume and Liquidity in Electronic Trading' (February 2018) 9.

1296 AMAFI (n 1284) 16.

1297 ibid 12.

Article 16a CDR (EU) 2017/565 as amended by the Commission Delegated Regulation (EU) 2017/2294 of 28 August 2017,[1298] the cause of this issue might still exist in the intransitive order for trading systems under MiFID II. Given the strict regulation of multilateral systems under MiFID II/MiFIR with regard to organization and trade transparency as well as the regulatory approach to use the positive definition of multilateral trading[1299] as an anchor for its regulatory framework while refraining from a definition for the OTC-space, it can be inferred that the EU legislator prefers to gather liquidity on multilateral trading systems over having bilateral trading. This is also congruent with the EU legislator's preference for organized lit trading over informal dark trading.[1300] This finds its expression in the definition of both the OTF and the SI which are subordinate to RMs and MTFs.[1301] However, the regulatory order becomes intransitive when considering that the OTF-operator has to explain why it does not operate as an SI, and the SI is by definition a system that cannot be an OTF. Unfortunately, this inconsistency with legislator's preferences leads to a predictable outcome: Since system operators prefer lighter regulation over stricter ones, they always choose the SI-regime if they wish to offer dark trading services.[1302]

Contrary to the legislative goal of closing the loophole between MTF- and SI-regulation that caused BCNs in the OTC-space, the introduction of the OTF and the fortification of the SI-regime under MiFID II/MiFIR may have shifted the issue from trading in equities to trading in non-equity

---

1298 Article 16a CDR (EU) 2017/565 as amended by CDR (EU) 2017/2294 of 28 August 2017. See also Humbel, *Die Regelung der Vor- und Nachhandelstransparenz in der Europäischen Union und der Schweiz* (n 50) 138.

1299 Under Article 4(1)(19) MiFID II of 2014, but the MiFID II/MiFIR-proposal of 2021 aims to move this definition to the new proposed Article 2(1)(11) MiFIR.

1300 See also Recital 6 MiFIR: '*It is important to ensure that trading in financial instruments is carried out as far as possible on organised venues and that all such venues are appropriately regulated. Under Directive 2004/39/EC, some trading systems developed which were not adequately captured by the regulatory regime. Any trading system in financial instruments, such as entities currently known as broker crossing networks, should in the future be properly regulated and be authorised under one of the types of multilateral trading venues or as a systematic internaliser under the conditions set out in this Regulation and in Directive 2014/65/EU (1).*' European Parliament (n 434) 4.

1301 Kumpan (n 125) WpHG § 2 para 108; Röh (n 1232) WpHG § 75 para 28.

1302 ESMA, 'MiFID II Review Report: MiFID II Review Report on the Functioning of Organised Trading Facilities (OTF)' (n 1246) 18–9; ESMA, 'MiFIR report on Systematic Internalisers in Non-Equity Instruments' (n 1282) 25 para 98; Röh (n 1232) WpHG § 75 para 28.

instruments.[1303] Thus, the chance for dark trading – or at least opaque trading – by circumventing the trading venue regime through merging multilateral and bilateral elements still exists under MiFID II/MiFIR.

2. Transposition into German Law

The definition of systematic internalizer has been transposed into German law under Section 2(8)(1)(2)(b) WpHG. Section 2(8)(4) WpHG also reflects that both prongs, 'frequently systematic' and 'substantial basis,' must be met in order to qualify as SI or that the investment firm can 'opt-in' by registering with BaFin.[1304]

3. Conclusion on New SI-Regime

In conclusion, the European Union has significantly amended the systematic internalizer regime to avoid the loophole that the qualitative definition created under MiFID I. It replaced those qualitative criteria with a complex array of quantitative criteria which principally clearly define the scope of the systematic internalizer regime. However, determining whether an investment firm falls within the scope requires a bulk of post-trade transparency data which is not (yet) available due to the difficulties in implementing a commercially operated consolidated tape that aggregates the post-trade transparency data of the trading activity in the entire EU but is supposed to be implemented under the MiFID II/MiFIR refit.[1305] While this is already a major hurdle for investment firms, conducting regular calculations for all financial instruments traded on individual basis makes the efforts to remain beneath the SI-threshold even more costly. It would therefore not be surprising if many investment firms evaded this task and used the 'voluntary' opt-in.

Nevertheless, financial markets law is an area of constant attempts for regulatory arbitrage. This is demonstrated by SI-networks setting up multi-

1303 ESMA, 'MiFID II Review Report: MiFID II Review Report on the Functioning of Organised Trading Facilities (OTF)' (n 1246) 19–20.

1304 Kumpan (n 125) WpHG § 2 para 104.

1305 European Commission, 'Proposal for a Regulation of the European Parliament and of the Council amending Regulation (EU) No 600/2014 as regards enhancing market data transparency, removing obstacles to the emergence of a consolidated tape, optimising the trading obligations and prohibiting receiving payments for forwarding client orders' (n 1146) 4.

lateral markets under a bilateral guise for non-equities trading replicating the issue of dark trading due to a loophole between the multilateral trading venue- and SI-regime under MiFID II/MiFIR.

IV. Trading Obligation to Shrink the OTC-Space

1. For Shares

For the purpose of bringing all organized trading back to organized venues and thereby restricting unregulated dark trading in the OTC-space, MiFID II/MiFIR already offers the new OTF-regime and the enhanced SI-definition. MiFID II/MiFIR, however, not only broadens the regulatory perimeter, especially with the OTF being restricted to non-equity instruments, which does not entirely close the regulatory gaps between the MTF- and SI-regime for equity instruments, but MiFID II/MiFIR also installed a device that forces liquidity in shares out of the OTC-realm onto the trading venues working as an additional line of defense against regulatory arbitrage. This additional device is the trading obligation for shares.[1306]

According to Article 23(1) MiFIR, the trading obligation requires an investment firm to ensure that the trades in shares admitted to trading on an RM or traded on a trading venue shall take place on an RM, MTF, SI or a third-country trading venue assessed to be equivalent.[1307] With the trading obligation, the EU demonstrates its shift from a facilitative to a more prescriptive regime: The trading obligation is a middle path between the pre-MiFID I era concentration rule regime that consolidated all liquidity in shares on the national exchanges and the free competition regime under MiFID I facilitative to all kinds of competition also from BCNs in the OTC-space.[1308] The trading obligation is, however, still consistent with the competition among markets ('markets for markets' approach) under MiFID I. Article 23(1) MiFIR merely requires trades in shares, as the most liquid financial instrument traded in an organized manner, make use of the array of trading systems that MiFID II provides. Regulated trading systems

1306 Kumpan and Schmidt (n 4) Art 23 paras 1, 5; Gomber and Nassauer (n 1086) 255.

1307 Article 23(1) MiFIR. NB: the German text of Article 23(1) MiFIR also lists the OTF as an eligible trading system which is incorrect due to the OTF being limited to non-equity instruments. It appears to be an editorial error that cannot be found in the English version. Kumpan and Schmidt (n 4) Art 23 para 5.

1308 Moloney, *EU Securities and Financial Markets Regulation* (n 4) 468.

are preferable to non-regulated systems because they ensure a balance between all interests involved while mitigating structural and operational risks, and support price discovery by being subject to trade transparency rules instead of allowing for opaque systems that combine a multitude of risks that are hard for national competent authorities to control.[1309]

Furthermore, the trading obligation accounts for exemptions. Trading in shares can occur outside a trading system in the OTC-space when the transaction is either (a) non-systematic, ad-hoc, irregular and infrequent, or (b) carried out between eligible and/or professional counterparties and does not contribute to the price discovery process.[1310] The specifics of those exemptions are left to the level 2 measure drafted by ESMA and enacted into a regulation by the Commission that culminated into the Commission Delegated Regulation (EU) 2017/587 of 14 July 2016. Under Article 2 CDR (EU) 2017/587, transactions that are executed at volume-weighted average prices or time-weighted average prices are considered to not contribute to price discovery.[1311] Moreover, the exemption encompasses an array of technical trades such as portfolio trades,[1312] give-in and give-up transactions.[1313]

This underlines again that one of the central issues of trading system regulation is providing for an entity that can aggregate organized trading in one place where it can be subjected to trade transparency obligations which eventually supports the price discovery mechanism. Whenever the orders or transactions are not organized, i.e., ad-hoc and irregular, or do not contribute to price discover because they are either subject to other circumstances as the rest of the market or pursue non-investment purposes, the trading venue regime does not have to incorporate such orders and transactions to eventually subject them to trade transparency.[1314]

Since the trading obligation is regulated under MiFIR, a regulation directly applicable in the Member States (Article 288 (2) TFEU), no national act of transposition is necessary.

1309 Cf. Kumpan and Schmidt (n 4) Art 23 paras 1, 5; Gomber and Nassauer (n 1086) 255.

1310 Article 23(1) MiFIR; Kumpan and Schmidt (n 4) Art 23 paras 8ff.

1311 Article 2(a) Commission Delegated Regulation (EU) No. 2017/587 of 14 July 2016.

1312 Article 2(b) Commission Delegated Regulation (EU) No. 2017/587 of 14 July 2016.

1313 Article 2(e) Commission Delegated Regulation (EU) No. 2017/587 of 14 July 2016. See also Kumpan and Schmidt (n 4) Art 23 para 10.

1314 Kumpan and Schmidt (n 4) Art 23 paras 13ff; Moloney, *EU Securities and Financial Markets Regulation* (n 4) 622.

2. For Derivatives

Article 28 MiFIR also contains a trading obligation for derivates. This obligation is also directly applicable in the Member States. There are two reasons for subjecting derivatives, as the only non-equity instrument, to a trading obligation: First, similar to shares, derivatives are actively traded instruments with liquid markets that can support organization and transparency.[1315] Second, having been regarded as a major cause of the Global Financial Crisis of 2008-09, the G20 Leaders agreed in their statement of the 2009 Pittsburgh Summit that *'(...) [a]ll standardized OTC derivative contracts should be traded on exchanges or electronic platforms, where appropriate, and cleared through central counterparties (...).'*[1316]

The trading obligation for derivates also shifts trading from the OTC-space onto organized trading systems, but unlike the trading obligation for shares, Article 28(1) MiFIR limits the eligible trading systems to regulated market, MTF, OTF or a recognized third-country trading venue. Systematic internalizers, however, do not qualify as an eligible trading system for derivatives under Article 28(1) MiFIR.[1317]

While also aiming at increasing trade transparency in the derivatives market, the trading obligation for derivatives, further aims at improving the orderly negotiating and enabling of the application of position limits.[1318] Therefore, the rationale of the trading obligation for derivatives is different from the one for shares: it is not only about trade transparency for the sake of price formation per se, but rather to avoid systematic risk building up in the OTC market beyond the sight of other market participants and the regulators. When other market participants induce a market reaction in case of risk building up in the derivatives markets, this is ultimately reflected in the market price and serves as a signal to the investing public and regulators alike.[1319] Thus, the trading obligation for derivatives aims for more transparency as well as facilitated regulatory monitoring, operational and risk-management efficiencies, and liquidity enhancements.[1320]

1315 Lehmann (n 1088) MiFIR Art 28 paras 1, 6–7.

1316 Lehmann (n 1088) MiFIR Art 28 paras 9–10; Gomber and Nassauer (n 1086) 255.

1317 Lehmann (n 1088) MiFIR Art 28 para 21; Gomber and Nassauer (n 1086) 255.

1318 Lehmann (n 1088) MiFIR Art 28 para 1.

1319 ibid MiFIR Art 28 paras 9–10.

1320 FSB, 'Implementing OTC Derivatives Market Reforms' (25 October 2010) 39–43; Moloney, *EU Securities and Financial Markets Regulation* (n 4) 623.

However, the trading obligation does not apply to all derivatives. Article 28(1) MiFIR ties the trading obligation only to standardized derivatives that are under the clearing obligation of EMIR. Only such standardized derivatives are considered to be sufficiently liquid to support organized trading on a trading venue.[1321] Consequently, the Commission first needs to impose the clearing obligation on a new derivative under EMIR before, in a second step, the Commission can adopt a delegated act in which it subjects the derivative to the trading obligation under Article 28 MiFIR.[1322] Which derivatives (or classes of derivatives) are standardized enough to be subjected to both clearing and trading obligations is also contingent on the liquidity levels of those derivatives.[1323] This is a calibration for the thinner liquidity levels that usually characterize the derivatives market compared to equity markets.[1324]

Since the trading obligation for derivatives is not universal but requires acts by the Commission to subject a new (class of) derivatives to Article 28(1) MiFIR, there is the risk of the Commission not performing this task in due time or at all. To allow for appropriate adaption to changed market conditions, ESMA is tasked with monitoring the activity in the derivatives not yet declared subject to the trading obligation. When ESMA identifies cases where derivatives may pose systematic risk or risk of regulatory arbitrage if not subjected to Article 28(1) MiFIR, it drafts a regulatory technical standard for the Commission to subject those instruments into the perimeter of the trading obligation.[1325]

The flipside of the trading obligation for derivatives is their eligibility to be admitted to regulated markets or any other trading venue as referred to in Article 28(1) MiFIR on a non-exclusive and non-discriminatory basis.[1326] By enabling efficient competition among trading venues, the legislator aims for cost reduction effects in liquid derivatives markets as achieved in the

1321 Recital 25 MiFIR. Lehmann (n 1088) MiFIR Art 28 para 20; Moloney, *EU Securities and Financial Markets Regulation* (n 4) 622.

1322 For the procedure see Article 32 MiFIR. See also Lehmann (n 1088) MiFIR Art 28 para 19.

1323 Recital 25 MiFIR. Lehmann (n 1088) MiFIR Art 28 para 20; Moloney, *EU Securities and Financial Markets Regulation* (n 4) 623.

1324 Moloney, *EU Securities and Financial Markets Regulation* (n 4) 623.

1325 Article 28(2) subpara 2, (5) MiFIR; Moloney, *EU Securities and Financial Markets Regulation* (n 4) 625.

1326 Lehmann (n 1088) MiFIR Art 28 para 22; Moloney, *EU Securities and Financial Markets Regulation* (n 4) 625.

market for shares under MiFID I.[1327] While this provision directly binds RMs, MTFs and OTFs within the EU, it cannot bind trading venues in third countries since the EU has no jurisdiction over them. However, when making the equivalence decision, the Commission must ensure such third-country trading venues actually meet those requirements.[1328]

In the Annex of CDR (EU) 2017/2417,[1329] the Commission subjected only a limited number of classes of derivatives to the trading obligation, i.e., fixed-to-float interest rate swaps denominated in Euro, British Pound Sterling, and US Dollar as well as index credit default swaps (Index CDS).[1330] The Commission chose those instruments because they have the highest levels of liquidity and therefore can sustain trading on a multilateral trading venue.[1331] Insofar, the Commission also shows a rather cautious approach since both the trading obligation for derivatives and the entailing trade transparency regime implemented for such instruments on the trading venues is a new adjustment for the market.[1332] This, too, is a calibration of MiFID II/MiFIR for the trade-off between liquidity and trade transparency.[1333]

Thus, the trading obligation for derivatives not only pursues the goal of improving price formation but also avoiding the unattended piling of risk in the OTC sector. Bringing liquid standardized derivatives onto trading venues should also generate more competition among organized trading venues and reduce spreads to ultimately benefit the investors.[1334]

1327 Gomber and others (n 1295) 7; Moloney, *EU Securities and Financial Markets Regulation* (n 4) 623.

1328 Lehmann (n 1088) MiFIR Art 28 paras 17, 25–6.

1329 Commission Delegated Regulation (EU) 2017/2417 of 17 November 2017.

1330 Lehmann (n 1088) MiFIR Art 28 para 24.

1331 Recitals 2–4 of Commission Delegated Regulation (EU) 2017/2417 of 17 November 2017.

1332 Lehmann (n 1088) MiFIR Art 28 para 24.

1333 See above Part II § 6 B.III.1.a).dd).

1334 Moloney, *EU Securities and Financial Markets Regulation* (n 4) 623.

C. Trade Transparency Regime under MiFID II/MiFIR

I. Role of the Trade Transparency Regime for Dark Trading under MiFID II/MiFIR

While it is the objective of the trading system regime to aggregate organized trading on trading venues and systematic internalizers, the trade transparency regime aims to enhance trade transparency by shining a light on those trading system marking the difference between lit and dark trading. However, the transparency regime only shines a light on certain orders and transactions while it spares others from the prying eyes of the investing public. The scope of the transparency regime decides how much trading remains untouched by pre- and post-trade transparency requirements, slipping through as unregulated dark trading. It also determines which trades support price formation as lit trading and which orders and trades should be privileged by an exemption from trade transparency. The latter describes how much regulated dark trading, created by a conscious regulatory decision, may occur on secondary markets.

Enforcing the trade transparency regime while avoiding high amounts of dark trading has also been a major objective in the review process of MiFID I.[1335] With MiFID II/MiFIR, the European Union aimed to strengthen trade transparency on financial markets after it identified loopholes and weaknesses under MiFID I before and during the Global Financial Crisis of 2008-09.[1336] A crucial step was moving the trade transparency regime into a separate Regulation, MiFIR, which complements the Directive MiFID II and is directly applicable in the Member States. This avoided deviations in the transposition process, increased harmonization, and created a single rulebook for trade transparency throughout the European Union.[1337] Another mechanism to elevate harmonization was to provide ESMA with

1335 European Commission, 'Commission Staff Working Paper Impact Assessment EU Commission, Impact Assessment' (n 382) 12–3; European Parliament (n 434) 4ff. See also Busch (n 1086) 130.

1336 Recital 1 MiFIR. Kumpan and Schmidt (n 4) Foreword MiFIR para 9; Busch (n 1086) 129–30.

1337 Recital 2, 3 MiFIR. Moloney, 'EU Financial Governance and Transparency Regulation' (n 3) para 12.02 who also sees the risk that there is little to no leeway to correct for regulatory errors on the member state level.

more power for proposing implementing measures and a new role in the coordination among NCAs.[1338]

Besides the instrument of harmonization, the transparency regime under MiFIR has been expanded compared to MiFID I so that less trading can occur outside the transparency regime. The expansion is most visible with regard to the instruments covered: while MiFID I only covered shares, MiFIR also covers other equity-like instruments,[1339] such as, depositary receipts, ETFs, certificates and other similar financial instruments, and non-equity instruments, such as, bonds, structured finance products, emission allowances and derivatives.[1340] This broad scope of the transparency regime was motivated by the commitments for increased transparency made during the G20 Summit in Pittsburgh as a reaction to the Global Financial Crisis of 2008-09.[1341] Another way the trade transparency regime has been broadened under MiFIR is by limiting the scope and usage of the exemptions from trade transparency, i.e., the waivers and deferrals from trade transparency discussed subsequently.[1342]

II. Pre-trade Transparency Regime for Trading Venues

The trade transparency regime under MiFIR reflects the ordering principles of the trading system regime under MiFID II. Like with MiFID II, the regulatory logic anchors its regime in the multilateral trading venues moving on to bilateral trading systems and the OTC-space. Unlike under its predecessor MiFID I, MiFIR provides for common pre-trade transparency rules for all multilateral trading venues (i.e., RM, MTF and OTF) reflecting the level-playing field among them. Within the trade transparency regime, MiFIR distinguishes between pre-trade transparency for equity instruments (Article 3) and non-equity instruments (Article 8) to tailor the transparen-

1338 Kumpan and Schmidt (n 4) MiFIR Art 4 para 26; Moloney, *EU Securities and Financial Markets Regulation* (n 4) 483; Moloney, 'EU Financial Governance and Transparency Regulation' (n 3) para 12.36; Salger (n 627) 194; Humbel, *Die Regelung der Vor- und Nachhandelstransparenz in der Europäischen Union und der Schweiz* (n 50) 240; Veil and Lerch, 'Auf dem Weg zu einem Europäischen Finanzmarktrecht' (n 1132) 1564.

1339 Recital 12 MiFIR.

1340 See Articles 3, 8 MiFIR. Ekkenga (n 96) § 7 para 136.

1341 Recital 1 MiFIR. Kumpan and Schmidt (n 4) Foreword MiFIR para 9.

1342 Kumpan and Schmidt (n 4) Foreword MiFIR para 10.

cy requirements and the subsequent exemptions to the respective asset class.[1343]

The pattern of trade transparency rules for equity instruments under Article 3 ff MiFIR begins with lit trading as the default rule, going to dark trading as the (regulated) exception, and ultimately, for certain exceptions, back to lit trading again. The pattern for non-equity instruments also starts out with lit trading as the default rule but has a more limited scope than trade transparency for equity instruments and goes to dark trading via regulated exceptions. These patterns will be laid out in the following.

1. Pre-Trade Transparency for Equity Instruments

a) Rule

Article 3(1) MiFIR requires market operators and investment firms operating a trading venue to make public the current bid and offer prices and the depth of the trading interest at those prices which are advertised through their systems for shares, depositary receipts, ETFs, certificates, and other similar financial instruments.[1344]

This provision makes lit trading the default rule for trading in equity instruments on trading venues. Every trading system operator is obliged to offer pre-trade transparent trading or has to find an exception from this default rule to offer dark trading services as seen after having discussed the scope of the pre-trade transparency rule of Article 3 MiFIR.

b) Addressee of Obligation

This obligation applies to market operators and investment firms that operate a regulated market or an MTF. Even though, OTFs also count among the definition of trading venues according to Article 4(1)(24) MiFID II, they cannot support trading in equity instruments since their definition is limited to non-equity instruments.[1345] Investment firms trading on the

1343 Recital 10 MiFIR; Kumpan and Schmidt (n 4) Foreword MiFIR para 9.

1344 Gebauer (n 94) MiFIR Art 3 para 2; Moloney, 'EU Financial Governance and Transparency Regulation' (n 3) para 12.18.

1345 Article 4(1)(23) MiFID II; Gebauer (n 94) MiFIR Art 3 para 8.

trading venue are not obligated to publish pre-trade information, since the system operators do it for them.[1346]

Under German law, the dualism of exchange as a public-law entity (Section 2(1) BörsG) and the exchange operator as a private-law entity (Sections 5, 52 BörsG)[1347] raises the question of which entity is obligated to publish pre-trade transparency information under Article 3(1) MiFIR. Since the exchange hosts the trading on the regulated market, it is the exchange that is obligated to publish pre-trade transparency information.[1348] However, the exchange can delegate the obligation to the exchange operator, who supplies the public-law exchange with staff and other operating equipment, while remaining the primary addressee of the obligation.[1349]

c) Scope of Pre-trade Transparency

aa) Equity Instruments

With regard to the captured instruments, it must be noted that the new pre-trade transparency rule for equity instruments is much broader than under MiFID I which was limited to shares admitted for trading on a regulated market only.[1350] The transposition of MiFID I into German law, former Section 31g WpHG and former Section 30(1) BörsG, also included depositary receipts since they are a functional equivalent to shares.[1351] Depositary receipts are traded as substitutes to shares by investors and should therefore be subject to the same transparency requirements.[1352] Such

---

1346 Thelen (n 147) 172.

1347 For further reading on the dualism under German law, see Klöhn, '§ 6 Kapitalmarktrecht' (n 68) § 6 paras 48–51.

1348 Cf. ibid § 6 paras 49–50; Lutter, Bayer and Schmidt (n 1090) § 32 para 32.37.

1349 Gebauer (n 94) MiFIR Art 3 para 11.

1350 Busch (n 1086) 130; Moloney, 'EU Financial Governance and Transparency Regulation' (n 3) para 12.18.

1351 Thomas Seiffert in Heribert Hirte and Thomas M J Möllers (eds), *Kölner Kommentar zum WpHG* (2nd edn, Carl Heymanns Verlag 2014) WpHG § 31g para 5. See for definition of depositary receipts Article 2(1)(25) MiFIR and Article 4(1)(45) of MiFID II: *"depositary receipts' means those securities which are negotiable on the capital market and which represent ownership of the securities of a non-domiciled issuer while being able to be admitted to trading on a regulated market and traded independently of the securities of the non-domiciled issuer'.*

1352 Gebauer (n 94) MiFIR Art 3 paras 2, 13; Seiffert (n 1351) WpHG § 31g para 5.

gold-plating of EU law by national law is, however, no longer feasible with a directly applicable regulation MiFIR.[1353]

Since subjecting additional asset classes to pre-trade transparency is the goal of MiFIR,[1354] Article 3(1) MiFIR provides pre-trade transparency information for orders in all equity instruments. This encompasses shares, depositary receipts, ETFs, certificates, and other similar financial instruments that are used by traders for similar economic purposes.[1355] Article 3(1) MiFIR even uses *'other similar financial instruments'* as a catch-all category to ensure broad pre-trade transparency for equity instruments and to capture new equity-like instruments created by financial innovation to prevent regulatory arbitrage in the future.[1356]

bb) Traded on a Trading Venue

Another way in which MiFID II/MiFIR broadened the scope of pre-trade transparency was by requiring pre-trade transparency data for all equity instruments that are traded on a trading venue (TOTV) from trading venue operators.[1357] This is a significant improvement over the scope of MiFID I which only required pre-trade transparency from shares that were admitted for trading on a regulated market, thus, excluding all shares that were only admitted to MTFs but not RMs at the time.[1358] This narrower scope enabled unregulated dark trading in a blind spot of MiFID I on otherwise regulated MTFs, which particularly effected shares of SMEs since those

1353 Recital 5 MiFIR.

1354 Recital 1 MiFIR.

1355 Recital 12 MiFIR; Gebauer (n 94) MiFIR Art 3 paras 13ff; Busch (n 1086) 130; Moloney, 'EU Financial Governance and Transparency Regulation' (n 3) para 12.18.

1356 Recital 12 MiFIR; Gebauer (n 94) MiFIR Art 3 para 17.

1357 Recitals 10, 11 MiFIR; Moloney, *EU Securities and Financial Markets Regulation* (n 4) 460–1; Christian Hoops, 'Das ToTV-Kriterium der MiFID II in der Rechtspraxis' [2018] ZBB 410; Christian Schmies and Alexander Sajnovits, 'Data Reporting: Market Structures and Regulatory Framework' (EBI Working Paper Series 2020 - No. 76, European Banking Institute, Frankfurt am Main, 6 November 2020) 10.

1358 ESMA, 'Opinion: OTC Derivatives Traded on a Trading Venue' (ESMA70-156-117, 22 May 2017) 2; Gebauer (n 94) MiFIR Art 3 para 18; Kumpan and Schmidt (n 4) MiFIR Art 3 paras 9ff.

shares most often were only admitted to trading on an MTF.[1359] The former limitation to shares admitted to trading on RMs tilted the level playing field in two ways: While dark MTFs benefitted from unregulated dark trading in shares not admitted to RMs, RMs themselves benefitted from the status of exchange trading being considered highly transparent.[1360] The new transparency regime corrects this uneven playing field and supports lit MTF trading over dark trading.

The enhanced trading infrastructure and the trading obligation for shares of large amounts of organized trading is brought back onto trading venues, OTC orders in equity instruments is a much smaller issue than it had been before.[1361]

d) Content of Publication

aa) Current Bid and Offer Prices

With regard to the content of the pre-trade transparency requirement, the market operators and investment firms operating a trading venue must publish the current bid and offer prices advertised through their system.[1362] Unlike with US-ATS, the phrase that the prices need to be 'advertised' does not mean that a trading venue can evade pre-trade transparency by simply not showing prices internally. While this interpretation was discussed for EU law, CESR already clarified that 'advertised' is to be understood generally: CESR considered all pieces of information that RMs and MTFs should generally display, like price and volume, as 'advertised' within the system subject to publication (or application for a waiver) regardless of whether the specific trading system displayed such information or not.[1363] Since prices are generally shown within a trading system, the rule does not alter

1359 Hoops, 'Das ToTV-Kriterium der MiFID II in der Rechtspraxis' (n 1357) 411; Moloney, *EU Securities and Financial Markets Regulation* (n 4) 455.

1360 Cf. Article 44(1)(1) MiFID I; Alexander, 'Market Structures and Market Abuse' (n 484) 388; Moloney, *EU Securities and Financial Markets Regulation* (n 4) 439 who stipulates that RMs and MTFs were only on a level-playing field with respect to trading in shares admitted to RMs but not regarding shares admitted only to MTFs.

1361 Kumpan and Schmidt (n 4) MiFIR Art 3 paras 9–10.

1362 Gebauer (n 94) MiFIR Art 3 para 20.

1363 CESR, 'CESR's Technical Advice on Possible Implementing Measures of the Directive 2004/39/EC on Markets in Financial Instruments' (CESR/05-290b, April 2005) 52.

whether or not the specific trading venue shows prices.[1364] With this rather prescriptive and result-oriented interpretation, EU law avoided opening up a major loophole in the pre-trade transparency regime.

bb) Depth of Trading Interest at Those Prices

In addition to price information, the trading venue operator must also publish the depth of the trading interest at that price. This means the volume, for instance, the number of shares, that should be sold or bought with the respective order at a specific price must be published as well.[1365] Only when price and volume of orders on both sides of the market are transparent, can investors assess the current market situation and make informed trading decisions.[1366]

cc) Actionable Indications of Interest

The new pre-trade transparency requirement captures not only orders in equity instruments but also 'actionable indications of interest' (Article 3(1)(2) MiFIR).[1367] According to Article 2(1)(33) MiFIR, an actionable IOI is a message from one member or participant to another within a trading system in relation to available trading interests that contains all necessary information to agree on a trade.[1368]

Unlike a fully-fledged order, an IOI is rather an invitation to the other party to place an order the inviting party may trade on. It is, thus, equivalent to an *invitatio ad offerendum* under German Contract Law.[1369] In this context, the *invitatio* is also meant to inform the market about the price and the product or service on offer. The only reason for not making a firm offer is that the 'inviting' party wishes to leave it to the bilateral negotiation if it wants to contract with the other party and in what quantity the 'inviting'

1364 ibid 52.

1365 Gebauer (n 94) MiFIR Art 3 para 21; Christoph Boschan, *Wertpapierhandelssysteme: Erscheinungsformen und Funktionsweisen, rechtliche Systematisierung und aufsichtsrechtliche Behandlung* (Ph.D.-Thesis TU Chemnitz 2007, Verlag Dr. Kovač 2007) 408.

1366 Gebauer (n 94) MiFIR Art 3 para 21.

1367 ibid MiFIR Art 3 para 22; Kumpan and Schmidt (n 4) MiFIR Art 3 para 6.

1368 Article 2(1)(33) MiFIR; Recital 7 MiFIR.

1369 Jan Busche in Franz J Säcker and others (eds), *Münchener Kommentar zum Bürgerlichen Gesetzbuch* (vol. 1, 9th edn, CH Beck 2021) BGB § 145 para 10.

party wants to enter into a trade with the offeror.[1370] However, in the context of contract law in general and in financial markets in particular, information about the reservation price and the general willingness to trade of the inviting party is revealed to all who learn about the invitation. Thus, this information should be public if broad transparency is the policy goal.

Since actionable IOIs do not formally fulfil the requirements of an order but still function in a technically similar manner, they were a means of unregulated dark trading since they did not (yet) trigger the pre-trade transparency obligation.[1371]

In dark pools, IOIs play an important role in increasing execution probability and execution speed, but they simultaneously raise issues of informational advantages and an uneven playing field.[1372] When an order is sent into a dark pool, it might well happen that no liquidity is currently available to execute this order. If the dark pool operator intends to accelerate the execution process, it can send an IOI to a frequent trader in the pool who appears suitable from the operator's perspective.[1373] As shown above, actionable IOIs are still used in US-ATS as a means to inform liquidity providers, such as HTFs, about available liquidity in the dark pool.[1374] This frequent trader, who is often an HFT, learns that there is a specific trading interest in the pool. The HFT then possesses an informational advantage because the dark pool is no longer fully opaque to them, and they can either use the trading opportunity provided by the dark pool operator or turn around and exploit the informational advantage on another market, or both.[1375]

Often, a trader in a dark pool formally consented to this practice of sending actionable IOIs to other privileged parties by accepting the terms and conditions of the trading system operator.[1376] Even though national contract law, in principle, offers protection to a certain extend via the law of terms and conditions (e.g., Sections 305 ff of the German Civil Code) suing the dark pool operator in court is insufficient to avoid loss in investor

1370 Cf. ibid 10.

1371 IOSCO, 'Principles for Dark Liquidity' (n 12) 4ff; Kumpan and Schmidt (n 4) MiFIR Art 3 para 6.

1372 Kumpan and Schmidt (n 4) MiFIR Art 3 para 6.

1373 IOSCO, 'Principles for Dark Liquidity' (n 12) 6 (fn 10), 23.

1374 See above Part II § 5 I.III.

1375 IOSCO, 'Principles for Dark Liquidity' (n 12) 23; Kumpan and Schmidt (n 4) MiFIR Art 3 para 6; Kasiske (n 11) 457.

1376 Kasiske (n 11) 457.

confidence. To avoid such detrimental effects, the new trade transparency regime also applies to actionable IOIs avoiding this type of unregulated dark trading. Including IOIs into the pre-trade transparency obligation is therefore a necessary step to avoid informational advantages used to the detriment of mostly unaware users of dark pools and other trading venues.[1377]

e) Modalities of Publication

Besides the broadening of the scope, Article 3(2) MiFIR requires the transparency requirements to be calibrated for the different types of trading systems.[1378] The defining the details was delegated to the level 2 measures[1379] and can be found in Article 3(1) MiFIR and Table 1 in Annex I of Commission Delegated Regulation (EU) 2017/587 of 14 July 2016. The five types of trading systems are trading systems operating a continuous auction order book, quote-driven, periodic auction, request for quote system, and hybrid systems which are systems that fall into two or more of the aforementioned categories.[1380]

Continuous auction order book trading systems do not have to make their entire order book transparent; it is usually sufficient if only the best five orders on the sell- and on the buy-side are published. In quote-driven systems, each market maker must make public the best bid and offer price and the volumes attached to those prices.[1381]

Furthermore, according to Article 3(1)(3) MiFIR and Article 3(1) Table I of Annex I CDR 2017/587, the trading venue operator has to publish the aforementioned pre-trade transparency information on a continuous basis during normal trading hours. The normal trading hours are determined by the trading venue itself.[1382] In this period, the trading venue needs to ensure a continuous and uninterrupted updating of the order flow and that

1377 Salger (n 627) 211.
1378 Moloney, 'EU Financial Governance and Transparency Regulation' (n 3) para 12.18.
1379 Article 4(6)(a) MiFIR; Gebauer (n 94) MiFIR Art 3 para 23.
1380 ibid MiFIR Art 3 para 23.
1381 ibid MiFIR Art 3 para 24.
1382 ibid MiFIR Art 3 para 25. For MTFs under German law see Section 72(1)(1)(2) WpHG.

all incoming orders are subject to pre-trade transparency unless a waiver applies.[1383]

However, publication of pre-trade transparency data does not necessarily mean that it is (immediately) disseminated free of charge to the investing public. According to Article 13(1)(1) MiFIR, the trading venue operator satisfies the pre-trade transparency requirement when it makes the information available on reasonable commercial basis and ensures non-discriminatory access to it.[1384] By asking for compensation for the data feed, the price formation service, which shares many features with a public good, receives an equivalent to a property right because others can be excluded from using it without paying the producer of the positive externality. Price referencing systems such as dark pools cannot free ride the price formation function of lit exchanges jeopardizing its production. Thus, MiFID II/MiFIR solves this central issue of dark trading and price formation in financial markets.[1385]

The fact that Article 13(1)(2) MiFIR requires publication of pre-trade transparency data free of charge 15 minutes after publication does not conflict with this assessment. In liquid and fast-moving markets such as equity trading markets, pre-trade transparency information from 15 minutes prior is almost uninformative and merely serves as a general source of information but cannot be exploited by investors to gain an informational edge via informed trading.[1386]

f) Access to Data and the System for Systematic Internalizers

Under Article 3(3) MiFIR, trading venue operators shall give access to their pre-trade transparency information to investment firms operating as a systematic internalizer on reasonable commercial terms and on a non-discriminatory basis as under Article 13(1)(1) MiFIR. In addition to Article 13(1)(1) MiFIR, a trading venue's obligation to publish the pre-trade transparency information also includes the obligation to publish quotes systematic internalizers have to publish according to Articles 14(1), 15(1)

1383 Gebauer (n 94) MiFIR Art 3 para 25; cf. Matthias Stötzel, 'High Frequency Trading: Einordnung in das Börsen- und Kapitalmarktrecht' [2011] RdF 156, 159.

1384 Gebauer (n 94) MiFIR Art 3 para 26.

1385 See on the issue of public goods, positive externalities and free riding by dark pools above Part I § 3 D.IV.

1386 Gebauer (n 94) MiFIR Art 3 para 26; Boschan (n 1365) 43.

MiFIR. This obligation, however, only applies if the trading venue also hosts trading in such financial instrument.[1387]

2. Pre-Trade Transparency for Non-Equity Instruments on Trading Venues

a) Paradigm Shift from MiFID I to MiFID II/MiFIR

Article 8 MiFIR introduced an entirely new transparency regime for non-equity instruments under EU law, marking a major change from MiFID I to MiFID II/MiFIR.[1388] When promulgating MiFID II/MiFIR, the European Union intended to create a comprehensive transparency framework for all relevant financial instruments which also includes non-equity instruments.[1389] After the Global Financial Crisis of 2008-09, the European Union considered it necessary to extend trade transparency also to bonds, structured finance products, emission allowances, derivatives traded on a trading venue and package orders to support the valuation and the efficient price formation in the markets for those products.[1390] A regulatory response to the Global Financial Crisis of 2008-09 was the application of trade transparency rules on secured finance products, which include asset backed securities, those financial instruments considered to be a cause of the crisis.[1391] Moreover, with the introduction of a transparency regime for non-equity instruments, the European Union fulfills the commitment it made to the G20 in the Pittsburgh Summit amidst the crisis to bring derivatives trading onto trading venues and increase trade transparency in such markets.[1392]

b) Article 8(1) MiFIR: The Rule

At first glance, Article 8(1) MiFIR mirrors the pre-trade transparency rule for equities under Article 3(1) MiFIR by requiring market operators and

1387 Gebauer (n 94) MiFIR Art 3 paras 28f.

1388 Kumpan and Schmidt (n 4) MiFIR Art 8 para 1; Busch (n 1086) 130; Moloney, *EU Securities and Financial Markets Regulation* (n 4) 485; Moloney, 'EU Financial Governance and Transparency Regulation' (n 3) para 12.22.

1389 Recital 14 MiFIR; Busch (n 1086) 130.

1390 Gebauer (n 94) MiFIR Art 8 paras 1–2; Kumpan and Schmidt (n 4) Foreword MiFIR para 9 and MiFIR Art 8 para 1; Gomber and Nassauer (n 1086) 254.

1391 Recital 15 MiFIR.

1392 Kumpan and Schmidt (n 4) Foreword MiFIR para 9.

investment firms operating a trading venue to make public the current bid and offer prices and their volume for bonds, structured finance products, emission allowances, derivatives traded on a trading venue and package orders.[1393] Unlike for equity instruments, however, in the non-equity context, 'trading venue' actually refers to all trading venues under Article 4(1)(24) MiFID II, which includes the OTF that is limited to non-equities trading only.[1394] Thus, a dark pool operator needs to find an exception from this general rule to offer dark trading services.[1395]

Like Article 3(1) MiFIR for equities, Article 8(1) MiFIR also pursues the rationale of providing investors with the necessary information to assess trading opportunities in the market and support the price formation process of non-equity markets. However, Article 8(1) MiFIR deviates in some respects from Article 3(1) MiFIR because the market for non-equities is subject to different economic restraints.[1396] Compared to markets for equity instruments, non-equity markets are generally less liquid and more volatile with fewer traders and therefore have a higher dependency on market makers who take over liquidity and market risk.[1397]

c) Content of Publication

As under Article 3(1) MiFIR, Article 8(1) MiFIR also requires the trading venue operator to publish the bid and offer prices and the depth of the orders at those prices which are advertised through their systems.[1398] Under Article 8(1)(2) the 2014 iteration of MiFIR currently in force, the pre-trade transparency obligation also extends to actionable indications of interest.[1399]

The MiFIR refit process, however, shows a worrying development: The first Draft Report by the Committee on Economic and Monetary Affairs of

1393 Gebauer (n 94) MiFIR Art 8 para 1; Busch (n 1086) 130; Moloney, *EU Securities and Financial Markets Regulation* (n 4) 485ff; Lutter, Bayer and Schmidt (n 1090) paras 32.57–8; Schmies and Sajnovits (n 1357) 11; Veil and Lerch, 'Auf dem Weg zu einem Europäischen Finanzmarktrecht' (n 1132) 1564.

1394 Gebauer (n 94) MiFIR Art 8 para 9.

1395 Cf. Busch (n 1086) 131.

1396 Recital 15 MiFIR. Gebauer (n 94) MiFIR Art 8 para 1.

1397 Moloney, *EU Securities and Financial Markets Regulation* (n 4) 431ff, 486; Moloney, 'EU Financial Governance and Transparency Regulation' (n 3) paras 12.13, 12.22.

1398 Gebauer (n 94) MiFIR Art 8 paras 3, 27–8.

1399 ibid MiFIR Art 8 para 29. See for details on IOIs above Part II § 6.C.II.1.d).cc).

the European Parliament dated 26 July 2022 deleted this extension on IOIs entirely,[1400] the Amendments 102 – 313 dated 20.10.2022 brought Article 8(1)(2) MiFIR as it currently is back into the report,[1401] only to delete it again in the final Report dated 2 March 2023 that was submitted to the European Parliament for the first plenary reading.[1402]

Unfortunately, no reason was given for either the initial deletion of Article 8(1)(2) MiFIR, its re-insertion, or its eventual deletion. An educated guess may be that the Committee on Economic and Monetary Affairs intended (if not deleted by mistake) to reduce complexity in the transparency regime and lift the burden pre-trade transparency in rather illiquid non-equity instruments that might benefit from some selected attention through IOIs without making big noise in the larger market.[1403]

Nevertheless, such good intentions may be misguided because leaving IOIs outside the scope of the transparency regime opens the door for an unwelcome erosion of the default rule that requires trading venues to show pre-trade transparency to the public. Moreover, it invites opportunistic behavior such as the signaling of available orders in dark pools by dark pool operators to select HFTs as has been the case in the US.[1404] This may tilt the level playing field at the detriment of unaware dark pool users and traders on lit pools equally unaware of the preferential treatment of some.[1405] This should be avoided by leaving Article 8(1)(2) MiFIR as it is and correct for adverse effects of pre-trade transparency by having appropriate waivers

1400 Committee on Economic and Monetary Affairs, 'Draft Report: on the proposal for a regulation of the European Parliament and of the Council amending Regulation (EU) No 600/2014 as regards enhancing market data transparency, removing obstacles to the emergence of a consolidated tape, optimising the trading obligations and prohibiting receiving payments for forwarding client orders (COM(2021)727 - C9-0440/2021 - 2021/0385(COD))' (2021/0385(COD), European Parliament, Rapporteur: Danuta Maria Hübner, 26 July 2022) 33.

1401 Committee on Economic and Monetary Affairs, 'Amendments 102 - 313: Amending Regulation (EU) No 600/2014 as regards enhancing market data transparency, removing obstacles to the emergence of a consolidated tape, optimising the trading obligations and prohibiting receiving payments for forwarding client orders Proposal for a regulation (COM(2021)727 - C9-0440/2021 - 2021/0385(COD))' (2021/0385(COD), European Parliament, 20 October 2022) 111.

1402 Committee on Economic and Monetary Affairs, 'Report' (n 1137) 22.

1403 Cf. Committee on Economic and Monetary Affairs, 'Draft Report' (n 1400) 100–1.

1404 See for instance: *ITG Inc.* (n 26) 9 paras 44–5.

1405 European Commission, 'Proposal for a Regulation of the European Parliament and of the Council on markets in financial instruments and amending Regulation [EMIR] on OTC derivates, central counterparties and trade repositories' (n 1124) 8, 31.

from pre-trade transparency that honor the default rule but allow in pre-defined cases for regulated dark trading under the supervision of the NCA and ESMA.

d) Captured Instruments

The financial instruments captured by pre-trade transparency are for bonds, structured finance products, emission allowances, derivatives traded on a trading venue and package orders. Non-equities are also subject to the TOTV approach discussed for equities including non-equities admitted to RMs, MTFs, and OTFs. This leaves only OTC instruments out of the scope of Article 8 MiFIR.[1406]

Although the principal functioning of pre-trade transparency is the same for equities and non-equities, Article 8(1) MiFIR refers only to specific non-equity instruments and lacks a catch-all category like the '*other similar financial instruments*' under Article 3(1) MiFIR. Due to this omission, financial innovation can create new non-equity instruments that may either fit under an existing category or fall outside the regulatory scope. This vulnerability has led to an amendment of Article 8(1) MiFIR by Article 1(5) of the amending Regulation (EU) 2016/1033 ('quick fix').[1407] In this process the phrase 'and package orders' has been added to Article 8(1) MiFIR.[1408] Package transactions, resulting from package orders, are transactions in derivatives and other financial instruments or assets that comprise of a number of interlinked, contingent trades, so-called 'exchange for physical' transactions.[1409] They have been added because such multifaceted risk-management transactions by investment firms should not build up risk outside the regulatory perimeter.[1410] This shows, while the pre-trade transparency regime for equities is no longer susceptible to being outrun by financial innovation, the newly added pre-trade transparency requirement for non-equities still is. However, this more lenient approach under Article 8 MiFIR designed to avoid automatic inclusion of instruments trading in

1406 Gebauer (n 94) MiFIR Art 8 para 25. See above Part II § 6 C.II.1.c).bb).

1407 Article 1(5) of Regulation (EU) 2016/1033 of the European Parliament and of the Council of 23 June 2016.

1408 Kumpan and Schmidt (n 4) MiFIR Art 8 para 2.

1409 Gebauer (n 94) MiFIR Art 8 paras 21ff.

1410 Recital 12 of Regulation (EU) 2016/1033 of the European Parliament and of the Council of 23 June 2016.

rather illiquid markets within the scope of pre-trade transparency is meant to protect such markets from drying up. This is important since the risk allocative function of the debt market should not be stifled.[1411]

e) Non-Equity Specific Exemptions of Pre-Trade Transparency

To account for the specifics of non-equity trading, Article 8(1)(4) MiFIR exempts derivative transactions of non-financial counterparties which are objectively measurable to reduce risks which directly relate to commercial activity or treasury financing activity of the non-financial counterparty or of the non-financial counterparty's group.[1412] The term non-financial counterparty is defined in Article 2(1)(9) EMIR[1413] as the opposite of central counterparties[1414] and financial counterparties,[1415] meaning it is any trader that is not an investment firm, alternative investment fund, UCIT etc.[1416] This is the first exception to the default rule of pre-trade transparency for trading in non-equities that allows for dark trading. With this exemption, the pre-trade transparency regime shall be calibrated for the special demands of non-equity instruments reflecting a fear within the European Union in the crisis-era that extension of the transparency regime may have

1411 Cf. Moloney, *EU Securities and Financial Markets Regulation* (n 4) 485ff.

1412 Gebauer (n 94) MiFIR Art 8 para 26; Moloney, 'EU Financial Governance and Transparency Regulation' (n 3) para 12.22.

1413 Regulation (EU) No 648/2012 of the European Parliament and of the Council of 4 July 2012.

1414 According to Article 2(1)(1) EMIR a central counterparty or *'(…) 'CCP' means a legal person that interposes itself between the counterparties to the contracts traded on one or more financial markets, becoming the buyer to every seller and the seller to every buyer'.*

1415 According to Article 2(1)(8) of EMIR a financial counterparty *'(…) means an investment firm authorised in accordance with Directive 2004/39/EC, a credit institution authorised in accordance with Directive 2006/48/EC, an insurance undertaking authorised in accordance with Directive 73/239/EEC, an assurance undertaking authorised in accordance with Directive 2002/83/EC, a reinsurance undertaking authorised in accordance with Directive 2005/68/EC, a UCITS and, where relevant, its management company, authorised in accordance with Directive 2009/65/EC, an institution for occupational retirement provision within the meaning of Article 6(a) of Directive 2003/41/EC and an alternative investment fund managed by AIFMs authorised or registered in accordance with Directive 2011/61/EU.'*

1416 According to Article 2(1)(9) of EMIR a non-financial counterparty *'(…) means an undertaking established in the Union other than the entities referred to in points (1) and (8).'*

adverse effects on the non-financial counterparties trading in the derivatives market to hedge their commercial risks.[1417] Since the trading venue operator has to recognize which transaction qualifies for the exemption of Article 8(1)(4) MiFIR in order to comply with it, the provision in effect requires the trading venue to implement a facility to flag those transactions in the first place.[1418]

f) Modalities of Publication

Parallel to Article 3(2) MiFIR, the modalities of publication for pre-trade transparency must also be calibrated to the trading system used for non-equity instruments (Article 8(2) MiFIR). They encompass the same order-book, quote-driven, hybrid and periodic auction systems that are used by equity instruments.[1419] Only the provision for voice trading systems is a special calibration for non-equity instruments. For voice trading systems, the level 2 measure requires publishing the bids and offers and the attached volumes from any member or participant which, if accepted, would lead to a transaction under the system's rules.[1420]

For the MiFIR refit, the Committee on Economic and Monetary Affairs proposed to limit the pre-trade transparency requirement to central limit order book and periodic auction systems only.[1421] The calibration would also only apply to those two system types, but no longer to request for quote and voice systems because the Committee is of the opinion that the benefit of pre-trade transparency calibration in those systems were of negligible value for end users which *'(...) has been informally recognised by supervisors.'*[1422] The rationale of removing a burden because calibrated pre-trade transparency seems less important when a consolidated tape is available[1423] neglects the fact that there is no consolidated tape as of now and that pre-trade transparency is not necessarily a burden that needs

1417 Kumpan and Schmidt (n 4) MiFIR Art 8 para 7; Moloney, *EU Securities and Financial Markets Regulation* (n 4) 485, 515ff.

1418 Gebauer (n 94) MiFIR Art 8 para 26.

1419 ibid MiFIR Art 8 paras 30-1; Moloney, 'EU Financial Governance and Transparency Regulation' (n 3) para 12.22.

1420 Table in Annex I of Commission Delegated Regulation (EU) 2017/583 of 14 July 2016 which was enacted upon the delegation in Article 9(5) MiFIR.

1421 Committee on Economic and Monetary Affairs, 'Report' (n 1137) 22.

1422 Committee on Economic and Monetary Affairs, 'Draft Report' (n 1400) 34

1423 ibid 34.

to be avoided right away if well calibrated waivers account for otherwise occurring hardship.

With regard to pre-trade transparency for non-equity instruments, the trading venue operator must also publish the pre-trade information on a continuous basis during normal trading hours (Article 8(1)(3) MiFIR). Furthermore, the trading venue operator must publish the data in accordance with Article 13 MiFIR on a reasonable commercial basis and ensure non-discriminatory access to the information.[1424]

3. Common Manner of Publishing Pre-Trade Transparency Data

For equity and non-equity instruments, Articles 3 and 8 MiFIR require the market operators and investment firms to make public the pre-trade transparency information on a continuous basis during normal trading hours. Moreover, the trading venue operators are required to provide access to transparency information on reasonable commercial terms on a non-discriminatory basis, ensuring both their compensation for the creation of the data and wide proliferation of information in the market. Under those principles, trading venue operators shall make the information public to systematic internalizers when they are obliged to publish quotes in the same instrument classes (Articles 3(3) and 8(3) MiFIR) and to the public (Article 13(1) MiFIR).

It can thus be concluded that both Article 3 MiFIR for equity instruments and Article 8(1) MiFIR for non-equity instruments, require broad trade transparency in their respective markets. Nevertheless, the scope of Article 8(1) MiFIR is more limited than that of Article 3(1) MiFIR which accounts for the particularities of the markets for non-equities but also leaves some orders beyond the scope of the pre-trade transparency regime. Choosing a more cautious approach, however, should not be seen as a weakness of the first non-equity transparency regime introduced in European markets.

1424 See already for Article 3 MiFIR above; Gebauer (n 94) MiFIR Art 8 para 33.

III. Waivers from Pre-Trade Transparency

From the default rule of pre-trade transparency under Articles 3 and 8 MiFIR, the waiver regime under Articles 4 and 9 MiFIR provides exceptions for orders that are vulnerable to trade transparency. These exceptions allow trading venue operators to offer dark trading services in a foreseen and, thus, regulated manner. The waivers from pre-trade transparency account for the trade-off between transparency and liquidity in pre-defined instances.[1425] To create an optimal amount of pre-trade transparency complimented by an optimal amount of dark trading, the European Union maintained its regime of waivers from pre-trade transparency that was first introduced under MiFID I. This regime comprised of four waivers namely waivers for systems using reference prices, for systems executing negotiated transactions, for orders that are large in scale, and for orders held in order management facilities pending disclosure.[1426]

In the MiFID revision process, the waiver regime – especially the reference price waiver – ignited controversial debate between the one group of Member States with an active (dark) trading market advocating for maintaining a facilitative waiver regime and the other group of Member States with strong national exchanges that lost liquidity to a growing dark pool industry elsewhere, who hoped to ban the reference price waiver entirely.[1427]

The result of this conflict was a compromise in which all four waivers from MiFID I were maintained but their scopes were significantly tightened to more clearly define the instances in which dark trading may occur with the result that dark trading became more difficult.[1428] The transition of the

1425 ibid MiFIR Art 4 para 1; Busch (n 1086) 130. See also Recital 13 MiFIR; Recital 2 CDR (EU) 2017/587.

1426 See for waivers under MiFID I: Gomber and Gvozdevskiy (n 43) paras 14.52ff; Hoops, *Verborgene Liquidität im Marktordnungsrecht der MiFID* (n 6) 122ff.

1427 Moloney, *EU Securities and Financial Markets Regulation* (n 4) 481, 454–5 on the dispute primarily occurred between the UK in favor of more dark trading since it already hosted a number of dark MTFs and France which wanted to support pre-trade transparency and the market share of incumbent exchanges.

1428 Council of the European Union, 'Progress Report - Revised rules for markets in financial instruments a) Proposal for a Directive of the European Parliament and of the Council on markets in financial instruments repealing Directive 2004/39/EC of the European Parliament and of the Council (Recast) (MiFID) b) Proposal for a Regulation of the European Parliament and of the Council on markets in financial instruments and amending Regulation [EMIR] on OTC derivatives, central counwaiver regime from MiFID I to MiFID II/MiFIR is generally described as moving from a 'principle based' approach, with only the broad lines of regulation laid out, to a 'rule based' approach, with specific and detailed regulations to ensure a predictable and uniform application.[1429]

Besides this rather heated discussion in the equity instruments realm, MiFID II/MiFIR also introduced an entirely new regime of waivers from pre-trade transparency for non-equity instruments.[1430] While the pre-trade transparency rule under Article 8(1) MiFIR already accounts for some particularities of non-equity instruments, the waiver regime further tailors the transparency regime to the needs of non-equity markets. When facing the task of defining the existing waivers for equities more precisely as well as finding appropriate new waivers for non-equity instruments, the European Union was guided by the following rationale: pre-trade transparency shall only be waived when the risk of prejudice to price formation is low, but the liquidity and position risk is high if the order was made public by pre-trade transparency.[1431]

1. Waivers for Equity Instruments, Article 4 MiFIR

The waivers from pre-trade transparency for equity and equity-like instruments are codified in Article 4 MiFIR. While maintaining the four waivers – i.e., the reference price, negotiated trade, large in scale, and order management facility waiver – first introduced under MiFID I, MiFIR imposed stricter and more detailed rules on their application.[1432]

terparties and trade repositories (MiFIR)' (2011/0296 (COD), 2011/0298 (COD), 16523/12, Brussels, 13 December 2012) 6 para 22; CESR, 'CESR Technical Advice to the European Commission in the Context of the MiFID Review - Equity Markets' (n 4) 6–7; Kumpan and Schmidt (n 4) MiFIR Art 4 paras 2, 8; Moloney, 'EU Financial Governance and Transparency Regulation' (n 3) paras 12.19 – 20.

1429 CESR, 'CESR Technical Advice to the European Commission in the Context of the MiFID Review - Equity Markets' (n 4) 10.

1430 Busch (n 1086) 131; Moloney, 'EU Financial Governance and Transparency Regulation' (n 3) para 12.23.

1431 Moloney, *EU Securities and Financial Markets Regulation* (n 4) 481; Moloney, 'EU Financial Governance and Transparency Regulation' (n 3) para 12.19; see also Kumpan and Schmidt (n 4) MiFIR Art 4 para 1.

1432 Council of the European Union (n 1428) 6 para 22; Kumpan and Schmidt (n 4) MiFIR Art 4 para 2; Schmies and Sajnovits (n 1357) 10.

The 2014 iteration of MiFIR already shows a relatively detailed approach when defining the waivers especially compared to the US[1433] and Switzerland[1434], which underlines its rather public-interest approach to regulation (rather than one caring only for correcting market failures).[1435] The proposed MiFIR refit follows this strand of regulation and becomes even more detailed in certain aspects. This will be discussed in conjunction with the current 2014 iteration of MiFIR.

a) Reference Price Waiver

Under the reference price waiver according to Article 4(1)(a) MiFIR, trading venues that do not have a mechanism for proprietary price discovery but rather import the prices at which they match their orders can dispense of showing pre-trade transparency. Since pre-trade transparency is meant to support the price formation process, requiring it on a trading venue that does not have one, but instead uses already publicly displayed prices, is futile.[1436]

aa) Prices that are 'Widely Published' and 'Regarded as Reliable by the Market'

Article 4(1)(a) MiFIR, however, requires the reference price used for order matching under this waiver to be widely published and to be regarded as reliable by market participants.[1437] These requirements ensure that the trading venue that uses the waiver matches orders at conditions that are already widely known in the market. Phrased differently, no order should be able to avoid trade transparency under this waiver if it seeks to be matched at a price different from the currently displayed market price that might bear new information and should better be imported in the price formation

1433 See above Part II § 5.E.III.
1434 See below Part II § 7.C.
1435 See above Part I § 1.E.IV.2.
1436 Kumpan and Schmidt (n 4) MiFIR Art 4 para 9; Moloney, 'EU Financial Governance and Transparency Regulation' (n 3) para 12.19.
1437 Gebauer (n 94) MiFIR Art 4 para 3; Kumpan and Schmidt (n 4) MiFIR Art 4 para 9.

mechanism.[1438] Both criteria were, however, already in the definition of the reference price waiver under MiFID I and failed to restrict the selection of reference prices by the trading venues operating under this waiver.[1439] As a paper by CESR showed, the national competent authorities were rather lenient and accepted as reference prices midpoint prices from one trading venue or from several trading venues, such as an average of all or a subset of the prices of the European trading venues as the EBBO.[1440]

bb) Market of First Admittance to Trading or Most Liquid Market

Instead of leaving the interpretation of which reference price meets the requirements of 'widely published' and 'regarded as reliable by the market' to the national competent authorities and the respective trading systems operators, as has been the case under MiFID I, MiFID II/MiFIR now provides a specification of both requirements: MiFID II/MiFIR complements the qualitative requirements of 'widely published' and 'regarded as reliable by the market' with the quantitative requirement that the reference price must be derived from either the trading venue where the financial instrument was first admitted to trading or from the most relevant market in terms of liquidity for the respective instrument (Article 4(2)(a) MiFIR).[1441] According to the level 2 provision of Article 4 CDR (EU) 2017/587, the most relevant market in terms of liquidity is the market with the highest turnover in the instrument.[1442] The calculation of the turnover data is conducted by the national competent authority responsible for the trading venue. In Germany this is either the Exchange Supervisory Authority of the respective State for regulated markets or BaFin for MTFs.[1443] The limitation to either of the two marketplaces mentioned above disallows the use of

1438 In this direction also aims the advice rendered by CESR for the predecessor under MiFID I, see: CESR, 'CESR's Technical Advice on Possible Implementing Measures of the Directive 2004/39/EC on Markets in Financial Instruments' (n 1363) 53. See also CESR, 'CESR Technical Advice to the European Commission in the Context of the MiFID Review - Equity Markets' (n 4) 10.

1439 CESR, 'CESR Technical Advice to the European Commission in the Context of the MiFID Review - Equity Markets' (n 4) 10–1.

1440 ibid 10–1.

1441 Gebauer (n 94) MiFIR Art 4 para 3.

1442 ibid MiFIR Art 4 para 3; Kumpan and Schmidt (n 4) MiFIR Art 4 para 9.

1443 Section 4(1) German Exchange Act (BörsG) and Section 6(1) German Securities Trading Act (WpHG); Kumpan and Schmidt (n 4) MiFIR Art 4 para 9.

'reference prices' synthetized from multiple trading venues' prices, such as the EBBO. The EBBO was frequently used by dark pool operators as a reference price to match orders at prices that were susceptible to their influence.[1444] Under MiFID II/MiFIR, the price for matching under the reference price waiver must reflect the price of a significant trading venue for the respective financial instrument.

cc) Pricing at the Midpoint

Moreover, Article 4(2) MiFIR narrows the scope of the reference price waiver even further: the provision sets out that the reference price under Article 4(1)(a) MiFIR shall be established by obtaining the midpoint within the current bid and offer prices of the trading venue where that financial instrument was first admitted to trading or the most relevant market in terms of liquidity.

The price importing trading venue can use the opening or closing price of the relevant trading session (Article 4(2)(b) MiFIR) only outside the phase of continuous trading on the lit trading venue can. In this period, the lit market does not produce new prices that can be used to calculate the midpoint. Thus, using the closing or opening price is yet the most accurate price to obtain.[1445]

Under the proposed MiFIR refit, the reference price for shares and ETFs can also be the price displayed on the consolidated tape, which appears reasonable given that it is a representation of the midpoint price of all displayed and reported prices.[1446]

dd) Reference Price Waiver captures Block Orders as well as other Orders

The fast growth of dark trading under the reference price waiver under MiFID I from 1 % in 2009 to 8 % in 2016[1447] showed that this waiver bears significant advantages for many traders. Dark pools using the reference price waiver remain attractive to traders because they execute orders at the

1444 CESR, 'CESR Technical Advice to the European Commission in the Context of the MiFID Review - Equity Markets' (n 4) 10; Banks (n 5) 117.

1445 ESMA, 'Final Report: Draft Regulatory and Implementing Technical Standards MiFID II/MiFIR' (ESMA/2015/1464, 28 September 2015) 17; Salger (n 627) 212.

1446 Committee on Economic and Monetary Affairs, 'Report' (n 1137) 20.

1447 Petrescu and Wedow (n 5) 5.

midpoint of the current bid-ask-spread of the lit trading venue. This allows traders to save half of the bid-ask-spread, which is also called the 'liquidity premium' for instant execution.[1448] While price improvements may have been greater under MiFID I where more exotic reference prices such as the EBBO or those reflecting maker-taker-schemes were allowed, pricing at the midpoint as under MiFID II/MiFIR is still a significant advantage for some traders.

Furthermore, the reference price matches all orders regardless of size at a uniform price. This is especially interesting for large block orders which incur market impact costs when sweeping down the order book on lit markets executing against ever inferior priced counter orders. In this context, the reference price waiver not only saves the liquidity premium but also the adverse price movement.[1449]

However, the reference price waiver has no restricting elements to narrow its scope to only block orders. In contrast, it applies to mid-sized and retail-sized orders as well which do not incur prohibitive market impact costs.[1450] Traders in those orders may seek the individual advantage of saving the liquidity premium (i.e., half of the bid-ask-spread).[1451] However, their orders may deteriorate prices on lit trading venues because market-makers need a certain number of uninformed traders to offset the costs incurred by adverse selection when trading against an informed trader. If those orders are pooled in dark pools, market makers may need to broaden their spread which renders prices less accurate and markets less liquid than before.[1452]

ee) Narrowing the Scope of the Reference Price Waiver under the MiFIR refit

The fact that the reference price waiver in its 2014 iteration could still be used by dark pools to lure smaller sized orders from lit venues still wor-

1448 Gomber and Gvozdevskiy (n 43) para 14.12; Gomber and Schweickert (n 265) 489.

1449 Gomber and Gvozdevskiy (n 43) para 14.12.

1450 CESR, 'CESR Technical Advice to the European Commission in the Context of the MiFID Review - Equity Markets' (n 4) 11.

1451 IOSCO, 'Principles for Dark Liquidity' (n 12) 12; Matteo Aquilina and others, 'Asymmetries in Dark Pool Reference Prices' (FCA Occasional Paper No. 21, FCA, September 2016) 32; Gomber and Gvozdevskiy (n 43) para 14.12; Gomber and Schweickert (n 265) 489; Preece (n 14) 12–3.

1452 Fox, 'MiFID II and Equity Trading' (n 53) paras 18.06ff, 18.100.

ries ESMA and the EU legislator in the MiFID II/MiFIR refit process.[1453] To further improve trade transparency and limit dark trading, the EU decided to clamp down on the scope of the waiver even further under the Article 4(1)(a) of the MiFIR refit which was proposed 25 November 2021.[1454] The proposed Article 4(1)(a) MiFIR required that the reference price waiver can only be used if the trading system is one that matches orders that are larger than twice the standard market size.[1455] Thus, smaller orders would no longer benefit from the waiver but rather support the price discovery mechanism on lit venues.

The Committee on Economic and Monetary Affairs, however, did not fully reflect the proposal by the Commission, but rather aims for a more flexible limitation of the reference price waiver in its report dated 2 March 2023.[1456] While the Committee does not reject the idea of a minimum size requirement to use the reference price waiver, it rather wants to place the determination of the minimum size in ESMA's hands (level 2 act) than having it in MiFIR.[1457] Since this is the more flexible approach in a rather technical matter, this is not unreasonable.

ff) Subject to Limitation by Article 5 MiFIR

The private gains of dark trading incentivize traders to make excessive use of the reference price waiver.[1458] Coupled with negative the externalities on market quality affecting all investors and the larger economy,[1459] the European Union saw the need to restrict the use of the reference price waiver when it promulgated Article 5 MiFIR under the 2014 iteration of

1453 European Commission, 'Proposal for a Regulation of the European Parliament and of the Council amending Regulation (EU) No 600/2014 as regards enhancing market data transparency, removing obstacles to the emergence of a consolidated tape, optimising the trading obligations and prohibiting receiving payments for forwarding client orders' (n 1146) 1.
1454 ibid 14.
1455 ibid 18f, 27.
1456 Committee on Economic and Monetary Affairs, 'Report' (n 1137) 20.
1457 ibid 20; Committee on Economic and Monetary Affairs, 'Draft Report' (n 1400) 32.
1458 See above Part I § 3.D.III.
1459 See above Part I § 3.D.IV.

MiFIR currently in force.[1460] Since not only the reference price waiver, but also the negotiated trade waiver, is subject to the limitation device under Article 5 MiFIR, the limitation device will be discussed after both affected waivers were outlined.

b) Negotiated Trade Waiver

According to Article 4(1)(b) MiFIR, national competent authorities can waive pre-trade transparency for trading venue operators for systems that formalize negotiated transactions. This definition describes the negotiated trade waiver for equity instruments that was already available for dark trading under MiFID I.[1461]

The negotiated trade waiver was retained under MiFIR to enable transactions between one or more members or participants of a trading venue that find superior execution quality outside the order book in bilaterally negotiated transaction but decide to subsequently formalize the transaction under the rules of a trading venue as a modern form of upstairs trading.[1462] The negotiated trade waiver applies in circumstances in which the trade could not be executed in other systems operated by the trading venue, such as the transparent limit order book, because the transaction is subject to special conditions or requirements like portfolio trades or contingent transactions like delta neutral equity hedges of a derivative.[1463]

In contrast to MiFID I, MiFIR applies a more detailed, 'rule'-based regulation to the negotiated trade waiver that sets stricter limits to its use with regard to admissible execution prices that are dependent on the type

1460 See below Part II § 6 C.III.1.c). See also Recital 17 MiFIR; Kumpan and Schmidt (n 4) MiFIR Art 5 para 1; Moloney, 'EU Financial Governance and Transparency Regulation' (n 3) para 12.20.

1461 Busch (n 1086) 130; Moloney, *EU Securities and Financial Markets Regulation* (n 4) 481–2; Moloney, 'EU Financial Governance and Transparency Regulation' (n 3) para 12.19.

1462 Article 5 CDR (EU) 2017/587; ESMA, 'Final Report: Draft Regulatory and Implementing Technical Standards MiFID II/MiFIR' (n 1445) 19 para 17; CESR, 'CESR Technical Advice to the European Commission in the Context of the MiFID Review - Equity Markets' (n 4) 11; Gebauer (n 94) MiFIR Art 4 para 5; Kumpan and Schmidt (n 4) MiFIR Art 4 para 14.

1463 ESMA, 'Final Report: Draft Regulatory and Implementing Technical Standards MiFID II/MiFIR' (n 1445) 19 para 17.

of the transaction and the characteristic of the financial instrument being traded.[1464]

To account for this more calibrated regulation, the negotiated trade waiver is now subdivided into three prongs under Article 4(1)(b)(i)-(iii) MiFIR: The first distinction is made between pre-negotiated transactions that are subject to conditions other than the current market price of the financial instruments, falling within Article 4(1)(b)(iii) MiFIR, and those that are subject to current market conditions (Article 4(1)(b)(i) and (ii) MiFIR).[1465]

aa) Transactions Subject to Conditions Other Than the Market Conditions (Article 4(1)(b)(iii) MiFIR)

Transactions subject to conditions other than the current market conditions can be executed at any price which is permitted under the rules of the trading venue and agreed upon by the parties to formalize the transaction.[1466] As the level 2 measure further defines under Article 6 Commission Delegated Regulation (EU) 2017/587, a list of nine types of transactions of a rather technical nature are given the privilege to waive pre-trade transparency and be priced at a different price than the current market price.[1467] Such technical trades are unlikely to bear non-public, material information, therefore, waiving the pre-trade transparency obligation for such trades which keeps their price information outside the price formation process has generally no adverse effects on market efficiency although their prices do not confirm the current market price. This is the case because technical trades are not motivated by an investment purpose and, thus, do not contribute to price formation.[1468] For this reason, this type of the negotiated trade waiver was not subjected to the limitations of the volume cap mechanism under Article 5 MiFIR since information about merely technical transactions with no investment purpose does not make the price

1464 ibid 20 para 19.
1465 ibid 20 para 20.
1466 ibid 20 para 20.
1467 Gebauer (n 94) MiFIR Art 4 para 7; cf. Kumpan and Schmidt (n 4) MiFIR Art 4 para 18.
1468 ESMA, 'Final Report: Draft Regulatory and Implementing Technical Standards MiFID II/MiFIR' (n 1445) 21 para 25.

formation process more informed when revealed to the public by trade transparency.[1469]

bb) Transactions Subject to Current Market Conditions in Liquid Markets (Article 4(1)(b)(i) MiFIR)

The rationale is different, however, for non-technical trades since they are subject to current market conditions. Those trades are conducted for an investment purpose. Within the transaction subject to current market conditions, it must be distinguished whether the market for the particular financial instrument is a liquid market or an illiquid one according to the following rules:[1470] Where according to Article 2(17)(b) MiFIR the free float, the average daily number of transactions and the average daily turnover warrants that there is a liquid market,[1471] the negotiated trade waiver is subject to the conditions under Article 4(1)(b)(i) MiFIR which requires the transaction to be executed within the current volume weighted spread reflected on the order book or the quotes of the market makers on the respective trading venue.[1472]

The execution at the current volume weighted spread binds the transaction price to the price level that would have been achievable had the order been sent into the transparent order book or to a market maker.[1473] Here, MiFIR tries to balance the interest of the traders that wish to enter private

1469 ibid 20–2.

1470 ibid 20 para 21.

1471 For definition of 'liquid market' and its calculation see Article 2(1)(17)(b) MiFIR.

1472 Gebauer (n 94) MiFIR Art 4 para 7; On the calculation of the 'current volume weighted spread reflected in the order book', see: ESMA, 'Questions and Answers: On MiFID II and MiFIR Transparency Topics' (ESMA70-872942901-35, 5 September 2022) 52:
'The volume weighted spread should be calculated as the spread between the volume weighted bid and offer prices of orders on the trading venue's public order book aggregated to the size of the negotiated transaction.
The volume weighted bid (offer) should be calculated considering all bid (sell) orders in the order book that would theoretically be executed if a sell (buy) order of a size equivalent to the negotiated transaction was introduced in the order book. Where the transaction size is larger than the volume of buy (sell) orders on the order book it will be the average price of the transaction assuming that a sell (buy) order is executed against all buy (sell) orders on the order book.
Orders benefitting from a pre-trade transparency waiver should not be included in the calculation.'

1473 Kumpan and Schmidt (n 4) MiFIR Art 4 para 15.

dark liquidity under the waiver and the public interest in having non-public information in possession of those traders seeking dark trading to be imported into the price formation process. Especially when the transaction is executed to market conditions, the parties' interest in a waiver for a private transaction is less persuasive since other traders would have been available for the transaction in a liquid lit market as well. The response of MiFIR is similar to the one for the reference price waiver: It does not bar access to this source of liquidity entirely but rather limits its supply by subjecting the waiver under Article 4(1)(b)(i) MiFIR to the volume cap mechanism under Article 5 MiFIR.[1474]

The overall skepticism towards this waiver can also be seen in the restrictions that Article 4(3) MiFIR places upon Article 4(1)(b)(i) MiFIR. In summary, the restrictions ensure that the transaction is carried out in accordance with the venue's rules. Furthermore, the venue must take appropriate measures to prevent or detect market abuse or attempted market abuse as well as to detect any attempt to circumvent the other rules under MiFID II and MiFIR, thus ensuring that the volume cap mechanism is not circumvented.[1475]

cc) Transactions Under Current Market Conditions but in an Illiquid Market (Article 4(1)(b)(ii) MiFIR)

The third prong of the negotiated trade waiver newly added to the waiver system under MiFID II/MiFIR concerns transactions that are under current market conditions but in an illiquid market.[1476] By implication of Article 2(1)(17)(b) MiFIR, an illiquid market is one that does not meet the requirements of a liquid market with regard to free float, the average daily number of transactions, and the average daily turnover in the respective financial instrument.[1477] According to Article 4(1)(b)(ii) MiFIR, those transactions can be executed at any price that is within a certain percentage of a suitable reference price set out by the trading venue. To maintain the objective nature of a multilateral, non-discretionary trading venue,

1474 Gebauer (n 94) MiFIR Art 4 para 7; Kumpan and Schmidt (n 4) MiFIR Art 4 para 15.

1475 Gebauer (n 94) MiFIR Art 4 para 9; Kumpan and Schmidt (n 4) MiFIR Art 4 para 16.

1476 Gomber and Gvozdevskiy (n 43) para 14.69.

1477 Gebauer (n 94) MiFIR Art 4 para 7.

the system operator of the venue must set both the reference price and the percentage in advance.[1478] The rational of this waiver from pre-trade transparency is that transactions in illiquid markets have to incur higher efforts to find contra side liquidity. If they can find it in negotiated trades, pre-trade transparency shall not cause the scarce liquidity to evaporate, even though the transaction is made under current market conditions meaning that there is a certain public interest in adding this information to the price formation process.[1479] In this facilitative spirit, MiFIR does not subject this alternative of the waiver to the volume cap mechanism to protect liquidity at the expense of reduced pre-trade transparency.

c) Limitation Devices: Double and Single Volume Cap Mechanisms

aa) Double Volume Cap Mechanism

The innovative tool to curb dark trading under the (at the time of writing) current 2014 iteration of MiFID II/MiFIR is the double volume cap mechanism (DVC) under Article 5 MiFIR.[1480] This mechanism functions as a reverse exception from the reference price and negotiated trade waivers. Under the DVC, only a certain amount of dark trading is allowed. When this amount is surpassed, the trading under the two waivers needs to revert back from dark to lit trading which reinstates the default rule of pre-trade transparency.[1481]

The DVC eventually brought peace to the dispute in the MiFID II/MiFIR process among the Member States of which one side was in favor of maintaining the reference price waiver while the other side wanted to abolish it entirely.[1482] In spite of the initial dispute revolving only around the reference price waiver, the negotiated trade waiver within the current market spread under Article 4(1)(b)(i) MiFIR also references the current market price of another trading system. Due to both systems 'free-riding'

1478 ibid MiFIR Art 4 para 7; ESMA, 'Final Report: Draft Regulatory and Implementing Technical Standards MiFID II/MiFIR' (n 1445) 20 para 21.
1479 Cf. ESMA, 'Final Report: Draft Regulatory and Implementing Technical Standards MiFID II/MiFIR' (n 1445) 19 para 17.
1480 Busch (n 1086) 130; Moloney, 'EU Financial Governance and Transparency Regulation' (n 3) para 12.20.
1481 Busch (n 1086) 130; Moloney, 'EU Financial Governance and Transparency Regulation' (n 3) para 12.20.
1482 Moloney, *EU Securities and Financial Markets Regulation* (n 4) 482–3.

the price formation of other markets, they are limited by the DVC.[1483] However, the other limbs of the negotiated trade waiver (Article 4(1)(b)(ii) and (iii) MiFIR) are excluded from the DVC as they would not contribute to price formation even if transparent.[1484] Equally, the large in scale and the order management facility waiver are not subject to Article 5 MiFIR because enhancing transparency in those orders would lead to increased market impact costs adversely affecting market efficiency.[1485]

ESMA also clarified the issue of the combination of waivers, especially the reference price waiver, subject to the DVC, and the large in scale waiver which is not. According to ESMA such combinations are possible but the trading venues applying for such combinations with the NCAs need to meet the requirements of all applied-for waivers.[1486] Moreover, the orders matched under the large in scale waiver must be matched at the same price as the orders matched under the reference price waiver. When an order under the large in scale waiver interacts with at least one order under the reference price waiver, ESMA holds that *'(...) any transaction resulting from the matching of orders where at least one order is not LIS [large in scale] is subject to Article 5 of MiFIR and counts for the double volume cap calculations.'*[1487]

The rationale of the DVC is to avoid negative impact on the price formation process only in those transactions that are less likely to suffer market impact and to limit the free riding of another marketplace's price formation process.[1488] The DVC applies on an instrument-by-instrument basis meaning that the thresholds are calculated specifically for each instrument.[1489] The first threshold of the DVC applies with regard to the specific trading venue and limits the trading under the restricted waivers to 4 % of

1483 Article 5(1) MiFIR; ESMA, 'Final Report: Draft Regulatory and Implementing Technical Standards MiFID II/MiFIR' (n 1445) 170 para 1.

1484 Recital 17 MiFIR; Kumpan and Schmidt (n 4) MiFIR Art 5 para 8.

1485 Kumpan and Schmidt (n 4) MiFIR Art 5 paras 1, 15; Petrescu and Wedow (n 5) 15 both not referring to the OMF-waiver, although it falls outside the scope of Art 5(1) MiFIR.

1486 ESMA, 'Opinion on the Assessment of Pre-Trade Transparency Waivers for Equity and Non-Equity Instruments' (ESMA70-155-6641, 23 March 2022) 13–4 paras 60–2.

1487 ibid 14 para 63.

1488 Recital 17 MiFIR; FCA, 'UK Equity Market Dark Pools' (n 6) 50; Kumpan and Schmidt (n 4) MiFIR Art 5 para 1; Thelen (n 147) 175.

1489 ESMA, 'Final Report: Draft Regulatory and Implementing Technical Standards MiFID II/MiFIR' (n 1445) 170 para 3.

the total trading volume in a specific financial instrument with respect to the trading volume over the previous 12 months.[1490] The second EU-wide threshold limits the overall Union trading under the restricted waivers to 8 % of the total trading volume in a specific financial instrument on all trading venues across the European Union over the previous 12 months.[1491] When the trading under the restricted waivers exceeds the 4 %-threshold on one trading venue, the NCA responsible for the specific trading venue suspends the use of those waivers for six months so that orders have to show pre-trade transparency again.[1492] When the EU-wide 8 %-threshold is exceeded, all NCAs have to suspend trading under the restricted waivers on all EU trading venues for six months in the respective instrument.[1493]

ESMA is responsible for the calculation of the volume data and receives data twice a month from the trading venues to issue a volume report once a month. Only when the dark trading under the restricted waivers has already reached 3.75 % with regard to the 4 %-threshold and 7.75 % with regard to the 8 %-threshold, does ESMA publish volume reports twice a month.[1494] Since the calculation of the double volume cap data hinges on the trading venues reporting to ESMA, Article 5(7) MiFIR requires trading venues to establish systems and procedures for tracking the trading under the restricted waivers and reporting the data to ESMA.[1495]

bb) Comparison with US law

The reference to a percentage in the regulatory text calls to mind the 5 %-threshold under US law. However, the US threshold and the EU DVC are aimed at opposite goals with regard to dark trading.

1490 Article 5(1)(a) MiFIR; ESMA, 'Final Report: Draft Regulatory and Implementing Technical Standards MiFID II/MiFIR' (n 1445) 170 para 3; Busch (n 1086) 130; Moloney, 'EU Financial Governance and Transparency Regulation' (n 3) para 12.20.

1491 Article 5(1)(b) MiFIR; ESMA, 'Draft Regulatory and Implementing Technical Standards MiFID II/MiFIR' (n 334) 170 para 3; Busch (n 1086) 130; Moloney, 'EU Financial Governance and Transparency Regulation' (n 3) para 12.20.

1492 Article 5(2) MiFIR; ESMA, 'Final Report: Draft Regulatory and Implementing Technical Standards MiFID II/MiFIR' (n 1445) 170 para 3.

1493 Article 5(3) MiFIR; ESMA, 'Final Report: Draft Regulatory and Implementing Technical Standards MiFID II/MiFIR' (n 1445) 171 para 4; Busch (n 1086) 130–1.

1494 ESMA, 'Final Report: Draft Regulatory and Implementing Technical Standards MiFID II/MiFIR' (n 1445) 172 paras 9–10; Kumpan and Schmidt (n 4) MiFIR Art 5 paras 10ff.

1495 Kumpan and Schmidt (n 4) MiFIR Art 5 para 9, 14.

In contrast to US law, the DVC's reference to the market share of dark trading in the entire European Union prevents an uncontrolled inflation of the dark sector as under US Regulation ATS. Regulation ATS allows ATS to execute transactions in a security with up to 5 % of the nationwide turnover on their trading venue without pre-trade transparency. However, Regulation ATS has no threshold limiting the nationwide amount of dark trading like the 8 %-threshold under the DVC. This led to ATS operators gaming the 5 %-threshold by operating several ATS in juxtaposition, each just below the 5 % turnover mark.[1496] This inflates the overall amount of dark trading in the market and defeats the purpose of the regulation to privilege small-sized market entrants by easing the regulatory requirements of pre-trade transparency to reduce initial operations costs.[1497] While European traders also search for unexhausted waiver capacity among trading venues, the second threshold limits the maximum amount of dark trading under the restricted waivers in the entire European Union to 8 %. Thus, circumventing the venue specific limitation of 4 % does not lead to an unlimited inflation of dark trading.

cc) Impact of the DVC on the Market

The DVC limits the availability of the reference price waiver and the negotiated trade waiver in case certain thresholds are breached within a 12-month period. Since the targeted reference price and negotiated trade waivers are the most versatile in the array of waivers offered by MiFIR, the DVC has a profound limiting effect on large volumes dark trading. At first sight, this result is unsurprising given that the EU aims to strengthen trade transparency and limit dark trading.[1498] But upon a closer look, it is striking that the EU frowns not only on unregulated dark trading by OTC BCNs, which are subject to less regulatory oversight, but also on regulated dark trading on well-regulated trading venues under waivers the EU-legislator itself designed.

Moreover, the DVC has ripple effects on an entire industry: for the trading venue operators who offer dark trading services, the clamp-down on the waivers for 6 months means that either a dark trading service is

1496 Cf. SEC, 'Regulation of Non-Public Trading Interest' (n 22) 74 FR 61208, 61229.
1497 See Hatch (n 783) 1045–6.
1498 Recitals 1, 5, 6 MiFIR.

harder to operate and leads to order streams shifting back and forth between dark trading and other forms of opaque trading.[1499] While restricting dark trading under the venue specific volume cap of 4 % may have some socially desirable steering effect of venues moderating their dark trading, the combination with the EU-wide 8 % does not have a steering effect on the individual venue, and it cannot successfully coordinate with others to remain below the 8 %. The EU-wide 8 %-threshold rather incentivizes traders to search for other sources of dark liquidity if the first is exhausted under the 4 % limit, imposing a coordination problem on both traders among themselves and traders and trading venues.[1500] No one wants to be the one who is too late to still use the waiver.

From a trader's perspective, the DVC makes using dark trading services unpredictable to some extent. If a waiver volume is on the brink of exceeding either threshold, the trader may be excluded from using the waiver for the next 6 months regardless of their prior trading activities. Even a new trader may bear the effects of other traders who consumed all available dark trading before them. This leads to a race for dark trading before the thresholds are exceeded, and might lead to more price volatility in this period. However, even though the DVC affects uninvolved parties who did not cause the DVC to be triggered, the effect on third 'innocent' parties is inherent to any quota rule and can hardly be avoided.[1501]

As a consequence of the DVC, trading venue operators and traders were incentivized to find new ways to access dark trading. The two most common strategies are to use the unrestricted large in scale waiver[1502] or to use frequent batch auctions.[1503]

1499 The volatility can be seen by the shifting between dark trading under the reference price and negotiated trade waiver and frequent batch auctions as found in: Claudia Guagliano and others, 'DVC Mechanism: The Impact on EU Equity Markets' (ESMA Working Paper No. 3, 2020, ESMA/2020/ WP-2020-3, Paris, September 2020) 11.

1500 ESMA, 'MiFID II/MiFIR Review Report: On the Transparency for Equity and Equity-Like Instruments, the Double Volume Cap Mechanism and the Trading Obligations for Shares' (ESMA70-156-2682, 16 July 2020) 15.

1501 ibid 15.

1502 ibid 14.

1503 ESMA, 'Opinion: On Frequent Batch Auctions (FBAs) and the Double Volume Cap Mechanism (DVCM)' (ESMA70-156-1355, 1 October 2019) 2 para 9; Guagliano and others (n 1499) 11.

dd) Circumventing the DVC: Frequent Batch Auctions

Frequent batch auctions are a market's reaction to the ripple effects of the DVC on regulated dark trading under the restricted waivers to circumvent the 6 months restriction period.[1504] ESMA suspected regulatory arbitrage and has identified two basic types of frequent batch auctions. In the first type, the auction is initiated upon receipt of the first order, but pre-trade transparency information is not disclosed until a counter order eligible for a possible match has been submitted during the auction call. Information about the indicative price and volume is disclosed when the counter order is submitted.[1505]

The second type of frequent batch auction systems initiate the auction even later only when a potential match has been identified. During the identification process of a possible match, no pre-trade transparency is disclosed. The auction is initiated when the potential match is found and then pre-trade transparency is disclosed, but some trading systems already lock the auction price at the beginning of the auction.[1506]

Frequent batch auctions are different from other periodic auctions with regard to the timing, the initiator, and the duration. Periodic auctions are typically held before continuous trading begins as an opening auction, when it ends as a closing auction, or before it restarts after a trading halt to increase liquidity so that trading can either resume or the order book is cleared. Those periodic auctions are initiated by the trading system operator and were not of such short duration as frequent batch auctions.[1507] Frequent batch auctions, however, occur during normal trading hours alongside continuous trading. They are initiated by the first incoming order and only last for a few milliseconds.[1508] ESMA's suspicion that frequent batch auctions are primarily driven by the objective to circumvent the waiver regime with the limits imposed by the DVC is most likely correct.[1509]

1504 ESMA, 'Opinion: On Frequent Batch Auctions (FBAs) and the Double Volume Cap Mechanism (DVCM)' (n 1503) 2 para 9.

1505 ESMA, 'Final Report: Call for Evidence on Periodic Auctions' (ESMA70-156-1035, 11 June 2019) 7 para 20; ESMA, 'Opinion: On Frequent Batch Auctions (FBAs) and the Double Volume Cap Mechanism (DVCM)' (n 1503) 4 para 20.

1506 ESMA, 'Final Report: Call for Evidence on Periodic Auctions' (n 1505) 7 para 22.

1507 ESMA, 'Opinion: On Frequent Batch Auctions (FBAs) and the Double Volume Cap Mechanism (DVCM)' (n 1503) 3 para 16.

1508 ESMA, 'Final Report: Call for Evidence on Periodic Auctions' (n 1505) 3–4 paras 4ff.

1509 ibid 6 para 15.

The traders hope if they can keep their initial order a secret through the rules of the frequent batch auction, they can have the advantages of a waiver without applying for one that might not be available due to the DVC.[1510]

Despite the novel structure, ESMA considered orders in frequent batch auctions to nevertheless be subject to the pre-trade transparency requirement under Article 3(1) MiFIR in its opinion rendered 1 October 2019.[1511]The initiating order is also subject to pre-trade transparency, and therefore risks causing market impact. Only when the orders in a frequent batch auction qualify for a waiver may they be exempted from pre-trade transparency requirements in accordance with Article 4, 5 MiFIR. The issue about applying for a waiver is that these types of orders would most likely qualify under reference price waiver or the negotiated trade waiver which are subject to the DVC that should have been circumvented. Moreover, the orders in frequent batch auctions are often pegged to the EBBO or other prices that do not qualify under the strict midpoint pricing under Article 4(2) MiFIR.[1512]

The example of frequent batch auctions shows how markets innovate to circumvent new regulations like the DVC.[1513] However, it also shows how responsive MiFID II/MiFIR has become by delegating significant competences to ESMA which can react quickly to new developments to prevent the regulation from being outrun by innovation as has been the case under MiFID I. With regard to the regulatory issue, this development begs the question whether this example of regulatory arbitrage was just an attempt of the market to carry on with dark trading despite new regulation or a sign that the DVC significantly increases transaction costs the market tries to remedy by innovative trading techniques.

ee) MiFID II/MiFIR Refit: Abandonment of the DVC

Since its implementation in 2018, the DVC has fallen out of favor with the regulated and the regulators alike. As described above, those regulated tried to circumvent the DVC when it clamped down on dark trading under

1510 ibid 4ff paras 8ff. and 6–7 paras 17ff.

1511 ESMA, 'Opinion: On Frequent Batch Auctions (FBAs) and the Double Volume Cap Mechanism (DVCM)' (n 1503) 4 paras 22–4.

1512 ibid 4–5 paras 25ff.

1513 ESMA, 'Final Report: Call for Evidence on Periodic Auctions' (n 1505) 4–5 paras 8ff; See also FCA (n 82).

the reference price and negotiated trade waiver through frequent batched auctions. The regulators and the EU legislator consider the DVC resource-intensive to administer, rigid, and unnecessarily complex.[1514] It may even harm the competitiveness of EU markets compared the markets abroad, especially in the United Kingdom after it left the EU.[1515]

In its initial proposal for the MiFIR refit, the European Commission suggested replacing the double volume cap with a single volume cap at 7 % (SVC) of trades that are executed under the reference price waiver and the negotiated trade waiver.[1516] This proposal adopts the suggestion by ESMA to have only a single threshold for the entire market (under the DVC the 8 %-threshold) because the trading venue specific (4 %-threshold) proved ineffective in limiting dark trading. If the 4 %-threshold was reached on one trading venue, dark trading in the instrument under the sanctioned waivers did not halt but rather re-distributed to those EU-venues where the 4 %-threshold had not yet been reached. There, dark trading went on until the EU-wide threshold of 8 % was exceeded.[1517] Thus, ESMA suggested to keep only the EU-wide threshold and set it at either 8 % or 7 %.[1518] The fact that ESMA and the Commission kept the volume cap as a limiting device shows that they principally consider dark trading, even the regulated kind, as a phenomenon that can very quickly impair the quality of trade transparency, price formation, and eventually the financial market.[1519]

1514 European Commission, 'Proposal for a Regulation of the European Parliament and of the Council amending Regulation (EU) No 600/2014 as regards enhancing market data transparency, removing obstacles to the emergence of a consolidated tape, optimising the trading obligations and prohibiting receiving payments for forwarding client orders' (n 1146) 4.

1515 Cf. Committee on Economic and Monetary Affairs, 'Draft Report' (n 1400) 32.

1516 European Commission, 'Proposal for a Regulation of the European Parliament and of the Council amending Regulation (EU) No 600/2014 as regards enhancing market data transparency, removing obstacles to the emergence of a consolidated tape, optimising the trading obligations and prohibiting receiving payments for forwarding client orders' (n 1146) 14, 28.

1517 ibid 19; ESMA, 'MiFID II/MiFIR Review Report: On the Transparency for Equity and Equity-Like Instruments, the Double Volume Cap Mechanism and the Trading Obligations for Shares' (n 1500) 15.

1518 ESMA, 'MiFID II/MiFIR Review Report: On the Transparency for Equity and Equity-Like Instruments, the Double Volume Cap Mechanism and the Trading Obligations for Shares' (n 1500) 15.

1519 Cf. European Commission, 'Proposal for a Regulation of the European Parliament and of the Council amending Regulation (EU) No 600/2014 as regards enhancing market data transparency, removing obstacles to the emergence of a consolidated

In the legislative process, the Committee on Economic and Monetary Affairs of the European Parliament suggests to rather suspend the DVC in its current form for a certain period while ESMA monitors the levels of dark trading under the waivers in the EU and limits dark trading if necessary.[1520]

The Committee's proposal is aligned with the recent actions the UK Financial Conduct Authority (FCA) took when it first suspended the DVC mechanism in its market and then asked the government to launch a legislative proposal to abolish the DVC entirely.[1521] Both the EU Committee and the UK FCA consider the thresholds as arbitrary and not founded in evidence, thus hindering beneficial amounts of regulated dark trading under the reference price waiver and the negotiated trade waiver.[1522] Empirical research by *Aquilina et al. 2017* on the UK market before Brexit supports this assumption because it found dark trading under the said waivers to be beneficial up to an amount of 11 % to 17 %.[1523]

Even though it would be the more internationally aligned path to suspend the DVC, the EU may decide to implement a single volume cap at 7 % instead. This would contradict the rationale to only fix the market when it is broken. In the case of moderate amounts of regulated dark trading under a waiver, there is no evidence that it will jeopardize the price formation process in a way that the price will no longer be sufficient for trading. This is most apparent if one considers that traders on a market are generally unable to identify the difference between the currently displayed market price and the non-observable fair value of an instrument.

However, the legislative process with regard to the MiFIR refit has not yet concluded and it remains to be seen which way the EU will ultimately choose.

---

tape, optimising the trading obligations and prohibiting receiving payments for forwarding client orders' (n 1146) 1.

1520 Committee on Economic and Monetary Affairs, 'Draft Report' (n 1400) 32.

1521 ibid 100–1; HM Treasury, 'Wholesale Markets Review: Consultation Response' (London, 1 March 2022) 12.

1522 HM Treasury, 'Wholesale Markets Review: Consultation' (London, July 2021) 2.

1523 Aquilina and others (n 275) 5.

e) Large in Scale Waiver

Under Article 4(1)(c) MiFIR, the national competent authority shall be able to waive pre-trade transparency for orders that are large in scale compared to the normal market size.[1524] With this waiver, MiFIR acknowledges that pre-trade transparency may be harmful for large orders (block orders) raising market impact costs and adverse price movement which may ultimately have adverse effects on market liquidity and the execution quality for end-investors.[1525] While Member States disagreed about the need for the reference price waiver and the negotiated trade waiver in the MiFID review process, it was common perception among the Member States that the large in scale waiver enhances market efficiency and should be maintained under MiFID II/MiFIR.[1526]

The level 2 measures of MiFID II/MiFIR define when an order qualifies as large in scale compared to normal market size.[1527] Article 7 CDR (EU) 2017/587 outlines what is to be understood by 'normal market size' as well as 'large in scale' by setting out thresholds of average daily turnover as a proxy for liquidity in a specific asset class.[1528] To determine whether the large in scale waiver applies to a specific order, the average daily turnover of the respective instrument has to be determined first to define a measuring stick for the overall market liquidity in the respective asset class, for instance shares. The average daily turnover for each asset class is calculated in annual intervals by the national competent authority.[1529] After that, the tables in the Annex II CDR (EU) 2017/587 set out a system of thresholds which assign every liquidity level with a certain threshold above which an order is deemed 'large in scale' and eligible for the waiver. Thus, also the

---

1524 Gebauer (n 94) MiFIR Art 4 para 10; Busch (n 1086) 130; Moloney, 'EU Financial Governance and Transparency Regulation' (n 3) para 12.19.

1525 CESR, 'CESR Technical Advice to the European Commission in the Context of the MiFID Review - Equity Markets' (n 4) 8; Gebauer (n 94) MiFIR Art 4 para 10; Kumpan and Schmidt (n 4) MiFIR Art 4 para 20.

1526 ESMA, 'Final Report: Draft Regulatory and Implementing Technical Standards MiFID II/MiFIR' (n 1445) 24 para 37; Moloney, *EU Securities and Financial Markets Regulation* (n 4) 481.

1527 See delegation in Article 4(6)(e) MiFIR.

1528 ESMA, 'Final Report: Draft Regulatory and Implementing Technical Standards MiFID II/MiFIR' (n 1445) 24 para 39.

1529 Article 7(1) Commission Delegated Regulation (EU) 2017/587.

large in scale waiver tries to strike a balance between transparency and market liquidity.[1530]

As with MiFID I, the order is considered large in scale under MiFID II/MiFIR when it meets the threshold of average daily turnover in its respective liquidity class. Unlike MiFID I, the tables that define the thresholds have been calibrated to reflect the liquidity levels more granularly, so that it is easier to qualify for a waiver in lower turnover instruments, especially for shares of SMEs, while it has become harder for the high turnover instruments to qualify.[1531] This is sensible since large orders need less protection from a waiver in a liquid, high turnover environment able to absorb the liquidity with no market impact costs, whereas in a less liquid market, orders above market standard struggled under MiFID I to qualify for the large in scale waiver.[1532]

Article 7(5) CDR (EU) 2017/587 also clarifies that order stubs, i.e., the remainder of a large in scale order that remains unexecuted after a partial execution of the initial order, still benefit from the waiver even if the size of the stub falls below the applicable threshold for the large in scale waiver.[1533] This has been discussed during the consultation period because the order stub itself does not show the order volume to justify the privilege of the large in scale waiver, especially compared to similarly sized orders in the lit order book that need to show pre-trade transparency information.[1534] Moreover, critics have also claimed that privileging large in scale traders for the extended period keeps important information away from the market at the expense of all other traders.[1535] The critics of an exemption for order stubs argued that ESMA's initial proposal should rather be followed so that only those order stubs that reach at least 75 % of the original large in scale threshold should further benefit from the waiver.[1536]

Even though it is true that large in scale orders receive prolonged privileges when also the stubs of partially executed orders remain dark, this

1530 See Annex of the thesis for threshold tables of Annex II of CDR (EU) 2017/587.

1531 ESMA, 'Final Report: Draft Regulatory and Implementing Technical Standards MiFID II/MiFIR' (n 1445) 26 paras 45ff.

1532 ibid 24–5 paras 37ff.

1533 Gebauer (n 94) MiFIR Art 4 para 10.

1534 ESMA, 'Final Report: Draft Regulatory and Implementing Technical Standards MiFID II/MiFIR' (n 1445) 29 para 60.

1535 ibid 29 para 61.

1536 Thelen (n 147) 179–80. See also ESMA, 'Final Report: Draft Regulatory and Implementing Technical Standards MiFID II/MiFIR' (n 1445) 29 para 61.

privilege is necessary to avoid large orders being withdrawn from organized markets entirely. Leaving the order stubs after a partial execution without the protection of the waiver would lead to information leakage before the market was able to absorb the entire trading interest of the large order's trader. Especially when only a small portion was executed, this would cause transaction costs with an effect as harmful as displaying the large order in the first place.[1537]

While the issue of leaving large parts of the block order unexecuted when only small amounts of a block order can be executed may have been avoided by ESMA's proposal to grant the large in scale waiver also to order stubs in the amount of 75 % of the original order. But implementing such a rule requires considerable effort and it may still force large block traders away from the market because their primary interest is to execute the entire order – not only a portion with the rest sitting in the order book – is not fully satisfied by this rule.[1538] Although the additional liquidity of the order stub may be only as big as another order in the market below such 75 %-threshold. In this case, requiring order stubs to show pre-trade transparency may result in losing the liquidity of the large order entirely. Furthermore, the fact that the large order could not be executed entirely under current market conditions shows that the order has to fear market impact, thus a prolonged waiver privilege is justified.[1539] For this reason, ESMA eventually decided to interpret the waiver in the way that all order stubs, regardless of their size, benefit from the large in scale waiver of the initial order and can remain dark liquidity until their full execution, alteration or deletion.[1540]

1537 ESMA, 'Final Report: Draft Regulatory and Implementing Technical Standards MiFID II/MiFIR' (n 1445) 29 para 62.

1538 ibid 29 para 62.

1539 Cf. ESMA, 'Discussion Paper: MiFID II/MiFIR' (n 1267) 63–4 paras 57–8.

1540 ESMA, 'Opinion on the Assessment of Pre-Trade Transparency Waivers for Equity and Non-Equity Instruments' (n 1486) 6 para 17; ESMA, 'Final Report: Draft Regulatory and Implementing Technical Standards MiFID II/MiFIR' (n 1445) 29 paras 62ff.

f) Using the Large-in-Scale Waiver to Circumvent the Volume Cap Mechanism

Although the large in scale waiver is meant for block orders only, intermediaries may also want to use the large in scale waiver to execute smaller orders by collecting them in their systems until the aggregate number qualifies for the large in scale waiver, particularly to avoid the impact of the volume cap mechanism on dark trading.[1541]

ESMA holds that those trading tactics do not qualify for the large in scale waiver and furthermore are manipulative under MAR.[1542] However, ESMA rests its evaluation on Article 28(2) MiFID II which requires prompt execution of client orders from investment firms. Waiting for other orders would violate this requirement. Here, ESMA uses a provision meant to protect the customer (ultimately the investor) to pursue the public means of delineating the large in scale waiver's scope of application to its actual purpose. However, ESMA does not consider the issue that the customer can waive the promptness requirement for the investment firm. Under this condition, a scheme that aggregates orders before the investment firm sends them as a large in scale order would be feasible.[1543]

Such circumvention of the volume cap mechanism is, however, incompatible with the purpose of the large in scale waiver and the volume cap mechanism. First, an exemption from the pre-trade transparency requirement for block traders is justified only if, on the one hand, the block trader suffers disadvantages and, on the other hand, the market in any case does not expect any advantages from keeping up the transparency requirement. Only then can the default rule of pre-trade transparency be waived and thus the requirement of equal access to market information of the other traders in the market be suspended.[1544] For actual block traders, the adverse effects of pre-trade transparency are market impact costs and adverse price

1541 ESMA, 'Final Report: ESMA's Technical Advice to the Commission on MiFID II and MiFIR' (n 1268) 181ff; Kumpan and Schmidt (n 4) MiFIR Art 5 para 16; Gomber and others (n 1295) 9.

1542 ESMA, 'Opinion on the Assessment of Pre-Trade Transparency Waivers for Equity and Non-Equity Instruments' (n 1486) 5 para 16 a); ESMA, 'Final Report: ESMA's Technical Advice to the Commission on MiFID II and MiFIR' (n 1268) 181ff.

1543 Thelen (n 147) 182.

1544 Kumpan and Schmidt (n 4) MiFIR Art 4 para 20: '(…) *Block orders are orders that are large in size and may have an adverse impact on the market price solely due to their size and the inability or difficulty in matching such a large order in the order book.*'

selection. For the market, on the other hand, the adverse effect is that large block traders will anticipate their vulnerability and refrain from sending large amounts of liquidity to the market.[1545] If this rationale for the large in scale waiver is no longer applicable because the large in scale order is merely an aggregation of small orders that would not suffer any adverse effects if executed individually, the NCA should not grant this waiver to this order or withdraw the large in scale waiver from trading systems that admit such orders into their system (see Article 4(5) MiFIR).[1546]

The second reason why this use of the large in scale waiver is not permissible is that the volume cap mechanism aims to bring back orders of retail-size to the lit markets so that information for price formation is supplied constantly.[1547] When the orders that are crucial for this purpose wait in an intermediary's system for aggregation simply to circumvent the purpose of the volume cap mechanism, such orders do not qualify for the large in scale waiver since the waiver regime for equities needs to be seen in conjunction with the volume cap mechanism. Only in tandem can the waivers and the volume cap mechanism achieve a tailored transparency regime for equity instruments. Hence, aggregating many retail-sized orders in an intermediary's systems to veil them under the large in scale waiver does not fall into the definition of the large in scale waiver.[1548]

g) Order Management Facility Waiver

The fourth waiver adopted from MiFID I is the waiver for orders held in an order management facility of the trading venue pending disclosure or, in short, the order management facility waiver (OMF-waiver) under Article 4(1)(d) MiFIR.[1549] Similar to the large in scale waiver, the OMF-waiver

1545 Liersch, *Regulierung des Blockhandels an den organisierten Aktienmärkten der Vereinigten Staaten, Großbritanniens und Deutschlands* (n 268) 62ff.

1546 Recital 13 MiFIR requires *'(…) to ensure a uniform application of the waivers from pre-trade transparency (…) for specific market models and types and sizes of orders (…)'* while aggregation would allow the opposite of a uniform application; ESMA, 'Opinion on the Assessment of Pre-Trade Transparency Waivers for Equity and Non-Equity Instruments' (n 1486) 5 para 16 a).

1547 Recital 17 MiFIR; Kumpan and Schmidt (n 4) MiFIR Art 5 para 6.

1548 ESMA, 'Opinion on the Assessment of Pre-Trade Transparency Waivers for Equity and Non-Equity Instruments' (n 1486) 5 para 16 a).

1549 Gebauer (n 94) MiFIR Art 4 para 11; Busch (n 1086) 130; Moloney, 'EU Financial Governance and Transparency Regulation' (n 3) para 12.19.

has been uncontroversial between the Member States in the MiFID review process and therefore has only been slightly adjusted under MiFID II/MiFIR.[1550] The purpose of the waiver is to enable traders, especially intermediaries, to insert a trading pattern into the order book that 'works' an order most efficiently through the market and thereby helps intermediaries fulfill their duty of best execution towards their customers.[1551]

The changes compared to MiFID I are on the level 2 measure. In Article 8 CDR (EU) 2017/587, the scope of the waiver is limited for reserve orders because those orders only qualify if the order volume is at least EUR 10,000 when the order first enters the order book or following any amendments.[1552] A reserve order, also called an 'iceberg order', is a (large) limit order where only one part of the order is sent to the order book as the visible tip of the iceberg ready for execution. The remainder of the order stays beneath the 'surface line' of trade transparency as dark liquidity, essentially hiding the full trading interest from the market to avoid market impact costs and other adverse price movements. Only when the 'tip of the iceberg' has executed will another small child order come to the surface for execution, this process repeats until the entire iceberg has 'melted' into the market.[1553]

To avoid misuse or overuse of this waiver, it is plausible to set a minimum size for the use of reserve orders under the OMF-waiver, because they are also used to 'work' (larger) orders through the market. Since the OMF-waiver is not restricted by the volume cap mechanism, such as the large in scale waiver, it happens to be the perfect candidate to also host dark trading in small and mid-sized orders, which formerly occurred under the reference price and negotiated trade waiver if no minimum size requirement applied. In the level 2 measure, ESMA tried to avoid misuse of the order management facility waiver by setting up the minimum order size of EUR 10,000. However, choosing a threshold even below the lowest large in scale threshold can only be explained by ESMA considering orders under the OMF-waiver less problematic with regard to its impact on the

1550 Moloney, *EU Securities and Financial Markets Regulation* (n 4) 481 fn 323.

1551 CESR, 'CESR Technical Advice to the European Commission in the Context of the MiFID Review - Equity Markets' (n 4) 12.

1552 Cf. ESMA, 'Final Report: Draft Regulatory and Implementing Technical Standards MiFID II/MiFIR' (n 1445) 24 para 36; Kumpan and Schmidt (n 4) MiFIR Art 4 para 25.

1553 Article 8(3) Commission Delegated Regulation (EU) 2017/587. ESMA, 'Discussion Paper: MiFID II/MiFIR' (n 1267) 74.

price formation process since at least the executable portion of the entire order (i.e., 'tip of the iceberg') shows pre-trade transparency.[1554]

For all other orders, it is sufficient if they meet the minimum tradable size quantity set in advance in the rules and protocols by the operator of the trading venue.[1555]

h) ESMA's Role in Granting and Withdrawing Waivers

aa) Granting a Waiver

The EU legislator has not only changed the scope of the waivers under MiFID II/MiFIR but also the administrative process granting the waivers. Under MiFID I, the waiver granting process lay solely in the hands of the NCA; any coordination with the NCAs in other Member States and ESMA's predecessor CESR was voluntary.[1556] Under Article 4(4), (5) MiFIR, this consultation process has been formalized:[1557] While the ultimate decision of granting a waiver remains under the sole discretion of the NCAs, it is mandatory for an NCA to notify ESMA and other NCAs of its intention to grant a waiver and explain the waiver's function.[1558] This notification has to be made at least four months before the waiver is intended to take effect. Two months after the notification, ESMA shall render a non-binding opinion assessing the compatibility of the waiver with the waiver regulation.[1559] Even though the notification process does not allow ESMA any formal power to decide over the matter whether to grant a waiver, it factually has a limiting effect on the NCA's discretion in the waiver granting process.[1560] The opinion rendered by ESMA compels the NCA to 'comply or explain',

1554 ibid 74.

1555 ESMA, 'Final Report: Draft Regulatory and Implementing Technical Standards MiFID II/MiFIR' (n 1445) 24 para 36; Kumpan and Schmidt (n 4) MiFIR Art 4 para 25.

1556 Moloney, *EU Securities and Financial Markets Regulation* (n 4) 483.

1557 ibid 483; see also Danny Busch and Guido Ferrarini, 'Who is Afraid of MiFID II?' in Danny Busch and Guido Ferrarini (eds), *Regulation of the EU Financial Markets: MiFID II and MiFIR* (1st edn, Oxford University Press 2017) para 1.32; Salger (n 627) 215.

1558 Article 4(4)(1) MiFIR; Moloney, 'EU Financial Governance and Transparency Regulation' (n 3) para 12.36.

1559 Recital 13 MiFIR; Gebauer (n 94) MiFIR Art 4 para 16.

1560 Gebauer (n 94) MiFIR Art 4 para 16.

thus curtailing the NCA's discretion in order to unifying the practice of granting waivers by the Member States.[1561]

Under Article 4(4) MiFIR, ESMA assumed the significant role as a coordinator among the NCAs of the Member States. This new supervisory role of ESMA is a response to the varying application of the waiver regime by the NCAs under MiFID I, which caused a dispute among the Member States during the recast of MiFID.[1562]

To further avoid misunderstandings among the Member States, the new coordination regime also grants an NCA that disagrees with a waiver granted by another Member State's NCA the right to refer the matter back to ESMA, which then may start a settlement of disagreement proceeding under Article 19 Regulation 1095/2010 (ESMA-Regulation).[1563] Additionally, ESMA also monitors the application of the waivers and submits an annual report to the Commission on the application of the waivers in practice.[1564] On the one hand, this task minimizes potential conflicts among the Member States because ESMA monitors the waiver applications so that the Member States do not need to call out on each other. On the other hand, this underlines a certain power shift from the Member States and their NCAs to ESMA and the European Union.[1565]

bb) Withdrawal of Waivers

According to Article 4(6) MiFIR, an NCA may either on its own initiative or upon request by another NCA, withdraw a waiver granted under Article 4(1) MiFIR if it observes that the waiver is being used in a way which deviates from its original purpose or if it believes that the waiver

1561 CESR, 'CESR Technical Advice to the European Commission in the Context of the MiFID Review - Equity Markets' (n 4) 7; ESMA, 'Waivers from Pre-trade Transparency' (n 1118) 3–4; Moloney, *EU Securities and Financial Markets Regulation* (n 4) 481; Busch and Ferrarini (n 1557) para 1.32.

1562 Moloney, *EU Securities and Financial Markets Regulation* (n 4) 481. See also ESMA, 'Waivers from Pre-trade Transparency' (n 1118) 3–4; CESR, 'CESR Technical Advice to the European Commission in the Context of the MiFID Review - Equity Markets' (n 4) 7.

1563 Gebauer (n 94) MiFIR Art 4 para 17.

1564 Article 4(4)(5) MiFIR; Moloney, 'EU Financial Governance and Transparency Regulation' (n 3) para 12.37.

1565 Cf. Busch and Ferrarini (n 1557) para 1.32; Moloney, *EU Securities and Financial Markets Regulation* (n 4) 483; Salger (n 627) 215.

is being used to circumvent the requirements established in this article.[1566] However, although ESMA may not be mentioned in Article 4(6) MiFIR, it retains a certain influence on whether a NCA withdraws a waiver through its annual report to the Commission on the application of the waivers in practice. Thereby ESMA may be the key figure initiating a withdrawal of a waiver. Member States also must inform ESMA about the withdrawal of a waiver. But, in contrast to the process of granting a waiver, they do not have to inform ESMA beforehand.[1567]

2. Waivers for Non-Equity Instruments, Article 9 MiFIR

The extension of pre-trade transparency to non-equity instruments under Article 8(1) MiFIR also requires the adoption of a waiver regime tailored to the needs of non-equity instruments. In fact, providing for waivers from pre-trade transparency is even more important for the trading in non-equity instruments because organized trading in such instruments greatly depends on dealers who would be susceptible to substantial liquidity risks under omnipresent trade transparency.[1568] The different characteristics of trading and price formation in non-equity instruments warrants the implementation of a tailored waiver regime separate from the one for equity instruments discussed above.[1569] Article 9 MiFIR provides for the waivers from pre-trade transparency for bonds, structured finance products, emission allowances, derivatives and package orders.[1570] Trading under those waivers also qualifies as regulated dark trading since MiFIR explicitly allows for those forms of dark trading and subjects them to supervision by the NCAs and ESMA.[1571]

1566 Article 4(6) MiFIR; Gebauer (n 94) MiFIR Art 4 paras 18ff; Kumpan and Schmidt (n 4) MiFIR Art 4 para 25.

1567 Gebauer (n 94) MiFIR Art 4 para 19.

1568 Recital 2 CDR (EU) 2017/583; Gebauer (n 94) MiFIR Art 9 para 1; Moloney, *EU Securities and Financial Markets Regulation* (n 4) 486.

1569 Recital 14 MiFIR; Gebauer (n 94) MiFIR Art 9 para 1.

1570 Package orders were added in the quick fix by Regulation (EU) 2016/1033.

1571 Cf. Moloney, 'EU Financial Governance and Transparency Regulation' (n 3) paras 12.19, 12.23.

a) Large in Scale Waiver (Article 9(1)(a) MiFIR)

Similar to Article 4(1)(c) MiFIR for equities, Article 9(1)(a) MiFIR adopted a waiver for orders in non-equities that are large in scale compared to normal market size.[1572] The large in scale waiver minimizes market impact costs for large orders in the non-equity market in a similar way as it does in the equity market.[1573] The scope of the waiver is determined by a threshold system outlined in the Tables of Annex III of Commission Delegated Regulation (EU) 2017/583.[1574] Those thresholds are calibrated for the liquidity levels of the specific non-equity instruments, i.e., for bonds, structured finance products, emission allowances, derivatives, and package orders (Article 3, 13 CDR (EU) 2017/583).[1575]

Also, parallel to the large in scale waiver for equity instruments is the treatment of order stubs that are left after partial execution of large orders.[1576] Even if those order stubs fall below the large in scale threshold, they remain protected by the waiver until they are either fully executed, altered, or cancelled.[1577]

The large in scale waiver for non-equity instruments only applies to orders, while indications of interests in a request for quote or voice trading system cannot benefit from this waiver. This, however, does not result in more transparency exposures for such indications of interest since Article 9(1)(b) MiFIR offers a waiver specifically applicable in such situations.[1578]

b) Order Management Facility Waiver (Article 9(1)(a) MiFIR)

Another waiver modelled after the waiver regime for equity instruments was the waiver for orders held in an order management facility of the

1572 Article 9(1)(a) MiFIR; Articles 3, 13 Commission Delegated Regulation (EU) 2017/583; Gebauer (n 94) MiFIR Art 9 para 3; Kumpan and Schmidt (n 1) MiFIR Art 9 para 7; Busch (n 1086) 131; Moloney, *EU Securities and Financial Markets Regulation* (n 4) 486.

1573 Gebauer (n 94) MiFIR Art 9 para 3; Moloney, 'EU Financial Governance and Transparency Regulation' (n 3) para 12.23.

1574 Gebauer (n 94) MiFIR Art 9 para 3.

1575 See Annex of the thesis for threshold tables of Annex II of CDR (EU) 2017/587.

1576 Gebauer (n 94) MiFIR Art 9 para 3.

1577 Kumpan and Schmidt (n 4) MiFIR Art 9 para 8.

1578 Gebauer (n 94) MiFIR Art 9 para 4.

trading venue pending disclosure.[1579] The rationale for this waiver is the same as for equity instruments, namely, allowing traders to protect order profiles entered into order management facilities executing the orders under the best possible market conditions.[1580] However, the immediately executable part of the order, the 'tip of the iceberg', must provide pre-trade transparency while the remainder is privileged in the dark.[1581] Under the same rationale, ESMA aligned the regulation of the equity and non-equity order management facility waiver.[1582]

The level 2 measures for non-equity instruments in Article 4 CDR (EU) 2017/587 are aligned to the level 2 measures for equity instruments requiring a minimum order size of EUR 10,000 or more for reserve orders (i.e., iceberg orders). For all other order types, however, the order size needs only to be equal or greater to the minimum tradable quantity set in advance by the system operator under its rules and protocols.[1583]

c) Indications of Interest That are Above the Size Specific to the Financial Instrument Waiver (Article 9(1)(b) MiFIR)

Under Article 9(1)(b) of the 2014 iteration of MiFIR, the pre-trade transparency requirement was waived for actionable indications of interest in request-for-quote and voice trading systems that are above a size specific to the financial instrument ('SSTI-waiver'), which would expose liquidity providers to undue risk.[1584]

Under the current 2014 iteration of MiFIR, the SSTI-waiver only applied to a subset of trading systems, namely request for quote and voice trading systems. Moreover, this waiver did not fully waive pre-trade transparency

1579 Article 9(1)(a) MiFIR; Article 4 Commission Delegated Regulation (EU) 2017/583; Gebauer (n 94) MiFIR Art 9 para 5; Kumpan and Schmidt (n 4) MiFIR Art 9 para 9; Busch (n 1086) 131; Moloney, *EU Securities and Financial Markets Regulation* (n 4) 486; Moloney, 'EU Financial Governance and Transparency Regulation' (n 3) para 12.23.

1580 Gebauer (n 94) MiFIR Art 9 para 5.

1581 ESMA, 'Consultation Paper: MiFID II/MiFIR' (ESMA/2014/1570, 19 December 2014) 211; ESMA, 'Discussion Paper: MiFID II/MiFIR' (n 1267) 74.

1582 ESMA, 'Consultation Paper: MiFID II/MiFIR' (n 1581) 212 para 25.

1583 Article 4(2)(a), (b) Commission Delegated Regulation (EU) 2017/583; Gebauer (n 94) MiFIR Art 9 para 6; Kumpan and Schmidt (n 4) MiFIR Art 9 para 10.

1584 ESMA, 'Discussion Paper: MiFID II/MiFIR' (n 1267) 183; Busch (n 1086) 131; Moloney, 'EU Financial Governance and Transparency Regulation' (n 3) para 12.23.

because trading venues still had to publish indicative information on the available price levels for the specific instrument.[1585]

The purpose of this waiver was to protect liquidity providers in the rather illiquid non-equity markets from market risk and prevent a situation in which liquidity providers withdraw from the market all together.[1586] In request-for-quote systems and voice trading systems, dealers are specifically exposed when offering a certain order size, i.e., above the SSTI-threshold, because they publish their indication of interest to the other party first so that this party can see all prices in the market and potentially front-run the trader posting the indication of interest.[1587]

In the review report of 2020, ESMA identified four major issues with the SSTI-waiver, namely:

> *'(...) a. it adds further complexity to an already complex pre-trade transparency regime by adding another threshold to be assessed;*
> *b. quotes benefitting from the SSTI waiver provide limited transparency to market participants;*
> *c. it grants a preferential treatment to RFQ and voice trading systems compared to other trading systems for no apparent reason;*
> *d. due to the many elements to be assessed, notifications for the SSTI waivers are burdensome to process for all: market participants, NCAs and ESMA.'*[1588]

Another issue may be seen in the waiver's vast success because trading under it accounted for 6 % of the total waiver notifications and roughly 8 % of the notional trading volume executed in 2018.[1589] Such high numbers, similar to those under the DVC, may have troubled ESMA. To avoid a situation in which dark trading becomes the default rule for markets in bonds,

---

1585 ESMA, 'MiFID II/MiFIR Review Report: MiFID II/MiFIR Review Report on the Transparency Regime for Non-Equity Instruments and the Trading Obligation for Derivatives' (ESMA70-156-3329, 25 September 2020) 18.

1586 ibid 19.

1587 Humbel, *Die Regelung der Vor- und Nachhandelstransparenz in der Europäischen Union und der Schweiz* (n 50) 321; Moloney, *EU Securities and Financial Markets Regulation* (n 4) 486–7; Verena Ross, 'MiFID II - Switching on the Light Without Turning-Off the Tap: Speech at ABA/Law Society Capital Markets Conference' (ESMA/2015/496, London, 26 February 2015) 10.

1588 ESMA, 'MiFID II/MiFIR Review Report: MiFID II/MiFIR Review Report on the Transparency Regime for Non-Equity Instruments and the Trading Obligation for Derivatives' (n 1585) 19.

1589 ibid 18.

credit derivatives, and interest rate derivatives, ESMA rather suggested to make lit trading the default rule by deleting the waiver. For compensation, ESMA suggests allowing more regulated dark trading at the other end of the order size spectrum under the large in scale waiver which would kick in for smaller-sized orders than before under the new level 2 measure protecting thin layers of liquidity.[1590]

In its review report on MiFIR, ESMA concluded that the waiver regime was too complicated and did not support trade transparency as desired.[1591] Following the proposal by ESMA, the Committee on Economic and Monetary Affairs also proposes to delete the SSTI-waiver in the transparency regime for non-equities trading.[1592] To minimize the adverse effects the deletion may have on liquidity providers in those markets, ESMA proposed to lower the threshold for the large in scale-waiver respectively in the subsequent level 2 measure.[1593]

d) Illiquid Financial Instruments Waiver (Article 9(1)(c) MiFIR)

Under Article 9(1)(c) MiFIR, orders in derivatives which are not subject to the trading obligation under Article 28 MiFIR as well as other financial instruments for which there is not a liquid market are exempt from showing pre-trade transparency. This waiver concerns all financial instruments trading in an illiquid market with particular reference to illiquid derivatives that fall outside the scope of the trading obligation.[1594]

The waiver for illiquid instruments applies to a large number of instruments since its wording does not apply to a specific order type or order size, but rather to illiquid non-equity instruments in general.[1595] For this

1590 ibid 18ff.

1591 ibid 20.

1592 Committee on Economic and Monetary Affairs, 'Report' (n 1137) 22. Cf. European Commission, 'Proposal for a Regulation of the European Parliament and of the Council amending Regulation (EU) No 600/2014 as regards enhancing market data transparency, removing obstacles to the emergence of a consolidated tape, optimising the trading obligations and prohibiting receiving payments for forwarding client orders' (n 1146) 8.

1593 ESMA, 'MiFID II/MiFIR Review Report: MiFID II/MiFIR Review Report on the Transparency Regime for Non-Equity Instruments and the Trading Obligation for Derivatives' (n 1585) 20.

1594 Gebauer (n 94) MiFIR Art 9 para 11; Busch (n 1086) 131; Moloney, 'EU Financial Governance and Transparency Regulation' (n 3) para 12.23.

1595 Kumpan and Schmidt (n 4) MiFIR Art 9 para 14.

reason, national competent authorities shall not grant the waiver on an instrument by instrument basis but rather for entire asset classes of instruments according to ESMA.[1596] The question of when a class of financial instruments is deemed not to trade in a liquid market is determined in accordance with Article 2(1)(17)(a) MiFIR.

According to Article 2(1)(17)(a) MiFIR, a liquid market in non-equity instruments is a market

> *'(...) where there are ready and willing buyers and sellers on a continuous basis, and where the market is assessed in accordance with the following criteria, taking into consideration the specific market structure of the particular financial instrument or of the particular class of financial instruments: (i) the average frequency and size of transactions over a range of market conditions, having regard to the nature and life cycle of products within the class of financial instrument, (ii) the number and type of market participants, including the ratio of market participants to traded financial instruments in a particular product; (iii) the average size of spreads, where available (...)'.*[1597]

Compared with the definition of a liquid market in equity instruments under Article 2(1)(17)(b) MiFIR,[1598] this definition provides much more leeway to calibrate the thresholds for a liquid market according to the 'specific market structure of the particular financial instrument.'[1599]

For the pre-trade transparency regime on trading venues, the threshold for a liquid market in non-equity instruments is to be determined by the level 2 measures of MiFIR (Article 9(5)(e) MiFIR). The convoluted regulation for determining whether or not an instrument trades in a liquid market can be found in Articles 6, 13 CDR (EU) 2017/583 which refer to a threshold model set out in the Tables of Annex III of CDR (EU)

1596 ESMA, 'Questions and Answers: On MiFID II and MiFIR Transparency Topics' (n 1472) 51; Kumpan and Schmidt (n 4) MiFIR Art 9 para 14.

1597 Article 2(1)(17)(a) MiFIR; Gebauer (n 94) MiFIR Art 9 para 12.

1598 Article 2(1)(17)(b) MiFIR: *''liquid market' means: (b) for the purposes of Articles 4, 5 and 14, a market for a financial instrument that is traded daily where the market is assessed according to the following criteria: (i) the free float; (ii) the average daily number of transactions in those financial instruments; (iii) the average daily turnover for those financial instruments'.*

1599 Humbel, *Die Regelung der Vor- und Nachhandelstransparenz in der Europäischen Union und der Schweiz* (n 50) 301.

2017/583.[1600] In particular, Article 13 CDR (EU) 2017/583 leaves no doubt that the determination of liquidity levels is a rather technical and multi-faceted endeavor with its many references to other provisions.[1601]

For illustrative purposes, the categorization logic of Article 13 CDR (EU) 2017/583 shall be briefly outlined. The assessment which financial instruments trade in a liquid or illiquid market is determined by a categorization into four groups according to economic characteristics of the instrument.[1602] The first category of asset classes contain such instruments for which the liquidity of the market can unequivocally be determined. These instruments are subject to a static determination because they either are regarded as liquid or illiquid without any periodic reassessment of this categorization. Foreign exchange derivatives which are considered to be illiquid fall within this group.[1603]

The second category comprises of asset classes of financial instruments which are determined with regard to quantitative liquidity criteria, such as, average daily turnover, average daily notional amount, and average daily number of trades (see for example Annex III Tables 2.1, 2.4). Where applicable, Article 13(1)(b) CDR (EU) 2017/583 complements the quantitative determination of a liquid market in a specific instrument with qualitative criteria. In contrast to the first category, the assessment in this category is not static but subject to periodic reassessment. The periods for reassessment, however, differ with respect to the specific financial instrument.[1604]

In spite of the fact that the second class uses both quantitative and qualitative criteria for determining the liquidity of the market, the third category uses qualitative characteristics alone. For the criteria and the assessment process see Tables 9.1 and 11.1 of Annex III of CDR (EU) 2017/583. The assessments in accordance with the qualitative criteria are subject to periodic reassessment.[1605]

1600 Kumpan and Schmidt (n 4) MiFIR Art 9 para 13.

1601 Humbel, *Die Regelung der Vor- und Nachhandelstransparenz in der Europäischen Union und der Schweiz* (n 50) 302.

1602 ibid 302.

1603 Humbel, *Die Regelung der Vor- und Nachhandelstransparenz in der Europäischen Union und der Schweiz* (n 50) 302–3; ESMA, 'Final Report: Draft Regulatory and Implementing Technical Standards MiFID II/MiFIR' (n 1445) 109–10.

1604 Humbel, *Die Regelung der Vor- und Nachhandelstransparenz in der Europäischen Union und der Schweiz* (n 50) 303.

1605 ibid 303.

The fourth category is for structured finance products only and uses a two-tiered test for liquidity. First, quantitative criteria are used for the assessment of the liquidity of an entire class of instruments. If the class of instruments is considered liquid, then another liquidity test is conducted on the instrument level according to quantitative criteria (see Table 3.1 of Annex III).[1606]

Although this waiver is very broad and might exempt the pre-trade transparency requirement for many classes of instruments, the waiver also accounts for the specific trading patterns in non-equity markets. Such markets are characterized by large liquidity risks where liquidity may vanish very quickly due to the different incentives to trade non-equities and the much smaller number of traders.[1607] Only practical experience will tell whether the waiver is too broad and overused by traders or the appropriate protective measure not to dry out markets.

e) Exchange for Physical Waiver (Article 9(1)(d) MiFIR)

The exchange for physical waiver and the following package order waiver both have been amended by Regulation 2016/1033 as a quick fix to the text of MiFID II/MiFIR. The amended Article 9(1)(d) MiFIR exempts orders in non-equity instruments from pre-trade transparency for the purpose of executing an exchange for physical.[1608] According to the also amended Article 2(1)(48) MiFIR, an 'exchange for physical' means a transaction in a derivative contract or other financial instrument contingent on the simultaneous execution of an equivalent quantity of an underlying physical asset. As ESMA clarified in the Q&A on transparency topics, the underlying physical asset can only be a truly physical asset, such as commodities, but not a financial instrument.[1609]

Exchange for physical orders, as a sub-category of package orders, serve the purpose of better managing risks for investment firms and their clients. Since the price of exchange for physical orders rather reflects the overall risk profile of the package order, of which it usually forms a part, rather

1606 ibid 303–4.

1607 Moloney, *EU Securities and Financial Markets Regulation* (n 4) 431ff, 486.

1608 Gebauer (n 94) MiFIR Art 9 para 15; Kumpan and Schmidt (n 4) MiFIR Art 9 para 15.

1609 ESMA, 'Questions and Answers: On MiFID II and MiFIR Transparency Topics' (n 1472) 32.

than the current market price, those orders do not support the price formation process. Thus, the waiver from pre-trade transparency is reasonable.[1610]

f) Package Order Waiver (Article 9(1)(e) MiFIR)

The last waiver is the waiver for package orders according to Article 9(1)(e) MiFIR. Package orders lead to transactions in which derivatives and other financial instruments or assets that comprise of a number of interlinked, contingent trades.[1611] According to Article 9(1)(e) MiFIR as amended by Regulation 2016/1033 (quick fix to MiFID II/MiFIR), a package order that meets one of the following three conditions is exempt from pre-trade transparency: (i) at least one of its components is a financial instrument for which there is not a liquid market, unless there is a liquid market for the package order as a whole; (ii) at least one of its components is large in scale compared with the normal market size, unless there is a liquid market for the package order as a whole; or (iii) all of its components are executed on a request-for-quote or voice system and are above the size specific to the instrument (Article 9(1)(e)(i)-(iii) MiFIR).[1612]

As with the sub-category of exchange for physical orders, investment firms and their clients use package orders to manage their risks. Therefore, transactions resulting from package orders comprise of multiple components of which the individual components reflect the overall risk profile

1610 Recital 12 of Regulation 2016/1033.

1611 Gebauer (n 94) MiFIR Art 9 para 16; Recital 12 of Regulation 2016/1033; cf. Article 2(1)(49) MiFIR as amended by Regulation 2016/1033:
'(49) 'package order' means an order priced as a single unit:
(a) for the purpose of executing an exchange for physical; or
(b) in two or more financial instruments for the purpose of executing a package transaction
(50) 'package transaction' means:
(a) an exchange for physical; or
(b) a transaction involving the execution of two or more component transactions in financial instruments and which fulfils all of the following criteria:
(i) the transaction is executed between two or more counterparties;
(ii) each component of the transaction bears meaningful economic or financial risk related to all the other components;
(iii) the execution of each component is simultaneous and contingent upon the execution of all the other components.'

1612 Gebauer (n 94) MiFIR Art 9 para 16; Kumpan and Schmidt (n 4) MiFIR Art 9 para 16.

of the package rather than the current market price for the component.[1613] Since the pricing of package orders does not support the price formation process for the instrument, the NCA can grant a waiver from pre-trade transparency either for the entire package order or for each individual component.[1614]

In the MiFIR refit process, the Committee on Economic and Monetary Affairs proposed in alignment with its proposal to exclude request for quote and voice systems from pre-trade transparency under Article 8(1) MiFIR to also delete the waiver under Article 9(1)(e)(iii) MiFIR. Where there is no pre-trade transparency obligation, no waiver is needed.[1615]

g) Temporary Suspension (Article 9(4) MiFIR)

The temporary suspension set out in Article 9(4) MiFIR is not a waiver but does suspend pre-trade transparency for a class of bonds, structured finance products, emission allowances, or derivatives.[1616] This temporary suspension can only be applied by a NCA that is responsible for supervision of at least one trading venue that trades these classes of instruments and where the liquidity of that respective class falls below a specified threshold. In Germany, this is BaFin for MTFs and OTFs and the respective Exchange Supervisory Authority for regulated markets.[1617]

The thresholds set out in Article 16 CDR (EU) 2017/583 distinguish between liquid and illiquid markets: For an instrument trading in a liquid market, the threshold for suspension is reached when the total volume as defined in Table 4 of Annex II calculated for the previous 30 calendar days represents less than 40 % of the average monthly volume calculated for the 12 calendar months preceding those 30 calendar days.[1618] Whereas, for an instrument trading in illiquid markets, the same calculation is made but the illiquidity threshold lies at 20 % of the average monthly volume

1613 Recital 12 of Regulation 2016/1033. Cf. Gebauer (n 94) MiFIR Art 9 paras 16–7.

1614 Article 9(2a) MiFIR as amended by Regulation 2016/1033; Gebauer (n 94) MiFIR Art 9 paras 16–7; Kumpan and Schmidt (n 4) MiFIR Art 9 para 17.

1615 Committee on Economic and Monetary Affairs, 'Report' (n 1137) 22.

1616 Gebauer (n 94) MiFIR Art 9 para 25; Busch (n 1086) 131; Moloney, 'EU Financial Governance and Transparency Regulation' (n 3) para 12.10.

1617 Article 9(4) MiFIR; Gebauer (n 94) MiFIR Art 9 para 27; Kumpan and Schmidt (n 4) MiFIR Art 9 para 22.

1618 Article 16(1) of Commission Delegated Regulation (EU) 2017/583 of 14 July 2016; Kumpan and Schmidt (n 4) MiFIR Art 9 para 22.

calculated for the 12 calendar months preceding the previous 30 calendar days.[1619] In its calculations, the NCA shall take into account the transactions on all venues in the European Union which trade the respective asset class.[1620] However, before the NCA suspends pre-trade transparency on merely quantitative reasons, it shall ensure that the decline in liquidity across all venues is not a result of a seasonal effect.[1621]

With regard to the suspension procedure, the NCA has to publish a notification of the temporary suspension on its website.[1622] The first suspension can only last for three months from the date of its publication on the website of the NCA, and it can only be renewed once for another three-month period. When it is not renewed, the suspension lapses automatically.[1623]

The procedure of first suspending or renewing a temporary suspension between the NCA and ESMA is parallel to the granting of a waiver:[1624] The NCA has to notify ESMA beforehand and provide an explanation. ESMA then renders a non-binding opinion which factually limits the leeway for the NCA since ESMA's views expressed in the opinion require the NCA to either comply or explain its divergence.[1625]

h) Granting and Withdrawal of Waivers

The process of the granting and withdrawing waivers among the NCAs and ESMA is the same for waivers from pre-trade transparency for non-equity instruments as for equity instruments discussed above in which ESMA exercises significant legal and factual powers.[1626]

1619 Article 16(2) Commission Delegated Regulation (EU) 2017/583 of 14 July 2016; Kumpan and Schmidt (n 4) MiFIR Art 9 para 22.

1620 Article 16(3) Commission Delegated Regulation (EU) 2017/583 of 14 July 2016; Kumpan and Schmidt (n 4) MiFIR Art 9 para 22.

1621 Article 16(4) Commission Delegated Regulation (EU) 2017/583 of 14 July 2016; Kumpan and Schmidt (n 4) MiFIR Art 9 para 22.

1622 Gebauer (n 94) MiFIR Art 9 para 27.

1623 Article 9(4) subpara 2 MiFIR; Gebauer (n 94) MiFIR Art 9 para 28; Kumpan and Schmidt (n 4) MiFIR Art 9 para 23.

1624 Article 9(4) subpara 3 MiFIR; Kumpan and Schmidt (n 4) MiFIR Art 9 para 23.

1625 Article 9(4) subpara 3 MiFIR. Gebauer (n 94) MiFIR Art 9 para 29.

1626 See above Part II § 6 C.III.1.h); cf. Article 9(2), (3) MiFIR.

i) Comparison to the Waiver Regime for Equity Instruments

As the European Union introduced the new transparency regime for non-equity instruments, it started on a clean slate with no predecessor under MiFID I. Yet, the European Union decided to import the transparency rules as well as the large in scale and the order management facility waivers from the transparency regime for equity instruments since the ongoing practice under MiFID I proved those waivers as sensible calibrations of the transparency regime, also for non-equity instruments.[1627]

Interestingly, neither a waiver similar to the reference price waiver nor to the negotiated trade waiver was adopted for the non-equity waiver regime. Only the exchange for physical waiver and package order waiver bear a certain resemblance to the negotiated trade waiver subject to conditions other than the current market conditions (Article 4(1)(b)(iii) MiFIR) that was not as controversial as the negotiated trade waiver subject to current market conditions, and is thus not restricted by the volume cap mechanism.[1628]

These omissions of controversial waivers may also explain why the non-equity waiver regime can operate without a device similar to the volume cap mechanism. However, the SSTI-waiver and the temporary suspension power under Article 9(4) MiFIR may prove to be similarly large loopholes but under stricter regulation with regard to indicative prices (SSTI-waiver) or the periods of application (temporary suspension), so that misuse may not be impossible but less likely than under MiFID I. Furthermore, the introduction of such liquidity exemptions appears to be a sensible mechanism for implementing new, strict transparency regulations while not jeopardizing that the organized trading of non-equities dries up entirely.[1629]

IV. Post-Trade Transparency for Trading Venues

As for pre-trade transparency, MiFIR distinguishes between post-trade transparency requirements for equity (Article 6 MiFIR) and non-equity instruments (Article 10 MiFIR).[1630] The content, however, of the post-trade

---

1627 Cf. Gebauer (n 94) MiFIR Art 9 paras 3ff.

1628 See above Part II § 6 C.III.1.b).aa).

1629 Cf. Moloney, *EU Securities and Financial Markets Regulation* (n 4) 486–7; Moloney, 'EU Financial Governance and Transparency Regulation' (n 3) paras 12.21, 12.25.

1630 Gebauer (n 94) MiFIR Art 6 para 1 and Art 10 para 1.

transparency rules is strongly aligned between equity and non-equity instruments as both require the market operator or investment firm operating a trading venue to make public the price, volume, and time of the transaction executed in the respective instrument traded on a trading venue.[1631] The trading venue operators must publish the post-trade information as close to real time as is technically possible.[1632] The level 2 measures set out the time limits for the real-time requirement, which is within one minute during normal trading hours for equity instruments traded on a trading venue.[1633] And for non-equity instruments the time-limit is 15 minutes for the first three years of application of MiFIR and 5 minutes after this initial time of adjustment and testing the market.[1634] This shows a more cautious approach in the non-equity markets that have lower liquidity levels compared to equities trading. It may also be considered a more cautious approach by the European Union since non-equity instruments have never before been under mandatory trade transparency requirements.

Trading venue operators must give access to post-trade transparency information on reasonable commercial terms and on a non-discriminatory basis to the systematic internalizers that must publish details of their transactions in equities or non-equities and to the public to create market transparency.[1635] However, only after 15 minutes from publication must such information be made available free of charge, providing the venue with enough time to market the service of price formation profitably before it becomes a (quasi-)public good.[1636]

Post-trade transparency in both equity and non-equity instruments serves the purpose of providing immediate and comprehensive information about market activity to promote price formation in financial instruments, including in fragmented markets across multiple trading systems.[1637]

1631 ibid MiFIR Art 6 para 10 and Art 10 para 10.

1632 Articles 6(1) and 10(1) MiFIR; Moloney, *EU Securities and Financial Markets Regulation* (n 4) 484, 487.

1633 See for all time limits in equity instruments trading Article 14 Commission Delegated Regulation (EU) 2017/587; Gebauer (n 94) MiFIR Art 6 para 11.

1634 Article 7(4) Commission Delegated Regulation (EU) 2017/583; Gebauer (n 94) MiFIR Art 10 para 11.

1635 Articles 6(2), 10(2), 13(1) MiFIR; Gebauer (n 94) MiFIR Art 6 paras 13ff and Art 10 paras 12ff.

1636 Article 13(1)(2) MiFIR; Gebauer (n 94) MiFIR Art 6 para 13 and Art 10 para 12.

1637 Gebauer (n 94) MiFIR Art 6 para 2 and Art 10 para 3.

V. Deferrals from Post-Trade Transparency

Post-trade transparency is necessary to support price formation and to integrate fragmented markets across multiple trading systems. However, in certain situations an overabundance of post-trade transparency may be detrimental since some transactions may suffer from liquidity and positing risks.[1638] When dispensing with post-trade transparency, however, one must be aware of the transaction costs incurred due to inaccurate, stale prices that do not (yet) reflect the exempted transaction.[1639] With Articles 7 and 11 MiFIR, the European Union attempted to strike a balance between both goals to maximize market efficiency.[1640]

1. Deferrals for Equity Instruments

According to Article 7(1) MiFIR, the NCA can authorize market operators and investment firms operating a trading venue to provide for deferred publication of the details of the transactions based on the type or size of the transaction.[1641] Unlike the waiver system for equity instruments, the deferral regime on the level 1 measure, i.e., MiFIR, is not exhaustive but only sets out that in particular transactions that are large in scale compared to the normal market size shall benefit from a deferred publication of post-trade transparency data.[1642] This may have been understood as leaving national competent authorities vast discretion over the issue of dispensing with post-trade transparency.[1643]

However, Article 7(2) subpara 1 lit c MiFIR requires that additional deferrals besides the large-in-scale deferral need to be specified in a commission delegated regulation. The relevant Commission Delegated Regulation (EU) 2017/587 only sets out a deferral for transactions that are large-in-scale according to Article 15 CDR (EU) 2017/587 with the thresholds defined in Tables 4, 5, and 6 of Annex II CDR (EU) 2017/587 but specify no

1638 Kumpan and Schmidt (n 4) MiFIR Art 7 para 1; cf. Gomber and Nassauer (n 1086) 255; Moloney, *EU Securities and Financial Markets Regulation* (n 4) 484.

1639 Cf. O'Hara, *Market Microstructure Theory* (n 45) 258–9.

1640 Recital 2 of CDR (EU) 2017/583; Gebauer (n 94) MiFIR Art 11 para 1.

1641 Article 7(1) MiFIR. See: Allgemeinverfügung Nachhandelstransparenz Handelsplätze, die nicht durch eine Börse betrieben werden/Eigenkapitalinstrumente 20 June 2023, WA 21-FR 1900/00006#00001 (BaFin).

1642 Article 7(1) subpara 2 MiFIR.

1643 Gebauer (n 94) MiFIR Art 7 para 3.

other deferral. Other deferrals are actually missing in CDR (EU) 2017/587, from which one must infer that the Commission did not wish to allow for additional deferrals in equity markets.[1644]

This decision appears sensible considering the goal of striking a trade-off between low transaction costs due to price accuracy and low transaction costs due to low market impact costs: When block orders are often traded on-venue instead of prearranged transactions, market makers often need to take over the block order from a certain seller, or in case of selling to a block order buyer, enter into a substantial short position. This basically shifts the risk of market impact costs to the market maker since it has to unwind its long or short position into the market. To do so, the prior transaction cannot become public beforehand.[1645]

Moreover, the NCA does not have to notify ESMA before granting a deferral to a trading venue. Nevertheless, ESMA monitors the application of the deferrals and submits an annual report to the Commission on their application.[1646] Parallel to the waiver regime, however, there is also an institutionalized conflict resolution mechanism if another Member State's NCA disagrees with the deferral or its effective application by an NCA. In this case, ESMA settles the disagreement under Article 19 Regulation (EU) No. 1095/2010 (ESMA-Regulation).[1647]

The level 2 measure outlines the maximum time allotted for the delay of publication of the details of the transaction. This time ranges from 60 minutes over 120 minutes to the end of the next trading day depending on the size of the transaction and the average daily turnover as proxy for liquidity in the respective instrument provided either (a) the transaction is between an investment firm dealing on own account other than matched principal trading and another party or (b) the size of the transaction is equal to or larger than the minimum sizes set out in the Tables 4, 5 or 6 of Annex II of CDR (EU) 2017/587.[1648] This again shows the narrow scope of the deferrals from post-trade transparency in equity instruments. A delay in

1644 ibid MiFIR Art 7 para 3.

1645 O'Hara, *Market Microstructure Theory* (n 45) 258–9.

1646 Article 7(1) subpara 3 MiFIR.

1647 Article 7(1) subpara 3 MiFIR.

1648 Article 15(1) and Tables 4, 5 and 6 of Annex II of Commission Delegated Regulation (EU) 2017/587; cf. Gebauer (n 94) MiFIR Art 6 para 1 and Art 7 para 3; Kumpan and Schmidt (n 4) MiFIR Art 7 para 9.

publication is only admissible if a liquidity provider or a large order trader took over liquidity and position risk with the past trade.[1649]

2. Deferrals for Non-Equity Instruments

a) Latest Developments

With the 2014 iteration of MiFID II/MiFIR, trade transparency rules for trading in non-equities has been introduced in EU markets. ESMA, however, identified issues with the post-trade transparency regime in its MiFID II/MiFIR review report wherein the EU legislator addresses in the MiFID II/MiFIR refit.[1650] The major objectives to make the new post-trade transparency regime work is to streamline the deferral regime and harmonize its application by the NCAs across the EU.[1651]

b) Functioning of the Deferrals for Non-Equity Trading

With regard to non-equity instruments, Article 11(1) MiFIR empowers the NCAs to allow market operators and investment firms to delay the publication of the details of the transactions concluded on their trading venues based on the type and size of the transaction.[1652]

Similar to Article 7(1) MiFIR, Article 11(1) MiFIR does not set out an exhaustive list of deferrals (*'In particular...'*). However, in contrast to the deferrals for equities, the deferrals for non-equities are much more detailed: Article 11(1) MiFIR sets out that NCAs may delay the publication of post-trade transparency for transactions (a) that are large in scale and (b) for

1649 Gebauer (n 94) MiFIR Art 6 para 1 and Art 7 para 3.

1650 ESMA, 'MiFID II/MiFIR Review Report: MiFID II/MiFIR Review Report on the Transparency Regime for Non-Equity Instruments and the Trading Obligation for Derivatives' (n 1585) 42–3; European Commission, 'Proposal for a Regulation of the European Parliament and of the Council amending Regulation (EU) No 600/2014 as regards enhancing market data transparency, removing obstacles to the emergence of a consolidated tape, optimising the trading obligations and prohibiting receiving payments for forwarding client orders' (n 1146) 8.

1651 ESMA, 'MiFID II/MiFIR Review Report: MiFID II/MiFIR Review Report on the Transparency Regime for Non-Equity Instruments and the Trading Obligation for Derivatives' (n 1585) 32.

1652 Article 11(1) MiFIR; Gebauer (n 94) MiFIR Art 6 para 1 and Art 11 para 1.

which there is no liquid market.[1653] This rule takes the rationale of the equity regime (Articles 4 and 7 MiFIR) that waivers from pre-trade transparency and deferrals from immediate post-trade transparency are necessary if liquidity risk are most prevalent as a blueprint and mirrors such rationale into the deferral regime for non-equities to determine when delays from real-time post-trade transparency are in order.[1654] These deferrals balance traders' interests in avoiding excessively high transaction costs due to stale prices with the market makers' interest in having enough time to unwind their inventory without undue market risk.[1655] However, the exception under the current Article 11(c) MiFIR for trades above a size specific to that instrument (SSTI) is proposed to be deleted in the MiFID II/MiFIR refit along with the corresponding SSTI-waiver.[1656]

c) Timing of the Deferrals and Deviating Practices across the EU

Under Article 8 CDR (EU) 2017/583, the publication of price, size, and time of the transaction can be deferred until 19:00 local time on the second working day after the date of the transaction. This sets a deadline until the information can be added to the price formation process.[1657] However, under Article 11(c), (d) CDR (EU) 2017/583, NCAs could allow for longer deferrals of either four weeks or indefinitely. In the MiFID II/MiFIR review report, ESMA found that many NCAs grant the four weeks deferral or even the indefinite deferral rather than the 2 days for transactions in non-equities, which undermines market transparency and, due to diverging NCA-practice, also leads to an uneven playing field across the EU.[1658]

1653 Article 11(1) subpara 2 (a)–(c) MiFIR; Gebauer (n 94) MiFIR Art 6 para 1 and Art 11 paras 1, 9ff.

1654 Cf. Kumpan and Schmidt (n 4) MiFIR Art 11 para 1.

1655 Cf. O'Hara, *Market Microstructure Theory* (n 45) 258–9.

1656 European Commission, 'Proposal for a Regulation of the European Parliament and of the Council amending Regulation (EU) No 600/2014 as regards enhancing market data transparency, removing obstacles to the emergence of a consolidated tape, optimising the trading obligations and prohibiting receiving payments for forwarding client orders' (n 1146) 8.

1657 Kumpan and Schmidt (n 4) MiFIR Art 11 para 8.

1658 ESMA, 'MiFID II/MiFIR Review Report: MiFID II/MiFIR Review Report on the Transparency Regime for Non-Equity Instruments and the Trading Obligation for Derivatives' (n 1585) 33ff.

The issue of non-aligned supervisory practice is exacerbated by the fact that the granting process of the deferrals by the NCAs does not require a notification of ESMA as it is the case for the granting of waivers from pre-trade transparency.[1659] Yet, ESMA monitors the application of the waivers and submits an annual report to the Commission on how the deferrals are used in practice. Interestingly, however, the deferral regime for non-equities also has no mechanism in which another Member State's NCA can refer back to ESMA if it disagrees with the content or application of the deferral granted by another NCA, as is the case under the regime for granting waivers from pre-trade transparency.[1660]

d) Proposed Changes under the MiFID II/MiFIR Refit

To streamline the post-trade transparency regime and to correct for the divergent application of the deferrals by the NCAs across the EU, the European Commission's proposal for the refit of MiFID II/MiFIR would shorten and harmonize the publication deferrals. The proposed new Article 11 under the MiFIR refit will only allow for either a deferral until the end of the day, or for the volume of the transaction for a maximum of two weeks.[1661] The Committee of Economic and Monetary Affairs' proposal is very similar but suggests a maximum deferral period of four weeks for very large transactions.[1662] An EU-wide threshold for determining which deferral period shall apply (end of day or two/four weeks) will take away the discretion of the NCAs and ensure uniform application.[1663] Since the legislative process is still ongoing, it remains to be seen how strong the alignment in post-trade transparency deferral will ultimately be.

1659 Gebauer (n 94) MiFIR Art 6 para 1 and Art 7 paras 18ff.

1660 Article 11(1) subpara 3 MiFIR; Gebauer (n 94) MiFIR Art 6 para 1 and Art 7 paras 18ff.

1661 European Commission, 'Proposal for a Regulation of the European Parliament and of the Council amending Regulation (EU) No 600/2014 as regards enhancing market data transparency, removing obstacles to the emergence of a consolidated tape, optimising the trading obligations and prohibiting receiving payments for forwarding client orders' (n 1146) 29.

1662 Committee on Economic and Monetary Affairs, 'Report' (n 1137) 23.

1663 European Commission, 'Proposal for a Regulation of the European Parliament and of the Council amending Regulation (EU) No 600/2014 as regards enhancing market data transparency, removing obstacles to the emergence of a consolidated tape, optimising the trading obligations and prohibiting receiving payments for forwarding client orders' (n 1146) 14.

e) Conclusion

The broader deferral regime for non-equity instruments compared to the one for equity instruments mirrors the regimes for waivers from pre-trade transparency for equity and non-equity instruments under MiFIR. This was, on the one hand, made to avoid imposing overly strict transparency requirements on the non-equity market newly captured by the trade transparency regime and, on the other hand, to account for the different liquidity levels between equity markets and non-equity markets.[1664] Insofar, the transparency regime for non-equity instruments allows for more dark trading compared to equity instruments. But this is justified due to the generally lower liquidity levels in markets for non-equities. With the MiFID II/MiFIR refit, the EU corrects for overbroad deferrals and divergent application of the deferrals by the NCAs across the EU. The latest iteration of MiFID II/MiFIR will enhance post-trade transparency but still protect the thinner levels of liquidity on non-equity markets.

VI. Implementation of a Consolidated Tape

The goal of MiFIR to support market transparency cannot be reached by merely publishing the trade transparency data, it is also important to collect and disseminate the data via a central institution. In the US, the consolidated tape fulfils this purpose.[1665] Under MiFID II/MiFIR, the EU aimed to set up a US-style consolidated tape to counter the fragmentation among the more than 279 trading venues and approved publication arrangements (APAs) and to propel the Capital Markets Union.[1666]

In ESMA's review report, the agency found that since the implementation of MiFID II/MiFIR no consolidated tape has yet been set up, which

1664 Gebauer (n 94) MiFIR Art 10 para 1; Moloney, *EU Securities and Financial Markets Regulation* (n 4) 486–7.

1665 See above Part II § 5.C.II.

1666 ESMA, 'MiFID II/MiFIR Review Report: MiFID II/MiFIR Review Report on the Transparency Regime for Non-Equity Instruments and the Trading Obligation for Derivatives' (n 1585) 40; European Commission, 'Proposal for a Regulation of the European Parliament and of the Council amending Regulation (EU) No 600/2014 as regards enhancing market data transparency, removing obstacles to the emergence of a consolidated tape, optimising the trading obligations and prohibiting receiving payments for forwarding client orders' (n 1146) 1–2; Committee on Economic and Monetary Affairs, 'Draft Report' (n 1400) 100.

significantly hinders trade transparency.[1667] The reason for this shortfall is the EU's reliance on private actors, so-called consolidated tape providers (CTP), while neglecting the costs such a service imposes on them. Private CTPs have not yet assumed the task themselves due to inhibitory costs.[1668]

For the MiFID II/MiFIR refit, the EU aims to create an environment in which a consolidated tape can emerge. The EU still relies on private actors, the CTPs, to create and run the consolidated tape. But instead of waiting for private actors to step up, ESMA would be able to select and appoint a CTP for each instrument for a five-years term.[1669] Moreover, the trading venues must make available the data to the CTP for incorporation into the consolidated tape and provide the CTP with harmonized data to lower the costs of data consolidation.[1670] Since a consolidated tape is crucial, especially for smaller- and medium-sized investors to navigate the market,[1671] the hope is that this time the EU can be successful in implementing it.

VII. Transparency Regime for Bilateral Systematic Internalizers and OTC Investment Firms

Trading beyond multilateral trading venues in the bilateral OTC-space can vary considerably with regard to the degree of organization. While investment firms trading in the OTC-market are generally exempt from

1667 European Commission, 'Proposal for a Regulation of the European Parliament and of the Council amending Regulation (EU) No 600/2014 as regards enhancing market data transparency, removing obstacles to the emergence of a consolidated tape, optimising the trading obligations and prohibiting receiving payments for forwarding client orders' (n 1146) 4.

1668 ESMA, 'MiFID II/MiFIR Review Report: MiFID II/MiFIR Review Report on the Transparency Regime for Non-Equity Instruments and the Trading Obligation for Derivatives' (n 1585) 42; European Commission, 'Proposal for a Regulation of the European Parliament and of the Council amending Regulation (EU) No 600/2014 as regards enhancing market data transparency, removing obstacles to the emergence of a consolidated tape, optimising the trading obligations and prohibiting receiving payments for forwarding client orders' (n 1146) 20.

1669 European Commission, 'Proposal for a Regulation of the European Parliament and of the Council amending Regulation (EU) No 600/2014 as regards enhancing market data transparency, removing obstacles to the emergence of a consolidated tape, optimising the trading obligations and prohibiting receiving payments for forwarding client orders' (n 1146) 15, 33.

1670 ibid 15, 31.

1671 ibid 2; Committee on Economic and Monetary Affairs, 'Draft Report' (n 1400) 100.

pre-trade transparency requirements as long as they trade in an ad-hoc and irregular manner, the regulatory treatment is different for those investment firms engaged in organized, frequent trading on a substantial basis. Those latter investment firms qualify as systematic internalizers because they offer trading services similar to those of trading venues.[1672] They are also capable of drawing liquidity from trading venues and exacerbating fragmentation in the market.[1673]

Since systematic internalizers aggregate liquidity in financial markets in a similar manner to trading venues, MiFID II/MiFIR subjects SIs to a pre-trade transparency obligation to achieve two goals: first, to enhance the market transparency for well-informed investor decision-making, and second, to prevent free-riding the price formation mechanism of trading venues since systematic internalizers often align the prices of their quotes with the prices displayed on trading venues.[1674] To prevent excessive trader migration from price forming trading venues to price importing OTC-trading systems which would leave the market with less informed prices, the transparency regime under MiFID II/MiFIR subjects those OTC-trading systems that trade frequently and on a substantial basis in a specific financial instrument to the systematic internalizer regime and tie a transparency regime to it which is calibrated for bilateral trading. While MiFID II/MiFIR adopted this regulatory practice from MiFID I, it strengthened and extended the formerly unsuccessful systematic internalizer regime significantly.[1675]

The MiFID II/MiFIR transparency regime for systematic internalizers reflects the compromise, found under MiFID I, between a regime functionally similar to that for trading venues and one that also accounts for the fact that SIs and OTC investment firms are taking on significant risk when trading bilaterally on their own account.[1676] Exposing SIs to the same pre-trade transparency requirements would expose them to liquidity and position risk when other traders either follow their trading pattern or engage in strategic behavior trading against the SI which renders the SI's hedging

1672 Moloney, *EU Securities and Financial Markets Regulation* (n 4) 488; Lutter, Bayer and Schmidt (n 1090) § 32 para 32.61; Schmies and Sajnovits (n 1357) 13.

1673 Schelling (n 1152) 222; Thelen (n 147) 195.

1674 Recital 18 MiFIR; Gebauer (n 94) MiFIR Art 14 paras 1–2; Schelling (n 1152) 222; Lutter, Bayer and Schmidt (n 1090) § 32 para 32.61.

1675 Recital 18 MiFIR; Gebauer (n 94) MiFIR Art 14 paras 1–2; Schelling (n 1152) 222; Lutter, Bayer and Schmidt (n 1090) § 32 para 32.61; Stefanski (n 1148) 131; Thelen (n 147) 195.

1676 Moloney, *EU Securities and Financial Markets Regulation* (n 4) 488.

transactions more expensive. Such risks specific to bilateral trading call for a calibrated transparency regime for systematic internalizers.[1677]

The calibrated transparency regime for systematic internalizers follows a familiar ordering pattern: It distinguishes between provisions for equity and non-equity instruments and within each category it distinguishes between rules for pre-trade and post-trade transparency and their respective exemptions.[1678] As with the transparency regime for trading venues, this examination starts with pre-trade transparency rules for equity instruments.

1. Pre-Trade Transparency in Equity Instruments

a) Rule

Pursuant to Article 14(1) MiFIR, investment firms shall make public firm quotes with respect to shares, depositary receipts, ETFs, certificates, and other similar financial instruments traded on a trading venue for which they qualify as a systematic internalizer and for which there is a liquid market.[1679] In case the respective market trades in an illiquid market, the systematic internalizer merely has to publish quotes to its clients upon request.[1680] This calibration to the liquidity level of the market for the financial instrument allows the systematic internalizer to manage the liquidity and position risk in such proprietary transactions.[1681]

aa) Firm Quotes and Obligation to Contract

The obligation for a systematic internalizer to publish 'firm quotes' if the instrument trades in a liquid market has an impact on the legal character of the quote. In terms of contract law, a firm quote needs to be a binding offer that can be accepted by the trading partner of the systematic internalizer. However, requiring the systematic internalizer to publish firm quotes sub-

1677 Thelen (n 147) 197–8.
1678 Gebauer (n 94) MiFIR Art 14 para 4.
1679 ibid MiFIR Art 14 paras 18ff; Kumpan and Schmidt (n 4) MiFIR Art 14 para 6.
1680 Gebauer (n 94) MiFIR Art 14 para 35; Kumpan and Schmidt (n 4) MiFIR Art 14 para 6; Lutter, Bayer and Schmidt (n 1090) § 32 para 32.62.
1681 Gebauer (n 94) MiFIR Art 14 para 20; Kumpan and Schmidt (n 4) MiFIR Art 14 paras 1, 6; Thelen (n 147) 197.

jects it to an obligation to contract.[1682] Traders admitted to trading with the systematic internalizer thus need to be able to trade at the quoted price with the systematic internalizer if they enter the published quote.[1683] This means a significant burden for the investment firm qualifying as a systematic internalizer. To account for this, the scope of the systematic internalizer regime is tied to the thresholds discussed above,[1684] the systematic internalizer can update and withdraw its quotes under Article 15 MiFIR and the obligation for firm quotes is limited to liquid markets only.[1685]

In an illiquid market, Article 14(1) MiFIR does not require systematic internalizers to quote continuously, but rather allows them to publish a quote upon request to its clients only. To other market participants than clients, a systematic internalizer does not have to publish a quote, not even upon request.[1686]

Dispensing with the requirement for firm quoting in illiquid markets serves a dual purpose. On the one hand, illiquid markets show less trading interest in the instrument which would render the effort to offer continuous quoting of current bid and offer prices burdensome for the systematic internalizer. On the other hand, exempting the systematic internalizer from the obligation to contract by not dispensing firm quoting protects the systematic internalizer from speculation and predatory trading by other market participants.[1687]

The definition of a liquid market in equity instruments according to Article 2(1)(17)(b) MiFIR represents the availability of continuous buyer- and seller-interest to enter into transactions.[1688] According to Article 5(1) CDR (EU) 2017/567 and Article 16 CDR (EU) 2017/590, the national competent authority of the most important market in terms of liquidity determines and publishes whether the market is liquid or illiquid in the respective instrument.[1689]

1682 Gebauer (n 94) MiFIR Art 14 paras 28ff.

1683 Cf. Articles 15(2), 17(1) MiFIR; Gebauer (n 94) MiFIR Art 14 para 28.

1684 See for the definition of systematic internalizer above Part II § 6 B.III.1.a).aa).

1685 Moloney, *EU Securities and Financial Markets Regulation* (n 4) 488ff.

1686 Cf. clients are admitted for internalization service according to Article 17(1) MiFIR; Gebauer (n 94) MiFIR Art 14 para 35.

1687 Gebauer (n 94) MiFIR Art 14 para 36.

1688 Moloney, *EU Securities and Financial Markets Regulation* (n 4) 493–4.

1689 Gebauer (n 94) MiFIR Art 14 para 31.

bb) Instruments Captured

Although the new Article 14(1) MiFIR closely resembles Article 27(1) MiFID I, its scope has been broadened to equity instruments other than shares to account for increased organized trading of equity-like instrument by systematic internalizers in the OTC-space, such as depositary receipts, ETFs, certificates, and other similar financial instruments, which already started under MiFID I.[1690] The new pre-trade transparency rule is further aligned with the goal under MiFID II/MiFIR to minimize unregulated dark trading of BCNs by bringing all organized trading within the scope of either the MTF- or SI-regulation.[1691]

cc) Modalities of Publication

According to Article 15(1) MiFIR, systematic internalizers must publish their quotes on a regular and continuous basis during normal trading hours.[1692] Systematic internalizers may update their quotes at any time and can withdraw their quotes under exceptional market conditions.[1693] To support transparency of the entire market, quotes shall be made public in a manner easily accessible to market participants other than merely the clients of an SI on a reasonable commercial basis.[1694]

dd) Minimum Size and Prevailing Market Conditions

Although the transparency regime for systematic internalizers must account for risks which are characteristic for bilateral proprietary trading, it also must ensure that published quotes are still meaningful for the market, so not only small orders but also orders below block size are executed, and that SIs inform traders about the price for trading interest of a relevant size.[1695] Under MiFID I, some SI quoted prices in quantities as small as

1690 Andreas Fuchs in Andreas Fuchs (ed), *Wertpapierhandelsgesetz (WpHG): Kommentar* (2nd edn, CH Beck 2016) WpHG § 32a para 2; Thelen (n 147) 197.

1691 Recital 6 MiFIR.

1692 Gebauer (n 94) MiFIR Art 15 para 4.

1693 ibid MiFIR Art 15 paras 5–6.

1694 Article 15(1) MiFIR; Gebauer (n 94) MiFIR Art 15 paras 7–8; Kumpan and Schmidt (n 4) MiFIR Art 15 paras 7–8.

1695 CESR, 'CESR Technical Advice to the European Commission in the Context of the MiFID Review - Equity Markets' (n 4) 14 para 58; Peter O Mülbert, 'Die one share which fulfilled the black-letter requirements but did not inform the market about the actual size of business the SI was willing to take on.[1696] MiFID I provided systematic internalizers with an inexpensive way to evade transactions with clients and to show no transparency for their meaningful quote sizes which is both problematic given that Article 17 MiFIR provides SIs with means to limit access to their quotes.[1697]

To make quotes more meaningful, Article 14(3) MiFIR limits the minimum size of quotes to at least 10 % of the standard market size of the respective equity(-like) instrument.[1698] According to Table 3 of Annex II CDR (EU) 2017/587, the standard market sizes span from EUR 10,000 for an average value of transaction (AVT) smaller than EUR 20,000 to EUR 130,000 for an AVT ranging between EUR 120,000 and EUR 140,000. A 10 % minimum order size means that systematic internalizers must quote at least in a size of EUR 1,000 up to EUR 13,000 depending on the liquidity class of the specific financial instrument.[1699]

However, some market comments on the minimum size prefer to align the minimum size to 100 % of the standard market size coupled with a withdrawal right in extreme situations.[1700] Their concern is that, despite the minimum size requirement under the MiFID II/MiFIR regime, systematic

---

neuen Transparenzregeln im Vorschlag einer Richtlinie über Wertpapierdienstleistungen und geregelte Märkte - insbesondere die Pre-Trade-Transparenzpflicht von systematischen Internalisierern: Arbeitspapiere 2003' (Institut für deutsches und internationales Recht des Spar-, Giro- und Kreditwesens an der Johannes Gutenberg-Universität Mainz, 2003) 23; Kumpan, *Die Regulierung außerbörslicher Wertpapierhandelssysteme im deutschen, europäischen und US-amerikanischen Recht* (n 8) 365.

1696 Kumpan, *Die Regulierung außerbörslicher Wertpapierhandelssysteme im deutschen, europäischen und US-amerikanischen Recht* (n 8) 364–5.

1697 CESR, 'CESR Technical Advice to the European Commission in the Context of the MiFID Review - Equity Markets' (n 4) 14 para 58; Kumpan, *Die Regulierung außerbörslicher Wertpapierhandelssysteme im deutschen, europäischen und US-amerikanischen Recht* (n 8) 365; Mülbert, 'Die neuen Transparenzregeln im Vorschlag einer Richtlinie über Wertpapierdienstleistungen und geregelte Märkte - insbesondere die Pre-Trade-Transparenzpflicht von systematischen Internalisierern' (n 1695) 23.

1698 CESR, 'CESR Technical Advice to the European Commission in the Context of the MiFID Review - Equity Markets' (n 4) 14 para 58; Kumpan and Schmidt (n 4) MiFIR Art 14 para 11; Moloney, *EU Securities and Financial Markets Regulation* (n 4) 488.

1699 Kumpan and Schmidt (n 4) MiFIR Art 14 para 11ff; Thelen (n 147) 203.

1700 Deutsche Börse Group, 'Response to Public Consultation: on the Review of Markets in Financial Instruments Directive (MiFID)' (Frankfurt am Main, 2 February internalizers would still provide only small quote sizes which allows them to evade significant amounts of trading interest, especially when even the retail order size is above the 10 % lot size. Only when the minimum order size is equal to the standard market size will trading on multilateral trading venues and bilateral systematic internalizers trading be truly aligned.[1701]

This concern may, however, be resolved by the obligation that the prices of quotes made by an SI shall reflect the prevailing market conditions under Article 14(3) MiFIR. This obligation would minimize the issue of SIs outperforming the prices trading venues can offer for their larger order sizes. SIs remain free to quote in sizes smaller than a multilateral market might produce, even though SIs often operate like market makers for the OTC-space.[1702] Yet, the fundamental difference between multilateral and bilateral markets with regard to proprietary risk cannot be neglected. Requiring a full ratchet alignment with multilateral trading venues represents a significant infringement of the freedom of contract for systematic internalizers, even if they can limit the number of transactions they want to enter with one or several traders.[1703] As reflected in the systematic internalizers' freedom to determine the price of their quotes, an overly restrictive bottom level for their quotes may not lead to an increase in liquidity provision in the OTC-space but rather to investment firms avoiding the SI regime entirely.

ee) Changes to the Minimum Size under the MiFID II/MiFIR Refit

For the MiFID II/MiFIR refit, the Commission proposed applying Articles 15, 16 and 17 MiFIR to SIs when they deal in sizes up to twice the standard market size and to exempt them from the said transparency obligations if they deal in sizes above twice the standard market size (proposed new Article 14(2) MiFIR).[1704] Furthermore, SIs shall in principle be allowed

2011) 17; ESMA, 'Final Report: Draft Regulatory and Implementing Technical Standards MiFID II/MiFIR' (n 1445) 34.

1701 Deutsche Börse Group, 'Response to Public Consultation' (n 1700) 17.

1702 Thelen (n 147) 203–4.

1703 Vgl. Hall (n 81) 500, 503.

1704 European Commission, 'Proposal for a Regulation of the European Parliament and of the Council amending Regulation (EU) No 600/2014 as regards enhancing market data transparency, removing obstacles to the emergence of a consolidated tape, optimising the trading obligations and prohibiting receiving payments for forwarding client orders' (n 1146) 30.

to quote any order size, but the minimum quote size shall be at least twice the standard market size for quotes in equity instruments that are traded on a trading venue (proposed new Article 14(3) MiFIR).[1705] SIs would also be prohibited from matching orders at the mid-point within the current bid and offer price (proposed new Article 14(6a) MiFIR).[1706]

These proposed amendments may fortify the shift of dark liquidity from the OTC-space into the SI-regime. While the EU designed the trading infrastructure regime to have all organized trading on multilateral trading venues (RM, MTF and OTF) rather than SIs, in part also to support trade transparency and price formation on such venues, it neglected the fact that the transparency regime set strong incentives to shift dark trading not onto multilateral venues under the carefully crafted waivers because on those waivers are limited by the volume cap mechanism. The more convenient option was to use SIs for this task.[1707]

The EU legislator frowns on this outcome for good reason, namely because multilateral trading venues provide the proper rules for this sort of trading while SIs tend not have such a detailed regime.[1708] But instead of suspending the volume cap mechanism to incentivize traders to use RMs, MTFs, or OTFs for their regulated dark trading under the waiver-system, the EU rather aligns the SI-regime to the trading venue regime. Under those amendments, both the reference price waiver for dark trading on trading venues and the quote threshold for equity trading on SIs apply a minimum size of twice the standard market size to disallow smaller sized orders from entering dark trading markets.[1709] This may be an issue to rethink. Incentivizing traders to use the trading venues by making their regulatory

1705 ibid 30.

1706 ibid 30.

1707 Gomber and others (n 1295) 19. Cf. ESMA, 'MiFID II/MiFIR Review Report: On the Transparency for Equity and Equity-Like Instruments, the Double Volume Cap Mechanism and the Trading Obligations for Shares' (n 1500) 27; European Commission, 'Proposal for a Regulation of the European Parliament and of the Council amending Regulation (EU) No 600/2014 as regards enhancing market data transparency, removing obstacles to the emergence of a consolidated tape, optimising the trading obligations and prohibiting receiving payments for forwarding client orders' (n 1146) 20.

1708 European Commission, 'Proposal for a Regulation of the European Parliament and of the Council amending Regulation (EU) No 600/2014 as regards enhancing market data transparency, removing obstacles to the emergence of a consolidated tape, optimising the trading obligations and prohibiting receiving payments for forwarding client orders' (n 1146) 14, 20.

1709 Committee on Economic and Monetary Affairs, 'Draft Report' (n 1400) 101.

regime more attractive is probably the better way than incentivizing traders to find new ways for dark trading.

ff) Access

The issue of access to quotes is crucial for a bilateral trading system since it exposes the system to market and information risks. Pursuant to Article 17(1) MiFIR, the systematic internalizer can decide which clients it will give access to its quotes. By referring to 'clients' instead of 'investors', as was the case under Article 27(5)(1) MiFID I, MiFIR enables the SI-operator not only to restrict access to only its clients, but to select even further among its clients those clients privileged with access to its quotes.[1710]

When restricting access, the systematic internalizer has to adhere to clear standards governing access in accordance with its commercial policy so that discretion is applied in a non-discriminatory way.[1711] Thus, refusal of access or discontinuation of a business relationship with a client shall be based on commercial considerations such as client credit status, the counterparty risks, and the final settlement of the transaction (Article 17(1) MiFIR).[1712] This allows systematic internalizers to filter clients and deny access to predatory traders, like HFTs, or other informed traders.[1713]

To limit its risk exposure further, a systematic internalizer can limit the number of transactions with one client or the total number of transactions from different clients as long as it is done in a non-discriminatory manner and upon conditions that have been published beforehand.[1714] The limitation of the total number of transactions from different clients must also comply with client order handling rules pursuant to Article 28 MiFID II. Additionally, the total number of transactions with different clients can only be limited when the number and/or volume of orders sought by clients considerably exceeds the norm (Article 17(2) MiFIR).[1715]

According to Article 15(1) CDR (EU) 2017/567, the number or volume of an order considerably exceeds the norm where the systematic internalizer

1710 Thelen (n 147) 199; cf. Kumpan and Schmidt (n 4) MiFIR Art 17 para 5.
1711 Gebauer (n 94) MiFIR Art 17 para 5; Kumpan and Schmidt (n 4) MiFIR Art 17 para 5.
1712 Kumpan and Schmidt (n 4) MiFIR Art 17 para 5.
1713 Thelen (n 147) 199–200.
1714 Article 17(2) MiFIR; Kumpan and Schmidt (n 4) MiFIR Art 17 paras 6–7.
1715 Kumpan and Schmidt (n 4) MiFIR Art 17 para 7.

cannot execute the order without exposing itself to undue risk.[1716] Since this determination is provided by the systematic internalizer itself, it is a possible loophole due to the qualitative character of 'undue risk' that can be used to evade the obligation to provide accessible liquidity. Despite the systematic internalizers' need for protection of their proprietary capital from extensive informed trading, this far-reaching and unclear access limitation may provide fertile ground for dark trading trying to avoid information trading, especially by HFTs. However, this may be limited by Article 14 MiFIR, which requires the systematic internalizer to provide non-discriminatory access to information to the public.[1717]

gg) Notification of NCA

Article 15(1) subpara. 2 MiFIR also requires an investment firm to notify the national competent authority when it meets the definition of a systematic internalizer for an instrument. This information is transmitted to ESMA which establishes a list of active systematic internalizers in the European Union.[1718] This notification process appears to be in an odd place within MiFIR, given that the other requirements of a systematic internalizer are laid down in MiFID II instead. However, the notification of SI in particular is strongly intertwined with transparency requirements, since SIs are the only investment firms in the OTC-space that need to publish their quotes. Thus, the notification ensures that there is no dark trading occurring on an 'organized, frequent systematic and substantial basis'[1719] within the OTC-space.[1720]

hh) Different Quality of Pre-Trade Transparency in Bilateral and Multilateral Trading Systems

This publication requirement of firm quotes is similar to pre-trade transparency on multilateral trading venues insofar as it informs traders about the trading opportunities offered to them on the trading system. Unlike the

1716 ibid MiFIR Art 17 para 7.
1717 ibid MiFIR Art 14 para 7.
1718 Gebauer (n 94) MiFIR Art 14 para 5.
1719 See definition of systematic internalizer under Article 4(1)(20) MiFID II.
1720 Kumpan and Schmidt (n 4) MiFIR Art 15 para 6.

information published by multilateral trading venues, however, it is not an aggregation of market interest of many third-party buyers and sellers but rather the quoted price of one systematic internalizer engaging in bilateral trading.[1721] In this regard the pre-trade transparency information informs traders where to find liquidity. However, the resulting pre-trade information may not be as unbiased price information as one may generally find on multilateral trading venues due to the proprietary interest taken by the systematic internalizer in the transaction and a lack of multiple selling and buying interests interacting to form a balanced price.[1722]

b) Exemptions

aa) No Quoting Obligation Above Standard Market Size

Systematic internalizers are exempt from publishing quotes when the order is above standard market size (Article 14(2)(2) MiFIR). The calculation of the standard market size is further determined under Article 11(3) subpara. 1(a)–(c) CDR (EU) 2017/587 and is performed by the national competent authorities in accordance with Table 3 of Annex II CDR (EU) 2017/587 that sets out the thresholds for the different liquidity levels in the market (Article 11(1) CDR (EU) 2017/587).[1723] A significant change from MiFID I to MiFID II/MiFIR was the deletion of the word 'only' in the phrase '*Systematic internalisers that only deal in sizes above standard market size (...)*'. This adjustment under Article 14(2) MiFIR clarifies that a systematic internalizer can benefit from the exemption from pre-trade transparency, even though, it does not exclusively ('only') execute orders above the standard market size but also occasionally.[1724] This brings the exemption for SIs closer to the large in scale waiver for trading venues and renders the SI category more versatile for firms that handle varying order sizes.[1725]

1721 Moloney, *EU Securities and Financial Markets Regulation* (n 4) 440; Schelling (n 1152) 222.

1722 See Ferrarini and Moloney (n 143) 592 criticizing the bilateral elements of the OTF category to be inferior to multilateral balancing of supply and demand under the supervision of an uninterested market operator.

1723 Cf. Kumpan and Schmidt (n 4) MiFIR Art 14 paras 8–10.

1724 Thelen (n 147) 204.

1725 ibid 204.

This exemption protects systematic internalizers from undue liquidity and position risk when trading either in an illiquid market or above standard market size.[1726] In both cases, a systematic internalizer takes on a position that cannot be sold off (or bought in) the SI's inventory quickly because the liquidity level of the market does not support it. Providing full transparency about the quotes would allow other traders to increase the systematic internalizer's costs by either following its trading strategy – assuming informed trading – or moving the market against his position.[1727]

Even though those exemptions resemble the large in scale waiver[1728] and the illiquid market waiver,[1729] the pre-trade transparency requirement for systematic internalizers is much lighter than the one for trading venues.[1730] Especially the fact that the exemption is triggered ipso iure without applying for a waiver with the national competent authority provides for broader exemptions. Under those exemptions, dark trading also at reference prices imported from price forming trading venues can be used without limitation of the volume cap mechanism that is not applicable to systematic internalizers.[1731]

bb) No Firm Quotes

In spite of illiquid markets, a systematic internalizer's obligation to publish firm quotes is also ipso iure dispensed under three cases according to Article 15 MiFIR.

1726 Moloney, *EU Securities and Financial Markets Regulation* (n 4) 488.

1727 CESR, 'CESR's Technical Advice on Possible Implementing Measures of the Directive 2004/39/EC on Markets in Financial Instruments' (n 1363) 61; Moloney, *EU Securities and Financial Markets Regulation* (n 4) 440, 488–9; Mülbert, 'Die neuen Transparenzregeln im Vorschlag einer Richtlinie über Wertpapierdienstleistungen und geregelte Märkte - insbesondere die Pre-Trade-Transparenzpflicht von systematischen Internalisierern' (n 1695) 21; Thelen (n 147) 197–8.

1728 Similar evaluation by CESR, 'CESR's Technical Advice on Possible Implementing Measures of the Directive 2004/39/EC on Markets in Financial Instruments' (n 1363) 69.

1729 Although it is only available for non-equity instruments on trading venues, see Article 9(1)(c) MiFIR.

1730 Moloney, *EU Securities and Financial Markets Regulation* (n 4) 467, 488–9.

1731 Thelen (n 147) 209–10.

(i) Price Improvement (Article 15(2) subpara. 2 MiFIR)

In the first case, systematic internalizers may execute orders – in justified cases – at a better price than the quoted price provided that the price falls within a public range close to market conditions. This allows the systematic internalizer to fulfill its duty of best execution under Article 27 MiFID II – Section 82 WpHG under German law – while also fulfilling its purpose as a market infrastructure in supporting the price formation process.[1732] According to Article 14(3) CDR (EU) 2017/567, a price 'close to market conditions' means a price within the bid and offer quotes of the systematic internalizer, thus ensuring that the transaction executed at the better price does not carry significant new price information.[1733]

Although the phrase 'in justified cases' under Article 15(2) subpara. 2 MiFIR is not further defined, it is not meaningless but rather a reminder that the quoting requirement shall not be dispensed of for insignificant price improvements, for instance, smaller than the tick size requirement of at least EUR 0.01 under Articles 49(1), 18(5) MiFID II.[1734]

(ii) Portfolio Transactions (Article 15(3) MiFIR)

The exemptions from the firm quoting requirement under Article 15(3) MiFIR are of a rather technical nature and only apply in transactions between an internalizer and a professional client.[1735] The first exemption applies to portfolio transactions in which several securities are executed as part of one transaction. Article 1(1) CDR (EU) 2017/587 sets out that only those transactions qualify as portfolio transactions that comprise of five or more different financial instruments where those transactions are traded at the same time by the same client and as a single lot against a specific reference price. Since such interconnected portfolio transactions are subject to their

1732 Gebauer (n 94) MiFIR Art 15 paras 11, 13.

1733 ibid MiFIR Art 15 para 13

1734 ESMA, 'Questions and Answers: On MiFID II and MiFIR Market Structures Topics' (n 1169) 61, No. 5.3 answer to question 29; Gebauer (n 94) MiFIR Art 15 para 14.

1735 According to Article 4(1)(10) and Annex II of MiFID II, a *'professional client is a client who possesses the experience, knowledge and expertise to make its own investment decisions and properly assess the risks that it incurs.'* For the specific criteria, see in Annex II of MiFID II.

specific price, it is warranted to allow systematic internalizers to deviate from their quoted price for any of the financial instruments the portfolio trade comprises of.[1736]

The second situation exempted under Article 15(3) MiFIR concerns orders that are subject to conditions other than the current market price. Those order types are further defined in Articles 2 and 6 CDR (EU) 2017/587 which contain a list of technical orders that are not subject to an investment purpose.[1737] Those orders can be exempted from pre-trade transparency since they do not contribute to price discovery and could risk investor confusion and would hinder best execution.[1738] This resembles the respective prong of the negotiated trade waiver under Article 4(b)(iii) MiFIR.

(iii) Client Quote is Bigger than Quoting Size (Article 15(4) MiFIR)

Another exemption from the requirement of firm quoting can be found in Article 15(4) MiFIR for instances in which the systematic internalizer is quoting only one quote or its highest quote is lower than the standard market size, and it receives a client order greater than its quote size, but smaller than standard market size. If the systematic internalizer decides to execute the order exceeding its highest quote, the systematic internalizer does not have to publish a firm quote in this instance and can deviate from the quoted price in accordance with Article 15(2), (3) MiFIR.[1739]

When the systematic internalizer is quoting in different sizes and receives a customer order that is placed between those sizes of its own quotes the systematic internalizer shall execute one of the quoted prices in compliance with Article 28 MiFID II, except where the SI may deviate from the firm quote in accordance with Article 15(2), (3) MiFIR.[1740]

1736 Gebauer (n 94) MiFIR Art 15 paras 15ff.
1737 ibid MiFIR Art 15 para 16.
1738 Recital 14 CDR (EU) 2017/587.
1739 Gebauer (n 94) MiFIR Art 15 para 18.
1740 ibid MiFIR Art 15 para 19.

2. Pre-Trade Transparency for Non-Equity Instruments

a) Rule

aa) Liquid Market

As for trading venues, Article 18 MiFIR also provides a pre-trade transparency requirement for systematic internalizers trading in non-equity instruments, setting trade transparency as the default rule for bilateral trading in non-equity instruments. Article 18(1) MiFIR requires the investment firm to make public firm quotes with respect to bonds, structured finance products, emission allowances, and derivatives traded on a trading venue for which the investment firm is a systematic internalizer and for which there is a liquid market. However, pre-trade transparency only needs to be provided when the systematic internalizer is prompted for a quote by a client and when the systematic internalizer agrees to provide a quote.[1741]

In comparison to the firm quoting requirement for systematic internalizers for equity instruments trading in a liquid market, Article 18(1) MiFIR is much lighter since the systematic internalizer can avoid a firm quote and the entailing obligation to contract if it does not agree to providing one. The systematic internalizer can refuse to provide a firm quote without providing a reason.[1742] The lighter pre-trade transparency requirement for systematic internalization of non-equity instruments accounts for the increased liquidity risks in this market compared to the more liquid equity markets. Possible reasons for refusing to provide firm quotes can be that the systematic internalizer does not have the respective instrument in stock and considers the risk of acquiring it too significant.[1743] Thus, the systematic internalizers' interest in being protected from adverse effect of continuous publication of quotes is justified.[1744]

In line with the requirements for trading equity instruments is a systematic internalizer's obligation under Article 18(5) MiFIR to make available to its other clients the firm quotes published in accordance with Article 18(1)

1741 Article 18(1) MiFIR; Gebauer (n 94) MiFIR Art 18 para 27; Kumpan and Schmidt (n 4) MiFIR Art 18 paras 6–7; Moloney, *EU Securities and Financial Markets Regulation* (n 4) 491.

1742 Gebauer (n 94) MiFIR Art 18 paras 2, 18, 27.

1743 ibid MiFIR Art 18 para 27.

1744 Moloney, *EU Securities and Financial Markets Regulation* (n 4) 491, 492, Thelen (n 147) 207.

MiFIR[1745] as well as the obligation to publish those quotes in a way that is easily accessible to other market participants on a reasonable commercial basis (Article 18(8) MiFIR).[1746]

bb) Illiquid Market

For non-equity instruments for which there is not a liquid market, a systematic internalizer only has to disclose quotes to its clients upon request when it agrees to provide a quote (Article 18(2) MiFIR).[1747] This is a strong protection from liquidity risks for the systematic internalizer since quoting is solely at its discretion; even when prompted for a quote by a client, the SI can refuse the publication of its trading interest.[1748]

This strong protection reflects in the fact that Article 18(5) MiFIR does not require quotes in illiquid instruments to be published for the systematic internalizer's clients. In the same vein, Article 18(8) MiFIR also does not require the systematic internalizer to publish its trading interest to other market participants since it only refers to quotes published pursuant to Article 18(1) and (5) but not Article 18(2) MiFIR.[1749]

Article 18(2) MiFIR does not clearly set out whether a systematic internalizer has to make public quotes in illiquid non-equity instruments towards other clients and other market participants when it agrees to provide a firm quote to one client upon request. Some argue that with reference to the use of plural '*(...) shall disclose quotes to their clients (...)*' would indicate that a systematic internalizer which agreed to provide a firm quote to just one requesting client must publish the firm quote to all its clients.[1750]

While this argument is not compelling since it disregards the fact that that Article 18(2) MiFIR also refers to '*systematic internalizers*' in the plural, its result is preferrable for other reasons: the systematic internalizer receives

---

1745 Gebauer (n 94) MiFIR Art 18 para 28.

1746 For the size specific for the financial instrument exemption see below 'ii) Exemptions'. Gebauer (n 94) MiFIR Art 18 para 28; Kumpan and Schmidt (n 4) MiFIR Art 18 para 20.

1747 Gebauer (n 94) MiFIR Art 18 para 31.

1748 ibid MiFIR Art 18 para 33.

1749 Moloney, *EU Securities and Financial Markets Regulation* (n 4) 492; Thelen (n 147) 207.

1750 See Christian Hoops, 'Das neue Regime für die systematische Internalisierung nach MiFID II: Auswirkungen auf den deutschen Zertifikatehandel' [2017] WM 319, 322–3; Thelen (n 147) 207.

broad protection by Article 18(2) MiFIR in deciding whether or not to agree to make a quote upon a client's request. When the systematic internalizer decides to make this quote, the remainder of the market participants should receive a quote as well. However, the modalities depend on the kind of trading system operated by the systematic internalizer. In a voice trading system, other clients need make a request themselves to receive the quote given to the initial requestor. The systematic internalizer cannot deny its agreement to provide a quote again. In electronic trading systems, the systematic internalizer likewise cannot refuse a quote upon request by another client, however, it can decline to post the quote in the electronic system for all clients to see without making a request.[1751]

Once the quote has been made to one requesting client, the systematic internalizer is required to treat other clients equally but it is within the SI's discretion whether it meets this obligation by providing other clients with access on a systematic basis or only upon request of those quotes.[1752] This interpretation of Article 18(2) MiFIR is preferrable since it is congruent with Article 18(8) MiFIR and the rationale to protect the systematic internalizer. The systematic internalizer is not discouraged from agreeing to provide a quote upon request of one client and depending on its choice with regard to the access regime for its other clients, the SI can regulate its own exposure to liquidity risk.

Furthermore, unlike Article 18(1) MiFIR, a firm quote is not required by Article 18(2) MiFIR. Since this wording is not incidental, the quote for illiquid shares is indicative and does not entail an obligation to contract.[1753] This is evidence of a far-reaching protection of systematic internalizers trading in non-equity instruments for which there is not a liquid market.[1754]

b) Exemptions

aa) Waivers under Article 9(1) MiFIR

In addition to the lighter requirements to publish quotes for illiquid instruments as discussed above, Article 18(2)(2) MiFIR privileges systematic

---

1751 Gebauer (n 94) MiFIR Art 18 para 33; Schelling (n 1152) 226.

1752 ESMA, 'Questions and Answers: On MiFID II and MiFIR Transparency Topics' (n 1472) 67–8, No. 7 Answer 5.d).

1753 Gebauer (n 94) MiFIR Art 18 para 34.

1754 Moloney, *EU Securities and Financial Markets Regulation* (n 4) 491.

internalizers trading in illiquid non-equity instruments even further by declaring the waivers under Article 9(1) MiFIR applicable.[1755] On this basis, national competent authorities can waive pre-trade transparency requirement for systematic internalizers trading in illiquid shares if the prongs of the waivers in Article 9(1) MiFIR are met.[1756]

Generally, before the national competent authority can grant a waiver, the SI needs to file a request for it.[1757] For Article 18(2)(2) MiFIR, ESMA is of the opinion that national competent authorities can waive pre-trade transparency for systematic internalizers under Article 18(2)(2) MiFIR in a generalized manner for all systematic internalizers that fall within the scope of Article 9(1) MiFIR without the need to file a request, although systematic internalizers may still make such filing.[1758] In response to ESMA's opinion, the French authority AMF,[1759] the UK authority FCA,[1760] and the German authority BaFin[1761] implemented some form of generalized exemption for systematic internalizers under the waivers of Article 9(1) MiFIR. Especially the German BaFin assumed that the interest in trade transparency and effective price formation is less significant in cases under Article 9(1) MiFIR than the systematic internalizers' interest in having effective means of risk regulation and negotiation of prices in the specific transaction at hand when liquidity levels are low.[1762]

1755 Kumpan and Schmidt (n 4) MiFIR Art 18 para 12.

1756 ibid MiFIR Art 18 para 12.

1757 Gebauer (n 94) MiFIR Art 18 para 35.

1758 ESMA, 'Questions and Answers: On MiFID II and MiFIR Transparency Topics' (n 1472) 56, No. 5 Answer 9; Konstantin Meljnik, 'Systematische Internalisierung: Eckpunkte des neuen Aufsichtsregimes nach MiFID II/ MiFIR' [2017] BaFin Journal 35, 38–9; Gebauer (n 94) MiFIR Art 18 para 36.

1759 General Regulation of the AMF (AMF) Article 315–25: While the version into force from 3 January 2018 to 22 April 2021 only allowed for a waiver '*following notification to the AMF of its request(s) for a waiver for each financial instrument concerned*', the AMF dropped this requirement in the version into force since 23 April 2021 allowing the granting of waivers in a more generalized manner.

1760 FCA Handbook (FCA) MAR 6.4A.

1761 Allgemeinverfügung - Befreiung systematischer Internalisierer von den Pflichten nach Art 18 Abs. 2 Satz 1 MiFIR in Bezug auf Kursofferten 2 January 2018, WA 21-FR 1900-2017/0002 (BaFin).

1762 Gebauer (n 94) MiFIR Art 18 para 37.

bb) Instruments Below the Liquidity Threshold of Article 9(4) MiFIR

Furthermore, systematic internalizers are not required to publish a firm quote for instruments within the scope of Article 18(1) MiFIR if the instruments' liquidity falls below the liquidity threshold set out in Article 9(4) MiFIR (Article 18(6) subpara. 2 MiFIR). This provision imports the calibration of the trading venue regime for the volatile liquidity levels into markets for non-equity instruments. Despite usually having a liquid market, liquidity levels can sometimes drop and render a temporary suspension of transparency necessary on trading venues. This rationale also exempts SIs from publishing quotes in otherwise liquid instruments when liquidity thins significantly.[1763]

cc) No Quoting Requitement for Orders Above the Size Specific for the Financial Instrument

Pursuant to Article 18(10) MiFIR, the quoting requirement for systematic internalizers does not apply when they deal in orders with sizes above the SSTI determined in accordance with Article 9(5)(d) MiFIR. Article 18(10) MiFIR applies to both instruments with liquid as well as illiquid markets.[1764] This provision exempts quotes from the requirement of publication that are of a size that is likely to cause undue liquidity risk for the systematic internalizer. The thresholds for the SSTI exception are determined in Articles 5(1), 13 and the Tables of Annex III CDR (EU) 2017/583. Functionally, the SSTI-exception operates like the exemption for deal sizes above the standard market size under Article 14(2)(2) MiFIR and the large in scale waiver for trading venues.

1763 For the determination of the drop of liquidity under Article 9(4) MiFIR see above Part II § 6 C.III.2.g); Kumpan and Schmidt (n 4) MiFIR Art 18 para 18; Gebauer (n 94) MiFIR Art 18 para 59 sees here a case of Article 18(2) MiFIR and considers Article 18(6) tautological. He neglects the fact that the decision about liquidity is made by an NCA on periodic basis and that liquidity levels of an instrument may drop significantly in between two liquidity assessments by the NCA rendering the exemption of Article 18(6) MiFIR necessary.

1764 Gebauer (n 94) MiFIR Art 18 para 59.

c) Price Improvements

Due to the bilateral character of transactions with a systematic internalizer, the SI is bound by the best execution obligation pursuant to Article 27 MiFID II. Moreover, it is under the obligation to make quotes that reflect the prevailing market conditions in relation to prices at which transactions are concluded on a trading venue in the same or a similar financial instrument (Article 18(9) subpara. 1 MiFIR). As under Article 15(2) subpara. 2 MiFIR, a systematic internalizer may quote better prices within a public range close to market conditions in justified cases.[1765]

Unlike Article 14(3) MiFIR which requires a minimum quote size, Article 18 MiFIR contains no such requirement. In a market where liquidity risks are prevalent, a minimum quote size is inappropriate.

d) Access

As for equity instruments under Article 17(1) MiFIR, Article 18(5) MiFIR enables systematic internalizers trading in non-equity instruments to refuse to enter or to discontinue the business relationship on the basis of commercial considerations, such as the client credit status, the counterparty risk, and the final settlement of the transaction.[1766] It is crucial that the process through which the systematic internalizer can limit the access to information rests on nondiscriminatory elements since information access is important for information arbitrage which in turn fuels the price formation and market efficiency.[1767] However, in cases in which negative indicators about a client's credit status, the counterparty risk, and the final settlement of the transaction motivate a systematic internalizer to limit access, this is not only in the interest of the systematic internalizer but also in the interest of its other clients.

1765 NB: the justified cases encompass the same cases as under Article 15(2) subpara 2 MiFIR; see also Kumpan and Schmidt (n 4) MiFIR Art 18 para 22.

1766 Gebauer (n 94) MiFIR Art 18 paras 42ff; Kumpan and Schmidt (n 4) MiFIR Art 18 para 21.

1767 Gebauer (n 94) MiFIR Art 18 para 45; Kumpan, *Die Regulierung außerbörslicher Wertpapierhandelssysteme im deutschen, europäischen und US-amerikanischen Recht* (n 8) 367; Seitz (n 132) 504.

3. Post-Trade Transparency Regime for Equity Instruments

Post-trade transparency in the bilateral OTC-space is regulated under Article 20 MiFIR for equity instruments traded on a trading venue.[1768] Article 20(1) MiFIR requires all investment firms, i.e., systematic internalizers and other OTC-investment firms not qualifying as a systematic internalizer, to publish price, volume and time of concluded transactions in equity instruments through an APA.[1769] Also, in the OTC-space, post-trade transparency supports price formation by informing the market about prices of actually concluded transactions and allows traders to compare their own transactions against other traders' transactions.[1770]

Article 20(2)(2) MiFIR aligns the scope of the post-trade transparency regime for systematic internalizers with that of trading venues because it declares Article 7 MiFIR applicable. This provision provides for deferred publication of post-trade transparency which is important when the transaction was large in scale.[1771] Thus, the deferral regime shall allow the systematic internalizer to unwind large positions into the market taken over in the previous transaction.[1772]

4. Post-Trade Transparency Regime for Non-Equity Instruments

For non-equity instruments traded on a trading venue, Article 21 MiFIR requires post-trade transparency also for systematic internalizers and other OTC-investment firms not qualifying as a systematic internalizer. The information about price, volume and time of the executed transaction shall be made public for each individual transaction through a single APA. This avoids aggregation of post-trade transparency data so that the data provid-

1768 Kumpan and Schmidt (n 4) MiFIR Art 20 para 9.
1769 Gebauer (n 94) MiFIR Art 20 para 14; Kumpan and Schmidt (n 4) MiFIR Art 20 para 9; Schmies and Sajnovits (n 1357) 16.
1770 Kumpan and Schmidt (n 4) MiFIR Art 20 paras 9ff; Moloney, *EU Securities and Financial Markets Regulation* (n 4) 491; Schelling (n 1152) 222; Thelen (n 147) 206.
1771 Gebauer (n 94) MiFIR Art 20 para 20.
1772 Kumpan and Schmidt (n 4) MiFIR Art 20 paras 18ff; Moloney, *EU Securities and Financial Markets Regulation* (n 4) 491; Thelen (n 147) 206.

ed is more granular and, hence, more informative for the price formation process.[1773]

Moreover, Article 21 MiFIR refers to the deferral regime of trading venues to provide it with deferred publication if the transaction was either large in scale, above the size specific for the financial instrument, or in an illiquid instrument.[1774]

VII. Systematic Internalizers: The New Home for Dark Trading?

In Recital 6 MiFIR, the EU legislator underlines its objective to bring unregulated dark trading nestling in the OTC-space, especially BCNs, within the regulatory perimeter. Under MiFID II/MiFIR, BCNs shall either comply with the regulatory requirements of the MTF- or SI-category.[1775] As discussed above, this objective is pursued by multiple measures: for instance, the improved definitions of MTF- and SI-classification as well as the introduction of the OTF-classification for non-equity trading, the introduction of trading obligations for shares and derivatives, and an enhanced transparency regime.

Before MiFID II/MiFIR went into force, commentators estimated that unregulated dark trading by BCNs and other dark OTC trading may prefer to be regulated under the new SI-regime instead of falling within the scope of the trading venue-regime.[1776] The mere increase in the numbers of SIs that notified ESMA, which soared from only 12 SIs under MiFID I[1777] to 188 SIs in July 2023 under MiFID II/MiFIR seems to confirm this assessment.[1778] The reason for this surge may be the less restrictive regulatory regime for SI compared to the regulatory regime for trading venues.

1773 Kumpan and Schmidt (n 4) MiFIR Art 21 paras 5ff; Moloney, *EU Securities and Financial Markets Regulation* (n 4) 492–3; Schelling (n 1152) 222, 227–8; Thelen (n 147) 209.

1774 Kumpan and Schmidt (n 4) MiFIR Art 21 paras 13–4; Moloney, *EU Securities and Financial Markets Regulation* (n 4) 492–3; Schelling (n 1152) 222, 227–8; Thelen (n 147) 209.

1775 Recital 6 MiFIR.

1776 Gomber and others (n 1295) 8–9; Gomber and Nassauer (n 1086) 258.

1777 Gomber and Nassauer (n 1086) 252.

1778 ESMA Database on MiFID Infrastructures (n 1264).

1. Advantages in the Transparency Regime

Compared to the strict transparency requirements for trading venues, systematic internalizers are under much less restrictive obligations. SIs that offer trading in equity instruments are allowed to offer dark trading when the size is above standard market size and less transparency in illiquid markets.[1779] When trading in non-equity instruments, there is no universal quoting obligation for systematic internalizers.[1780] Even in liquid markets, the discretion of the SI to publish quotes is quite profound compared to trading venues.[1781]

Even more important, however, is the fact that trading equity instruments at a reference price is not restricted by the volume cap mechanism under the SI-regime.[1782] Although systematic internalizers cannot waive their pre-trade transparency requirements by means of the reference price waiver, pre-trade transparency can be avoided by aggregating many retail-sized orders into one large order above the standard market size. This order is exempted from pre-trade transparency requirements because clients can exempt SIs from the obligation of prompt execution under Article 28(2) MiFID II.[1783] The ability of SIs to host unlimited amounts of reference price trading may even cause a migration from dark trading on trading venues to systematic internalizers.[1784]

Unlike under the large in scale waiver, aggregation of order flow in SIs does not encounter the same concerns as under Article 4(1)(c) MiFIR because there is no tension between the scope of the reference price waiver and the volume cap mechanism.[1785] The exemption for systematic internalizers from the requirement to publish quotes is not motivated by the goal of inducing liquidity providers to place their large block orders on a multilateral trading venue, but rather it is a calibration for the bilateral

1779 Kumpan and Schmidt (n 4) MiFIR Art 14 paras 6, 8; Moloney, *EU Securities and Financial Markets Regulation* (n 4) 488.

1780 Gebauer (n 94) MiFIR Art 18 para 2.

1781 Cf. Thelen (n 147) 209–10.

1782 Gomber and others (n 1295) 9.

1783 Martin Brenncke in Matthias Lehmann and Christoph Kumpan (eds), *European Financial Services Law: Article-by-Article Commentary* (1st edn, Nomos; CH Beck; Hart Publishing 2019) MiFID II Art 28 para 6.

1784 Gomber and others (n 1295) 8f, 27; Gomber and Nassauer (n 1086) 258; Thelen (n 147) 210; Christer Wennerberg, 'Double Volume Caps in MiFID II: What Are the Effects?' (bobsguide 30 November 2015).

1785 See discussion above Part II § 6 C.II.1.f).

character of SIs to avoid exposure to undue liquidity risk. Since an SI is also free to quote at sizes of its choosing (Article 14(3) MiFIR), actively quoting in large sizes cannot be considered an undue circumvention of the transparency regime. However, if regulatory mindsets change for the next revision of MiFID II/MiFIR, it may well be considered undue regulatory arbitrage to aggregate multiple smaller orders within the systems of the SI. A market response to this may however be the introduction of another investment firm into the order execution process that aggregates the orders before sending them as a large order to the SI.[1786]

An additional advantage of the transparency regime for SIs is that the transparency requirements are much narrower in scope than for trading venues so that it is often not dependent on waivers. And where waivers can be granted, this is done on a generalized basis. This enables systematic internalizers to avoid the lengthy process among the NCAs and ESMA according to Articles 4(4) and 9(2) MiFIR which carries the additional risk of being denied a waiver. Moreover, the fact that investment firms only need to notify their NCA of their SI status, without any further control mechanism before they can begin dark trading, also allows the investment firms to choose NCAs that have a 'lighter regulatory touch'. The lack of the process among NCAs and ESMA leads to less convergent application of MiFIR – despite ESMA's annual reports to the Commission – and allows for a strategic choice of the most 'SI-friendly' NCA. Since the lack of convergence has already led to major confrontation among the Member States in the review process of MiFID I, an extension of such coordination mechanisms should be considered.

2. Advantage in Order Pricing

In a continuous trading system on a trading venue operating under price/time-priority, a trader can only receive priority over an earlier order by posting a better priced order. If the price increments in a trading system are not standardized, a trader can front-run earlier orders by posting insignificant price improvements of a fraction of a cent. This strategy is most often used by HFTs.[1787] To avoid this, Articles 49(1), 18(5) MiFID II

1786 Gomber and others (n 1295) 7ff.

1787 Marcus Lerch, '§ 25 Algorithmic Trading and High-Frequency Trading' in Rüdiger Veil (ed), *European Capital Markets Law* (3rd edn, Hart Publishing 2022) § 25 para 41; Salger (n 627) 225.

and the Annex of CDR (EU) 2017/588 set out the minimum tick sizes, i.e., the minimum increment of price deviation, with regard to the traded instrument, market liquidity, and price range.[1788] The scope of this tick size regime is confined to trading venues only and is not applicable to trading in systematic internalizers and the OTC-space.[1789] Thus, when price increments on a trading venue must be, for instance, at least EUR 0.01, an SI would allow any increment, even EUR 0.000001 or less. Such trivial price improvements enable the SI to execute within the public spread and to free-ride public price formation, which makes front running almost cost free.[1790] Moreover, liquidity providers have little incentive to provide competitive quotes on lit markets, which deteriorates the price formation process even further. The miniscule price advantage also prioritizes SIs over transparent trading venues so that brokers need to route their clients' liquidity to systematic internalizers to meet the duty of best execution which drains liquidity on lit markets.[1791] In comparison, the similar US tick size rule captures all trading including by dealers, and therefore precludes such form of front running.[1792]

Having become aware of this potential loophole, ESMA offered a broader definition of the criterion of 'quoting at prevailing market conditions' under Article 14(3) MiFIR.[1793] Article 10 CDR (EU) 2017/587 therefore requires the quotes of SIs to reflect the prevailing market conditions, which means that their prices need to be close to those prices for the same instrument at the most relevant market in terms of liquidity. ESMA is of the opinion that prevailing market conditions not only refer to the current market prices but also to the price increments applied on this market. Since systematic internalizers supply liquidity in a similar manner to market makers on a regulated market who are under the tick size obligation, both should be

1788 Kumpan and Schmidt (n 4) MiFID II Art 45 paras 1, 5ff.
1789 Gomber and others (n 1295) 8.
1790 ibid 8.
1791 ibid 9.
1792 See Rule 612(a), (b) of US Regulation NMS (17 CFR § 242.612(a), (b)); Thelen (n 147) 210–1.
1793 ESMA, 'Final Report: Draft Regulatory and Implementing Technical Standards MiFID II/MiFIR' (n 1445) 32ff paras 70ff.

treated equally by extending the tick size regime through the meaning of 'prevailing market conditions' into systematic internalizer regime.[1794]

Despite the validity of the argument of a comparable situation, neither MiFID II/MiFIR nor the text of Article 10 CDR (EU) 2017/587 must unequivocally be understood as an extension of the tick size requirement into the SI-regime. ESMA admits that it lacks the power to change the level 1 text of MiFID II/MiFIR, an act even ESMA seems to consider necessary to rectify the problem.[1795] Moreover, Article 10 CDR (EU) 2017/587 requires only a quote that is *'(...) [close] in price (...) to quotes of equivalent sizes for the same financial instrument on the most relevant market in terms of liquidity (...)'*.[1796] Therefore, a price that is the slightest increment better than the current market price fulfils the requirement of being (very) close to this price. Especially due to the lack of an administrative process, like in the waiver granting process (Article 4(4) MiFIR), ESMA cannot efficiently ensure that the price increments of quotes by SIs reflect the standard tick size at trading venues. Extending the tick size regime to SIs similar to the US regime would be preferable in the revision of MiFID II/MiFIR. Thus, the equivocal provision of Article 10 CDR (EU) 2017/587 coupled with less effective oversight may induce dark pools to take advantage of the SI-regime.

3. Issue of Bringing Together Client Orders

The SI regime, while suitable for dark trading with regard to the transparency regime, may be disadvantageous as a regulatory category for dark pools, especially BCNs, due to systematic internalizers being conceptualized as bilateral trading systems. The bilateral character requires systematic internalizers to always form the other part of the transaction using their proprietary capital.[1797] Combining bilateral trading with matching client orders, as BCNs did to disperse liquidity and position risk, is not possible because it would qualify as multilateral trading pushing the system into the

1794 ESMA, 'Consultation Paper: Amendments to Commission Delegated Regulation (EU) 2017/587 (RTS 1)' (ESMA70-156-275, 9 November 2017) 6ff; Thelen (n 147) 211.

1795 ESMA, 'Final Report: Draft Regulatory and Implementing Technical Standards MiFID II/MiFIR' (n 1445) 32 para 70.

1796 Article 10 CDR (EU) 2017/587 (emphasis added).

1797 Kumpan (n 125) WpHG § 2 para 103.

scope of an MTF[1798] or OTF; only the occasional bringing together of client orders shall not be harmful for the SI-classification.[1799]

The combined effects of the volume cap mechanism and the rigid differentiation between multilateral trading venues and bilateral systematic internalizers may force dark pools into the SI-regime potentially so they can use reference pricing without limitations which may have unwelcome effects on market resilience.[1800] Since only the lenient SI transparency regime allows for dark pools to carry out their operations using unlimited reference pricing, they may choose to become an SI.[1801] This also means dark pools under the SI regime have to execute all trades against their proprietary capital because matching client orders in the amount they did under MiFID I would bring them back into the now unfavorable multilateral trading venue regime under the volume cap mechanism. Thus, for the sake of enhanced trade transparency, MiFID II/MiFIR is willing to have investment firms, usually run by banks, to accumulate large amounts of proprietary risk which otherwise would have been borne by many investors in the market. In a time of crisis, this may have massive backlashes not only onto the OTC markets, for which SIs are almost the exclusive provider of liquidity, but also into other parts of the financial system, like the banking system.

Trading the gains of trade transparency achieved by stricter waivers and a clear distinction between neutral multilateral systems and interested bilateral systems to manage conflict of interests, appears to be a decision that may need to be reformed in the future. Moreover, the issue of conflict of interests when introducing multilateral elements into bilateral systems can be resolved by conduct rules and fraud law as is the case for broker-dealers. Hence, softening the multilateral-bilateral-distinction for SIs may still keep multilateral trading venues free of conflicts of interest but simultaneously allow for a more resilient market by dispersing risk on multiple shoulders.

Considering the advantages of the SI-regime for dark pool-operators and the fact that systemic risks would most likely not have to be borne by such operators alone, it is most likely that the SI-regime is the new home for dark pools. From a market resilience perspective, this decision should induce second thoughts with regulators.

1798 Cf. Article 23(2) MiFIR.

1799 Kumpan (n 125) WpHG § 2 para 103; Kumpan, *Die Regulierung außerbörslicher Wertpapierhandelssysteme im deutschen, europäischen und US-amerikanischen Recht* (n 8) 286.

1800 Gomber and others (n 1295) 9.

1801 ibid 9.

4. Trading Obligation and Dark Trading under the SI-regime: An Unlucky Combination?

The trading obligation and the enhanced SI-regime are both intended to shrink the OTC-space significantly to dry up BCNs populating this market.[1802] Those fortifications against OTC trading shall induce liquidity in those markets to migrate to trading venues increasing market efficiency and driving down costs. The high ambition of the European legislator may, however, be disappointed if trading migrated from the OTC-space, especially dark trading in BCNs, to find a new home in systematic internalizers.

A study conducted by *Gomber et al. (2018)* sought to predict the effects of the liquidity migration on market quality for equity trading under the trading obligation for shares (Article 23 MiFIR). They distinguished three scenarios where liquidity may move when the trading obligation for shares is adopted and calculated the bid-ask-spread and round-trip costs for trading EUR 50,000 as measures for market liquidity as a proxy for market efficiency.[1803]

Even though this prospective study has been conducted before MiFID II/ MiFIR went into force on 3 January 2018, the subsequent market development, and the review process by ESMA found similar results that a larger amount of the unregulated OTC dark trading migrated in the SI-regime whereas only small amounts were repatriated onto the trading venues. The reason for the migration into SIs but not onto the trading venues as intended can be mainly found in the strict regulation of dark trading on trading venues by the volume cap mechanism.[1804]

In the MiFID II/MiFIR assessment for the MiFID II refit, ESMA found that this prediction by *Gomber et al. (2018)* was fulfilled. The liquidity once gathered by BCNs in the OTC-space did not migrate onto the trading venues as planned by the legislator, but rather chose the more permissive SI-regime as the new home.[1805] The current proposals intends to correct

---

1802 ibid 7.

1803 ibid 19. For the scenarios see Gomber and others (n 1295) 10–11 and for the results see Gomber and others (n 1295) 22–25.

1804 ESMA, 'MiFID II/MiFIR Review Report: On the Transparency for Equity and Equity-Like Instruments, the Double Volume Cap Mechanism and the Trading Obligations for Shares' (n 1500) 27.

1805 ESMA, 'Consultation Paper: MiFID II/ MiFIR Review Report on the Transparency Regime for Equity and Equity-Like Instruments, the Double Volume Cap Mechanism and the Trading Obligations for Shares' (ESMA70-156-2188, 4 Februfor this issue discussed above[1806] and include in the SI-regime a minimum quoting size of twice the standard market size (sms) and limits matching at the midpoint price to order sizes between order sizes above this minimum of twice the sms and up to the large in scale size.[1807] Those measures should align the SI-regime with the trading venue regime and take away the incentive to use the SI-regime for dark trading.[1808]

However, the main reason for using the SI-regime is the fact that the volume cap mechanism does not apply and therefore dark trading services can be used more predictably. While the Commission proposed to simplify the DVC to an SVC,[1809] it may be advisable to follow the Committee on Economic and Monetary Affairs of the European Parliament who proposed suspending the DVC.[1810] This approach worked well for the UK which suspended the DVC as well.[1811] This would introduce a positive incentive to use the trading venue regime under the carefully crafted waivers instead of the SI-regime.

D. Access Regime under MiFID II/MiFIR and German law

To examine the reach of dark trading, it is also important to examine the access rules of trading systems in European Union and German law. Especially since the rise of high-frequency traders, many traders have sought shelter in dark trading to limit their exposure to the arbitrage strategies employed by most HFTs.[1812]

One way to limit exposure is of course by dispensing trade transparency. If, however, HFTs use so-called 'predatory' strategies, such as pinging and

---

ary 2020) 48; ESMA, 'MiFID II/MiFIR Review Report: On the Transparency for Equity and Equity-Like Instruments, the Double Volume Cap Mechanism and the Trading Obligations for Shares' (n 1500) 27.

1806 See above Part II § 6.C.III.1).c).ee) on the DVC and § 6.C.VII.1).a).ee) on the SI-regime.

1807 European Commission, 'Proposal for a Regulation of the European Parliament and of the Council amending Regulation (EU) No 600/2014 as regards enhancing market data transparency, removing obstacles to the emergence of a consolidated tape, optimising the trading obligations and prohibiting receiving payments for forwarding client orders' (n 1146) 14, 20, 30.

1808 Cf. ibid 20.

1809 ibid 14.

1810 Committee on Economic and Monetary Affairs, 'Draft Report' (n 1400) 100.

1811 HM Treasury, 'Wholesale Markets Review' (n 1521) 12.

1812 Cf. Haeberle (n 459) 824.

electronic front running, information can be extracted from the dark pool which renders mere non-transparency insufficient. In such cases, traders wish to trade on those dark pools which also limit the access rights to their trading facility in order to keep HFTs away. In how far a trading system is able to deny access depends on whether they can discriminate regarding whom they grant access.

While denying HFTs access to certain trading systems like dark pools in which block traders and information traders try to hide their order information from the public eye, admitting HFTs to dark pools can even be in the public interest because they can detect pieces of private information and bring it to light. Especially intermarket arbitrage strategies performed by HFTs may benefit market quality at large. If, for instance, HFTs can probe a dark pool's liquidity by sending ping orders at different price points into the market, it may unveil an informed trader's informational advantage and impound it sooner into the price discovery process on lit markets. Thus, while the informed trader forfeits its exclusive right of information usage, the price inaccuracy is decreased sooner, and transaction costs last for a shorter period of time. If such intermarket arbitrage does not become so excessive as to render the information search futile, granting HFTs access to dark pools is efficiency enhancing.[1813]

The law on access to trading systems in the European Union and its transposition into German law both show the familiar differentiation between multilateral trading venues and bilateral trading systems used in the trading systems regime as well as the trade transparency regime.

I. Access to Trading Venues

According to Article 18(3), 53(1) MiFID II, access for traders to multilateral trading venues – RMs, MTFs, and OTFs – must be granted on the basis of transparent and non-discriminatory rules. Under German law, Section 19 BörsG and Section 72(1)(1) WpHG implement this standard for regulated markets, MTFs and OTFs seated in Germany.[1814] This provision aims to protect the functioning of financial markets by allowing traders

1813 Cf. Fox, Glosten and Rauterberg, 'The New Stock Market' (n 88) 244.

1814 Gebauer (n 152) WpHG § 72 para 13; Kumpan (n 125) BörsG § 19 para 1; Röh (n 1232) WpHG § 72 para 10.

equal access to trading venues to facilitate efficient interaction among multiple trading interests driving the price formation process.[1815]

Trading venue operators must thus not intervene in the interaction of supply and demand on their marketplaces by excluding unwelcome traders such as arbitrageurs, as HFTs often are. If a trading venue operator had such discriminatory powers, it might close off its trading system and propel market fragmentation.[1816] Accordingly, the access regime under MiFID II does not primarily aim to set out competition rules among traders but rather provisions to protect the functioning of financial markets.[1817]

The requirement for trading venue operators to offer non-discriminatory access may, however, not be misunderstood in a way that operators cannot set up requirements to limit access to eligible traders only. On the contrary, the operator can define requirements that traders have to meet in order to receive access to the trading venue. Those requirements may not be grounded in extraneous considerations but have to be motivated by legitimate interests. Examples for extraneous considerations are nationality of the trader, whether the trader engages in arbitrage or other legitimate trading strategies such as electronic front running.[1818] Whereas, legitimate interests are strategies like distinguishing between retail clients, professional clients, and eligible counterparties because trading venue operators can determine to which of the aforementioned client-category they wish to offer their services. While discriminating between client-categories serves legitimate reasons, it will prove significantly more challenging to find a legitimate reason to distinguish within one of the established client-categories, since such discrimination is generally regarded as discriminatory among equals.[1819]

According to Section 74 WpHG, access to MTFs shall only be granted to traders who meet the proficiency requirements set out for trading participants at German exchanges according to Section 19(2), (4) BörsG. Those requirements limit access to German exchanges to professional traders and eligible counterparties, such as credit institutions (Section 1(1) KWG), financial service institutions (Section 1(1a) KWG) and financial companies (Section 1(3) KWG), excluding retail customers who do not trade in a

1815 Röh (n 1232) WpHG § 72 para 10.
1816 ibid WpHG § 72 para 12.
1817 ibid WpHG § 72 para 10.
1818 ibid WpHG § 72 para 12.
1819 ibid WpHG § 72 para 12.

professional manner (*'gewerbsmäßig'*).[1820] However, high-frequency traders and other algorithmic traders fulfil the requirements of Section 19(2), (4) BörsG and cannot be excluded.[1821] Those proficiency requirements are considered non-discriminatory since they serve the legitimate interest of the trading venue operator to limit access to trading to traders who can vouch for their professional competence, personal integrity, and solvency.[1822]

This levels the playing field among regulated markets and MTFs under German law, inducing fair competition.[1823] Nevertheless, retail investors can also gain indirect access to trading on trading venues through the brokerage services of the professional traders who qualify as trading participants on trading venues.[1824]

Consequently, while operators of RMs, MTFs, and OTFs can limit access to their trading venues with regard to proficiency, they cannot exclude traders engaging in certain trading strategies, such as HFTs. Even when trading venues operate a dark pool due to waivers from pre-trade transparency, they still have to grant access in compliance with non-discriminatory rules.[1825] European and German law in this regard lack an exemption from the duty of fair access like the 5 %-threshold for ATS according to Rule 301(b)(5)(i) Regulation ATS under US law.[1826] Since US law uses the same 5 %-threshold for the trade transparency requirements and the duty of fair access to apply, US dark pools can offer dark trading services as well as protection from certain traders such as HFTs. EU and German law, on the other hand, only provide exemptions from trade transparency but not from exposure to other traders through limited system access, even for HFTs. This approach is preferable over the US approach, since the increased protection under US law interferes with price formation and exacerbates market fragmentation, whereas EU and German law can avoid such severely adverse effects on trading venues.

1820 Gebauer (n 94) WpHG § 72 para 19; Röh (n 1232) WpHG § 74 para 2.
1821 Kumpan (n 56) BörsG § 19 para 22.
1822 Kumpan (n 125) BörsG § 19 para 23.
1823 Röh (n 1232) WpHG § 72 para 12; Gebauer (n 94) WpHG § 72 para 18.
1824 Cf. Kumpan (n 125) BörsG § 19 paras 5, 6.
1825 Gebauer (n 94) WpHG § 72 para 13.
1826 Bošković, Cerruti and Noël (n 70) 10–1.

II. Access to Systematic Internalizers

The access regime for bilateral systematic internalizers is not part of MiFID II but can rather be found in Articles 17(1) and 18(5) MiFIR. Since EU regulations are directly applicable within the Member States' jurisdictions, there is no transposition into national law in Germany.

To account for proprietary risk assumed in bilateral trading, investment firms can generally choose with whom they wish to transact. Also, systematic internalizers are under no obligation to transact under every market condition or in unlimited numbers with any market participant at their published quotes.[1827] Systematic internalizers are only under an obligation to contract if they have to publish the quote and if the other party is a client of the systematic internalizer in the first place. Systematic internalizers can, however, decide whom they grant access to their quotes beyond mere informational purposes as one of their clients.[1828]

Nevertheless, systematic internalizers are subject to stricter regulation compared to other investment firms because they account for a significant amount of the off-venue market share. Accordingly, Article 17(1) MiFIR requires systematic internalizers to grant access to their quotes in equity instruments on the basis of their commercial policy and in an objective non-discriminatory way.[1829] This decision requires clear standards for governing access to their quotes. To base the decision about access on objective, non-discriminatory criteria, the SI has to meet the same standard as trading venues with regard to the criteria used in the commercial policy: those criteria need to be based on legitimate reasons and cannot be based on extraneous considerations.[1830] It is, however, a legitimate reason to limit access to either professional or retail clients only.[1831] However, the systematic internalizer cannot limit access due to trading strategies like those used by high-frequency traders who engage in regulatory arbitrage, since this would qualify as discriminatory criteria to fend off competitors from other traders and would undermine the price formation process by exacerbating market fragmentation.[1832] If a trader fulfills the requirements set up by the

---

1827 Gebauer (n 94) MiFIR Art 17 para 1.
1828 ibid MiFIR Art 17 para 1.
1829 ibid MiFIR Art 17 para 8.
1830 ibid MiFIR Art 17 para 8.
1831 ibid MiFIR Art 17 para 7.
1832 ibid MiFIR Art 17 para 1; Kumpan, *Die Regulierung außerbörslicher Wertpapierhandelssysteme im deutschen, europäischen und US-amerikanischen Recht* (n 8)

systematic internalizers, the SI is under the obligation to grant the trader access to its quotes.[1833]

According to Article 17(1)(3) MiFIR, systematic internalizers may refuse to enter into or discontinue business relationships with their clients on the basis of commercial considerations such as the client credit status, the counterparty risk and the final settlement of the transaction. This reflects the proprietary risk assumed by systematic internalizers in bilateral trading.[1834]

To further limit the proprietary risk exposure for systematic internalizers, Article 17(2) MiFIR allows, on the one hand, limiting, in a non-discriminatory way, the number of transactions from the same client, and on the other hand, limiting the total number of transactions from different clients if the number and/or volume of orders sought by clients considerably exceeds the norm. The thresholds for the latter are laid out in Article 15 CDR (EU) 2017/567.[1835]

While Article 17 MiFIR applies to equity instruments only, Article 18(5) MiFIR sets out a similar standard tailored for non-equity instruments, essentially requiring the same non-discriminatory access to quotes as the access regime for equity instruments.[1836]

Thus, the access regime for systematic internalizers is calibrated for their bilateral character and the associated proprietary risks. But similar to the access regime for trading venues, it does not allow dark trading to be sealed off from HFTs as under US law.[1837]

In conclusion, EU and German law on access to trading systems require trading system operators to grant fair and non-discriminatory access. This, however, does not mean that there cannot be any requirements with regard to proficiency and solvency. EU law also accounted for proprietary risks in bilateral trading to protect the trading system operator. The legislative decision in favor of fair and non-discriminatory access will most certainly often prevent trading venue operators from offering dark trading without HFT intervention. As a result, the EU rather opts for consolidation of

---

367; Seitz (n 132) 504; Heiko Beck and Lars Röh in Eberhard Schwark and Daniel Zimmer (eds), *Kapitalmarktrechts-Kommentar* (4th edn, CH Beck 2010) WpHG § 32 para 2.

1833 Gebauer (n 94) MiFIR Art 17 para 5.

1834 ibid MiFIR Art 17 para 9.

1835 ibid MiFIR Art 17 paras 12–3.

1836 ibid MiFIR Art 18 para 45.

1837 Kumpan and Schmidt (n 4) MiFIR Art 17 paras 5ff.

market information in a fragmented market, instead of granting informed traders an exclusive right of information usage for a prolonged period of time. Whereas block orders are protected, the price for the block order and all other orders in the dark pool shall reflect an accurate market price.

E. Conclusion and Criticism

After having seen a steep increase in overall dark trading and a significant growth in the number of dark pools under MiFID I, the European Union aimed to put limits on dark trading under the MiFID II/MiFIR-regime.[1838] The regulatory framework reveals that repatriating organized trading from the OTC-space to regulated trading systems was a major objective.[1839] The European Union frowned upon the liquidity that BCNs lured into the OTC-space by evading MiFID I's regulatory framework and undermining its trading system categorization, and thus subjected dark trading to stricter regulation.[1840] The EU wanted to regulate dark trading, especially BCNs, which had slipped through the cracks of regulation under MiFID I.[1841]

By clarifying the definitions of MTF and SI with quantitative definitions as well as by introducing the OTF-category for trading in non-equity instruments, the trading system regime under MiFID II/MiFIR has become much more capable of capturing trading patterns used by BCNs and other dark trading in the OTC-space and have drawn them into the regulatory perimeter. Although measuring the exact liquidity that was repatriated is difficult and a matter for economists, the increase in the number of registered systematic internalizers and the acceptance of the OTF category since MiFID II/MiFIR went into force indicates that the regulatory perimeter in fact captures more trading than before, although not in under the indented regulatory category of trading venues.

Tying a more ambitious trade transparency regime to the broader trading system regime has also increased the transparency in the overall market and simultaneously has limited dark trading. By extending pre-trade and

1838 ibid Foreword MiFIR paras 9ff.

1839 Recitals 8, 10 MiFIR; Moloney, *EU Securities and Financial Markets Regulation* (n 4) 461.

1840 Recital 6 MiFIR; Hoops, 'Bedeutung des organisierten Handelssystems in der gegenwärtigen Marktinfrastruktur' (n 131) 14; Kumpan and Schmidt (n 4) Forword MiFIR paras 5ff; Moloney, *EU Securities and Financial Markets Regulation* (n 4) 458.

1841 Kumpan and Schmidt (n 4) Forword MiFIR paras 9ff.

post-trade transparency requirements to equity instruments other than shares as well as non-equity instruments, MiFID II/MiFIR succeeding in making trading under trade transparency the default setting at trading system. Only for non-equity instruments does the calibrated transparency regime allow for certain exemptions from the trade transparency in case an instrument trades in an illiquid market. But nevertheless, trade transparency has been significantly improved.

The vast majority of cases are under the obligation to show pre-trade transparency unless they have requested and received a waiver from the national competent authority. This form of on-venue, regulated dark trading is considered less problematic than unregulated dark trading in the OTC-space, since trading systems operate under vast regulations and the cases in which dark trading can occur is limited to the scope of the waivers from pre-trade transparency and the deferrals from post-trade transparency.[1842] While the European Union retained all four waivers for equity instruments that were already in use under MiFID I, it significantly narrowed the scope of the controversial reference price waiver and the negotiated trade waiver to allow for less dark trading under those waivers and for less divergence in the application of the waivers among the national competent authorities limiting regulatory arbitrage.[1843]

Furthermore, MiFID II/MiFIR introduced an active limitation device on regulated dark trading, the double volume cap mechanism, which was designed to ensure that dark trading at one trading venue and in the entire European Union does not surpass certain thresholds. Interestingly, the EU's regulation is closely aligned with empirical findings by *Comerton-Forde/Putniņš (2015)*[1844] and *Foley/Putniņš (2016)*[1845] discussed above: MiFID II/MiFIR does not limit those waivers dedicated to large block order trading, which is considered efficiency enhancing by economists but restrains excessive use of the reference price waiver and the negotiated trade waiver. Those waivers allow for so-called 'one-sided' dark trading which, in a certain amount, is efficiency enhancing; but when the optimum is surpassed is detrimental for market efficiency.[1846] Putting a certain limit to those means of dark trading is thus sensible and an interesting implementation of economic research into law.

1842 Recital 13 MiFIR; Gomber and Gvozdevskiy (n 43) paras 14.16ff, 14.104.
1843 Moloney, *EU Securities and Financial Markets Regulation* (n 4) 481–2.
1844 Comerton-Forde and Putniņš (n 382) 70ff.
1845 Foley and Putniņš (n 389) 456ff.
1846 See Comerton-Forde and Putniņš (n 382) 90; Foley and Putniņš (n 389) 478–9.

However, the findings of *Comerton-Forde/Putniņš (2015)* and *Foley/Putniņš (2016)* were based on data from the Canadian and Australian financial markets and may therefore not be directly applicable to the European market as a study by *Aquilina et al. (2017)*[1847] suggests. The data by *Aquilina et al. (2017)* suggests that the thresholds under Article 5 MiFIR are actually lower than the empirical models for the optimum amount of dark trading might suggest. Economically, this may cause losses in market efficiency which is also in contrast to regulatory principals. Moreover, overregulating markets in order to 'err on the side of caution' with the implemented regulation may unduly curtail the fundamental freedoms of market participants and investors and should be reconsidered for calibration.[1848]

The strict regulation of waivers by the double volume cap mechanism, while in isolation may have been efficiency enhancing if calibrated for European markets, may have caused a problematic cocktail of regulatory measures considering that the trading obligation for shares and derivatives also applies. Both trading obligations effectuate the repatriation of dark liquidity from the OTC-space to regulated trading systems. Given that some dark trading is necessary and efficiency enhancing, it is also sensible to implement a regulatory regime that guides liquidity away from unregulated dark trading in the OTC-space into regulated dark trading under waivers. Restricted by the double volume cap, dark trading looked for remaining niches where dark trading can occur. As it turned out, systematic internalizers offer an attractive regime for dark trading having caused the EU legislator to close certain loopholes already.[1849]

Since the EU insists on a strict differentiation between multilateral and bilateral trading systems to make a clear distinction between neutral multilateral trading venues and bilateral systematic internalizers potentially under conflicts of interest, systematic internalizers need to incur position risks when trading against their proprietary capital because matching client orders would push them into the MTF or OTF category. In isolation, this is not problematic. But given that those systematic internalizers are also the systems most attractive for dark trading due to the limitations put on unregulated dark trading in the OTC-space and the volume cap for regulated dark trading on trading venues, this policy leads to a trade-off between trade transparency and market resilience. It appears doubtful that

1847 Aquilina and others (n 275) 5ff.
1848 ibid 5, 27.
1849 Gomber and others (n 1295) 9, 27.

more trade transparency on trading venues by implementing a volume cap is preferrable over having dark trading – even in large amounts – on multilateral RMs, MTFs, and OTFs where position risk is dispersed among many investors rather than accrued by few systematic internalizers who are often banks.

Insofar, MiFID II/MiFIR is a tremendous improvement over MiFID I with a much clearer regulation due to the shift from principle-based to rule-based regulation aiding regulatory convergence among 27 Member States. It is also a significant improvement with regard to the trading systems regime and trade transparency regime.

In the MiFID II/MiFIR refit process, which is still ongoing at the time of this writing in mid-2023, the EU is about to address the pressing issues with the double volume cap and the use of the SI regime for regulated dark trading. With regard to the volume cap mechanism, however, the move from a double to a single volume cap only lifts the administrative burden of such a limiting device for ESMA which now only needs to gather data to calculate a single threshold. But the issue of an overly restrictive regulation that is neither efficiency enhancing nor risk reducing and, at best, futile because the market circumvents it by frequent batch auctions and using SI rather than trading venues, has not been addressed. While the strengthening of the SI regime is a welcome reform in the MiFID II/MiFIR refit process, it is rather a band aid to patch the larger issue of having a volume cap mechanism which sets incentives to avoid trading venues with their well calibrated transparency regime; an outcome that should worry everyone who sees merit in regulated dark trading. The United Kingdom, a critic of the volume cap when it still was in the EU, abolished the DVC and did not suffer adverse effects due to an increase in (regulated) dark trading under the reference price waiver. This measure should be and is currently considered in the EU as well. When the refit process brings new rules into law, a final assessment on this reform act must be made.

§ 7. Regulation of Dark Trading under Swiss Law

A. A New Regime for Swiss Financial Markets

On 1 January 2016, the Swiss trading landscape changed when the new parliamentary act, the Financial Market Infrastructure Act (*'Finanzmarktinfrastrukturgesetz'* – FinfraG), and the accompanying ordinance, the Financial Market Infrastructure Ordinance (*'Finanzmarktinfrastrukturverordnung'* – FinfraV), went into force.[1850]

Unlike MiFID II/MiFIR in the European Union, the Swiss reform was not primarily driven by the intention to close regulatory loopholes revealed during the Global Financial Crisis of 2008-09. The Swiss legislator even concluded that Swiss financial infrastructures had rather proven resilient during the crisis.[1851] Nevertheless, the subsequent wave of regulatory measures, spearheaded by the G20 and their decisions at the Pittsburgh Summit of 2009 to close the loopholes in the regulation of OTC-derivatives trading, eventually washed over Switzerland.[1852] Although Switzerland is not a member of the G20, it still adheres to G20 policies because it is a member to the Financial Stability Board (FSB) which was tasked with monitoring the implementation of the Pittsburgh measures.[1853]

Another driver for reform was to maintain access to the financial markets of the European Union with which Swiss financial markets were tradition-

1850 Sethe (n 196) SK FinfraG Einleitung paras 2, 11; however, significant provisions regarding trade transparency were delayed until 1 January 2018 when also MiFID II/MiFIR went into force (3 January 2018) in the EU, see Article 129 FinfraV und Article 58a former version of BEHV.

1851 Bundesrat, 'Botschaft zum Finanzmarktinfrastrukturgesetz (FinfraG)' (n 22) BBl. 2014, 7483, 7512; Alexander Vogel, Christoph Heiz and Reto Luthiger, *OFK FinfraG/BEG Kommentar: Finanzmarktinfrastrukturgesetz und Bucheffektengesetz mit HWpÜ und weiteren Erlassen* (Orell Füssli Kommentar (OFK), 1st edn, Orell Füssli Verlag 2019) Art 1 para 4.

1852 Bundesrat, 'Botschaft zum Finanzmarktinfrastrukturgesetz (FinfraG)' (n 22) BBl. 2014, 7591ff; Vogel, Heiz and Luthiger, *OFK FinfraG/BEG Kommentar* (n 1851) OFK FinfraG Art 1 para 5.

1853 Bundesrat, 'Botschaft zum Finanzmarktinfrastrukturgesetz (FinfraG)' (n 22) BBl. 2014, 7497; Hans Kuhn, 'Die Regulierung des Derivatehandels im künftigen Finanzmarktinfrastrukturgesetz' [2014] GesKR 161, 162.

ally deeply intertwined.[1854] Since the European Union tied market access to an equivalency test applied by the European Commission under Articles 23 and 25(4) MiFIR, Swiss law had to adapt to the reforms being implemented by the European Union.[1855] Despite the efforts undertaken with FinfraG, the European Union did not prolong the equivalency status for Swiss regulation on trading venues in mid-2019, which barred access of Swiss exchanges and other trading venues to EU markets, and led to counter-measures from the Swiss government banning EU trading systems from offering trading in Swiss shares.[1856] At least on the Swiss side, the decision was widely conceived as a political one rather than a regulatory necessity because the decision about equivalency has been regarded as a means to put pressure on the Swiss government in the negotiations about the EU-Swiss Institutional Framework Agreement which eventually failed.[1857] However, the following analysis and comparison shall not comment on

---

1854 Bundesrat, 'Botschaft zum Finanzmarktinfrastrukturgesetz (FinfraG)' (n 22) BBl. 2014, 7513; Watter (n 196) BSK FinfraG Art 1 para 4; Vogel, Heiz and Luthiger, *OFK FinfraG/BEG Kommentar* (n 1851) OFK FinfraG Art 1 para 8. See also Bundesrat, 'Bericht zur Finanzmarktpolitik des Bundes' (19 December 2012) 22–3; Bundesrat, 'Finanzmarktpolitik für einen wettbewerbsfähigen Finanzplatz Schweiz: Bericht des Bundesrates' (October 2016) 15–6; Aymo Brunetti and others, 'Expertengruppe zur Weiterentwicklung der Finanzmarktstrategie: Schlussbericht' (1 December 2014) 22–3.

1855 Sethe (n 196) SK FinfraG Einleitung para 32; Bahar Rashid and Bianca Nedwed, 'Grenzüberschreitendes Angebot von Finanzdienstleistungen und -produkten: Die Eidgenossenschaft schlägt zurück' [2019] SZW 618ff; Mirjam Eggen and Rupert Schaefer, 'Regulierung grenzüberschreitender Tätigkeiten im Finanzmarktrecht' [2013] GesKR 368, 372–3, 380; Susan Emmenegger and Andrea Bigler, 'Fortress Europe: Die Äquivalenzverfahren der EU im Bereich der Finanzdienstleistungen' [2019] SZW 155ff; Rolf Sethe, 'Das Drittstaatenregime von MiFIR und MiFID II' [2014] SZW 615ff.

1856 Benedikt Pirker and Livia Matter, 'Europarecht: Schweiz - Europäische Union' [2019] SRIEL 101, 106; Benedikt Pirker and Livia Matter, 'Europarecht: Schweiz-Europäische Union' [2020] SRIEL 75, 82; Urs Zulauf and Hans Kuhn, *Finanzmarktrecht* (2nd edn, Dike 2021) 84–5. See also: Michael Ferber, 'Sechs Wochen nach dem Auslaufen der Börsenäquivalenz zeigt sich: Der grosse Knall ist ausgeblieben' *Neue Zürcher Zeitung* (9 August 2019).

1857 Bahar Rashid and Nedwed (n 1855) 620; Franca Contratto, 'Sanktionen - Neue Gretchenfrage im Ringen um den Marktzugang in die EU' [2018] SZW 653, 654ff; Emmenegger and Bigler (n 1855) 158ff; Charlotte Sieber-Gasser, 'Offene strategische Autonomie in der EU-Handelspolitik: Auswirkungen auf europäische Drittstaaten' [2021] EuZ 222, 235; Zulauf and Kuhn (n 1856) 85; Mehreen Khan and Philip Stafford, 'EU-Based Traders Caught in Swiss 'Equivalence' Spat: Breakdown in Talks Leaves Investors in Cross-Border Limbo' *Financial Times* (30 June 2019); European Commission, *Press Release: Commission Statement on the*

the equivalency test and the politics behind the EU's decision in 2019, but rather shine a light on the Swiss regulation of dark trading and examine how it used the European regulatory framework as a blueprint to build its own regulatory regime that addresses an internationally shared problem.

With FinfraG and FinfraV, the Swiss legislator not only abandoned its former trading system regime which differentiated between 'exchanges' and 'exchange-like'[1858] facilities, a distinction that is considered outdated, but also overhauled its trade transparency regime.[1859] Article 1(2) FinfraG even mentions transparency of securities and derivative markets as a principal objective of Swiss financial infrastructure law next to ensuring the proper functioning of the market as well as investor protection. Even though this reference to transparency does not qualify as an end of financial market regulation equal to the functioning of the market and investor protection, but rather a means to achieve such ends, the highlighting of transparency underlines the Swiss legislator's determination to address dark trading with a new, enhanced transparency regime.[1860]

While the first Swiss dark pool – Swiss Block, operated by SIX Swiss Exchange from 2007 to 2011[1861] – occurred almost simultaneously with the soaring of dark pools in the European Union, dark trading in Switzerland has never stirred up similar regulatory attention as it has in the European Union.[1862] The regulatory objective may also be seen as an import into

decision by the Swiss Federal Council to terminate the negotiations of the EU-Swiss Institutional Framework Agreement (2021).

1858 i.e., '*börsenähnliche Einrichtung*' in German.

1859 Bundesrat, 'Botschaft zum Finanzmarktinfrastrukturgesetz (FinfraG)' (n 22) BBl. 2014, 7483, 7530; Schott and Winkler (n 70) SK FinfraG Art 26 para 34.; René Bösch and Stean Kramer, 'Schweizer Finanzmarktrecht im Umbruch: Das Finanzmarktinfrastrukturgesetz als eine der neuen Säulen' [2014] SJZ 249, 252; Humbel, *Die Regelung der Vor- und Nachhandelstransparenz in der Europäischen Union und der Schweiz* (n 50) 441.

1860 Bundesrat, 'Botschaft zum Finanzmarktinfrastrukturgesetz (FinfraG)' (n 22) BBl. 2014, 7485; Sethe (n 196) SK FinfraG Art 1 para 3; differently Holger Fleischer and Hanno Merkt, 'Empfiehlt es sich, im Interesse des Anlegerschutzes und zur Förderung des Finanzplatzes Deutschland das Kapitalmarkt- und Börsenrecht neu zu regeln?: Gutachten F/G für den 64. Deutschen Juristentag' in Hrsg. von der Ständigen Deputation des Deutschen Juristentages (ed), *Verhandlungen des vierundsechzigsten Deutschen Juristentages* (CH Beck 2002) F 26ff.

1861 Hochstrasser (n 11) 308.

1862 See EFD and SIF, 'Evaluation des Finanzmarktinfrastrukturgesetzes - FinfraG-Review: Bericht des EFD' (30 September 2022) 12 who see the current trading infrastructure and trade transparency regime fit to grapple with effects of dark trading on the Swiss financial markets.

Swiss law via G20 policy and European Union adaptation for market access. Nevertheless, the question remains whether FinfraG provides a proper regulatory framework for dark trading in Switzerland or whether the new trading systems and transparency regime show flaws similar to MiFID I which had caused large amounts of unregulated dark trading in the European Union.

The FinfraG-Review report by the Swiss Ministry of Finance ('*Eidgenössisches Finanzdepartement*' – EFD) of 30 September 2022 is rather content with the regulation of dark trading under FinfraG and sees no need for immediate regulatory action.[1863] If this optimism is grounded in the regulatory regime or other factors, will be examined below.

However, the report also reveals a shift in the regulatory goals of Switzerland from primarily containing dark trading with the expectation to be granted access to EU markets to a more liberal approach. While Switzerland wants to allow for dark trading only in a prudent amount so it cannot jeopardize its price formation process at lit markets, it is also concerned that the business of dark trading may leave Switzerland, especially for the United Kingdom which offers a more permissive trading environment than the EU and a more attractive marketplace than Switzerland.[1864] This balancing between prudence and competitiveness may result in a more lenient regulatory environment as well.

B. Trading Infrastructure Regime

I. Ordering Principles

FinfraG is reminiscent of EU law in the way it echoes the structural principles of the trading infrastructure regime since FinfraG also structures its trading systems along the lines of multilateral vs. bilateral trading, on the one hand, and non-discretionary vs. discretionary trading, on the other hand.[1865]

1863 ibid 12.

1864 ibid 12.

1865 Daniel Daeniker and Stefan Waller in Rolf Watter and Rashid Bahar (eds), *Basler Kommentar Finanzmarktaufsichtsgesetz, Finanzmarktinfrastrukturgesetz* (3rd edn, Helbing & Lichtenhahn Verlag 2019) FinfraG Art 26 paras 1–2.

1. Multilateral vs. Bilateral Trading

Multilateral trading is defined pursuant to Article 22 FinfraV as trading that brings together the selling and buying interest of multiple participants in securities (*'Effekten'*) or other financial instruments within a trading system for contract formation.[1866] Although not defined in FinfraG nor FinfraV, bilateral trading is trading in securities or other financial instruments where the trading system operator always forms the counterparty for transactions with other traders.[1867]

2. Non-Discretionary vs. Discretionary Trading

Pursuant to Article 23 FinfraV, the rules of a trading system are non-discretionary if they do not allow for discretion with regard to the order matching decision for the trading system operator. The matching decision is solely based on the pre-defined rules of the trading system.[1868]

In contrast, discretionary systems allow the trading system operator to exercise discretion when matching orders. The discretion can occur on different levels: A trading system operator may exercise discretion with regard to placing or withdrawing the order. Furthermore, system operators can decide whether and when an order may be matched with other orders in the trading system (subject to investor specifications and the duty of best execution). Especially when trading bilaterally, a trading system operator has the discretion to decide whether to match with an incoming order or to reject it.[1869]

1866 FINMA, 'Circular 2018/1 Organised trading facilities: Duties of operators of organised trading facilities (OTF)' (Bern, 1 January 2018) 5 para 20; Patrick Schleiffer and Patrick Schärli, 'Organisation und Betrieb einzelner Finanzmarktinfrastrukturen' in Peter Sester and others (eds), *St. Galler Handbuch zum Schweizer Finanzmarktrecht: Finanzmarktaufsicht und Finanzmarktinfrastrukturen* (1st edn, Dike 2017) § 22 para 140; Schott and Winkler (n 70) SK FinfraG Art 26 para 24.

1867 FINMA, 'Circular 2018/1 Organised trading facilities' (n 1866) 6 para 23; Schleiffer and Schärli, 'Organisation und Betrieb einzelner Finanzmarktinfrastrukturen' (n 1866) § 22 para 141; Favre and Kramer (n 566) SK FinfraG Art 46 para 27.

1868 FINMA, 'Circular 2018/1 Organised trading facilities' (n 1866) 5 para 16; Schleiffer and Schärli, 'Organisation und Betrieb einzelner Finanzmarktinfrastrukturen' (n 1866) § 22 para 142.

1869 FINMA, 'Circular 2018/1 Organised trading facilities' (n 1866) 5 para 17; Schleiffer and Schärli, 'Organisation und Betrieb einzelner Finanzmarktinfrastrukturen' (n 1866) § 22 para 143.

3. Securities (*'Effekten'*) and Other Financial Instruments

Comparable to EU law, Swiss law determines that only certain types of financial instruments are eligible for trading on certain types of trading systems. Insofar, both systems use asset classes as a differentiating factor to determine the scope of different trading systems. While the European Union differentiates between equity and non-equity financial instruments, Swiss law differentiates between securities and other financial instruments.[1870]

Pursuant to Article 2(b) FinfraG and Article 3(b) Financial Services Act (*'Finanzdienstleistungsgesetz'* – FIDLEG), securities (*'Effekten'*) are defined as standardized, certificated and uncertificated securities, derivatives and intermediated securities, which are suitable for mass trading.[1871] Such instruments qualify as suitable for mass standardized trading if they are publicly offered for sale in the same structure and denomination or are placed with more than twenty clients, unless the instruments are specifically created for the particular counterparty (Article 2(1) FinfraV).[1872] Although the definition of securities is similar to the definition of transferrable security under Article 4(1)(44) MiFID II, EU law does not use it to structure its trading system regime or its trade transparency regime, but instead uses the categories of 'equity' and 'non-equity instruments' instead.[1873] The use of 'securities' as a regulatory category is rather comparable to US law, where a similarly broad definition of securities under Section 3(a)(1) Exchange Act defines the scope of the law and of the SEC's regulatory power in contrast to the scope of the Commodities Exchange Act and the jurisdiction of the CFTC.[1874]

The term 'financial instrument' has not been legally defined until FIDLEG went into force on 1 January 2020. Since FIDLEG, FinfraG and Financial Institutions Act (*'Finanzinstitutsgesetz'* – FINIG) are meant to jointly form the new legislative framework to govern Swiss financial markets, the other codes, such as FinfraG, also refer to the term financial instruments, even though FinfraG preceded FIDLEG by four years.[1875] Pur-

1870 Schott and Winkler (n 70) SK FinfraG Art 29 paras 40ff.
1871 Favre and Kramer (n 566) SK FinfraG Art 2 lit B para 1. See also Kägi (n 50) BSK FinfraG Art 29 paras 17, 56.
1872 Daeniker and Waller (n 1865) BSK FinfraG Art 2 lit B para 1.
1873 See above Part II § 6 C.I.
1874 Daeniker and Waller (n 1865) BSK FinfraG Art 2 lit B para 28, Loss, Seligman and Paredes (n 631) 183ff, 299ff.
1875 FinfraG went into force on 1 January 2016.

suant to Article 3(a) FIDLEG, the category *'financial instrument'* is broader than securities and also encompasses instruments that are not suitable for mass standardized trading.[1876] Thus, the level of liquidity has no impact on the qualification as a financial instrument but on the qualification as a security.[1877] However, the term 'financial instrument' is the umbrella term that also catches securities since Article 42 FinfraG speaks of securities and other financial instruments of which securities form a part.[1878] While the term 'financial instrument' is generally defined broadly and can also encompass bespoke instruments like OTC-derivatives, which are not sold in identical form to more than 20 counterparties, certain types of re-purchasable life insurances, and deposits,[1879] it does not include currency and precious metal spot-transactions.[1880] Those latter transactions remain outside the trading venue regime and therefore also outside of the transparency regime tied to the trading venue regime. Those transactions often occur as dark trading, where price formation must be handled between the transacting parties.

II. Trading Infrastructure

The Swiss trading infrastructure under FinfraG comprises of three trading systems, i.e., exchanges (*'Börsen'*), multilateral trading systems or 'CH-MTF' (*'multilaterale Handelssysteme'*) and organized trading systems or

---

1876 Schleiffer and Schärli, 'Organisation und Betrieb einzelner Finanzmarktinfrastrukturen' (n 1866) § 22 para 149. See also Daeniker and Waller (n 1865) BSK FinfraG Art 2 lit B para 19; Favre and Kramer (n 566) SK FinfraG Art 42 para 23; Lukas Fahrländer, 'Das Schweizer Börsenrecht' in Christian Bovet (ed), *Finanzmarktaufsicht/ Surveillance des marchés financiers* (Schweizerisches Bundesverwaltungsrecht Band XV, 1st edn, Helbing Lichtenhahn Verlag 2016) 355 para 84; Simon Schären, Günther Dobrauz-Saldapenna and Martin Liebi, 'Organisierte Handelssysteme im neuen FinfraG: Versuch einer regulatorischen Kategorisierung' [2016] SZW 194, 196–7.

1877 FINMA, 'Circular 2018/1 Organised trading facilities' (n 1866) 6 para 24; Daeniker and Waller (n 1865) BSK FinfraG Art 2 lit B para 19.

1878 Daeniker and Waller (n 1865) BSK FinfraG Art 2 lit B para 19.

1879 ibid BSK FinfraG Art 2 lit B para 19; Favre and Kramer (n 566) SK FinfraG Art 2 lit B para 12.

1880 FINMA, 'Circular 2018/1 Organised trading facilities' (n 1866) 6 para 24: *'(…) The term "financial instruments" is to be understood as broadly defined, but it does not include currency and precious metals spot-transactions. (…)'.*

'CH-OTF' ('*organisierte Handelssysteme*').[1881] In the new trading infrastructure set out in FinfraG, only exchanges and CH-MTFs qualify as trading venues ('*Handelsplatz*', Article 26(a) FinfraG) and 'financial market infrastructures' ('*Finanzmarktinfrastruktur*', Article 2(a) FrinfraG).[1882] Although, CH-OTF were also included into both classifications in the draft version of FinfraG (*Draft-FinfraG*),[1883] the CH-OTF was excluded from both categories in the final version.[1884] The *Botschaft* explains this change of mind with the fact that they do not fall within the general licensing obligations as do the other financial market infrastructures.[1885]

1. Exchanges

a) Definition

Pursuant to Article 26(b) FinfraG an exchange is a facility for the multilateral trading of securities ('*Effekten*') where offers of multiple participants can interact simultaneously and contracts are formed according to non-discriminatory rules. A characteristic of exchanges is their ability to list securities ('*Kotierung von Effekten*'), which is an important gatekeeping function on the primary markets.[1886]

b) Multilateral, Non-Discretionary Trading

Like regulated markets under EU law and exchanges under US law, Swiss exchanges are purely multilateral, non-discretionary trading systems.[1887] A system that qualifies for this category cannot engage in any sort of bilateral

1881 Hochstrasser (n 11) 312–3; Baisch, Baumann and Weber (n 11) 197; Zulauf and Kuhn (n 1856) 81.

1882 Hochstrasser (n 11) 312–3; Zulauf and Kuhn (n 1856) 81.

1883 See Article 3(1)(c) and Article 25(1) Draft-FinfraG.

1884 Bundesrat, 'Botschaft zum Finanzmarktinfrastrukturgesetz (FinfraG)' (n 22) BBl. 2014, 7501, 7530.

1885 ibid BBl. 2014, 7513.

1886 Daeniker and Waller (n 1865) BSK FinfraG Art 26 paras 8ff; Schott and Winkler (n 70) SK FinfraG Art 26 paras 23ff; Vogel, Heiz and Luthiger, *OFK FinfraG/BEG Kommentar* (n 1851) OFK FinfraG Art 26 paras 3ff; Zulauf and Kuhn (n 1856) 82.

1887 Cf. Zulauf and Kuhn (n 1856) 82.

trading against its proprietary capital[1888] nor can it exercise discretion, meaning that the order matching process must be subject to pre-defined rules.[1889]

c) Trading of Securities

A central difference to EU law, but rather a resemblance to the US exchange, is the fact that Swiss exchanges are limited to the trading of securities, instead of financial instruments as a whole.[1890] As discussed above, securities (*'Effekten'*) are defined as standardized, certificated and uncertificated securities, derivatives and intermediated securities, which are suitable for mass trading.[1891] Such instruments qualify as suitable for mass standardized trading if they are publicly offered for sale in the same structure and denomination or are placed with more than twenty clients, unless the instruments are specifically created for the particular counterparty (Article 2(1) FinfraV) which shall ensure that those instruments trade in a liquid market that can sustain a multilateral market with trade transparency supporting price formation for those instruments.[1892]

Every instrument falling outside the scope of the securities (*'Effekten'*) definition – particularly when not meeting the threshold requirements in Article 2(1) FinfraV – is no longer eligible to trade on an exchange (or CH-MTF). Such instruments may be traded as other financial instruments within the systems of a CH-OTF.[1893] Despite the difference on the surface, the scope of the exchange system is very similar to the one in the European Union, where financial instruments as defined under Article 4(1)(15) MiFID II and Section C of Annex I of MiFID II also encompass instruments

1888 Daeniker and Waller (n 1865) BSK FinfraG Art 26 paras 9, 13, 19; Schott and Winkler (n 70) SK FinfraG Art 26 para 24.

1889 Daeniker and Waller (n 1865) BSK FinfraG Art 26 para 13; Schott and Winkler (n 70) SK FinfraG Art 26 para 27; Vogel, Heiz and Luthiger, *OFK FinfraG/BEG Kommentar* (n 1851) OFK FinfraG Art 26 para 7.

1890 Cf. Daeniker and Waller (n 1865) BSK FinfraG Art 26 para 26. See also on the difference between Swiss securities and EU financial instruments: Schott and Winkler (n 70) SK FinfraG Art 29 paras 40ff.

1891 See above Part II § 7 B.I.3.

1892 Daeniker and Waller (n 1865) BSK FinfraG Art 2 lit B para 1.

1893 Schott and Sester (n 57) § 22 para 4.

that are fungible and are offered to the public.[1894] Consequently, Swiss law might lack the clear-cut differentiation for equity and non-equity instruments, which might be less advantageous for the transparency regime, but with regard to the breadth of the exchange definition, the limitation to securities trading does not make a significant difference.[1895]

d) Conclusion of Contracts within the System

Furthermore, a contract for the sale of a security must be concluded within the system.[1896] This distinguishes trading systems – including exchanges – from mere communication and information systems, such as, bulletin boards.[1897] This definition is also slightly narrower than the EU's definition of a regulated market which can also be a system that merely facilitates the bringing together of sellers and buyers.[1898] Because a contract is usually formed, this does not make a large difference.

e) Listing of Securities

Besides multilateral trading of securities, Swiss exchanges also serve an important function as gatekeepers on the primary markets when they are listing securities.[1899] Pursuant to Article 2(f) FinfraG, the listing of securities is the admission of a security to trading on an exchange in accordance with a standardized procedure in which the exchange verifies the issuer's and its issued securities' compliance with requirements set out by the exchange.[1900] This form of standardized reputation lending provided by the exchange as a highly regarded repeat player in the market distinguishes the

---

1894 See Daeniker and Waller (n 1865) BSK FinfraG Art 2 lit B para 28; Schott and Winkler (n 70) SK FinfraG Art 29 paras 40ff.

1895 Schott and Winkler (n 70) SK FinfraG Art 29 para 42.

1896 ibid SK FinfraG Art 29 para 24.

1897 Daeniker and Waller (n 1865) BSK FinfraG Art 26 para 16; Schott and Sester (n 57) § 22 para 12; Kumpan, *Die Regulierung außerbörslicher Wertpapierhandelssysteme im deutschen, europäischen und US-amerikanischen Recht* (n 8) 19ff.

1898 See Lutter, Bayer and Schmidt (n 1090) § 32 para 32.36.

1899 Daeniker and Waller (n 1865) BSK FinfraG Art 26 para 12; Schott and Winkler (n 70) SK FinfraG Art 26 para 25; Vogel, Heiz and Luthiger, *OFK FinfraG/BEG Kommentar* (n 1851) OFK FinfraG Art 26 para 5; Zulauf and Kuhn (n 1856) 82.

1900 Schott and Sester (n 57) § 22 paras 7ff; Schott and Winkler (n 70) SK FinfraG Art 26 para 25.

listing of securities from the mere admission to trading that CH-MTFs can offer.[1901] Also in this regard Swiss exchanges are similar to their peers in the US and EU.[1902]

2. Swiss Multilateral Trading Facility (CH-MTF)

A multilateral trading facility under Article 26(b) FinfraG is an institution for multilateral trading of securities (*'Effekten'*) for the purpose of the simultaneous exchange of orders among multiple participants and the conclusion of contracts based on non-discretionary rules without listing securities.[1903]

As the definition sets out, CH-MTFs are functionally equivalent to exchanges except for the ability to list securities. This primary market function is reserved for exchanges only, CH-MTFs can merely admit but not list securities to trading, which carries less weight with regard to the standard the new market entrant has to pass (at least in the eyes of other market participants).[1904] With regard to the common defining criteria between exchanges and CH-MTFs, see the explanations for exchanges above.[1905]

1901 Cf. Gilson and Kraakman (n 62) 620: In the listing process, exchanges take on a similar function as underwriters with regard that both players are repeat players in securities markets who lend their 'reputation bond' to the issuer signally a certain amount of quality investors can put their trust in.

1902 See above Part II § 5 D.II. and § 6 B.II.1.

1903 Schleiffer and Schärli, 'Organisation und Betrieb einzelner Finanzmarktinfrastrukturen' (n 1866) § 22 para 135.

1904 Bundesrat, 'Botschaft zum Finanzmarktinfrastrukturgesetz (FinfraG)' (n 22) BBl. 2014, 7499; see also Schleiffer and Schärli, 'Organisation und Betrieb einzelner Finanzmarktinfrastrukturen' (n 1866) § 22 para 153 describing that the difference between listing of securities at exchanges and their mere admittance to trading at CH-MTFs. While listing securities at an exchange is also an admittance to trading, like the admittance at CH-MTFs, the listing is different because of the particularly high requirements imposed on the issuer and the securities in the listing procedure as well as with regard to the ongoing obligations as, for example, providing for ad hoc and periodic disclosure. That marks the difference between exchanges and CH-MTFs.

1905 Bundesrat, 'Botschaft zum Finanzmarktinfrastrukturgesetz (FinfraG)' (n 22) BBl. 2014, 7499; Zulauf and Kuhn (n 1856) 82.

According to Articles 2(a) and 26(a) FinfraG, exchanges and multilateral trading facilities qualify as financial market infrastructures and trading venues.[1906]

3. Gaps in the Regulatory Regime

The similarity of Swiss exchanges and CH-MTFs to RMs and MTFs under EU law raise the question of whether there is a similar gap between the multilateral systems and bilateral trading as under MiFID I.[1907] If this is the case, there is the chance that trading slips through these gaps and market participants may offer trading systems similar to BCNs in the European Union combining multilateral and bilateral trading in a manner that does not fall in the scope of any trading system. Ultimately, this would lead to unregulated dark trading.[1908]

To assess this question, the focus must shift to the scope of the third category of trading system: the CH-OTF.

4. Swiss Organized Trading System (CH-OTF)

a) Definition

The naming of the Swiss organized trading facility or CH-OTF is reminiscent of its counterpart under EU law.[1909] Unlike Swiss exchanges and CH-MTFs, CH-OTFs do not qualify as financial market infrastructures or as trading venues.[1910] Thus, they are not under direct supervision of Swiss Financial Market Supervisory Authority ('*Eidgenössischen Finanzmarktauf-*

1906 Bundesrat, 'Botschaft zum Finanzmarktinfrastrukturgesetz (FinfraG)' (n 22) BBl. 2014 7498–9, 7513, 7529ff.

1907 See above Part II § 6 A.II.2.

1908 Easthope and Ray (n 5) 16; Moloney, *EU Securities and Financial Markets Regulation* (n 4) 428.

1909 Cf. Zulauf and Kuhn (n 1856) 83.

1910 See Article 2(a) and Article 26(1) FinfraG. Ueli Studer and Marino Vollenweider in Rolf Watter and Rashid Bahar (eds), *Basler Kommentar Finanzmarktaufsichtsgesetz, Finanzmarktinfrastrukturgesetz* (3rd edn, Helbing & Lichtenhahn Verlag 2019) FinfraG Art 42 para 2; Favre and Kramer (n 566) SK FinfraG Art 42 paras 1–2; Vogel, Heiz and Luthiger, *OFK FinfraG/BEG Kommentar* (n 1851) OFK FinfraG Art 42 para 3; Zulauf and Kuhn (n 1856) 87–8.

sicht' – FINMA), the Swiss regulatory authority.[1911] Only their operators, which are limited to authorized banks, securities traders, Distributed Ledger Technology (DLT) trading facilities, or trading venues, need to register with FINMA and fall under FINMA supervision.[1912]

However, while the EU-OTF is modelled as a residual trading infrastructure for the trading of non-equity instruments that is best defined negatively as a multilateral trading system which is not a RM or a MTF,[1913] the CH-OTF is an even broader catch-all category.[1914] Since Swiss law lacks a dedicated trading system for bilateral trading, such as the systematic internalizer under EU law, the CH-OTF also absorbs this functionality.[1915] For this reason, Article 42 FinfraG sets out three different types of CH-OTFs which all lack one feature of a trading venue (i.e., Swiss exchanges and CH-MTF).[1916] Thus, a facility not fulfilling the trading venue definition can qualify as a CH-OTF if it either offers (a) multilateral trading of securities or other financial instruments under discretionary rules – lacking the element of non-discretionary trading rules which trading venues must have.[1917] A facility under the CH-OTF umbrella can also offer (b) multilateral trading in financial instruments other than securities under non-discretionary rules – because trading venues only allow for trading of securities (CH-OTFs are the only facilities for multilateral, non-discretionary trading in financial instruments other than securities).[1918] Or, a facility can operate under the CH-OTF regime if it offers (c) bilateral trading – lacking the element of multilateral trading which is characteristic for trading venues.[1919]

While the combination of multilateral, bilateral, and discretionary trading in one regulatory category appears to be similar to the US-ATS category as well as the BCNin the EU under MiFID I which both fostered

1911 Vogel, Heiz and Luthiger, *OFK FinfraG/BEG Kommentar* (n 1851) OFK FinfraG Art 42 para 3; Zulauf and Kuhn (n 1856) 87.

1912 Article 43(1) FinfraG. Studer and Vollenweider (n 1910) BSK FinfraG Art 43 para 1; Favre and Kramer (n 566) SK FinfraG Art 43 para 1; Vogel, Heiz and Luthiger, *OFK FinfraG/BEG Kommentar* (n 1851) OFK FinfraG Art 43 para 1.

1913 Cf. Article 4(1)(23) MiFID II.

1914 Bundesrat, 'Botschaft zum Finanzmarktinfrastrukturgesetz (FinfraG)' (n 22) BBl. 2014, 7539; Schleiffer and Schärli, 'Organisation und Betrieb einzelner Finanzmarktinfrastrukturen' (n 1866) § 22 paras 150–1; Zulauf and Kuhn (n 1856) 87–8.

1915 Zulauf and Kuhn (n 1856) 83, 88.

1916 ibid 87–8.

1917 ibid 88.

1918 ibid 88.

1919 ibid 88; see Article 42 FinfraG.

large amounts of dark trading, the Swiss regulator considers each of the abovementioned types of CH-OTF individual and separate types. Those three types of CH-OTF need to be distinguished and operated separately from each other.[1920] This distinction may foster dark pool growth in the shape of BCNs under Swiss law. The multilateral types of CH-OTF can be subdivided into the discretionary and the non-discretionary type.

b) Multilateral CH-OTFs

aa) CH-OTF under Article 42(a) FinfraG

The discretionary type of CH-OTF under Article 42(a) FinfraG is open for both trading in securities and other financial instruments.[1921] The system operator may exercise its discretion with regard to the decision to execute or cancel an order and to decide whether an order of a user will not match with other executable orders in the system, provided that the discretion is executed in accordance with the user's instructions and complies with the duty of best execution.[1922]

The multilateral, discretionary CH-OTF closely resembles the EU-OTF which also operates as a multilateral but discretionary trading venue.[1923] In contrast to the CH-OTF, MiFID II/MiFIR limits the EU-OTF to trading in non-equity instruments.[1924] While initially proposed as a trading system capable of hosting trading in both equity and non-equity instruments, the EU-OTF was eventually cut back to only host non-equity trading. Critics regarded the discretionary element as adversely effecting price discovery and harmful for equities trading on EU-RMs and EU-MTFs. Moreover,

---

1920 FINMA, 'Circular 2018/1 Organised trading facilities' (n 1866) 7 para 26; cf. Patrick Schleiffer and Patrick Schärli, 'New Rules for Organized Trading Facilities' [2017] CapLaw 44.

1921 Studer and Vollenweider (n 1910) BSK FinfraG Art 42 para 20; Schären, Dobrauz-Saldapenna and Liebi (n 1876) 196.

1922 Bundesrat, 'Botschaft zum Finanzmarktinfrastrukturgesetz (FinfraG)' (n 22) BBl. 2014, 7531; FINMA, 'Circular 2018/1 Organised trading facilities' (n 1866) 5 para 17; Favre and Kramer (n 566) SK FinfraG Art 42 para 20; Schären, Dobrauz-Saldapenna and Liebi (n 1876) 196; Schleiffer and Schärli, 'Organisation und Betrieb einzelner Finanzmarktinfrastrukturen' (n 1866) § 22 para 147.

1923 Studer and Vollenweider (n 1910) BSK FinfraG Art 42 paras 39–40.

1924 Schleiffer and Schärli, 'Organisation und Betrieb einzelner Finanzmarktinfrastrukturen' (n 1866) § 22 para 311; Favre and Kramer (n 566) SK FinfraG Art 42 para 9; Hall (n 81) 498.

discretionary trading was considered only necessary in non-equity markets since such markets are usually dealer-based markets due to their volatility and, at times, thin liquidity levels.[1925] Equity markets, instead, were considered sufficiently liquid to sustain non-discretionary, multilateral trading capable of producing price information unbiased by discrete matching decisions of the venue operator.[1926]

Surprisingly, this is a limitation that is lacking under Swiss law which means that a multilateral, discretionary CH-OTF can also offer trading in equity instruments, such as shares, which trade in a highly liquid market. Insofar, the Swiss legislator created a trading infrastructure that is modelled after the BCNs in the EU under MiFID I which traded instruments in liquid markets multilaterally and under discretionary rules as unregulated OTC dark pools.[1927]

However, an important aspect of those BCNs is banned under the CH-OTF regime: an operator of a multilateral CH-OTF cannot engage in bilateral trading in its own trading system. Although a multilateral CH-OTF can perform matched principal trading where it matches two opposite client orders simultaneously without assuming risk or gaining a profit besides pre-defined fees, this sort of trading is not considered to carry the same risk as bilateral trading since the position risk of each order does not linger for long (if at all) on the proprietary capital of the CH-OTF.[1928]

The CH-OTF operator is even obliged to separate the operation of the CH-OTF from other business activities.[1929] Even different CH-OTFs that are run by one operator are barred from interaction. Different types of CH-OTFs according to Article 42(a)-(c) FinfraG must be operated separately. Especially the transfer of orders between multilateral and bilateral CH-OTFs must be prevented by the operator.[1930] This is important to ensure the neutrality of the operator of a multilateral CH-OTF and is

1925 Moloney, *EU Securities and Financial Markets Regulation* (n 4) 431–2.
1926 Deutsche Börse Group, 'Review of the Markets in Financial Instruments Directive: Questionnaire on MiFID/MiFIR 2 by Markus Ferber MEP' (13 January 2012) 5; Ferrarini and Moloney (n 143) 562–3; Moloney, *EU Securities and Financial Markets Regulation* (n 4) 428, 431, 466.
1927 Studer and Vollenweider (n 1910) BSK FinfraG Art 42 para 40; Ferrarini and Moloney (n 143) 584ff; Moloney, *EU Securities and Financial Markets Regulation* (n 4) 466.
1928 FINMA, 'Circular 2018/1 Organised trading facilities' (n 1866) 6 para 21.
1929 ibid 6 para 22.
1930 ibid 7 para 26.

insofar in alignment with the regulatory requirements for OTFs under EU law which are also barred from interacting with bilateral systematic internalizers to protect the operator's neutrality.[1931]

Moreover, this separation of operations also includes market making activities by a proprietary trading desk. While such proprietary trading desks do perform bilateral trading, they are considered eligible if they are fully separated from the operation of the trading system itself organizationally and informationally, for example by setting up information barriers (so-called 'Chinese Walls').[1932] The CH-OTF must also disclose the operation of a proprietary trading desk for market making.[1933] By these means, the neutrality of the CH-OTF operator shall be maintained while liquidity levels can be elevated through a market making division that shall not gain an informational advantage over other traders.[1934] Compared to EU and German law, the Swiss regulation is slightly more lenient because Article 20(1) MiFID II and Section 75(1)(1) WpGH only allow market making by firms separate from the EU-OTF or their affiliate firms, also aiming to ensure the operators neutrality while elevating liquidity levels.[1935] The EU-OTF must also disclose the market making activities of another firm to the NCA, in Germany to BaFin.[1936] While both regulatory approaches are viable, FINMA should pay special attention that indirectly supervised CH-OTFs are not tempted to slip information through Chinese Walls to tip-off their trading desks as has been the case in the US in the SEC enforcement measure of Pipeline LLC. In this case, the operator of the dark ATS of Pipeline LLC matched client orders via a propriety trading desk of a wholly-owned subsidiary against its proprietary capital without disclosing this practice.[1937]

Whether the introduction of a discretionary multilateral trading venue in equity instruments actually jeopardizes the price discovery mechanism as

1931 See above Part II § 6 B.III.1.a).hh).

1932 FINMA, 'Circular 2018/1 Organised trading facilities' (n 1866) 6–7 paras 22, 26–7.

1933 ibid 6 para 22.

1934 ibid 6 para 22; Studer and Vollenweider (n 1910) BSK FinfraG Art 42 para 29.

1935 Röh (n 1232) WpHG § 75 para 22; ESMA, 'Questions and Answers: On MiFID II and MiFIR Market Structures Topics' (n 1169) 49 No 5.2, Answer 14.

1936 Art 6 lit a Commission Implementing Regulation (EU) 2016/824; Röh (n 1232) WpHG § 75 para 22.

1937 *Pipeline Trading Systems LLC* (n 26) 1, 15ff.

some critics feared, must be studied in the Swiss example by economists.[1938] Despite the more lenient separation requirements for market making under FinfraG/FinfraV, the Swiss legislator created a multilateral CH-OTF that preserves the neutrality of the system operator and can avoid fraudulent behavior as in the Pipeline LLC case if the rules are applied properly. Thus, even when the CH-OTF may make use of waiver from trade transparency, it can be considered as a regulated dark pool with less potential to harm investor trust.

bb) CH-OTF under Article 42(b) FinfraG

Under Article 42(b) FinfraG, the other type of multilateral CH-OTF is the one operating under non-discretionary rules. In its basic architecture, it rather resembles a Swiss exchange or a CH-MTF, which are non-discretionary, multilateral venues for trading in securities. However, the CH-OTF is limited to trading financial instruments other than securities, i.e., it lacks the element of trading in securities.[1939] By this limitation, the Swiss regulator creates a catch-all trading system to prevent liquidity from slipping through the regulatory cracks due to the limitation of Swiss exchanges and CH-MTFs to trading in securities, but also ensures that this type of CH-OTF does not propel market fragmentation through direct competition with Swiss exchanges and CH-MTFs. The limitation of this type of CH-OTF to financial instruments other than securities assigns this trading system to another market rather than the one of Swiss trading venues. Whether there is a sizable market in financial instruments other than securities, however, remains to be seen, given that even OTC-derivatives need to be offered to less than 20 counterparties to fail the qualification as a security under Article 2(1) FinfraV, unless the instruments are specifically created for the particular counterparty.[1940]

1938 See Ferrarini and Moloney (n 143) 591ff; Moloney, *EU Securities and Financial Markets Regulation* (n 4) 466.

1939 Schären, Dobrauz-Saldapenna and Liebi (n 1876) 197; Vogel, Heiz and Luthiger, *OFK FinfraG/BEG Kommentar* (n 1851) OFK FinfraG Art 42 paras 16–7.

1940 See above B.I.3. and Article 2(1) FinfraV. Cf. Schären, Dobrauz-Saldapenna and Liebi (n 1876) 197; Vogel, Heiz and Luthiger, *OFK FinfraG/BEG Kommentar* (n 1851) OFK FinfraG Art 42 para 17.

c) Bilateral CH-OTF

The versatile character of the CH-OTF becomes most apparent with its third type: pursuant to Article 42(c) FinfraG, an CH-OTF can also be a facility for bilateral trading in securities or other financial instruments for the purpose of exchanging orders.[1941] Counting a bilateral system within the OTF-category is inconsistent with the scope of the EU-OTF because it resembles the category of systematic internalizer under EU law. The bilateral CH-OTF thereby completes the regulatory scope of the trading infrastructure regime.[1942]

However, compared to the systematic internalizer in the European Union, the definition of the CH-OTF does not have any trading-specific requirements that delineate the regulated entity from any other bilaterally trading firm in the OTC-space selling financial instruments. For instance, EU law requires that the trading of an investment firm falling within the scope of SI-regulation must be 'frequent systematic' and 'substantial' in a specific instrument.[1943] Any investment firm not triggering those thresholds, i.e., those who trade ad hoc, remain outside the regulatory scope of the SI-regime in the unregulated OTC-space.[1944] Since the qualitative determination of those thresholds has caused the regulatory gap used by BCNs to set up shop in the OTC-space as unregulated dark pools, the EU fortified those weak points by introducing quantitative thresholds.[1945]

The bilateral CH-OTF definition does not have comparable limitations for its scope of application. Only the limitation of the eligible operating entity to either be authorized as a bank, a securities dealer or a DLT trading facility, or a trading venue delineates the scope of the bilateral CH-OTF.[1946] However, this limitation may also be gamed by any operator who is not one of the eligible entities to offer bilateral trading services outside of

1941 Studer and Vollenweider (n 1910) BSK FinfraG Art 42 para 30; Favre and Kramer (n 566) SK FinfraG Art 42 para 27; Schären, Dobrauz-Saldapenna and Liebi (n 1876) 198; Vogel, Heiz and Luthiger, *OFK FinfraG/BEG Kommentar* (n 1851) OFK FinfraG Art 42 para 19.

1942 Studer and Vollenweider (n 1910) BSK FinfraG Art 42 para 39; Favre and Kramer (n 566) SK FinfraG Art 42 para 14; Schären, Dobrauz-Saldapenna and Liebi (n 1876) 198.

1943 Favre and Kramer (n 566) SK FinfraG Art 42 para 10; Kumpan (n 125) WpHG § 2 para 104.

1944 Kumpan (n 125) WpHG § 2 para 104.

1945 Moloney, *EU Securities and Financial Markets Regulation* (n 4) 446ff; See above Part II §6 B.III.1.a).cc).(ii).

1946 Article 43 FinfraG.

the regulatory perimeter as unregulated dark trading simply because their bilateral trading is not captured by the CH-OTF regime.

This issue becomes even more pressing given that FINMA also considered it useful to limit the scope of the bilateral CH-OTF to those trading systems that offer bilateral trading on a regular basis. When FINMA realized in the consultation process that there is no legislative delegation of power under FinfraG that would allow FINMA the implementation of quantitative thresholds similar to those under MiFID II/MiFIR, it anchored qualitative limitations in the definition of the CH-OTF itself: A CH-OTF requires trading that is governed by a set of standardized and binding rules.[1947] According to FINMA, for this kind of trading under a standardized and binding set of rules, trading must be planned in advance and conducted through recurring processes.[1948] Consequently, '*(...) [a] facility designed exclusively for spontaneous trading that is not planned in advance (ad-hoc trading) on the basis of rules that are not defined in advance is not covered by the OTF rules.*'[1949]

However, the limitation under Swiss law is imprecise in two ways: First, it does not assess trading on an instrument-by-instrument basis like the threshold system for determining SI-status under MiFID II/MiFIR. Second, using quantitative criteria has proven prone to regulatory arbitrage under MiFID I due to its imprecise delineation in a case-by-case application. Unregulated dark pools gamed MiFID I's permissive qualitative criteria to create a large number of dark pools in the OTC-space. To prevent such activities, the EU has introduced (clear-cut) quantitative threshold under MiFID II/MiFIR.[1950]

So far, there is no evidence that the Swiss qualitative definition causes issues of unregulated dark trading comparable to those under MiFID I. Nevertheless, FINMA should remain vigilant for market developments like BCNs in the OTC-space and the Swiss legislator should consider delegating to FINMA the power to promulgate quantitative thresholds comparable to those under MiFID II/MiFIR for systematic internalizers. Nevertheless, this susceptibility to gaming may be less of an issue in Switzerland than in the European Union, since Swiss financial regulation is federal law administered by a federal agency, FINMA, which avoids the issue of multiple NCAs

1947 FINMA, 'Circular 2018/1 Organised trading facilities' (n 1866) 3 para 5.
1948 ibid 4 para 7.
1949 ibid 4 para 7.
1950 See above Part II § 6 B.III.1.a).dd)ff.

in 27 Member States applying the transposed national law in a different manner as was the case under MiFID I.

III. Authorization

1. Authorization of Exchanges and CH-MTFs

According to Article 4(1) FinfraG, financial market infrastructures require authorization from FINMA.[1951] With regard to trading systems, only exchanges and CH-MTF count among financial market infrastructures pursuant to Article 2(a) FinfraG.[1952] An exchange or CH-MTF seeking authorization must comply with both the general authorization requirements pursuant to Articles 4ff FinfraG as well as the authorization requirements specific to trading venues pursuant to Article 27ff and Article 36ff FinfraG.[1953] When the entity fulfils the requirements, the trading venue is entitled to receive authorization. In this instance, FINMA cannot exercise discretion since it is an administrative authorization (*'Polizeibewilligung'*).[1954]

2. For CH-OTFs

Since CH-OTFs do not qualify as financial market infrastructures (e contrario Article 2(a) FinfraG), they need not seek authorization from FINMA before commencing their operations; they only need to notify FINMA (Article 29 FINMAG).[1955] Nevertheless, Article 43(1) FinfraG restricts the entities eligible to operate a CH-OTF to authorized banks, securities traders,

1951 Article 4(1) FinfraG. Winzeler (n 196) BSK FinfraG Art 4 paras 1, 9; Sarah Jungo, Oliver Zibung and Daniel Roth in Rolf Sethe and others (eds), *Kommentar zum Finanzmarktinfrastrukturgesetz FinfraG* (SK FinfraG, 1st edn, Schulthess 2017) Art 4 para 12.

1952 Jungo, Zibung and Roth (n 1951) SK FinfraG Art 4 para 16; Zulauf and Kuhn (n 1856) 82–3.

1953 Schleiffer and Schärli, 'Organisation und Betrieb einzelner Finanzmarktinfrastrukturen' (n 1866) § 22 paras 162–3.

1954 Schott and Sester (n 57) § 22 para 24; Alois Rimle, *Recht des schweizerischen Finanzmarktes: Ein Grundriss für die Praxis* (Schulthess 2004) 25.

1955 Bundesrat, 'Botschaft zum Finanzmarktinfrastrukturgesetz (FinfraG)' (n 22) BBl. 2014 7516, 7540; FINMA, 'Rundschreiben 2018/xx „Organisierte Handelssysteme": Erläuterungsbericht' (Bern, 28 September 2016) 41; Favre and Kramer (n

DLT trading facilities or trading venues as well as recognized (foreign) trading venues. Thus, an indirect form of supervision is exercised by FINMA.[1956] Under Article 43(2) FinfraG, no authorization is required for the operation of a CH-OTF within a financial group if the entity operating the CH-OTF is controlled directly by a financial market infrastructure and is subject to consolidated FINMA supervision. In this case, group supervision substitutes the entity supervision.[1957]

The authorization as a bank, securities dealer, DLT trading facility, trading venue or another financial market infrastructure also allows for the operation of a CH-OTF.[1958] Article 43 FinfraG ties the oversight of the operator to the oversight of the CH-OTF and subjects the operator to the additional requirements under Article 44ff FinfraG. The operator's authorization as a bank, securities trader, trading venue or another financial market infrastructure is contingent upon the compliance with the OTF-specific requirements just as much as on the requirements under the operator's specific regime.[1959] For banks the general authorization requirements are set out in BankG, for securities firm in FINIG, and for trading venues in FinfraG.[1960]

IV. Trading Obligations for Shares and Derivatives

Regulating dark trading requires multiple regulatory means. Besides creating a broad landscape of trading systems that can capture all organized trading and subject such trading systems with organized trading to trade transparency rules to fuel the price formation process, regulators can use trading obligations as another means to limit unregulated dark trading in the OTC-space.[1961] In modern financial markets with multiple trading systems competing for order flow, concentration rules that favor pivotal

---

566) SK FinfraG Art 43 paras 1, 17; Schären, Dobrauz-Saldapenna and Liebi (n 1876) 199.

1956 Hochstrasser (n 11) 312; Vogel, Heiz and Luthiger, *OFK FinfraG/BEG Kommentar* (n 1851) OFK FinfraG Art 43 paras 1ff.

1957 Vogel, Heiz and Luthiger, *OFK FinfraG/BEG Kommentar* (n 1851) OFK FinfraG Art 43 para 5; Favre and Kramer (n 566) SK FinfraG Art 43 para 18.

1958 Bundesrat, 'Botschaft zum Finanzmarktinfrastrukturgesetz (FinfraG)' (n 22) BBl. 2014, 7540; Favre and Kramer (n 566) SK FinfraG Art 43 para 2.

1959 Favre and Kramer (n 566) SK FinfraG Art 43 para 2.

1960 ibid SK FinfraG Art 43 para 16.

1961 See, for instrance, Article 23 MiFIR under EU law.

(national) exchanges are no longer feasible to avoid liquidity from seeping into the OTC-space.[1962] To maintain competition but favor trading on organized trading systems over trading in the OTC-space, trading obligations for shares and derivates are a proper and less intrusive measure since they have a steering effect on liquidity away from less regulated OTC markets towards organized trading systems.[1963] The European Union uses this tool under MiFID II/MiFIR by having a trading obligation for both shares (Article 23 MiFIR) and derivatives (Article 28 MiFIR).[1964]

1. No Trading Obligation for Shares under Swiss Law

In spite of FinfraG's general objective closely aligning with MiFID II/MiFIR under EU law for attaining market access through an equivalence decision by the EU Commission, Swiss law did not adopt the trading obligation for shares pursuant to Article 23 MiFIR under EU law. This provision was introduced under MiFID II/MiFIR as an additional measure to limit unregulated dark trading by BCNs in the OTC-space.[1965] Article 23 MiFIR was also the vehicle through which the European Union denied Swiss trading systems the classification as an equivalent third-country trading venue eligible for trading EU financial instruments bound by the trading obligation and thereby blocked the Swiss access to the EU market.[1966] The political reasons behind this are, however, more complex and strongly influenced by political negotiations over the EU-Swiss Institutional Framework Agreement which ultimately failed.[1967]

By not implementing a similar trading obligation for shares, Swiss law does not have a similarly strong mechanism for consolidation of trading in shares on transparent trading systems as EU law does. Despite this

1962 Moloney, *EU Securities and Financial Markets Regulation* (n 4) 434.

1963 ibid 468.

1964 On the trading obligations for shares and derivates under EU law see above Part II § 6 B.IV.2 and C.VII.4.

1965 Cf. Recital 11 MiFIR.

1966 Zulauf and Kuhn (n 1856) 84–5; Marco Toni and Lea Hungerbühler, 'Neue Handelspflicht für Aktien in der EU: Ist der Schweizer Rechtsrahmen für Handelsplätze äquivalent?' [2017] GesKR 205.

1967 Zulauf and Kuhn (n 1856) 85; Khan and Stafford (n 1857); European Commission, *Press Release: Commission Statement on the decision by the Swiss Federal Council to terminate the negotiations of the EU-Swiss Institutional Framework Agreement* (n 1857).

lack, Swiss law provides a more extensive CH-OTF category that does not rely on limiting minimum thresholds with regard to its trading activity.[1968] Thus, the CH-OTF, by design, reaches further in the OTC-space and captures trading on a trading system that would have been steered from the OTC-realm to a trading system under Article 23 MiFIR in the EU market.[1969] However, this effect is rather a passive one which may not have the same draining effect on OTC dark trading as the trading obligation for shares. If, therefore, the legislator or FINMA finds rising levels of OTC dark trading in Swiss shares trading, it should consider whether implementing a trading obligation may improve market efficiency, especially regarding price formation. This could become necessary if the qualitative CH-OTF definition which does not include spontaneous trading that is not planned in advance (ad hoc-trading)[1970] is gamed by BCNs in a similar manner as the SI-definition has been under MiFID I.[1971]

2. Trading Obligation for Derivatives under Swiss Law

Under EU law, the second trading obligation is the trading obligation for derivatives pursuant to Article 28 MiFIR.[1972] Swiss law adopted a trading obligation for derivatives under Articles 112 ff FinfraG.[1973] Unlike the trading obligation for shares, the trading obligation for derivatives was agreed upon by the G20 at the 2009 Pittsburgh Summit as a response to the concurrently unfolding the Global Financial Crisis of 2008-09.[1974] After the investment bank Lehman Brothers defaulted and the insurance company AIG got into financial turmoil due to activities in bilaterally traded OTC-derivatives

---

1968 Schären, Dobrauz-Saldapenna and Liebi (n 1876) 198.

1969 Studer and Vollenweider (n 1910) BSK FinfraG Art 42 para 44; Favre and Kramer (n 566) SK FinfraG Art 42 para 15.

1970 FINMA, 'Circular 2018/1 Organised trading facilities' (n 1866) 4 para 7.

1971 Moloney, *EU Securities and Financial Markets Regulation* (n 4) 446ff; See above Part II § 6 A.II.2.

1972 Rashid Bahar in Rolf Watter and Rashid Bahar (eds), *Basler Kommentar Finanzmarktaufsichtsgesetz, Finanzmarktinfrastrukturgesetz* (3rd edn, Helbing & Lichtenhahn Verlag 2019) FinfraG Art 112 para 3; See above Part II § 6 B.V.2.

1973 ibid BSK FinfraG Art 112 para 2.

1974 Kuhn, 'Die Regulierung des Derivatehandels im künftigen Finanzmarktinfrastrukturgesetz' (n 1853) 176; Marco Häusermann and Bertrand G Schott in Rolf Sethe and others (eds), *Kommentar zum Finanzmarktinfrastrukturgesetz FinfraG* (SK FinfraG, 1st edn, Schulthess 2017) Art 112 para 5.

thrusting risk into the entire market, the G20 decided to take aligned regulatory action.[1975]

For the crucial management of counterparty risk, rules for central clearing have been adopted.[1976] Furthermore, the G20 also agreed that the opacity of the OTC-derivatives markets also added to the instability of the system because regulators and other market participants were unable to fully anticipate the amount of trading occurring and the risk building up in those markets.[1977] To allow a clearer view, certain trading in derivatives should be brought to trading systems where they can be subjected to trade transparency rules. Thus, the trading obligation also serves the purpose of limiting dark trading in derivatives.[1978]

Even though not a member of the G20, Switzerland adopted the trading obligation for derivatives because the United States and the European Union were frontrunners in this field and Swiss derivatives trading occurs largely with foreign counterparties, at that time, primarily with counterparties in the European Union, to which Switzerland aimed to maintain market access.[1979]

Pursuant to Article 112 FinfraG, counterparties must trade all derivatives[1980] in accordance with Article 113 FinfraG either via a FINMA-authorized or -recognized trading venue or a FINMA-authorized or -recognized operator of a CH-OTF.[1981] This duty however does not apply to transactions

1975 Häusermann and Schott (n 1974) SK FinfraG Art 112 para 5; Seema G Sharma, 'Over-the-Counter Derivatives: A New Era of Financial Regulation' (2011) 17 Law and Business Review of the Americas 279, 280.

1976 Under Swiss law see Articles 97ff FinfraG.

1977 Häusermann and Schott (n 1974) SK FinfraG Art 112 para 9. See also Hans Kuhn, 'Kollisionsrechtliche Aspekte der Derivateregulierung' [2014] SZW 362, 364; Kuhn, 'Die Regulierung des Derivatehandels im künftigen Finanzmarktinfrastrukturgesetz' (n 1853) 162; Rashid Bahar, 'Derivative Trading under the Federal Act on Financial Markets Infrastructure' [2015] GesKR 479ff.

1978 Bundesrat, 'Botschaft zum Finanzmarktinfrastrukturgesetz (FinfraG)' (n 22) BBl. 2014, 7491–2, 7580; Häusermann and Schott (n 1974) SK FinfraG Art 112 paras 2, 5.

1979 Bahar (n 1972) BSK FinfraG Art 112 para 4; Favre and Kramer (n 566) SK FinfraG. Vor Art 93 paras 5ff; Kuhn, 'Die Regulierung des Derivatehandels im künftigen Finanzmarktinfrastrukturgesetz' (n 1853) 162.

1980 Swiss law defines "derivatives" under Article 2(c) FinfraG as *'(...) financial contracts whose value depends on one or several underlying assets and which are not cash transactions.'*

1981 Bahar (n 1972) BSK FinfraG Art 112 para 11; Häusermann and Schott (n 1974) SK FinfraG Art 112 paras 41, 47.

with small counterparties or transactions between such counterparties.[1982] In spite of the voluntary adaption to EU law, the Swiss legislator allowed for the trading obligation for derivatives to be deferred to be able to monitor its international development, especially with regard to the implementation of the trading obligation for derivatives under EU law (Article 164 FinfraG).[1983]

Although Switzerland enacted the trading obligation on 1 August 2017,[1984] the practical effects of Article 112 FinfraG depend on FINMA who shall determine which derivatives have to be traded via a trading venue or a trading facility under Article 113 FinfraG.[1985] In doing so, it shall take into account the derivatives' degree of legal and operational standardization, their liquidity, their trading volume, the availability of pricing information in the given category and the counterparty risks associated with them.[1986] However, no trading duty may be imposed for derivatives that are not admitted for trading by any corresponding trading venue or trading facility since this indicates that those derivatives are not able to sustain multilateral trading due to an illiquid market.[1987] Moreover, currency swaps and forward transactions, provided they are not settled on a payment versus payment basis, are also not eligible to be subjected to the trading obligation by FINMA.[1988]

After the Federal Council announced its review of FinfraG in the coming years in September 2018, FINMA decided to refrain from determining any classes of derivatives that shall be subject to the trading obligation until this revision process will have been completed.[1989] Thus, currently, Swiss law merely offers a legal provision setting out a trading obligation for

---

1982 Article 112(2) FinfraG; Häusermann and Schott (n 1974) SK FinfraG Art 112 para 47.

1983 Bundesrat, 'Botschaft zum Finanzmarktinfrastrukturgesetz (FinfraG)' (n 22) BBl. 2014, 7580.

1984 FINMA, 'FINMA-Aufsichtsmitteilung 01/2020: Finanzmarktinfrastrukturgesetz und -verordnung: Derivatehandel' (Bern, 20 March 2020) 3.

1985 Häusermann and Schott (n 1974) SK FinfraG Art 112 para 50.

1986 Article 113(1)(2) FinfraG; Bahar (n 1972) BSK FinfraG Art 113 paras 9ff.; Häusermann and Schott (n 1974) SK FinfraG Art 113 para 11.

1987 Bahar (n 1972) BSK FinfraG Art 113 para 7; Häusermann and Schott (n 1974) SK FinfraG Art 113 paras 17ff; Delphine Meylan and Ariel Ben Hattar, 'Le concept de dérivé dans la LIMF: Les contours flous d'une notion au coeur de la réglementation financière' [2018] GesKR 205, 212.

1988 Article 113(3) FinfraG; Häusermann and Schott (n 1974) SK FinfraG Art 113 paras 17ff.

1989 FINMA, 'FINMA-Aufsichtsmitteilung 01/2020' (n 1984) 3.

derivatives but, in practice, it has not yet been implemented. Consequently, the OTC-derivatives market has not been regulated in a manner similar to the European Union and the United States, thus allowing large amounts of unregulated dark trading in those instruments beyond the regulatory perimeter of FinfraG.

V. Self-Regulatory Powers

1. Article 27 FinfraG: Principle of Self-Regulation

According to Article 27(1) FinfraG, trading venues shall establish their own regulatory and supervisory organization which is appropriate for their activities and is subject to FINMA supervision. With this provision, Swiss financial markets law follows the tradition of self-regulation which was formerly a domain of Swiss exchanges,[1990] but has been broadened to trading venues, i.e., Swiss exchanges and CH-MTFs (Article 26(a) FinfraG).[1991] While CH-OTFs do not possess self-regulatory powers, they must perform similar organizational functions (cf. Articles 43ff FinfraG).[1992]

The Swiss brand of self-regulation does not give free rein to trading venues. It sets two distinct limits: first, with regard to Article 27 FinfraG, FINMA uses the term of 'obligatory self-regulation'[1993] to emphasize that the transferal of self-regulatory power is coupled with an obligation of the trading venues to use their self-regulatory power, instead of leaving matters unregulated to provide them with more liberties.[1994] The second limitation is the subjection of self-regulatory powers to FINMA's supervision which is primarily exercised by the obligation of trading venues to submit their regulations and amendments to FINMA for approval (Article 27(4) FinfraG).[1995] FINMA's approval process for newly drafted and amended regulations is laid out in Article 25 FinfraV. The right of approval, however,

1990 See former Article 4 BEHG.

1991 Schott and Winkler (n 70) SK FinfraG Art 27 paras 1, 11.

1992 See below Part II § 7 C.III; Schott and Winkler (n 70) SK FinfraG Art 28 para 6. Differently: Studer and Vollenweider (n 1910) BSK FinfraG Art 42 para 14 who see self-regulatory powers with CH-OTFs despite not falling in the scope of Article 27(1) FinfraG.

1993 Schott and Winkler (n 70) SK FinfraG Art 27 para 6: *'obligatorische Selbstregulierung'*.

1994 ibid SK FinfraG Art 27 para 6.

1995 ibid SK FinfraG Art 27 paras 1, 27.

does not encompass all regulations. FINMA's approval is only required for regulations which are important to fulfill the purposes of Article 1(2) FinfraG.[1996] No separate, additional approval is required for downstream regulations, such as operational or technical regulations. It is sufficient if these are based on already-approved regulations which are linked to the legal purpose of protection.[1997]

While Article 27 FinfraG only sets out the principle of self-regulation, the individual self-regulatory powers are conferred by special provisions scattered throughout FinfraG: inter alia, trading venues have to issue regulations concerning the organization of orderly and transparent trading (Article 28 FinfraG), the admission of participants (Article 34 FinfraG) and the admission of securities to trading on either an exchange or a CH-MTF (Articles 35, 36 FinfraG).[1998]

2. Article 28 FinfraG: Self-Regulation and Dark Trading

Of special importance for the issue of lit and dark trading are the regulations on the organization of orderly and transparent trading according to Article 28 FinfraG. Those regulations are important to fulfill the purposes of Article 1(2) FinfraG, where transparency is particularly mentioned. And thus, those regulations are subject to FINMA's approval.[1999]

As the rules for pre-trade and post-trade transparency under Article 29 FinfraG show, the legislator sets limitations on self-regulatory power by setting the ground-rules of trade transparency marking the difference between lit and dark trading.[2000] Only the details of trade transparency are left to the self-regulatory power of the trading venue. Nevertheless, those details may have a significant effect on how much dark trading can occur in a trading system and whether or not the price discovery process is affected by these decisions.

1996 Bundesrat, 'Botschaft zum Finanzmarktinfrastrukturgesetz (FinfraG)' (n 22) BBl. 2014, 7532; Schott and Winkler (n 70) SK FinfraG Art 27 para 27.

1997 Schott and Winkler (n 70) SK FinfraG Art 27 para 27.

1998 Schleiffer and Schärli, 'Organisation und Betrieb einzelner Finanzmarktinfrastrukturen' (n 1866) § 22 para 175. On the legal nature of regulations see the comprehensive description in Schott and Winkler (n 70) SK FinfraG Art 25 para 23.

1999 Kägi (n 50) BSK FinfraG Art 28 paras 10, 14; Schott and Winkler (n 70) SK FinfraG Art 28 paras 7–8.

2000 The transparency regime under Article 29 FinfraG is discussed in detail below, see Part II § 7 C.II.2.

While the detailed discussion is left to the subsequent part on trade transparency, it shall be noted that the Swiss system of self-regulation puts the regulatory regime closer to the United States which employs self-regulation through SROs to include the subjects of regulatory measures into the regulatory process.[2001] Often, self-regulation is motivated by the objectives of including specific knowledge that is assumed to be concentrated in the hands of the industry rather than regulatory agencies, increased approval rates from the ones regulated if they have had a say in the promulgation of the rules, and faster and less bureaucratic adaptation to changes in the business and technology.[2002]

The European Union, on the other hand, rather frowns upon self-regulatory elements. Neither MiFID II nor MiFIR refer to self-regulatory elements and its incorporation would contradict its approach of a single rulebook and a level-playing field among different jurisdictions.[2003] The often identified disadvantages of self-regulation are conflicts between public and private interests, especially if the regulating private entities and the regulated entities have similar interests that are at odds with public interests, an uneven playing field due to several different regulations; and the risk of regulatory arbitrage.[2004]

The issue of non-alignment of public and private interests might be problematic with trade transparency and dark trading: While the public has an interest in high levels of transparency and the publication of market prices to use both trade transparency and market prices as beacons that guide the investing public through the rough waters of the market much like lighthouses that provide a common good of safety for maritime traffic, the private interests of trading systems can be different. Trading venues prefer to create at least some pre- and post-trade transparency to enable trading on the trading venue (disregarding price-importing trading systems for a moment). However, they are not interested in sharing their trading and price information with the public for free, since others could free-ride

2001 Schott and Winkler (n 70) SK FinfraG Art 27 paras 8–9; Peter Nobel, *Aktienrecht: Systematische Darstellung* (Berner Kommentar, Stämpfli Verlag 2017) 417–8.

2002 Schott and Winkler (n 70) SK FinfraG Art 27 para 3. See also Wohlers Wolfgang, 'Selbstregulierung – Aufsichtsrecht – Strafrecht: (Ziel-) Konflikte und Interdependenzen' in Jürg-Beat Ackermann and Wolfgang Wohlers (eds), *Finanzmarkt ausser Kontrolle?: Selbstregulierung - Aufsichtsrecht - Strafrecht.* 3. Zürcher Tagung zum Wirtschaftsstrafrecht (Schulthess 2009) 289.

2003 Daeniker and Waller (n 1865) BSK FinfraG Art 27 para 57; Schott and Winkler (n 70) SK FinfraG Art 27 para 3.

2004 Schott and Winkler (n 70) SK FinfraG Art 27 para 10.

their price information, which is a costly endeavor for them and for which they want to charge their traders. Assigning a right of exclusive usage, a 'property right', may solve this issue of a (quasi-)public good for trading venues. In addition, as offering lit trading is a service worth selling for trading venues, offering dark trading services are too. It is therefore in the trading venues' interest to define exemptions from trade transparency that serve their clients rather than the public or even market quality. Thus, it can be expected from a regulatory design, as the one in Switzerland, that trading venues will adopt exceptions from pre-trade transparency that maximize their fee-revenue from selling dark trading services. A limitation to block orders only or even a device like the volume cap mechanism under Article 5 MiFIR in the European Union cannot be expected.

C. Trade Transparency Regime

I. Introduction

The Swiss trade transparency regime enhances efficient price discovery as well as public trust in fair and orderly financial markets.[2005] Since its scope decides which orders and trades fuel the price formation process and which remain hidden from the public eye, the Swiss transparency regime also differentiates between lit and dark trading.[2006] Structurally, the Swiss transparency regime can be sub-divided into requirements for trading venues under Article 29 FinfraG and requirements for CH-OTFs under Article 46 FinfraG.

Under FinfraG, Swiss law is closely aligned with international standards as well as foreign law – especially EU law – which was a central objective for reforming the transparency regime.[2007] This alignment rests on two motifs: first, in anticipation of MiFID II/MiFIR in the European Union, the Swiss legislator sought to implement a similar transparency regime to the one in the European Union to receive market access via the recognition of

2005 See Art 1(2) FinfraG; Bundesrat, 'Botschaft zum Finanzmarktinfrastrukturgesetz (FinfraG)' (n 22) BBl. 2014, 7532; Schott and Winkler (n 70) SK FinfraG Art 29 para 9.

2006 See Schott and Winkler (n 70) SK FinfraG Art 29 para 16.

2007 See Bundesrat, 'Botschaft zum Finanzmarktinfrastrukturgesetz (FinfraG)' (n 22) BBl. 2014, 7533.

equivalency.[2008] As discussed above, this expectation was frustrated when the European Union denied equivalency status after the negotiations over the EU-Swiss Institutional Framework Agreement stalled and eventually failed.[2009] Nevertheless, EU law remains an important source for the interpretation of the Swiss trade transparency regime.[2010] The second motif for an alignment with international standards is that Switzerland and its institutions are members to international standard setters such as IOSCO.[2011] In order for the Swiss financial market to maintain a good reputation, it is important for the Swiss legislator to ensure high international standards for financial markets.[2012] Insofar, the principles of IOSCO, especially the principles for dark liquidity, will provide valuable insights on the transparency regime under FinfraG.[2013]

II. Trade Transparency for Trading Venues

1. Structure of Trade Transparency Rules

a) Three Layers of Regulation

The trade transparency regime for trading venues under Article 29 FinfraG must be regarded as an aspect of the objective of transparent trading under Article 28(1) FinfraG which binds trading venues when they promulgate their trading regulations.[2014] Insofar, Article 28(1) FinfraG sets out that, in principle, transparent trading is a matter of self-regulation. Article 29 FinfraG, on the other hand, defines core obligations for the provision of trade transparency and delegates certain aspects to the Federal Council

2008 ibid BBl. 2014, 7496; Kägi (n 50) BSK FinfraG Art 29 para 13; Schott and Winkler (n 70) SK FinfraG Art 29 paras 65, 68; see also Nina Arquint, 'Internationalisierung der Finanzmarktaufsicht' [2014] GesKR 131 132; Brunetti and others (n 1854) 25.

2009 See above Part II § 7 A.

2010 See Kägi (n 50) BSK FinfraG Art 29 para 14; Schott and Winkler (n 70) SK FinfraG Art 29 paras 69ff.

2011 Kägi (n 50) BSK FinfraG Art 29 para 12.

2012 Bundesrat, 'Botschaft zum Finanzmarktinfrastrukturgesetz (FinfraG)' (n 22) BBl. 2014, 7490ff; Kägi (n 50) BSK FinfraG Art 29 para 12.

2013 Kägi (n 50) BSK FinfraG Art 29 para 12.

2014 ibid BSK FinfraG Art 29 para 9.

(*'Bundesrat'*) under its ordinance power, Article 29(3) FinfraG.[2015] Thus, to grasp the full scope of trade transparency for trading venues under Swiss law, three layers must be considered: the stipulations under federal law (FinfraG), the stipulations of the Federal Council under the federal ordinance (FinfraV), and the stipulations of the trading regulations set out by the trading venues within their residual self-regulatory power.

Because of this three-layer-approach, the stipulations of Swiss federal law do not conclusively inform about the actual scope of both lit and dark trading in Swiss financial markets. Instead, Swiss trading venues often have to close the 'last mile' of regulation.[2016] Putting the regulatory responsibility in the hands of trading venues may result in rules that do not restrict dark trading in a way that fully reflects the public interest in having transparent markets but rather allows for deviating regulations between multiple trading venues, thus opening the door to regulatory arbitrage.

b) Pre- and Post-Trade Transparency

While the differentiation between pre- and post-trade transparency rules is familiar from both US and EU law, the introduction of a dedicated provision for pre-trade transparency under Article 29(1) FinfraG is a novelty under Swiss law and shows its motivation to promote pre-trade as well as post-trade transparency, which has its own provision under Article 29(2) FinfraG.[2017] While Article 5 of the former Swiss Federal Act on Exchange and Securities Trading (*'Bundesgesetz über den Börsen und Effektenhandel'* - BEHG) only had a dedicated rule for post-trade transparency,[2018] the new legal framework shows the Swiss motivation to align with foreign law, especially EU law,[2019] and its willingness to abide by international standards since the IOSCO principles also recommend promoting both pre-trade and

2015 ibid BSK FinfraG Art 29 paras 9–10.

2016 Schott and Winkler (n 70) SK FinfraG Art 29 para 38.

2017 Kägi (n 50) BSK FinfraG Art 29 paras 2, 16; Schott and Winkler (n 70) SK FinfraG Art 29 para 25.

2018 Rolf Watter and Urs Kägi in Rolf Watter and Nedim P Vogt (eds), *Basler Kommentar Börsengesetz, Finanzmarktaufsichtsgesetz, Art. 161, 161bis, 305bis und 305ter Strafgesetzbuch* (2nd edn, Helbing & Lichtenhahn Verlag 2011) BEHG Art 5 paras 46, 49ff; Kägi (n 50) BSK FinfraG Art 29 para 2; Schott and Winkler (n 70) SK FinfraG Art 29 para 23.

2019 Bundesrat, 'Botschaft zum Finanzmarktinfrastrukturgesetz (FinfraG)' (n 22) BBl. 2014, 7533; Schott and Winkler (n 70) SK FinfraG Art 29 para 25.

post-trade transparency.[2020] With the implementation of an unequivocal pre-trade transparency rule – which does not leave the matter of pre-trade transparency mostly to the self-regulatory power of trading venues – the Swiss legislator made a significant step towards containing dark trading, which is also a central objective of FinfraG.[2021]

2. Pre-Trade Transparency Rule

a) General Scope of Article 29(1) FinfraG

Under Article 29(1) FinfraG, the trading venue shall publish the bid and offer prices for shares and other securities in real time, as well as the sizes of the trading position at these prices.[2022] As the addressee of the provision, FinfraG broadened the scope from Swiss exchanges, which were the sole addressees under the former Article 5 BEHG, to trading venues, which encompasses Swiss exchanges and CH-MTFs.[2023] With this uniform rule, FinfraG creates a level playing field among incumbent exchanges and new market entrants, which are commonly CH-MTFs, to allow for fair competition to unfold. Moreover, the scope of Article 29(1) FinfraG avoids a blind spot in the transparency regulation where organized trading can slip through the cracks of the regulation and operate as unregulated dark trading. Even though CH-OTFs do not count among trading systems, the Swiss transparency regime accounts for this form of organized trading under Article 46 FinfraG, which is discussed below.[2024]

As the marketplace operator, a trading venue must publish the trading interests on both the bid and offer side of the market with its price and size, which means the overall volume of either the order or quotation, under Article 29(1) FinfraG.[2025] The Federal Council determined in Article 27(2) FinfraV that the trading venue must publish the five best bid and offer

2020 IOSCO, 'Principles for Dark Liquidity' (n 12) 25; Kägi (n 50) BSK FinfraG Art 29 para 12.
2021 Bundesrat, 'Botschaft zum Finanzmarktinfrastrukturgesetz (FinfraG)' (n 22) BBl. 2014, 7532–3.
2022 Article 29(1) FinfraG.
2023 Schott and Winkler (n 70) SK FinfraG Art 29 para 4.
2024 See below Part II § 7 C.III. Schott and Winkler (n 70) SK FinfraG Art 29 para 4.
2025 Bundesrat, 'Botschaft zum Finanzmarktinfrastrukturgesetz (FinfraG)' (n 22) BBl. 2014, 7532–3.

prices for shares and their respective order volumes.[2026] This is similar to the pre-trade transparency requirements for quote-driven systems under Article 3(1) and Table 1 of Annex I of CDR (EU) 2017/587 the European Union,[2027] which requires publishing 'at least' the five best bid and offer prices allowing deeper insights into the order book. Despite this greater flexibility under EU law compared to the strictness of Swiss law, showing the top five bid and offer prices appears to be a reasonable compromise to allow enough transparency with regard to the depth of the order book but also to protect orders that possess limit prices further off the midpoint of the bid-ask-spread from adverse effects caused by pre-trade transparency, since those orders are often larger.[2028] It is therefore also common for trading venues in the European Union to provide pre-trade transparency for no more than the top five bid and offer prices in their order books.[2029]

However, the strict obligation to show the top five bid and offer prices under Article 27(2) FinfraV does not account for trading systems other than order-driven ones. For instance, market makers in quote-driven systems often show only one bid and one offer quote for an instrument for which Article 3(1) and Table 1 of Annex I of CDR (EU) 2017/587 accounts under EU law.[2030] Since Swiss law does not have a similar calibration of the trade transparency regime while it is supposed to align with EU law, Article 27(2) FinfraV is to be interpreted narrowly in this regard requiring no more than EU law.[2031] This interpretation should also be adopted by Swiss trading venues in their trading regulations.

2026 Kägi (n 50) BSK FinfraG Art 29 para 27; Schott and Winkler (n 70) SK FinfraG Art 29 para 27.

2027 Gebauer (n 94) MiFIR Art 3 para 24; Kägi (n 50) BSK FinfraG Art 29 para 27; Schott and Winkler (n 70) SK FinfraG Art 29 para 27.

2028 Cf. Picot, Bortenlänger and Röhrl (n 77) 24; Rudolph and Röhrl (n 51) 208.

2029 See for instance the Exchange Rules for the Frankfurter Wertpapierbörse, § 117(1) Exchange Rules for the Frankfurter Wertpapierbörse (FWB) 1 July 2019 (Frankfurter Wertpapierbörse).

2030 Kägi (n 50) BSK FinfraG Art 29 para 27; Schott and Winkler (n 70) SK FinfraG Art 29 para 27.

2031 Kägi (n 50) BSK FinfraG Art 29 para 27; Schott and Winkler (n 70) SK FinfraG Art 29 para 27.

b) Indications of Interest

Furthermore, Article 27(3) FinfraV requires the same pre-trade transparency information that applies to orders and quotes for actionable indications of interests. Also under Swiss law, the term 'actionable IOI' refers to a message about a limit order residing in the market which is sent to one or several selected counterparties to enable transactions with those orders.[2032] As discussed under US and EU law, those IOIs have been used by dark pool operators to lure liquidity to rather illiquid markets and have caused an uneven playing field with regard to information and eroded investor trust.[2033] For this reason, IOSCO recommended that national regulation should include IOIs into the scope of the pre-trade transparency regime, which both the EU and Switzerland have done, while the US still fails to implement this measure.[2034] Insofar, Switzerland also delivered on its promise to take measures to address the issues of dark pools which motivated FinfraG.[2035]

c) Traded on the Trading Venue

A striking difference to Article 3(1) MiFIR under EU law is that Article 29(1) FinfraG does not limit the scope of pre-trade transparency to shares and other securities that are traded on the trading venue in question.[2036] Nevertheless, by way of a narrow interpretation of the provision, this requirement must be read into the wording of Article 29(1) FinfraG to avoid an overbroad and unreasonable obligation of pre-trade transparency. Since pre-trade transparency serves the purpose of orderly operations on the trading venue, it only has to publish pre-trade transparency for instruments that are actually traded within its systems not any shares traded somewhere.[2037]

2032 Schott and Winkler (n 70) SK FinfraG Art 29 para 28; IOSCO, 'Principles for Dark Liquidity' (n 12) 27 fn 89.

2033 IOSCO, 'Principles for Dark Liquidity' (n 12) 23.

2034 ibid 15, 27. See Mahoney and Rauterberg (n 118) 244.

2035 Bundesrat, 'Botschaft zum Finanzmarktinfrastrukturgesetz (FinfraG)' (n 22) BBl. 2014, 7499.

2036 Kägi (n 50) BSK FinfraG Art 29 para 17.

2037 ibid BSK FinfraG Art 29 para 17.

d) Subjected Instruments: Lit Trading for Shares, Dark Trading for other Securities

According to Article 29(1) FinfraG, trading venues must publish pre-trade transparency data for shares and securities other than shares. However, this broad scope, similar to the pre-trade transparency requirements for equity and non-equity instruments under Articles 3 and 8 MiFIR in the European Union, is limited by Article 29(3) FinfraG.[2038] Since Article 29(3) (a) FinfraG defers the regulatory power to the Federal Council to determine whether securities other than shares are subject to pre-trade transparency, only pre-trade transparency in shares is mandatory under Article 29(1) FinfraG.[2039] The Federal Council enacted Article 27(1) FinfraV which only requires pre-trade transparency for shares traded on trading venues leaving the trading in other securities in the dark since no mandatory pre-trade transparency rule applies under Swiss federal law. A rather rudimentary rule like this is not comparable to the vast pre-trade transparency regime under MiFIR,[2040] and also lags behind the pre-trade transparency rules in US law which apply to all NMS securities.[2041]

Thus, Swiss law only sets up lit trading as the default rule for trading in shares; whereas for trading other securities, the default rule is dark trading as far as the government-made law is concerned. Originally, the Swiss legislator planned a more ambitious pre-trade transparency regime which is documented by the draft-version of FinfraG that had a pre-trade transparency rule for both shares and other securities.[2042] In the consultation process, however, the industry feared that the implementation of a far-reaching pre-trade transparency rule stretching beyond the liquid markets for shares was too risky, given that the EU also debated the scope of its then still planned pre-trade transparency rule for non-equity

2038 ibid BSK FinfraG Art 29 para 16; Schott and Winkler (n 70) SK FinfraG Art 29 paras 39ff.

2039 Bundesrat, 'Botschaft zum Finanzmarktinfrastrukturgesetz (FinfraG)' (n 22) BBl. 2014, 7501; Kägi (n 50) BSK FinfraG Art 29 para 17.

2040 See above Part II § 6 C.

2041 See above Part II § 5 E.

2042 See Article 27 of Draft-FinfraV; EFD, 'Erläuterungsbericht zur Verordnung über die Finanzmarktinfrastrukturen und das Marktverhalten im Effekten- und Derivatehandel: (Finanzmarktinfrastrukturverordnung, FinfraV)' (20 August 2015) 15–6; Schott and Winkler (n 70) SK FinfraG Art 29 para 39.

instruments.[2043] Since the level 2 measures that calibrated the pre-trade transparency rules had not been enacted yet, the Swiss legislator decided to enact a pre-trade transparency rule for shares only and tasked the Federal Council with enacting a properly calibrated pre-trade transparency rule for other securities when the European Union had tested the waters with their new rule.[2044] This way, the legislator wanted to account for the investors' interest in transparent trading – especially addressing dark trading – while avoiding adopting a rule from EU law that was yet unclear with regard to its scope.[2045]

Despite the European Union operating under the new transparency regime since 3 January 2018 without experiencing adverse effects, the Federal Council has not yet broadened the scope of pre-trade transparency under Article 29(3)(a) FinfraG and Article 27(1) FinfraV sofar. One reason for this may be the denied market access by the European Union which rendered further adaptations to foreign law futile. Another aspect is, however, that the most important trading venues, SIX Swiss Exchange and BX Swiss, adopted pre-trade transparency rules in their respective regulations that encompass shares and other securities for their transparent trading segment.[2046] The Swiss exchange, thus, aligned with EU law and international standards within their self-regulatory powers and avoided having significant amounts of liquidity turn into dark trading on their venues. Insofar, the initial skepticism towards the alignment of public and private

2043 Bundesrat, 'Botschaft zum Finanzmarktinfrastrukturgesetz (FinfraG)' (n 22) BBl. 2014, 7501–2; EFD, 'Bericht des Eidgenössischen Finanzdepartements EFD über die Anhörung zur Finanzmarktinfrastrukturverordnung (FinfraV)' (25 November 2015) 6; EFD, 'Erläuterungsbericht zur Verordnung über die Finanzmarktinfrastrukturen und das Marktverhalten im Effekten- und Derivatehandel: (Finanzmarktinfrastrukturverordnung, FinfraV)' (25 November 2015) 6; Kägi (n 50) BSK FinfraG Art 29 paras 17–8; Schott and Winkler (n 70) SK FinfraG Art 29 para 39.

2044 Bundesrat, 'Botschaft zum Finanzmarktinfrastrukturgesetz (FinfraG)' (n 22) BBl. 2014, 7501–2; EFD, 'Erläuterungsbericht zur Verordnung über die Finanzmarktinfrastrukturen und das Marktverhalten im Effekten- und Derivatehandel' (n 2043) 5–6; Kägi (n 50) BSK FinfraG Art 29 paras 17–8; Schott and Winkler (n 70) SK FinfraG Art 29 para 61; Vogel, Heiz and Luthiger, *OFK FinfraG/BEG Kommentar* (n 1851) OFK FinfraG Art 29 paras 6–7.

2045 Bundesrat, 'Botschaft zum Finanzmarktinfrastrukturgesetz (FinfraG)' (n 22) BBl. 2014, 7501–2.

2046 SIX Swiss Exchange, 'Trading Rules' (6 December 2021) Rule 10.8; BX Swiss, 'Handelsreglement der BX Swiss AG' (4 May 2018) Rule 9; BX Swiss, 'Weisung zum Handel an der BX Swiss AG' (20 July 2018) 3ff.

interests in the self-regulatory process appears to be unwarranted. Thus, the Swiss trading venues altered the decision of Swiss government-made law and set lit trading as the general default rule for trading in both shares and other securities.

Nevertheless, trusting in trading venues to 'close the last mile of regulation' may result in new market entrants that deviate from the welcome practice of the major exchanges and only offer pre-trade transparency for trading in shares but not for other securities. In this case, also the last line of defense, FINMA's approval of trading regulations under Article 27(4) FinfraG, will fail since FINMA will find it difficult to deny approving trading regulations that mirror the stipulations of FinfraG/FinfraV. Such events open the door not only to large amounts of dark trading but also to a fragmentation of the regulatory environment. This outcome should be avoided by amending Article 27(1) FinfraV.

3. Waivers from Pre-Trade Transparency

From the default rule of lit trading for shares, the Swiss transparency regime offers certain waivers from pre-trade transparency that allow for dark trading on trading venues. While FinfraG does not contain the waivers itself, the Swiss legislator tasked the Federal Council with determining exceptions from pre-trade and post-trade transparency, particularly in relation to securities transactions involving large volumes or those that are executed by the Swiss National Bank (SNB) according to Article 29(3) FinfraG.[2047] When determining such exceptions, the Federal Council shall also take recognized international standards and legal developments in foreign jurisdictions into account which shall allow for a flexible alignment with EU law on waivers as well.[2048]

a) Waivers

The Federal Council exercised its ordinance power when it formulated four waivers from pre-trade transparency under Article 27(4) FinfraV which a trading venue can adopt into its trading regulations. These waivers com-

2047 Bundesrat, 'Botschaft zum Finanzmarktinfrastrukturgesetz (FinfraG)' (n 22) BBl. 2014, 7533; Schott and Winkler (n 70) SK FinfraG Art 29 para 61.

2048 See Article 27(3) FinfraG; Schott and Winkler (n 70) SK FinfraG Art 29 para 61.

prise of *prima facie* old acquaintances under EU law: (a) a reference price waiver, (b) a negotiated trade waiver, (c) an order management facility waiver, and (d) a large in scale waiver.[2049]

Since the trading venue only can – but is not obliged to – adopt the enumerated waivers, the waiver regime of a trading venue can comprise of no waiver, some, or all of the abovementioned. However, different waivers from the ones enumerated under Article 27(4) FinfraV cannot be chosen since the enumeration is exhaustive.[2050]

aa) Reference Price Waiver

Pursuant to Article 27(4)(a) FinfraV, a trading venue can adopt a waiver from pre-trade transparency for reference price systems if the reference prices are widely published and considered as reliable by participants. By reference price system, the Federal Council means a trading system, i.e., a set of trading rules under which orders can be matched to a trade, that does not possess an internal price discovery mechanism. Instead, the trading system imports the price for order matching from one or several reference markets, for instance a transparent exchange.[2051]

Insofar, the Swiss reference price waiver is congruent with its sibling under EU law according to Article 4(1)(a) MiFIR. It even serves the same fundamental purpose of facilitating (larger) transactions of institutional investors and fund managers without incurring market impact costs.[2052] The rationale behind the waiver is that traders that set orders at an already known price do not have to offer pre-trade transparency because their price information is already reflected in the price.[2053]

In the MiFID I-review process, the reference price waiver was heavily debated and almost abolished because some Member States considered it prone to misuse.[2054] It was not only used to facilitate vulnerable (large)

2049 Kägi (n 50) BSK FinfraG Art 29 paras 21ff; Schott and Winkler (n 70) SK FinfraG Art 29 paras 32ff; Schott and Sester (n 57) § 22 para 101; Hochstrasser (n 11) 313.

2050 Kägi (n 50) BSK FinfraG Art 29 para 19; Schott and Winkler (n 70) SK FinfraG Art 29 paras 30–1.

2051 Kägi (n 50) BSK FinfraG Art 29 para 21; Schott and Winkler (n 70) SK FinfraG Art 29 para 32.

2052 Schott and Winkler (n 70) SK FinfraG Art 29 para 32.

2053 CESR, 'CESR Technical Advice to the European Commission in the Context of the MiFID Review - Equity Markets' (n 4) 10.

2054 Moloney, *EU Securities and Financial Markets Regulation* (n 4) 481.

orders that would otherwise have suffered market impact costs, but the reference price waiver was a welcome means for trading venue operators to offer dark trading for all sorts of financial instruments, regardless of its susceptibility to market impact costs.[2055] This issue is also present with the Swiss reference price waiver since it is not contingent to any order size requirement or any other measure that would suggest the propensity of suffering market impact. Using the reference price waiver solely requires a price import from another venue.

As restricting requirements may serve the prongs that demand the reference price to be 'widely published' and 'considered as reliable by participants', one might argue that those requirements disqualify prices that are taken from an insignificant venue, prices derived and merged from several trading venues, or prices at which the trading venue no longer matches orders, i.e., stale prices. The initial reference price waiver according to Article 18(1)(a) CR (EC) 1287/2006 under EU law also had the abovementioned restricting requirements and they proved to be insufficient to limit dark trading under this waiver.[2056] In the MiFID I-era, multiple reference prices were admitted by the national competent authorities, such as prices from smaller markets, prices that either represented the midpoint price, the volume weighted average price, the opening or closing price even during normal trading hours, the Primary Best Bid and Offer (PBBO) as well as a combination of multiple reference prices into an European Best Bid and Offer, which is an unofficial price unlike the US National Best Bid and Offer. With such variation in 'reference' prices, dark pools managed to offer significant price improvements under MiFID I rendering their services even more attractive.[2057] Since those prices were slightly different, it could no longer be argued that the price information of the dark orders is already known to the market. It could not be ruled out that some traders even targeted certain dark pools because they offered stale prices, such as the opening price, while the current price had already changed.

2055 CESR, 'CESR Technical Advice to the European Commission in the Context of the MiFID Review - Equity Markets' (n 4) 11.

2056 Schott and Winkler (n 70) SK FinfraG Art 29 para 32; Moloney, *EU Securities and Financial Markets Regulation* (n 4) 482. See also Recital 13 MiFIR; CESR, 'CESR Technical Advice to the European Commission in the Context of the MiFID Review - Equity Markets' (n 4) 10–1, 29–30; ESMA, 'Consultation Paper: MiFID II/MiFIR' (n 1581) 51.

2057 Banks (n 5) 108ff, 113–4; Francotte, Valiante and Lannoo (n 71) 60–1; Gomber and Gvozdevskiy (n 43) paras 14.53f.

For this reason, Article 4(1)(a), (2) MiFIR restricted the reference price waiver to midpoint prices of the most liquid trading venue for the respective instrument. And only if there is no such market, could the price be imported from the trading venue of first admittance to trading.[2058] Opening and closing prices can only be used outside the normal trading hours of the referenced trading venue.[2059] Artificial prices such as the EBBO can no longer be used.[2060]

Article 27(4)(a) FinfraV makes no such limitation to the eligibility of a reference price. Unlike the rule-based Article 4(1)(a), (2) MiFIR under current EU law, the Swiss waiver rather resembles its principle-based predecessor pursuant to Article 18(1)(a) CR (EC) 1287/2006 which was consciously abandoned by the European Union.[2061] Since Swiss law only points out which waivers trading venues may adopt in their regulations, trading venues could offer more detailed rules under their self-regulatory power.

The primary dark pools run by a Swiss trading venue are SwissAtMid and SwissEBBO both operated by SIX Swiss Exchange. The trading directive No. 5 on 'alternative trading' based on the SIX trading regulation shows that there are no limiting features comparable to those under Article 4(1)(a), (2) MiFIR rendering the Swiss reference price waiver more facilitative to dark trading than its EU counterpart.[2062] While SwissAtMid functions similar to a dark pool under the reference price waiver in the European Union by taking the midpoint price from the central limit order book of SIX Swiss Exchange, which is generally both the most liquid market in Switzerland as well as the market of first admittance to trading,[2063] SwissEBBO uses a midpoint price aggregated from several trading venues in the European Union by an independent provider.[2064] A function like SwissEBBO would no longer be eligible under EU law.

2058 Kumpan and Schmidt (n 4) MiFIR Art 4 paras 9–10; Gebauer (n 94) MiFIR Art 4 para 3.

2059 Article 4(2)(b) MiFIR.

2060 Aquilina and others (n 1451) 9, 13; ESMA, 'Questions and Answers: On MiFID II and MiFIR Transparency Topics' (n 1472) 51–2, Answer 3.

2061 Kägi (n 50) BSK FinfraG Art 29 para 21; Schott and Winkler (n 70) SK FinfraG Art 29 para 32.

2062 See SIX Swiss Exchange, 'Directive 5: Alternative Trading' (23 November 2022) Rule 9.10.2 (SwissAtMid) and Rules 10.4 and 10.10 (SwissEBBO).

2063 See ibid Rule 9.10.2.

2064 See ibid Rule 10.4.

Due to the few limitations which Article 27(4)(a) FinfraV imposes on the use of the reference price waiver, there is an actual risk of trading venues abusing this waiver by luring additional liquidity into their dark pool to earn fees from them. An unregulated growth could harm both investor trust and price accuracy if the amount of dark liquidity exceeds a certain threshold. Those risks are, furthermore, not contained by a limiting mechanism like the volume cap mechanism pursuant to Article 5 MiFIR as under EU law.[2065]

In spite of the striking resemblance to MiFID I, Swiss financial markets are not in a similarly troubling position as the European Union before MiFID II/MiFIR's enactment was enacted. The reason for this, however, is not a superior regulatory framework but rather more favorable market conditions. The fact that the market for lit and dark trading is both concentrated in the hands of only a few trading venues which offer both trading services ensures that the trading venues will not allow for their lit services to be eroded by dark trading. Moreover, Swiss financial markets are under the supervision of FINMA not multiple national competent authorities of 27 Member States. This and the fact that the trading venues are organizationally concentrated in almost one hand prevents different interpretations of the same waiver such as the reference price waiver under MiFID I. Nevertheless, Switzerland should reconsider its regulation of the reference price waiver once additional competition enters the market.

bb) Negotiated Trade Waiver

The Federal Council also provided the trading venues with the choice to implement a waiver from pre-trade transparency for systems that exist only to formalize transactions already negotiated.[2066] The brief definition is complemented by the legislative materials revealing that the general situation in which this waiver is applicable, i.e., privately negotiated trades eventually formalized by a trading venue, is similar to the negotiated trade waiver pursuant to Article 4(1)(b) MiFIR.[2067]

2065 Kägi (n 50) BSK FinfraG Art 29 para 21. See on EU law above Part II § 6 C.III.1.c).

2066 Article 27(4)(b) FinfraV.

2067 EFD, 'Erläuterungsbericht zur Verordnung über die Finanzmarktinfrastrukturen und das Marktverhalten im Effekten- und Derivatehandel' (n 2042) 15; Kägi (n 50) BSK FinfraG Art 29 para 22; Humbel, *Die Regelung der Vor- und Nachhandelstransparenz in der Europäischen Union und der Schweiz* (n 50) 503.

Although not expressly stated, the Swiss version of the waiver serves the same purpose as the EU's version given their similarity.[2068] CESR initially introduced the negotiated trade waiver to allow for privately negotiated trades outside the order book when those transactions result in a better execution than within the systems of the trading venue, i.e., modern form of 'upstairs trading'. By way of example, CESR thought of transactions that may not be fully executed within the order book or may not qualify for execution in the order book due to minimal size requirements, such as a 'round lot'-requirement.[2069] In practice, the negotiated trade waiver enables institutional traders with portfolio trades or transactions in connection with delta-neutral equity hedges of a derivative, thus, rather technical transactions.[2070]

When comparing the very nuanced negotiated trade waiver under Article 4(1)(b), (3) MiFIR and even its predecessor Article 18(1)(b) CR (EC) 1287/2006, it becomes apparent that only specific negotiated transactions shall be exempted from pre-trade transparency. Both, the MiFID I and the MiFID II/MiFIR version of the waiver distinguish between pre-negotiated transactions being subject to current market conditions,[2071] on the one hand, and those subject to conditions other than the current market price of the financial instrument, on the other hand, i.e., technical trades without an investment purpose.[2072] For those transactions under current market conditions, the waiver is only available if the price is within a percentage of a suitable reference price set in advance by the system operator which is not required for trades outside current market conditions.[2073] The EU

2068 Humbel, *Die Regelung der Vor- und Nachhandelstransparenz in der Europäischen Union und der Schweiz* (n 50) 503; Schott and Winkler (n 70) SK FinfraG Art 29 para 33.

2069 CESR, 'CESR Technical Advice to the European Commission in the Context of the MiFID Review - Equity Markets' (n 4) 11: Round lot-requirement often means that orders can only be entered in the order book of a trading venue if the order is at least in the amount of 100 shares or a multiple of this.

2070 ESMA, 'Final Report: Draft Regulatory and Implementing Technical Standards MiFID II/MiFIR' (n 1445) 19; Schott and Winkler (n 70) SK FinfraG Art 29 para 33.

2071 i.e., the negotiated transaction is made within the current volume weighted spread in the order book or quotes, cf. Article 4(1)(b)(i), (ii) MiFIR and Article 18(1)(b)(i) CR (EC) 1287/2006.

2072 Cf. Article 4(1)(b)(iii) MiFIR and Article 18(1)(b)(ii) CR (EC) 1287/2006.

2073 Kumpan and Schmidt (n 4) MiFIR Art 4 para 15; Gebauer (n 94) MiFIR Art 4 para 7. See also Article 18(1)(b)(i) CR (EC) 1287/2006.

legislator considered this distinction necessary to avoid an overuse of this waiver.[2074] While technical trades – not at current market conditions – can occur at any price, trades for an investment purpose – at current market conditions – can only be exempt from pre-trade transparency if the price for their transaction is at least approximately known to the public and thus does not need to be added to the price formation process.[2075] Hence, it has to occur at a suitable reference price set in advance by the trading venue operator.[2076]

This differentiation is crucial to allow the necessary leeway for technical transactions, such as the one mentioned above that is used for hedging risk but restricting dark trading that occurs at prices that would have informed the market and should therefore fuel the price formation process.

Currently, Swiss law does not require trading venues to adopt a similar distinction in their trading venues when implementing the negotiated trade waiver, although trading venues could do so within their self-regulatory powers. To avoid unintended overuse of the waiver which might potentially be draining important pricing information into dark trading, the trading venues should either by themselves implement a distinction similar to the one under EU law, or FINMA should specifically require such limitations in the approval process under Article 27(4) FinfraG.[2077]

The additional distinction between liquid and illiquid instruments traded at current market conditions in a pre-negotiated transaction under Article 4(1)(b)(i) and (ii) MiFIR solely serves the purpose of subjecting frequent trading under the waiver to the volume cap mechanism, while not burdening illiquid markets with this new restriction.[2078] Since Swiss law does not provide for a volume cap mechanism, this distinction is not relevant under Article 27(4)(b) FinfraV. If a trading venue considers

---

2074 ESMA, 'Final Report: Draft Regulatory and Implementing Technical Standards MiFID II/MiFIR' (n 1445) 20ff.

2075 Kumpan and Schmidt (n 4) MiFIR Art 4 para 15; Gebauer (n 94) MiFIR Art 4 para 7.

2076 ESMA, 'Final Report: Draft Regulatory and Implementing Technical Standards MiFID II/MiFIR' (n 1445) 21.

2077 Whether such limitations are modelled after MiFID I or MiFID II/MiFIR is not of paramount importance, since both regimes avoided unintended overuse with regard to scope. The overuse with regard to quantity is, however, regulated by the volume cap under Article 5(1) MiFIR which is absent under Swiss law.

2078 ESMA, 'Final Report: Draft Regulatory and Implementing Technical Standards MiFID II/MiFIR' (n 1445) 20.

adopting a mechanism similar to Article 5 MiFIR,[2079] a parallel distinction to Article 4(1)(b)(i) and (ii) MiFIR to protect illiquid markets might be in order.

cc) Order Management Facility Waiver

Parallel to Articles 4(1)(d) and 9(1)(a) MiFIR under EU law, Article 27(4)(c) FinfraV sets out that pre-trade transparency can be waived for orders held in an order management facility of the trading venue pending disclosure.[2080] Such orders benefitting from the OMF-waiver allow for price- and cost-efficient execution of institutional investors' orders.[2081] The orders qualifying for this waiver are generally iceberg orders, also called reserve orders, which show only a small fraction of the entire order size. Once this fraction has been executed another fraction or 'peak' comes to the surface of the order book under a new time stamp.[2082]

Choosing the OMF-waiver is sensible for traders that have a somewhat larger order and wish 'to work' it through the market with minimal market impact costs, thus, they slice the large order into smaller child orders. This rationale is comparable to the one of the large in scale waiver that aims to protect large amounts of liquidity from market impact as well. However, *prima facie*, the OMF-waiver would also apply if a trader decided to slice up smaller orders to make use of this waiver. To contain dark trading in orders that would not suffer market impact, EU law introduced a minimum order size for reserve orders, i.e., iceberg orders, that require a minimum threshold of EUR 10,000 order volume pending for disclosure to use the OMF-waiver.[2083] Although Swiss law does not implement a similar threshold requirement, the trading venues can implement such requirement and

2079 However, introducing a volume cap mechanism would potentially limit the turnover on a trading venue and therefore directly contradicts its primary objective to maximize profits by earning fees per order and transaction. A trading venue is, thus, highly unlikely to implement a double volume cap mechanism.

2080 Kägi (n 50) BSK FinfraG Art 29 para 23.

2081 Schott and Winkler (n 70) SK FinfraG Art 29 para 34.

2082 Banks (n 5) 172; Gomber and Gvozdevskiy (n 43) para 14.56.

2083 Article 8 CDR (EU) 2017/587.

SIX did so for its reserve order service called 'Iceberg Plus orders' requiring a minimum order value of CHF 10,000.[2084]

Another issue left for interpretation is the question of whether a trader can still influence how and when a hidden part is sent to the order book for display or if it is subject to objective, pre-defined rules. Although neither the law nor the legislative materials address this issue, considering the OMF-waiver's purpose to enable traders to trade in certain liquidity providing order types points in the direction that the transition shall not be subject to the trader's discretion. If the trader was to decide when a fraction of the order enters into the order book for display, the OMF waiver would share similarities to the reference price waiver. As under the reference price waiver, traders would use the OMF-waiver to trade at a certain (reference) price that is independent of the market impact that their (entire) order might produce. If the trader under the OMF-waiver had discretion, it could wait for a suitable price as under the reference price waiver. Under EU law, this separation of the purposes of the RP- and OMF-waiver is crucial because otherwise a trader could circumvent the volume cap mechanism that is only applicable to the RP- and NGT-waiver. Although preventing regulatory arbitrage is not an issue under Swiss law, which does not have such a mechanism, the trader still should not have discretion over the issue of when a fraction of an order is sent to the order book. The waivers shall protect liquidity providers that would suffer market impact if the order was displayed (entirely). In exchange for this privilege, the traders have to commit their liquidity to the market for execution without discretion. The only discretion left is to cancel (the remainder of) the order.

The second aspect of the Swiss OMF-waiver that is not clearly regulated in Article 27(4)(c) FinfraV is the question of whether the hidden part of an iceberg order can interact with a lit order pending disclosure. Under EU law, Article 8(1)(b) CDR (EU) 2017/587 bars all orders under the OMF-waiver to do that and repeats this prohibition under Article 8(3) CDR (EU) 2017/587 for reserve orders in particular.[2085] EU law rests this decision on two factors. First, it considers the OMF-waiver less detrimental for price discovery and fairness to other market participants because the

2084 SIX Swiss Exchange, 'SWXess Maintenance Release 7.1 (SMR7.1): Participant Readiness (Version 4.00)' (3 May 2018) 10: *'Note that for Iceberg Plus orders the Minimum Order Value of CHF 10'000 applies.'*

2085 Humbel, *Die Regelung der Vor- und Nachhandelstransparenz in der Europäischen Union und der Schweiz* (n 50) 508–9.

fraction that is executable becomes subject to pre-trade transparency when it is sent into the order book for display. Although the market is ignorant with regard to the entire trading interest of the trader, it at least can estimate market depth that is currently available. The second aspect is that OMF-waiver may become a less regulated substitute for the reference price waiver restricted by the volume cap mechanism if orders could execute their displayed and their hidden fraction when the preferred price is hit by another order.[2086]

Although Swiss law does not have a volume cap mechanism and therefore the issue of regulatory arbitrage is not as prevalent as under EU law, allowing the hidden fraction to execute when the volume of the displayed fraction is exhausted at a given price is contrary to the rationale of the OMF-waiver. While this practice is favorable also for the trader crossing with the order hidden by the OMF-waiver since it does not have to accept the next best order in the order book at an inferior price as long as there is still liquidity at a better price, it unduly favors the user of the OMF-waiver compared to both the RP- and LIS-waiver. The user of the OMF-waiver can avoid market impact as effectively as the users of the RP- and the LIS-waiver since the displayed order size is small enough to avoid stirring up the market. In contrast to the RP- and LIS-waiver, however, the OMF-waiver can benefit from attracting trading interest by displaying a fraction of its actual order which may have a superior time stamp compared to the other waivers if the trading venue awards dark orders inferior priority to lit orders.[2087] Furthermore, under the OMF-waiver a trader does not have to accept the midpoint price but can set its own limit price for the displayed part of the order and still consume the entire liquidity of a large enough counter order. This is not the case under the RP- and LIS-waiver. Additionally, using the OMF-waiver may be favorable compared to the LIS-waiver because a trader does not have to meet the higher LIS-thresholds but receives full execution of its entire trading interest when a large enough order crosses the displayed and hidden fraction of its order.

Consequently, also allowing the hidden fraction of an order under the OMF-waiver to execute with a large order that is not exhausted when executing with the lit fraction combines the best out of two worlds in one waiver. To avoid arbitrage effects with many traders using the OMF-waiver

2086 ibid 509.
2087 NB: This is rather often the case.

instead of the RP- or LIS-waiver, the OMF-waiver must require a sequential execution of the displayed fraction only.[2088] Then the next fraction receives a new time stamp when it is sent to the order book falling to the end of the queue under price/time-priority rules providing a level playing field for other displayed orders.

dd) Large in Scale Waiver

The final pre-trade transparency waiver under Swiss law is the large in scale waiver found in Article 27(4)(d) FinfraV. Comparable to its peers under Article 4(1)(d) MiFIR and Article 9(1)(a) MiFIR in the EU, the Swiss large in scale waiver exempts orders from the obligation to show pre-trade transparency if their volume is large in scale compared to standard market size.[2089] Together with the OMF-waiver, the large in scale-waiver serves (institutional) traders who want to execute large orders without incurring market impact costs, and it supports market quality by encouraging those traders to make their liquidity available for other traders.[2090] In contrast to the OMF-waiver, the large in scale waiver exempts the entire order from pre-trade transparency, thus, providing a higher degree of protection.

The central factor for the application of the large in scale waiver is when an order is deemed to exceed the standard market size and how to determine the latter. EU law solves this issue by determining tables for each asset class, i.e., shares, ETFs, certificates, etc., in which different thresholds are defined when an order is deemed to exceed the standard market size and is therefore large in scale. These thresholds are dependent on the average daily turnover in the instrument.[2091] The result is a quite elaborate but objective and predictable threshold system.

Swiss law, however, remains silent on the vital question of defining when an order is large compared to normal market size and delegates this task

2088 Cf. Gomber and Gvozdevskiy (n 43) para 14.56 on the OMF-Waiver under EU law.

2089 Kägi (n 50) BSK FinfraG Art 29 para 24; Schott and Winkler (n 70) SK FinfraG Art 29 para 35.

2090 Kägi (n 50) BSK FinfraG Art 29 para 24; Schott and Winkler (n 70) SK FinfraG Art 29 para 35; Hochstrasser (n 11) 311; Humbel, *Die Regelung der Vor- und Nachhandelstransparenz in der Europäischen Union und der Schweiz* (n 50) 514.

2091 See Article 7 CDR (EU) 2017/587 and Annex I; Kumpan and Schmidt (n 4) MiFIR Art 4 paras 21–2; Gebauer (n 94) MiFIR Art 4 para 10.

to the self-regulatory efforts of trading venues.[2092] The Federal Council only pointed out in the materials of FinfraV that the classification of orders qualifying for the waiver should be made with regard to the average daily turnover.[2093] Although this is also the measure used under EU law, it is non-binding to the trading venues since it is not in the black letter law.[2094]

Also, for the large in scale waiver, the SIX Swiss Exchange picked up the task and closed the last mile of regulation.[2095] In this case, however, SIX did not adopt the EU's approach of drawing up extensive threshold systems for each asset class but rather determines the threshold for trading large in scale by publishing the minimum volume for block orders per security in conjunction with the core data of the security.[2096] In practice, this results in a table on the SIX website where the traded securities are listed with their bid-ask-prices with two categories attached, one showing the minimum volume for orders to be accepted as large in scale under the SwissAtMid rules and another for the SwissEBBO rules.[2097]

While this approach is certainly well-tailored to the individual level of liquidity of different securities, including non-equity securities suffering from lower levels of liquidity, this approach is also unpredictable and opaque to a certain extent. The EU thresholds are set out in law and remain unaltered over a period of time, whereas SIX's system just tells the result of a computation done by the exchange and is subject to constant alteration over the trading day. It is therefore hard for an institutional investor to plan dark trading under the large in scale waiver ahead of time. Since the computation of the threshold is not determined in the trading regulation nor in the directive No. 5 on alternative trading, FINMA will find it hard to exercise its approval power over this piece of self-regulation if SIX chooses to contest it.

This distance to regulatory oversight and the fact that every trading venue could eventually determine its own threshold system could lead to regulatory fragmentation that could invite regulatory arbitrage which ultimately leads to large amounts of dark trading. Currently, however, Swiss law

2092 EFD, 'Erläuterungsbericht zur Verordnung über die Finanzmarktinfrastrukturen und das Marktverhalten im Effekten- und Derivatehandel' (n 2042) 15.

2093 ibid 15.

2094 Humbel, *Die Regelung der Vor- und Nachhandelstransparenz in der Europäischen Union und der Schweiz* (n 50) 514–5.

2095 Cf. SIX Swiss Exchange, 'Directive 5: Alternative Trading' (n 2062) Rule 9.7 e).

2096 See ibid Rule 9.12(2)(2).

2097 See SIX Swiss Exchange, 'SIX Share Explorer' (3 April 2022).

can operate with this degree of vagueness because of its highly concentrated market in which SIX plays a pivotal role.

b) Omitted Waivers during the Legislative Process

As said before, the term 'shares and other securities' under Swiss law spans roughly the same number of instruments as 'equity and non-equity financial instruments' under EU law. While the European Union created a transparency regime with both transparency requirements and the ancillary waivers for equity and non-equity instruments, Swiss federal law restricts its scope to shares only (Article 27(1) FinfraV). This decision is reflected in the waiver regime under Article 27(4) FinfraV because it mirrors only those waivers that EU law implemented under Article 4(1) MiFIR for equity instruments but omits the waivers for non-equity instruments under Articles 8(4) and 9 MiFIR. The waivers the European Union designed for non-equity instruments to account for their lower liquidity levels were accounted for in the legislative process in the draft of FinfraV (Draft-FinfraV), but eventually discarded.[2098]

The Draft-FinfraV adopted the waiver for actionable indications of interests communicated in voice trading and request-for-quote systems but, as the original under Articles 9(1)(b) and 8(4) MiFIR, it required market makers to make at least indicative quotes close to the actual bid and offer prices (Article 27(3) Draft-FinfraV).[2099] Furthermore, Draft-FinfraV prepared a waiver for derivatives not subject to the trading platform obligation under Article 112 FinfraG (Article 27(2)(b) Draft-FinfraV) and transactions in derivatives with non-financial counterparties (Article 27(4) Draft-FinfraV).[2100] Those transactions are usually made by companies to hedge their market risks.[2101] Additionally, the draft waiver regime for other securities held ready a waiver for instruments without a liquid market

2098 EFD, 'Erläuterungsbericht zur Verordnung über die Finanzmarktinfrastrukturen und das Marktverhalten im Effekten- und Derivatehandel' (n 2042) 8, 15–6; See also Schott and Sester (n 57) § 22 para 102.

2099 Schott and Winkler (n 70) SK FinfraG Art 29 para 44.

2100 Similar to the waiver under Article 9(1)(c) MiFIR.

2101 EFD, 'Erläuterungsbericht zur Verordnung über die Finanzmarktinfrastrukturen und das Marktverhalten im Effekten- und Derivatehandel' (n 2042) 15–6; Schott and Winkler (n 70) SK FinfraG Art 29 para 45.

(Article 27(2)(b) second clause Draft-FinfraV).[2102] Lacking was, however, a dedicated large in scale waiver. This was potentially considered redundant having the waiver under Article 27(4)(d) FinfraV which could be broadened by the trading venues for orders large in scale in other instruments than shares under their self-regulatory powers.

In general, the Federal Council's first approach using EU law as a blueprint for a waiver regime was sensible considering that Swiss law already adapted to EU law's pre-trade transparency regime. However, EU law puts great emphasis on the difference between liquid and illiquid markets and ties a complex mechanism to determine liquidity to it.[2103] When taking over the waivers for securities other than shares, Swiss law would have to introduce a similar distinction. When reintroducing the waivers that were once in the Draft-FinfraV, it would be advisable to also define a liquid market and set out liquidity thresholds instead of delegating this task to the trading venues. In this case, the Federal Council should set out clear rules applicable to all trading venues in other securities to avoid regulatory arbitrage. With certain adjustments, the EU law will provide a vital source of inspiration.

When the waivers for other securities are eventually adopted into FinfraV, the Federal Council may want to reconsider the homogeneous application to a heterogenous group as the one of 'other securities than shares.' Under EU law, the abovementioned waivers apply to non-equity instruments which is merely a subcategory to the Swiss category of 'other securities than shares' because the latter also includes equity-like instruments, such as depository receipts. Here, the Federal Council should try to distinguish between equity-like instruments that trade in a market as liquid as those for shares – which should also qualify for the waivers currently under Article 27(4) FinfraG – and non-equity instruments that trade in a less liquid market and are in need of the waivers similar to Articles 8(4) and 9 MiFIR. This would also require introducing a large in scale waiver dedicated to non-equity instruments. Insofar, Swiss law would have to abandon

2102 EFD, 'Erläuterungsbericht zur Verordnung über die Finanzmarktinfrastrukturen und das Marktverhalten im Effekten- und Derivatehandel' (n 2042) 15; Schott and Winkler (n 70) SK FinfraG Art 29 para 46.

2103 See Article 2(1)(17) MiFIR; ESMA, 'Consultation Paper: MiFID II/MiFIR' (n 1581) 98ff.

its traditional differentiation between shares, securities, and other financial instruments for the sake of the transparency regime under FinfraV.[2104]

Currently, however, the trading venues fulfil their self-regulatory function well by subjecting both shares and other securities to pre-trade transparency and by creating a well-adjusted waiver system for all securities by determining the threshold for the large in scale waiver on a security-by-security basis as, for instance, SIX did. This way, the trading venues found a proper balance between lit and dark trading at least on their venues. Nevertheless, reconsideration is in order if new market entrants set foot into Swiss markets and provide the chance for regulatory arbitrage.

c) No Volume Cap Mechanism under Swiss law

Unlike EU law, Swiss law has not adopted a mechanism to limit dark trading similar to the double or single volume cap mechanism pursuant to Article 5 MiFIR.[2105] By lacking this central limitation on dark trading, FinfraG is much closer to MiFID I than to MiFID II/MiFIR.

However, given that the EU regulation not only repatriates orders from OTC-BCNs onto regulated trading systems by means of the trading obligation for shares under Article 23 MiFIR but also restricts regulated dark trading on those trading venues with the volume cap mechanism, EU law may create an overly restrictive environment for advantageous dark trading. Moreover, the EU's approach has led to a shift from OTC trades into the less regulated bilateral systematic internalizer regime which is also sub-optimal compared to having trading occur on multilateral trading venues. Thus, Swiss law may not be worse off by not having adopted the volume cap mechanism.

In spite of the adverse effects when a trading obligation for shares and a volume cap mechanism coincide, the absence of a volume cap mechanism alone does not render Swiss law per se superior to its EU counterpart.

2104 Cf. Schott and Winkler (n 70) SK FinfraG Art 29 paras 43ff.

2105 Kägi (n 50) BSK FinfraG Art 29 para 21; Baisch, Baumann and Weber (n 11) 190; Hochstrasser (n 11) 311ff.

d) Process: Waiver decision is with the Trading Venue not FINMA

Just as the individual waivers under Swiss law already differ from their counterparts under MiFID II/MiFIR, the waiver granting process also shows significant deviations. The European Union chose the legislative means of a regulation with MiFIR that is directly applicable in the Member States to ensure uniform application of law, it requires national competent authorities to grant waivers without discretion if the requirements under Articles 4(1) and 9(1) MiFIR are met.[2106] On the other hand, Swiss law only sets out the high-level principles in the act of parliament, FinfraG, leaving the definition of the individual waivers for the executive to define in FinfraV. Moreover, FinfraV sets out a much more lenient waiver regime.[2107]

Under Article 27(4) FinfraV, it is the trading venues that may make provisions for exceptions in their trading regulations for the abovementioned waivers. The character as a 'may'-provision leaves trading venues a large amount of discretion in the waiver implementation process on their trading venue.[2108] Granting trading venues discretion over the waiver implementation process bears the potential risk of admitting high-levels of dark trading into the financial markets because trading venues offer dark trading as a service to maximize their fees.

Furthermore, FINMA as the national competent authority is also involved in the waiver implementation process because every trading regulation as well as every major amendment has to be approved by FINMA pursuant to Article 27(4) FinfraG.[2109]

Yet, this process is different to the EU's: When giving its approval, FINMA usually has to review an entire trading regulation, thus, it does not make a specific decision in an independent process on the waiver regime as under Articles 4(4) and 9(2) MiFIR.[2110] FINMA does not even decide on each individual waiver for a trading venue on a case-by-case basis but for the entire waiver regime of a trading venue in its trading regulations *en bloc*. This is, by design, a substantially less granular review process charged with overlapping and diverging interests in which the waiver regime does not play a pivotal role.

2106 See Gebauer (n 94) MiFIR Art 4 paras 13ff.

2107 Schott and Winkler (n 70) SK FinfraG Art 29 paras 30–1.

2108 ibid SK FinfraG Art 29 para 31.

2109 Article 27(4) FinfraG; Schott and Winkler (n 70) SK FinfraG Art 27 para 22; Schott and Sester (n 57) § 22 para 43.

2110 Cf. See Gebauer (n 94) MiFIR Art 4 paras 13ff.

Even though the Swiss transparency regime deals with domestic issues instead of coordination among Member State institutions, the interests involved are comparable. Think of two trading venues under Swiss law that adopt diverging waiver regimes or execute their waiver regimes in a different way. Despite the initial approval required from FINMA that is similar to ESMA's opinion under Article 4(4) MiFIR, of course, without the constitutive effect, there is no motion of recourse for one trading venue to complain about the waiver practice of the other. Even worse, there is also no means for FINMA to rectify deviating application practices among trading venues since the waiver application is within the trading venues' self-regulatory power.

Regarding the comparability to MiFID II/MiFIR, Article 27(4) FinfraG sets out a process for granting waivers that does not ensure uniform application among multiple venues and shows little governmental control in the review that FINMA can exercise during the approval of the entire trading regulation. The self-regulatory element of Article 27(4) FinfraG essentially places the Swiss waiver regime on the opposite end of the spectrum from the paternalistic regime under MiFID II/MiFIR.[2111]

Despite this inherent conflict of interest between regulating dark trading and generating earnings from offering the service, the issue of excessive rates of dark trading is not raised in Swiss financial markets. Trading venues and other market participants appear not to complain about the jeopardizing effects on price discovery or market quality as a whole. This might be due to a special market structure present in Swiss financial markets which is absent in the US and EU: Swiss financial markets are still highly concentrated with SIX as the pivotal supplier of both lit and dark trading services for trading in Swiss securities. While SIX has an interest in maximizing its revenue from dark trading services, it certainly has a larger incentive in protecting its main service of lit exchange trading. This means that it is less likely that waivers for dark trading are provided in a manner that jeopardizes the price formation at the lit exchange, and thereby aligns the private interest of fee maximization with the public interest of having primarily lit trading with a certain (small) amount of dark trading for vulnerable orders. It can thus be concluded that a rather concentrated market can have dark trading under less restrictive rules than markets in which the level of fragmentation is high in which dark trading needs to be regulated more rigorously. This is especially true for the US and EU markets

2111 See Schott and Winkler (n 70) SK FinfraG Art 29 para 38.

but may also become an issue in Swiss markets if new competitors enter the market and begin to offer primarily dark trading services. Those trading system operators may not have an incentive to protect the price formation on lit markets. Then more restrictive regulation would be warranted in Switzerland, with regard to both the formulation and application of the waivers, which then should be administered by FINMA.

4. Post-Trade Transparency

Article 29(2) FinfraG regulates post-trade transparency on trading venues. This provision requires the trading venue to immediately publish information on trades executed on the trading venue and on trades reported to it outside the trading venue in all securities admitted to trading on this trading venue.[2112] In particular, the trading venue must publish the price, volume, and time of the transaction.[2113]

In essence, Article 29(2) FinfraG is an amended version of the former Article 5(3) former BEHG which set out post-trade transparency for exchanges.[2114] However, Article 29(2) FinfraG's expanded scope to cover CH-MTFs is significant for providing a level playing field among the trading venues and avoiding unintended blind spots for dark trading.[2115]

Strikingly, Article 29(2) FinfraG demands a higher degree of post-trade transparency than Article 29(1) FinfraG and Article 27(1) FinfraV for pre-trade transparency by requiring information about transactions in all securities not merely shares.[2116] With minor deviations due to the reference to securities, post-trade transparency has an equally broad scope under Swiss law as under EU law pursuant to Articles 6(1), 10(1) MiFIR.[2117]

The broader post-trade transparency regime shows that the Swiss legislator favors lit trading also for securities other than shares but has refrained from expanding the scope of pre-trade transparency in order to spare

2112 Kägi (n 50) BSK FinfraG Art 29 paras 31–2; Schott and Winkler (n 70) SK FinfraG Art 29 paras 48–9; Schott and Sester (n 57) § 22 para 103.

2113 Kägi (n 50) BSK FinfraG Art 29 paras 32ff; Schott and Winkler (n 70) SK FinfraG Art 29 para 48.

2114 Kägi (n 50) BSK FinfraG Art 29 para 2.

2115 Cf. Bundesrat, 'Botschaft zum Finanzmarktinfrastrukturgesetz (FinfraG)' (n 22) BBl. 2014, 7516, 7532.

2116 Kägi (n 50) BSK FinfraG Art 29 para 33.

2117 ibid BSK FinfraG Art 29 paras 32, 57; Schott and Winkler (n 70) SK FinfraG Art 29 para 42.

traders the disproportional burdens.[2118] Since such traders' execution quality is generally no longer affected by post-trade transparency and due to the importance of post-trade data for the price formation process, the Swiss regulator followed the regulatory advice of IOSCO to subject even those securities to post-trade transparency obligations that have not shown pre-trade transparency information before.[2119]

Post-trade transparency is also broader than pre-trade transparency with regard to the kind of transactions that need to be published: while pre-trade transparency was satisfied with only providing bid and offer prices that occurred on the trading venue, post-trade transparency demands publication of both information of on-venue transactions as well as off-venue transactions by its participants reported to the trading venue pursuant to Article 28(2) FinfraG.[2120] This allows a certain consolidation of post-trade transparency data underlining its importance for the public.[2121]

Another issue is to whom post-trade transparency data needs to be published. As said above, Swiss law only requires disseminating pre-trade transparency data among participants and parties paying for the service due to its limited objective to assess current trading opportunities.[2122] Also for post-trade transparency, the details of the publication lie within the trading venue's self-regulatory power.[2123] Post-trade transparency information is important not only for traders on the respective trading venue but for the investing public as well. To account for this, post-trade transparency needs to be disseminated in a broader manner. This refers to the issue of the price information being a (quasi-)common good that is costly for the trading venue to produce, thus, requires some exclusivity for the producer to recoup the production costs. However, extensive exclusivity is also detrimental because it leads to information asymmetry in the market. For this reason, a middle path must be found for post-trade data dissemination

2118 Bundesrat, 'Botschaft zum Finanzmarktinfrastrukturgesetz (FinfraG)' (n 22) BBl. 2014, 7533; Kägi (n 50) BSK FinfraG Art 29 para 33; Schott and Sester (n 57) § 22 para 103.

2119 Cf. Principle 2 in: IOSCO, 'Principles for Dark Liquidity' (n 12) 27–8.

2120 EFD, 'Erläuterungsbericht zur Verordnung über die Finanzmarktinfrastrukturen und das Marktverhalten im Effekten- und Derivatehandel' (n 2042) 16; Schott and Winkler (n 70) SK FinfraG Art 29 para 49.

2121 Bundesrat, 'Botschaft zum Finanzmarktinfrastrukturgesetz (FinfraG)' (n 22) BBl. 2014, 7533.

2122 Kägi (n 50) BSK FinfraG Art 29 paras 1, 29.

2123 ibid BSK FinfraG Art 29 para 37.

under Swiss law: Whereas selling the latest data appears justified given the production costs, pre-trade transparency data should be made public free of charge at a later point in time. While the exact regulation of the modalities of publication is in the self-regulatory power of the trading venues, the rationale of post-trade transparency seems to require, at least at a later point in time, a publication to the public. SIX Swiss Exchange provides post-trade transparency free of charge to the public on its website service 'Share-Explorer' 15 minutes after the trade has taken place.[2124] However, a clear legal obligation as in the European Union under Article 13(1)(2) MiFIR would be preferable.[2125]

With regard to the timing of the publication of post-trade transparency data, Article 29(2) FinfraG requires publication 'immediately' but both FinfraG and FinfraV fail to provide an exact definition how long the publication process can take.[2126] EU law, however, requires publication no later than one minute after the transaction occurred.[2127] Swiss exchanges will certainly be able to meet this requirement and be even faster but ask a price that will reflect the information advantage gained by such real-time access. Those services are only profitable for institutional traders.[2128]

5. Deferrals from Post-Trade Transparency

Article 29(3) FinfraG also delegates the power to define exemptions from post-trade transparency to the Federal Council. It used this power to implement a deferral regime similar to the one under EU law under Article 28(4) FinfraV.[2129] This deferral regime comprises of three exemptions from immediate publication of post-trade transparency information: one for transactions that are large in scale, one for transactions above the standard size for

2124 See SIX Swiss Exchange (n 2097).
2125 Kägi (n 50) BSK FinfraG Art 29 paras 37ff.
2126 Schott and Winkler (n 70) SK FinfraG Art 29 para 51.
2127 Article 14(1)(a) CDR (EU) 2017/587; Gebauer (n 94) MiFIR Art 4 para 11.
2128 Kägi (n 50) BSK FinfraG Art 29 para 40; Schott and Winkler (n 70) SK FinfraG Art 29 para 51.
2129 EFD, 'Erläuterungsbericht zur Verordnung über die Finanzmarktinfrastrukturen und das Marktverhalten im Effekten- und Derivatehandel' (n 2042) 16; Schott and Sester (n 57) § 22 para 104; Vogel, Heiz and Luthiger, *OFK FinfraG/BEG Kommentar* (n 1851) OFK FinfraG Art 29 paras 6–7.

the transactions in the instrument, and one for transactions in securities for which there is no liquid market.[2130]

The rationale for allowing deferred publication is the same under Swiss and EU law.[2131] Also the general legal consequence of deferring the publication of post-trade information to a later point in time is the same. However, there are two main aspects in which the deferral regime under Swiss and EU law differ from each other.

First, while EU law is much more detailed and technical with respect to deferrals comprising of vast regulatory technical standards to determine what kind of transaction can be deferred for how long, Swiss law lacks this degree of detail and delegates this task to the trading venues and their self-regulatory power.[2132] In an effort to determine the permissible time for deferral, legal scholars hold that the post-trade transparency data can only be deferred until the likelihood for an adverse impact of the publication on the parties involved and the market price is low.[2133] They, however, also admit that this point in time may not be precisely defined[2134] and therefore it leaves much discretion to trading venues which may lead to multiple different regulations resulting in an uneven playing field.

The second aspect in which Swiss law deviates from its EU model is with regard to the scope of the deferrals. Although Swiss law used the deferrals set out under EU law as a blueprint, it neglected the fact that Article 29(2) FinfraG universally applies to securities comprising of both equity and non-equity instruments. Parallel to the waiver regime from pre-trade transparency, post-trade transparency also sets out the entire array of deferrals a trading venue may adapt into its regulations in one provision blending deferrals for transactions in equity instruments with those in non-equity instruments. Whether this is detrimental will be discussed in the examination of each deferral below.

2130 Article 28(4) FinfraV; Schott and Sester (n 57) § 22 para 104; Schott and Winkler (n 70) SK FinfraG Art 29 paras 55ff.

2131 See above Part II § 6 C.V.1 and VI.3.-4.

2132 Schott and Winkler (n 70) SK FinfraG Art 29 paras 57ff.

2133 ibid SK FinfraG Art 29 para 57.

2134 Kägi (n 50) BSK FinfraG Art 29 para 51; Schott and Sester (n 57) § 22 para 104; Schott and Winkler (n 70) SK FinfraG Art 29 para 57.

a) Large in Scale

The only exception from immediate post-trade transparency that is already indicated under Article 29(3)(b) FinfraG is the one for transactions that are large in scale.[2135] The Swiss legislator considered both large orders and concluded large transactions eligible for dark trading to protect them from adverse market effects since Article 29(3)(b) FinfraG refers to both pre- and post-trade transparency. This interlacing between the large in scale exceptions in the pre- and post-trade context has been adopted under FinfraV because the deferral from post-trade transparency for transactions that are large in scale directly refers to its counterpart among the pre-trade transparency waivers under Article 27(4)(d) FinfraV.[2136]

This, however, raises the question of whether a trading venue must apply the same standards for the large in scale orders in the pre-trade transparency context as for transactions in the post-trade transparency context. While the reference may suggest so, the rationale of the large in scale exception in the pre-trade context compared to the post-trade context suggests otherwise. When an order is seeking for liquidity, it is much more vulnerable to adverse market impact than already completed transactions. It can also not be disregarded that pre-trade transparency currently only applies to shares while post-trade transparency encompasses all securities. Having an equal standard for the large in scale waiver as well as for the large in scale deferral therefore seems to be sub-optimal. This is also supported by comparing the pre-trade waiver and post-trade deferral system under EU law which also has different standards for determining the thresholds.[2137]

Considering the different rationales of the large in scale exception in the pre-trade and post-trade context, an independent interpretation of the post-trade transparency deferral for transactions that are large in scale seems warranted. Thus, trading venues should set up a tailored post-trade transparency regime for transactions that are large in scale, independent from their regime set out for the large in scale waiver from pre-trade transparency. Trading venues should also adjust their requirements to the classes of instruments that may qualify for the deferral that may differ

2135 Kägi (n 50) BSK FinfraG Art 29 para 48; Schott and Winkler (n 70) SK FinfraG Art 29 para 55.

2136 Article 28(4)(a) FinfraV; Schott and Winkler (n 70) SK FinfraG Art 29 para 55.

2137 See, Annex below for tables 1 and 4 of Annex II of CDR (EU) 2017/587 under EU law.

from the ones they have found for shares under the waiver from pre-trade transparency.[2138]

b) Size Specific to the Instrument

Pursuant to Article 28(4)(b) FinfraV, trading venues may defer the publication of transactions that are above the size specific to the securities in question.[2139] This waiver is similar to Article 11(1)(c) MiFIR which allows for deferred publication if the transaction is above the specific size for the instrument, the so-called SSTI-deferral.[2140] The Swiss version of this deferral also requires that, on the one hand, the deferral is only available for transactions for which a liquidity provider would be exposed to undue risk, and on the other hand, the deferral requires taking into consideration whether the transaction has been made with a retail or a wholesale investor.[2141]

Both prongs are also present under EU law but are considered to be of minor significance – rather in the sense of marginal conditions – compared to the central requirement of the transaction being above the size specific to the security in question.[2142] Under Swiss law, those two prongs also serve a secondary role to the first prong but are necessary to delineate this deferral from the large in scale deferral.[2143] At first glance both deferrals are simply for large-sized transactions, however, the second prong of the SSTI-deferral referring to a situation of a liquidity provider being exposed to inappropriate risks further defines the scope of the deferral. The SSTI-deferral is meant for markets in which market makers primarily supply liquidity. Since market makers take on principal risk, they need to be protected from the public eye even before the large in scale waiver applies. Without this

2138 Humbel, *Die Regelung der Vor- und Nachhandelstransparenz in der Europäischen Union und der Schweiz* (n 50) 535ff. Especially using the average daily turnover (ADT) as proxy for liquidity may not prove to be the best proxy for other instruments than shares.

2139 Kägi (n 50) BSK FinfraG Art 29 para 49; Schott and Winkler (n 70) SK FinfraG Art 29 para 56.

2140 Schott and Winkler (n 70) SK FinfraG Art 29 para 56; Kumpan and Schmidt (n 4) MiFIR Art 11 para 6.

2141 Kägi (n 50) BSK FinfraG Art 29 para 49; Schott and Winkler (n 70) SK FinfraG Art 29 para 56.

2142 Cf. Kumpan and Schmidt (n 4) MiFIR Art 11 para 6.

2143 Schott and Winkler (n 70) SK FinfraG Art 29 para 56.

privilege, market makers anticipate that they will find it difficult to unwind larger positions into the market after a transaction, and as a result will not take a client's order above standard market size on their books in the first place. This will render markets dominated by less-liquid market makers if there is additional post-trade transparency, thus deferring post-trade transparency not only privileges the market maker but benefits the entire market.[2144]

Considering that this deferral was originally designed for markets dominated by market makers and can be found in Article 11(1)(c) MiFIR, it becomes clear that this waiver is tailored to the specific needs of markets for non-equity instruments that often show low levels of liquidity.[2145] When adopting this deferral to their trading regulations, trading venues might want to limit the deferral to non-equity instruments only, since otherwise liquidity providers in equity instruments may also use this deferral despite the high levels of liquidity in such markets where market makers face little to no risk of not being able to unwind their holdings into the market. This would increase dark liquidity unduly because the private interest in dark trading does not outweigh the public interest in having disclosure of post-trade transparency information of such transactions.[2146]

Also striking is the mentioning of retail and wholesale investors in the third prong of Article 11(1)(c) MiFIR. This is a rather uncritical adoption of the differentiation of retail and wholesale investors under MiFID II/ MiFIR that initially had no counterpart under Swiss law as FinfraG was introduced. Fortunately, however, Article 4(1) FIDLEG introduced a similar differentiation into Swiss law distinguishing among retail clients, professional clients, and institutional clients.[2147] Trading venues need to align the blunt adoption of EU law with the new requirements of FIDLEG in their regulations, while the Federal Council should merely take account of international standards and developments in foreign laws (Article 29(3) FinfraG), and need not import foreign law without any adaptations.

2144 Kägi (n 50) BSK FinfraG Art 29 para 49; Schott and Winkler (n 70) SK FinfraG Art 29 para 56. Humbel, *Die Regelung der Vor- und Nachhandelstransparenz in der Europäischen Union und der Schweiz* (n 50) 537–8.

2145 Kumpan and Schmidt (n 4) MiFIR Art 11 para 5.

2146 Humbel, *Die Regelung der Vor- und Nachhandelstransparenz in der Europäischen Union und der Schweiz* (n 50) 537–8.

2147 Kägi (n 50) BSK FinfraG Art 29 para 49; Schott and Winkler (n 70) SK FinfraG Art 29 para 56; Humbel, *Die Regelung der Vor- und Nachhandelstransparenz in der Europäischen Union und der Schweiz* (n 50) 538–9.

c) Illiquid Securities

The third deferral from post-trade transparency is available for transactions in securities for which there is no liquid market.[2148] Again, under EU law, the deferral is meant for non-equity instruments only, while Swiss law includes both equity and non-equity instruments in its overbroad scope.[2149] However, the drafting history show that the Federal Council also meant to limit the scope of the deferral to non-equity instruments because it was adopted to exempt corporate bonds from post-trade transparency.[2150] Trading venues would be well advised to rectify this issue when adopting the deferral into their regulations.

Furthermore, Article 28(4)(c) FinfraV leaves unanswered the question of how to determine a liquid market, whereas EU law has very detailed provisions on this issue. Under Swiss law, there is only a definition of a liquid market for shares with regard to bilaterally trading CH-OTFs by FINMA in its circular.[2151] This measure, however, is tailored to shares and should not be directly transferred for application to other securities which need a different measure.[2152] Furthermore, this definition of a liquid market by FINMA was introduced to find balance between lit and dark bilateral trading, whereas for trading venues that host multilateral trading instead, the threshold for lit trading does not have to be as high as under Article 42(c) FinfraG.[2153] When promulgating their trading regulations, trading venues would be well advised to use the EU law definition of a liquid market as a blueprint for finding an adequate version under Swiss law.[2154] However, the issue with this extent of self-regulation may again be regulatory arbitrage, when trading venues choose high thresholds to allow their traders prolonged dark trading in the post-trade phase. Although FINMA must approve the regulations of trading venues, FINMA has shown that it considers liquidity thresholds that might be rather high for some

2148 Article 28(4)(c) FinfraV.

2149 EFD, 'Erläuterungsbericht zur Verordnung über die Finanzmarktinfrastrukturen und das Marktverhalten im Effekten- und Derivatehandel' (n 2042) 16.

2150 Kägi (n 50) BSK FinfraG Art 29 para 50; EFD, 'Erläuterungsbericht zur Verordnung über die Finanzmarktinfrastrukturen und das Marktverhalten im Effekten- und Derivatehandel' (n 2042) 16.

2151 FINMA, 'Circular 2018/1 Organised trading facilities' (n 1866) paras 38–9.

2152 Cf. Moloney, *EU Securities and Financial Markets Regulation* (n 4) 431–2.

2153 Cf. Kägi (n 50) BSK FinfraG Art 29 para 50.

2154 Humbel, *Die Regelung der Vor- und Nachhandelstransparenz in der Europäischen Union und der Schweiz* (n 50) 539–40.

non-equity instruments in compliance with the objective of FinfraG. This can be seen through its definition of a liquid market for bilateral trading as being compliant with Article 42 FinfraG if the instrument is traded at least 100 times per day on average.[2155]

The post-trade transparency regime, especially the deferrals under Article 28(4) FinfraV, show that the uncritical adoption of EU law under Swiss law causes several conflicts. Those conflicts must be resolved by the trading venues within their self-regulatory power. In comparison to EU law, Swiss law is even more liberal with exceptions from immediate post-trade transparency which puts Swiss law into stark contrast to US law which insists on immediate publication of post-trade transparency data, especially if it derives from multilateral trading systems, such as exchanges.

6. Exception for SNB Transactions, Article 29 FinfraV

Besides the waivers and deferrals under Articles 27f FinfraV, the Federal Council also fulfilled the second mandate under Article 29(3)(b) FinfraG to create exceptions from trade transparency for securities transactions that are executed by the SNB. Pursuant to Article 29(1) FinfraV, pre- and post-trade transparency obligations do not apply to securities transactions for public purposes instead of investment purposes if they are conducted by either the Swiss Confederation, the Cantons, municipalities, the SNB, the Bank for International Settlement (BIS), or multilateral development banks.[2156]

While trading venues were free to adopt or exclude the waivers and deferrals under Articles 27–28 FinfraV, the exception from pre- and post-trade transparency for sovereign market transactions under Article 29 FinfraV is mandatory.[2157] The exception is considered necessary for governmental institutions, especially the SNB, since the publication of the orders and

2155 FINMA, 'Circular 2018/1 Organised trading facilities' (n 1866) paras 38–9.

2156 Kägi (n 50) BSK FinfraG Art 29 para 25; Schott and Winkler (n 70) SK FinfraG Art 29 para 36.

2157 EFD, 'Erläuterungsbericht zur Verordnung über die Finanzmarktinfrastrukturen und das Marktverhalten im Effekten- und Derivatehandel' (n 2042) 16; Kägi (n 50) BSK FinfraG Art 29 para 25.

transactions could jeopardize the public purpose of the transaction, such as transactions by the SNB to implement monetary policy.[2158]

Such a rule is not unique to Swiss law since EU law also has a similar provision under Article 1(6), (7) MiFIR, although it is restricted to non-equity instruments and to members of the European System of Central Banks.[2159]

To delineate the scope of the exception under Article 29 FinfraV, it appears *prima facie* sensible to distinguish between transactions motivated by public purposes, to which the exception applies, and transactions motivated by investment purposes, which are subject to trade transparency. The delineation between transactions made in the public interest and for investment purposes shall be based on the classification of the assets used in the transaction. If the assets used in the transactions are classified as financial assets,[2160] the transaction is regarded as serving investment purposes and shall therefore be subject to trade transparency like any other investor's transaction. If, however, the assets are classified as administrative assets,[2161] the transaction is regarded as serving the public interest and is eligible for the privilege under Article 29(1) FinfraV to be exempted from pre- and post-trade transparency.[2162]

In practice, however, neither FINMA nor the trading venue exercises scrutiny over such transactions since they are lacking the legal capacity to do so. Moreover, trading venues are under no obligation to check whether the transaction may fall within the scope of Article 29 FinfraV. The eligible entity, for instance, the SNB or BIS, simply tells the trading venue that the entered order or transaction benefits from the exception under Article 29(1) FinfraV.[2163] Since governmental institutions have little incentive to disrupt

2158 Bundesrat, 'Botschaft zum Finanzmarktinfrastrukturgesetz (FinfraG)' (n 22) BBl. 2014, 7533.

2159 Schott and Winkler (n 70) SK FinfraG Art 29 para 36.

2160 EFD, 'Erläuterungsbericht zur Verordnung über die Finanzmarktinfrastrukturen und das Marktverhalten im Effekten- und Derivatehandel' (n 2042) 16 uses the term '*Finanzvermögen*'.

2161 ibid 16 uses the term '*Verwaltungsvermögen*'.

2162 ibid 16; Ulrich Häfelin, Georg Müller and Felix Uhlmann, *Allgemeines Verwaltungsrecht* (8th edn, Dike 2020) paras 2203ff; Humbel, *Die Regelung der Vor- und Nachhandelstransparenz in der Europäischen Union und der Schweiz* (n 50) 480–1.

2163 EFD, 'Erläuterungsbericht zur Verordnung über die Finanzmarktinfrastrukturen und das Marktverhalten im Effekten- und Derivatehandel' (n 2042) 17; cf. Kägi (n 50) BSK FinfraG Art 29 para 25.

the financial market and its price formation process, the issue of overuse of this exception is negligible.

Under Article 29(2) FinfraV, the same exception from pre- and post-trade transparency can be granted to foreign national banks, the European Central Bank (ECB), governmental entities administering national debt, the European Financial Stability Facility (EFSF), and the European Stability Mechanism (ESM). Those foreign sovereign entities are, however, only granted the same privilege if Swiss sovereign entities are granted reciprocal rights and the exception does not contradict the legislative purpose. Thus, foreign sovereign entities also have to act in the public interest and not upon investment purposes when using the exception.[2164]

The exemption of foreign entities requires motion by the Swiss entity that wishes to be granted reciprocal rights under foreign law, i.e., either the Confederation, a canton, a municipality, and/or the SNB. The decision lies with the Swiss Department of Finance (EFD), specifically the State Secretariat for International Finance ('*Staatssekretariat for Internationale Finanzfragen*' – SIF) which also publishes a list of exempted jurisdictions.[2165] By the time of this writing, the SIF appears not to have granted the privilege under Article 29(2) FinfraV to a foreign jurisdiction.

III. Trade Transparency for CH-OTFs

1. Pre-Trade Transparency for CH-OTFs

With the introduction of the new trading category CH-OTF, the Swiss legislator aimed to subject trading that could not be hosted on a Swiss trading venue to trade transparency.[2166] This increased transparency aims to improve the problems raised by dark pools under Swiss law.[2167]

In 2016, the Swiss legislator took EU law as a blueprint for FinfraG but also had concerns over subjecting its domestic financial markets to untested transparency rules while the European Union had not yet implemented its

2164 EFD, 'Erläuterungsbericht zur Verordnung über die Finanzmarktinfrastrukturen und das Marktverhalten im Effekten- und Derivatehandel' (n 2042) 16f.

2165 ibid 16–7; cf. Kägi (n 50) BSK FinfraG Art 29 para 26.

2166 See above Part II § 7 B.II.4.

2167 Bundesrat, 'Botschaft zum Finanzmarktinfrastrukturgesetz (FinfraG)' (n 22) BBl. 2014, 7541; Studer and Vollenweider (n 1910) BSK FinfraG Art 46 para 1; Favre and Kramer (n 566) SK FinfraG Art 46 para 2.

new transparency framework under MiFID II/MiFIR.[2168] The precaution was, however, not fully justified: While the introduction of the EU-OTF and the transparency rules for non-equity instruments were an untested novelty at that time, the CH-OTF also encompasses the category of the bilateral EU-SI which was already implemented and showed pre-trade transparency for shares since the implementation of MiFID I.[2169] Insofar, the Swiss legislator was overly cautious when it created the transparency regime for CH-OTFs which resulted in a framework under Article 46 FinfraG and Article 42 FinfraV that deviates from its EU-counterpart.[2170]

Because of this excessive caution, Article 46 FinfraG does not set out a pre-trade transparency rule for CH-OTFs. Article 46(1) FinfraG requires the publication of information on the transactions carried out on the trading facility and thus only addresses post-trade transparency.[2171] To allow for an amendment of the transparency regime, the Swiss legislator charged the Federal Council with creating a pre-trade transparency rule in accordance with recognized international standards in an ordinance.[2172]

In Article 42(1) FinfraV, the Federal Council determined that Articles 27 and 29 FinfraV shall apply *mutatis mutandis* for both multilateral trading and bilateral trading, where a liquid market exists. The Federal Council considered the extension of pre-trade transparency to multilateral CH-OTFs necessary since their trading mechanisms are closely aligned to those of Swiss exchanges and CH-MTF.[2173] This assumption is correct given that multilateral CH-OTFs provide either non-discretionary, multilateral trading in financial instruments other than securities or discretionary, multilateral trading in securities and other financial instruments according to Article 42(a), (b) FinfraG.

For bilateral CH-OTFs, however, the Federal Council also correctly realized that a direct application of the pre-trade transparency rules for multi-

2168 Bundesrat, 'Botschaft zum Finanzmarktinfrastrukturgesetz (FinfraG)' (n 22) BBl. 2014, 7541; Favre and Kramer (n 566) SK FinfraG Art 46 para 3.

2169 See Article 24(1)(a) Commission Regulation (EC) 1287/2006.

2170 Favre and Kramer (n 566) SK FinfraG Art 46 paras 3ff.

2171 Studer and Vollenweider (n 1910) BSK FinfraG Art 46 paras 2, 12; Favre and Kramer (n 566) SK FinfraG Art 46 para 3.

2172 Bundesrat, 'Botschaft zum Finanzmarktinfrastrukturgesetz (FinfraG)' (n 22) BBl. 2014, 7541; Studer and Vollenweider (n 1910) BSK FinfraG Art 46 para 2; Favre and Kramer (n 566) SK FinfraG Art 46 para 3.

2173 EFD, 'Erläuterungsbericht zur Verordnung über die Finanzmarktinfrastrukturen und das Marktverhalten im Effekten- und Derivatehandel' (n 2043) 25.

lateral trading systems is unsuitable. It therefore only requires application *mutatis mutandis* if the bilateral CH-OTF trades instruments for which there is a liquid market.[2174] If, however, there is no liquid market in bilateral trading, quotes on request are sufficient in accordance with Article 42(2) FinfraV. The Federal Council did not define when a market qualifies as liquid, and it did not further specify what a *mutatis mutandis*-application of Articles 27 and 29 FinfraG means with regard to bilateral trading. This creates an array of issues for both the definition of pre-trade transparency as well as the determination of the necessary leeway to resolve those issues in an area where clear rules should balance lit and dark trading to lower transaction costs to the minimum.[2175]

a) Entity Subject to Pre-Trade Transparency

Article 42 FinfraV leaves open who the addressee of the pre-trade transparency requirement shall be. While under Article 29 FinfraG this was the trading venue itself, this is not possible for the CH-OTF because it does not fall in the scope of the definition of 'financial markets infrastructure' pursuant to Article 2(a) FinfraG subject to authorization under Articles 4ff FinfraG. In the case of Article 42 FinfraV, Article 46(1) FinfraG provides valuable insight because the addressee for post-trade transparency is the operator of the trading system, i.e., either a bank, a securities firm (formerly securities dealer), a DLT trading system, or an authorized or recognized trading venue (Article 43(1) FinfraG). Since the addressee of pre- and post-trade transparency is the same entity as under Article 29 FinfraG, the same must be true under Article 46 FinfraG and Article 42 FinfraV, so that the operator of a CH-OTF is under the obligation to provide pre-trade transparency in analogy to Articles 27 and 29 FinfraV.[2176]

2174 ibid 25; Bundesrat, 'Botschaft zum Finanzmarktinfrastrukturgesetz (FinfraG)' (n 22) BBl. 2014, 7541; Studer and Vollenweider (n 1910) BSK FinfraG Art 46 para 9; Favre and Kramer (n 566) SK FinfraG Art 46 para 23.

2175 Cf. Schären, Dobrauz-Saldapenna and Liebi (n 1876) 199–200; Favre and Kramer (n 566) SK FinfraG Art 46 para 18.

2176 Humbel, *Die Regelung der Vor- und Nachhandelstransparenz in der Europäischen Union und der Schweiz* (n 50) 550–1; Jacques Iffland and Ariel Ben Hattar, 'Les systèmes organisés de négociation' [2016] GesKR 458, 462–5; Favre and Kramer (n 566) SK FinfraG Art 46 paras 1ff; Schären, Dobrauz-Saldapenna and Liebi (n 1876) 199–200.

Compared to EU law, the bilateral CH-OTF definition lacks the quantitative requirements that distinguish systematic internalizers from mere investment firms trading in the OTC-space.[2177] Due to this overbroad definition, the bilateral CH-OTF brings more pre-trade transparency into the (former) OTC-space beyond the scope of systematic internalization compared to EU law because EU law does not require pre-trade transparency from its bilaterally trading investment firms unless they qualify as a systematic internalizer.[2178]

b) Instruments Subject to Pre-Trade Transparency

With regard to the captured instruments, the reference to Articles 27 and 29 FinfraV results in pre-trade transparency for shares only under Article 42(1) FinfraV. Unlike trading venues under Article 27 FinfraG, CH-OTFs do not possess self-regulatory powers which would allow them to broaden the scope of pre-trade transparency by way of their trading regulations as SIX has done. Thus, for CH-OTFs, pre-trade transparency is limited to only shares until the Federal Council amends FinfraV.[2179]

Pre-trade transparency for shares also applies under Article 42(2) FinfraV which declares price quotes on demand sufficient for bilateral systems where there is no liquid market.[2180] Under Article 42(2) FinfraV, quotes upon request are sufficient for bilateral trading in illiquid markets. This obligation also only applies to shares despite the lacking reference to Articles 27 and 29 FinfraV since Article 42(1) and (2) FinfraV are clearly interrelated.[2181] Thus, the scope of Article 42(2) FinfraV, which is designed as an alleviation

2177 Studer and Vollenweider (n 1910) BSK FinfraG Art 42 para 41; Favre and Kramer (n 566) SK FinfraG Art 42 paras 11, 15; Schären, Dobrauz-Saldapenna and Liebi (n 1876) 198.

2178 Cf. Favre and Kramer (n 566) SK FinfraG Art 42 paras 11, 15; Schären, Dobrauz-Saldapenna and Liebi (n 1876) 198.

2179 Studer and Vollenweider (n 1910) BSK FinfraG Art 46 para 6; Favre and Kramer (n 566) SK FinfraG Art 46 para 16.

2180 Studer and Vollenweider (n 1910) BSK FinfraG Art 46 para 11; Favre and Kramer (n 566) SK FinfraG Art 46 para 25.

2181 Studer and Vollenweider (n 1910) BSK FinfraG Art 46 para 11; Favre and Kramer (n 566) SK FinfraG Art 46 para 25.

of pre-trade transparency when markets are illiquid, cannot be broader than under Article 42(1) FinfraV.[2182]

Given, however, that the multilateral non-discretionary type of the CH-OTF (Article 42(b) FinfraG) can only trade in financial instruments other than securities, a broadening of the scope of the pre-trade transparency should be aimed for in the long run. Otherwise, this type of CH-OTF operates without pre-trade transparency qualifying it as a dark pool which contradicts the initial objective of FinfraG to implement the CH-OTF and an accompanying transparency regime to limit dark pools.[2183]

2. Pre-Trade Transparency for Multilateral CH-OTFs

Despite the categorization of multilateral CH-OTFs as outside of the trading venue regime, the two types of CH-OTF under Article 42(a) and (b) FinfraG are functionally similar to the multilateral trading venues under Article 26 FinfraG. Both classifications of trading systems bring together multiple buy- and sell-side trading interests of third parties. Therefore, those CH-OTFs should be subject to the same pre-trade transparency requirement and the same waiver regime as trading venues.[2184] To avoid redundancy, the outlines made for Articles 27 and 29 FinfraV apply for multilateral CH-OTF accordingly.[2185]

With this reference, the Federal Council rectified the decision during the legislative process by the Swiss legislator to pull the multilateral CH-OTF

2182 EFD, 'Erläuterungsbericht zur Verordnung über die Finanzmarktinfrastrukturen und das Marktverhalten im Effekten- und Derivatehandel' (n 2043) 25; Favre and Kramer (n 566) SK FinfraG Art 46 para 16; Humbel, *Die Regelung der Vor- und Nachhandelstransparenz in der Europäischen Union und der Schweiz* (n 50) 551; Schären, Dobrauz-Saldapenna and Liebi (n 1876) 200; Schleiffer and Schärli, 'New Rules for Organized Trading Facilities' (n 1920) 44.

2183 Bundesrat, 'Botschaft zum Finanzmarktinfrastrukturgesetz (FinfraG)' (n 22) BBl. 2014, 7499, 7541.

2184 Studer and Vollenweider (n 1910) BSK FinfraG Art 46 para 7; Favre and Kramer (n 566) SK FinfraG Art 46 paras 18ff.

2185 See above Part II § 7 C.II.3 – 6. Cf. Humbel, *Die Regelung der Vor- und Nachhandelstransparenz in der Europäischen Union und der Schweiz* (n 50) 551–2. See also EFD, 'Erläuterungsbericht zur Verordnung über die Finanzmarktinfrastrukturen und das Marktverhalten im Effekten- und Derivatehandel' (n 2043) 25; Favre and Kramer (n 566) SK FinfraG Art 46 para 5; Hall (n 81) 498.

out of the trading venue regime and subject it to an independent body of laws.[2186]

3. Pre-Trade Transparency for Bilateral CH-OTFs

a) Issues Raised by the Reference to Article 27 FinfraV

The extension of the pre-trade transparency regime under Article 27 FinfraV may work for the multilateral CH-OTFs, but it becomes more difficult to determine the scope of pre-trade transparency for bilateral CH-OTFs pursuant to Articles 42(1) and 27 FinfraG. Bilateral CH-OTFs do not bring together multiple buying and selling interests in an instrument without being a party to the transaction like multilateral trading systems do. Thus, there is no aggregation of price-forming information in a neutral manner but rather an offer to either buy or sell an instrument to the operator of the bilateral trading system as the counterparty to the transaction.[2187]

Since there are no multiple buy- and sell-offers for an instrument, an application *mutatis mutandis* of Article 27 FinfraV cannot result in showing the five best sell and buy orders pursuant to Article 27(2) FinfraV because those are unavailable.[2188] It is only possible for the bilateral CH-OTF to display quotes for buying as well as selling for each instrument.[2189]

If such quotes shall have a price informing character comparable to showing the five best bid and offer prices on a multilateral system, those quotes must be firm quotes, i.e., firm offers to enter into a contract with the bilateral CH-OTF.[2190] This result is supported by a comparison with EU law: under Article 14(1) MiFIR, the systematic internalizer, which is a bilateral trading system comparable to the bilateral CH-OTF, is generally bound

2186 Cf. Bundesrat, 'Botschaft zum Finanzmarktinfrastrukturgesetz (FinfraG)' (n 22) BBl. 2014, 7530.

2187 Hall (n 81) 499, 502; Favre and Kramer (n 566) SK FinfraG Art 46 para 6.

2188 Favre and Kramer (n 566) SK FinfraG Art 46 paras 6, 22, 24; Hall (n 81) 499, 502; Humbel, *Die Regelung der Vor- und Nachhandelstransparenz in der Europäischen Union und der Schweiz* (n 50) 522–3; Claude Humbel, 'Organisierte Handelssysteme in der Schweiz – Quo vadis?: Handlungsspielräume de lege lata und Gestaltungsoptionen de lege ferenda im Lichte aktueller Entwicklungen' [2021] GesKR 25, 35.

2189 Hall (n 81) 499–500. See also Favre and Kramer (n 566) SK FinfraG Art 46 para 6.

2190 EFD, 'Erläuterungsbericht zur Verordnung über die Finanzmarktinfrastrukturen und das Marktverhalten im Effekten- und Derivatehandel' (n 2043) 25; FINMA, 'Circular 2018/1 Organised trading facilities' (n 1866) para 37; Hall (n 81) 502–3.

to make firm quotes.[2191] Only if the SI offers trading in illiquid non-equity instruments is it eligible to limit its offers to non-binding indicative quotes to offer some information about the SI's reservation price (Articles 18(2)(2) and 9(1) MiFIR).[2192] Despite the different naming scheme, the systematic internalizer under EU law was the blueprint for the bilateral version of the CH-OTF.[2193]

Because the Swiss legislator aimed for a close alignment with EU law for market access but did not adopt EU law under MiFID II/MiFIR to its full extent, it is heavily debated whether the pre-trade transparency requirement for bilateral CH-OTFs requires firm offers by the system operator or merely indicative quotes that qualify as indications of interest (*invitatio ad offerendum*).[2194] Despite the objective of feeding the price discovery mechanism, a firm offer would face two challenges. First, requiring firm offers from the system operator by means of pre-trade transparency would mean an obligation to contract, thus curtailing fundamental freedoms of the CH-OTF under the Swiss federal constitution.[2195] This would require a sufficient legal basis to withstand the test of constitutionality.[2196]

The second issue of a firm offer would also circle around the question of constitutionality. The resulting obligation to contract can only be constitutional if it is limited to the necessary scope which excludes those situations in which the CH-OTF operator would jeopardize its financial soundness. EU law shows that important limitations can be volume-thresholds above which firm quotes are no longer required since the CH-OTF would take over additional risk, like position risk and risk of market impact

2191 Humbel, *Die Regelung der Vor- und Nachhandelstransparenz in der Europäischen Union und der Schweiz* (n 50) 553; Humbel, 'Organisierte Handelssysteme in der Schweiz – Quo vadis?' (n 2188) 35–6.

2192 Humbel, *Die Regelung der Vor- und Nachhandelstransparenz in der Europäischen Union und der Schweiz* (n 50) 553; Humbel, 'Organisierte Handelssysteme in der Schweiz – Quo vadis?' (n 2188) 35–6.

2193 Favre and Kramer (n 566) SK FinfraG Art 46 para 25; Humbel, *Die Regelung der Vor- und Nachhandelstransparenz in der Europäischen Union und der Schweiz* (n 50) 553.

2194 See, for instance, Favre and Kramer (n 566) SK FinfraG Art 46 paras 6, 25; Humbel, *Die Regelung der Vor- und Nachhandelstransparenz in der Europäischen Union und der Schweiz* (n 50) 553ff; Humbel, 'Organisierte Handelssysteme in der Schweiz – Quo vadis?' (n 2188) 35; Hall (n 81) 503ff.

2195 Studer and Vollenweider (n 1910) BSK FinfraG Art 46 para 10; Favre and Kramer (n 566) SK FinfraG Art 46 para 25; Hall (n 81) 502.

2196 Studer and Vollenweider (n 1910) BSK FinfraG Art 46 para 10; Favre and Kramer (n 566) SK FinfraG Art 46 para 6.

costs.[2197] Systematic internalizers in the European Union can further limit the number of transactions that they need to enter with one client because otherwise they would face the risk falling prey to strategic behavior of, for instance, informed traders and HFTs.[2198] Bilateral traders should also retain the liberty to deny a transaction with parties that are not creditworthy.[2199]

Thus, the following section first answers whether Swiss law requires a firm offer or merely an indication of interest. Second, if a firm offer is required, it must be determined if Articles 42(1) and 27(1) FinfraV implement the obligation to contract in a constitutional manner.

b) Firm Offer or Indication of Interest

Since Swiss law does not specifically speak of firm offers or firm quotes like Articles 14(1), 18(1) MiFIR under EU law, an application *mutatis mutandis* of Article 27(1) FinfraV is open to interpretation and can also mean a mere indication of interest (*invitatio ad offerendum*).

Those who favor the interpretation that Articles 42(1) and 27(1) FinfraV merely mean an indication of interest argue that a CH-OTF cannot publish a firm offer because not every essential term of the contract is yet given, i.e., the *essentialia negotii* are incomplete.[2200] According to this theory, CH-OTF only publish the price for selling and buying a specific financial instrument, but the quantity of any eventual contract is still undefined. Thus, a potential customer of a bilateral CH-OTF cannot bring the contract to a conclusion by simply accepting the price offered by the CH-OTF, but rather they must also add their preferred quantity.[2201] And thereby it is the customer who is making the offer which is then accepted by the CH-OTF.[2202] Under this interpretation, however, the publication of the price is non-binding which

2197 See Article 14(3)(1) MiFIR; Hall (n 81) 504–5.

2198 See Article 17(1)(2) MiFIR; Hall (n 81) 503.

2199 See Article 17(1)(2) MiFIR.

2200 Favre and Kramer (n 566) SK FinfraG Art 46 para 25. Different: Hall (n 81) 502–3; Humbel, *Die Regelung der Vor- und Nachhandelstransparenz in der Europäischen Union und der Schweiz* (n 50) 556ff.

2201 The situation is also different to a buyer at a vending machine because the vending machine shows either through a window or by other means (e.g., flashing a red light) if there are still enough products left to conclude another sales contract.

2202 Cf. Favre and Kramer (n 566) SK FinfraG Art 46 para 25; Humbel, *Die Regelung der Vor- und Nachhandelstransparenz in der Europäischen Union und der Schweiz* (n 50) 556.

puts it closer to a publication of indicative quotes like under Article 9(1) MiFIR.[2203]

Since Article 42(2) FinfraV considers the obligation of a CH-OTF to publish quotes only upon request in illiquid markets as an easing of the default requirement in liquid markets under Article 42(1) FinfraV, the actual *ratio legis* is to require a firm offer.[2204]

The stipulation found in FINMA's circular on CH-OTF also points in the direction of a firm quote requirement: a bilateral CH-OTF must exercise its discretion on the issue whether to enter into a contract or reject it upon pre-defined rules.[2205] If the quote was non-binding this effort would be futile because it would be the CH-OTF operator who would receive the offers upon its indication of interests and could then freely choose if it wishes to transact.[2206]

Moreover, the comparison to EU law is also persuasive evidence of Article 42(1) FinfraV requiring a firm quote. For systematic internalizers under EU law, Articles 14(1), 18(1) MiFIR require a firm quote. Swiss law used the SI-regime as blueprint for its bilateral CH-OTF and therefore aims for a comparable regulation. Swiss law even aimed to align with the regulatory standard under EU law when FinfraG and FinfraV were enacted to receive market access.[2207] If Swiss law satisfied itself with mere indications of interests, it would remain far behind the transparency level of MiFID II/ MiFIR.[2208]

2203 Humbel, *Die Regelung der Vor- und Nachhandelstransparenz in der Europäischen Union und der Schweiz* (n 50) 553.

2204 FINMA, 'Circular 2018/1 Organised trading facilities' (n 1866) 9 paras 37, 40; Humbel, *Die Regelung der Vor- und Nachhandelstransparenz in der Europäischen Union und der Schweiz* (n 50) 555; Humbel, 'Organisierte Handelssysteme in der Schweiz – Quo vadis?' (n 2188) 35.

2205 FINMA, 'Circular 2018/1 Organised trading facilities' (n 1866) 5 paras 17–8; Humbel, *Die Regelung der Vor- und Nachhandelstransparenz in der Europäischen Union und der Schweiz* (n 50) 555.

2206 Humbel, *Die Regelung der Vor- und Nachhandelstransparenz in der Europäischen Union und der Schweiz* (n 50) 555; Humbel, 'Organisierte Handelssysteme in der Schweiz – Quo vadis?' (n 2188) 35.

2207 Humbel, *Die Regelung der Vor- und Nachhandelstransparenz in der Europäischen Union und der Schweiz* (n 50) 556; Humbel, 'Organisierte Handelssysteme in der Schweiz – Quo vadis?' (n 2188) 35.

2208 Humbel, *Die Regelung der Vor- und Nachhandelstransparenz in der Europäischen Union und der Schweiz* (n 50) 556; Humbel, 'Organisierte Handelssysteme in der Schweiz – Quo vadis?' (n 2188) 35.

To combine the rationale of the law with the issue of a non-defined quote quantity, *von Hall* suggests a dynamic interpretation of *essentialia negotii* to account for the functioning of contemporary trading systems. In a bilateral setting, a firm quote is sufficient for making an offer which can be accepted by any trader and ultimately result in a contract.[2209] While this interpretation supports the rationale of Article 42(1) FinfraV, the issue raised by *Humbel* is even more persuasive: it is rather a misperception that CH-OTF will only offer a price – without quantity – when they are quoting a sell and an offer price. Since they take over risk, it is generally the case that bilateral trading systems quote prices with an attached volume. Due to the position risk bilateral traders take on, they will quote more competitive prices for smaller volumes and less competitive one for larger volumes.[2210] Moreover, it is hard to imagine a quote for individualizable financial instruments that does not at least show the price for the minimum quantity of one instrument.[2211] Further, Article 27(1) FinfraV also mentions that the volume of a buy or sell order must be determined when providing pre-trade transparency. The CH-OTF will display multiple quotes of different sizes rather than quoting prices without any specified volume. The published information is therefore not an *invitatio ad offerendum* which lacks the offeror's willingness to be bound but rather is an offer to an unspecified number of offerees (i.e., an *offerta ad incertas personas*).[2212] Thus, CH-OTFs publish every information that counts among the *essentialia negotii* making its quotes rather firm quotes than mere indications of interest.[2213]

c) Sufficient Legal Basis

After having established that quotes in bilateral systems qualify as binding offers resulting in an obligation to contract for CH-OTFs, it must be examined whether there is a sufficient legal basis under Swiss law to

2209 Hall (n 81) 502–3; see also Humbel, *Die Regelung der Vor- und Nachhandelstransparenz in der Europäischen Union und der Schweiz* (n 50) 556–7.

2210 Humbel, *Die Regelung der Vor- und Nachhandelstransparenz in der Europäischen Union und der Schweiz* (n 50) 557–8.

2211 ibid 557–8; see also Humbel, 'Organisierte Handelssysteme in der Schweiz – Quo vadis?' (n 2188) 36.

2212 Corinne Zellweger-Gutknecht in Corinne Widmer Lüchinger and David Oser (eds), *Basler Kommentar Obligationenrecht I* (7th edn, Helbing & Lichtenhahn Verlag 2020) Art 3 para 13.

2213 Humbel, *Die Regelung der Vor- und Nachhandelstransparenz in der Europäischen Union und der Schweiz* (n 50) 556ff.

proportionally curtail the freedom to contract and the economic freedom of the CH-OTF.

Article 46(3) FinfraG only delegates the power to the Federal Council to implement pre-trade transparency for CH-OTFs. The Federal Council used this power by implementing pre-trade transparency pursuant to Articles 42, 27, 29 FinfraV. When considering all three Articles together, there is a sufficient legal basis for limiting the fundamental freedoms of CH-OTFs. The fact that major elements of this rule are on the level of the regulation does not harm this interpretation because in Swiss financial markets law, it is common for the laws by Parliament to contain only the high-level principles, while the details are to be determined by the Federal Council within its delegated powers.[2214]

Another issue is, however, whether the legal basis is sufficiently specified. Due to the limiting effects on CH-OTF operators' fundamental freedoms (i.e., because they are subject to an obligation to contract), a legal basis is necessary. CH-OTFs are uniformly subject to pre-trade transparency requirements by these requirements. However, only bilateral (and not multilateral) CH-OTF are limited. This is not clearly identified in the provision under Article 42(1) FinfraV. Therefore, the degree of specificity in those provision is marginal with regard to the obligation to contract despite a very complex and technical matter that would normally require the legislator to formulate an unequivocal rule to ensure that the addressee can comply with it.

The Swiss Federal Court determined that the degree of specificity is contingent upon the subject matter and the addressees of the law.[2215] Despite the complex subject matter, the law only addresses the small group of eligible operators of CH-OTFs which all have sufficient experience evidenced by their authorization as either bank, securities firm (securities trader), or trading venue to understand the consequences of an obligation to publish firm quotes in a bilateral system. Thus, the legal basis for imposing an obligation to contract on bilateral CH-OTFs is sufficiently specified as well.

2214 Peter V Kunz, *Kreuzfahrt durch's schweizerische Finanzmarktrecht* (Stämpfli 2014) 31: *'die finanzmarktrechtlichen Rahmenerlasse die verfassungsmässigen Anforderungen an eine gesetzliche Basis zur Einschränkung der Wirtschaftsfreiheit ohne weiteres [erfüllen]'*; Humbel, *Die Regelung der Vor- und Nachhandelstransparenz in der Europäischen Union und der Schweiz* (n 50) 560.

2215 BGE 128 I 327 E. 4.2.

Nonetheless, the Federal Council may wish to use a future occasion to increase the degree of specificity to elevate this issue beyond any doubt.[2216]

d) Proportionality

An obligation to contract limits the fundamental freedom of the bilateral trading system operator. To balance its interests with those of the (investing) public, the law may only limit the bilateral trading system operator insofar as it is necessary for the achievement of a decent amount of transparency fueling price discovery and eventually supporting an efficient and resilient market. In this proportionality test, the interests of the bilateral trading system operator to choose its contracting parties may be limited, but the system operator cannot be obligated to jeopardize its own financial well-being by entering into risky transactions or falling prey to predatory trading. At a certain point, the public interest even swings to the side of the system operator because pre-trade transparency is meant to serve the creation of market liquidity. If too much pre-trade transparency, however, renders offering bilateral trading services inefficient, the system operators will cease to offer it and thereby pre-trade transparency will dry up liquidity.

aa) Elements Mitigating the Infringement of CH-OTF's Freedom

Since EU law stood as a model for Swiss law and faces the same issue, the measures taken under Swiss law to mitigate the effects of the obligation to contract will be compared with those taken under EU law.

(i) No Quoting Requirement for Illiquid Instruments

An explicit limitation of the effects of an obligation to contract can be found in Article 42(2) FinfraV which only requires to publish quotes upon request for bilateral systems when trading in an illiquid market. Conversely, this means that Article 42(1) FinfraV states an obligation for quoting on a continuous basis in liquid markets. This provision adopts the differentia-

2216 Humbel, *Die Regelung der Vor- und Nachhandelstransparenz in der Europäischen Union und der Schweiz* (n 50) 558ff.

tion between quoting requirements for liquid and illiquid markets under Article 14 MiFIR.[2217]

Unlike EU law, Swiss law does not define the concept of a liquid market in FinfraG nor in FinfraV. Only FINMA provides a guideline in its circular on CH-OTF where the thresholds for liquidity shall be drawn. In a rather coarse and simplified assumption, FINMA determines that financial instruments not admitted to trading on a trading venue are per se illiquid without any regard to market size or turnover.[2218] This is a particularly broad exemption given the limitations of the trading venue classification to exchanges and CH-MTF. It disregards that multilateral trading on CH-OTFs and internalization services of bilateral CH-OTFs can create significant liquidity, with regard to financial instruments other than securities, the only organized liquidity in the market. Thus, especially for bespoke derivatives, so called OTC-derivatives, a bilateral CH-OTF will only have to quote upon request even when pre-trade transparency is eventually expanded from shares to all financial instruments.

Conversely, this means that only financial instruments admitted to trading on a trading venue can qualify to trade in a liquid market. Among those, FINMA determined that the market for a financial instrument qualifies as liquid if the instrument was traded on average at least 100 times per trading day in the previous calendar year measured on the trading venue on which the instrument was first admitted.[2219] With this definition, FINMA introduced a relatively high threshold which SIX estimated to qualify less than 10 % of financial instruments to trade in a liquid market, further reducing the light pre-trade transparency can shine into bilateral markets.[2220] However, EU law also uses a more nuanced approach to define a liquid market under Article 2(1)(17) MiFIR.[2221]

2217 FINMA, 'Circular 2018/1 Organised trading facilities' (n 1866) 9 paras 37ff; Favre and Kramer (n 566) SK FinfraG Art 46 para 25; Humbel, *Die Regelung der Vor- und Nachhandelstransparenz in der Europäischen Union und der Schweiz* (n 50) 561; Humbel, 'Organisierte Handelssysteme in der Schweiz – Quo vadis?' (n 2188) 36; Hall (n 81) 502ff.

2218 FINMA, 'Circular 2018/1 Organised trading facilities' (n 1866) 9 para 39.

2219 ibid 9 para 38; Favre and Kramer (n 566) SK FinfraG Art 46 para 23.

2220 Studer and Vollenweider (n 1910) BSK FinfraG Art 46 para 10.

2221 Humbel, *Die Regelung der Vor- und Nachhandelstransparenz in der Europäischen Union und der Schweiz* (n 50) 562; Schären, Dobrauz-Saldapenna and Liebi (n 1876) 200. See Article 2(1)(17) MiFIR:
"liquid market' means:

To increase transparency when a CH-OTF refrains from publishing quotes due to an illiquid market, FINMA requires the system operator to document its analysis of the market liquidity so that a knowledgeable third party can make a reliable judgement of the situation later on. This increases accountability and curbs regulatory arbitrage in the system.[2222]

With this provision, Swiss law significantly mitigates the impact of the obligation to contract by alleviating bilateral CH-OTFs from publishing quotes for instruments with a potentially volatile market due to the lack of liquidity. Although this narrow definition of a liquid market leaves a large portion of instruments outside the pre-trade transparency regime, it also supports the existence of a market for illiquid instruments and thereby adds to the overall liquidity. Despite the positive effects on proportionality for the CH-OTF operators, a future revision of FINMA's liquidity definition may lead to a more ambitious definition of the term 'liquid market' after more experience has been gained with pre-trade transparency.

(ii) Quoting Requirement above Standard Market Size and Below a Minimum Size

In order to further protect the operator of a bilateral trading system from the adverse effects of the publication of quotes, Article 14(2) MiFIR in the European Union limits the requirement to publish quotes for systematic internalizers when the deal size is above standard market size. Under Swiss

for the purposes of Articles 9, 11, and 18, a market for a financial instrument or a class of financial instruments, where there are ready and willing buyers and sellers on a continuous basis, and where the market is assessed in accordance with the following criteria, taking into consideration the specific market structures of the particular financial instrument or of the particular class of financial instruments:
(i) the average frequency and size of transactions over a range of market conditions, having regard to the nature and life cycle of products within the class of financial instrument;
(ii) the number and type of market participants, including the ratio of market participants to traded financial instruments in a particular product;
(iii) the average size of spreads, where available;
(b) for the purposes of Articles 4, 5 and 14, a market for a financial instrument that is traded daily where the market is assessed according to the following criteria:
the free float;
(ii) the average daily number of transactions in those financial instruments;
(iii) the average daily turnover for those financial instruments;'

2222 FINMA, 'Circular 2018/1 Organised trading facilities' (n 1866) 9 para 40.

law, however, there is no explicit exemption from the publication requirement for its bilateral CH-OTFs.[2223]

The publication of order sizes above standard market size has adverse effects because this information shows the market that the system operator has taken on a large short- or long-position that it needs to unwind into the market in reasonable time. To prevent other market participants from using such knowledge privileges the operators of CH-OTFs to incentivize them to supply liquidity also in large order lots to the market.[2224]

Given this rationale of the exemption from publishing quotes above standard market size, it is reasonable to assume that this exemption is the functional equivalent to the large in scale waiver for multilateral trading venues.[2225] Since Article 42(1) FinfraV declares Article 27 FinfraV applicable by analogy, so too can the large in scale waiver under Article 27(4)(d) FinfraV be applied to bilateral CH-OTF to create an exemption similar to the one pursuant to Article 14(2) MiFIR in the European Union.[2226]

Even though the large in scale waiver is applicable to this situation, it must be noted that the Federal Council only set out the principles of the large in scale waiver under Article 27(4)(d) FinfraV, while it left the details to the self-regulatory powers of the trading venues. In particular, the issue of defining the thresholds that determine the average daily turnover above which an order qualifies for the waiver was left to the self-regulatory power.[2227] This permissive approach becomes concerning in the context of CH-OTF, which the Swiss legislator denied the status of a trading venue and thereby denied self-regulatory powers under Article 27 FinfraG.[2228] For CH-OTFs, FINMA must define many technical details and, especially with regard to the functioning of the CH-OTF, the operator must be given at

2223 Hall (n 81) 504–5; Humbel, *Die Regelung der Vor- und Nachhandelstransparenz in der Europäischen Union und der Schweiz* (n 50) 563; Humbel, 'Organisierte Handelssysteme in der Schweiz – Quo vadis?' (n 2188) 37.

2224 Hall (n 81) 504.; Humbel, *Die Regelung der Vor- und Nachhandelstransparenz in der Europäischen Union und der Schweiz* (n 50) 563; Humbel, 'Organisierte Handelssysteme in der Schweiz – Quo vadis?' (n 2188) 37.

2225 Humbel, *Die Regelung der Vor- und Nachhandelstransparenz in der Europäischen Union und der Schweiz* (n 50) 564; Humbel, 'Organisierte Handelssysteme in der Schweiz – Quo vadis?' (n 2188) 37.

2226 Humbel, *Die Regelung der Vor- und Nachhandelstransparenz in der Europäischen Union und der Schweiz* (n 50) 564; Humbel, 'Organisierte Handelssysteme in der Schweiz – Quo vadis?' (n 2188) 37.

2227 Cf. Schott and Winkler (n 70) SK FinfraG Art 29 para 38.

2228 Different Studer and Vollenweider (n 1910) BSK FinfraG Art 42 para 14.

least some power to define certain technical details to provide a properly operating trading system. Regarding the thresholds of the large in scale waiver, the reference in Article 42(1) FinfraV which declares Article 27(4)(d) FinfraV applicable *mutatis mutandis* must include the power to define thresholds for when an order qualifies as large in scale. Nevertheless, FINMA should add more details for CH-OTFs with regard to the scope of application of the pre-trade transparency rule and its exceptions under Articles 42(1) and 27 FinfraV.

Furthermore, Article 14(3) MiFIR sets out minimum quote sizes.[2229] This provision has been added under MiFID II/MiFIR to prevent systematic internalizers from publishing best priced quotes in an economically meaningless small size (i.e., only a couple of instruments). Such a strategy helped bilateral trading systems to push in front of other trading systems for order flow that is routed under the duty of best execution, whereas only committing little capital. The European Union considered such bait and switch tactics to bias the price formation mechanism with exaggerated prices and to disadvantage those who supply the market with meaningful liquidity at competitive prices (i.e., order sizes that match the demands of the market but at slightly inferior prices because of the additional position risk).[2230]

In spite of the desirability of such minimum quote sizes, it is currently not part of the regulatory regime for CH-OTFs under Swiss law. First, there is no provision that would point out such an obligation, not even the waiver regime under Article 27(4) FinfraV; and second, implementing such an obligation would require implementing measures setting up a standard for 'standard market size' of classes of financial instruments. Both are currently absent under Swiss law but would be desirable to add in the next revision of FinfraV.[2231]

However, with regard to the proportionality of the requirement to publish quotes, the absence of a minimum quoting requirement provides the bilateral CH-OTFs additional leeway to exercise their fundamental freedoms. Depending on how large the minimum quote size may be, implementing this requirement will not necessarily render the publication of

2229 Gebauer (n 94) MiFIR Art 14 para 25; Kumpan and Schmidt (n 4) MiFIR Art 14 para 11.

2230 Gebauer (n 94) MiFIR Art 14 para 27; Gomber and Nassauer (n 1086) 254.

2231 Hall (n 81) 504; Humbel, *Die Regelung der Vor- und Nachhandelstransparenz in der Europäischen Union und der Schweiz* (n 50) 563ff; Humbel, 'Organisierte Handelssysteme in der Schweiz – Quo vadis?' (n 2188) 37–8.

quotes a disproportional measure if it only prevents economically insignificant quote sizes.[2232]

(iii) Discretion with regard to Access to Quotes

Pursuant to Article 17(1) MiFIR, a systemic internalizer in the European Union may decide on the clients to whom it gives access to its quotes. The decision shall be made based on the SI's commercial policy and in an objective non-discriminatory way.[2233]

Under Swiss law, neither FinfraG nor FinfraV have a similar provision setting out this discretionary power for bilateral CH-OTFs. However, FINMA deduced this power from the bilateral character of this type of CH-OTF and most likely with regard to its model under EU law. In its circular, FINMA outlined that the CH-OTF can have discretion to enter into a contract with a client.[2234] This power includes the discretion to decide whom the CH-OTF operator provides with access to certain quotes.[2235]

Similar to EU law, FINMA requires the operator of an CH-OTF to disclose the principles for the exercise of its discretion to its clients. Those principles should be based on objective criteria and shall be non-discriminatory.[2236] Thus, with regard to access to quotes, Swiss and EU law are very closely aligned.

(iv) Limiting the Number of Transactions

Some methods of trading, especially algorithmic and high frequency trading, expose bilateral trading systems to high levels of risk. Bilateral trading systems are vulnerable to high frequency trading since they are obliged

2232 Cf. Hall (n 81) 504.; Humbel, *Die Regelung der Vor- und Nachhandelstransparenz in der Europäischen Union und der Schweiz* (n 50) 563ff; Humbel, 'Organisierte Handelssysteme in der Schweiz – Quo vadis?' (n 2188) 37–8.

2233 Gebauer (n 94) MiFIR Art 17 para 1; Kumpan and Schmidt (n 4) MiFIR Art 17 para 5.

2234 FINMA, 'Circular 2018/1 Organised trading facilities' (n 1866) 5 para 17.

2235 Hall (n 81) 503; Humbel, *Die Regelung der Vor- und Nachhandelstransparenz in der Europäischen Union und der Schweiz* (n 50) 566; Humbel, 'Organisierte Handelssysteme in der Schweiz – Quo vadis?' (n 2188) 37–8.

2236 FINMA, 'Circular 2018/1 Organised trading facilities' (n 1866) 5 para 18.

to publish firm quotes and thus can fall prey to short trading peaks by high frequency traders. High frequency traders are constantly screening the market for price changes and when they pick one up at one venue they will turn around and trade against the stale price of the bilateral trading system that has not yet realized the price change.[2237] However, when leaving the bilateral trading system exposed to such kind of trading, it might either widen the spread or stop offering larger order sizes to hedge its risk which, in result, increases transaction costs.[2238]

Since the EU legislator considered the liquidity supplied by (bilateral) systematic internalizers more important than a fast price correction by high frequency traders using informed trading, the European Union implemented the limitation under Article 17(2) MiFIR. Under this provision the systematic internalizer can limit in a non-discriminatory way the number of transactions from either one client or several different clients.[2239]

Although having a similar degree of automation in the capital markets, Swiss law does not protect its bilateral CH-OTF with a provision similar to Article 17(2) MiFIR.[2240] Trying to embed this provision within the CH-OTFs discretionary power would mean renouncing the nature of the quote as a binding offer, and is therefore not possible for the reasons mentioned above.[2241] This is hence another situation in which FinfraG and FinfraV replicate the law under MiFID I instead of implementing the new features introduced by MiFID II/MiFIR. This time, to the detriment of the CH-OTF which will probably respond to this vulnerability by quoting best prices in in miniscule size, thus compromising trade transparency.

2237 Cf. Monsch (n 90) 74.

2238 See, for instance, Fox, 'MiFID II and Equity Trading' (n 53) paras 18.72ff.

2239 Gebauer (n 94) MiFIR Art 17 para 12; Kumpan and Schmidt (n 4) MiFIR Art 17 paras 6–7.

2240 Humbel, *Die Regelung der Vor- und Nachhandelstransparenz in der Europäischen Union und der Schweiz* (n 50) 566; Humbel, 'Organisierte Handelssysteme in der Schweiz – Quo vadis?' (n 2188) 37–8.

2241 Humbel, *Die Regelung der Vor- und Nachhandelstransparenz in der Europäischen Union und der Schweiz* (n 50) 566; Humbel, 'Organisierte Handelssysteme in der Schweiz – Quo vadis?' (n 2188) 37–8.

(v) Updating or Withdrawing Quotes

Capital markets are dynamic and so are their prices for financial instruments. Under EU law, Article 15(1) MiFIR accounts for this fact by allowing systematic internalizers to update their quotes at any time. This means that a once-published quote can be overwritten by another quote with an adjusted price or volume whenever the systematic internalizer sees fit.[2242]

Although Swiss financial markets law lacks a provision similar to Article 15(1) MiFIR, Swiss contract law allows for the same result to void a prior, not yet accepted offer when a new offer is made.[2243]

Article 15(1) MiFIR, however, goes further by allowing not only replacing a prior quote with a new one, but withdrawing a quote leaving the market without a new quote for the instrument. This provision is meant to cover situations of exceptional market conditions which, for instance, means a situation in which trading in the respective instrument has been ceased by the most important market in terms of liquidity or a market the bilateral trading system used as a reference market.[2244] Thus, this provision is crucial with regard to market resilience containing market volatility.

Under Swiss law, there is no comparable provision and therefore experts are of the opinion that bilateral CH-OTFs cannot react to such situations.[2245] While other experts advocate applying Article 7(1) OR in combination with objective criteria for determining exceptional market conditions developed by FINMA.[2246] Before reverting to contract law principles, it shall be examined whether principles of financial markets law may apply.

One option for the bilateral CH-OTF to react to such situations might be to update its orders with prices so high that no one is incentivized to trade anymore. This would also bring trading to an end as on multilateral markets but may cause a certain amount of volatility along the way.

2242 Gebauer (n 94) MiFIR Art 15 paras 4–5.

2243 Humbel, *Die Regelung der Vor- und Nachhandelstransparenz in der Europäischen Union und der Schweiz* (n 50) 566–7; Humbel, 'Organisierte Handelssysteme in der Schweiz – Quo vadis?' (n 2188) 38.

2244 Beck and Röh (n 1832) WpHG § 32a para 27; Gebauer (n 94) MiFIR Art 15 paras 4–5.

2245 Humbel, *Die Regelung der Vor- und Nachhandelstransparenz in der Europäischen Union und der Schweiz* (n 50) 566–7.

2246 Hall (n 81) 504. Cf. Humbel, *Die Regelung der Vor- und Nachhandelstransparenz in der Europäischen Union und der Schweiz* (n 50) 567.

Humbel advocates to interpret Article 42(1) FinfraV which requires that the transparency rules apply *mutatis mutandis* in the way that bilateral CH-OTF must be granted discretion to withdraw their quotes and to update them when the market is in turmoil.[2247] Another option would be to apply Article 42(2) FinfraV analogously in situations in which the primary multilateral market halts its trading due to volatility. In situations in which a bilateral CH-OTF references this multilateral market's price for its trading, the scenario is comparable to a market in which there is no liquid market for the instrument in the first place because the liquid multilateral market(place) no longer operates. However, the issue with this solution is that CH-OTFs would still be obliged to publish their quotes upon request, but there is no limitation in the statutory text that requires the CH-OTF to publish a stale quote upon request; it might as well be a current one which takes the market turmoil in consideration.

While none of these options is ideal, an analogy to Article 42(2) FinfraV is the best option under current Swiss law and provides the bilateral CH-OTF with a perspective in exceptional market situations. Nevertheless, the critics in the literature are correct that the Swiss legislator should provide the CH-OTF with the ability to withdraw its quotes under exceptional market conditions and to determine what is meant by exceptional market conditions.[2248]

bb) Overall Evaluation of Proportionality

After having established that the requirement to publish firm quotes results in an obligation to contract which limits the bilateral CH-OTFs fundamental freedoms, examining Swiss law further has shown that there are also multiple exceptions that mitigate the impact of the limitation of the fundamental freedoms. Even though the exceptions may not always reach as far as under MiFID II/MiFIR, they replicate very closely what MiFID I set out for systematic internalizers. This may not always produce the best trade transparency data given that bilateral CH-OTFs can freely choose minis-

2247 Humbel, *Die Regelung der Vor- und Nachhandelstransparenz in der Europäischen Union und der Schweiz* (n 50) 567; Humbel, 'Organisierte Handelssysteme in der Schweiz – Quo vadis?' (n 2188) 38.

2248 Humbel, *Die Regelung der Vor- und Nachhandelstransparenz in der Europäischen Union und der Schweiz* (n 50) 567. Cf. Favre and Kramer (n 566) SK FinfraG Art 46 para 24; Hall (n 81) 504.

cule sizes or extremely high prices to protect themselves, but it does not lead to the verdict that the obligation to publish quotes is an infringement of fundamental freedoms.[2249]

As under MiFID I, this framework will render providing bilateral liquidity a profitable business model for market makers and will also provide more pre-trade transparency data than under the preceding law. Nevertheless, the Swiss legislator should amend both FinfraG and FinfraV with clearer and more detailed provisions. In certain cases, such as the withdrawal of quotes under exceptional market conditions and the limitation of the number of transactions with one or several different clients, the Swiss legislator may consider further alignment with EU law to account for modern methods of trading and the occasional disruptions that result from those.[2250]

4. Post-Trade Transparency for CH-OTF

Article 46(1) FinfraG sets out that an operator of a CH-OTF shall publish the information on transactions carried out on the trading facility, in particular, price, volume and the time of the transaction.[2251]

Although this provision does not subject other securities firms in the OTC-space to post-trade transparency as do Articles 20, 21 MiFIR, the scope is approximately similar, since the scope of the CH-OTF lacks the quantitative requirements of the systematic internalizer definition under EU law and is therefore broader in scope.[2252]

Even though this provision is closely aligned with post-trade transparency for trading venues pursuant to Article 29(2) FinfraG, Article 46(1) FinfraG tailors post-trade transparency with respect to both the entity subject to the obligation and the instruments captured.[2253] Under Article 46(1) FinfraG, the operating entity has to ensure that post-trade information

2249 Cf. Humbel, *Die Regelung der Vor- und Nachhandelstransparenz in der Europäischen Union und der Schweiz* (n 50) 567.

2250 Cf. ibid 568–9.

2251 Studer and Vollenweider (n 1910) BSK FinfraG Art 46 para 12; Favre and Kramer (n 566) SK FinfraG Art 46 para 27.

2252 Humbel, *Die Regelung der Vor- und Nachhandelstransparenz in der Europäischen Union und der Schweiz* (n 50) 569–70.

2253 Studer and Vollenweider (n 1910) BSK FinfraG Art 46 paras 12–3; Favre and Kramer (n 566) SK FinfraG Art 46 para 27.

is published.[2254] Furthermore, Article 46(1) FinfraG does not specify the instruments captured by post-trade transparency because, unlike with pre-trade transparency, there is no limitation to shares, and, unlike post-trade transparency on trading venues, there is also no limitation to securities either. Hence, post-trade transparency on CH-OTFs applies to all financial instruments.[2255] This also fulfils the requirement under the IOSCO principles on dark liquidity to capture even these financial instruments via post-trade transparency that have not been subject to prior pre-trade trade transparency to contain the adverse effects of dark trading.[2256]

For further details on the scope of post-trade transparency on CH-OTFs, Article 46(2) FinfraG delegates power to the Federal Council. In its implementing measure, the Federal Council distinguished once more between the multilateral and bilateral type of this trading system.

a) Post-Trade Transparency for Multilateral CH-OTFs

Pursuant to Article 43(1) FinfraV, for multilateral trading on CH-OTF the requirements under Article 28(1), (4) and 29 FinfraV apply by analogy. While Article 28(1) FinfraV concerns the publication, the reference to Article 28(4) FinfraV allows multilateral CH-OTF to defer publication for the specified transactions.[2257] On both, see the outlines made above with regard to trading venues.[2258]

Post-trade transparency of multilateral CH-OTFs, however, differs in comparison to trading venues with respect to publication of off-venue transactions. Since Article 43(1) FinfraV only refers to Article 28(1) FinfraV but not to Article 28(2), (3) FinfraV, multilateral CH-OTFs do not have to publish post-trade data of off-venue transactions. This is only sensible considering that CH-OTFs have customers instead of participants and that those customers are not obliged to report the off-venue transactions to the CH-OTFs pursuant to Article 39 FinfraG and Article 37 FinfraV.[2259]

2254 Favre and Kramer (n 566) SK FinfraG Art 46 para 28.

2255 Studer and Vollenweider (n 1910) BSK FinfraG Art 46 para 12; Favre and Kramer (n 566) SK FinfraG Art 46 para 27.

2256 IOSCO, 'Principles for Dark Liquidity' (n 12) 27–8.

2257 Studer and Vollenweider (n 1910) BSK FinfraG Art 46 paras 13–4; Favre and Kramer (n 566) SK FinfraG Art 46 paras 28–9.

2258 See above Part II § 7 C.II.4 – 5.

2259 Favre and Kramer (n 566) SK FinfraG Art 46 para 29.

With this reference, the Federal Council managed to align post-trade transparency requirements and exceptions with those that apply to multilateral trading venues, and succeeded in subjecting functionally similar trading systems to functionally similar regulation.[2260]

b) Post-Trade Transparency for Bilateral CH-OTFs

While the content of Article 46(1) FinfraG has been widely preserved for multilateral CH-OTFs, the Federal Council's provision for bilateral CH-OTFs is a broad interpretation of Article 46(1) FinfraG. Pursuant to Article 43(2) FinfraV, it shall suffice if bilateral CH-OTFs make aggregate publication of post-trade transparency data at the end of the trading day.[2261]

In comparison to EU law, the provision under Swiss law lags behind the granular publication requirements for post-trade information under MiFIR. Pursuant to Articles 20(1), (2) and 21(1), (2) MiFIR, post-trade transparency by bilateral trading systematic internalizers and investment firms trading OTC shall be made public on a trade-by-trade basis in as close to real-time as possible.[2262] Systematic internalizers and investment firms trading OTC can delay the publication only under the special circumstances described by the deferrals under Articles 7 and 11 MiFIR.[2263] Unlike Swiss law, only transactions in non-equity instruments under special circumstances laid out in Article 11 MiFIR justify aggregated publication of post-trade transparency,[2264] whereas Article 43(2) FinfraV sets this as the default rule under Swiss law.[2265]

However, Article 43(2) FinfraV can be interpreted as a minimal requirement only due to the phrasing 'shall suffice'.[2266] This can be understood in

2260 Humbel, *Die Regelung der Vor- und Nachhandelstransparenz in der Europäischen Union und der Schweiz* (n 50) 574.

2261 Studer and Vollenweider (n 1910) BSK FinfraG Art 46 para 15; Favre and Kramer (n 566) SK FinfraG Art 46 para 32.

2262 Gebauer (n 94) MiFIR Art 20 paras 16ff and Art 21 paras 11ff.

2263 ibid MiFIR Art 20 paras 20ff and Art 21 paras 15ff.

2264 Cf. Article 21(4) MiFIR.

2265 Cf. Humbel, *Die Regelung der Vor- und Nachhandelstransparenz in der Europäischen Union und der Schweiz* (n 50) 573.

2266 The original versions of Article 43(2) FinfraV in German, French and Italian similarly suggest a minimal requirement: German '*Beim bilateralen Handel genügt eine aggregierte Publikation am Ende eines Handelstages.*'; French '*En cas de négociation bilatérale, une publication agrégée à la fin d'un jour de négociation suffit.*'; Italian a manner that the bilateral CH-OTF may also go beyond this requirement and demand a more granular publication of post-trade transparency data.

Minimal requirements are, however, only a useful regulatory technique if the market is characterized by competition with regard to the quality of the respective criterion ('*Qualitätswettbewerb*'). In this case, this would require competition for more post-trade transparent bilateral trading, then, some CH-OTFs may want to offer more (granular) post-trade transparency data to attract additional customers. In this context, this is a very problematic assumption which may not hold up to an empirical test by economists. The reason is the incentive structure which incentivizes bilateral CH-OTFs to provide no more than the post-trade data required by Article 43(2) FinfraV. Aggregate post-trade data is beneficial when CH-OTFs wish to protect the identity of their customers. This is often welcomed by customers, especially institutional investors, who reward such favorable conditions by sending even more liquidity to this trading system. Furthermore, bilateral CH-OTFs may want to keep post-trade transparency data unpublished for as long as possible to protect their own position in the transaction. When only published at the end of the trading day, post-trade transparency data is less informative for the purpose of (present) price discovery during the trading day and is less useful for parties to the transaction to monitor their transaction quality by comparing it with other trades made around the same time. Both factors may favor the bilaterally trading CH-OTF that benefits from an informational advantage during the trading day and is less vulnerable to customer complaints when transactions did not fully meet their expectations. Moreover, customers have little to gain from more post-trade transparency since their trading interest has been satisfied, i.e., they do not need to attract another trader to fill their order. In this regard, post-trade transparency is very similar to a public good that the public wishes for, but, on the other hand, no traders and no trading systems wants to pay for.[2267]

Since an aggregate publication of post-trade information protects the position of the bilateral CH-OTFs, they are less likely to divert from the minimal rule under Article 43(2) FinfraV to offer better post-trade trans-

'*Nel caso di negoziazione bilaterale è sufficiente una pubblicazione aggregate alla fine della giornata di negoziazione*.'

2267 Moloney, *EU Securities and Financial Markets Regulation* (n 4) 432: '*everyone likes transparent markets but nobody likes to contribute*'. On public goods, see Baldwin, Cave and Lodge (n 541) 20.

parency. So, the minimal standard set out under Article 43(2) FinfraV is, in practice, the level of post-trade transparency bilateral CH-OTFs will offer.

In comparison to EU law, bilateral CH-OTFs allow for much more dark trading in their systems during the trading day. Additionally, the data published at the end of the trading day either fails to support market functions and efficiency or has a much less significant impact than an immediate, trade-by-trade publication as under MiFIR.

Simultaneously, Article 43(2) FinfraV is particularly harsh to transactions that may need deferred publication but occur towards or at the very end of the trading day. From them, Article 43(2) FinfraV demands something more closely related to immediate publication compared to transactions earlier in the day. Vulnerable transactions may then only hope to be hidden from the public eye due to the aggregation with other transactions.

D. Access to Trading Systems

Also, under Swiss law, the impact dark trading may have on market efficiency, particularly on price discovery, not only depends on the regimes of trading systems and trade transparency, but also on the access regime to trading systems. As in the United States and the European Union, the rise of arbitrageurs who use high-frequency trading incentivizes traders to hide in dark pools to manage their exposure to high-frequency traders.[2268] This allows traders of large orders vulnerable to market impact costs as well as informed traders to lower their transaction costs. Informed traders may even receive a right of exclusive usage for a new piece of price-relevant information for the time the information has not yet been disclosed and added to the displayed price on lit trading systems.

Since HFTs probe dark pools for new information by sending ping orders into the market, only dark pools that can limit access to their trading system can effectively protect informed traders.[2269] On the other hand, sealing off dark pools from certain traders such as HFTs may limit the chances of intermarket arbitrage and render the displayed price less informed for a longer period of time raising transaction costs for all traders.[2270]

Thus, it is important to see how access to trading systems is regulated under Swiss law as well. Swiss law again follows the distinction between

2268 See, for instance, IOSCO, 'Principles for Dark Liquidity' (n 12) 11–2.
2269 ibid 22ff.
2270 ibid 22ff.

trading venues like exchanges and CH-MTFs, on the one hand, and CH-OTFs, on the other hand.

I. Access to Trading Venues

1. Article 18 FinfraG

According to Article 2(a) FinfraG, financial market infrastructures include trading venues, i.e., exchanges and CH-MTF.[2271] Pursuant to Article 18(1) FinfraG, a financial infrastructure shall ensure fair and open access to its services. Access is considered 'open' if the barriers of access are kept as low as possible.[2272] Access qualifies as 'fair' or 'non-discriminatory' if the access rules are objectively justified by reasonable interests.[2273] All access rules which aim to enhance security or efficiency of the market are objectively justified; whereas access rules which distort fair competition among traders do not qualify as objectively justified. Access rules also do not qualify as non-discriminatory if they set out overly strict or extraneous criteria for access or if excessive fees are charged by the trading venue operator.[2274]

However, access can be limited without violating the principle of open and non-discriminatory access for the purposes of Article 18(2) FinfraG.[2275] This provision allows for restrictions for the purposes of security and efficiency of the financial market infrastructures if other measures are not capable of achieving the same effect (Article 18(2)(a) FinfraG).[2276] Access

2271 Ansgar Schott in Rolf Sethe and others (eds), *Kommentar zum Finanzmarktinfrastrukturgesetz FinfraG* (SK FinfraG, 1st edn, Schulthess 2017) Art 2 lit A para 5.

2272 Hans Kuhn in Rolf Watter and Rashid Bahar (eds), *Basler Kommentar Finanzmarktaufsichtsgesetz, Finanzmarktinfrastrukturgesetz* (3rd edn, Helbing & Lichtenhahn Verlag 2019) FinfraG Art 18 para 14; Committee on Payment and Settlement Systems and Technical Committee of the International Organizations of Securities Commissions, 'Principles for Financial Market Infrastructures: Final Version' (BIS/IOSCO, April 2012) para 3.18.1.

2273 Kuhn (n 2272) BSK FinfraG Art 18 para 14; Oliver Zibung, Sarah Jungo and Daniel Roth in Rolf Sethe and others (eds), *Kommentar zum Finanzmarktinfrastrukturgesetz FinfraG* (SK FinfraG, 1st edn, Schulthess 2017) Art 18 para 4.

2274 Kuhn (n 2272) BSK FinfraG Art 18 para 14; Bundesrat, 'Botschaft zum Finanzmarktinfrastrukturgesetz (FinfraG)' (n 22) BBl. 2014, 7523.

2275 Kuhn (n 2272) BSK FinfraG Art 18 paras 17ff; Zibung, Jungo and Roth (n 2273) SK FinfraG Art 18 paras 12–3.

2276 Kuhn (n 2272) BSK FinfraG Art 18 para 18; Zibung, Jungo and Roth (n 2273) SK FinfraG Art 18 para 12.

can also be restricted if admitting certain traders would jeopardize either the business operations of the financial market infrastructure or its participants (Article 18(2)(b) FinfraG).[2277] Article 17(2) FinfraV further specifies that access to financial market infrastructures can be conditioned on the participant fulfilling certain operational and technical proficiency requirements.[2278]

Considering Article 18(2)(b) FinfraG, restricting access to high-frequency traders on dark trading venues appears feasible if the trading venue operator can argue that HFTs on its trading system would jeopardize either its own business operations or that of one of its participants. Given how HFTs use electronic front running and other strategies discussed above to earn profits from other traders, it appears a viable justification for limiting access to trading venues under Article 18(2)(b) FinfraG. However, Article 34 FinfraG supplements Article 18 FinfraG and shines a different light on this issue.

2. Article 34 FinfraG

Article 34 FinfraG requires trading venues to set out rules for admission of participants to their trading venue in their trading regulations within their self-regulatory power observing in particular the principle of equal treatment.[2279] Article 34(2) FinfraG restricts the parties that are eligible for access to trading venues to securities firms,[2280] other parties supervised by FINMA, foreign participants authorized by FINMA in accordance with Article 40 FinfraG, and the SNB.[2281]

A trading venue's regulation containing the access regime is subject to approval by FINMA according to Article 27(4) FinfraG. In the approval process, FINMA is required to review whether the regulations ensure trans-

---

2277 Kuhn (n 2272) BSK FinfraG Art 18 para 22; Zibung, Jungo and Roth (n 2273) SK FinfraG Art 18 para 12.

2278 Kuhn (n 2272) BSK FinfraG Art 18 para 17.

2279 Roland Truffer in Rolf Watter and Rashid Bahar (eds), *Basler Kommentar Finanzmarktaufsichtsgesetz, Finanzmarktinfrastrukturgesetz* (3rd edn, Helbing & Lichtenhahn Verlag 2019) FinfraG Art 34 para 1.

2280 According to Article 2(d) Financial Institutions Act.

2281 Truffer (n 2279) BSK FinfraG Art 34 para 5c; Philippe Borens and Phil Baumann in Rolf Sethe and others (eds), *Kommentar zum Finanzmarktinfrastrukturgesetz FinfraG* (SK FinfraG, 1st edn, Schulthess 2017) Art 34 para 12.

parency and equal treatment of investors as well as the functioning of the securities markets (Article 25(1) FinfraV).[2282]

According to the rationale of the legislator, the duty of equal treatment primarily serves fair competition among traders. This means that comparable traders ought to receive equal access to the *'production factor'* trading venue.[2283] In contrast, this means that traders who are not comparable have to be treated differently.[2284] This may only allow for differentiation among classes of traders such as retail and professional traders. Within one class of traders, such as within professional traders, high-frequency traders and other traders may use different strategies, but they are not different per se, i.e., with regard to their risk profile and trading proficiency. However, while excluding algorithmic traders may not be warranted, some consider it viable to ask higher fees from algorithmic traders if they incur higher costs for the trading venue, for instance, due to high order placement and cancellation ratios.[2285] Since those measures can only be implemented to internalize the costs of the strategies employed by algorithmic traders and HFTs, it will not keep them away from trading venues as some dark pool users might hope for. Consequently, trading venues are not able to exclude HFTs, even if the trading venue operates as a dark pool.

HFTs can therefore engage in intermarket arbitrage retrieving price information from dark pools and impound them into the price formation process of lit trading systems. Thus, under Swiss law, dark trading on trading venues only protects orders vulnerable to market impact costs but shows little protection for informed traders. Whenever a HFT sends a ping order to a dark pool receiving execution at a specific price point, it can infer the information of the informed trader so that the informed trader's exclusive right of usage is forfeited.[2286]

This result is aligned with the functioning of access regime under EU and German law. Both EU and Swiss law, however, deviate from US-ATS

2282 Truffer (n 2279) BSK FinfraG Art 34 para 4.

2283 ibid BSK FinfraG Art 34 paras 7–8.

2284 ibid BSK FinfraG Art 34 para 8; Borens and Baumann (n 2281) SK FinfraG Art 34 para 11; Zibung, Jungo and Roth (n 2273) SK FinfraG Art 18 para 4; Monsch (n 90) 681, 701; Zobl and Kramer (n 51) para 67.

2285 Zibung, Jungo and Roth (n 2273) SK FinfraG Art 18 para 5; EFD, 'Erläuterungsbericht zur Verordnung über die Finanzmarktinfrastrukturen und das Marktverhalten im Effekten- und Derivatehandel' (n 2043) 21.

2286 See similar under EU law above Part II § 6 C. VII. 2.

operating below the 5 %-threshold, which can limit their access to traders at their discretion, such as HFTs, and, in effect, also protect informed traders.

II. Access to CH-OTF

Since the Swiss legislator decided in the legislative process of FinfraG that the CH-OTF shall not qualify as financial market infrastructure nor as a trading venue, the CH-OTF comprises as a class of its own. The consequences of this decision also resonate in the access regime. The access regime for CH-OTF is not subject to the general provision of Article 18 FinfraG which is applicable to financial market infrastructures nor the trading venue-specific Article 34 FinfraG.[2287] Thus, CH-OTFs can choose whom they want to provide with access to their trading system. Moreover, unlike trading venues, they are not restricted to certain categories of eligible traders.

This is troublesome insofar as the CH-OTF combines functions of multilateral and bilateral trading that encompass functions of an MTF, OTF, and SI under EU law. The regulation of the CH-OTF therefore denies the non-discriminatory access to the liquidity hosted in multilateral trading systems, whereas EU law requires trading systems qualifying as MTF or OTF to grant non-discriminatory access to eligible traders. Unlike other misalignments with the model under EU law, this issue has also not been fixed by the Federal Council under FinfraV. This potentially risks an uneven playing field with regard to access to liquidity, both lit and dark, that has the potential to further propel market fragmentation.

This may have adverse effects on both investor trust and the reputation of the Swiss financial market. Thus, those CH-OTFs operating a multilateral trading system should be subjected to a provision similar to Article 34 FinfraG requiring them to grant access to their systems in a non-discriminatory manner as has been the case under the Draft-FinfraG. Under the Draft-FinfraG multilateral CH-OTFs qualified as trading venues. Currently, however, CH-OTFs have discretion over the access to their trading system regardless of whether it is multilateral or bilateral.

2287 Cf. Zibung, Jungo and Roth (n 2273) SK FinfraG Art 18 para 1; Borens and Baumann (n 2281) SK FinfraG Art 34 para 1.

E. Conclusion and Criticism

With the new FinfraG/FinfraV-framework, Swiss law introduced a regime for trading systems and trade transparency that used the EU's MiFID II/MiFIR as a blueprint. Swiss law structures its trading systems regime in accordance with the same principles as EU law, i.e., bilateral and multilateral systems as well as discretionary and non-discretionary systems. In spite of the far-reaching similarities, the Swiss trading systems' regime only comprises of three categories, exchanges, CH-MTFs, and CH-OTFs, lacking a dedicated systematic internalizer category for bilateral trading as under EU law.

Swiss law, however, merges functions of the multilateral EU-OTF and the bilateral EU-SI into the catch-all category of the CH-OTF. Moreover, the CH-OTF is defined by more permissive qualitative criteria which rather resembles the SI definition under MiFID I, not the new and stricter quantitative definition used under MiFID II/MiFIR. Thus, the CH-OTF category may also be susceptible to regulatory arbitrage as was the EU-SI category under MiFID I, creating a loophole for unregulated dark trading occurring in the OTC-space.

With regard to the trade transparency regime, FinfraG and FinfraV also resemble the scope of MiFID I rather than the one under MiFID II/MiFIR: First, the scope of pre-trade transparency is limited to shares, leaving the remainder of the equity and non-equity instruments to dark trading even when occurring within trading systems. However, the Swiss trading venues broadened their scope of pre-trade transparency within their self-regulatory powers and aligned with EU standards. Due to a lack of self-regulatory powers this is, however, not possible for CH-OTFs. EU law sets pre-trade transparency as the default for all trading in equity and non-equity instruments on trading venues. Post-trade transparency under Swiss law is, however, broader capturing transactions in all securities (*Effekten*). Nevertheless, post-trade transparency under MiFID II/MiFIR is still slightly broader since it requires post-trade transparency for equity and non-equity instruments which encompasses more instruments than securities (*Effekten*).

Also, regarding the waivers and deferrals from trade transparency, Swiss law appears to aim for a regulation equivalent to the EU's MiFID II/MiFIR, but ultimately rather compares to the less restrictive regulation applicable under MiFID I. Swiss law for instance adopted the waivers from pre-trade transparency for equity instruments as set out by Article 4 MiFIR. However, FinfraG and FinfraV ultimately fail to also adopt the new, more restrictive details which distinguish the MiFID II/MiFIR waiver regime from its facilitative predecessor under MiFID I. Particularly, the restrictions that were adopted on the calculation of the reference price waiver and the more nuanced regulation of the negotiated trade waiver are lacking under Swiss law. Swiss law also did not adopt a volume cap mechanism.

A rather surprising adoption from MiFID I is that Swiss law imported the issue of having diverging applications of the waivers by tasking multiple institutions with further defining and granting the waiver. Under MiFID I, the multiple national competent authorities in the Member States came to different conclusions about how far the scope of the waiver actually reaches which left a broad field for regulatory arbitrage. Under FinfraG and FinfraV, the broad, often unspecified waivers are not applied by FINMA as the central authority but by the trading venues. This appears to resemble the situation under MiFID I where a decentralized system of institutions applied the waivers at their discretion. This becomes well visible with the large in scale waiver, for which each trading venue can assign its own definition and cannot utilize a threshold system defined by the legislator; an imprecision in application of a legal standard that was not even considered under the rather permissive MiFID I.

If multiple trading venues decide individually how waivers shall be applied, the conflicts of interest are very similar to the ones which national competent authorities had when they tried to exert a light touch of regulation to protect their national financial markets. Swiss law may only be able to carry on with this practice not pestered by the same negative consequences that the European Union experienced under MiFID I because the Swiss financial market is highly concentrated with only a few major trading venues deciding upon waivers.

In consequence, Swiss law may have used MiFID II/MiFIR as its blueprint but failed to transfer the crucial details which distinguished the new framework under EU law from MiFID I. Thus, FinfraG and FinfraV are a modern version of MiFID I which allows for broad exemptions in which both regulated and unregulated dark trading can flourish. This is in stark contrast to the motivation of the legislator who intended to contain dark pools with FinfraG.

If Swiss financial markets do not suffer consequences similar to the European Union under MiFID I, it is not due to a superior regulatory framework but rather grounded in its less vulnerable market structure.

Insofar the evaluation of the EFD in the FinfraG-Review of 30 September 2022 is correct that no (immediate) action is necessary to further regulate dark trading in Switzerland.[2288] However, if and when more competition enters the market in the future, as it happened under MiFID I in the European Union, the Swiss legislator may wish to implement a stricter regime on trading systems and trade transparency more closely aligned with its blueprint MiFID II/MiFIR.

2288 EFD and SIF (n 1862) 12.

Part III: Comparison and Conclusion

§ 8. Comparison

A. Causes and Regulation of Dark Trading in the Three Jurisdictions

I. The Rise of Dark Trading

The architecture of financial markets has undergone fundamental changes in the last decades turning from manual to automated markets and from centralized to decentralized markets.[2289] These drastic shifts were accompanied by both widely-welcomed innovation as well as detrimental developments frowned-upon by market participants and regulators. The rise of dark trading, while not entirely new, was steep and did not go unnoticed. While some market participants, like incumbent stock exchanges, who lost their dominant market position, frowned upon their new competitors, others, like block traders, welcomed new cost-efficient trading opportunities that dark trading brought to the market. Regulators were and remain undecided on whether to welcome or frown upon the new forms of dark trading.[2290]

II. Economic Theory of Dark Trading

1. Defining and Categorizing the Subject Matter

As has been discussed in Chapter § 2, dark trading is trading in financial instruments on secondary markets which shows no pre-trade transparency and, in some instances, shows reduced, incomplete, or deferred post-trade transparency.[2291] Analogously, dark orders are orders that share the said qualities. Dark orders can occur in otherwise pre-trade transparent markets, like exchanges, as a special-order type, or in fully non-transparent

2289 SEC, 'Concept Release on Equity Market Structure' (n 6) 75 FR 3594; FCA, 'UK Equity Market Dark Pools' (n 6) 7. On the application of artificial intelligence in trading see: ESMA, 'ESMA TRV Risk Analysis: Artificial Intelligence in EU Securities Markets' (n 6) 12ff.

2290 Jordan (n 8) 258.

2291 Cf. IOSCO, 'Principles for Dark Liquidity' (n 12) 4.

trading venues where only dark orders are permitted for trading.[2292] These venues are dubbed dark pools.[2293] When non-transparent liquidity is concerned, it is often referred to as dark liquidity.[2294]

Among dark pools and dark trading services, one should differentiate between regulated and unregulated dark pools according to the classification by *Gomber/Gvozdevskiy*.[2295] A regulated dark pool is one that is operated by a regulated entity, i.e., a regulated trading infrastructure of the concerned jurisdiction such as RM, MTF, or OTF in the EU.[2296] Whereas unregulated dark pools are those not operated by a regulated trading infrastructure but instead are operated in the OTC-space.[2297] Since regulated dark pools are already subject to regulation and are easier to monitor and sanction by the regulator, they are considered less troublesome than unregulated dark pools where misconduct is more difficult to address.

2. Regulatory Goals and the Roles of Lit and Dark Trading

In Chapter § 3, the reasons for having trade transparency and for dispensing of it in the case of dark trading are discussed in conjunction with the regulatory goals of financial markets regulation. Although different jurisdictions are examined, the United States, the European Union, Germany, and Switzerland all share the common financial market regulation goals of protecting and promoting the functioning of the financial markets and protecting investors.[2298]

Given the insights of the *ECMH*, trade transparency is vital for the proper functioning of financial markets and investor protection because it fosters informational efficiency as a necessary pre-condition for a well-

---

2292 Cf. ibid 4; Davies and Sirri (n 12) 167.

2293 Cf. IOSCO, 'Principles for Dark Liquidity' (n 12) 4–5. Here it appears that IOSCO sees dark orders limited to orders in otherwise lit pools. However, given that dark pools are characterized by hosting only dark orders, according to the IOSCO definition, dark orders can appear on both dark and lit pools.

2294 Cf. ibid 4.

2295 Gomber and Gvozdevskiy (n 43) paras 14.16ff.

2296 ibid para 14.17.

2297 ibid para 14.19.

2298 Sethe (n 196) SK FinfraG Art 1 para 3; Buck-Heeb (n 196) § 1 paras 6ff; Pan (n 196) 190–1; Veil, '§ 2 Concept and Aims of Capital Markets Regulation' (n 196) § 2 paras 7, 11.

functioning price formation process.[2299] Only when the signals of trading on (new pieces of) information are poured into the market where everyone can observe them, can market participants come to an intersubjectively agreed upon market price that is as close as possible to the (non-observable) fair value of the instrument in question. If a market performs this valuation function well, it will eventually be able to achieve allocative efficiency, a state in which capital is allocated to those in most urgent need of it and risk is allocated to those who can bear it best.[2300]

In economics, however, the assumption that more trade transparency will always create more valuation and allocative efficiency is disproven by the *Information Paradox* which postulates that fully transparent markets cannot achieve a stable price equilibrium, but rather create volatile prices instead.[2301] The reason for this lies in the individual incentives of informed traders who want to offset their costs of information discovery by generating a profit from trades against uninformed traders at a stale price (*information arbitrage*). If all information were already reflected in the displayed market price, no trader would incur the expenses for finding new information which would instantaneously be reflected before they can generate a profit from it.[2302] Thus, a certain amount of dark trading is necessary for the market to operate properly and to reach its highest level of efficiency.[2303]

Moreover, *behavioral finance* found that the assumption of well-informed, rational traders under the *ECMH* does not apply to all market participants. Some are either uninformed or myopic traders trading on false information or rumors and thereby create *noise trading* which rather distorts than supports price discovery.[2304] Sending a certain amount of noise trading into dark trading might rather support market efficiency because it raises the relative share of informed trading on lit markets, so

2299 IOSCO, 'Principles for Dark Liquidity' (n 12) 15; Picot, Bortenlänger and Röhrl (n 77) 23–4.

2300 Hendrik Brinckmann, '§ 16 Foundations' in Rüdiger Veil (ed), *European Capital Markets Law* (3rd edn, Hart Publishing 2022) § 16 para 5; Veil, '§ 2 Concept and Aims of Capital Markets Regulation' (n 196) § 2 para 8.

2301 Grossmann and Stiglitz, 'Information and Competitive Price Systems' (n 249) 246ff; Grossmann and Stiglitz, 'On the Impossibility of Informationally Efficient Markets' (n 249) 393ff; Picot, Bortenlänger and Röhrl (n 77) 23.

2302 Picot, Bortenlänger and Röhrl (n 77) 23.

2303 ibid 24–5.

2304 Langevoort (n 205) 868; Merritt B Fox, 'Measuring Share Price Accuracy' (2004) 1 Berkeley Business Law Journal 113, 119–20.

long as enough uninformed traders remain, in order for informed traders to generate their profit.[2305]

From an individual trader's perspective, dark trading may grant price improvements, lower costs of trading, present an opportunity to minimize market impact costs (especially for large orders), minimize information leakage, increase anonymity, and avoid trading practices by HFTs.[2306] On the flipside, dark trading means less transparency for individual traders which may have detrimental effects on price accuracy and market liquidity, may increase transaction costs due to exacerbated fragmentation, result in free-riding of the information production and regulation of others, result in information asymmetry and principal-agent-conflicts to the detriment of investors. Further, it may allow unaware traders to be taken advantage of by unnoticed HFT activity in a dark pool.[2307] This may jeopardize the proper functioning of the market as well as investor trust.

3. Regulatory Issues when Regulating Dark Trading

Considering the complex interrelation of transparency and non-transparency, the regulatory goal is to regulate towards an optimum of both lit and dark trading at the same time.[2308] However, defining the proper amount of dark trading is difficult for regulators who must put their policy into pre-set legal requirements but do not know which amount of dark trading is still efficiency enhancing and which is already harmful. This optimal amount of dark trading depends on assets class and market liquidity and may fluctuate.[2309]

Chapter § 4 discussed an additional predicament: Individual interests and the needs of the market at large may not align. While everyone wants price formation to work properly, no one wants to support it with their own trade transparency information. This describes a situation of potential

2305 Zhu (n 186) 779.

2306 IOSCO, 'Principles for Dark Liquidity' (n 12) 11–2; Davies and Sirri (n 12) 169.

2307 Those concerns are described in detail in Part I.§ 3.D.IV. above. See also IOSCO, 'Principles for Dark Liquidity' (n 12) 20; Jordan (n 8) 258–9; Kasiske (n 11) 456ff.

2308 Davies and Sirri (n 12) 168 speak of a tipping point. Picot, Bortenlänger and Röhrl (n 77) 25 speak of optima.

2309 Cf. Picot, Bortenlänger and Röhrl (n 77) 24–5.

underproduction of trade transparency and free riding of the displayed market price understood as a (quasi-)public good.[2310]

4. In-Depth Analysis of the Regulatory Regimes

Chapters §§ 5–7 discuss the extent of the different jurisdictions capabilities to support the positive effects of dark trading while limiting their adverse effects to a minimum.[2311] The results of this discussion will be analyzed in the following section B.

B. Comparing the Findings on the Three Regulatory Regimes

In this final Part III, the regulatory responses of the examined jurisdictions are compared and evaluated with regard to the trading infrastructure regimes, the trade transparency regimes, the access regimes, the price protection rules, and the supervisory structure (Chapter § 8). Finally, Chapter § 9 will conclude with an evaluation of whether an ideal regulatory regime for dark trading can be identified, suggestions for future improvements to the individual regimes, and a summary of the findings.

I. Trading Infrastructure Regime

1. Requirements for a Proper Trading Infrastructure Regime

The examination of the trading infrastructure regime in the three jurisdictions is crucial to answer the question how much of the overall order flow generated in a financial market is gathered within the regulatory perimeter and how much can operate outside of it. This breadth of the trading infrastructure regime decides how much trading can be lit trading and regulated dark trading, on the one hand, and how much is left in the less regulated OTC-space as unregulated dark trading, on the other hand.[2312]

Since it is much easier for regulators to tie conduct rules and transparency requirements to regulated trading venues and to police those rules, a

2310 See above Part I § 4. See also Moloney, *EU Securities and Financial Markets Regulation* (n 4) 432.
2311 See above Part II §§ 5–7.
2312 Cf. Gomber and Gvozdevskiy (n 43) paras 14.16ff.

regulatory regime is well equipped to regulate dark trading if the trading infrastructure regime is broad and does not have loopholes.

A sound trading systems regime aims to capture as much organized trading as possible, leaving the remaining irregular and ad hoc trading for the OTC-space. The rationale behind this is that organized trading is generally driven by investment purposes, whereas irregular and ad hoc trading is often driven by other, more technical purposes. Only trading driven by investment purposes is sensitive to prices because it is driven by economic factors.[2313] This sort of trading should therefore be poured in the price formation process by means of the trade transparency rules tied to the different trading systems.[2314] If the trading system regime is too narrow, large amounts of organized trading may slip into the OTC-space, no longer supporting the price formation process.[2315]

A secondary goal is that the regulatory categories keep multilateral, non-discretionary trading apart from bilateral, discretionary trading, because for multilateral trading the market operator is an uninterested party to all trades and therefore the price data rather resembles an undistorted interaction of supply and demand unveiling the equilibrium price. Discretionary trading, however, is price data warped by the trading interest of the operator that can match orders subject to their discretion. Additionally, the operator of bilateral, discretionary systems decides how much and at which price to take over as principal risk. This is a much less informative source for price discovery.[2316]

2. Findings in the Three Jurisdictions

The trading infrastructure under the Exchange Act and the Securities Act Amendments of 1975 under the federal securities laws of the United States show a trading system regime comprising of national securities exchanges and broker-dealers.[2317] This rather outdated regime designates the role of

2313 Cf. ESMA, 'Final Report: ESMA's Technical Advice to the Commission on MiFID II and MiFIR' (n 1268) 200 para 15

2314 Cf. Kumpan and Schmidt (n 4) MiFIR Art 23 paras 13ff; Moloney, *EU Securities and Financial Markets Regulation* (n 4) 446ff, 623.

2315 See Gomber and Nassauer (n 1086) 252–3; Moloney, *EU Securities and Financial Markets Regulation* (n 4) 446–7.

2316 Ferrarini and Moloney (n 143) 592–3.

2317 Mahoney and Rauterberg (n 118) 227–9.

a marketplace to the exchange and the role of market participant or intermediary to broker-dealers. Under Regulation ATS, the SEC, as the body responsible for administering the Exchange Act, implemented the category of ATS.[2318] This category introduces rules suited for marketplaces other than exchanges. However, the ATS must fit into the regulatory regime provided by the Exchange Act and, thus, the ATS is regulated as a broker-dealer as long as it does not register as an exchange.[2319]

The European Union and Germany have a more nuanced trading system regime which distinguishes between multilateral, non-discretionary trading systems, which include RMs, MTFs and OTFs, and bilateral, discretionary trading systems which are regulated as SIs.[2320] When the European legislator introduced MiFID II/MiFIR, it specifically addressed unregulated dark trading in the OTC-space, particularly in BCNs.[2321] A cornerstone to repatriate this form of unregulated dark trading to trading systems was to strengthen the trading system regime. The most apparent adaptation in regard to this goal is the adoption of the new trading venue category of OTF.[2322] With its differentiated array of trading systems, EU law is well equipped to capture all organized trading.

Like the European Union, the Swiss legislator reformed its trading system regime to implement modern regulatory categories that correspond to modern ways of trading and to keep unregulated dark trading at bay. Swiss law took EU law as a blueprint for its trading systems regime and implemented a slightly deviating variant of the regime found under MiFID II/MiFIR.[2323] This can be regarded as a form of a Brussels effect for the sake of market access to EU markets,[2324] which Switzerland was later denied.[2325] The Swiss trading landscape comprises of exchanges, CH-

2318 Colby and Sirri (n 605) 183–4; Mahoney and Rauterberg (n 118) 228.

2319 Colby and Sirri (n 605) 183–4; Mahoney and Rauterberg (n 118) 228.

2320 Moloney, *EU Securities and Financial Markets Regulation* (n 4) 462.

2321 ESMA, 'Final Report: On ESMA's Opinion on the Trading Venue Perimeter' (ESMA70-156-6360, 2 February 2023) 6; Gomber and Nassauer (n 1086) 252–3; Moloney, *EU Securities and Financial Markets Regulation* (n 4) 446ff, 461.

2322 Recitals 6, 8 MiFIR; Hoops, 'Bedeutung des organisierten Handelssystems in der gegenwärtigen Marktinfrastruktur' (n 131) 14ff.

2323 Sethe (n 196) SK FinfraG Einleitung para 38; Schott and Winkler (n 70) SK FinfraG Art 26 paras 18–9.

2324 Bradford, 'The Brussels Effect' (n 49) 3ff.

2325 Simon Schären and Thomas Jutzi, 'Schweizer Finanzmarktrecht im europäischen Kontext - Aufbruch in eine neue Ära' [2021] GesKR 466, 468; Khan and Stafford (n 1857).

MTFs, and CH-OTFs.[2326] Exchanges and CH-MTFs have to be multilateral, non-discretionary trading systems.[2327] While the EU-systematic internalizer category is missing under Swiss law, the CH-OTF combines the functions of the multilateral OTF and the bilateral SI under EU law in one class of trading systems.[2328]

3. Evaluation of the Similarities and Differences

a) Issues with Overbroad Categories

The comparison shows that the EU, Germany, and Switzerland have very nuanced trading regimes with many categories to capture all organized trading, whereas the US regime merely comprises of three categories. One of these, the ATS, is merely a subcategory of the broker-dealer with special conduct rules better suited for a rising marketplace.

The rather outdated trading system regime under US law has difficulties capturing modern ways of trading, which may cause large amounts of unregulated dark trading in the OTC-space. There broker-dealers, as a category for market intermediaries, internalize large amounts of order flow like a marketplace, while the exchange as the primary category for a marketplace does not receive any of the internalized order flow.[2329] Broker-dealers assuming the role of a marketplace even though they were originally designed as intermediaries is troublesome because the rules for broker-dealers are not equally well-equipped to moderate conflicts of interest as the rules for exchanges. This is most apparent when broker-dealers mingle bilateral internalization with matching client orders in a market maker-style at their discretion.[2330] While there is certainly also a difference in the manner of exercise of supervisory power between the US and the EU, Germany, and Switzerland, the larger number of enforcement measures against US dark pools may not only be founded in this difference, but also indicate that those conflicts of interest lead to detrimental outcomes for traders that are followed by enforcement measures.

2326 Studer and Vollenweider (n 1910) BSK FinfraG Art 42 para 1.
2327 Schott and Winkler (n 70) SK FinfraG Art 26 paras 24, 35.
2328 Studer and Vollenweider (n 1910) BSK FinfraG Art 42 para 39.
2329 Mahoney and Rauterberg (n 118) 228–9.
2330 SEC, 'Concept Release on Equity Market Structure' (n 6) 75 FR 3599f; Mahoney and Rauterberg (n 118) 259ff.

Under the aspect of fair competition, the goal of US law should be to subject similar trading to similar rules while trading that is not similar should be subject to different rules. Or put differently, privileging some organized trading to trade in a less regulated manner in the dark OTC-space, instead of trading on regulated lit trading systems where the majority of organized trading takes place, contradicts the goals of the National Market System of fair competition under Section 11A Exchange Act.

b) Issues with Highly Specific Categories

On the other end sit the European Union and Germany with their very detailed trading system regime. The primary issue under MiFID I was that the strict distinction between multilateral MTFs and bilateral SIs coupled with a qualitative definition for the SI-regime allowed for regulatory arbitrage. Operators of hybrid forms of trading could seep through the regulatory net under MiFID I and set up shop as BCNs in the OTC-space offering unregulated dark trading.[2331]

For non-equity instruments, the OTF category patched this regulatory loophole under MiFID II/MiFIR but, despite the initial draft of MiFID II, the OTF category is not eligible to host equities trading. While this limitation is sensible because equities trading on an OTF would allow for discretionary trading in highly liquid markets and thereby distort the price discovery data as well as undermine the MTF and SI category because the OTF is an attractive combination of both categories, the issue of the loophole between MTF and SI still needs to be addressed by another measure.[2332]

MiFID II/MiFIR is able to tighten the regulatory net by shifting from ambiguous qualitative definitions open for deviating interpretation to the new clear-cut set of quantitative definitions dependent on (large amounts of) market data.[2333] While a quantitative approach has the advantage of a clearer scope of application, it also has significant disadvantages: market data may simply not be available or inaccurate rendering the regulatory measure futile. On the other hand, a complex system as the one set out by

2331 Moloney, *EU Securities and Financial Markets Regulation* (n 4) 446ff, 461.

2332 Cf. Ferrarini and Moloney (n 143) 592–3; Moloney, *EU Securities and Financial Markets Regulation* (n 4) 451.

2333 Recital 18, 19 MiFIR; Kumpan (n 125) WpHG § 2 paras 106ff; Moloney, *EU Securities and Financial Markets Regulation* (n 4) 467.

MiFID II/MiFIR is on the verge of creating massive costs no longer justified by the risks which it attempts to regulate.[2334]

Undisputedly, law governing complex fact patterns, such as financial markets, may itself arise to a certain degree of complexity. However, the increase of complexity from MiFID I to MiFID II/MiFIR has been enormous and it should be avoided that any successor to MiFID II/MiFIR becomes even more complex.[2335]

An illustrative example are the minimal thresholds for systematic internalizers: the thresholds for 'frequent systematic' and 'on substantial basis' require so many resources to calculate that many firms are rather willing to use the opt-in option and 'voluntarily' subject themselves to the SI regulation to avoid the burden of monitoring compliance in the first place. ESMA explains the high levels of voluntary opt-ins as a result of clients' preference to delegate the reporting requirement of post-trade transparency onto the SI entirely, thus clients only want to transact with SIs rather than mere OTC-investment firms.[2336] However, it cannot be overlooked that the effort to monitor the regulatory thresholds may be too burdensome compared to opt-in the SI regime right away. Uncertainty and burdensome regulations as incentives for seeking 'voluntary' regulation is a warning sign for any liberal legal system.

Nevertheless, the trading system regime under EU law is in general very differentiated and fit to capture all organized trading which should be the basis for the price formation process. It is also capable of avoiding or at least managing conflicts of interest by separating among neutral multilateral trading venues and interested bilateral trading systems, both attributes which US law is lacking.

c) Issues with a Detailed Regime using Qualitative Definitions

The Swiss trading systems regime is closely aligned with the one under EU law and should therefore be able to capture broad amounts of organized

---

2334 Cf. Moloney, *EU Securities and Financial Markets Regulation* (n 4) 498–9.

2335 ibid 499 on the data-dependence of MiFID II/MiFIR: *'The related data collection exercise will be massive in scale, not least given the need to assess the quality and accuracy of the data available and to draw robust conclusions.'*

2336 Cf. ESMA, 'Consultation Paper: MiFIR Report on Systematic Internalisers in Non-Equity Instruments' (n 1282) 12; ESMA, 'MiFIR report on Systematic Internalisers in Non-Equity Instruments' (n 1282) 11; Kumpan (n 125) WpHG § 2 para 104.

trading leaving only little to unregulated dark trading in the OTC-space. However, Swiss law is much less prescriptive, using qualitative regulatory categories instead of quantitative like EU law. This incentivizes market actors to find loopholes in the qualitative definition of the trading systems to escape the regulatory perimeter and trade in the OTC-space as demonstrated by the history of BCNs under MiFID I in the EU.[2337] It remains an open question for additional empirical research in how far Swiss markets suffer from unregulated dark trading in the OTC-space. If unregulated dark trading proves to cause issues comparable to those under MiFID I, the Swiss legislator may want to adjust its approach and align with the more prescriptive framework under MiFID II/MiFIR. If such measures become necessary in the future, the Swiss legislation needs to weigh carefully whether such complex regulation is necessary in the much smaller Swiss financial market as can be observed in the EU financial market. Currently, however, Switzerland appears to be content with its regulation of dark trading and rather fears the migration of dark trading to the United Kingdom as its biggest rival for order flow after Brexit.[2338]

4. Conclusion

In conclusion, the US regime still appears to work reasonably well for the market but is no longer able to bring all organized trading into the regulatory perimeter to subject it to trade transparency rules. It therefore allows for large amounts of unregulated dark trading in the OTC-space. It also mingles multilateral and bilateral trading logics, making the venue operators more susceptible to conflicts of interest at the detriment of most investors.

EU law, on the other hand, is very differentiated and has closed its regulatory loopholes under MiFID II/MiFIR. With its complex system, its primary concern is no longer whether it has enough devices to capture all organized trading, but rather whether the data is available to fuel the system and if the NCAs are capable to operate such an extensive of regulatory machinery. Such broad regulation appears only feasible because its burdens

2337 Moloney, *EU Securities and Financial Markets Regulation* (n 4) 467 fn 263. See on the early criticism of the qualitative SI-definition under EU law: Mülbert, 'Die neuen Transparenzregeln im Vorschlag einer Richtlinie über Wertpapierdienstleistungen und geregelte Märkte - insbesondere die Pre-Trade-Transparenzpflicht von systematischen Internalisierern' (n 1695) 15; Spindler and Kasten (n 134) 1756.

2338 Cf. EFD and SIF (n 1862) 12.

are shouldered by many Member States and such extensive regulation is justified as a large counterweight to heavy centrifugal forces that may cause divergence among the Member States.

Swiss law is on a middle path between US and EU law since it adopted a more differentiated principle-based trading systems regime inspired by the EU's but refrained from the complex rule-based approach heavily reliant on vast amounts of data, more like the US. Whether this allows for most organized trading to be within the regulatory perimeter and subject to trade transparency remains to be seen. The fact that Swiss law has to work for only one country and not many as in the case of EU law certainly weighs in Switzerland's favor.

II. Trade Transparency Regime

1. Requirements for a Proper Trade Transparency Regime

At the center of the regulatory attention for regulating dark trading must be the trade transparency regime because it eventually decides which orders must display trade transparency and which can remain hidden. This is a central issue because only lit orders and trades support the price formation process. The assessment of the trade transparency regimes of the jurisdictions needs to distinguish three levels of regulation.

a) First Level: Set Trade Transparency as Default Rule

On the first level, it must be assessed how broad the scope of the transparency regime is and if it is capable of shining a bright light on all or at least most of the orders and trades. On this level, the transparency regime decides whether its default rule is lit or dark trading.

A trade transparency regime that aims for a high degree of informational efficiency needs to have a broad scope which covers all types of financial instruments.[2339] When both equity and non-equity instruments are captured, the trade transparency regime needs to be calibrated for the asset classes and the liquidity levels in the respective markets.[2340]

2339 Cf. Recitals 10, 15 MiFIR. IOSCO, 'Principles for Dark Liquidity' (n 12) 26.
2340 Cf. Recital 16 MiFIR.

The trade transparency regime should also avoid any loopholes or blind spots where traders can evade trade transparency without showing due reason for being treated differently than comparable traders who are subject to trade transparency rules.[2341]

Moreover, a proper transparency regime should ensure that the wide availability of trade transparency information in real time is the default rule. If the reporting occurs with no or minimal delay, algorithmic traders and HFTs will find it more difficult to take advantage of other traders by means of latency arbitrage. This supports investor trust in the lit markets and minimizes incentives for an overuse of dark markets.[2342]

b) Second Level: Implement Clear-Cut Exceptions from the Default Rule

On the second level, the trade transparency regimes must be assessed on how exemptions from pre-trade and post-trade transparency can achieve an advantageous degree of dark trading.[2343] A proper trade transparency regime will allow for some dark trading because, according to the *Information Paradox*, excessive levels of trade transparency will lead to volatile prices.[2344] Furthermore, a certain amount of dark trading can divert some noise trading from the lit markets rendering displayed prices more informed.[2345] Consequently, a sound trade transparency regime design should have non-transparent trading as the exception from the default rule of transparency.[2346]

In the process of defining and applying exceptions from trade transparency, the regulator faces the issue of setting clear and reasonable requirements for the use of such exemptions as well as applying them uniformly. A deviation from the default rule of transparency should only be allowed if there is due reason for both the trader and the market.[2347] This means that dispensing from trade transparency should have a benefit for the trader and

2341 IOSCO, 'Principles for Dark Liquidity' (n 12) 26–7.
2342 ibid 26.
2343 Cf. ibid 27.
2344 Grossmann and Stiglitz, 'Information and Competitive Price Systems' (n 249) 246ff; Grossmann and Stiglitz, 'On the Impossibility of Informationally Efficient Markets' (n 249) 393ff; Picot, Bortenlänger and Röhrl (n 77) 23.
2345 Zhu (n 186) 779.
2346 IOSCO, 'Principles for Dark Liquidity' (n 12) 26.
2347 Cf. ibid 26.

at least no harm for the market at large (*Pareto optimal*).[2348] Alternatively, a regulation that allows for an exemption if there is a benefit for the trader so large that they could (theoretically) offset the losses suffered by all others and the market at large (*Kaldor-Hicks optimal*),[2349] is not desirable. Although theoretically efficient, this approach to trade transparency neglects that the issue of providing a trading environment for secondary markets is a closed system comparable to a zero-sum game (since there is only one piece of informational advantage that is not increasing if shared but rather decreasing).[2350] Investor trust must be earned at the marketplace at hand or it is lost. There is no other place where those who use the trading infrastructure can hope to benefit from any efficiency enhancements created by dark trading of others and there is also no guarantee that they may end up on the benefactor side if they play the game long enough as well. Traders who realize that they are providing all the data for price formation and may have suspicions of being taken advantage of by others will likely move to dark markets or leave the market entirely. Then, the market at large will suffer under increasing information asymmetry with the price becoming ever less accurate over time.[2351]

Furthermore, in the design of exemptions and the granting of such exemptions, the regulator needs to distinguish the different qualities of pre-trade and post-trade transparency. Pre-trade transparency informs about the reservation price of a trader posting a limit order that is not immediately filled. When the trader is susceptible to undue position risk while their order is sitting in the order book, the regulator can grant an exemption.

With exemptions from post-trade transparency, however, the regulator needs to be more cautious because post-trade transparency shares the qualities of a quasi-public good that might suffer from underproduction.[2352] Only post-trade transparency is non-rivalrous and non-exclusive if a certain amount of transparency is available in the first place, because everyone can use the information as a reference price for their future trades. In this regard, pre-trade transparency is rather rivalrous because the order itself

2348 Stefan Magen, '§ 4 - Spieltheorie' in Emanuel V Towfigh and Niels Petersen (eds), *Ökonomische Methoden im Recht: Eine Einführung für Juristen* (2nd edn, Mohr Siebeck 2017) § 4 para 199.

2349 ibid § 4 para 200.

2350 ibid § 4 para 207.

2351 Cf. Moloney, *EU Securities and Financial Markets Regulation* (n 4) 432 referring to the issue that *'everyone likes transparent markets but nobody likes to contribute'*.

2352 Cf. ibid 432. On the qualities of a public good, see Magen (n 2348) § 4 paras 222ff.

cannot be used again for trading once it is filled. The mere information about a reservation price of an order via pre-trade transparency could in theory be used for pricing one's own order but in this regard, traders would rather use the displayed mid-point price for reference. Pre-trade transparency shall rather inform about available liquidity than inform about a proper price. Thus, only post-trade transparency is similar to a public good and should therefore only be limited if there is a due reason for the parties involved and it should only be delayed, not dispensed entirely.

c) Third Level: Consider a Reverse-Exception to Support the Default Rule

On the third level, it must be examined to what extent a risk for overuse of an exception in its transparency regime exists, and therefore it must be considered to introduce a reverse-exception to limit the application of this exception from trade transparency.[2353] If a transparency regime manages to set up broad trade transparency rules covering large amounts of trading and has a wide exceptions regime, a reverse exception might be a tool to manage unwanted uses of the exceptions (e.g., a waiver from pre-trade transparency). A reverse-exception supporting the default rule of trade transparency might be a method for regulators to grapple with the issue that the exact amount of harmful dark trading is not (yet) fully understood.[2354] By implementing a reverse-exception, the regulator may even set a maximum amount of permissible dark trading, not knowing whether it is already harmful, but in any case, avoiding an outright ban on a certain form of dark trading as a more intrusive measure. Nevertheless, implementing a reverse-exception also contains the legislative verdict that dark trading above a certain amount is socially undesirable because dark trading adversely affects the social goals of a proper functioning market and investor protection. Whether such precautious regulation is warranted needs to be assessed by the respective legislator.[2355]

2353 On the development of some jurisdictions restricting dark trading, see Davies and Sirri (n 12) 170–1.

2354 On the mixed academic opinions on dark trading see Part I § 3.D.IV.1. above.

2355 See Calliess (n 528) 139–41.

2. Findings in the Three Jurisdictions

The transparency regimes of the examined jurisdictions all aim at having trade transparency as their default rule and grant specific exceptions for dark trading, but they vary in execution.

a) Trade Transparency Rules in the United States

aa) First Level: Transparency Rules

The transparency regime in the United States is set out in Regulation NMS and Regulation ATS. Regulation NMS implements a trade transparency rule which requires the publication of quotes and limit orders (pre-trade transparency) and the reporting of all transactions (post-trade transparency).[2356] An issue regarding the scope of pre-trade transparency is that US law does not require pre-trade transparency for actionable IOIs which is a certain kind of signal to the market that does not qualify as an order but serves a similar economic purpose of informing traders about available liquidity in the market. Although the SEC proposed changes to Regulation NMS to include IOIs, those changes have not yet been adopted into law.[2357]

On the post-trade transparency side, however, US law is very strict and does not allow for any deferrals from reporting in real time.[2358] The reporting infrastructure is also very well designed in the US because the US market has a consolidated tape mechanism that combines all post-trade information of the multiple trading venues and makes this information available to the investing public.[2359] The issue with its latency times which may allow for algorithmic and HFTs to front-run the tape and thus overtake the investing public, however, signals the need for future improvements.[2360]

2356 See above Part II § 5.E.I. and II.
2357 Colby and Sirri (n 605) 186.
2358 Haeberle (n 459) 819; cf. O'Hara, *Market Microstructure Theory* (n 45) 258–9.
2359 Kumpan, *Die Regulierung außerbörslicher Wertpapierhandelssysteme im deutschen, europäischen und US-amerikanischen Recht* (n 8) 126; Beny (n 51) 415–7.
2360 Fox, Glosten and Rauterberg, 'The New Stock Market' (n 88) 238–9; Mattli (n 799) 115ff; Lewis (n 800) 97–8.

bb) Second Level: Exceptions

The US trade transparency regime, however, has more pressing issues with exceptions from pre-trade transparency. In principle, US law has rules that follow the rule-exception-pattern described above because Regulation NMS has exceptions for specific transactions that are either block orders, technical orders, or orders that are subject to trade transparency at another venue.[2361] While these specific exceptions are well-designed, they cannot perform their limiting and steering effect on dark trading as a form of regulated dark trading because all dark trading pours out of the regulatory perimeter as unregulated dark trading due to an overbroad loophole initially implemented for another purpose.

This loophole is the 5 %-threshold in Regulation ATS. Under the 5 %-threshold rule, an ATS is not obliged to comply with the pre- or post-trade transparency rules under Regulation NMS if the ATS stays below the threshold of 5 % of the average daily turnover in the specific NMS stock or does not publish quotes to more than one person.[2362] This exception was initially designed to foster competition among marketplaces under the National Market System by breaking the (quasi-)monopolies of incumbent exchanges. The 5 %-threshold was meant to apply more permissive regulation on new market entrants so they could flourish at the beginning and would grow into the stricter regulatory regime for larger ATS once they have gained sufficient market share.[2363]

The current use of the 5 %-threshold for unregulated dark trading was not intended. ATS operators have even gone so far as to run several dark ATS parallel to each other to stay below the individual threshold of 5 % or they avoid transparency by communication trading interest through indications of interest that, other than orders, do not trigger the transparency requirement.[2364] Since there is no overall threshold restricting dark trading across all venues to a certain level for the market as a whole, like the 8 %-threshold of the DVC under EU law, unregulated dark trading could grow from a small phenomenon to a large industry in the US. Due to this rather broad and unrestricted exception, the default rule for US law is rather dark trading because its transparency regime can be easily circum-

2361 See above Part II § 5.E.I.1.b).
2362 Colby and Sirri (n 605) 185.
2363 Cf. Mahoney and Rauterberg (n 118) 244.
2364 SEC, 'Regulation of Non-Public Trading Interest' (n 22) 74 FR 61214; Mahoney and Rauterberg (n 118) 244.

vented and its specific exceptions from trade transparency are rendered futile. Nevertheless, US law is very strict on the post-trade transparency side where transparency rules apply. Thus, it can be dubbed a post-trade transparency heavy system.

cc) Third Level: Reverse Exceptions

On the third level of limitation measures, the US tested the implementation of a trade-at rule similar to the ones implemented in Australia and Canada. The trade-at rule requires trading systems displaying only quotes at inferior prices to the NBBO to either route an incoming order to the trading venue that displays orders at the NBBO or to offer a new order at a price significantly better than the NBBO on their trading system. Merely refraining from trading is no longer an option to avoid trading at the NBBO.[2365] The test also showed that dark trading at the midpoint was curbed by the measure while lit trading was enhanced. Nevertheless, the US has not yet implemented the trade-at rule into law.

b) Trade Transparency Rules in the European Union and Germany

aa) First Level: Transparency Rules

EU law aims to make trade transparency the default rule for all organized trading to enhance market efficiency and to limit unregulated dark trading, especially by BCNs in the OTC-space.[2366] To achieve this, EU law broadened its scope to integrate all equity and non-equity instruments into its transparency regime and introduced common rules for pre-trade and post-trade transparency for all multilateral systems to create a level playing field among similar trading infrastructures.[2367] The trade transparency regime is also granularly calibrated for different sorts of asset classes within both equity and non-equity instruments and, if necessary, for different liquidity levels within the respective asset classes.[2368] In contrast to US law, the EU pre-trade transparency regime also captures actionable IOIs to avoid

2365 SEC, 'Concept Release on Equity Market Structure' (n 6) 75 FR 3613; SEC, 'National Securities Exchanges and FINRA' (n 1028) 6–7.

2366 Recitals 10, 11 MiFIR.

2367 Moloney, *EU Securities and Financial Markets Regulation* (n 4) 480.

2368 ibid 480, 485–6.

regulatory arbitrage by market signals similar to traditional orders.[2369] This results in a vast regulatory regime which tries to balance the interest of having broad transparency with the interest of protecting markets with lower levels of liquidity from undue risk caused by too much transparency. MiFIR also calibrates the transparency regime for bilateral trading systems, such as SIs, to protect them from adverse effects of excessive trade transparency when assuming proprietary risk while trading.[2370]

In spite of the strengths of the calibrated trade transparency regime under MiFID II/MiFIR as crafted in 2014, ESMA and the EU legislator identified certain issues that they aimed to correct with the MiFID II/MiFIR refit process started in 2021. The first issue is one driven by regulatory arbitrage. When MiFID II/MiFIR was crafted, the EU legislator aimed to repatriate organized unregulated dark trading from the OTC-space onto lit multilateral trading venues by closing the gap between the MTF and SI category.[2371] But the EU frowned not only on unregulated dark trading but also on regulated dark trading occurring under one of the pre-defined waivers on multilateral trading venues and, thus, implemented a limiting device, the double volume cap mechanism.[2372] With the DVC, regulated dark trading became unattractive for traders because its availability depended on whether the DVC was currently suspending dark trading or not. The industry avoided this limitation by moving dark trading at the midpoint price to SIs to whom the DVC does not apply. This migration from unregulated dark trading in the OTC-space to more permissively regulated dark trading under the SI-regime, however, undermines the categories of multilateral trading systems and leads to an uneven playing field. To correct for this development, the EU aligns the regulation for SI matching at the midpoint with those of the reference price waiver and requires double the standard market size.[2373]

Another issue with trade transparency in the EU is that there is no consolidated tape comparable to the one in the US which combines the trading information of all trading venues. Although the EU wants to set up

---

2369 ibid 480.

2370 Recital 1 MiFIR; Kumpan and Schmidt (n 4) Foreword MiFIR para 9.

2371 Moloney, *EU Securities and Financial Markets Regulation* (n 4) 467 fn 263.

2372 Discussed below § 8.B.II.2.b).cc).

2373 ESMA, 'Consultation Paper: MiFID II/ MiFIR Review Report on the Transparency Regime for Equity and Equity-Like Instruments, the Double Volume Cap Mechanism and the Trading Obligations for Shares' (n 1805) 48ff.

such a service, it has not yet been realized and this impairs the transparency level for the investing public on a rather practical level.[2374]

To correct for the failure of MiFID II/MiFIR in setting up a consolidated tape, the MiFIR refit will move away from the idea to have several consolidated tape providers competing with one another, at least for now, because no consolidated tape provider has yet stepped up to perform the task.[2375] Instead, the MiFIR refit will entrust ESMA with assigning the task to a consolidated tape provider for each asset class in a selection process.[2376] This assignment will be for a period of five years before it is repeated.[2377]

bb) Second Level: Exceptions

Nevertheless, EU law also recognizes the need for dark trading in specific situations but only supports regulated dark trading and only wants regulated dark trading to occur in instances in which MiFIR deems it necessary.[2378] Therefore, MiFIR provides for a calibrated regime of waivers from pre-trade transparency and deferrals from immediate post-trade transparency. Similar to the transparency rules, the waivers and the deferrals are granularly calibrated to equity and non-equity instruments, the asset classes falling within them, and their respective liquidity levels. MiFIR only grants waivers and deferrals where it deems it useful for the individual trader and at least not harmful for the market at large.[2379] By way of example, the pre-trade transparency obligation for equities is only waived in four

2374 European Commission, 'Proposal for a Regulation of the European Parliament and of the Council amending Regulation (EU) No 600/2014 as regards enhancing market data transparency, removing obstacles to the emergence of a consolidated tape, optimising the trading obligations and prohibiting receiving payments for forwarding client orders' (n 1146) 4–5; John Armour, Martin Bengtzen and Luca Enriques, 'Globalization' in Merritt B Fox and others (eds), *Securities Market Issues for the 21st Century* (Columbia University 2018) 448.

2375 European Commission, 'Proposal for a Regulation of the European Parliament and of the Council amending Regulation (EU) No 600/2014 as regards enhancing market data transparency, removing obstacles to the emergence of a consolidated tape, optimising the trading obligations and prohibiting receiving payments for forwarding client orders' (n 1146) 4, 11.

2376 ibid 15–6, 20, 31.

2377 ibid 33.

2378 Recital 13 MiFIR.

2379 Moloney, *EU Securities and Financial Markets Regulation* (n 4) 481.

instances:[2380] under the reference price waiver, the negotiated trade waiver, the order management facility waiver, and the large in scale waiver.[2381] For instance, the large in scale waiver is useful to raise overall liquidity on the market and to spare block traders from position risk, thus supporting overall market quality and execution quality for the individual trader.[2382] The reference price waiver, on the other hand, is attractive for traders who want to trade at the midpoint price but is of no further interest for the market if the price information is already added to the midpoint price, thus the waiver improves execution quality for the individual trader and, although not benefitting the market, it is considered not to harm the market either.[2383]

Since the reference price waiver has already been frowned upon by some NCAs in the MiFID II/MiFIR negotiations and was on the brink of being abolished,[2384] the issue came up in the MiFID II/MiFIR review process again. It was once more argued that it allows orders of small size to evade pre-trade transparency which may erode the price formation process.[2385] Thus, the current proposal for a MiFID II/MiFIR refit plans to tighten the scope of the reference price waiver to orders which are at least double the standard market size.[2386] The source of the data should preferably be the data from the yet to be implemented consolidated tape providers; another large issue under the refit.[2387]

Moreover, under the latest MiFIR-refit, the trade transparency regime for non-equities which has been implemented by the 2014 iteration of MiFIR for the first time, will be tightened to allow for more trade transparency.

2380 For details on all waivers, see above Part II § 6.C.III. and V.

2381 Moloney, *EU Securities and Financial Markets Regulation* (n 4) 481.

2382 Cf. ibid 482.

2383 ibid 482. NB: it is a matter of debate whether the reference price waiver, if used extensively, is harmful for overall market quality. Nevertheless, the regulatory rationale was that non-displayed trading at a price already known to the market cannot be harmful and should therefore be allowed.

2384 ibid 481–2.

2385 ESMA, 'MiFID II/MiFIR Review Report: On the Transparency for Equity and Equity-Like Instruments, the Double Volume Cap Mechanism and the Trading Obligations for Shares' (n 1500) 12.

2386 European Commission, 'Proposal for a Regulation of the European Parliament and of the Council amending Regulation (EU) No 600/2014 as regards enhancing market data transparency, removing obstacles to the emergence of a consolidated tape, optimising the trading obligations and prohibiting receiving payments for forwarding client orders' (n 1146) 14.

2387 ibid 27; see proposed Article 4(1)(a) MiFIR.

To achieve this, the SSTI-waiver from pre-trade transparency under Article 9(1)(b) MiFIR and the corresponding SSTI-deferral under Article 11(1)(c) MiFIR will be deleted.[2388] Also, the deferral times will be shorted and streamlined to minimize the discretion of the NCAs, which have applied different practices in similar cases with regard to the deferrals.[2389] ESMA suggested those steps because it found that the current regime was overly complicated and did not deliver effective regulation in every instance.[2390]

cc) Third Level: Reverse Exception

In spite of the careful crafting of the waivers, the EU is still skeptical about the reference price waiver and the negotiated trade waiver because those waivers exempt orders regardless of their size and propensity to suffer adverse effects when showing pre-trade transparency.[2391] To avoid an outright ban of the two waivers, which can be used for detrimental as well as beneficial purposes, MiFIR introduced the DVC to limit an overuse of the two controversial waivers.[2392] The DVC limits dark trading under the two waivers if trading under it amounts to more than 4 % of the total trading in the instrument on the specific trading venue and more than 8 % of total trading on all trading venues in the entire EU in the last 12 months.[2393] If those thresholds are met, trading is suspended for 6 months under the specific waiver.[2394] The DVC forces trading to be lit trading if no

2388 ibid 8, 19–20.
2389 ibid 8–9.
2390 ibid 8.
2391 Recital 13 MiFIR; Kumpan and Schmidt (n 4) Foreword MiFIR para 10; ESMA, 'MiFID II/MiFIR Review Report: On the Transparency for Equity and Equity-Like Instruments, the Double Volume Cap Mechanism and the Trading Obligations for Shares' (n 1500) 12.
2392 Cf. Moloney, *EU Securities and Financial Markets Regulation* (n 4) 481–2.
2393 ESMA, 'MiFID II/MiFIR Review Report: On the Transparency for Equity and Equity-Like Instruments, the Double Volume Cap Mechanism and the Trading Obligations for Shares' (n 1500) 14.
2394 On the new Recital 7 of proposed MiFIR, see European Commission, 'Proposal for a Regulation of the European Parliament and of the Council amending Regulation (EU) No 600/2014 as regards enhancing market data transparency, removing obstacles to the emergence of a consolidated tape, optimising the trading obligations and prohibiting receiving payments for forwarding client orders' (n 1146) 19.

other waiver applies. This mechanism has been criticized because it is very data dependent making it costly to administer.[2395]

For this reason, the MiFIR refit will transform the double volume cap into a single volume cap (SVC) limiting the reference price waiver and the negotiated trade waiver when its trading in the whole of the EU exceeds 7 % of trading in the instrument.[2396] Whether this new SVC mechanism will bring the intended advantages and be easier to administer remains to be seen.

As a consequence of this analysis, it can be observed that EU law goes to great lengths to ensure a high degree of pre-trade transparency adjusted with a regulated amount of dark trading that should be kept at bay by the waiver system itself and the limitation device of the DVC/SVC. Thus, EU law can be dubbed pre-trade transparency heavy.

c) Trade Transparency Rules in Switzerland

aa) First Level: Transparency Rules

A major goal of the Swiss trade transparency regime is to limit dark trading similarly to the legislative efforts in the EU.[2397] The Swiss pre-trade transparency regime, however, has a narrower scope than the EU's since it only applies to shares.[2398] All orders in other equity instruments besides shares and all orders in non-equity instruments, which are subject to pre-trade transparency rules under EU law, remain dark orders under Swiss law. Thus, lit trading is the default rule only for shares, and for all other orders the default rule is dark trading.

With this narrow scope, the Swiss pre-trade transparency regime rather resembles the former pre-trade transparency regime under MiFID I in the EU than the new, broad regime under MiFID II/MiFIR. However, Swiss financial markets regulation has a strong self-regulatory tradition which originally saw pre-trade transparency rules as a matter of the trading venues' self-regulatory power.[2399] Thus, also the trade transparency regime

2395 ibid 4.

2396 ibid 14, 28.

2397 Bundesrat, 'Botschaft zum Finanzmarktinfrastrukturgesetz (FinfraG)' (n 22) BBl. 2014, 7499.

2398 Schott and Winkler (n 70) SK FinfraG Art 29 para 39.

2399 Watter and Kägi (n 2018) BSK BEHG Art 5 paras 35, 50.

under FinfraG/FinfraV allows trading venues to exceed the narrow scope set out by law and to subject equity instruments other than shares and non-equity instruments to pre-trade transparency requirements in their regulations.[2400]

The post-trade transparency regime under FinfraG, however, is far broader than the pre-trade transparency regime and requires all trades in securities (*'Effekten'*) to inform about price, size, and time of a transaction.[2401] This is, on the one hand, similar to the broad trade transparency regime under MiFID II/MiFIR in the EU because the regulatory term 'securities' also includes all equity instruments even beyond shares and non-equity instruments. On the other hand, the broader post-trade transparency rule adds the trading information of instruments other than shares into the price formation process, although at a later point in time compared to shares.[2402]

bb) Second Level: Exceptions

On the second level concerned with exceptions from trade transparency rules, Swiss law also follows EU law, in principle, but differs from it in important details. Swiss law also applies a waiver system comprising of the four waivers known from the EU for equity trading, i.e., the reference price waiver, the negotiated trade waiver, the order management facility waiver, and the large in scale waiver.[2403] Interestingly, the modern Swiss waiver system reflects the EU waiver system used under MiFID I, but lacks the new waivers for non-equity instruments introduced under MiFID II/MiFIR.

At first sight, this is unsurprising because Swiss law does not provide for a transparency rule for non-equity instruments, and thus does not need to provide waivers from it either. Upon second thought however, the Swiss pre-trade transparency regime allows for the trading venues to implement pre-trade transparency rules for non-equity instruments by way of their self-regulatory power but creates no common framework for waivers from such transparency rules to steer the amount of transparency in this market.

2400 Kägi (n 50) BSK FinfraG Art 29 paras 9–10.
2401 ibid BSK FinfraG Art 29 para 33; Schott and Winkler (n 70) SK FinfraG Art 29 para 49.
2402 Kägi (n 50) BSK FinfraG Art 29 para 33.
2403 Schott and Winkler (n 70) SK FinfraG Art 29 para 30.

Even though FINMA may steer the admissible non-equities waivers in some regard in the approval process of the trading regulations by a venue, it cannot ban innovative new waivers in the same way the legislator is able to do. This uncertainty may impair fair and orderly competition among the venues.[2404]

Moreover, unlike the EU, the scope of Swiss pre-trade transparency waivers is rather roughly described. Swiss law does not describe any details of when and how the waivers shall apply. Under EU law, for instance, the large in scale waiver is applied according to a detailed threshold system for different levels of liquidity in a specific asset class which is outlined in the level 2 measures to MiFIR (i.e., quantitative definitions of the waivers). The corresponding ordinance to FinfraG, the FinfraV, only contains the waivers' general principles but not any detailed description or quantitative definition of the waivers' scope. Insofar, the Swiss government delegates this task to the trading venues to choose which of the outlined waivers they want to incorporate into their trading regulations and how they want to apply them.[2405]

This broad delegation of regulatory power on the subsequent regulatory level with little quantitative guidelines is comparable to the regulatory system under MiFID I. MiFID I only contained the very principles of regulation and delegated the details to the Member States in their legislative power by their parliaments and administrative power by their NCAs. This led to divergences among the Member States where some had more permissive and others more restrictive rules.[2406] This may also happen in Switzerland, because FinfraG/FinfraV only provides the principles for regulation and leaves the trading venues with both their rule-making power and their market policing power to pick and choose the scope of the trade transparency rules as well as the waivers and their scope of application. Currently, however, Switzerland is not in the same dilemma as the EU faced under MiFID I because the Swiss market is highly centralized between two major exchanges which also run the largest dark trading service. The exchanges therefore have no incentive to allow for dark trading that harms their price formation process. If the Swiss market becomes more fragmented in the future, the Swiss regulator should be aware of the pitfalls in its

2404 Cf. ibid SK FinfraG Art 29 paras 38, 43ff.

2405 ibid SK FinfraG Art 29 paras 37–8.

2406 Moloney, *EU Securities and Financial Markets Regulation* (n 4) 481.

regulatory design and may consider more detailed regulation similar to that under MiFID II/MiFIR.

cc) Third Level: Reverse Exception

On the third level of the transparency regime, Swiss law has no limiting device like the DVC in the EU, or the trade-at rule proposed but not implemented in the US. The reason for this more permissive regulation in Switzerland may also be found in the more centralized market which bears a smaller risk of market failure due to excessive dark trading.

That said, the Swiss trade transparency regime can be dubbed self-regulatory heavy because the ultimate scope of the transparency regime depends on the trading venue's choice within their self-regulatory power.

3. Evaluation of the Similarities and Differences

a) Issues with Overbroad Exceptions

US law demonstrates that even a well-crafted transparency regime can be rendered futile if an exception designed for another purpose is overbroad in scope and misused in practice. While US law follows the Common law tradition of correcting market failures while refraining from comprehensive, all-encompassing systems of regulation aligned with public policy concerns like the EU rather does, it still created an elaborate transparency regime to correct for the issue of underproduction of information. The National Market System as a policy set out in Section 11A Exchange Act, however, also introduces another goal – enhancing competition – which in practice conflicts with trade transparency to some extent.

The 5 %-threshold under Regulation ATS is an overbroad exception from the trade transparency rules which was implemented to foster competition under more permissive rules. The rule maker did not anticipate its current use of offering dark trading services. Although the SEC has discussed lowering the threshold to 0.25 %[2407] of the daily average turnover of the respective NMS stock, this has not yet been implemented and would also lead to more dispersion among an increased number of dark ATS of smaller size. The SEC should consider abandoning the minimal threshold

2407 Mahoney and Rauterberg (n 118) 244.

exception and rather consider a calibration of the transparency rules for liquidity levels on a specific trading venue. To avoid this calibration for liquidity from also being misused to set up multiple smaller ATS with low liquidity levels by the same operator, the liquidity levels of one de facto ATS operator (regardless of the corporate shell) should be added to identify the actual liquidity level in this marketplace. This way, the elaborate system of transparency rules and exceptions under Regulation NMS would apply and steer liquidity either to the lit or to the regulated dark markets.

A change to the better would however be the implementation of the 2022 proposal of a broader Rule 605 Regulation NMS that would require (at least) post-trade transparency from large broker-dealers and single dealer platforms that are currently operating in the dark.[2408]

b) Issues with a Limitation Device

An issue addressed by the US and the EU is the issue of implementing a limitation device. While the US tested but did not implement the trade-at rule, the EU implemented the DVC mechanism but is planning on changing it to a single volume cap mechanism because of the high cost of administering such a complex limitation instrument.[2409] The idea of a limiting mechanism for regulated dark trading using waivers has come under further pressure when the FCA announced it would no longer automatically apply the DVC to UK and EU equities in 2021.[2410] HM Treasury supported this step and argued that the FCA's empirical market analysis in 2017 found that dark trading is not harmful up to a level of 11 %-17 %.[2411] Furthermore, HM Treasury refers to market participants who reported that they rather experienced market improvements and no negative effect on price improvement since the DVC no longer applied. The market participants feel that the thresholds of the DVC were arbitrary.[2412] For this reason, HM Treasury

---

2408 SEC, 'Fact Sheet Disclosure of Order Execution Information' (n 1077) 2.

2409 European Commission, 'Proposal for a Regulation of the European Parliament and of the Council amending Regulation (EU) No 600/2014 as regards enhancing market data transparency, removing obstacles to the emergence of a consolidated tape, optimising the trading obligations and prohibiting receiving payments for forwarding client orders' (n 1146) 19.

2410 HM Treasury, 'Wholesale Markets Review' (n 1521) 12.

2411 Aquilina and others (n 275) 27; HM Treasury, 'Wholesale Markets Review' (n 1522) 19.

2412 HM Treasury, 'Wholesale Markets Review' (n 1521) 12.

will bring forward legislation to remove the DVC entirely under UK law.[2413] This decision appears reasonable because it is unclear at which point the amount of dark trading turns from useful to harmful for market quality, but it seems to be rather certain that the actual threshold lies above 4 % and 8 % (at approximately 11 %-17 %) as the FCA research suggests.[2414]

There is also the possibility that dark trading levels will find an equilibrium by themselves which means markets are not broken and need no fixing by regulation. This seems to be the case under US law where the market share for dark trading seems to have found an equilibrium at around 10 % according to HM Treasury.[2415] This plateauing of dark trading levels may also be the reason why the SEC did not pursue the idea of a trade-at rule.

Moreover, the EU also decided to further clamp down on the reference price waiver which will apply only to orders of twice the standard market size if the MiFIR refit comes into law.[2416] This is also a limiting device for regulated dark trading by narrowing the scope of permissible dark trading.

This strong distrust against the reference price waiver and its adherence to a limitation device, now the SVC, shows that the EU will only accept a transparency regime that is *Pareto* efficient for their markets. One trader can only benefit from regulated dark trading if one has a personal gain, but the market at large does not suffer adverse effects. According to the EU, it can be assumed that no adverse effects will be created from up to 4 % and 8 % dark trading under the DVC, and 7 % under the SVC. This is supported by *Anquliar* who found that the thresholds for harmful dark trading may lie even higher at 11 %-17 %, so the EU is also overcautious.[2417] The EU, however, rejects the idea of *Kaldor-Hicks* efficiency where a trader can use dark trading if they gain a benefit large enough to (theoretically) offset the losses suffered by all others.[2418] This shows the rather public

2413 ibid 12.

2414 Aquilina and others (n 275) 27; HM Treasury, 'Wholesale Markets Review' (n 1522) 19.

2415 HM Treasury, 'Wholesale Markets Review' (n 1522) 20.

2416 European Commission, 'Proposal for a Regulation of the European Parliament and of the Council amending Regulation (EU) No 600/2014 as regards enhancing market data transparency, removing obstacles to the emergence of a consolidated tape, optimising the trading obligations and prohibiting receiving payments for forwarding client orders' (n 1146) 18–9.

2417 Aquilina and others (n 275) 27.

2418 Otherwise, the EU would abandon a limiting device like the DVC/SVC because the benefit of the few using dark trading would be efficiency enhancing if they (theoretically) were able to offset the many who use lit trading.

policy-oriented regulation characteristic for Civil law jurisdictions under EU law because the EU tries to actively regulate towards an (economically) ideal market with far-reaching transparency by having the volume cap mechanism.[2419] This mechanism is supposed to propel the price formation process towards a non-observable fair value.[2420] This goal of reaching an ideal market according to economic theory does (at best) benefit the public but not the individual trader seeking for dark trading opportunities under a capped waiver.

Since the US market, on the other hand, has witnessed a plateauing of dark trading levels, it does not see a reason for regulatory intervention with a limitation device like a trade-at rule.[2421] It can, thus, be argued that the US system would be rather open to *Kaldor-Hicks* efficiency, under which certain traders can use a privilege (i.e., dark trading) at the cost of others (the investing public) so long as it is in total an efficiency gain for the market. Even though, the US has some waivers implemented under the more recent Regulation NMS which shows its intention to preferably have regulated dark trading under such waivers, it still keeps the loophole of the 5 %-threshold under the older Regulation ATS, originally designed for easier market access for ATS, knowing that it can be used for unlimited dark trading by market participants.[2422] This observation aligns with the Common law tradition of only promulgating new regulations in order to correct for market failure, i.e., only if certain groups of investors or the investing public is prone to suffer harm.[2423]

The same is true for Swiss law. The fact that Swiss law also intends to have only regulated dark trading under waivers shows that Swiss law only allows for dark trading if there is no harm for the market. Moreover, the Swiss regulator has no need to have stricter rules because dark trading is a relatively small phenomenon in Swiss markets.[2424] For a Civil law jurisdiction, it is uncommon to have such a regulatory approach that rather wants to correct for market failures.[2425] However, it is unsurprising that Switzerland tries to create a permissive market environment to attract

2419 Siems (n 29) 53; Ogus, 'Comparing Regulatory Systems' (n 48) 148–9.

2420 Recital 17 MiFIR. See also Ekkenga (n 96) § 7 para 135.

2421 HM Treasury, 'Wholesale Markets Review' (n 1522) 20. See also SEC, 'Concept Release on Equity Market Structure' (n 6) 75 FR 3598.

2422 See above Part II § 5.E.

2423 Cf. Siems (n 29) 53; Ogus, 'Comparing Regulatory Systems' (n 48) 148–9.

2424 EFD and SIF (n 1862) 12.

2425 Siems (n 29) 53; Ogus, 'Comparing Regulatory Systems' (n 48) 148–9.

foreign investors in order to compete with the large financial markets in the US and the UK which, as Common law systems, also operate under the logic to merely correct for market failures than building a colossal regulatory system like the EU's MiFID II/MiFIR.[2426]

The volume cap mechanism in the EU is an example of precautious regulation that may to be reassessed because dark trading in its current form and size appears not have adverse effects on financial stability in a sense a failing bank may have. Nevertheless, the EU's example shows that precautious regulation is primarily a political question in which the legislator decides how much risk it is willing to accept in its financial markets.[2427]

c) Issues with Lean Regulation

Compared to the vast trade transparency regimes in the US and EU, the lean Swiss regulation shows that setting out the mere principles of trade transparency may leave an open field for the self-regulating trading venues to implement trading regulations that may vary significantly from each other. In Switzerland, this has not led to any practical issues so far because FINMA needs to approve the trading regulations and, most importantly, the market is rather small and centralized.

However, with regard to the waivers, the comparison showed that it is not clear what order size qualifies as large in scale and if this should be dependent on liquidity levels as under EU law. Moreover, Swiss law leaves even more room for self-regulatory rule making if a trading venue decides to implement pre-trade transparency for equity instruments other than shares and non-equities. In this case, Swiss law does not even provide mere principles for the waiver. A market less centralized than the Swiss today should rather provide for more government made law on the matter to avoid uncertainty and eventually the creation of an uneven playing field among multiple venues.

d) Categorizing the Trade Transparency Regimes

In an effort to categorize the individual trade transparency regimes, the discussion above leads to the following categorizations. The is US is a

2426 Cf. EFD and SIF (n 1862) 12.

2427 Commission of the European Communities, 'Communication from the Commission on the precautionary principle' (n 527) 15 para 5.2.1.; Calliess (n 528) 140.

'market failure-minded regime' with a tendency to create *Kaldor-Hicks* efficiency. The EU regime can be dubbed a 'public policy-minded regime' aiming for *Pareto* efficiency. The Swiss regime, however, is also a 'public policy-minded regime' but one which does not quite so much aim for *Pareto* efficiency as it is more permissive than the EU regime lacking a limitation device (like the DVC/SVC) and has more lenient regulation due to strong self-regulatory elements.

4. Conclusion

With regard to the transparency regime, all jurisdictions aim to ensure a certain amount of trade transparency and try to moderate dark trading.

Despite a differentiated transparency and waiver regime in Regulation NMS, the 5 %-threshold in Regulation ATS can be used by ATS multiple times to circumvent the regulatory effect of US law entirely. Dark trading under US law is almost unrestricted when it makes use of the 5 %-threshold and is available for all sorts of trading whether vulnerable to trade transparency or not.

The European Union imposes a very strict and differentiated regime that steers liquidity to lit venues if the liquidity cannot qualify for one of the limited and specified exemptions. Moreover, the double volume cap (and the single volume cap under the new law) keeps the application of the reference price waiver and negotiated trade waiver in check. Some say the double volume cap is overly restrictive and may leave traders who need to use dark liquidity to search for it elsewhere although dark trading on regulated trading venues has not yet reached its full potential. This criticism will likely not be muted under the new SVC.

Swiss law walks a middle path with its trade transparency regime. It does not capture as many instruments as the European Union under the pre-trade transparency regime, but leaves room for vast amounts of dark trading which is, however, rectified by a broad post-trade transparency rule. With regard to exemptions, Swiss law follows a similarly restrictive path as the European Union but not as complex as under MiFID II/MiFIR.

III. Access Regime

1. Requirements for a Proper Access Regime

For the regulation of dark trading, the regulators must also consider the access regime. Access, in this regard, means access to trading information as well as access to trading venues. In a trading environment with fragmented markets dispersed among multiple marketplaces, a first important step for traders is knowing where they can find liquidity at the best price in the market. The trade transparency regime can only determine if information is produced but the access regime decides who is granted access to it. Thus, the introduction of a system to disseminate information throughout the market becomes increasingly important in a more decentralized market with multiple trading venues.[2428]

However, it is not enough to merely know where the best trading opportunities are, traders also need to have access to those trading venues to tap into the available liquidity. The presumption is that a financial market should allow for interaction between investors on the buy-side and the sell-side with as little restriction as possible to increase liquidity which eventually supports the price discovery process. Under this presumption, the regulatory goal needs to be allowing equal access for every trader unless there is sound justification to ban certain traders from the market.[2429]

2. Findings in the Three Jurisdictions

a) Access to Information

The access to trading information is regulated by a rather broad access rule in the US. In an effort to consolidate a fragmented market, Rule 610 of Regulation NMS requires access to quotations on other trading venues through private linkages without imposing unfairly discriminatory terms. Regulation NMS even caps the fees that trading venues can charge for access to their trading information.[2430] Moreover, US law requires a consolidated tape in which all major trading venues publish and disseminate their trading data. This consolidated tape has been set up and, despite

2428 IOSCO, 'Principles for Dark Liquidity' (n 12) 22–3.
2429 ibid 23.
2430 Mahoney and Rauterberg (n 118) 246.

needing some upgrades with regard to speed, functions well for the market at large.[2431]

In the European Union and Switzerland, regulators also aim for fair access to trading data to minimize the adverse effects of market fragmentation. Under MiFID II/MiFIR, RMs, MTFs, and OTFs must provide access to their displayed prices on reasonable commercial terms and on a non-discriminatory basis.[2432] The quotes of bilateral SIs shall be made public in a manner which is easily accessible to other market participants on a reasonable commercial basis.[2433] The detailed requirements for the criteria 'easily accessible' quotes and access upon 'reasonable commercial basis' are further defined in the commission delegated regulation (EU) 2017/567 of 18 May 2016.[2434] Although EU law requires the implementation of a consolidated tape similar to the one in the US, the mere legal requirement was not enough to incentivize private actors to set one up.[2435] Under the MiFID II/MiFIR refit, ESMA now assigns this task to private actors as the sole consolidated tape providers for a specific instrument, and the trading venues are now obliged to give those private actors their data for dissemination.[2436] This assignment will be for a period of five years before it is repeated.[2437]

Although Swiss law does not explicitly set out that access to price information has to be provided on reasonable commercial terms and on a non-discriminatory basis as under EU law, FINMA applies this standard in the approval process for trading regulations of trading venues. If trading venues do not provide for access on reasonable commercial terms on a non-discriminatory basis, FINMA will not approve the trading regulation

2431 Beny (n 51) 415–7; Mattli (n 799) 115ff; Lewis (n 800) 97ff.

2432 Moloney, *EU Securities and Financial Markets Regulation* (n 4) 473–4, 477.

2433 Article 15(1) subpara 3 MiFIR.

2434 Articles 6–11 of Commission Delegated Regulation (EU) 2017/567 of 18 May 2016. See also Kumpan and Schmidt (n 4) MiFIR Art 13 paras 4ff.

2435 European Commission, 'Proposal for a Regulation of the European Parliament and of the Council amending Regulation (EU) No 600/2014 as regards enhancing market data transparency, removing obstacles to the emergence of a consolidated tape, optimising the trading obligations and prohibiting receiving payments for forwarding client orders' (n 1146) 4.

2436 ibid 15–6, 20, 31.

2437 ibid 33.

preventing the trading venue from commencing or continuing its operations.[2438]

b) Access to Trading Venues

In all three jurisdictions, only professional investors can access trading venues whereas retail investors have to use brokerage services. This differentiation is, however, justified because only professional traders have the capabilities to participate in the highly sophisticated trading environment.[2439]

Under US law, the trading venue regime generally requires operators to provide fair and non-discriminatory access. As with the transparency regime, however, ATS operating below the 5 %-threshold are exempt from the fair access requirement. Since this coincides with the loophole used for dark trading, US dark pools are not required to provide fair access to traders. They even differentiate themselves from lit exchanges by their capability to exclude HFTs from their venue for the benefit of their other traders. As the enforcement measures have shown, this is not always a true claim.[2440]

EU and Swiss law are very similar regarding access to trading systems. Trading systems need to provide fair and non-discriminatory access. Within this requirement, only bilateral trading systems that assume proprietary risk when trading can exclude some traders due to commercial considerations such as credit status.[2441] Thus, trading systems in the EU and in Switzerland cannot exclude HFTs just by staying below a certain turnover threshold.

3. Evaluation and Conclusion

The access regimes in all three jurisdictions are, in principle, well equipped to allow for fair and non-discriminatory access to trading venues. The motif

2438 Humbel, *Die Regelung der Vor- und Nachhandelstransparenz in der Europäischen Union und der Schweiz* (n 50) 490–1.

2439 See, for example, Moloney, *EU Securities and Financial Markets Regulation* (n 4) 473–4, 477.

2440 Haeberle (n 459) 823ff.

2441 Gebauer (n 94) MiFIR Art 17 para 8; Kuhn (n 2272) BSK FinfraG Art 18 para 14; Truffer (n 2279) BSK FinfraG Art 34 para 4.

of the 5 %-thresholds undermining the well-designed US regulatory regime surfaces again in this context which allows dark ATS to offer trading systems from which HFTs may be excluded. On the one hand, this exclusion is not necessarily efficiency enhancing if intermarket arbitrage by fast traders is no longer possible. On the other hand, the trading venues' discretion over access rights and their need for liquidity creates a conflict of interest which may lead to a situation in which HFTs might still be invited into a dark pool that is sold to other investors as supposedly free of HFT.[2442]

While the obvious disadvantage is the discouragement of further technological innovation, it remains doubtful if an arms race for the last split seconds improves market quality at a level noticeable to either the financial market or the real economy.

IV. Price Protection Rules

1. Further Measures to Protect Price Formation

Besides the central instruments of a well-designed trading venue regime, trade transparency regime, and access regime, some jurisdictions have implemented certain conduct rules that aim to protect the price formation process. To find a universal standard to measure those conduct rules is, however, not possible because there are a number of measures that can be implemented but none are mandatory. Those rules should rather be evaluated before the backdrop of their regulatory regimes and then be contrasted with the other jurisdictions.

2. Findings in the Three Jurisdictions

a) Order Protection Rule, Sub-Penny Rule, and Speed Bumps in the United States

Under US law, the Order Protection Rule per Rule 611 of Regulation NMS protects the best bid and best offer prices to encourage traders to post best

2442 SEC, *Press Release: SEC Charges UBS Subsidiary With Disclosure Violations and Other Regulatory Failures in Operating Dark Pool* (n 26); *UBS Securities LLC* (n 26) 1ff; Kasiske (n 11) 456–7.

priced limit orders into the lit market. The Order Protection Rule, however, only protects the NBBO against trade-throughs at inferior prices.[2443]

To prevent liquidity providers who post limit orders from being outperformed by a superior quote of insignificant volume, the United States also implemented the Sub-Penny Rule.[2444] The Sub-Penny Rule quoting and accepting quotes in smaller increments than a penny (USD 0.01) for all stocks traded at a price higher than USD 1.[2445] While those rules were principally capable of bringing together trading interests at the best available prices without being front-run by arbitrageurs at a lit pool, dark trading is not restricted by this rule because the Sub-Penny Rule only restricts the quoting and accepting of quotes but not the execution of (dark) orders (not showing quotes) in increments smaller than a penny.[2446]

Therefore, the 2022 proposal of an amendment to the Sub-Penny Rule, as a new Tick Size Rule, would be welcome if it came into law in 2023. The SEC proposed a new tick size rule that has a tiered minimum price increment system reaching from USD 0.01 for stocks with a bid-ask-spread greater than USD 0.04 down to USD 0.001 for stocks with a bid-ask-spread at or below USD 0.008.[2447] This proposed rule change could make lit markets much more attractive as they have been in recent years compared to their dark pool competition because orders on lit markets could be priced more competitively which would make using a dark pool no longer necessary.[2448]

Another measure to protect the price formation process from potentially harmful practices by algorithmic traders and HFTs is the implementation of a so-called 'speed bumps'. A speed bump is a kind of trading rule of a venue that allows incoming orders to match only after a certain period of time has elapsed. This way, the technological advantage of HFTs is levelled out so that they in effect trade like any other trader.[2449] In the US, the Investors Exchange (IEX) uses this technique and appears to attract traders with their 'speed bump' rule.[2450]

2443 Mahoney and Rauterberg (n 118) 244–5.
2444 Rule 612 Regulation NMS (17 CFR § 242.612).
2445 Mahoney and Rauterberg (n 118) 246–7.
2446 ibid 247.
2447 SEC, 'Fact Sheet Tick Size, Access Fees, and Transparency of Better Priced Orders' (n 1074) 2.
2448 ibid 1.
2449 Mahoney and Rauterberg (n 118) 271.
2450 ibid 271–2.

b) Tick-Size Rule in the European Union

EU and Swiss law do not provide for a similar rule as the Order Protection Rule under Regulation NMS. The European Union, however, has a Tick Size Rule under Article 49 MiFID II which operates similarly to the US Tick Size Rule and also aims to avoid front running of best priced limit orders by insignificant margins. Unlike US law, the Tick-Size Rule under EU law applies to individual financial instrument and, thus, does also apply to dark orders although those orders do not show a limit price.[2451] However, the Tick-Size Rule does not apply to systematic internalizers despite their increased importance since the introduction of the volume cap mechnism for waivers on trading venues.[2452]

c) Obligation to Trade on a Trading Venue in the European Union

Additionally, EU law also forces trading in shares and derivatives from the OTC-space onto regulated trading systems subject to trade transparency via the trading obligations under Articles 23 and 28 MiFIR. The rationale of both rules is to ensure that orders in highly liquid instruments support the price formation process on regulated trading systems since they are unlikely to suffer adverse effects when subjected to trade transparency.[2453] If those transactions are, however, still vulnerable to trade transparency, they may seek protection by a waiver from pre-trade transparency or a deferral of post-trade transparency.

3. Evaluation and Conclusion

The Order Protection Rule is a sensible rule to avoid trade-throughs which may hinder fair competition among different trading venues competing for the best displayed bid and offer prices. However, the issue with the Order Protection Rule is that it does not prevent traders to avoid a specific lit market simply by refraining to route their order to the market with the best NBBO at a given time. Such trader can rather sit idle in their own trading venue waiting for orders priced closer to their own limit order to

---

2451 Kumpan and Schmidt (n 4) MiFID II Art 49 paras 1ff.
2452 ibid MiFIR Art 23 para 5.
2453 ibid MiFIR Art 23 paras 5ff; Lehmann (n 1088) MiFIR Art 28 paras 1, 9–10.

come to their venue. Avoiding this was the goal of the trade-at rule by mandating the routing of an order to the best priced contra-side order at the NBBO but it has not yet been adopted in the US.[2454]

The Sub-Penny Rule in the US and the Tick-Size Rule in the EU are useful tools to avoid front running by insignificant margins, especially by algorithmic traders and HFTs. Those rules appear to function according to their intended purpose and should be kept in place. In the US, however, the Sub-Penny Rule should also apply to dark orders, while in the EU, the Tick-Size Rule may be extended to systematic internalizers, given their increased importance under the volume cap mechanism.[2455] Another improvement would be the proposed Tick Size Rule that would make minimum price increments, formerly only available on dark pools, also available on lit market.[2456]

The implementation of a speed bump-rule appears sensible to avoid potentially harmful HFT-strategies but may hinder innovation. Currently, it may be the best strategy for the regulator to allow for those rules but not require them by law, and then seeing how many trading venues implement such rules. If the trading venues see a need to protect less technically sophisticated traders, they will implement those rules to cater to their needs.

V. Supervisory Structure

The regulatory frameworks in the United States, the European Union, Germany, and Switzerland differ significantly from each other with regard to the supervisory structure and the role of self-regulation.

1. United States

In the United States, the SEC is entrusted with the administration of the Exchange Act.[2457] However, in a federal system such as the United States, enforcement measures can also be brought by State officials, such

2454 Cf. Committee on Capital Markets Regulation, 'Enhancing U.S. Equity Market Structure for Retail Investors' (n 650) 7–8.

2455 Cf. Kumpan and Schmidt (n 4) MiFIR Art 23 para 5.

2456 SEC, 'Fact Sheet Tick Size, Access Fees, and Transparency of Better Priced Orders' (n 1074) 1.

2457 Barr, Jackson and Tahyar (n 596) 445–6; Pan (n 196) 204.

as the Attorney General of New York. But even within the Exchange Act's framework, the SEC is not the only institution assuming regulatory tasks. Additionally, the SROs, comprising of national exchanges and FINRA, play an important role as self-regulatory bodies. National exchanges and FINRA are also the addressees of the transparency rules in Regulation NMS and need to ensure that their members comply with such rules.[2458]

2. European Union and Germany

In the European Union, the regulatory power lies primarily in the hands of the NCAs of the Member States. For Germany, these are BaFin and the several State Exchange Authorities.[2459] In contrast to US law, ESMA, as the central agency on the EU level, cannot exert regulatory power but rather drafts the commission delegated regulations and other implementing standards in the first place and renders its opinions and reports on the regulatory actions of national competent authorities in the Member States. While ESMA can exert a certain amount of 'soft power' through 'comply or explain' policies, the EU's supervisory system still rests upon the Member States' administrative apparatus which can result in deviating regulatory decision making.[2460]

In the context of dark trading, this became apparent in the deviating practices of national competent authorities in granting waivers, allowing for incoherent waiver application and regulatory arbitrage. For this reason, the European Union saw the need to implement strict waiver rules.[2461]

Also, the skepticism towards self-regulatory measures may be founded in the belief that adding another level of regulatory power may undermine the harmonization of law in the European Union.[2462] While some claim that this lack of self-regulation often costs the European Union valuable time since self-regulation can often react faster than the government, this opinion disregards the Lamfalussy process in EU legislation. In the Lamfalussy

2458 Barr, Jackson and Tahyar (n 596) 449–50.

2459 Fabian Walla, '§ 11 Capital Markets Supervision' in Rüdiger Veil (ed), *European Capital Markets Law* (3rd edn, Hart Publishing 2022) § 11 paras 1, 22; Fabian Walla, *Die Konzeption der Kapitalmarktaufsicht in Deutschland* (Nomos 2012) 19ff.

2460 Moloney, *EU Securities and Financial Markets Regulation* (n 4) 483.

2461 ibid 481.

2462 Rüdiger Veil and Marcus Lerch, 'Auf dem Weg zu einem Europäischen Finanzmarktrecht: die Vorschläge der Kommission zur Neuregelung der Märkte für Finanzinstrumente - Teil II -' [2012] WM 1605, 1607.

process, only the level 1 measures, i.e., MiFID II/MiFIR, are promulgated by the European Parliament and the Council upon recommendation by the Commission, all other levels, which are more detailed and technical in nature, are delegated to ESMA and the Commission. In case of an abrupt market development, this means that ESMA and the Commission can adjust their delegated acts within the boundaries of MiFID II/MiFIR. This may often be as efficient as self-regulatory interventions.[2463]

3. Switzerland

In Switzerland, the administration of financial markets regulation is vested in FIMNA as the competent federal agency. Despite Switzerland's alignment with EU law, Swiss law is characterized by far-reaching elements of self-regulation. With only the principles of the trading systems and trade transparency regimes determined in FinfraG, trading venues assume a key role in further defining and applying the law through the promulgation of their trading regulations.[2464] Even though FINMA can exert some oversight over the trading regulations through the approval process, FINMA has to accept a variety of regulations, even deviating ones, so long as they fall within the broad definitions of FinfraG. The broad self-regulatory powers of trading venues are particularly troublesome with regard to the implementation of waivers because FinfraG does not specify any details regarding their application. And trading venues have an interest in providing trading services that are attractive to their users, but not necessarily services that support efficient price formation. Insofar the Swiss supervisory structure is characterized by a facilitative rather than restrictive impact on dark trading.

C. Conclusion

In this chapter, the key variables for the issue of dark trading, i.e., the trading venue regime, the transparency regime, the access regime, the price protection rules, the supervisory structures, were examined against a pre-defined standard for regulation and then compared among the three

---

2463 Cf. Rüdiger Veil, '§ 1 History' in Rüdiger Veil (ed), *European Capital Markets Law* (3rd edn, Hart Publishing 2022) § 1 para 18.

2464 Winzeler, 'Selbstregulierung' (n 540) § 7 paras 12ff.

jurisdictions. After that, the advantages and disadvantages were discussed. This showed us that the US is a post-trade transparency heavy system, the EU is a pre-trade transparency heavy system, and Switzerland is self-regulatory heavy system.

In the final chapter, the question of whether an ideal regulatory regime can be identified shall be answered, suggestions for future improvements in the jurisdiction will be made, and the findings on the research questions will be summarized.

§ 9. Conclusion

A. The Issue of Identifying an Ideal Regulatory Regime

I. No Blueprint Available

In the introduction, this study raised the question of whether an ideal regulation for the phenomenon of dark trading can be identified. The in-depth analysis and the comparison of the examined jurisdictions have shown that there is no single set of rules to be found in one jurisdiction that is superior to all others. All regulatory responses given by the jurisdictions left some aspects to be desired. It is also not possible to synthesize an ideal regulation from the jurisdictions by taking the 'best bits' of each regulatory regime and combine them into a new regulatory regime. This approach would neglect the individual characteristics of both the jurisdictions' historically developed patterns of their financial markets and their legal systems. For instance, a market's degree of decentralization, the degree of self-regulatory power, or the potential for deviating interpretations of the law by the regulators are all issues that demand widely different approaches for the regulation of dark trading. Although desirable, the regulation of dark trading cannot be condensed to a blueprint applicable to all jurisdictions in the sense that individual rules can be formulated that fit all sizes.

II. Principles for Regulation

This result, however, does not mean that dark trading can and should be regulated as the national regulator sees fit. The absence of a roadmap with every street, corner, or junction clearly marked does not mean that this study cannot provide for a nautical chart where waterways are marked to some degree and the way forward highly depends on where you want to go, what vessel you are steering, and how the weather conditions are during your voyage. Translated into terms of financial regulation, the proper regulation for your market depends on your policy goals, the structure of your market, and the circumstances in which your financial market is embedded.

As to the policy goals, the fact that financial markets, at least in the examined jurisdictions, serve the purpose of allocation of capital and risk for the economy and that they all pursue the protection of the functioning of the market and investor protection with their financial markets regulation shows that all jurisdictions are sailing in the same direction.[2465] This allows for the distillation of the meta-goals of regulation to common principles for the regulation for dark trading.

Those principles have already been outlined above to facilitate the comparison between the jurisdictions as a standard to measure them against. The standards above can also be understood as objectives for a proper regulation of dark trading. To evaluate jurisdiction against the standard, the individual characteristics need to be taken into account. In the following, the different principles for proper regulation shall be briefly outlined. Against this standard, the jurisdictions' strengths and shortfalls will be outlined.

B. Principles for Proper Regulation and Suggestions for Future Improvements

I. Principle 1: Have a Broad Trading Infrastructure Regime

The first principle outlined above is that the trade infrastructure regime should be broad to capture all organized trading. The rationale is to prevent organized trading which contains price-relevant information from slipping through the regulatory net into the OTC-space creating unregulated dark trading.[2466]

While the EU and the Swiss trade infrastructure regimes are very detailed and capable of capturing organized trading to a sufficient degree, the US trade infrastructure regime should be re-evaluated. The differentiation between national securities exchanges, broker-dealers, and ATS does not capture all organized trading as the large proportion of broker-dealer internalization shows. Also, the US trading infrastructure does not clearly distinguish between venues for non-discretionary, multilateral systems, and discretionary, bilateral systems which makes US venues more susceptible to

2465 See above Part I § 3.A.

2466 Cf. ESMA, 'Final Report: On ESMA's Opinion on the Trading Venue Perimeter' (n 2321) 6.

conflicts of interest.[2467] This could be remedied by a clear-cut trading venue categorization like under EU law.

II. Principle 2: Have a Broad Transparency Regime

The second principle suggests a broad but balanced trade transparency regime to counter an unwanted growth of dark trading. For liquid markets, the default rule for all instruments, both equity and non-equity, should be lit trading because it supports both a level playing field among the traders and the price formation process.[2468] For rather illiquid markets, the default rule should rather be dark trading because otherwise the market may dry up, like in illiquid bonds markets.[2469]

1. US law

Despite a nuanced trade transparency regime, US law does not manage to make pre-trade transparency the default rule for all organized trading because of the 5 %-threshold. While this permissive rule was once designed to encourage new market participants to enter into competition with large stock exchanges, it is currently used as a loophole that allows unregulated dark trading in a way that orders can vanish in dark pools not being subject to any pre-trade transparency rule whatsoever. Such orders do not need to seek exemption from the transparency rules, they remain spared from it in the first place. No control is exerted whether the ATS or the orders within it need to use dark trading because they would otherwise face market risk. Even the proposal to lower the threshold from 5 % to 0.25 % would not close this loophole, but would rather thin liquidity even further on those dark ATS. The minimum-threshold rule needs to be abolished entirely so that the nuanced trade transparency regime under US law would apply to all organized trading as an inevitable default rule. In this case, the carefully crafted exceptions from pre-trade transparency under US law would apply

2467 Having both ATS and broker-dealer internalization regulated under the broker-dealer category, see Mahoney and Rauterberg (n 118) 228–9.
2468 Recital 10 MiFIR; IOSCO, 'Principles for Dark Liquidity' (n 12) 26–8.
2469 Moloney, *EU Securities and Financial Markets Regulation* (n 4) 431–2, 486.

and can begin steering liquidity from lit to dark as the regulator deemed necessary.[2470]

2. EU law

In this regard the EU has a very broad transparency regime which sets up pre-trade and post-trade transparency rules for both equity and non-equity instruments as the default rule. Only for illiquid non-equities markets does the EU suspend the rule to protect the thin layer of liquidity from market risks. This regulatory decision meets the above standard quite well and should be maintained. Whether having a limiting device, like the volume cap mechanism, coupled with a requirement to trade on a trading venue is sensible, is not a question of setting transparency as a default rule.[2471] It will be dealt with under principle 4.

3. Swiss law

Swiss law should reconsider its approach to set pre-trade transparency as the default rule only for shares, leaving trading in other equity instruments and non-equity instruments in the dark. Although the Swiss trading venues remedied these shortfalls by implementing broader rules in their trading regulations via self-regulatory power, a default rule for trade transparency under Swiss law would insulate the market from future market entrants who do not implement the same rules in their trading venues in order to run an unregulated dark pool. This would create an uneven playing field, and can be avoided by expanding Article 27(1) FinfraV. In this regard Swiss law lacks the breadth and the detail of regulation the standard suggests which favors dark trading. The fact that this susceptibility of Swiss law is counterbalanced by self-regulatory measures should not satisfy the Swiss legislator and regulator.[2472]

2470 See above Part III § 8.B.I. and II.
2471 See above Part III § 8.B.II.
2472 See above Part III § 8.B.II.

III. Principle 3: Provide for Clear-cut Exceptions from Trade Transparency where Beneficial for Trader and Market

The third principle for proper regulation of dark trading touches upon the bedrock of regulated dark trading. Proper regulation should provide clear-cur exceptions from pre-trade and post-trade transparency in instances in which it benefits the individual trader and at least does not harm the market at large (*Pareto optimal*).[2473] Because of the *Information Paradox*, full transparency is not desirable.[2474] Empirical research also shows that a certain amount of dark trading alleviates the burden of noise trading from the price formation process; only large quantities, which cannot currently be identified with full certainty, harm market quality. It, thus, appears sensible to craft exceptions for situations in which the regulator expects dark trading to be *Pareto optimal*. If such exceptions have a limiting character, i.e., they cannot apply to everyone, they may already be sufficient to steer dark trading to a proper amount.

1. US law

Under US law, the 5 %-threshold cannot distinguish between orders in need of dark trading because they would otherwise face market risk in lit markets and those orders perfectly capable of showing transparency. The 5 %-threshold is a mere loophole which should be closed. The remaining exceptions under Regulation NMS, however, are a proper regulation of dark trading because they can exempt orders like block orders from pre-trade transparency which would otherwise face market risk. Thus, it is recommended to abolish the 5 %-threshold under US law.[2475]

2. EU law

Even in its MiFID II/MiFIR-refit, the EU legislator one-sidedly aims to enhance trade transparency and appears to frown on any form of dark trading as a disruptive element.[2476] The EU legislator once more identified the

---

2473 Magen (n 2348) § 4 para 199.

2474 Picot, Bortenlänger and Röhrl (n 77) 23.

2475 See above Part III § 8.B.II.3.a).

2476 European Commission, 'Proposal for a Regulation of the European Parliament and of the Council amending Regulation (EU) No 600/2014 as regards enhancing reference price waiver as a problematic exception propelling dark trading. For that reason, the reference price waiver can only apply to orders that are twice the standard market size under the proposed Article 4(1)(a) MiFIR for the MiFIR refit to prevent dark trading in small trade sizes.[2477] Even though this particular adaption may be useful, it shows that the EU has difficulties accepting dark trading as a valuable phenomenon in its financial market and acknowledging that it may serve and not harm its goal to have an internationally competitive financial market.[2478] The EU legislator appears to be trapped in the discussion over abolishing the reference price waiver it already had in the legislative process of MiFID II/MiFIR[2479] when especially France was in favor of this proposal. The former opponent in this discussion, the UK, has eased the restrictions on the waiver after Brexit and sees no point in limiting this waiver as it appears to benefit the market.[2480]

From an academic point of view, it appears as if the EU condemns regulated dark trading under waivers just as much as it condemns unregulated dark trading in the OTC-space. The risks of regulated dark trading are however much smaller because waivers can be retracted if market quality suffers. The argument of the EU that small order sizes are not prone to suffer any market risk when subjected to pre-trade transparency and should therefore not benefit from the reference price waiver appears compelling at first glance. Upon second thought, the decision by the UK FCA not to limit the waiver is more useful under the current circumstances. The rationale appears to be that a trader of small orders that decides for dark trading to only save half of the bid-ask-spread in exchange for a longer waiting time for execution has nothing more to gain from their trade, thus, they are likely uninformed. Taking this noise trading from the lit market improves price discovery as long as there is still enough liquidity left for information arbitrage. Since these mechanisms are not impaired as to the opinion of the FCA, there is no reason for (further) regulatory intervention ('if it's not broken, don't fix it').[2481]

---

market data transparency, removing obstacles to the emergence of a consolidated tape, optimising the trading obligations and prohibiting receiving payments for forwarding client orders' (n 1146) 4.

2477 ibid 14.

2478 ibid 1.

2479 Cf. Moloney, *EU Securities and Financial Markets Regulation* (n 4) 435, 481 fn 323.

2480 HM Treasury, 'Wholesale Markets Review' (n 1521) 12.

2481 ibid 12; Davies and Sirri (n 12) 168–9; Zhu (n 186) 779.

As a future suggestion, the EU may consider embracing regulated dark trading under the waivers it designed for the market, and allow the market some breathing space to unfold its market powers. Even though it may not sit well with an initial sense of justice that small orders use dark trading under the reference price waiver, the EU may reconsider if the risk it poses to market quality justifies a regulatory intervention, especially when no other jurisdiction sees a benefit in doing the same.

3. Swiss Law

Under Swiss law, the EU waiver system for equity instrument has been adopted but there are two issues to address. The first issue is that the waivers are only described in principle under Article 27(4) FinfraV but no further explanation on their application is given.[2482] To delegate this task to trading venues in their self-regulatory power with the approval process by FIMNA may work for a handful of venues, especially if the large exchanges also run the dark pools. This delegation of power may however present difficulties if more trading venues arise that only run dedicated dark pools because there is a potential for deviation in the interpretation of the waivers and their application that even FINMA may no longer be able to monitor. In this regard, a more nuanced waiver description may be recommended that explains, for instance, when an order shall be deemed large in scale.

The second issue is that there are no waivers for non-equity instruments laid out in FinfraV because it does not state a pre-trade transparency rule for non-equities.[2483] Trading venues however could demand pre-trade transparency for non-equities within their self-regulatory power and then had to come up with their own waivers for vulnerable orders. This practice bears the potential of deviating waiver application in it and should be remedied by the Swiss legislator defining at least the waivers it would see fit for non-equities trading. This is the only way a clear-cut transparency regime can support a level playing field in the Swiss market.

2482 Schott and Winkler (n 70) SK FinfraG Art 29 para 38.
2483 ibid SK FinfraG Art 29 paras 39–47.

IV. Principle 4: Be Cautious with Limiting Devices

The fourth principle is to be cautious with limiting devices for regulated dark trading. As mentioned, a certain amount of dark trading is useful, but becomes detrimental after passing that optimum. The issue is that the optimum cannot be identified a priori and might be subject to change.[2484] Even though it is understandable that regulators try to limit even regulated dark trading to avoid overuse, law is always a pre-defined set of rules which cannot adjust instantaneously to changing market conditions. Increased flexibility comes with increased complexity to administer such a rule. Ultimately, a limiting device may aim to support the default rule of trade transparency, but at very high costs to administer the device with little chance to hit the target and high social costs if the device cuts off socially desirable dark trading too early.

The US and Switzerland therefore refrained from implementing a limiting device, although the US tested the trade-at rule but did not consider it worth the effort. As the example of the EU shows, the US may have made the better decision under current circumstances.

With MiFID II/MiFIR, the EU implemented the double volume cap mechanism for the reference price waiver and the negotiated trade waiver which limits dark trading in those waivers if the 4 %- or 8 %-threshold is met. In its review process of MiFID II/MiFIR, the EU realized that

> *'(...) [s]uch provisions, apart from being resource-intensive to administer on the part of the regulators, have proven to be rigid and collectively introduce unnecessary complexity in the operation of the equity markets.'*[2485]

This admission of an ill-advised regulation did not lead to the EU to abolish the DVC, but rather to replace it with a single volume cap at 7 % of overall trading in the EU,[2486] a number yet far off from the empirically-found 11 %-17 % of beneficial dark trading under the reference price waiver.[2487]

2484 Cf. Picot, Bortenlänger and Röhrl (n 77) 23–5.

2485 European Commission, 'Proposal for a Regulation of the European Parliament and of the Council amending Regulation (EU) No 600/2014 as regards enhancing market data transparency, removing obstacles to the emergence of a consolidated tape, optimising the trading obligations and prohibiting receiving payments for forwarding client orders' (n 1146) 4.

2486 ibid 14.

2487 Aquilina and others (n 275) 27.

The verdict of the UK FCA on the DVC reads as follows:

> '(...) *The double volume cap was well-intentioned but has no basis in evidence. We need to tackle failures in market data provision to make it available to all. Many rules around transparency and disclosure serve to reduce price formation while needlessly raising costs.*'[2488]

It is therefore unsurprising that the UK suspended the application of the DVC and abolished it under UK law.[2489]

It cannot yet be predicted whether the EU or the UK will have better market quality, but the EU would be well advised to re-think its very restrictive approach towards the reference price waiver and the negotiated trade waiver. The fact that no other jurisdiction has such a rule and their markets suffer no measurable hardship under regulated dark trading may be an indicator for costly overregulation, even under the new single volume cap. Furthermore, a volume cap mechanism combined with an obligation to trade on a trading system may fail the goal to repatriate organized trading on trading venues that are well-equipped to handle lit and regulated dark trading. The outcome the EU saw after the implementation of MiFID II/ MiFIR was that dark trading sought its way to the least regulated trading system, i.e., the SI.[2490] This is potentially sub-optimal to a situation in which there is simply slightly more than 4 % or 8 % regulated dark trading on trading venues.

V. Principle 5: Ensure Fair Access

The fifth principle for proper regulation of dark trading is to ensure fair access both to trading venues and to information.[2491]

While all examined jurisdictions have rules that ensure both fair access to trading venues and to trade transparency information, the US again falls short of this principle because its rule to fair access to trading venues does not apply to those ATS that operate below the 5 %-threshold of the daily turnover in the stock. Parallel to the suggestion in the transparency

2488 HM Treasury, 'Wholesale Markets Review' (n 1522) 2.

2489 HM Treasury, 'Wholesale Markets Review' (n 1521) 12.

2490 ESMA, 'Consultation Paper: MiFID II/MiFIR Review Report on the Transparency Regime for Equity and Equity-Like Instruments, the Double Volume Cap Mechanism and the Trading Obligations for Shares' (n 1805) 48ff.

2491 IOSCO, 'Principles for Dark Liquidity' (n 12) 22–3.

regime, this 5 %-threshold is a mere loophole and the suggestion for future improvement is to abolish it. However, the access to information is relatively fair in the US due to the consolidated tape that operates quite well but might need some technical update to minimize the advantage of private data feeds.[2492]

The EU has no issue with fair access to trading venues but its rule to provide fair access to trade transparency information suffers under the fact that no consolidated tape has yet been implemented although the law requires it. The reason for this shortfall is that initially the EU thought private market actors would step up for the job themselves, but this never happened because it was too costly.[2493] The EU however realized that this situation needed to be remedied and implemented a rule that allows ESMA to appoint a private market actor as consolidated tape provider for each instrument.[2494] Setting up a consolidated reporting tape is a much needed and welcome addition in a market as fragmented as the EU's.

Swiss law also manages to grant fair access to their trading venues through their trading regimes subject to FINMA approval.

VI. Principle 6: Consider Price Protection Rules

As said in Chapter § 8, there is no universal standard for price protection rules. Nevertheless, the jurisdictions have found different sorts of price protection rules. Most prominent is the Sub-Penny rule in the US and the Tick Size rule in the EU which determines the minimum price increments for orders to avoid front running especially by HFTs.[2495] This is a very important rule for achieving a fair trading environment in both lit and dark markets.

Moreover, the introduction of rules that reduce the advantages of HFTs, such as speed bumps, appears to be a politically motivated issue. The fact that none of the three examined jurisdictions require a speed bump mecha-

2492 See above Part III § 8.B.III.

2493 European Commission, 'Proposal for a Regulation of the European Parliament and of the Council amending Regulation (EU) No 600/2014 as regards enhancing market data transparency, removing obstacles to the emergence of a consolidated tape, optimising the trading obligations and prohibiting receiving payments for forwarding client orders' (n 1146) 4.

2494 ibid 15.

2495 See above Part III § 8.B.IV.

nism, but rather allow the trading venues to implement such a mechanism if they see a competitive advantage in this service, shows that there is no clear regulatory need to have a device that might limit both innovation and liquidity in the market. Regulators should however be vigilant if algorithmic trading and HFTs is still producing any benefit or if it already exerts detrimental effects on the market as a whole.[2496] This question needs to be addressed by studies dealing with algorithmic trading and HFTs.

VII. Principle 7: Ensure a Sound Supervisory Regime

The seventh principle for proper regulation of dark trading is to ensure a sound supervisory regime. As stated in Chapter § 8 above, neither systems with strong self-regulatory elements nor systems emphasizing government regulation have an advantage by design. The strength of a supervisory regime depends on its ability to respond quickly and appropriately to regulatory issues while avoiding conflicts of interest.[2497]

1. US law

While the supervision by the SEC under US law is generally quick and appropriate as well as free of conflicts of interest, it is striking that the SEC did not promulgate its proposed rule changes in recent years. Both the lowering of the 5 %-threshold to 0.25 % as well as the trade-at rule did not come to fruition. Taking the above evaluation of those policies into account, those rule changes might not have been ultimately desirable.[2498] Although desirable from a scholar's point of view, the SEC will most likely not consider publicly announcing when it ultimately abandons a proposed rule change to avoid limiting its future maneuvering space.

2. EU law

The fact that the supervision in the EU is exercised by the NCAs whereas ESMA rather plays a coordinating role through means of 'comply or

2496 See above Part III § 8.B.IV.
2497 Cf. IOSCO, 'Principles for Dark Liquidity' (n 12) 31–2.
2498 See above Part II § 5.K. and Part III § 8.B.II.2. and 3.

explain' is often criticized as being too slow and susceptible to deviating practice among the different NCAs.[2499] While this was certainly the case under MiFID I where ESMA did not yet exist, and its predecessor CESR had less coordinative power, this changed with the adoption of MiFID II/ MiFIR. ESMA plays a major role in the coordinative process.[2500] Moreover, the discretion of the NCAs has been limited further and further, once again in the MiFID II/MiFIR-refit with regard to the deferrals form immediate post-trade transparency for non-equities trading.[2501] In this regard, EU law leaves little to be desired given the fact that it coordinates 27 Member States; the flaws under MiFID I have been addressed and corrected. A greater centralization of supervisory power at the EU level like with the banking supervision for systematically important institutions at the ECB under the Single Supervisory Mechanism is not necessary because trade transparency matters do not carry the same (if any) systematic risk as is characteristic for large banks defaulting.[2502]

The EU's skepticism towards self-regulation has also been criticized as being too rigid and not capable of reacting swiftly to upcoming issues.[2503] It is certainly true that the promulgation of level 1 measures takes significant amounts of time and is a matter of broad consensus among the Member States. It is however a strength rather than a weakness to have the Lamfalussy-process.[2504] The level 2 measures suggested by ESMA and promulgated by the Commission are the instrument of choice in a supranational organization. All lags in this process need to be accepted for the benefit of having a much larger market under the capital markets union.

Whether an economic cost-benefit-analysis justifies a complex regulatory system like the transparency regime under MiFID II/MiFIR must be examined by economists. It has been stated that some data-hungry regulatory tools like the DVC border on overregulation and should be

2499 Salger (n 627) 247–8.

2500 Moloney, *EU Securities and Financial Markets Regulation* (n 4) 459–60.

2501 European Commission, 'Proposal for a Regulation of the European Parliament and of the Council amending Regulation (EU) No 600/2014 as regards enhancing market data transparency, removing obstacles to the emergence of a consolidated tape, optimising the trading obligations and prohibiting receiving payments for forwarding client orders' (n 1146) 19.

2502 Cf. Moloney, *EU Securities and Financial Markets Regulation* (n 4) 460.

2503 Salger (n 627) 247–8.

2504 See Walla, '§ 4 Rule-Making Process' (n 1137) § 4 paras 4ff.

reconsidered.[2505] Even the EU appears to realize this and corrects it with a less complex single volume cap. Here, an outright deletion might have been the better choice.

3. Swiss law

The Swiss supervisory system has strong elements of self-regulation which is not in itself troublesome. However, the fact that Swiss law leaves so many core questions for dark trading unanswered, like the composition of the waivers for equities, which waivers apply for non-equities, and the maximum amount post-trade transparency can be deferred, bears the risk of conflicts of interest. If a market entrant who only runs a dark pool wants to use this flexibility, they could probably implement far reaching waivers which FINMA could not oppose in the approval process of the trading rules because the black letter law may allow for such waivers. This risk has not yet materialized only because the major trading venues run both the major lit exchanges and the major dark pools at the same time which aligns the interests of the regulator to protect the lit exchanges and the interests of the regulated. Such a favorable market structure can change quickly, thus leaving Swiss law susceptible to conflicts of interest that should be remedied by more nuanced rules in the black letter law.[2506]

C. Summary of the Findings on the Research Questions

In this concluding section, the findings of this study on the research questions posed at the beginning will be summarized in the form of theses.

2505 European Commission, 'Proposal for a Regulation of the European Parliament and of the Council amending Regulation (EU) No 600/2014 as regards enhancing market data transparency, removing obstacles to the emergence of a consolidated tape, optimising the trading obligations and prohibiting receiving payments for forwarding client orders' (n 1146) 4.

2506 See above Part III. § 8.B.V.3.

I. What is the definition and purpose of trade transparency and dark trading before the backdrop of the regulatory goal of the three examined jurisdictions?

1. Trade transparency is transparency about market information. It can be subdivided into pre-trade transparency, which informs about price, size, and volume of an order; and post-trade transparency, which informs about price, size, and volume of an executed trade.
2. Dark trading is trading in financial instruments on secondary markets which shows no pre-trade transparency and, in some instances, shows reduced, incomplete, or deferred post-trade transparency.
3. The three jurisdictions share the two goals of financial markets regulation, which are the protection and promotion of the functioning of financial markets and investor protection.
4. Significance of trade transparency for the regulatory goals: given the insights of the *ECMH*, trade transparency is significant for the proper functioning of financial markets and investor protection because it fosters informational efficiency as a necessary pre-condition for a well-functioning price formation process. Only a proper informational efficiency with an informative price allows the market to perform its valuation function and its allocation function.
5. Dark trading is also important for keeping information arbitrage as the conveyer belt for informational efficiency running, because full trade transparency would render the costly endeavor of information discovery unprofitable (*Information Paradox*). Dark trading also clears the process of price discovery of an overabundance of uninformed noise trading making the prices more accurate.

II. What are the issues with dark trading?

1. Dark trading is said to have detrimental effects on both price accuracy and market liquidity. Economists have reached different conclusions on this issue. Empirical research suggests that dark trading, like transparent trading, has an optimum. This means that certain amounts of dark trading are beneficial for both price accuracy and market liquidity, but when an optimal amount of dark trading is surpassed, every additional amount of dark trading deteriorates market quality.

2. In some instances, HFTs are capable of gaining more information in a dark pool than the other traders in the pool. When HFTs exploit their informational advantage to the detriment of the other traders this undermines investor trust and ultimately the functioning of the market if traders exit the market.
3. Some dark pools under US law, may limit the access of certain traders (often HFTs). This discretionary access to large pools of liquidity raises the issue of market fragmentation and a two-tiered market which may harm investor trust and ultimately the functioning of the market if traders decide to leave the market.
4. In a market environment in which liquidity is dispersed among different marketplaces, transparency is key to consolidate the financial market as one. Dark pools undermine this consolidating force of transparency information because they do not provide any pre-trade transparency information, thus making it harder for traders to identify available trading opportunities.
5. Dark trading is free-riding the price formation process of lit trading venues. The chance to enjoy the benefits of price formation without providing for its production (quasi-common good) may lead to an underproduction of price relevant data which in turn harms the price formation process.
6. Dark pools are also accused of being more lightly regulated than exchanges although they perform similar trading functions in the market. This is primarily true for unregulated dark trading in the OTC-space. In those instances, dark trading is free-riding the regulatory efforts of self-regulating entities, like exchanges for example in some jurisdictions. Those self-regulatory entities may exercise their supervisory function less zealously if they anticipate that dark pools as their competitors for order flow benefit from their efforts but do not compensate them for it.
7. Dark trading also creates information asymmetry between the traders on a dark pool, who know nothing about the order flow, and the dark pool operator, who knows everything. If the dark pool operator is allowed to trade in the dark pool, too, it may raise principal-agent-conflicts because the operator may take advantage of the uninformed traders.

III. Where in the three jurisdictions can dark trading occur and does it serve a regulatory purpose? Or is it rather an exploitation of a loophole and regulatory gaps?

1. For the in-depth analysis of the three jurisdictions, see Part II above.
2. To see where dark trading occurs, unregulated dark trading in the OTC-space and regulated dark trading on trading systems must be distinguished. To evaluate the scope of regulated trading, the trading infrastructure regime has been examined. The US trading system regime is rather dated, narrow, and allows for unregulated dark trading especially through broker-dealer internalization. The trading system regime in the EU and Switzerland is nuanced and captures organized trading very well. Only the qualitative definition of bilateral CH-OTFs under Swiss law may allow for some unregulated dark trading in the OTC-space.
3. With regard to the transparency regime, all jurisdictions aim to ensure a certain amount of trade transparency and try to moderate dark trading.
4. While US law has a very nuanced transparency regime, its default rule is rather dark trading because under the ATS regime, traders can exploit the 5 %-threshold as a loophole in the transparency regime for unregulated dark trading.
5. The EU trade transparency regime, on the other hand, has trade transparency as the default rule for both equities and non-equities trading. It even captures IOIs which remain outside of the regulatory perimeter in the US. Dark trading under EU law requires the application of waivers which are regulated in detail and granted by the NCAs. The EU also has a limitation device for two waivers which originally was a double volume cap but becomes simplified to a single volume cap under the MiFIR-refit. This complex limitation device may however not be justified given that the risk for market failure is rather small.
6. Under Swiss law, pre-trade transparency is only the default rule for trading in shares, the remainder is left in the dark if the trading venue does not require pre-trade transparency in its trading rules. The waiver regime is similar to the one for equities in the EU but only contains the principles of the waivers' functioning while the trading venue needs to further define its scope in practice.
7. The access regime in all three jurisdictions grants fair access to trading venues and information. In the US, however, ATS are also exempt from granting fair access if they stay below the 5 %-threshold.

8. The US and the EU also implemented price protection rules to support the price discovery mechanism.
9. The supervisory structures in the jurisdictions differs from one another but do not support dark trading or an uneven playing field among the trading venues.

IV. Can an ideal regulatory framework for dark trading be identified among the examined jurisdictions? If not, are there common principles of regulation that may serve as a standard for proper regulation of dark trading?

1. Due to the different market characteristics, no jurisdiction can be identified as an ideal regulatory framework that can be used as a blueprint for others.
2. However, there are common principles that all jurisdictions can aim for to achieve proper regulation of dark trading.
3. Principle 1: Have a broad trading infrastructure regime.
4. Principle 2: Have a broad trade transparency regime.
5. Principle 3: Provide for clear-cut exceptions from trade transparency where beneficial for the trader and not harmful for the market.
6. Principle 4: Be cautious with limiting devices.
7. Principle 5: Ensure fair access to trading venues and information.
8. Principle 6: Consider price protection rules.
9. Principle 7: Ensure a sound supervisory regime.

Annex

ANNEX II CDR (EU) 2017/587: Orders large in scale compared with normal market size, standard market sizes and deferred publications and delays

Average daily turnover (ADT) in EUR	ADT < 50 000	50 000 ≤ ADT < 100 000	100 000 ≤ ADT < 500 000	500 000 ≤ ADT < 1 000 000	1 000 000 ≤ ADT < 5 000 000	5 000 000 ≤ ADT < 25 000 000	25 000 000 ≤ ADT < 50 000 000	50 000 000 ≤ ADT < 100 000 000	ADT ≥ 100 000 000
Minimum size of orders qualifying as large in scale compares with normal market size in EUR	15 000	30 000	60 000	100 000	200 000	300 000	400 000	500 000	650 000

Table 1: Orders large in scale compared with normal market size for shares and depositary receipts[2507]

Average daily turnover (ADT) in EUR	ADT < 50 000	ADT ≥ 50 000
Minimum size of orders qualifying as large in scale compared with normal market size in EUR	15 000	30 000

Table 2: Orders large in scale compared with normal market size certificates and other similar financial instruments[2508]

Average value of transaction (AVT) in EUR	AVT < 20 000	20 000 ≤ AVT < 40 000	40 000 ≤ AVT < 60 000	60 000 ≤ AVT < 80 000	80 000 ≤ AVT < 100 000	100 000 ≤ AVT < 120 000	120 000 ≤ AVT < 140 000	Etc.
Standard market size[3*]	10 000	30 000	50 000	70 000	90 000	110 000	130 000	Etc.

Table 3: Standard market sizes[2509]

2507 Table taken from Annex II of CDR (EU) 2017/587.
2508 Table taken from Annex II of CDR (EU) 2017/587.
2509 Table taken from Annex II of CDR (EU) 2017/587.

Average daily turnover (ADT) in EUR	Minimum qualifying size of transaction for permitted delay in EUR	Timing of publication after the transaction
> 100 m	10 000 000	60 minutes
	20 000 000	120 minutes
	35 000 000	End of the trading day
50 m – 100 m	7 000 000	60 minutes
	15 000 000	120 minutes
	25 000 000	End of the trading day
25 m – 50 m	5 000 000	60 minutes
	10 000 000	120 minutes
	12 000 000	End of the trading day
5 m – 25 m	2 500 000	60 minutes
	4 000 000	120 minutes
	5 000 000	End of the trading day
1 m – 5 m	450 000	60 minutes
	750 000	120 minutes
	1 000 000	End of the trading day
500 000 – 1 m	75 000	60 minutes
	150 000	120 minutes
	225 000	End of the trading day
100 000 – 500 000	30 000	60 minutes
	80 000	120 minutes
	120 000	End of the trading day
50 000 – 100 000	15 000	60 minutes
	30 000	120 minutes
	50 000	End of the trading day
< 50 000[5*]	7 500	60 minutes
	15 000	120 minutes
	25 000	End of the next trading day

Table 4: Deferred publication thresholds and delays for shares and depositary receipts[2510]

2510 Table taken from Annex II of CDR (EU) 2017/587.

Minimum qualifying size of transaction for permitted delay in EUR	Timing of publication after the transaction
15 000 000	60 minutes
50 000 000	End of the trading day

Table 5: Deferred publications thresholds and delays for ETFs[2511]

Average daily turnover (ADT) in EUR	Minimum qualifying size of transaction for permitted delay in EUR	Timing of publication after the transaction
ADT < 50 000	15 000	120 minutes
	30 000	End of the trading day
ADT ≥ 50 000[8*]	30 000	120 minutes
	60 000	End of the trading day

Table 6: Deferred publications thresholds and delays for certificates and other similar financial instruments[2512]

2511 Table taken from Annex II of CDR (EU) 2017/587.
2512 Table taken from Annex II of CDR (EU) 2017/587.

Bibliography

Abdel-Qader A, 'Dark Pool Operator Liquidnet Activates Dublin MTF Ahead of Brexit: Liquidnet began preparations to open an EEA-based presence as a post-Brexit base of operations in early 2017' (Finance Magnates 2 December 2020) <https://www.financemagnates.com/institutional-forex/execution/dark-pool-operator-liquidnet-activates-dublin-mtf-ahead-of-brexit/> accessed 4 July 2023.

Adrian J, 'Informational Inequality: How High Frequency Traders Use Premier Access to Information to Prey on Institutional Investors' (2016) 14 Duke Law & Technology Review 256.

Akerlof GA, 'The Market for "Lemons": Quality Uncertainty and the Market Mechanism' (1970) 84(3) The Quarterly Journal of Economics 488.

Aldridge I, *High-frequency trading: A practical guide to algorithmic strategies and trading systems, second edition* (2nd edn, Wiley 2013).

Alexander K, 'Market Structures, Technologie and European Regulation' in Brigitte Strebel-Aerni (ed), *Finanzmärkte im Banne von Big Data: Einfluss der modernen Informations- und Kommunikationstechnologie auf die Geschäftsmodelle der Finanzdienstleister und auf die Finanzmärkte, die Politik, Regulierungsbehörden und die Souveränität der Schweiz* (Schulthess 2012).

Alexander K, 'Market Structures and Market Abuse' in Gerard Caprio (ed), *Handbook of safeguarding global financial stability: Political, social, cultural, and economic theories and models* (1st edn, Elsevier 2013).

Allgemeinverfügung – Befreiung systematischer Internalisierer von den Pflichten nach Art. 18 Abs. 2 Satz 1 MiFIR in Bezug auf Kursofferten 2 January 2018, WA 21-FR 1900–2017/0002 (BaFin).

Allgemeinverfügung Nachhandelstransparenz Handelsplätze, die nicht durch eine Börse betrieben werden/Eigenkapitalinstrumente 20 June 2023, WA 21-FR 1900/00006#00001 (BaFin).

AMAFI, 'Impact of the MiFIR Volume Cap Mechanism on the Microstructure of European Equity Markets' (Paris, 28 October 2019) AMAFI/19–103 <http://82.223.27.163/download/pages/rb2LBc6XXLaKreHkwoyxTgk8S5aHldcs4WAWSJz2.pdf> accessed 31 May 2023.

Angel J, Harris L and Spatt CS, 'Equity Trading in the 21st Century' (Marshall Research Paper Series, Working Paper FBE 09–10, 18 May 2010) <https://www.sec.gov/spotlight/emsac/equity-trading-in-the-21st-century.pdf> accessed 1 May 2023.

Aquilina M and others, 'Asymmetries in Dark Pool Reference Prices' (FCA Occasional Paper No. 21, FCA, September 2016) <https://www.fca.org.uk/publication/op16-21.pdf> accessed 3 April 2022.

Aquilina M and others, 'Aggregate Market Quality Implications of Dark Trading' (FCA Occasional Paper No. 29, FCA, August 2017) <https://www.fca.org.uk/publications/occasional-papers/no-29-aggregate-market-quality-implications-dark-trading> accessed 3 April 2022.

Armour J and others, *Principles of Financial Regulation* (1st edn, Oxford University Press 2016).

Armour J, Bengtzen M and Enriques L, 'Globalization' in Merritt B Fox and others (eds), *Securities Market Issues for the 21st Century* (Columbia University 2018).

Arnuk S and Saluzzi J, *Broken Markets: How High Frequency Trading and Predatory Practices on Wall Street Are Destroying Investor Confidence and Your Portfolio* (2nd edn, Addison Wesley 2014).

Arquint N, 'Internationalisierung der Finanzmarktaufsicht' [2014] GesKR 131.

ASIC, 'Dark Liquidity and High-Frequency Trading' (Report 331, March 2013) <https://download.asic.gov.au/media/1344182/rep331-published-18-March-2013.pdf> accessed 9 March 2022.

—— 'Review of High-Frequency Trading and Dark Liquidity' (Report 452, October 2015) <https://download.asic.gov.au/media/3444836/rep452-published-26-october-2015.pdf> accessed 9 March 2022.

Assmann H-D in Heinz-Dieter Assmann, Uwe H Schneider and Peter O Mülbert (eds), *Wertpapierhandelsrecht: Kommentar* (7th edn, Otto Schmidt 2019).

Assmann H-D and Buck-Heeb P, 'Kapitalanlagerecht im Regelungsgefüge des Kapitalmarkt- und Finanzmarktrechts' in Heinz-Dieter Assmann, Rolf A Schütze and Petra Buck-Heeb (eds), *Handbuch des Kapitalanlagerechts* (5th edn, CH Beck 2020).

Ayres I and Braithwaite J, *Responsive Regulation: Transcending the Deregulation Debate* (Oxford University Press 1992).

Baberis N and Thaler RH, 'A Survey of Behavioral Finance' in Richard H Thaler (ed), *Advances in Behavioral Finance* (Princeton University Press 2005).

Bachmann G, *Private Ordnung: Grundlagen ziviler Regelsetzung* (Mohr Siebeck 2006).

BaFin, 'Merkblatt: Tatbestand des Betriebs eines multilateralen Handelssystems gemäß § 1 Abs. 1a Satz 2 Nr. 1b KWG' (7 December 2009, changed on 27 April 2023) <https://www.bafin.de/SharedDocs/Veroeffentlichungen/DE/Merkblatt/mb_091208_tatbestand_multilaterales_handelssystem.html> accessed 8 July 2023.

—— 'Hinweise zu den Tatbeständen des Eigenhandels und des Eigengeschäfts' (22 March 2011, changed on 15 May 2019) <https://www.bafin.de/SharedDocs/Veroeffentlichungen/DE/Merkblatt/mb_110322_eigenhandel_eigengeschaeft_neu.html> accessed 11 February 2022.

—— 'Hinweise zu Finanzinstrumenten nach § 1 Abs. 11 Sätze 1 bis 5 KWG (Aktien, Vermögensanlagen, Schuldtitel, sonstige Rechte, Anteile an Investmentvermögen, Geldmarktinstrumente, Devisen, Rechnungseinheiten, Emissionszertifikate, Kryptowerte und Schwarmfinanzierungsinstrumente)' (20 December 2011, changed on 1 December 2022) <https://www.bafin.de/SharedDocs/Veroeffentlichungen/DE/Merkblatt/mb_111220_finanzinstrumente.html> accessed 23 May 2023.

—— 'Studie zur Ausführung an ausgewählten deutschen Handelsplattformen: WA-Datenanalyseeinheit' (11 April 2022) <https://www.bafin.de/SharedDocs/Downloads/DE/dl_Studie_WA_Ausfuehrungsqualitaet_Handelsplattformen.html> accessed 23 May 2023.

Bahar R, 'Derivative Trading under the Federal Act on Financial Markets Infrastructure' [2015] GesKR 479.

—— in Rolf Watter and Rashid Bahar (eds), *Basler Kommentar Finanzmarktaufsichtsgesetz, Finanzmarktinfrastrukturgesetz* (3rd edn, Helbing & Lichtenhahn Verlag 2019).

—— and Nedwed B, 'Grenzüberschreitendes Angebot von Finanzdienstleistungen und -produkten: Die Eidgenossenschaft schlägt zurück' [2019] SZW 618.

Baisch R, Baumann S and Weber RH, '"Shades of grey" in Dark Pools' [2014] GesKR 183.

Bak J and Bigus J, 'Kapitalmarkteffizienz versus zwingender Anlegerschutz im Aktienrecht' (2006) 18(6) ZBB 430.

Baldwin R, Cave M and Lodge M, *Understanding Regulation: Theory, Strategy, and Practice* (2nd edn, Oxford University Press 2012).

Banks E, *Dark Pools: Off-Exchange Liquidity in an Era of High Frequency, Program, and Algorithmic Trading* (2nd edn, Palgrave Macmillan UK 2014).

Barr MS, Jackson HE and Tahyar ME, *Financial Regulation: Law and Policy* (University Casebook Series, Foundation Press 2018).

Baruch S, 'Who Benefits from an Open Limit-Order Book?' (2005) 78(4) The Journal of Business 1267.

Batista E, 'A Shot in the Dark: An Analysis of the SEC's Response to the Rise of Dark Pools' (2014) 14 Journal of High Technology Law 83.

Baxter BP, 'The Securities Black Market: Dark Pool Trading and the Need for a More Expansive Regulation ATS-N' (2017) 70 Vanderbilt Law Review 311.

Bayram M, *Manipulative Handelspraktiken gem. Art. 12 MAR* (Ph.D.-Thesis University of Erlangen-Nuremberg 2019, Duncker & Humblot 2020).

—— and Meier D, 'Pinging, Front Running und Quote Matching – Verbotene Handelspraktiken nach der Marktmissbrauchsverordnung?' [2018] WM 1295.

Beck H and Röh L in Eberhard Schwark and Daniel Zimmer (eds), *Kapitalmarktrechts-Kommentar* (4th edn, CH Beck 2010).

Becker B and others, 'Automated Securities Trading' (1992) 6(4) Journal of Financial Services Research 327.

Benston GJ, 'Required Disclosure and the Stock Market: An Evaluation of the Securities Exchange Act of 1934' (1973) 63(1) The American Economic Review 132.

Beny LN, 'U.S. Secondary Stock Markets: A Survey of Current Regulatory and Structural Issues and a Reform Proposal to Enhance Competition' (2002) 2002(2) Columbia Business Law Review 399.

Bernard C, 'MiFID II: The new market structure paradigm' (February 2014) <https://studylib.net/doc/8233557/mifid-ii--the-new-market-structure-paradigm> accessed 20 March 2022.

Bialluch SM, 'Systematische Internalisierung de lege lata' [2015] WM 2030.

Bienert H, *Der Marktprozeß an Aktienbörsen: Bewertungseffizienz und Umverteilung* (Gabler Verlag 1996).

Birdthistle W and Henderson MT, 'Becoming a Fifth Branch' (2013) 99 Cornell Law Review 1.

Black F, 'Noise' (1986) 41 The Journal of Finance 529.

Blanc RD, 'Intermarket Competition and Monopoly Power in the U.S. Stock Markets' (2007) 1(2) Brooklyn Journal of Corporate, Financial & Commercial Law 273.

Bloomfield R and O'Hara M, 'Market Transparency: Who Wins and Who Loses?' (1999) 12(1) Review of Financial Studies 5.

—— 'Can Transparent Markets Survive?' (2000) 55(3) Journal of Financial Economics 425.

Bloomfield R, O'Hara M and Saar G, 'Hidden Liquidity: Some New Light on Dark Trading' (2015) 70(5) The Journal of Finance 2227.

Boehmer E, Saar G and Yu L, 'Lifting the Veil: An Analysis of Pre-trade Transparency at the NYSE' (2005) 60(2) The Journal of Finance 783.

Bogard V, 'TABB Equity Digest: Q2–2016, TABB Group' (8 December 2016) <https://research.tabbgroup.com/report/v14-071-tabb-equity-digest-q2-2016> accessed 13 January 2022.

Boni LA, Brown DC and Leach JC, 'Dark Pool Exclusivity Matters' (19 December 2013) <https://dx.doi.org/10.2139/ssrn.2055808> accessed 27 February 2023.

Bonin A and Glos A, 'Die neuere Rechtsprechung der europäischen Gerichte im Bereich des Bank- und Kapitalmarktrechts' [2013] WM 1201.

Borens P and Baumann P in Rolf Sethe and others (eds), *Kommentar zum Finanzmarktinfrastrukturgesetz FinfraG* (SK FinfraG, 1st edn, Schulthess 2017).

Borrelli M, 'Market Making in the Electronic Age' (2001) 32(4) Loyola University Chicago Law Journal 815.

Bortenlänger C, *Börsenautomatisierung: Effizienzpotentiale und Durchsetzbarkeit* (Gabler Verlag, Deutscher Universitätsverlag 1996).

Bortoli L and others, 'Limit Order Book Transparency, Execution Risk, and Market Liquidity: Evidence from the Sydney Futures Exchange' (2006) 26(12) Journal of Future Markets 1147.

Bösch R and Kramer S, 'Schweizer Finanzmarktrecht im Umbruch: Das Finanzmarktinfrastrukturgesetz als eine der neuen Säulen' [2014] SJZ 249.

Boschan C, *Wertpapierhandelssysteme: Erscheinungsformen und Funktionsweisen, rechtliche Systematisierung und aufsichtsrechtliche Behandlung* (Ph.D.-Thesis TU Chemnitz 2007, Verlag Dr. Kovač 2007).

Bošković T, Cerruti C and Noël M, 'Comparing European and U.S. Securities Regulations: MiFID versus Corresponding U.S. Regulations' (World Bank Working Paper No. 184, The World Bank, Washington, D.C., 2009) <https://openknowledge.worldbank.org/bitstream/handle/10986/13528/52460.pdf?sequence=1&isAllowed=y> accessed 13 February 2022.

Boston Consulting Group, 'Securities and Exchange Commission: Organizational Study and Reform' (10 March 2011) <https://www.sec.gov/files/967study.pdf> accessed 10 March 2022.

Boulatov A and George TJ, 'Hidden and Displayed Liquidity in Securities Markets with Informed Liquidity Providers' (2013) 26(8) Review of Financial Studies 2095.

Bradford A, 'The Brussels Effect' (2012) 107(1) Northwestern University Law Review 1.

—— *The Brussels Effect: How the European Union rules the world* (Oxford University Press 2020).

Brandeis LD, *Other People's Money and How the Bankers Use It* (Stokes 1914).

Brannon VC, 'Statutory Interpretation: Theories, Tools, and Trends' (Congressional Research Service, 18 May 2022) <https://crsreports.congress.gov/product/pdf/R/R45153/4> accessed 20 February 2023.

Brealey R, Myers S and Allen F, *Principles of Corporate Finance* (12th edn, McGraw Hill Education 2016).

Bremer H, *Grundzüge des deutschen und ausländischen Börsenrechts* (Enzyklopädie der Rechts- und Staatswissenschaft, Springer 1969).

Brenncke M in Matthias Lehmann and Christoph Kumpan (eds), *European Financial Services Law: Article-by-Article Commentary* (1st edn, Nomos; CH Beck; Hart Publishing 2019).

Breyer SG, *Regulation and Its Reform* (Harvard University Press 1982).

Brinckmann H, '§ 16 Foundations' in Rüdiger Veil (ed), *European Capital Markets Law* (3rd edn, Hart Publishing 2022).

Brugler J, 'Into the Light: Dark Pool Trading and Intraday Market Quality on the Primary Exchange' (Staff Working Paper No. 545, Bank of England, September 2015) <https://www.bankofengland.co.uk/-/media/boe/files/working-paper/2015/into-the-light-dark-pool-trading-and-intraday-market-quality-on-the-primary-exchange.pdf?la=en&hash=16AA4DE665BEC69AA3FA712F28275F54EFFFB056> accessed 25 February 2023.

Brummer C, 'Disruptive Technology and Securities Regulation' (2015) 84 Fordham Law Review 977.

Brunetti A and others, 'Expertengruppe zur Weiterentwicklung der Finanzmarktstrategie: Schlussbericht' (1 December 2014) <https://www.admin.ch/gov/de/start/dokumentation/medienmitteilungen.msg-id-55545.html> accessed 21 March 2023.

Buck-Heeb P, *Kapitalmarktrecht* (12th edn, C.F. Müller Verlag 2022).

Buck-Heeb P and Dieckmann A, *Selbstregulierung im Privatrecht* (Mohr Siebeck 2010).

Bumke C, 'Regulierung am Beispiel der Kapitalmärkte' in Klaus J Hopt, Rüdiger Veil and Jörn A Kämmerer (eds), *Kapitalmarktgesetzgebung im europäischen Binnenmarkt* (Mohr Siebeck 2008).

Bundesrat, 'Bericht zur Finanzmarktpolitik des Bundes' (19 December 2012) <https://www.newsd.admin.ch/newsd/message/attachments/35762.pdf> accessed 27 March 2022.

—— 'Botschaft zum Finanzmarktinfrastrukturgesetz (FinfraG)' (3 September 2014) <https://www.fedlex.admin.ch/eli/fga/2014/1633/de> accessed 13 January 2022.

—— 'Finanzmarktpolitik für einen wettbewerbsfähigen Finanzplatz Schweiz: Bericht des Bundesrates' (Oktober 2016) <https://www.newsd.admin.ch/newsd/message/attachments/45749.pdf> accessed 21 March 2023.

Busch D, 'MiFID II and MiFIR: Stricter Rules for the EU Financial Markets' (2017) 11 Law and Financial Markets Review 126.

—— and Ferrarini G, 'Who is Afraid of MiFID II?' in Danny Busch and Guido Ferrarini (eds), *Regulation of the EU Financial Markets: MiFID II and MiFIR* (1st edn, Oxford University Press 2017).

Busche J in Franz J Säcker and others (eds), *Münchener Kommentar zum Bürgerlichen Gesetzbuch* (vol. 1, 9th edn, CH Beck 2021).

Buti S, Rindi B and Werner IM, 'Diving Into Dark Pools' (Fisher College of Business Working Paper Series, June 2010) <https://files.fisher.osu.edu/department-finance/public/2010-10.pdf> accessed 6 March 2022.

—— 'Dark Pool Trading Strategies, Market Quality and Welfare' (2017) 124(2) Journal of Financial Economics 244.

BX Swiss, 'Handelsreglement der BX Swiss AG' (4 May 2018) <https://www.bxswiss.com/downloads/regulatory-information/de/BX%20Handelsreglement_04.05.2018.pdf> accessed 3 April 2022.

—— 'Weisung zum Handel an der BX Swiss AG' (20 July 2018) <https://www.bxswiss.com/downloads/regulatory-information/de/BX%20Weisung%20zum%20Handel_20.07.2018.pdf> accessed 3 April 2022.

Calliess C, 'Finanzkrisen als Herausforderung der internationalen, europäischen und nationalen Rechtssetzung' in Christian Calliess, Georg Lienbacher and Bernd Grzeszick (eds), *Grundsatzfragen der Rechtsetzung und Rechtsfindung: Referate und Diskussionen auf der Tagung der Vereinigung der Deutschen Staatsrechtslehrer in Münster vom 5. bis 8. Oktober 2011* (Veröffentlichungen der Vereinigung der Deutschen Staatsrechtslehrer Band 71. De Gruyter 2012).

Cao C, Hansch O and Wang X, 'The Information Content of an Open Limit-Order Book' (2009) 29(1) Journal of Futures Markets 16.

Carney G, 'Comparative Approaches to Statutory Interpretation in Civil Law and Common Law Jurisdictions' (2015) 36(1) Statute Law Review 46.

Caspari K-B, 'Anlegerschutz in Deutschland im Lichte der Brüsseler Richtlinie' [2005] NZG 98.

Cave T, 'European Equities Liquidity Matrix January 2020' <https://research.tabbgroup.com/report/v17-400-european-equities-liquiditymatrix-january-2020> accessed 22 May 2023.

CESR, 'Proposed Standards for Alternative Trading Systems: Paper for final Consultation' (CESR/02–001, 14 January 2002) <http://www.cnmv.es/cnmvdia/decetes/02-001.pdf> accessed 22 May 2023.

—— 'CESR's Technical Advice on Possible Implementing Measures of the Directive 2004/39/EC on Markets in Financial Instruments' (CESR/05–290b, April 2005) <https://www.esma.europa.eu/sites/default/files/library/2015/11/05_290b.pdf> accessed 27 March 2022.

—— 'CESR's Response to the Commission on Non-Equities Transparency' (CESR/07-284b, July 2007) <https://www.esma.europa.eu/sites/default/files/library/2015/11/07_284b.pdf> accessed 26 March 2022.

—— 'Report: Impact of MiFID on equity secondary markets functioning' (CESR/09-355, 10 June 2009) <https://www.esma.europa.eu/sites/default/files/library/09_355_0.pdf> accessed 26 March 2022.

—— 'CESR Technical Advice to the European Commission in the Context of the MiFID Review – Equity Markets: Consultation Paper' (CESR/10-394, April 2010) <https://www.esma.europa.eu/sites/default/files/library/2015/11/10_394.pdf> accessed 22 May 2023.

—— 'CESR Technical Advice to the European Commission in the Context of the MiFID Review – Equity Markets' (CESR/10-802, 29 July 2010) <https://www.esma.europa.eu/sites/default/files/library/2015/11/10_802_technical_advice_mifid_review_equity_markets.pdf> accessed 9 March 2022.

—— 'CESR Technical Advice to the European Commission in the Context of the MiFID Review: Non-Equity Markets Transparency' (CESR/10-799, 29 July 2010) <https://www.esma.europa.eu/sites/default/files/library/2015/11/10_799_technical_advice_mifid_review_non_equity_markets_transparency_u_2_.pdf> accessed 20 March 2022.

—— 'CESR Response to Questions 1–14 and 19 of the European Commission Request for Additional Information in Relation to the Review of MiFID' (CESR/10-1254, October 2010) <https://www.esma.europa.eu/sites/default/files/library/2015/11/1-10_1254.pdf> accessed 20 March 2022.

CFA Institute, 'Trade-At Rules in Australia and Canada: A Mixed Bag for Investors' (November 2014) <https://www.cfainstitute.org/-/media/documents/issue-brief/policy-brief-trade-at-rules.ashx> accessed 11 March 2022.

Chaboud AP and others, 'Rise of the Machines: Algorithmic Trading in the Foreign Exchange Market' (2014) 69(5) The Journal of Finance 2045.

Choi SJ and Pritchard AC, *Securities Regulation* (5th edn, Foundation Press 2019).

Clausen NJ and Sørensen KE, 'Reforming the Regulation of Trading Venues in the EU under the Proposed MiFID II: Levelling the Playing Field and Overcoming Market Fragmentation?' (2012) 9(3) European Company and Financial Law Review 275.

Cliff D, Brown D and Treleaven P, 'Technology Trends in the Financial Markets: A 2020 Vision' (The Future of Computer Trading in Financial Markets Driver Review – DR 3, London, 2010) <https://assets.publishing.service.gov.uk/government/uploads/system/uploads/attachment_data/file/289029/11-1222-dr3-technology-trends-in-financial-markets.pdf> accessed 23 May 2023.

Coase RH, 'The Nature of the Firm' (1937) 4(16) Economica 386.

—— 'The Problem of Social Cost' (1960) 3(1) The Journal of Law & Economics 1.

—— 'The Nature of the Firm: Origin' (1988) 4(1) Journal of Law, Economics, and Organization 3.

Coffee JC, Sale HA and Henderson MT, *Securities Regulation: Cases and Materials* (13th edn, Foundation Press 2015).

Cohen PD, 'Securities Trading via the Internet' (1999) 4 Stanford Journal of Law, Business & Finance 1.

Cohn D, 'Alternative Handelssysteme: Ein Beitrag zur Neufassung der §§ 58 ff BörsG' [2002] ZBB 365.

Cohn-Heeren D, *Kapitalmarktrechtliche Regulierungskonzepte für Alternative Handelssysteme* (Ph.D.-Thesis University of Freiburg 2004, Duncker & Humblot 2006).

Colby RL and Sirri ER, 'Consolidation and Competition in the US Equity Markets' (2010) 5 Capital Markets Law Journal 169.

Collins AL, 'Regulation of Alternative Trading Systems: Evolving Regulatory Models and Prospects for Increased Regulatory Coordination and Convergence' (2002) 33 Law and Policy in International Business 481.

Comerton-Forde C, 'Current Issues in Market Design' in H. K Baker and Halil Kiymaz (eds), *Market Microstructure in Emerging and Developed Markets: Price Discovery, Information Flows, and Transaction Costs* (John Wiley & Sons, Inc 2013).

—— 'Shedding Light on Dark Trading in Europe' (August 2017) <https://drive.google.com/file/d/18P9KSp4c3hoLaB1JruvXq57YarXnAYVs/view> accessed 22 May 2023.

Comerton-Forde C, Frino A and Mollica V, 'The Impact of Limit Order Anonymity on Liquidity: Evidence from Paris, Tokyo and Korea' (2005) 57(6) Journal of Economics and Business 528.

Comerton-Forde C and Putniņš TJ, 'Dark Trading and Price Discovery' (2015) 118(1) Journal of Financial Economics 70.

Comerton-Forde C and Tang KM, 'Anonymity, Liquidity and Fragmentation' (2009) 12(3) Journal of Financial Markets 337.

Commission of the European Communities, 'Communication from the Commission on the precautionary principle' (COM(2000) 1 final, Brussels 2 February 2000) <https://eur-lex.europa.eu/LexUriServ/LexUriServ.do?uri=COM:2000:0001:FIN:EN:PDF> accessed 10 March 2022.

—— 'Proposal for a Directive of the European Parliament and of the Council on Investment Services and Regulated Markets, and amending Council Directives 85/611/EEC, Council Directives 93/6/EEC and European Parliament and Council Directive 2000/12/EC' (COM(2002) 625 final, 2002/0269 (COD), Brussels, 19 November 2002) <https://www.europarl.europa.eu/registre/docs_autres_institutions/commission_europeenne/com/2002/0625/COM_COM(2002)0625_EN.pdf> accessed 24 June 2023.

Committee on Capital Markets Regulation, 'The U.S. Equity Markets: A Plan for Regulatory Reform' (July 2016) <https://capmktsreg.org/committee-releases-u-s-equity-market-structure-report/> accessed 6 July 2023.

—— 'Enhancing U.S. Equity Market Structure for Retail Investors' (September 2021) <https://capmktsreg.org/committee-report-on-enhancing-u-s-equity-market-structure-for-retail-investors/> accessed 6 July 2023.

Committee on Economic and Monetary Affairs, 'Draft Report: on the proposal for a regulation of the European Parliament and of the Council amending Regulation (EU) No 600/2014 as regards enhancing market data transparency, removing obstacles to the emergence of a consolidated tape, optimising the trading obligations and prohibiting receiving payments for forwarding client orders (COM(2021)727 – C9–0440/2021 – 2021/0385(COD))' (2021/0385(COD), European Parliament, Rapporteur: Danuta Maria Hübner, 26 July 2022) <https://www.europarl.europa.eu/doceo/document/ECON-PR-731644_EN.pdf> accessed 24 June 2023.

—— 'Amendments 102 – 313: Amending Regulation (EU) No 600/2014 as regards enhancing market data transparency, removing obstacles to the emergence of a consolidated tape, optimising the trading obligations and prohibiting receiving payments for forwarding client orders Proposal for a regulation (COM(2021)727 – C9–0440/2021 – 2021/0385(COD))' (2021/0385(COD), European Parliament, 20 October 2022).

—— 'Report: on the proposal for a regulation of the European Parliament and of the Council amending Regulation (EU) No 600/2014 as regards enhancing market data transparency, removing obstacles to the emergence of a consolidated tape, optimising the trading obligations and prohibiting receiving payments for forwarding client orders (COM(2021)0727 – C9–0440/2021 – 2021/0385(COD))' (A9–0040/2023, European Parliament, Rapporteur: Danuta Maria Hübner, 2 March 2023).

Committee on Payment and Settlement Systems and Technical Committee of the International Organizations of Securities Commissions, 'Principles for Financial Market Infrastructures: Final Version' (BIS/IOSCO, April 2012) <https://www.bis.org/cpmi/publ/d101a.pdf> accessed 3 April 2022.

Contratto F, 'Hochfrequenzhandel und systemische Risiken: Risikovorsorge im Finanzmarktrecht gestützt auf das Vorsorgeprinzip' [2014] GesKR 143.

—— 'Sanktionen – Neue Gretchenfrage im Ringen um den Marktzugang in die EU' [2018] SZW 653.

Cooter R and Ulen TS, *Law and Economics* (6th edn, Addison-Wesley 2012).

Coridaß B and Dreyer D, 'Hochfrequenzhandel – was ist noch erlaubt?: Anforderungen und Gefahren des Hochfrequenzhandels' in Ralf Temporale (ed), *Europäische Finanzmarktregulierung: Handbuch zu EMIR, MiFID II/MiFIR, PRIIPs, MAD/MAR, OTC-Derivaten und Hochfrequenzhandel* (1st edn, Schäffer-Poeschel 2015).

Council of the European Union, 'Progress Report – Revised rules for markets in financial instruments a) Proposal for a Directive of the European Parliament and of the Council on markets in financial instruments repealing Directive 2004/39/EC of the European Parliament and of the Council (Recast) (MiFID) b) Proposal for a Regulation of the European Parliament and of the Council on markets in financial instruments and amending Regulation [EMIR] on OTC derivatives, central counterparties and trade repositories (MiFIR)' (2011/0296 (COD), 2011/0298 (COD), 16523/12, Brussels, 13 December 2012) <https://www.eumonitor.eu/9353000/1/j9vvik7m1c3gyxp/vj5i5cpxp6yt> accessed 1 May 2023.

Cox JD and others, *Securities Regulation: Cases and Materials* (8th edn, Wolters Kluwer 2017).

Cremer H-J, 'Regulierung und Freiheit' in Michael Fehling and Matthias Ruffert (eds), *Regulierungsrecht* (Mohr Siebeck 2010).

Crone HC von der, Maurer M and Hoffmann JH, 'Revision Börsendelikte und Marktmissbrauch: Der Entwurf zur Änderung des Börsengesetzes' [2011] SZW 533.

Crudele N, 'Dark Pool Regulation: Fostering Innovation and Competition while Protecting Investors' (2015) 9 Brooklyn Journal of Corporate, Financial & Commercial Law 569.

Czervionke E, 'Making Markets Work: The Critical Role of Market Infrastructure' in Gary Strumeyer and Sarah Swammy (eds), *The Capital Markets: Evolution of the Financial Ecosystem* (Wiley finance series. John Wiley & Sons 2017).

Daeniker D and Waller S in Rolf Watter and Rashid Bahar (eds), *Basler Kommentar Finanzmarktaufsichtsgesetz, Finanzmarktinfrastrukturgesetz* (3rd edn, Helbing & Lichtenhahn Verlag 2019).

Damrau J, *Selbstregulierung im Kapitalmarktrecht: Eine rechtsökonomische Analyse der Normsetzung der deutschen Börsen und ihrer Träger* (Ph.D.-Thesis University of Göttingen 2003, TENEA-Verlag 2003).

Daniëls TR, Dönges J and Heinemann F, 'Crossing Network versus Dealer Market: Unique Equilibrium in the Allocation of Order Flow' (2013) 62 European Economic Review 41.

Davies RJ and Sirri ER, 'The Economics and Regulation of Secondary Trading Markets' in Merritt B Fox and others (eds), *Securities Market Issues for the 21st Century* (Columbia University 2018).

De Long JB and others, 'Noise Trader Risk in Financial Markets' (1990) 98 Journal of Political Economy 703.

Dean JVC, 'Paradigm Shifts & Unintended Consequences: The Death of the Specialist, the Rise of High Frequency Trading & the Problem of Duty-Free Liquidity in Equity Markets' (2012) 8 Florida International University Law Review 217.

Degryse H and others, 'Dark Trading' in H. K Baker and Halil Kiymaz (eds), *Market Microstructure in Emerging and Developed Markets: Price Discovery, Information Flows, and Transaction Costs* (John Wiley & Sons, Inc 2013).

Degryse H and others, 'Two Shades of Opacity: Hidden Orders and Dark Trading' (June 2021) <https://papers.ssrn.com/sol3/papers.cfm?abstract_id=2669447> accessed 23 February 2023.

Degryse H, Achter M von and Wuyts G, 'Shedding Light on Dark Liquidity Pools' [2008] TILEC Discussion Paper <https://deliverypdf.ssrn.com/delivery.php?ID=128099110002125067005106000019122105016045018003062006097073073089097024011084021091009055049008126055027075101030064104111085010034047002017100029018086068116010010040087101093009094108089027095074112020080122079099092015113081107108101125070071009&EXT=pdf&INDEX=TRUE> accessed 14 February 2022.

Degryse H, Jong F de and van Kervel V, 'The Impact of Dark Trading and Visible Fragmentation on Market Quality' (2015) 19(4) Review of Finance 1587.

Deutsche Börse Group, 'Response to Public Consultation: on the Review of Markets in Financial Instruments Directive (MiFID)' (Frankfurt am Main, 2 February 2011) <https://www.deutsche-boerse.com/resource/blob/61186/f90716f5181223118250cd69ebe5421c/data/20110202_dbg-response-to-mifid-review-consultation_de.pdf> accessed 27 March 2022.

—— 'Review of the Markets in Financial Instruments Directive: Questionnaire on MiFID/MiFIR 2 by Markus Ferber MEP' (13 January 2012) <https://www.deutsche-boerse-cash-market.com/resource/blob/291954/b5a8124c2799283b4825c09d360b2ad0/data/Stellungnahme-der-Gruppe-Deutsche-B-rse-zum-Fragebogen-zur-berarbeitung-der-Richtlinie-ber-M-rkte-f-r-Finanzinstrumente-von-Markus-Ferber-Mitglied-des-Europ-ischen-Parlaments-Januar-2012-.pdf> accessed 3 April 2022.

Deutscher Bundestag – Wissenschaftliche Dienste, 'Das Federal Reserve System: Entstehungsgeschichte, Grundlagen, Aufbau' (2008) <https://www.bundestag.de/resource/blob/408364/1df598fe4b02f2c4eb15a8df3b303464/WD-4-037-08-pdf-data.pdf> accessed 11 March 2022.

Di Fabio U, 'Gefahr, Vorsorge, Risiko: Die Gefahrenabwehr unter dem Einfluß des Vorsorgeprinzips' [1996] Jura 566.

Döhmel D in Heinz-Dieter Assmann, Uwe H Schneider and Peter O Mülbert (eds), *Wertpapierhandelsrecht: Kommentar* (7th edn, Otto Schmidt 2019).

Dolgopolov S, 'Securities Fraud Embedded in the Market Structure Crisis: High-Frequency Traders as Primary Violators' (2018) 9(3) William & Mary Business Law Review 551.

Domowitz I and Lee R, 'On the Road to Reg ATS: A Critical History of the Regulation of Automated Trading Systems' (2001) 4(2) International Finance 279.

Duve C and Keller M, 'MiFID: Die neue Welt des Wertpapiergeschäfts' [2006] BB 2537.

Easthope D and Ray A, 'Dark Pools: In the Eye of the Storm' (April 2014) <https://tfetimes.com/wp-content/uploads/2014/04/Celent_darkpools_eyeofthestorm_2013-11-20.pdf> accessed 6 July 2023.

EFD, 'Erläuterungsbericht zur Verordnung über die Finanzmarktinfrastrukturen und das Marktverhalten im Effekten- und Derivatehandel: (Finanzmarktinfrastrukturverordnung, FinfraV)' (20 August 2015) <https://www.newsd.admin.ch/newsd/message/attachments/40659.pdf> accessed 3 April 2022.

—— 'Bericht des Eidgenössischen Finanzdepartements EFD über die Anhörung zur Finanzmarktinfrastrukturverordnung (FinfraV)' (25 November 2015) <https://fedlex.data.admin.ch/filestore/fedlex.data.admin.ch/eli/dl/proj/6015/70/cons_1/doc_5/de/pdf-a/fedlex-data-admin-ch-eli-dl-proj-6015-70-cons_1-doc_5-de-pdf-a.pdf> accessed 3 April 2022.

—— 'Erläuterungsbericht zur Verordnung über die Finanzmarktinfrastrukturen und das Marktverhalten im Effekten- und Derivatehandel: (Finanzmarktinfrastrukturverordnung, FinfraV)' (25 November 2015) <https://www.newsd.admin.ch/newsd/message/attachments/41938.pdf> accessed 3 April 2022.

EFD and SIF, 'Evaluation des Finanzmarktinfrastrukturgesetzes – FinfraG-Review: Bericht des EFD' (30 September 2022) <https://www.newsd.admin.ch/newsd/message/attachments/73356.pdf> accessed 6 July 2023.

Eggen M and Schaefer R, 'Regulierung grenzüberschreitender Tätigkeiten im Finanzmarktrecht' [2013] GesKR 368.

EG-Kommission, 'Vorschlag für neue Wertpapierdienstleistungsrichtlinie' [2002] ZBB 518.

Eifert M, 'Regulierungsstrategien' in Andreas Voßkuhle, Martin Eifert and Christoph Möllers (eds), *Grundlagen des Verwaltungsrechts Gesamtwerk: In 2 Bänden* (3rd edn, CH Beck 2022).

Ekkenga J, '§ 7. Wertpapierhandel' in Carsten P Claussen and Roland Erne (eds), *Bank- und Kapitalmarktrecht* (6th edn, CH Beck 2023).

Emmenegger S and Bigler A, 'Fortress Europe: Die Äquivalenzverfahren der EU im Bereich der Finanzdienstleistungen' [2019] SZW 155.

Entwurf eines Gesetzes zur Umsetzung der Richtlinie über Märkte für Finanzinstrumente und der Durchführungsrichtlinie der Kommission (Finanzmarkt-Richtlinie-Umsetzungsgesetz) 12 January 2007, BT-Drucks. 16/4028 (Deutscher Bundestag).

Eom KS, Ok J and Park J-H, 'Pre-Trade Transparency and Market Quality' (2007) 10(4) Journal of Financial Markets 319.

ESMA, 'Discussion Paper: MiFID II/MiFIR' (ESMA/2014/548, 22 May 2014) <https://www.esma.europa.eu/sites/default/files/library/2015/11/2014-548_discussion_paper_mifid-mifir.pdf> accessed 26 March 2022.

—— 'Consultation Paper: MiFID II/MiFIR' (ESMA/2014/1570, 19 December 2014) <https://www.esma.europa.eu/sites/default/files/library/2015/11/2014-1570_cp_mifid_ii.pdf> accessed 6 July 2023.

—— 'Final Report: ESMA's Technical Advice to the Commission on MiFID II and MiFIR' (ESMA/2014/1569, 19 December 2014) <https://www.esma.europa.eu/sites/default/files/library/2015/11/2014-1569_final_report_-_esmas_technical_advice_to_the_commission_on_mifid_ii_and_mifir.pdf> accessed 26 March 2022.

—— 'Final Report: Draft Regulatory and Implementing Technical Standards MiFID II/MiFIR' (ESMA/2015/1464, 28 September 2015) <https://www.esma.europa.eu/sites/default/files/library/2015/11/2015-esma-1464_-_final_report_-_draft_rts_and_its_on_mifid_ii_and_mifir.pdf> accessed 27 March 2022.

—— 'Waivers from Pre-trade Transparency: CESR Positions and ESMA Opinions' (ESMA/2011/241h, 20 June 2016) <https://www.esma.europa.eu/sites/default/files/library/2011-241h_esma_opinions_cesr_positions_on_pre-trade_waivers_0.pdf> accessed 20 March 2022.

—— 'Opinion: OTC Derivatives Traded on a Trading Venue' (ESMA70–156–117, 22 May 2017) <https://www.esma.europa.eu/sites/default/files/library/esma70-156-117_mifir_opinion_on_totv.pdf> accessed 27 March 2022.

—— 'Consultation Paper: Amendments to Commission Delegated Regulation (EU) 2017/587 (RTS 1)' (ESMA70–156–275, 9 November 2017) <https://www.esma.europa.eu/sites/default/files/library/esma70-156-275_cp_on_revised_rts_1.pdf> accessed 6 July 2023.

—— 'Final Report: Call for Evidence on Periodic Auctions' (ESMA70–156–1035, 11 June 2019) <https://www.esma.europa.eu/sites/default/files/library/esma70-156-1035_final_report_call_for_evidence_periodic_auctions.pdf> accessed 6 July 2023.

—— 'Opinion: On Frequent Batch Auctions (FBAs) and the Double Volume Cap Mechanism (DVCM)' (ESMA70–156–1355, 1 October 2019) <https://www.esma.europa.eu/sites/default/files/library/esma70-156-1355_opinion_frequent_batch_auctions.pdf> accessed 6 July 2023.

—— 'Consultation Paper: MiFIR Report on Systematic Internalisers in Non-Equity Instruments' (ESMA70–156–1757, 3 February 2020) <https://www.esma.europa.eu/sites/default/files/library/esma70-156-1757_consultation_paper_-_mifir_report_on_si.pdf> accessed 6 July 2023.

—— 'Consultation Paper: MiFID II/MiFIR Review Report on the Transparency Regime for Equity and Equity-Like Instruments, the Double Volume Cap Mechanism and the Trading Obligations for Shares' (ESMA70–156–2188, 4 February 2020) <https://www.esma.europa.eu/sites/default/files/library/cp_review_report_transparency_equity_dvc_tos.pdf> accessed 8 June 2023.

—— 'MiFID II/MiFIR Review Report: On the Transparency for Equity and Equity-Like Instruments, the Double Volume Cap Mechanism and the Trading Obligations for Shares' (ESMA70–156–2682, 16 July 2020) <https://www.esma.europa.eu/sites/default/files/library/esma70-156-2682_mifidii_mifir_report_on_transparency_equity_dvc_tos.pdf> accessed 6 July 2023.

—— 'MiFIR report on Systematic Internalisers in Non-Equity Instruments' (ESMA70–156–2756, 16 July 2020) <https://www.esma.europa.eu/sites/default/files/library/esma70-156-2756_mifidii_mifir_report_on_systematic_internalisers.pdf> accessed 26 March 2022.

—— 'MiFID II/MiFIR Review Report: MiFID II/MiFIR Review Report on the Transparency Regime for Non-Equity Instruments and the Trading Obligation for Derivatives' (ESMA70–156–3329, 25 September 2020) <https://www.esma.europa.eu/sites/default/files/library/esma70-156-3329_mifid_ii_mifir_review_report_on_the_transparency_regime_for_non-equity_instruments.pdf> accessed 6 July 2023.

—— 'MiFID II Review Report: MiFID II Review Report on the Functioning of Organised Trading Facilities (OTF)' (ESMA70–156–4225, 23 March 2021) <https://www.esma.europa.eu/sites/default/files/esma70-156-4225_mifid_ii_final_report_on_functioning_of_otf.pdf> accessed 26 March 2022.

—— 'Questions and Answers: On MiFID II and MiFIR Market Structures Topics' (ESMA70–872942901–38, 6 April 2021) <https://www.esma.europa.eu/sites/default/files/library/esma70-872942901-38_qas_markets_structures_issues.pdf> accessed 26 March 2022.

—— 'Opinion on the Assessment of Pre-Trade Transparency Waivers for Equity and Non-Equity Instruments' (ESMA70–155–6641, 23 March 2022) <https://www.esma.europa.eu/sites/default/files/library/esma70-155-6641_opinion_on_the_assessment_of_pre-trade_transparency_waivers.pdf> accessed 6 July 2023.

—— 'Questions and Answers: On MiFID II and MiFIR Transparency Topics' (ESMA70–872942901–35, 5 September 2022) <https://www.esma.europa.eu/sites/default/files/library/esma70-872942901-35_qas_transparency_issues.pdf> accessed 30 March 2023.

—— 'ESMA TRV Risk Analysis: Artificial Intelligence in EU Securities Markets' (ESMA50-164-6247, 1 February 2023) <https://www.esma.europa.eu/sites/default/files/library/ESMA50-164-6247-AI_in_securities_markets.pdf> accessed 22 May 2023.

—— 'Final Report: On ESMA's Opinion on the Trading Venue Perimeter' (ESMA70-156-6360, 2 February 2023) <https://www.esma.europa.eu/sites/default/files/library/ESMA70-156-6383%20Final%20Report%20on%20ESMA%27s%20Opinion%20on%20the%20trading%20venue%20perimeter.pdf> accessed 6 July 2023.

ESMA Database on MiFID Infrastructures <https://registers.esma.europa.eu/publication/searchRegister?core=esma_registers_upreg> accessed 8 July 2023.

European Commission, 'Commission Staff Working Paper Impact Assessment EU Commission, Impact Assessment: Accompanying the document Proposal for a Directive of the European Parliament and of the Council on Markets in financial instruments [Recast] and the Proposal for a Regulation of the European Parliament and of the Council on Markets in financial instruments' (SEC(2011) 1226 final, Brussels, 20 October 2011) <https://ec.europa.eu/smart-regulation/impact/ia_carried_out/docs/ia_2011/sec_2011_1226_en.pdf> accessed 9 March 2022.

—— 'Proposal for a Directive of the European Parliament and of the Council Parliament and of the Council on markets in financial instruments repealing Directive 2004/39/EC of the European Parliament and of the Council (Recast)' (COM(2011) 656 final, 2011/0298 (COD), Brussels, 20 October 2011) <https://eur-lex.europa.eu/LexUriServ/LexUriServ.do?uri=COM:2011:0656:FIN:en:PDF> accessed 20 March 2022.

—— 'Proposal for a Regulation of the European Parliament and of the Council on markets in financial instruments and amending Regulation [EMIR] on OTC derivates, central counterparties and trade repositories' (COM(2011) 652 final, 2011/0296 (COD), Brussels, 20 October 2011) <https://eur-lex.europa.eu/LexUriServ/LexUriServ.do?uri=COM:2011:0652:FIN:EN:PDF> accessed 20 March 2022.

—— 'Press Release: Commission Statement on the decision by the Swiss Federal Council to terminate the negotiations of the EU-Swiss Institutional Framework Agreement' (Brussels, 26 May 2021) <https://ec.europa.eu/commission/presscorner/detail/en/statement_21_2683> accessed 27 March 2022.

—— 'Press Release: Capital Markets Union: Commission proposes new measures to boost Europe's capital markets' (Brussels, 25 November 2021) <https://ec.europa.eu/commission/presscorner/detail/en/ip_21_6251> accessed 24 June 2023.

—— 'Proposal for a Regulation of the European Parliament and of the Council amending Regulation (EU) No 600/2014 as regards enhancing market data transparency, removing obstacles to the emergence of a consolidated tape, optimising the trading obligations and prohibiting receiving payments for forwarding client orders' (COM(2021) 727 final, 2021/0385 (COD), Brussels, 25 November 2021) <https://eur-lex.europa.eu/legal-content/EN/TXT/?uri=CELEX:52021PC0727> accessed 24 June 2023.

European Parliament, 'Report on Regulation of Trading in Financial Instruments – 'Dark Pools' etc. (2010/2075(INI))' (A7–0326/2010, Committee on Economic and Monetary Affairs, Rapporteur: Kay Swinburne, 16 November 2010) <https://www.europarl.europa.eu/meps/en/96920/KAY_SWINBURNE/all-activities/reports/7> accessed 1 May 2023.

European Union Committee, *MiFID II: Getting it Right for the City and EU Financial Services Industry* (HL 2012–13, HL Paper 28).

Exchange Rules for the Frankfurter Wertpapierbörse (FWB) 1 July 2019 (Frankfurter Wertpapierbörse).

Fahrländer L, 'Das Schweizer Börsenrecht' in Christian Bovet (ed), *Finanzmarktaufsicht/ Surveillance des marchés financiers* (Schweizerisches Bundesverwaltungsrecht Band XV, 1st edn, Helbing Lichtenhahn Verlag 2016).

Fama EF, 'The Behavior of Stock-Market Prices' (1965) 38(1) The Journal of Business 34.

Fama EF and others, 'The Adjustment of Stock Prices to New Information' (1969) 10(1) International Economic Review 1.

Fama EF, 'Efficient Capital Markets: A Review of Theory and Empirical Work' (1970) 25(2) The Journal of Finance 383.

—— 'Efficient Capital Markets: Reply' (1976) 31(1) The Journal of Finance 143.

—— 'Efficient Capital Markets: II' (1991) 46(5) The Journal of Finance 1575.

Fama EF and Laffer AB, 'Information and Capital Markets' (1971) 44(3) The Journal of Business 289.

Favre O and Kramer S in Rolf Sethe and others (eds), *Kommentar zum Finanzmarktinfrastrukturgesetz FinfraG* (1st edn, Schulthess 2017).

FCA, 'UK Equity Market Dark Pools: Role, Promotion and Oversight in Wholesale Markets' (Thematic Review TR 16/5, July 2016) <https://www.fca.org.uk/publication/thematic-reviews/tr16-05.pdf> accessed 22 May 2023.

—— 'Periodic Auctions: With MiFID II Altering the Landscape of Equity Markets, We Take a Look at this Emerging Trading Format – With the Help of Data' (25 June 2018) <https://www.fca.org.uk/publications/research/periodic-auctions> accessed 22 January 2022.

FCA Handbook (FCA) <https://www.handbook.fca.org.uk/> accessed 11 March 2022.

Federal Reserve Bank of New York, 'Foreign Exchange Operations' <https://www.newyorkfed.org/markets/international-market-operations/foreign-exchange-operations> accessed 11 March 2022.

—— 'FAQs Treasury Purchases' (11 February 2022) <https://www.newyorkfed.org/markets/treasury-reinvestments-purchases-faq> accessed 11 March 2022.

Ferber M, 'Sechs Wochen nach dem Auslaufen der Börsenäquivalenz zeigt sich: Der grosse Knall ist ausgeblieben' *Neue Zürcher Zeitung* (9 August 2019) <https://www.nzz.ch/finanzen/aufhebung-boersenaequivalenz-der-grosse-knall-ist-ausgeblieben-ld.1500834?reduced=true> accessed 27 March 2022.

Fernholz F, *Börse und ihre Alternativen: Eine Transaktionskostensicht* (Josef Eul Verlag 2005).

Ferran E, 'Institutional Design: The Choices for National Systems' in Niamh Moloney, Eilís Ferran and Jennifer Payne (eds), *The Oxford Handbook of Financial Regulation* (Oxford University Press 2015).

Ferrarini G, 'Exchange Governance and Regulation: An Overview' in Guido Ferrarini (ed), *European Securities Markets: The Investment Services Directive and Beyond* (Kluwer Law International 1998).

Ferrarini G and Moloney N, 'Reshaping Order Execution in the EU and the Role of Interest Groups: From MiFID I to MiFID II' (2012) 13(4) European Business Organization Law Review 557.

Ferrarini G and Saguato P, 'Reforming Securities and Derivatives Trading in the EU: from EMIR to MiFIR' (2013) 13(2) Journal of Corporate Law Studies 319.

—— 'Regulating Financial Market Infrastructures' in Niamh Moloney, Eilís Ferran and Jennifer Payne (eds), *The Oxford Handbook of Financial Regulation* (Oxford University Press 2015).

Ferrell A, 'A Proposal for Solving the "Payment for Order Flow" Problem' (2001) 74 Southern California Law Review 1027.

FINMA, 'Rundschreiben 2013/8 Marktverhaltensregeln: Aufsichtsregeln zum Marktverhalten im Effektenhandel' (Bern, 1 October 2013) <https://www.finma.ch/de/~/media/finma/dokumente/rundschreiben-archiv/2013/rs-13-08/rs-13-08-letzte-aenderung-20160812.pdf?sc_lang=de&hash=FDF566CEA72AA1148E44959899D08354> accessed 6 July 2023.

—— 'Rundschreiben 2018/xx „Organisierte Handelssysteme": Erläuterungsbericht' (Bern, 28 September 2016) <https://www.finma.ch/de/~/media/finma/dokumente/dokumentencenter/anhoerungen/laufende-anhoerungen/rs-effektenhandel/20160928-eb-rs-ohs.pdf?la=de> accessed 6 July 2023.

—— 'Circular 2018/1 Organised trading facilities: Duties of operators of organised trading facilities (OTF)' (Bern, 1 January 2018) <https://www.finma.ch/en/~/media/finma/dokumente/dokumentencenter/myfinma/rundschreiben/finma-rs-2018-01.pdf?sc_lang=en&hash=48D9F7DA704A734128371018D9818767> accessed 6 July 2023.

—— 'FINMA-Aufsichtsmitteilung 01/2020: Finanzmarktinfrastrukturgesetz und -verordnung: Derivatehandel' (Bern, 20 March 2020) <https://www.finma.ch/~/media/finma/dokumente/dokumentencenter/myfinma/4dokumentation/finma-aufsichtsmitteilungen/20200320-finma-aufsichtsmitteilung-01-2020.pdf?sc_lang=de> accessed 6 July 2023.

Fioravanti SF and Gentile M, 'The Impact of Market Fragmentation on European Stock Exchanges' (Working Paper No 69, Commissione Nazionale per le Società e la Borsa (CONSOB), Rome, July 2011) <https://papers.ssrn.com/sol3/papers.cfm?abstract_id=1997419> accessed 22 May 2023.

Fleckner AM and Hopt KJ, 'Stock Exchange Law: Concept, History, Challenges' (2013) 7(3) Virginia Law & Business Review 513.

Fleischer H, *Informationsasymmetrie im Vertragsrecht: Eine rechtsvergleichende und interdisziplinäre Abhandlung zu Reichweite und Grenzen vertragsschlussbezogener Aufklärungspflichten* (Habilitation-Thesis University of Cologne 1999, CH Beck 2001).

Fleischer H and Merkt H, 'Empfiehlt es sich, im Interesse des Anlegerschutzes und zur Förderung des Finanzplatzes Deutschland das Kapitalmarkt- und Börsenrecht neu zu regeln?: Gutachten F/G für den 64. Deutschen Juristentag' in Hrsg. von der Ständigen Deputation des Deutschen Juristentages (ed), *Verhandlungen des vierundsechzigsten Deutschen Juristentages* (CH Beck 2002).

Flood MD and others, 'Quote Disclosure and Price Discovery in Multiple-Dealer Financial Markets' (1999) 12(1) Review of Financial Studies 37.

Foley S and Putniņš TJ, 'Should We Be Afraid of the Dark?: Dark Trading and Market Quality' (2016) 122(3) Journal of Financial Economics 456.

Foresight, 'The Future of Computer Trading in Financial Markets: An International Perspective' (Final Project Report, The Government Office for Science, London, 2012) <https://www.gov.uk/government/publications/future-of-computer-trading-in-financial-markets-an-international-perspective> accessed 22 May 2023.

Foucault T, Moinas S and Theissen E, 'Does Anonymity Matter in Electronic Limit Order Markets?' (2007) 20(5) The Review of Financial Studies 1707.

Foucault T, Pagano M and Röell A, *Market Liquidity: Theory, Evidence, and Policy* (Oxford University Press 2013).

Fox MB, 'Measuring Share Price Accuracy' (2004) 1 Berkeley Business Law Journal 113.

—— 'MiFID II and Equity Trading: A US View' in Danny Busch and Guido Ferrarini (eds), *Regulation of the EU Financial Markets: MiFID II and MiFIR* (1st edn, Oxford University Press 2017).

Fox MB, Glosten LR and Rauterberg GV, 'The New Stock Market: Sense and Nonsense' (2015) 65(2) Duke Law Journal 191.

—— 'High-Frequency Trading and the New Stock Market: Sense And Nonsense' (2017) 29(4) Journal of Applied Corporate Finance 30.

—— 'Informed Trading and Its Regulation' (2018) 43(4) The Journal of Corporation Law 817.

—— 'Stock Market Manipulation and Its Regulation' (2018) 35 Yale Journal on Regulation 67.

—— *The New Stock Market: Law, Economics, and Policy* (Columbia University Press 2019).

Fox MB and Haeberle KS, 'Evaluating Stock-Trading Practices and Their Regulation' (2017) 42 The Journal of Corporation Law 887.

Francotte P, Valiante D and Lannoo K, *MiFID 2.0 – Casting New Light on Europe's Capital Markets: Report of the ECMI-CEPS Task Force on the MiFID Review* (Centre for European Policy Studies (CEPS) 2011).

Frey S and Sandås P, 'The Impact of Iceberg Orders in Limit Order Books' (CFR-Working Paper No. 09–06, 17 May 2009) <https://www.econstor.eu/bitstream/10419/41392/1/605038759.pdf> accessed 13 February 2022.

Fritsch M, *Marktversagen und Wirtschaftspolitik: Mikroökonomische Grundlagen staatlichen Handelns* (10th edn, Vahlen 2018).

Frutos MÁ de and Manzano C, 'Market transparency, market quality, and sunshine trading' (2014) 17 Journal of Financial Markets 174.

FSB, 'Implementing OTC Derivatives Market Reforms' (25 October 2010) <https://www.fsb.org/wp-content/uploads/r_101025.pdf> accessed 27 March 2022.

Fuchs A in Andreas Fuchs (ed), *Wertpapierhandelsgesetz (WpHG): Kommentar* (2nd edn, CH Beck 2016).

Funke S, 'Reaktion auf die Finanzmarktkrise: Teil 2: MiFID und MiFIR machen das Frühwarnsystem perfekt!' [2012] CCZ 54.

Gannon J, 'Developments in Banking and Financial Law 2009–2010: The Shadow Financial System' (2009) 29 Review of Banking & Financial Law 1 ff.

Gebauer M in Heinz-Dieter Assmann, Uwe H Schneider and Peter O Mülbert (eds), *Wertpapierhandelsrecht: Kommentar* (7th edn, Otto Schmidt 2019).

General Regulation of the AMF (AMF) <https://www.amf-france.org/en/regulation/general-regulation/general-regulation-user-guide> accessed 11 March 2022.

Gilson RJ and Kraakman RH, 'The Mechanisms of Market Efficiency' (1984) 70 Virginia Law Review 549.

Gomber P, *Elektronische Handelssysteme: Innovative Konzepte und Technologien im Wertpapierhandel* (Ph.D.-Thesis Justus-Liebig-University Gießen 2000, Physica-Verlag 2000).

Gomber P and others, 'High-Frequency Trading' (April 2011) Policy Platform White Paper <https://safe-frankfurt.de/fileadmin/user_upload/editor_common/Policy_Center/Gomber_et_al_High_Frequency_Trading.pdf> accessed 6 March 2022.

Gomber P and others, 'Competition Between Equity Markets: A Review of the Consolidation Versus Fragmentation Debate' (2017) 31 Journal of Economic Surveys 792.

Gomber P and others, 'The MiFIR Trading Obligation: Impact on Trading Volume and Liquidity in Electronic Trading' (February 2018) <https://papers.ssrn.com/sol3/papers.cfm?abstract_id=3133161> accessed 6 July 2023.

Gomber P and Gvozdevskiy I, 'Dark Trading under MiFID II' in Danny Busch and Guido Ferrarini (eds), *Regulation of the EU Financial Markets: MiFID II and MiFIR* (1st edn. Oxford University Press 2017).

Gomber P and Jäger B, 'MiFID: Eine systematische Analyse der Zielerreichung' (2014) 26 ZBB 40.

Gomber P and Nassauer F, 'Neuordnung der Finanzmärkte in Europa durch MiFID II/MiFIR' (2014) 26 ZBB 250.

Gomber P and Pierron A, 'MiFID: Spirit and Reality of a European Financial Markets Directive' (September 2010) <https://safe-frankfurt.de/fileadmin/user_upload/editor_common/Policy_Center/Gomber_Pierron_MiFID_report.pdf> accessed 22 May 2023.

Gomber P and Schweickert U, 'Der Market Impact: Liquiditätsmaß im elektronischen Wertpapierhandel' [2002] Die Bank 485.

Gresse C, 'Market Fragmentation in Europe: Assessment and Prospects for Market Quality' (UK Government's Foresight Project, Government Office for Science, Driver Report DR 19, London, 30 March 2012) <https://assets.publishing.service.gov.uk/government/uploads/system/uploads/attachment_data/file/289026/12-1052-dr19-market-fragmentation-in-europe-assessment-for-quality.pdf> accessed 22 May 2023.

Groß W, *Kapitalmarktrecht: Kommentar zum Börsengesetz, zur Börsenzulassungs-Verordnung, zum Wertpapierprospektgesetz und zur Prospektverordnung* (8th edn, CH Beck 2022).

Grossmann SJ, 'On the Efficiency of Competitive Stock Markets: Where Traders Have Diverse Information' (1976) 31(2) The Journal of Finance 573.

Grossmann SJ and Stiglitz JE, 'Information and Competitive Price Systems' (1976) 66(2) The American Economic Review 246.

—— 'On the Impossibility of Informationally Efficient Markets' (1980) 70(3) The American Economic Review 393.

Grzeszick B in Günter Dürig, Roman Herzog and Rupert Scholz (eds), *Grundgesetz: Kommentar* (99th edn, CH Beck 2022).

Guagliano C and others, 'DVC Mechanism: The Impact on EU Equity Markets' (ESMA Working Paper No. 3, 2020, ESMA/2020/ WP-2020–3, Paris, September 2020) <Guagliano, Guillaumie, Reiche, Spolaore, Zanon, DVC mechanism - The impact on EU equity markets, ESMA Working Paper No. 3, 2020.pdf> accessed 6 July 2023.

Güllner M, 'MiFID II: Die neue Handelsplatzarchitektur in der EU' [2017] WM 938.

Haeberle K, 'Stock Market Law and the Accuracy of Public Companies' Stock Prices' (2015) 2015(1) Columbia Business Law Review 121.

Haeberle KS, 'Discrimination Platforms' (2017) 42(4) The Journal of Corporation Law 809.

Häfelin U, Müller G and Uhlmann F, *Allgemeines Verwaltungsrecht* (8th edn, Dike 2020).

Hall P von, 'Vorhandelstransparenzpflichten für Systematische Internalisierer' [2015] GesKR 497.

Hallak I, 'Amendments to MiFID II and MiFIR: The EU's Markets in Financial Instruments' (Briefing - EU Legislation in Progress, European Parliamentary Research Service, April 2023) <https://www.europarl.europa.eu/thinktank/en/document/EPRS_BRI(2022)733546> accessed 24 June 2023.

Harris L, *Trading and exchanges: Market microstructure for practitioners* (Oxford University Press 2003).

Hasbrouck J and Saar G, 'Low-Latency Trading' (2013) 16(4) Journal of Financial Markets 646.

Hatch R, 'Reforming the Murky Depths of Wall Street: Putting the Spotlight on the Securities and Exchange Commission's Regulatory Proposal Concerning Dark Pools of Liquidity' (2010) 78 The George Washington Law Review 1032.

Häusermann M and Schott BG in Rolf Sethe and others (eds), *Kommentar zum Finanzmarktinfrastrukturgesetz FinfraG* (1st edn, Schulthess 2017).

Hayek FA, 'The Use of Knowledge in Society' (1945) 35 The American Economic Review 519.

Heidelbach A in Eberhard Schwark and Daniel Zimmer (eds), *Kapitalmarktrechts-Kommentar: Börsengesetz mit Börsenzulassungsverordnung, Wertpapierprospektgesetz, Wertpapierhandelsgesetz, Wertpapiererwerbs- und Übernahmegesetz, Europäische Marktmissbrauchsverordnung* (5th edn, CH Beck 2020).

Hellgardt A, 'Europäisches Kapitalmarktrecht und Corporate Governance' in Harald Baum and others (eds), *Perspektiven des Wirtschaftsrechts: Deutsches, europäisches und internationales Handels-, Gesellschafts- und Kapitalmarktrecht. Beiträge für Klaus J. Hopt aus Anlass seiner Emeritierung* (De Gruyter 2008).

Hendershott T and Jones CM, 'Island Goes Dark: Transparency, Fragmentation, and Regulation' (2005) 18(3) The Review of Financial Studies 743.

Hendershott T, Jones CM and Menkveld AJ, 'Does Algorithmic Trading Improve Liquidity?' (2011) 66(1) The Journal of Finance 1.

Hendershott T and Mendelson H, 'Crossing Networks and Dealer Markets: Competition and Performance' (2000) 55(5) The Journal of Finance 2071.

Hinterleitner G and Hornung P, *Marktqualität und Insiderhandel auf Kapitalmärkten: Eine experimentelle Untersuchung unterschiedlicher Handelsformen* (Springer Gabler 2016).

Hintz A, 'Lost in the Dark: An Analysis of the SEC's Regulatory Response to Dark Pools' (2015) 13(2) DePaul Business & Commercial Law Journal 329.

HM Treasury, 'Wholesale Markets Review: Consultation' (London, July 2021) <https://assets.publishing.service.gov.uk/government/uploads/system/uploads/attachment_data/file/998165/WMR_condoc_FINAL_OFFICIAL_SENSITIVE_.pdf> accessed 6 July 2023.

—— 'Wholesale Markets Review: Consultation Response' (London, 1 March 2022) <HM Treasury, Wholesale Markets Review - Consulation Response, 1 March 2022.pdf> accessed 6 July 2023.

Ho TSY and Michaely R, 'Information Quality and Market Efficiency' (1988) 23(1) Journal of Financial and Quantitative Analysis 53.

Hochstrasser T, 'Dark Pools im Spannungsfeld zwischen Transparenz und Anonymität' [2016] AJP 305.

Hoffmann J, 'Elektronische Handelssysteme nach dem 4. Finanzmarktförderungsgesetz' [2003] WM 2025.

Holzborn T and Israel A, 'Die Neustrukturierung des Finanzmarktrechts durch das Finanzmarktrichtlinienumsetzungsgesetz (FRUG)' [2008] NJW 791.

Hoops C, 'Bedeutung des organisierten Handelssystems in der gegenwärtigen Marktinfrastruktur' [2017] RdF 14.

—— 'Das neue Regime für die systematische Internalisierung nach MiFID II: Auswirkungen auf den deutschen Zertifikatehandel' [2017] WM 319.

—— 'Das ToTV-Kriterium der MiFID II in der Rechtspraxis' [2018] ZBB 410.

—— 'Die Regulierung von Marktdaten nach der MiFID II' [2018] WM 205.

—— *Verborgene Liquidität im Marktordnungsrecht der MiFID* (Ph.D.-Thesis Johann Wolfgang Goethe-University Frankfurt 2018, Peter Lang 2018).

Hope B, 'NYSE, Nasdaq Join to Push for Trading Rule' *The Wall Street Journal* (10 March 2014) <https://www.wsj.com/articles/SB10001424052702304020104579431300583920332> accessed 11 March 2022.

Hopt KJ, *Der Kapitalanlegerschutz im Recht der Banken: Gesellschafts-, bank- und börsenrechtliche Anforderungen an das Beratungs- und Verwaltungsverhalten der Kreditinstitute* (Habilitation-Thesis University of Munich 1973, CH Beck 1975).

—— 'Grundsatz- und Praxisprobleme nach dem Wertpapierhandelsgesetz – insbesondere Insidergeschäfte und Ad-hoc-Publizität' (1995) 159 ZHR 135.

Humbel C, 'Beyond human response time – Prävention und Freiheitlichkeit im Hochfrequenzhandel' in Anna Coninx, Ege Gian and Julian Mausbach (eds), *Prävention und freiheitliche Rechtsordnung* (Dike 2017).

—— *Die Regelung der Vor- und Nachhandelstransparenz in der Europäischen Union und der Schweiz* (Ph.D.-Thesis University of Zurich 2019, Schulthess 2019).

—— 'Organisierte Handelssysteme in der Schweiz – Quo vadis?: Handlungsspielräume de lege lata und Gestaltungsoptionen de lege ferenda im Lichte aktueller Entwicklungen' [2021] GesKR 25.

Iffland J and Ben Hattar A, 'Les systèmes organisés de négociation' [2016] GesKR 458.

IOSCO, *Transparency on Secondary Markets: A Synthesis of the IOSCO Debate* (Il Sole 24 Ore Libri 1993).

—— 'Transparency and Market Fragmentation: Report from the Technical Committee of the International Organization of Securities Commissions' (November 2001) <https://www.iosco.org/library/pubdocs/pdf/IOSCOPD124.pdf> accessed 22 May 2023.

—— 'Issues Raised by Dark Liquidity: Consultation Report' (CR05/10, October 2010) <https://www.iosco.org/library/pubdocs/pdf/IOSCOPD336.pdf> accessed 22 May 2023.

—— 'Principles for Dark Liquidity: Final Report' (FR06/11, May 2011) <https://www.iosco.org/library/pubdocs/pdf/IOSCOPD353.pdf> accessed 22 May 2023.

—— 'Regulatory Issues Raised by the Impact of Technological Changes on Market Integrity and Efficiency: Final Report' (FR09/11, October 2011) <https://www.iosco.org/library/pubdocs/pdf/IOSCOPD361.pdf> accessed 22 May 2023.

—— 'Objectives and Principles of Securities Regulation' (May 2017) <https://www.iosco.org/library/pubdocs/pdf/IOSCOPD561.pdf> accessed 22 May 2023.

Jarrell GA, 'Change at the Exchange: The Causes and Effects of Deregulation' (1984) 27 The Journal of Law & Economics 273.

Jiang CX, McInish TH and Upson J, 'Market Fragmentation and Information Quality: The Role of TRF Trades' (March 2012) <https://dx.doi.org/10.2139/ssrn.1960115> accessed 27 February 2023.

Jickling M, 'The Trade-Through Rule' (Congressional Research Service, 6 June 2005) <https://crsreports.congress.gov/product/pdf/RS/RS21871/3> accessed 11 March 2022.

Jolls C, Sunstein CR and Thaler RH, 'A Behavioral Approach to Law and Economics' in Cass R Sunstein (ed), *Behavioral Law and Economics* (Cambridge University Press 2000).

Jordan C, *International Capital Markets: Law and Institutions* (Jeffrey Golden ed, 1st edn, Oxford University Press 2014).

Jung P and Bischof E, *Europäisches Finanzmarktrecht: Die Regulierung von Märkten, Unternehmen und Dienstleistungen durch die Europäische Union* (Nomos 2015).

Jungo S, Zibung O and Roth D in Rolf Sethe and others (eds), *Kommentar zum Finanzmarktinfrastrukturgesetz FinfraG* (1st edn, Schulthess 2017).

Kägi U in Rolf Watter and Rashid Bahar (eds), *Basler Kommentar Finanzmarktaufsichtsgesetz, Finanzmarktinfrastrukturgesetz* (3rd edn, Helbing & Lichtenhahn Verlag 2019).

Kasiske P, 'Compliance-Risiken beim Wertpapierhandel in Dark Pools' [2015] BKR 454.

Khan M and Stafford P, 'EU-Based Traders Caught in Swiss 'Equivalence' Spat: Breakdown in Talks Leaves Investors in Cross-Border Limbo' *Financial Times* (30 June 2019) <https://www.ft.com/content/41091f2c-9ad0-11e9-9c06-a4640c9feebb> accessed 31 March 2023.

Klock M, 'The SEC's New Regulation ATS: Placing the Myth of Market Fragmentation Ahead of Economic Theory and Evidence' (1999) 51 Florida Law Review 753.

Klöhn L, *Kapitalmarkt, Spekulation und Behavioral Finance: Eine interdisziplinäre und vergleichende Analyse zum Fluch und Segen der Spekulation und ihrer Regulierung durch Recht und Markt* (Ph.D.-Thesis University of Göttingen 2006, Duncker & Humblot 2006).

—— 'Wertpapierhandelsrecht diesseits und jenseits des Informationsparadigmas' (2013) 177 ZHR 349.

—— in Heribert Hirte and Thomas M J Möllers (eds), *Kölner Kommentar zum WpHG* (2nd edn. Carl Heymanns Verlag 2014).

—— in Lars Klöhn (ed), *Marktmissbrauchsverordnung: Verordnung (EU) Nr. 596/2014 über Marktmissbrauch* (1st edn, CH Beck 2018).

—— '§ 6 Kapitalmarktrecht' in Katja Langenbucher (ed), *Europäisches Privat- und Wirtschaftsrecht* (5th edn, Nomos 2022).

Köndgen J, 'Effizienzorientierung im Kapitalmarktrecht?' in Holger Fleischer and Daniel Zimmer (eds), *Effizienz als Regelungsziel im Handels- und Wirtschaftsrecht* (Verlag Recht und Wirtschaft 2008).

König D and Kleinlein T, '§ 2 Gesetzgebung' in Reiner Schulze, André Janssen and Stefan Kadelbach (eds), *Europarecht: Handbuch für die deutsche Rechtspraxis* (4th edn, Nomos 2020).

Korhonen K, 'Securities Market ATSs Concepts, Their Roles and Related Policy Issues' (Bank of Finland Discussion Papers 24/2001, Helsinki, 20 November 2001) <https://www.econstor.eu/bitstream/10419/211902/1/bof-rdp2001-024.pdf> accessed 11 February 2022.

Korsmo CR, 'High-Frequency Trading: A Regulatory Strategy' (2014) 48 University of Richmond Law Review 523.

Kotzur M in Rudolf Geiger, Daniel-Erasmus Khan and Markus Kotzur (eds), *EUV - AEUV Kommentar: Vertrag über die Europäische Union – Vertrag über die Arbeitsweise der Europäischen Union* (6th edn, CH Beck 2017).

Kovaleva P and Iori G, 'The Impact of Reduced Pre-Trade Transparency Regimes on Market Quality' (2015) 57 Journal of Economic Dynamics and Control 145.

Kress S, *Effizienzorientierte Kapitalmarktregulierung: Eine Analyse Aus Institutionenökonomischer Perspektive* (Ph.D.-Thesis Johann Wolfgang Goethe-University Frankfurt 1995, Gabler 1996).

Kuhn H, 'Die Regulierung des Derivatehandels im künftigen Finanzmarktinfrastrukturgesetz' [2014] GesKR 161.

—— 'Kollisionsrechtliche Aspekte der Derivateregulierung' [2014] SZW 362.

—— in Rolf Watter and Rashid Bahar (eds), *Basler Kommentar Finanzmarktaufsichtsgesetz, Finanzmarktinfrastrukturgesetz* (3rd edn, Helbing & Lichtenhahn Verlag 2019).

Kumpan C, *Die Regulierung außerbörslicher Wertpapierhandelssysteme im deutschen, europäischen und US-amerikanischen Recht* (Ph.D.-Thesis University of Hamburg 2005, De Gruyter 2006).

—— 'Transparenz als Mittel der Kapitalmarktregulierung: Die neuen Transparenzvorschriften der Richtlinie über Märkte für Finanzinstrumente' [2006] WM 797.

—— in Eberhard Schwark and Daniel Zimmer (eds), *Kapitalmarktrechts-Kommentar: Börsengesetz mit Börsenzulassungsverordnung, Wertpapierprospektgesetz, Wertpapierhandelsgesetz, Wertpapiererwerbs- und Übernahmegesetz, Europäische Marktmissbrauchsverordnung* (5th edn, CH Beck 2020).

Kumpan C and Müller-Lankow H, 'Ein-Market-Maker-Systeme in der neuen Kapitalmarktregulierung - Abgrenzung zwischen multilateralen und bilateralen Systemen' [2017] WM 1777.

Kumpan C and Schmidt F in Matthias Lehmann and Christoph Kumpan (eds), *European Financial Services Law: Article-by-Article Commentary* (1st edn, Nomos; CH Beck; Hart Publishing 2019).

Kümpel S and Wittig A (eds), *Bank- und Kapitalmarktrecht* (4th edn, Otto Schmidt 2011).

Kunz PV, *Kreuzfahrt durch's schweizerische Finanzmarktrecht* (Stämpfli 2014).

Kutscheid E, 'Immissionsschutzrechtliche Vorsorge und Drittschutz' in Bernd Bender and others (eds), *Rechtsstaat zwischen Sozialgestaltung und Rechtsschutz: Festschrift für Konrad Redeker zum 70. Geburtstag* (CH Beck 1993).

Kwan A, Masulis R and McInish TH, 'Trading Rules, Competition for Order Flow and Market Fragmentation' (2015) 115 Journal of Financial Economics 330.

Kyle AS, 'Continiuous Auctions and Insider Trading' (1985) 53 Econometrica 1315.

Lambert TA, *How to Regulate: A Guide for Policymakers* (Cambridge University Press 2017).

Langevoort DC, 'Theories, Assumptions, and Securities Regulation: Market Efficiency Revisited' (1992) 140 University of Pennsylvania Law Review 851.

Lee R, *What is an Exchange?: The Automation, Management, and Regulation of Financial Markets* (Oxford Universty Press 2000).

—— *Running the World's Markets: The Governance of Financial Infrastructure* (Princeton University Press 2011).

Lehmann M, *Finanzinstrumente* (Mohr Siebeck 2009).

—— in Matthias Lehmann and Christoph Kumpan (eds), *European Financial Services Law: Article-by-Article Commentary* (1st edn, Nomos; CH Beck; Hart Publishing 2019).

—— 'Internationales Finanzmarktrecht' in Jan von Hein (ed), *Münchener Kommentar zum Bürgerlichen Gesetzbuch: Internationales Privatrecht II, Internationales Wirtschaftsrecht, Einführungsgesetz zum Bürgerlichen Gesetzbuche (Art. 50–253)* (vol. 13, 8th edn, CH Beck 2021).

Lemke TP, 'The SEC No-Action Letter Process' (1987) 42 The Business Lawyer 1019.

Lenenbach M, *Kapitalmarktrecht und kapitalmarktrelevantes Gesellschaftsrecht* (2nd edn, RWS-Verlag 2010).

Lepsius O, 'Verfassungsrechtlicher Rahmen der Regulierung' in Michael Fehling and Matthias Ruffert (eds), *Regulierungsrecht* (Mohr Siebeck 2010).

Lerch M, '§ 25 Algorithmic Trading and High-Frequency Trading' in Rüdiger Veil (ed), *European Capital Markets Law* (3rd edn, Hart Publishing 2022).

LeRoy SF, 'Efficient Capital Markets and Martingales' (1989) 27 Journal of Economic Literature 1583.

Leschke M, 'Regulierungstheorie aus ökonomischer Sicht' in Michael Fehling and Matthias Ruffert (eds), *Regulierungsrecht* (Mohr Siebeck 2010).

Lev B and Villiers M de, 'Stock Price Crashes and 10b-5 Damages: A Legal, Economic, and Policy Analysis' (1994) 47(1) Stanford Law Review 7.

Lewis M, *Flash Boys* (Allen Lane 2014).

Liersch J, *Regulierung des Blockhandels an den organisierten Aktienmärkten der Vereinigten Staaten, Großbritanniens und Deutschlands* (Ph.D.-Thesis Johann Wolfgang Goethe-University Frankfurt 2001, Peter Lang 2002).

—— 'Nachteile für den Finanzplatz durch außerbörslicher Wertpapiergeschäfte' [2003] WM 473.

Lin Y, Ma T and Chen H-K, 'Does Information Content Necessarily Increase with Greater Pre-Trade Transparency?' (2008) 11(4) Review of Pacific Basin Financial Markets and Policies 531.

Linnainmaa JT and Saar G, 'Lack of Anonymity and the Inference from Order Flow' (2012) 25(5) The Review of Financial Studies 1414.

London Economics, 'Quantification of the Macro-Economic Impact of Integration of EU Financial Markets: Final Report to The European Commission Directorate General for the Internal Market' (November 2002) <https://londoneconomics.co.uk/wp-content/uploads/2011/09/103-Quantification-of-the-Macro-economic-Impact-of-Integration-of-EU-Financial-Markets.pdf> accessed 26 March 2022.

Lopez L, 'New York's Attorney General Has Declared War on Cheating High-Frequency Traders' *Business Insider* (24 September 2013) <https://www.businessinsider.com/schneiderman-targets-hft-front-running-2013-9> accessed 27 February 2023.

Loss L, Seligman J and Paredes T, *Fundamentals of Securities Regulation* (7th edn, Wolters Kluwer Law & Business 2018).

Lubben SJ, *Corporate Finance* (2nd edn, Wolters Kluwer Law & Business 2017).

Lutter M, Bayer W and Schmidt J, *Europäisches Unternehmens- und Kapitalmarktrecht: Grundlagen, Stand und Entwicklung; nebst Texten und Materialien* (6th edn, De Gruyter 2018).

Macey JR and Haddock DD, 'Shirking at the SEC: The Failure of the National Market System' (1985) 1985(2) University of Illinois Law Review 315.

Macey JR and O'Hara M, 'Regulating Exchanges and Alternative Trading Systems: A Law and Economics Perspective' (1999) 28(1) The Journal of Legal Studies 17.

—— 'From Markets to Venues: Securities Regulation in an Evolving World' (2005) 58 Stanford Law Review 563.

MacIntosh JG, 'Revisioning Revisionism: A Glance at HFT's Critics' in Greg N Gregoriou (ed), *Handbook of High Frequency Trading* (Academic Press/Elsevier 2015).

Madhavan A, 'Market Microstructure: A Survey' (2000) 3 Journal of Financial Markets 205.

Madhavan A, Porter D and Weaver D, 'Should Securities Markets Be Transparent?' (2005) 8(3) Journal of Financial Markets 265.

Magen S, '§ 4 – Spieltheorie' in Emanuel V Towfigh and Niels Petersen (eds), *Ökonomische Methoden im Recht: Eine Einführung für Juristen* (2nd edn, Mohr Siebeck 2017).

Mahoney P and Rauterberg G, 'The Regulation of Trading Markets' in Merritt B Fox and others (eds), *Securities Market Issues for the 21st Century* (Columbia University 2018).

Maijoor S, 'Letter of Steven Maijoor to Olivier Guernsent – Ref: MiFID II – SIs Operating Broker Crossing Networks' (ESMA70-872942901-19, 1 February 2017) <https://www.hba.gr/UplDocs/mifidII-mifir/esma_letter_SI_%20Feb%202017.pdf> accessed 26 March 2022.

Marciello JM, 'Are You Afraid of the Dark: How the New York Attorney General is Shedding Light on Dark Pools and High Frequency Trading' (2016) 49 Suffolk University Law Review 163.

Markham JW, '"Confederate Bonds," "General Custer," and the Regulation of Derivative Financial Instruments' (1994) 25 Seton Hall Law Review 1.

Mattig D, 'Kurze Leitungswege für den Handel in Milli- und Mikrosekunden – Zu den latenzminimierenden Infrastrukturen an Börsen und multilateralen Handelssystemen' [2014] WM 1940.

Mattli W, *Darkness by Design: The Hidden Power in Global Capital Markets* (Princeton University Press 2019).

Matus G, 'The Regulation of Alternative Trading Systems: Market Fragmentation and the New Market Structure' (2000–2001) 44 New York Law School Law Review 583.

Maynard TH, 'What is an "Exchange?" – Proprietary Electronic Securities Trading Systems and the Statutory Definition of an Exchange' (1992) 49(3) Washington and Lee Law Review 833.

McDowell H, 'The Only Game in Town' (The Trade News 6 January 2020) <https://www.thetradenews.com/the-only-game-in-town/> accessed 13 January 2022.

McNamara S, 'The Stock Exchange as Multi-Sided Platform and the Future of the National Market System' (2019) 2018(5) Brigham Young University Law Review 969.

Meljnik K, 'Systematische Internalisierung: Eckpunkte des neuen Aufsichtsregimes nach MiFID II/MiFIR' [2017] BaFin Journal 35 <https://www.bafin.de/SharedDocs/Downloads/DE/BaFinJournal/2017/bj_1704.pdf;jsessionid=A146B2890F7B1574B47900E6FE2362DF.2_cid501?__blob=publicationFile&v=5> accessed 6 July 2023.

Mendelson M and Peake JW, 'Whose Market Is It Anyway? Intermediaries' or Investors'' (1994) 19 Journal of Corporate Law 443.

Menkveld AJ, Yueshen BZ and Zhu H, 'Shades of Darkness: A Pecking Order of Trading Venues' (2017) 124(3) Journal of Financial Economics 503.

Mercurio C, 'Dark Pool Regulation' (2013–2014) 33 Review of Banking & Financial Law 69.

Meylan D and Ben Hattar A, 'Le concept de dérivé dans la LIMF: Les contours flous d'une notion au coeur de la réglementation financière' [2018] GesKR 205.

Michaels D, 'Trading Rebates Skew Markets, NYSE and Allies Tell SEC' (Bloomberg 21 February 2014) <https://www.bloomberg.com/news/articles/2014-02-21/trading-rebates-skew-markets-nyse-and-allies-tell-sec> accessed 9 March 2022.

—— 'U.S. Exchanges Get Test to Curb Dark Trading in SEC Program' (Bloomberg 25 June 2014) <https://www.bloomberg.com/news/articles/2014-06-24/exchanges-get-test-to-curb-dark-trading-in-sec-program> accessed 6 July 2023.

Moloney N, *EU Securities and Financial Markets Regulation* (3rd edn, Oxford University Press 2016).

—— 'EU Financial Governance and Transparency Regulation: A Test for the Effectiveness of Post-Crisis Administrative Governance' in Danny Busch and Guido Ferrarini (eds), *Regulation of the EU Financial Markets: MiFID II and MiFIR* (1st edn, Oxford University Press 2017).

Monsch M, *Hochfrequenzhandel: Eine rechtsökonomische Analyse des Phänomens sowie eine rechtsdogmatische Betrachtung des schweizerischen Aufsichtsrechts unter funktionaler Berücksichtigung des europäischen Rechts* (Ph.D.-Thesis University of Zurich 2018, Schulthess 2018).

Moon JG, 'Dangerous Territoriality of American Securities Law: A Proposal for an Integrated Global Securities Market' (2000) 21(1) Northwestern Journal of International Law & Business 131.

Morell A, '§ 3 – Nachfrage, Angebot und Märkte' in Emanuel V Towfigh and Niels Petersen (eds), *Ökonomische Methoden im Recht: Eine Einführung für Juristen* (2nd edn, Mohr Siebeck 2017).

Mülbert PO, 'Anlegerschutz und Finanzmarktregulierung: Grundlagen' (2013) 177 ZHR 160.

—— 'Empfiehlt es sich, im Interesse des Anlegerschutzes und zur Förderung des Finanzplatzes Deutschland das Kapitalmarkt- und Börsenrecht neu zu regeln?' [2002] JZ 826.

—— 'Die neuen Transparenzregeln im Vorschlag einer Richtlinie über Wertpapierdienstleistungen und geregelte Märkte – insbesondere die Pre-Trade-Transparenzpflicht von systematischen Internalisierern: Arbeitspapiere 2003' (Institut für deutsches und internationales Recht des Spar-, Giro- und Kreditwesens an der Johannes Gutenberg-Universität Mainz, 2003) <https://institut-kreditrecht.de/wp-content/uploads/2021/06/institut_isd2003.pdf> accessed 27 March 2022.

Nagy DM, 'Judicial Reliance on Regulatory Interpretations in SEC No-Action Letters: Corrent Problems and a Proposed Framework' (1998) 83 Cornell Law Review 921.

NASDAQ, 'Midpoint Liquidity' (2018) <https://www.nasdaqtrader.com/content/productsservices/trading/midpointpeg.pdf> accessed 11 March 2022.

Nimalendran M and Ray S, 'Informational Linkages Between Dark and Lit trading Venues' (2014) 17 Journal of Financial Markets 230.

Nobel P, *Aktienrecht: Systematische Darstellung* (Berner Kommentar, Stämpfli Verlag 2017).

Nyquist P, 'Failure to Engage: The Regulation of Proprietary Trading Systems' (1995) 13 Yale Law & Policy Review 281.

Oechsler J, 'Das Verbot der Marktmanipulation durch Aktienrückkauf im Licht der neueren Kritik an der klassischen Kapitalmarkttheorie' in Jens C Dammann, Wolfgang Grunsky and Thomas Pfeiffer (eds), *Gedächtnisschrift für Manfred Wolf* (CH Beck 2011).

Oesterhelweg O and Schiereck D, 'Meßkonzepte für die Liquidität von Finanzmärkten' [1993] Die Bank 390.

Ogus AI, 'Comparing Regulatory Systems: Institutions, Processes and Legal Forms in Industrialised Countries' in Paul Cook and others (eds), *Leading Issues in Competition, Regulation and Development* (Edward Elgar 2004).

—— *Regulation: Legal Form and Economic Theory* (Hart Publishing 2004).

O'Hara M, *Market Microstructure Theory* (Blackwell Publishing 1995).

—— 'High Frequency Market Microstructure' (2015) 116(2) Journal of Financial Economics 257.

O'Malley G, 'Diving into Dark Pools: An Analysis of Hidden Liquidity with Regard to the Proposed Markets in Financial Instruments Directive' (2014) 17 Trinity College Law Review 94.

'Opinion of the European Economic and Social Committee on the 'Proposal for a Regulation of the European Parliament and of the Council on markets in financial instruments and amending Regulation (EMIR) on OTC derivatives, central counterparties and trade repositories': COM(2011) 652 final — 2011/0296 (COD), (2012/C 143/14)' [2012] OJ C143/74.

Owens A and others, 'SEC Adopts Significant Changes to Regulation ATS' (Securities Alert, 11 September 2018) <https://www.wilmerhale.com/-/media/files/shared_content/editorial/publications/wh_publications/client_alert_pdfs/20180911-sec-adopts-significant-changes-to-regulation-ats.pdf> accessed 6 July 2023.

Pagano M and Röell A, 'Transparency and Liquidity: A Comparison of Auction and Dealer Markets with Informed Trading' (1996) 51(2) Journal of Finance 579.

Pan EJ, 'Organizing Regional Systems: The US Example' in Niamh Moloney, Eilís Ferran and Jennifer Payne (eds), *The Oxford Handbook of Financial Regulation* (Oxford University Press 2015).

Patterson S, *Dark pools: The Rise of the Machine Traders and the Rigging of the U.S. Stock Market* (1st edn, Crown Business 2013).

Petrescu M and Wedow M, 'Dark Pools in European Equity Markets: Emergence, Competition and Implications' (Occasional Paper Series No. 193, European Central Bank, July 2017) <https://www.ecb.europa.eu/pub/pdf/scpops/ecb.op193.en.pdf> accessed 22 May 2023.

Pfüller M in Thomas Hoeren, Ulrich Sieber and Bernd Holznagel (eds), *Handbuch Multimedia-Recht: Rechtsfragen des elektronischen Geschäftsverkehrs* (date of issue: January 2018, CH Beck 2014).

Picot A, Bortenlänger C and Röhrl H, *Börsen im Wandel: Der Einfluß von Informationstechnologie und Wettbewerb auf die Organisation von Wertpapiermärkten* (Knapp 1996).

Pirker B and Matter L, 'Europarecht: Schweiz – Europäische Union' [2019] SRIEL 101.

—— 'Europarecht: Schweiz-Europäische Union' [2020] SRIEL 75.

Pistor K, 'A Legal Theory of Finance' (Columbia Law School Public Law & Legal Theory Working Paper Group, 9 May 2013) <https://scholarship.law.columbia.edu/cgi/viewcontent.cgi?article=3286&context=faculty_scholarship> accessed 6 July 2023.

Poelzig D, 'Insider- und Marktmanipulationsverbot im neuen Marktmissbrauchsrecht' [2016] NZG 528.

—— *Kapitalmarktrecht* (2nd edn, CH Beck 2021).

Poser NS, 'Restructuring the Stock Markets: A Critical Look at the SEC's National Market System' (1981) 56 New York University Law Review 883.

Preece R, 'Dark Pools, Internalization, and Equity Market Quality' (CFA Institute, October 2012) <https://www.cfainstitute.org/en/advocacy/policy-positions/dark-pools-internalization-and-equity-market-quality> accessed 22 May 2023.

Preece RG and Rosov S, 'Dark Trading and Equity Market Quality' (2014) 70(6) Financial Analysts Journal 33.

Reiser N, 'Anlegerschutz durch Trennung?: Segregierung von Eigen- und Kundenbeständen bei der Drittverwahrung von Bucheffekten' [2017] SZW 452.

—— *Durchsetzung heterogener börsengesellschaftsrechtlicher Normen* (Dike 2017).

Reuschle F and Fleckner AM, 'Börsenähnliche Einrichtungen – die privatrechtliche Organisation einer Börse im materiellen Sinne' [2002] BKR 617.

Rimle A, *Recht des schweizerischen Finanzmarktes: Ein Grundriss für die Praxis* (Schulthess 2004).

Röh L in Eberhard Schwark and Daniel Zimmer (eds), *Kapitalmarktrechts-Kommentar: Börsengesetz mit Börsenzulassungsverordnung, Wertpapierprospektgesetz, Wertpapierhandelsgesetz, Wertpapiererwerbs- und Übernahmegesetz, Europäische Marktmissbrauchsverordnung* (5th edn, CH Beck 2020).

Ross V, 'MiFID II – Switching on the Light Without Turning-Off the Tap: Speech at ABA/Law Society Capital Markets Conference' (ESMA/2015/496, London, 26 February 2015) <https://www.esma.europa.eu/sites/default/files/library/2015/11/2015-496_mifid_ii_-_switching_on_the_light_without_turning-off_the_tap_-_verena_ross_executive_director_esma.pdf> accessed 27 March 2022.

Rudolph B, 'Computerbörse für den Finanzplatz Deutschland' [1994] Die Betriebswirtschaft 426.

Rudolph B and Röhrl H, 'Grundfragen der Börsenorganisation aus ökonomischer Sicht' in K. Hopt, B. Rudolph and H. Baum (eds), *Börsenreform: Eine ökonomische, rechtsvergleichende und rechtspolitische Untersuchung* (Schäffer-Poeschel 1997).

Ruffert M in Christian Calliess and Matthias Ruffert (eds), *EUV/AEUV-Kommentar: Das Verfassungsrecht der Europäischen Union mit Europäischer Grundrechtecharta* (6th edn, CH Beck 2022).

Salger A-C, *Dark Trading: Shedding Light on US and EU Regulation of the Securities Markets' Dark Sector* (Ph.D.-Thesis University of Freiburg 2018/19, De Gruyter 2020).

Sapien B, 'Financial Weapons of Mass Destruction: From Bucket Shops to Credit Default Swaps' (2010) 19 Southern California Interdisciplinary Law Journal 411.

Sapusek A, *Informationseffizienz auf Kapitalmärkten: Kozepte und empirische Ergebnisse* (Gabler Verlag 1998).

Schären S, Dobrauz-Saldapenna G and Liebi M, 'Organisierte Handelssysteme im neuen FinfraG: Versuch einer regulatorischen Kategorisierung' [2016] SZW 194.

Schären S and Jutzi T, 'Schweizer Finanzmarktrecht im europäischen Kontext – Aufbruch in eine neue Ära' [2021] GesKR 466.

Scheffrahn R, *Gestaltung einer wettbewerbsfähigen Börse Schweiz* (Ph.D.-Thesis University of Zurich, P. Haupt 1992).

Schelling H, 'Die systematische Internalisierung in Nichteigenkapitalinstrumenten nach MiFID II und MiFIR' [2015] BKR 221.

Schizer DM, 'Benign Restraint: The SEC's Regulation of Execution Systems' (1992) 101(7) Yale Law Journal 1551.

Schleiffer P and Schärli P, 'Organisation und Betrieb einzelner Finanzmarktinfrastrukturen' in Peter Sester and others (eds), *St. Galler Handbuch zum Schweizer Finanzmarktrecht: Finanzmarktaufsicht und Finanzmarktinfrastrukturen* (1st edn, Dike 2017).

—— 'New Rules for Organized Trading Facilities' [2017] CapLaw 44.

Schmidhuber M, *Verhaltenskodizes im nationalen und grenzüberschreitenden elektronischen Geschäftsverkehr: Zur Frage der Integration der Selbstregulierung durch Private in die staatliche Rechtsordnung* (Ph.D.-Thesis University of Heidelberg 2004, Peter Lang 2004).

Schmies C and Sajnovits A, 'Data Reporting: Market Structures and Regulatory Framework' (EBI Working Paper Series 2020 – No. 76, European Banking Institute, Frankfurt am Main, 6 November 2020) <https://deliverypdf.ssrn.com/delivery.php?ID=27607302900801008200712011609208612002203704002905905109010008700700408907506707207703805500501211903303206901009000007309712405508104408306712112502008510308700709800501307308810800111100112702111300712202509012410706710001409911812506809411903007608 5&EXT=pdf&INDEX=TRUE> accessed 27 March 2022.

Schmolke KU, '§ 5 – Vertragstheorie und ökonomische Analyse des Vertragsrechts' in Emanuel V Towfigh and Niels Petersen (eds), *Ökonomische Methoden im Recht: Eine Einführung für Juristen* (2nd edn, Mohr Siebeck 2017).

—— in Lars Klöhn (ed), *Marktmissbrauchsverordnung: Verordnung (EU) Nr. 596/2014 über Marktmissbrauch* (1st edn, CH Beck 2018).

Schott A in Rolf Sethe and others (eds), *Kommentar zum Finanzmarktinfrastrukturgesetz FinfraG* (1st edn, Schulthess 2017).

Schott A and Sester P, 'Organisation und Betrieb einzelner Finanzmarktinfrastrukturen' in Peter Sester and others (eds), *St. Galler Handbuch zum Schweizer Finanzmarktrecht: Finanzmarktaufsicht und Finanzmarktinfrastrukturen* (1st edn, Dike 2017).

Schott A and Winkler M in Rolf Sethe and others (eds), *Kommentar zum Finanzmarktinfrastrukturgesetz FinfraG* (1st edn, Schulthess 2017).

Schulte AA, *Die Regulierung der deutschen Effektenbörsen: Eine Analyse staatlicher Maßnahmen im deutschen Börsenwesen seit der Währungsreform* (Ph.D.-Thesis University of Münster 1994, Peter Lang 1995).

Schultheiß T, 'Die Neuerungen im Hochfrequenzhandel' [2013] WM 596.

Schwark E and Zimmer D in Eberhard Schwark and Daniel Zimmer (eds), *Kapitalmarktrechts-Kommentar: Börsengesetz mit Börsenzulassungsverordnung, Wertpapierprospektgesetz, Wertpapierhandelsgesetz, Wertpapiererwerbs- und Übernahmegesetz, Europäische Marktmissbrauchsverordnung* (5th edn, CH Beck 2020).

Schwartz RA, *Reshaping the Equity Markets: A Guide for the 1990s* (Harper Collins 1991).

Schwartz RA and Francioni R, *Equity Markets in Action: The Fundamentals of Liquidity, Market Structure & Trading* (John Wiley & Sons 2004).

Scopino G, *Algo Bots and the Law* (Cambridge University Press 2020).

SEC, 'Form 1: Application for, and Amendments to Application for, Registration as a National Securities Exchange or Exemption from Registration Pursuant to Section 5 of the Exchange Act' <https://www.sec.gov/files/form1.pdf> accessed 10 March 2022.

—— 'Form BD: Uniform Application for Broker-Dealer Registration' <https://www.sec.gov/files/formbd.pdf> accessed 6 July 2023.

—— 'Hidden Volume Ratios: Market Structure Data Highlight' (9 October 2013) <https://www.sec.gov/marketstructure/research/highlight-2013-02.html#.Yitc4omZO3B> accessed 25 May 2023.

—— 'Order Directing the Exchanges and the Financial Industry Regulatory Authority to Submit a Tick Size Pilot Plan' (Release No. 34-72460, 30 June 2014) 79 FR 36840.—— 'Payment for Order Flow' (17 CFR Part 240, Release No. 34–33026, File No. S7–29–93, 13 October 1993) 58 FR 52934.

—— 'Market 2000 Report: An Examination of Current Equity Market Developments' (Washington, D.C., January 1994) <https://www.sec.gov/divisions/marketreg/market2000.pdf> accessed 6 July 2023.

—— 'Order Execution Obligations: Final Rules' (17 CFR Part 240, Release No. 34–37619A, File No. S7–30–95, 12 September 1996) 61 FR 48290.

—— 'Concept Release' (17 CFR Part 240, Release No. 34–38672, File No. S7–16–97, 4 June 1997) 62 FR 30485.

—— 'Regulation of Exchanges and Alternative Trading Systems: Final Rules' (17 CFR Parts 202, 240, 242 and 249, Release No. 34–40760, File No. S7–12–98, 22 December 1998) 63 FR 70844.

—— 'Regulation NMS: Proposed rules and amendments to joint industry plans' (17 CFR Parts 200, 230, 240, 242, and 249, Release No. 34–49325, File No. S7–10–04, 9 March 2004) 69 FR 11126.

—— 'Regulation NMS: Final Rules' (17 CFR Parts 200, 201, 230, 240, 242, 249, and 270, Release No. 34–51808, File No. S7–10–04, 29 June 2005) 70 FR 37496.

—— 'Regulation of Non-Public Trading Interest: Proposed Rules and Amendments to Joint-industry Plans' (17 CFR Part 242, Release No. 34–60997, File No. S7–27–09, 23 November 2009) 74 FR 61208.

—— 'Concept Release on Equity Market Structure' (17 CFR Part 242, Release No. 34–61358, File No. S7–02–10, 21 January 2010) 75 FR 3594.

—— 'Order Granting Approval to Proposed Rule Changes, as Modified by Amendments Nos. 1 and 2, Adopting NYSE Rule 107C to Establish a Retail Liquidity Program for NYSE-Listed Securities on a Pilot Basis until 12 Months From Implementation Date, and Adopting NYSE Amex Rule 107C to Establish a Retail Liquidity Program for NYSE Amex Equities Traded Securities on a Pilot Basis Until 12 Months From Implementation Date, and Granting Exemptions Pursuant to Rule 612(c) of Regulation NMS' (Release No. 34–67347, File Nos. SR–NYSE-2011–55, SR–NYSEAmex-2011–84, 3 July 2012, 10 July 2012) 77 FR 40673.

—— 'Press Release: SEC Charges New York-Based Dark Pool Operator With Failing to Safeguard Confidential Trading Information' (Washington, D.C., 6 June 2014) <https://www.sec.gov/news/press-release/2014-114> accessed 16 January 2023.

—— 'Regulation Systems Compliance and Integrity' (17 CFR Parts 240, 242, and 249, Release No. 34–73639, File No. S7–01–13, 5 December 2014) 79 FR 72252.

—— 'Press Release: SEC Charges UBS Subsidiary With Disclosure Violations and Other Regulatory Failures in Operating Dark Pool' (Washington, D.C., 15 January 2015) <https://www.sec.gov/news/pressrelease/2015-7.html> accessed 16 February 2023.

—— 'Memorandum to SEC Market Structure Advisory Committee: Rule 611 of Regulation NMS' (SEC Division of Trading and Markets, 30 April 2015) <https://www.sec.gov/spotlight/emsac/memo-rule-611-regulation-nms.pdf> accessed 25 May 2023.

—— 'Press Release: SEC Charges ITG With Operating Secret Trading Desk and Misusing Dark Pool Subscriber Trading Information' (Washington, D.C., 12 August 2015) <https://www.sec.gov/news/pressrelease/2015-164.html> accessed 16 February 2023.

—— 'Press Release: SEC Proposes Rules to Enhance Transparency and Oversight of Alternative Trading Systems' (Washington, D.C., 18 November 2015) <https://www.sec.gov/news/pressrelease/2015-261.html> accessed 11 March 2022.

—— 'Shedding Light on Dark Pools: Statement by Commissioner Luis A. Aguilar' (18 November 2015) <https://www.sec.gov/news/statement/shedding-light-on-dark-pools.html> accessed 14 January 2022.

—— 'Regulation of NMS Stock Alternative Trading Systems: Proposed Rule' (17 CFR Parts 240, 242, 249, Release No. 34–76474, File No. S7–23–15, 28 December 2015) 80 FR 80998.

—— 'Responses to Frequently Asked Questions Concerning Large Trader Reporting' (2016) <https://www.sec.gov/divisions/marketreg/large-trader-faqs.htm> accessed 15 April 2023.

—— 'Memorandum to Equity Market Structure Advisory Committee: Certain Issues Affecting Customers in the Current Equity Market Structure' (Division of Trading and Markets, 26 January 2016) <https://www.sec.gov/spotlight/equity-market-structure/issues-affecting-customers-emsac-012616.pdf> accessed 6 July 2023.

—— 'Press Release: Barclays, Credit Suisse Charged With Dark Pool Violations: Firms Collectively Paying More Than $150 Million to Settle Cases' (Washington, D.C., 31 January 2016) <https://www.sec.gov/news/pressrelease/2016-16.html> accessed 16 February 2023.

—— 'Press Release: Deutsche Bank Settles Charges of Misleading Clients About Order Router' (Washington, D.C., 16 December 2016) <https://www.sec.gov/news/pressrelease/2016-264.html> accessed 16 February 2023.

—— 'National Securities Exchanges and FINRA: Assessment of the Plan to Implement a Tick Size Pilot Program' (3 July 2018, revised 2 August 2018) <https://www.finra.org/sites/default/files/tick-size-pilot-assesment.pdf> accessed 11 March 2022.

—— 'Regulation of NMS Stock Alternative Trading Systems: Final Rule' (17 CFR Parts 232, 240, 242, and 249, Release No. 34–83663, File No. S7–23–15, 7 August 2018) 83 FR 38768 <https://www.govinfo.gov/content/pkg/FR-2018-08-07/pdf/2018-15896.pdf> accessed 11 March 2022.

—— 'Press Release: SEC Charges Citigroup for Dark Pool Misrepresentations' (Washington, D.C., 14 September 2018) <https://www.sec.gov/news/press-release/2018-193> accessed 16 February 2023.

—— 'Press Release: SEC Adopts Rules That Increase Information Brokers Must Provide to Investors on Order Handling' (Washington, D.C., 2 November 2018) <https://www.sec.gov/news/press-release/2018-253> accessed 11 March 2022.

—— 'Disclosure of Order Handling Information: Final Rules' (17 CFR Parts 240 and 242, Release No. 34–84528, File No. S7–14–16, 19 November 2018) 83 FR 58338.

—— 'Fact Sheet Disclosure of Order Execution Information' (Washington, D.C., 14 December 2022) <https://www.sec.gov/files/34-96493-fact-sheet.pdf> accessed 8 July 2023.

—— 'Fact Sheet Proposed Rule to Enhance Order Competition' (Washington, D.C., 14 December 2022) <https://www.sec.gov/files/34-96495-fact-sheet.pdf> accessed 8 July 2023.

—— 'Fact Sheet Regulation Best Execution' (Washington, D.C., 14 December 2022) <https://www.sec.gov/files/34-96496-fact-sheet.pdf> accessed 8 July 2023.

—— 'Fact Sheet Tick Size, Access Fees, and Transparency of Better Priced Orders' (Washington, D.C., 14 December 2022) <https://www.sec.gov/files/34-96494-fact-sheet.pdf> accessed 8 July 2023.

—— 'SEC Proposals: Market Structure' (14 December 2022) <https://www.sec.gov/newsroom/market-structure-proposals-december-2022> accessed 8 July 2023.

Seibert S, *Dark Pools – schwarze Goldgrube der Betreiber?: Eine Untersuchung verdeckter Liquiditätsplattformen im deutschen Aktienhandel* (GRIN Verlag 2010).

Seiffert J and Lembke LA, 'Handelstransparenz' in Jürgen Ellenberger and Peter Clouth (eds), *Praktikerhandbuch Wertpapier- und Derivategeschäft* (5th edn, Finanz Colloquium Heidelberg 2018).

Seiffert T in Heribert Hirte and Thomas M J Möllers (eds), *Kölner Kommentar zum WpHG* (2nd edn, Carl Heymanns Verlag 2014).

Seitz J, 'Die Regulierung von Wertpapierhandelssystemen in der EU' [2004] AG 497.

Seligman J, *The Transformation of Wall Street: A History of the Securities and Exchange Commission and Modern Corporate Finance* (3rd edn, Aspen Publishing 2003).

—— 'Cautious Evolution or Perennial Irresolution: Stock Market Self-Regulation During the First 70 Years of the Securities and Exchange Commission' (2004) 59(4) The Business Lawyer 1347.

Sethe R, 'Das Drittstaatenregime von MiFIR und MiFID II' [2014] SZW 615.

—— in Rolf Sethe and others (eds), *Kommentar zum Finanzmarktinfrastrukturgesetz FinfraG* (1st edn, Schulthess 2017).

Sethe R and others (eds), *Kommentar zum Finanzmarktinfrastrukturgesetz FinfraG* (1st edn, Schulthess 2017).

Sharma SG, 'Over-the-Counter Derivatives: A New Era of Financial Regulation' (2011) 17 Law and Business Review of the Americas 279.

Shiller RJ, *Market Volatility* (MIT Press 1989).

Shleifer A, *Inefficient Markets: An Introduction to Behavioral Finance* (Oxford University Press 2000).

Shleifer A and Summers LH, 'The Noise Trader Approach to Finance' (1990) 4 The Journal of Economic Perspectives 19.

Shorter G and Miller RS, 'High-Frequency Trading: Background, Concerns, and Regulatory Developments' (Congressional Research Service, 19 June 2014) <https://sgp.fas.org/crs/misc/R43608.pdf> accessed 9 March 2022.

—— 'Dark Pools in Equity Trading: Policy Concerns and Recent Developments' (Congressional Research Service, 26 September 2014) <https://sgp.fas.org/crs/misc/R43739.pdf> accessed 11 February 2022.

Sieber-Gasser C, 'Offene strategische Autonomie in der EU-Handelspolitik: Auswirkungen auf europäische Drittstaaten' [2021] EuZ 222.

Siems MM, *Comparative Law* (3rd edn, Cambridge University Press 2022).

Simaan Y, Weaver DG and Whitcomb DK, 'Market Maker Quotation Behavior and Pretrade Transparency' (2003) 58 The Journal of Finance 1247.

SIX Swiss Exchange, 'SWXess Maintenance Release 7.1 (SMR7.1): Participant Readiness (Version 4.00)' (3 May 2018) <https://www.six-group.com/dam/download/the-swiss-stock-exchange/trading/participation/SWXess-maintenance-releases/smr71_participant_readiness.pdf> accessed 3 April 2022.

—— 'Directive 3: Trading' (10 March 2021) <https://www.ser-ag.com/dam/downloads/regulation/trading-revisions/directive03/2021-06-21-dir03-en.pdf> accessed 23 February 2023.

—— 'Trading Rules' (6 December 2021) <https://www.ser-ag.com/dam/downloads/regulation/trading/rule-books/rb-en.pdf> accessed 3 April 2022.

—— 'SIX Share Explorer' (3 April 2022) <https://www.six-group.com/en/products-services/the-swiss-stock-exchange/market-data/shares/share-explorer.html> accessed 3 April 2022.

—— 'Directive 5: Alternative Trading' (23 November 2022) <https://www.ser-ag.com/dam/downloads/regulation/trading/directives/dir05-en.pdf> accessed 10 June 2023.

—— 'SwissAtMid: Ihre Liquiditätsquelle für Schweizer Aktien' (Factsheet, 2023) <https://www.six-group.com/de/products-services/the-swiss-stock-exchange/trading/markets/swissatmid.html> accessed 16 February 2023.

Sliskovic V, 'MiFID II-Anforderungen an den algorithmischen Handel aus der Perspektive eines Energiehandelsunternehmens' [2020] CB 145.

Smith A, 'Goldman Sachs to go live with SIGMA X Europe MTF on 21 December: The SIGMA X EU MTF will launch on 21 December in Paris at Goldman Sachs ahead of the end of the Brexit transition period on 31 December' (The Trade News 17 December 2020) <https://www.thetradenews.com/goldman-sachs-to-go-live-with-sigma-x-europe-mtf-on-21-december/> accessed 14 February 2022.

Spindler G, 'Elektronische Finanzmärkte und Internet-Börsen – Teil I: Grundlegende Risiken und Reform des nationalen Kapitalmarktrechts' [2002] WM 1325.

—— 'Elektronische Finanzmärkte und Internet-Börsen – Teil II: Regulierungsvorhaben auf der europäischen Ebene' [2002] WM 1365.

—— and Hüther M, 'Börse ohne Parkett - oder: Alternative Trading Systems: Elektronische Handelssysteme in den USA' [2002] RIW 649.

—— and Kasten RA, 'Der neue Rechtsrahmen für den Finanzdienstleistungssektor – die MiFID und ihre Umsetzung – Teil I -' [2006] WM 1749.

Stahl R, *Capital Asset Pricing Model und Alternativkalküle: Analyse in der Unternehmensbewertung mit empirischem Bezug auf die DAX-Werte* (Springer Gabler 2016).

Stefanski A, *Eigenhandel für andere: Market-Making und Internalisierung im deutschen, europäischen und US-amerikanischen Recht* (Nomos 2009).

Steffen P in Urs B Lendermann, Heinrich Nemeczek and Ulrich G Schroeter (eds), *Wertpapierinstitutsgesetz: WpIG-Kommentar* (1st edn, CH Beck 2024).

Stiglitz JE, 'Information and the Change in the Paradigm in Economics' (2002) 92(3) The American Economic Review 460.

Stoll HR, 'Electronic Trading in Stock Markets' (2006) 20(1) The Journal of Economic Perspectives 153.

Stötzel M, 'High Frequency Trading: Einordnung in das Börsen- und Kapitalmarktrecht' [2011] RdF 156.

Stout LA, 'Irrational Expectations' (1997) 3 Legal Theory 227.

—— 'Why the Law Hates Speculators: Regulation and Private Ordering in the Market for OTC Derivatives' (1999) 48 Duke Law Journal 701.

Studer U and Vollenweider M in Rolf Watter and Rashid Bahar (eds), *Basler Kommentar Finanzmarktaufsichtsgesetz, Finanzmarktinfrastrukturgesetz* (3rd edn, Helbing & Lichtenhahn Verlag 2019).

Teall JL, *Financial Trading and Investing* (2nd edn, Elsevier Academic Press 2018).

The Federal Reserve System, 'Purposes & Functions' (10th edn, Federal Reserve System Publication, Washington, D.C., 2016) <https://fraser.stlouisfed.org/files/docs/historical/federal%20reserve%20history/bog_publications/bog_frs_purposes_2016.pdf?utm_source=direct_download> accessed 11 March 2022.

Thelen MK, *Dark Pools: Schattenbörsen im Lichte US-amerikanischer, europäischer und deutscher Kapitalmarktregulierung* (Ph.D.-Thesis University of Bonn 2019, Duncker & Humblot 2019).

Thiel M, *Die Entgrenzung der Gefahrenabwehr: Grundfragen von Freiheit und Sicherheit im Zeitalter der Globalisierung* (Mohr Siebeck 2011).

Thompson AR, 'Taming the Frontier?: An Evaluation of the SEC's Regulation of Internet Securities Trading Systems' (1999) 1999 Columbia Business Law Review 165.

Thomsen EF, *Prices and Knowledge: A Market-Process Perspective* (Routledge 1992).

Tobin J, 'On the Efficiency of the Financial System' [1984] Lloyds Bank Review 1.

Toni M and Hungerbühler L, 'Neue Handelspflicht für Aktien in der EU: Ist der Schweizer Rechtsrahmen für Handelsplätze äquivalent?' [2017] GesKR 205.

Truffer R in Rolf Watter and Rashid Bahar (eds), *Basler Kommentar Finanzmarktaufsichtsgesetz, Finanzmarktinfrastrukturgesetz* (3rd edn, Helbing & Lichtenhahn Verlag 2019).

Tuch AF, 'Self-Regulation of Investment Bankers' (2014) 83 The George Washington Law Review 101.

Valiante D, 'Setting an Institutional and Regulatory Framework for Trading Platforms: Is There a Case for a New Trading Venue Under MiFID?' (2013) 21(1) Journal of Financial Regulation and Compliance 69.

Vaupel FC, 'Die aufsichtsrechtliche Behandlung automatisierter Handelssysteme in den USA' [1995] RIW 568.

Veil R, '§ 1 History' in Rüdiger Veil (ed), *European Capital Markets Law* (3rd edn, Hart Publishing 2022).

—— '§ 2 Concept and Aims of Capital Markets Regulation' in Rüdiger Veil (ed), *European Capital Markets Law* (3rd edn, Hart Publishing 2022).

—— '§ 3 Legislative Power for Regulating and Harmonising Capital Markets in Europe' in Rüdiger Veil (ed), *European Capital Markets Law* (3rd edn, Hart Publishing 2022).

—— '§ 5 Sources of Law and Principles of Interpretation' in Rüdiger Veil (ed), *European Capital Markets Law* (3rd edn, Hart Publishing 2022).

Veil R and Lerch M, 'Auf dem Weg zu einem Europäischen Finanzmarktrecht: die Vorschläge der Kommission zur Neuregelung der Märkte für Finanzinstrumente – Teil I -' [2012] WM 1557.

—— 'Auf dem Weg zu einem Europäischen Finanzmarktrecht: die Vorschläge der Kommission zur Neuregelung der Märkte für Finanzinstrumente – Teil II -' [2012] WM 1605.

Vogel A, Heiz C and Luthiger R, *OFK FinfraG/BEG Kommentar: Finanzmarktinfrastrukturgesetz und Bucheffektengesetz mit HWpÜ und weiteren Erlassen* (Orell Füssli Kommentar (OFK), 1st edn, Orell Füssli Verlag 2019).

—— *OFK FIDLEG/FINIG Kommentar: Bundesgesetz über die Finanzdienstleistungen und Bundesgesetz über die Finanzinstitute* (Orell Füssli Kommentar (OFK), 1st edn, Orell Füssli Verlag 2020).

Vollmuth C and Seifert J, 'Handelstransparenz differenziert nach Marktform: geregelte Märkte, multilaterale Handelssysteme, systematische Internalisierer' in Peter Clouth and Volker Lang (eds), *MiFID Praktikerhandbuch: Neue Verhaltenspflichten für Banken und Sparkassen durch Gesetzgeber und Bankenaufsicht* (Bank-Verlag Medien 2007).

Walla F, *Die Konzeption der Kapitalmarktaufsicht in Deutschland* (Nomos 2012).

—— '§ 11 Capital Markets Supervision' in Rüdiger Veil (ed), *European Capital Markets Law* (3rd edn, Hart Publishing 2022).

—— '§ 4 Rule-Making Process' in Rüdiger Veil (ed), *European Capital Markets Law* (3rd edn, Hart Publishing 2022).

Watter R in Rolf Watter and Rashid Bahar (eds), *Basler Kommentar Finanzmarktaufsichtsgesetz, Finanzmarktinfrastrukturgesetz* (3rd edn, Helbing & Lichtenhahn Verlag 2019).

Watter R and Kägi U in Rolf Watter and Nedim P Vogt (eds), *Basler Kommentar Börsengesetz, Finanzmarktaufsichtsgesetz, Art. 161, 161bis, 305bis und 305ter Strafgesetzbuch* (2nd edn, Helbing & Lichtenhahn Verlag 2011).

Weaver DG, 'The Trade-At Rule, Internalization, and Market Quality' (17 April 2014) <https://deliverypdf.ssrn.com/delivery.php?ID=284123064090007000107083114103097065040086057015091007085094112078112071011006089069106114044017059048002098031122113099016085060078047087052021071010087122098112092020060079029086071126085001119101071011118066014101098105119090068071089094081017031125&EXT=pdf&INDEX=TRUE> accessed 11 March 2022.

Weber M, 'Börsenkursbestimmung aus ökonomischer Perspektive' [2004] ZGR 280.

—— 'Die Entwicklung des Kapitalmarktrechts im Jahre 2007' [2007] NJW 3688.

Wennerberg C, 'Double Volume Caps in MiFID II: What Are the Effects?' (bobsguide 30 November 2015) <https://www.bobsguide.com/double-volume-caps-in-mifid-ii-what-are-the-effects/#:~:text=Double%20Volume%20Caps%20in%20MiFID%20II:%20What%20are%20the%20effects?> accessed 27 March 2022.

Werlen T, *Konzeptionelle Grundlagen des schweizerischen Kapitalmarktrechts* (Ph.D.-Thesis University of Zurich 1994, Schulthess 1994).

White LJ, 'International Regulation of Securities Markets: Competition or Harmonization?' in Andrew W Lo (ed), *The Industrial Organization and Regulation of the Securities Industry* (The University of Chicago Press 1996).

White MJ, 'SEC Enhancing Our Equity Market Structure' (5 June 2014) <https://www.sec.gov/news/speech/2014-spch060514mjw> accessed 13 January 2022.

Winzeler C, 'Selbstregulierung: Grenzen und Möglichkeiten' in Peter Sester and others (eds), *St. Galler Handbuch zum Schweizer Finanzmarktrecht: Finanzmarktaufsicht und Finanzmarktinfrastrukturen* (1st edn, Dike 2017).

—— in Rolf Watter and Rashid Bahar (eds), *Basler Kommentar Finanzmarktaufsichtsgesetz, Finanzmarktinfrastrukturgesetz* (3rd edn, Helbing & Lichtenhahn Verlag 2019).

Wohlers Wolfgang, 'Selbstregulierung – Aufsichtsrecht – Strafrecht: (Ziel-) Konflikte und Interdependenzen' in Jürg-Beat Ackermann and Wolfgang Wohlers (eds), *Finanzmarkt ausser Kontrolle?: Selbstregulierung – Aufsichtsrecht – Strafrecht.* 3. Zürcher Tagung zum Wirtschaftsstrafrecht (Schulthess 2009).

Yadav Y, 'The Failure of Liability in Modern Markets' (2016) 102 Virginia Law Review 1031.

—— 'Oversight Failure in Securities Markets' (2019) 104 Cornell Law Review 1799.

Yamamoto R, 'Order Aggressiveness, Pre-Trade Transparency, and Long Memory in an Order-Driven Market' (2011) 35(11) Journal of Economic Dynamics and Control 1938.

Ye L, 'Understanding the Impacts of Dark Pools on Price Discovery' (October 2016) <https://arxiv.org/pdf/1612.08486.pdf> accessed 27 February 2023.

Ye M, 'A Glimpse into the Dark: Price Formation, Transaction Cost and Market Share of the Crossing Network' (9 June 2011) <https://dx.doi.org/10.2139/ssrn.1521494> accessed 27 February 2023.

Zaza K, 'A Fiduciary Standard as a Tool for Dark Pool Subscribers' (2013) 18 Stanford Journal of Law, Business & Finance 319.

Zellweger-Gutknecht C in Corinne Widmer Lüchinger and David Oser (eds), *Basler Kommentar Obligationenrecht I* (7th edn, Helbing & Lichtenhahn Verlag 2020).

Zhu H, 'Do Dark Pools Harm Price Discovery?' (2014) 27(3) Review of Financial Studies 747.

Zibung O, Jungo S and Roth D in Rolf Sethe and others (eds), *Kommentar zum Finanzmarktinfrastrukturgesetz FinfraG* (1st edn, Schulthess 2017).

Zobl D and Kramer S, *Schweizerisches Kapitalmarktrecht* (Schulthess 2004).

Zulauf U, 'Koregulierung statt Selbstregulierung: Erfahrungen mit der Selbstregulierung im Schweizer Finanzmarktrecht seit der Finanzkrise von 2007' (Jusletter 4 November 2013) <https://urszulauf.ch/wp-content/uploads/2018/07/Zulauf.-2013.-Koregulierung-statt-Selbstregulierung.-Jusletter-Nov-13.pdf> accessed 6 July 2023.

Zulauf U and Kuhn H, *Finanzmarktrecht* (2nd edn, Dike 2021).

Züll T, *Regulierung im politischen Gemeinwesen: Zur demokratischen Legitimation von Wirtschaftsregulierung nach dem Grundgesetz und dem Europäischen Primärrecht* (Mohr Siebeck 2014).

Zweigert K and Kötz H, *Introduction to Comparative Law* (Tony Weir tr, 3rd edn, Oxford University Press 1998).

Zyskind M, 'Fighting for Market Share: How a Trade-at Rule Can Improve Market Efficiency' (2016) 91(1) Chicago-Kent Law Review 411.

List of Cases

Barclays Capital Inc. (2016) Exchange Act Release No. 77001, 113 SEC Docket 1548, 2016 WL 369813 (SEC).

Barclays Liquidity Cross and High Frequency Trading Litigation (2015) 126 F. Supp. 3d 342 (S.D.N.Y. 2015) (US District Court for the Southern District of New York).

Board of Trade of the City of Chicago v. Securities and Exchange Commission (1991) 923 F.2d 1270 (7th Cir. 1991) (US Court of Appeals for the 7th Circuit).

Citigroup Global Markets, Inc. (2018) Exchange Act Release No. 84124, 2018 WL 4382852 (SEC).

Deutsche Bank Securities Inc. (2016) Exchange Act Release No. 79576, 115 SEC Docket 4333, 2016 WL 7324405 (SEC).

EBX, LLC (2012) Exchange Act Release No. 67969, 104 SEC Docket 2844, 2012 WL 4580151 (SEC).

ITG Inc. (2015) Exchange Act Release No. 75672, 112 SEC Docket 887, 2015 WL 4748216 (SEC).

ITG Inc. (2018) Exchange Act Release No. 84548, 2018 WL 5818281 (SEC).

ITG Inc. (2015) Exchange Act Release No. 75672, 112 SEC Docket 887, 2015 WL 4748216 (SEC).

Lanier v. BATS Exchange, Inc. (2016) 838 F.3d 139 (2d Cir. 2016) (US Court of Appeals for the 2nd Circuit).

Liquidnet, Inc. (2014) Exchange Act Release No. 72339, 109 SEC Docket 10, 2014 WL 2547522 (SEC).

Nilaş and Others, ECLI:EU:C:2012:166 (2012) C-248/11 (CJEU).

Opper v. Hancock Securities Corporation (1966) 250 F. Supp. 668 (S.D.N.Y. 1966) (US District Court for the Southern District of New York).

Pipeline Trading Systems LLC (2011) Exchange Act Release No. 65609, 102 SEC Docket 1062, 2011 WL 5039038 (SEC).

Securities and Exchange Commission v. Daniel Bergin (2013) 2013 WL 2400793 (N.D.Tex.) (Trial Pleading) (US District Court for the Northern District of Texas Dallas Division).

Securities and Exchange Commission v. Robert L. Ridenour (1990) 913 F.2d 515 (8th Cir. 1990) (US Court of Appeals for the 8th Circuit).

UBS Securities LLC (2015) Exchange Act Release No. 74060, 110 SEC Docket 3471, 2015 WL 179551 (SEC).